THE RETT SYNDROME HANDBOOK

SECOND EDITION

By KATHY HUNTER

Parent, Founder and President
International Rett Syndrome Association

*With contributions from the best Rett experts
around the globe and heartfelt stories
of love and courage
from fellow families everywhere*

INTERNATIONAL RETT SYNDROME ASSOCIATION
9121 PISCATAWAY ROAD, SUITE 2B
CLINTON, MARYLAND 20735
PHONE: (800) 818-RETT
(301) 856-3334
FAX: (301) 856-3336
WWW.RETTSYNDROME.ORG

Published by IRSA Publishing
9121 Piscataway Road, Suite 2B
Clinton, MD 20735

Publisher's Cataloging-in-Publication Data
Hunter, Kathy.

The Rett Syndrome handbook / by Kathy Hunter. – 2nd ed. - Clinton, MD : IRSA Publishing, © 2007.

p. ; cm.
Includes index.
ISBN: 0-9770644-0-9
ISBN13: 978-0-9770644-0-3

1. Rett syndrome-Handbooks, manuals, etc. 2. Children with mental disabilities-Handbooks, manuals, etc. I. Title.

RJ506.R47 H86 2006
618.92/85884-dc22   2005937239

Printed in the United States of America
11 10 09 08 07 • 5 4 3 2 1

DEDICATION

To my daughter, Stacie, for giving my life purpose and inspiration ...

To my family for their continued patience, understanding and sacrifice ...

To the medical experts who give of themselves tirelessly and with determination to conquer RS ...

To the dedicated teachers and therapists who use loving hands and who recognize small wonders ...

To the contributors to this book, whose gifts of knowledge and experience light the way ...

*To Kim Poulos Lieberz, who always understands how to illustrate what I want to say,
and whose help with editing was an immeasurable gift of love ...*

*To the families in Rettland everywhere, who live ordinary lives yet meet extraordinary difficulties
with courage and conviction day in and day out ...*

*And to our loved ones with RS, who rise above the challenges every moment of their lives,
and through whose generous gifts of unconditional love
we find the hope and inspiration to go on ...*

ACKNOWLEDGMENTS

A warm and special thanks to

Christopher and Dana Reeve
Paralysis Resource Center

Christopher Reeve Foundation

Rett Syndrome
Association of Illinois

16 Years of
Caring & Sharing
1989-2005

The Christopher Reeve Foundation
and the Rett Syndrome Association of Illinois
for generously providing grants toward the publication of this book.
http://www.christopherreeve.org/

Interior/cover design and art production by Kim Poulos Lieberz • www.kgidesigngroup.com
Interior typesetting and production by Stephen Tiano Page Design & Production
Production coordination by Jenkins Group, Inc. • www.BookPublishing.com

Copy Editors Kathy Pryor, Claudia Weisz, Penny Horsfall, Maureen Walther,
Judy Fry, Susan McLoughlin and Diane Ross

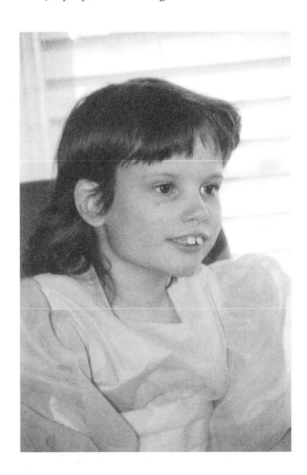

The Rett Syndrome Handbook
Second Edition

GENERAL CONTENTS

Rett Syndrome Handbook
Second Edition

DETAILED CONTENTS

Rett Syndrome Handbook
Second Edition
CONTENTS Continued

SECTION TWO | FAMILY ISSUES

Rett Syndrome Handbook
Second Edition
CONTENTS Continued

Three
SECTION THREE | COMMON PROBLEMS

Rett Syndrome Handbook
Second Edition
CONTENTS Continued

Rett Syndrome Handbook
Second Edition
CONTENTS Continued

Four
SECTION FOUR CARE AND MANAGEMENT

Rett Syndrome Handbook
Second Edition
CONTENTS Continued

Rett Syndrome Handbook
Second Edition

Rett Syndrome Handbook
Second Edition
CONTENTS Continued

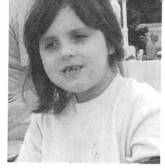

Rett Syndrome Handbook
Second Edition
CONTENTS Continued

Seven
SECTION SEVEN | RESOURCES

Rett Syndrome Handbook
Second Edition

CONTENTS Continued

SECTION EIGHT | THE FUTURE

FOREWORD

How fortunate is the Rett community to have Kathy Hunter, founder and president of the International Rett Syndrome Association (IRSA), put together a new edition of the Rett Syndrome Handbook. This handbook will be useful to everyone who has been touched by Rett syndrome: parents, relatives, friends, neighbors, teachers, caregivers, physicians, and scientists.

Twenty years ago our knowledge about the child with Rett syndrome and her needs were very limited, but Kathy and parents like her shared their observations and experiences to inspire physicians and scientists to study this syndrome and to help other parents provide the best care for their children and cope with the challenges of this disorder. Today, there are over 1,230 medical and scientific publications on Rett syndrome. The amount of knowledge that a parent has to sift through or comprehend is overwhelming. This handbook introduces the reader to the nervous system and how it is affected in Rett syndrome, summarizes what medical research has informed us about this disorder and shares the best management options for some of the symptoms. The book provides practical advice about how to cope with the medical challenges and how to enjoy life with Rett syndrome.

It is written beautifully (as we have grown to expect from Kathy) and is easy to read. The book is rich with the experiences and the wisdom of many parents who want to share lessons they learned to help new generations of patients with Rett syndrome and families. The book also provides the reader with resources to find the necessary equipment, financial and community support, and up-to-date information. It concludes with updates on the latest research findings and ongoing research activities giving the reader a sense of what the future might hold. Kathy and IRSA have played a major role in increasing awareness about Rett syndrome, ensuring research support, providing families with up-to-date information, and sharing resources for support. On a personal note, I can say that their help went beyond advocacy and family support. I learned quite a bit about Rett syndrome from Kathy and the IRSA family, and their support helped us to identify the gene in 1999.

Watching all the exciting discoveries on Rett and the gene (*MECP2*), one can't help but wonder how much more this disease and its causative gene are going to teach us about the brain and the magic of its workings. The Rett Syndrome Handbook certainly captures all of this and leaves the reader wanting more. At the pace research is moving, we hope that more discoveries will come soon, and we can bet that Kathy will be happy to write a new edition to share exciting advances, and hopefully, effective treatments.

Huda Y. Zoghbi, M.D., Ph.D.
Investigator, Howard Hughes Medical Institute
Professor, Baylor College of Medicine

❖ ❖ ❖

Who better to produce a comprehensive handbook on Rett syndrome than the Founder and President of the International Rett Syndrome Association? Kathy Hunter has more than thirty years of experience as a personal practitioner in the world of Rett syndrome, dedicated to providing the best and most current information for parents, extended family members, and other caretakers. This is a world that was never envisioned by her or any parent, but one that was faced directly in order to deal with the daily aspects of this relatively new neurodevelopmental disorder that affects predominantly girls and women. This handbook contains a wealth of information from persons, including physicians and scientists, therapists and educators, but of equal importance, parents of children with Rett syndrome, whose daily experiences surely qualify them as "experts."

This handbook should serve as a valuable resource when needed. Not every aspect will pertain to every child, but virtually every aspect of Rett syndrome is covered in detail. The handbook is written with sensitivity and objectivity, but from the perspective that it is better to shed light on a subject than to curse the unknown. The Rett Syndrome Handbook is a treasure chest of useful and important information that should serve the reader well and advance the lives of those affected by this disorder.

Alan K. Percy, M.D.
Associate Director, Civitan International Research Center
Director, Civitan-Sparks Clinic
University of Alabama at Birmingham

INTRODUCTION

In 1954, Dr. Andreas Rett of Vienna, Austria, noticed two girls sitting together with their mothers in his waiting room. The girls made the same unusual handwashing movements, and he discovered after examining them that their clinical and developmental histories were strikingly alike. After consulting with his nurse, Dr. Rett found six others like them in his practice and made a film of the girls, which he took all over Europe trying to find other cases. His findings were published in several obscure German language medical journals, which unfortunately never reached the attention of the worldwide medical community.

In 1960, Dr. Bengt Hagberg observed several girls who had similar behaviors in his busy practice in Sweden. He put these interesting cases in a special box under his desk, vowing to look further into the nature of this unusual and unknown disorder. In 1978, Dr. Ishikawa and colleagues from Japan described three girls in a brief note which also went unnoticed. Many years went by before Drs. Hagberg and Rett realized they were reporting the same disorder. In a generous gesture, Dr. Hagberg deferred his original descriptive title and submitted the name Rett syndrome for the first English language article on the disorder, published in late 1983. Until his death in 1996, Dr. Rett worked ceaselessly to unite parents and professionals in a community of care to bring a better life to the girls whose disorder bore his name. Dr. Hagberg, now in his eighties, continues today as a world leader in the field. His energy and enthusiasm in the research arena are only surpassed by his gentle spirit and compassion at the human level of the lives he works to improve.

"I can only express my gratitude to all the parents for their love and the affection they give to their children, and my admiration for all their efforts and services they deliver to their girls. Don't lose heart in your work, keep your love for the children, and remember what I have always tried to say: watch the wonderful expression of the eyes of these girls, an expression which makes them so lovable."

- PROFESSOR ANDREAS RETT

Shortly before the first paper on RS was published, my daughter, Stacie, who was ten years old at the time, was given the diagnosis of RS. She became the thirty-sixth documented case in the world. Stacie had developed normally until fifteen months of age, then began a regression that led to a loss of the few words she had developed, aloofness, withdrawal and irritability most of the time. She began mouthing and wringing her hands constantly. Over the years, and like many of your daughters, Stacie had a number of diagnoses, including autism and Angelman (Happy Puppet) syndrome. However, she never fit neatly into any category. She was always one of a kind.

Two important events changed me for-ever. To this day, my spirit stays afire to keep the Rett movement alive—just so this will *never* happen to others. One is the young doctor who told me to just give up, saying that Stacie would never know what it was like to be normal and that I had to accept that and try to keep my own life normal. He said I must give up. The other was a child

Kathy and Scott Hunter. Below, the Hunter family

psychologist who told me that it was possible I had caused the "autism," according to an outdated theory on autism that blamed "cold" mothers in the face of no other explanation for their child's regression. You can be sure that these were the first two people to receive information about RS. Their insensitive comments launched me on a journey to prevent others from ever having to hear the same unfortunate advice. It

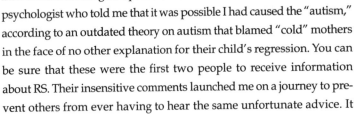

was a broken road that led me to the diagnosis of RS, but the path forward from that news has been rewarding and hopeful.

Since IRSA began more than twenty years ago on my kitchen table, I have longed for this book—a tangible resource to put into the hands of families new to the diagnosis of RS. Usually exhausted from the diagnostic process, they ask in so many different ways, "So, where do we go from here? What do we do while we wait for the cure?" As Stacie was growing up, there were no answers for our questions. It was important to direct energy at finding those answers and giving them to families everywhere as they arrived in "Rettland." Authors are often told to keep the reader wanting more. *The Rett Syndrome Handbook* does not follow this rule. It was created for those who want it, and deserve *it all*. Hopefully, it will give you answers, spark your thoughts, fire up your imagination, and provide you with as much information as possible to give your loved one the best life she can have. You are where I was more than thirty years ago; to be able to give you this leaves me with remarkable rewards and immeasurable happiness.

Some of the advice in this book is sprinkled in more one than one flower bed. If you find the advice repeated but worded differently in more than one chapter, that's because like fertilizer, it needs repeating. Just as RS has many stages, coming to terms with RS comes in stages. You are not done with the emotional stuff when you finish "Welcome to Rettland." Keep turning the pages, and when you get stuck in a hard place, take pause … then read on. You will find that the wisdom and insight of others who blazed the path before you cultivated some rich soil that will be like salve on your tender heart.

There may be forks in the road, a number of bumpy spots, and some rough obstacles in Rettland. But for all of the low places, there are magnificent high places to round out the view. With the experience and suggestions of others who have already been there, we are able to map out our journeys. We can be safe in the knowledge that we are not alone. It may take some time to adjust to the new scenery in Rettland, but once we fully arrive, the vista is spectacular.

Your experience with Rett syndrome will be a lasting journey of love. It may take awhile to realize, but you'll come to know it in time. As you listen gently to the words that come from the hearts of those who have been there, you will recognize how much we share.

THE BOOK OF LIFE

It's too bad that the Book of Life doesn't come with a first draft so you can edit out the bad stuff and double the good stuff. But it doesn't work that way. You didn't choose to have a chapter on RS included in your life. Nevertheless, it is a part of you that you can't edit out or white-out. This is the plot you got. You have to make your own happy ending. Whether your Book of Life is a tragedy, a horror story, a drama, or a true life adventure is all up to you.

And you can do that because it's not what happens, but how you choose to *look at what happens* that makes your life what it is. Attitude is paramount. Every experience can be seen as an obstacle or an opportunity, depending on your outlook. You can choose to remain *bitter* or you can choose to get *better*. You can *complain* because rosebushes have thorns, or you can *rejoice* because thornbushes have roses. Life is more than what you are handed. It's what you *do* with what is placed in your hands.

Do you ever wonder why something can happen to two different people with radically different outcomes? I have two lifelong friends who had troubled upbringings. Both were children of alcoholics. Both grew up poor. Both became teachers. One committed suicide and the other built his own successful business. Each had the same difficult childhood, but one was not defeated by it.

You can't choose how you are born or how you die, but you can choose *how you live*. Your attitude is your most important possession. To say it another way, what happens *to you* is less significant than what happens *within you*. I often hear from parents when they are at their lowest point, just having learned their daughter's diagnosis. Many times I hear them say, "I don't know what else can happen." I say gently and quietly, "a lot." And the truth is, Rett syndrome is not the worst thing that could happen to them. Someday, down the road after it has had time to settle, they will realize that there are worse things than the diagnosis of RS. A lot worse.

WE WITHER

When you hear the words Rett syndrome for the first time, they bring on bewilderment, confusion, and sadness. Your heart droops, your hopes shrink, and your spirit wilts to the ground. You go through the universal stages of grief, no less than if your child had died. You may wonder what you did to make this happen and stay awake at night wondering how to make it go away. And then you have to face a couple of universal truths: 1) you didn't make it happen and 2) it won't go away.

Then, you get angry. Real, deep down gut-wrenching angry. Angry at God, angry at fate, angry at life. But you pull yourself together and keep moving forward, doing what needs to be done. Pretty soon you realize that there are not enough hours in the day to do what you need to do, and guilt enters the picture. There are so many competing emotions it's sometimes hard to separate them out. Many days, it's hard to see a patch of blue sky through the heavy clouds and there seems to be no silver lining, much less one you can see.

Over each door to the Rett family home could hang a sign with the Chinese proverb: "No one can say of this house, there is no trouble here." RS is hard. It hurts. It bewilders. It confounds. It defies reason. It shouldn't be this way. You would gladly trade a king's riches to take away RS. It will take some time before you realize that, just as Helen Keller said, "When one door of happiness closes, another opens; but often we look so long at the closed door that we do not see the one which has been opened for us."

Many times, I've thought to myself that I'd rather be a rotten person than have to deal with all this growth and greater wisdom stuff that comes from the suffering. But I can't change what RS has done to my daughter. I can only change what it does to me. If I don't choose the growth and greater wisdom stuff, I'm guaranteed to wither.

The playwright Henry Miller wrote, "Life has no other discipline to impose, if we would but realize it, than to accept life unquestioningly. Everything we shut our eyes to, everything we run away from, everything we deny, denigrate, or despise, serves to defeat us in the end. What seems nasty, painful, evil, can become a source of beauty, joy, and strength, if faced with an open mind. Every moment is a golden one for him who has the vision to recognize it as such." Those golden moments come in time, when we learn to thank God, thank fate and be thankful for life. We learn that happiness does not require perfection and performance, only acceptance and love. This awareness does not come easily. We don't wake up a few days after the diagnosis and have a revelation. We meet hurt after hurt, challenge after challenge, and crisis after crisis. Then we are able to put a real name on hurt, on challenge, on crisis. We learn that the big things in life really are, after all, the little things.

Each of us has to learn to change what we can, accept what we can't, and go on. Those of us who have been crushed can attest to this: we grow stronger in the broken places. We gain so many valuable insights and gather so much courage. As one mother told me, "I am no longer afraid of anything." At the same time, we learn the true meaning of unconditional love and see the enormous power of the powerless.

Don't you find it amusing what other people think is a problem? It makes me chuckle out loud sometimes. I just smile and remember my own philosophy about problems … "if little kids don't die from it, it ain't a problem." When I've been in line a long time and have exercised incredible patience with delays or bumbled transactions, the clerk often thanks me for my composure while others are flying off the handle around me. I usually reply, "Well, you know, I learned patience in the Hard School. I have a child with multiple handicaps. She can't do anything for herself. I've had a lot of practice. And you know what? This is small stuff. In fact, if this is the worst thing that happens to me today, I'll still be way ahead." It usually brings introspection to others who take a moment to reconsider what's important and what's not.

People have always amazed me when they comment about my patience with Stacie. I find it amusing to begin with, because Stacie is the one with patience. She has to wait to be fed until I think she is hungry, put to bed when I think she is tired. Too often, she has to put up with people who either act like she isn't there or treat her like she's an infant. People often remark that they "couldn't do it." I usually smile and say, "Well, what would you do?" Of course, love does not diminish with the diagnosis. It grows.

WE GROW

We don't grow overnight. We grow in little spurts. We don't learn it all in books. Experience is the best teacher. When my first child was born, I looked at him and said to the doctor, "I've never been a mother before. I don't know what to do." The doctor smiled and said, "You'll be fine. He's never been a baby before, either."

The story I am about to tell is true. While I was pregnant with Stacie, I took a college course called Psychology of the Exceptional Child. For some reason, one phrase jumped out from the course textbook with the chilling words, "autism is the most severely debilitating disorder of childhood." I shuddered as I thought about what a wrenching experience it must be to have such a child. Then, with my vast experience as mother of two healthy youngsters and my newly found education from this informative course, I decided to write my final paper on "How to Counsel Parents of Disabled Children." I read all the right books, brought together the needed resources, and wrote the paper. I figured I must have said all the right things. I got an "A" on the paper. I was excused from the final exam because I was giving birth, but my good grades earned me an "A" in the class anyway. I thought

I knew everything there was to know. Then, about ten years later, I was cleaning out the basement when I came upon a box of old books and papers. There it was staring up at me: "How to Counsel Parents of Disabled Children." My mouth dropped open as I stared down at the "A" paper. I started to read what I had written, and then with sudden rage, I tore it into a thousand pieces and threw it in the trash. Bitter tears flooded my face as I realized how prophetic it was that I would choose this subject so long before, and how preposterous that I could even begin to pretend to know what to say before I had lived through it.

I think this is why as parents, our souls are so connected. Others can think about it, study it, teach about it, and write about it, but they don't live it. They don't really know it. We are a fraternity, a sorority, blood brothers and sisters, unrelated, but so very related. We come from many roads away and much distance apart, speaking any number of dialects, and observing different customs but we are one. An old Swedish proverb tells us that "shared joy is double joy, and shared sorrow is half sorrow." That's what joins our hearts. It hurts me to know that your child also has RS, but it helps me to know that we can get through it together.

We grow from this experience. Like the trees, we learn to bend with the wind before the force breaks us. And like some of the most beautiful flowers in the garden that bloom even more brilliantly after their blossoms are pinched off, we grow more from living with adversity than when everything is "perfect." The lucky ones learn to count their *blessings* instead of their burdens. Have you ever wondered what it would be like to have a child with RS and live in a country where there was little medical care and no special education? No family to help out? It's hard to imagine how some people survive without some lifesaving items we all take for granted, like disposable diapers, washing machines, Velcro, VCRs and DVD players, McDonald's French fries, Walkmen, IDEA and of course, Barney. We can't count our burdens without remembering our blessings.

BLOOM WHERE YOU ARE PLANTED

No matter what the circumstances, we can choose to be *alive*, to *thrive*, and to *survive*. Choose to grow and bloom where you are planted, as the saying goes. Throughout it all, it is important to always keep your sense of humor. Laughter gets the blood bubbling, swells the chest, jolts the nerves, sweeps the cobwebs from the brain, and cleans out the whole system. Laughter is physical therapy for the soul. You've come a long way when you can laugh at some of life's predicaments. It's good that we can laugh. And it's healthy for us to cry now and then.

REACH FOR THE STARS

Above it all, it is important to hope, and I'd like to share my own hope with you. I hope to soon be out of work. I hope to make RS something no one ever heard of, not because it is *unknown*, but because it is *conquered.* I hope the next book I write will be titled, RS: The Cure. My hopes are very high. Once I didn't even have ordinary hope, and now I have "high, apple pie in the sky" hope. Hope is faith, reliance, and trust. We have every reason to be hopeful. We are so close to finding answers. It hasn't been easy. We've seen the misfortune of RS strike more than once in a family, but have seen the fortunate turnaround of families willing to overlook their own tragedy to participate vigorously in research. We have seen the sadness of girls lost to early death, yet have had our hearts warmed by parents who consented to autopsy so that the rest of us could be spared the same anguish. We've had bake sales, craft sales, car washes, races, dances, dinners, auctions, and concerts for the cause. It all adds up to hope. We are closer than we have ever been to solving the puzzle of RS. Just when you are about to give up or lose hope, remember that the world is round—the end is often the beginning. We are going to come full circle. It's going to happen. We are joined hand in hand, by Carl Sandburg's promise, "where there is life, there is hope."

BELIEVE IN YOURSELF: BELIEVE IN HER

The insights we gain on the Rett journey are invaluable. While some may see our daughters as powerless, we know of the enormous power they have to change us. She may not walk, yet she helps us walk taller. As she struggles to move, she moves many hearts. She may need to be fed, yet she feeds our spirits. We seek to understand her, yet in so doing, we begin to understand far more. She may not speak to us in words, but she speaks to us in the silent language of love.

Your daughter brings so many blessings. She may never talk, but she will never talk back. She may never run, but she will never run away from home. She may need drugs to sustain life, but she will never take drugs to escape life. She may never use her hands for skills, but she will not use those hands for violence or evil. Look into her eyes and you can't help but have hope. She lives through her eyes. She loves through her eyes. As Dr. Alan Percy says, "The eyes have it." Her eyes, windows to the soul, take us to cherished places within her heart. Her eyes do more than see us. They *touch* us. Every human emotion is whispered, sung, shouted by her dancing, sparkling eyes.

While there may be confusion in her head, make no mistake, there is a lot of understanding in her head. She may have many obstacles to learning, but she can learn many things. Just because she can't *show* it doesn't mean she doesn't *know* it. It's in there. She's in there. Keep looking. You'll see.

It is most appropriate that this is called a "handbook," for hands are the trademark of RS. It is with our hands that we touch, feel, grasp, stroke, carry, comfort, and we give and receive. When we hold hands, we connect, and we double our strength. Our goal is to join our hands together, extending the circle ever wider until the day when others ask, "What *was* RS?" I could continue to write forever, for no book on the subject could include everything. For now, I hope this book lights your path.

Kathy Hunter

Kathy Hunter
Parent, Founder and President, IRSA

To Julianna

My daughter is my mentor, my daughter is my strength.

My daughter is the center of my world, each and every day.

She taught me how to laugh, when times get really tough.

She taught me how to say "I'm sorry" when I say things that aren't okay.

She has taught me not to dwell on every little thing.

She has taught me how to be happy, when inside I felt like dying.

She has taught me there's more to life than perfect, normal or sane,

things like beautiful, stunning, surprising, and great.

She has taught me to hold my head up high,

to not be ashamed, to not want to cry.

She has taught me to love unconditionally, wholeheartedly, and sure,

to thank my lucky stars above, for a special daughter like her.

- PAM JORDAN

Special note to readers: For the sake of continuity and space, and as RS occurs almost exclusively in females, individuals with RS in this text are referred to in the female gender. It is acknowledged that RS can occur occasionally in males.

1

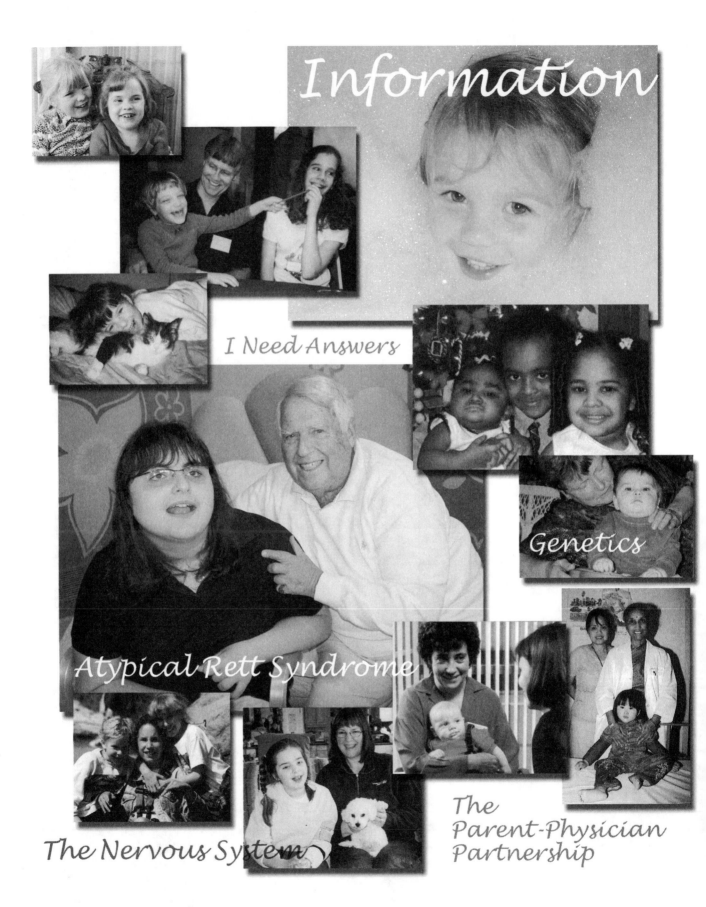

Information

I Need Answers

Genetics

Atypical Rett Syndrome

The Nervous System

The Parent-Physician Partnership

I Need Answers

WHAT IS RETT SYNDROME?

RETT SYNDROME (RS) IS A UNIQUE developmental disorder that is first recognized in infancy and seen almost always in girls. It is found in all racial and ethnic groups throughout the world, and in every socioeconomic class.

SHE SEEMED TO DEVELOP SO NORMALLY. WHAT HAPPENED?

RS RESULTS FROM A CHAIN of events beginning with a genetic mutation (change in a specific piece of DNA), which occurs at the time of conception. The name of the mutated gene is *MECP2* (*methyl CpG binding protein 2*), and it is pronounced "**meck**-pea-two)." It is always found at the end of the long arm of the X chromosome. When it is written with a capital "E" and italicized, *MECP2* stands for the gene itself. The protein made by the *MECP2* gene is pronounced the same way, but it is written MeCP2 with a small "e" and no italics.

"The important thing is to never stop questioning."

– ALBERT EINSTEIN

WHAT DOES THE *MECP2* MUTATION DO?

THE *MECP2* GENE IS A "HOUSEKEEPING GENE," responsible for telling downstream genes when to shut off. Scientists believe that lack of a properly functioning *MECP2* gene allows other genes to come on or stay on at inappropriate times, disturbing the precisely regulated pattern necessary for proper development of the central nervous system.

Different *MECP2* mutations result in the overproduction, shortage, or absence of some specific "factor" (usually a protein or an enzyme) needed for normal development. When any disruption in the amount or type of "factors" needed occurs, selected regions of the brain responsible for cognitive, sensory, emotional, motor, and autonomic function are impacted. Development appears to be normal in early infancy until the time when the disrupted and normal brain development is altered. Without any of these specific factors, or with too much of any of them, selected regions of the brain remain developmentally immature, or are flooded with an overproduction of proteins and enzymes that are toxic to the central nervous system. The child appears to be developing normally in the first months of life because her early jobs do not demand much work from these factors until later in development. We now believe that the type of mutation and the number of cells impacted determine the stage when normal development will cease.

DID I DO SOMETHING TO CAUSE THE MUTATION?

WE DO NOT KNOW WHY THIS MUTATION OCCURS. Mutations occur naturally in everyone all the time and most do not cause problems. In fact, some mutations can result in improvements, like a better protein for using oxygen. Unfortunately, a mutation on the *MECP2* gene results in Rett syndrome. Studies to date have not revealed any pattern in exposure to chemicals or radiation, or any correlation with demographics (where you live). The most likely explanation for the *MECP2* mutation is that while the

I Need Answers

gene is forming and going through thousands of rapid duplications, it just stutters or burps, causing a change in the normal pattern of DNA. When this happens in much of the other of billions of pairs of DNA pieces, it just isn't noticeable.

IS IT POSSIBLE TO CHANGE THIS MUTATION?

IT IS IMPOSSIBLE TO JUST REMOVE THE MUTATION. Although the *MECP2* gene is expressed in every cell in the body, only one X chromosome is active in any cell at any time, so some cells will have the mutated copy of *MECP2* active and others will have the normal copy of the gene active. This presents a very complex situation and one that is not immediately amenable to gene therapy using stem cells. At this point, stem cells hold little immediate promise for "reseeding" the brain with "good" MeCP2, a hope for other disorders where only a small portion of the brain is affected. Researchers are working on ways to have another gene "take over" for the mutated *MECP2* gene, but this will require more knowledge of the downstream relationships *MECP2* has with other genes and proteins.

IS THE *MECP2* MUTATION FOUND ONLY IN RS?

WE HAVE RECENTLY LEARNED THAT MUTATIONS in the same gene are involved in a number of other more well-known disorders, including autism, mental retardation, learning disorders, schizophrenia, and bipolar disorder. This finding greatly increases our chances of finding the treatment and cure for RS, because researchers in other more prominent fields are also very interested in *MECP2*. Federal funding will increase because mutations on the *MECP2* gene could account for millions of affected people.

AT WHAT AGE DOES RETT SYNDROME BEGIN?

THE AGE WHEN RS BEGINS AND THE SEVERITY of different symptoms may vary. The child with RS is usually born healthy and shows an early period of apparently normal or near normal development until six to eighteen months of life, when there is a slowing down or stagnation of skills. A period of regression then follows when she loses communication skills and purposeful use of her hands. Soon, stereotyped hand movements, gait disturbances, and slowing of the normal rate of head growth become apparent. Other problems may include seizures and disorganized breathing patterns while she is awake. There may be a period of isolation or withdrawal when she is irritable and cries inconsolably. Over time, motor problems may increase, while other symptoms may decrease or improve.

At fifteen months, Heather started having more gastrointestinal problems such as severe constipation. At this time she was walking independently and continued for one year. Since then she has mostly walked with various assistance and up to fifty steps independently again for a brief time. Heather regressed from fifteen months to twenty-six months. Before regression, she could say single words, finger feed, open packages, turn pages in a book, take things in and out of containers, and was a very happy child.

HOW WILL THE MUTATION AFFECT WHAT SHE CAN DO?

THE MECP2 PROTEIN CAN BE FOUND IN ALL CELLS of the body, but it is most prevalent in the brain. Therefore, RS causes problems in brain function that are responsible for cognitive, sensory, emotional, motor and autonomic function. These can include learning, speech, sensory sensations, mood, movement, breathing, cardiac function, and even chewing, swallowing, and digestion.

I Need Answers

WHAT IS THE GREATEST HANDICAP IN RS?

APRAXIA (DYSPRAXIA), THE INABILITY or difficulty to program the body to perform motor movements, is the most fundamental and severely handicapping aspect of RS. It can interfere with every body movement, including eye gaze and speech, making it difficult for the girl with RS to do what she wants to do. Due to this apraxia and her inability to speak, it may be very difficult to make an accurate assessment of her intelligence. Most traditional testing methods require her to use her hands and/or speech, which may be impossible for the girl with RS.

IS RS DEGENERATIVE?

RESEARCHERS NOW AGREE THAT RS is a developmental disorder and *not* a degenerative disorder with continuous downward progression as once thought. Girls can learn throughout their lives and barring illness or complications, survival into adulthood is expected.

HOW OFTEN DOES RS OCCUR?

WHILE MANY HEALTH PROFESSIONALS may not be familiar with RS, it is a relatively frequent cause of delayed development in girls. The prevalence rate in various countries is from 1:10,000 to 1:23,000 live female births, making it three times more common in females than phenylketonuria (PKU), a congenital error of metabolism that is tested for in every newborn.

HOW IS RS DIAGNOSED?

RS HAS BEEN MOST OFTEN MISDIAGNOSED as autism, cerebral palsy, or non-specific developmental delay. In the past, making the correct diagnosis called not only for a long list of diagnostic tests and procedures to rule out other disorders, but it also took from months to years waiting to confirm the diagnosis as new symptoms appeared over time.

Today, we have a simple blood test to confirm the diagnosis. However, since we know that the *MECP2* mutation is also seen in other disorders, the presence of the *MECP2* mutation in itself is not enough for the diagnosis of RS. Diagnosis requires either the presence of the mutation (a molecular diagnosis) or fulfillment of the diagnostic criteria (a clinical diagnosis, based on signs and symptoms that you can observe) or both.

DIAGNOSTIC CRITERIA FOR RS

Necessary criteria

1. apparently normal prenatal and perinatal history
2. psychomotor development largely normal through the first six months or may be delayed from birth
3. normal head circumference at birth
4. postnatal deceleration of head growth in the majority
5. loss of achieved purposeful hand skill between ages $1/2$–$2 1/2$ years
6. stereotypic hand movements such as hand wringing/squeezing, clapping/tapping, mouthing and washing/rubbing automatisms

I Need Answers

7. emerging social withdrawal, communication dysfunction, loss of learned words, and cognitive impairment

8. impaired (dyspraxic) or failing locomotion

Supportive criteria

1. awake disturbances of breathing (hyperventilation, breath-holding, forced expulsion of air or saliva, air swallowing)

2. teeth grinding (bruxism)

3. impaired sleep pattern from early infancy

4. abnormal muscle tone successively associated with muscle wasting and dystonia

5. peripheral vasomotor disturbances (cold, blue hands and feet)

6. scoliosis/kyphosis progressing through childhood

7. growth retardation

8. hypotrophic (small) feet; small, thin hands

Exclusion criteria

1. enlarged organs or other signs of storage disease

2. retinopathy, optic atrophy, or cataract

3. evidence of brain damage before or after birth

4. existence of identifiable metabolic or other progressive neurological disorder

5. acquired neurological disorder resulting from severe infections or head trauma

HOW DOES RS DIFFER FROM AUTISM?

WHILE RS OCCURS PRIMARILY IN GIRLS, autism occurs much more frequently in boys. In both conditions, there is loss of speech and emotional contact. However, symptoms seen in RS and not in autism include deceleration of the rate of head growth and loss of purposeful hand skills and mobility. While hand "flapping" is seen frequently in autism as visual stimulation, the wider range of compulsive, purposeless hand stereotypes common to RS are not seen in autism. The girl with RS almost always prefers people to objects, but the opposite is seen in autism. Unlike those with autism, the RS girl often enjoys affection. While girls with RS often have autistic tendencies at an early age, these features decrease over time.

WHAT ABOUT MALES WITH RS?

IN ORDER FOR A MALE TO HAVE THE DIAGNOSIS of RS, he must fulfill the diagnostic criteria. While there have been reports of males with the *MECP2* mutation, only a very few of them actually fulfill the diagnostic criteria for RS. The few who have been given the diagnosis of RS are either Klinefelter's syndrome (XXY) or mosaic (some cells with normal *MECP2* and some cells with mutated *MECP2*). Most males with the *MECP2* mutation are affected much more severely than females, and die very early in life. Others with the *MECP2* mutation are much milder, lack features of Rett syndrome, and are diagnosed with severe mental retardation.

I Need Answers

IS RETT SYNDROME SEEN PREDOMINANTLY IN ONE RACE?

NO, RS IS SEEN IN ALL RACES AND ALL ETHNIC GROUPS. A statewide population study in Texas has revealed that the incidence of RS in the African-American and Hispanic population in the United States is comparable to that in Caucasian Americans.

WHAT ARE THE STAGES OF RS AND WHAT DO THEY MEAN?

STAGE 1 USUALLY BEGINS BETWEEN SIX AND EIGHTEEN MONTHS, and is often overlooked, because the symptoms of RS are just beginning and are somewhat vague. Parents and physicians may not notice the subtle slowing of development at first. The infant may have progressed and gained new skills, but at a slower rate or later date than expected. She may have a "floppy" body and a poor suck. Her development then slows down and seems to stagnate. This stage usually lasts a few months, but can last more than a year. The infant may show less eye contact and have reduced interest in toys. She is often described as a "good" baby, calm and quiet. There may be delays in some gross motor milestones, such as sitting, crawling, or pulling to stand. Gradually, her lack of attention is noticed and she may have non-specific hand movements. The rate of her head growth may be slowed, but may not be significant enough to cause notice.

The only difference between Megan and her brother was the way they played. The world acted on Meg, while Connor acted on the world. It's a hard distinction to make, but generally Meg accepted that things happened and didn't try to figure them out.

Amy seemed to be developing normally. She met her early milestones, sitting at six months and walking at fourteen months. She smiled at people but sometimes looked through them. Then, her eye contact began to decline and she looked more at objects. She didn't really play with toys like other babies. She just sort of "batted" at them.

Our first clues for Angela that something was up was that her behavior until thirteen months was pretty good, although she seemed to "rule" the family with demands at times. She met her milestones on time or before, particularly with social interaction and fine motor skills. Gross motor skills were within the normal range, though at the later end. Although she was quick to smile or laugh, she was never happy traveling, seldom happy shopping, and loved to be home. She couldn't handle any variation on her routine unless it was her choice. Her only comfort was breastfeeding, and we did it every forty-five minutes for what seemed like ages.

STAGE 2 begins from one to four years and usually lasts from weeks to months. A general developmental decline is seen with regression and loss of acquired skills. This stage can have a rapid onset or it can be more gradual as acquired finger and hand skills and spoken language are lost. Stereotyped hand movements begin and often include hand-to-mouth movements and clapping first. Movements which follow are most often midline hand wringing or hand washing. These hand movements persist while the girl is awake but disappear during sleep. Hands are sometimes clasped behind the back or held at the sides in a specific pose, with random touching, grasping and releasing. Breathing irregularities may be noticed, and may include episodes of breath holding and hyperventilation (overbreathing) associated with vacant spells. Puffing, air expulsion, or spitting may precede these. However, breathing is normal during sleep. Some girls appear autistic-like with loss of social interaction and communication. A lack of imitative or imaginative play is seen. General irritability and sleep irregularity may be seen, and some girls awaken with inappropriate laughing or crying spells. Periods of shakiness may be obvious, especially

I Need Answers

when they are excited. Gait patterns are unsteady with uncoordinated, jerky movements. Initiating motor movements can be difficult. Tooth grinding is common. Further slowing of head growth is usually noticed from three months to four years, when the girl's head circumference growth rate decelerates on a percentile chart when compared with other children at the same age.

At thirteen months things started to slowly change, and it seemed like she was having horrible temper tantrums. Looking back, it was really a combination of two things: 1) reflux that we didn't yet realize she had, and 2) her own realization that her skills were slipping. That beautiful pincer grip that astounded her pediatrician was deteriorating and that frustrated her. She couldn't roll where she wanted to go anymore. Her words had stopped coming; she'd had nine to that point. It became difficult for her to manipulate her toys and, worst of all, to hold her beloved books. Angela's regression/screaming lasted between the ages of thirteen to twenty-six months.

When she was 2 1/2, she withdrew, would not respond to her name, would not give eye contact, and resisted cuddles and hugs. She went through some terrible crying and screaming spells. Her dad would hold her, and she'd cling so tightly to him, it seemed that she was trying to crawl inside him. It always seemed to come with a new situation she didn't want to be in, like company at the house, loud children, homes of friends who were once so loved by her. Any closed-in space freaked her out, yet she would be as happy as ever in a grocery store, or riding in the car. When she was 3 1/2, she appeared to snap out of this, began to babble again, and became lovable, gave eye contact again, became playful, and loved to be hugged.

STAGE 3 usually begins from two to ten years following the rapid destructive period, and can last for many years. Regression is now over, and she reaches a stable period. Apraxia, motor problems, scoliosis, and seizures may be more prominent. However, improvement is seen in behavior with less irritability and crying, fewer autistic features and good eye contact. She shows more interest in her surroundings, and her alertness, attention span, and communication skills improve. Many girls with RS remain in Stage 3 for most or all of their lifetime.

Ashley has continued to advance, however slowly, in communication, alertness, and in social skills. She is still able to walk, assists in dressing by raising her arms and pushing her sleeves on, and assists in eating and drinking. She can take the utensil with food on it and put it in her mouth, eat, and hand back the utensil. She assists in holding a glass and still uses the toilet appropriately. She just seems more overall "with it."

Kendall started off like a typical little girl. She crawled on time, pulled to a stand on time, babbled, giggled, and cooed. Then, things started to decline. She was a late walker at eighteen months and withdrew into her own little world. For an agonizing period of time, I thought all was lost. But then, shortly before Kendall's second birthday, she learned eye contact, could point to things she wanted, the screaming spells began to subside and we began to get our lovely little girl back.

The term "floppy" was used when she was a baby. She was late in meeting her developmental milestones during her first year and by the second year her progress was slowing down. By her third year she had lost all of her speech (well except the word NO, which she retained for a few more years). She also lost her balance and the ability to sit without assistance and to stand up. Her hands became her obsession and she began wringing and mouthing them constantly. She screamed and cried most of the time and refused any eye contact. She started having seizures and reflux, and scoliosis also appeared. We dealt with all these issues the best we could and thankfully by the time Rachel started elementary school, she was a different child. By age five, her constant crying had stopped and she became a happy girl, her eye gaze improved and her face became very expressive. Her seizures and reflux were under control and her overall health improved. By age ten, Rachel's hypotonia was changing to spasticity.

I Need Answers

STAGE 4, which usually begins after age ten, is characterized by reduced mobility. Stage 4-A is used to describe those who once walked and stopped. Stage 4-B describes those who were never able to walk. In this stage, muscle weakness, rigidity, spasticity and scoliosis are prominent features which contribute to loss of movement skills. Feet are often swollen, cold, and bluish. However, there is no further decline in cognition, communication, or hand skills. Emotional contact and eye gaze are improved. Hand movements may decrease in frequency and intensity. Puberty begins at the expected age in most girls. In general, women with RS appear younger than their actual age.

Alice walked by herself until she was twelve and until fifteen with assistance. She began to get very shaky when standing, and then began to refuse to bear weight. She makes intense eye contact and seems to take in all of the activity around her. She doesn't wring her hands as much because of contractures in her arms. She seems happier than ever in her life, and enjoys being with people and going on outings.

"He who asks a question is a fool for five minutes; he who does not ask a question remains a fool forever."

– CHINESE PROVERB

DO ALL GIRLS MOVE THROUGH THE STAGES SIMILARLY?

NO. THE STAGES OF RETT SYNDROME are simply provided to help understand the natural history of the disorder. It is important to recognize that the ages within stages are averages. All girls go through Stage 1 (appearance of normal development) and Stage 2 (regression) in about the same way. But some individuals with RS may remain in Stage 3 for all of their lives and never pass to Stage 4. And, children may be in Stage 4 during childhood because they never developed the ability to walk.

WHAT DETERMINES THE SEVERITY OF RS?

THE COURSE OF RS IS PREDETERMINED by the location, type and severity of her mutation and X-inactivation (more in Genetics). Therefore, two girls of the same age can appear quite different.

WHAT IS THE RANGE OF SEVERITY IN RS?

JUST AS IN ANY OTHER DISORDER, there can be a wide range of disability ranging from mild to severe. It is difficult to predict the intensity of symptoms in any individual child. Many girls begin walking within the normal range, while others show significant delay or inability to walk independently. Some begin walking and lose this skill, while others continue to walk throughout life. Still others do not walk until late childhood or adolescence. The same range holds true for using her hands and other skills she may acquire.

WHAT WILL SHE BE ABLE TO DO?

ALTHOUGH SHE WILL NEED HELP for most activities of daily living, she can learn some independent skills. Most girls can learn to use the toilet and many can learn to feed themselves by hand or with utensils with some assistance. She may learn to assist in dressing by raising her arm or leg. Some girls can learn to use augmentative devices to

I Need Answers

communicate. Despite their difficulties, girls and women with RS can continue to learn and enjoy family and friends well into middle age and beyond. They experience a full range of emotions and show their engaging personalities as they take part in social, educational, and recreational activities at home and in the community.

I never dreamed that dealing with Rett was going to be so hard and at the same time I can't imagine life without Amelia. I once asked my husband, "What is Amelia capable of? I don't know anymore," and Don replied, "love." I never knew what unconditional love was until Rett syndrome came through our door.

IS ANY TREATMENT AVAILABLE?

CURRENTLY, TREATMENT IS PALLIATIVE, including drugs aimed at treating the symptoms of RS for seizures, reflux, breathing, and mood. Other therapies are aimed at improving movement and function. These include physical and occupational therapy, music therapy, sensory integration therapy, hydrotherapy, and horseback therapy.

WHAT DRUGS HAVE BEEN TRIED IN RESEARCH TRIALS?

L-DOPA IS A SYNTHETIC FORM OF DOPAMINE. It has been found to improve rigidity during the motor deterioration stage (4), but otherwise failed to provide improvement on a consistent basis.

Naltrexone (Revia) is an opiate antagonist, used to alleviate the drug "high" in addicts. It was tried in RS due to the unusually high level of naturally occurring opium-like brain chemicals called endorphins in the spinal fluid of girls with RS and their diminished response to pain. The study was limited to the dose of 1 mg/kg/day and did not show dramatic results. However, independent studies have shown that use of naltrexone in higher or lower doses may be beneficial in controlling irregular breathing and seizures, and in alleviating screaming spells. This may be due to the drug's sedative effects. One negative aspect of the study was that performance on the Bayley Scales of Infant Development was significantly worse during the administration of the drug compared to placebo, also possibly due to its sedative effect. Another negative side effect is loss of appetite.

Bromocriptine (Parlodel) is a drug which improves the functioning of the dopamine system in the brain. One drug trial showed initial improvements in communication, decreased agitation, and reduced hand movements in the first phase; however, when the drug was stopped symptoms reappeared, and the reintroduction of the drug did not bring back the initial improvements. The drug was found to be most effective in those girls who had milder symptoms.

Tyrosine (dopamine and noradrenalin) and **Tryptophan** (serotonin) are amino acids, used to boost neurotransmitter levels. The study indicated no differences in clinical performance or EEG patterns.

L-Carnitine is a derivative of the essential amino acid lysine, and is often found to be deficient in those who take anticonvulsants. A single case report of one child indicated improvements in language and awareness. However, the child was atypical, and these results have not been replicated. In another study of thirty-five girls, carnitine supplements (100 mg/kg/day) did not lead to any major neurological improvements in the group as a whole. However, approximately seventy-five percent of the families involved in the study reported subtle but important improvements to their quality of life while on the

I Need Answers

drug, including increased alertness, increased mobility, less daytime sleeping, increased energy, and improvement in constipation. Some parents reported their daughter saying a word for the first time in a number of years. L-carnitine has been found beneficial in a large group of girls with RS in increasing muscle mass, energy, and strength. A beneficial side effect is loose stools.

Supplementation with **Folate** and **Betaine** was recently evaluated in a clinical trial, and studies revealed that those on the supplements were more alert, had better muscle tone, and fewer/shorter seizures than those on either Betaine alone or placebo. These supplements can now be used in open trials by having your doctor contact Dr. Alan Percy at the University of Alabama at Birmingham.

A study with **Folinic Acid** showed early promise in the original study, based on the finding of low levels of folate in CSF. In a large-scale follow-up study, CSF folate levels were normal. However, we can now tell parents with confidence that their daughters are unlikely to be suffering from folate deficiency, but that a multivitamin (Flintstones) which includes folic acid is a good idea.

WHAT IS LIFE EXPECTANCY?

WE EXPECT MOST GIRLS WITH RS to live well into the fourth decade at least.

WHAT ARE THE CAUSES OF DEATH?

IT IS IMPORTANT TO NOTE THAT ONLY SEVEN PERCENT of cases reported to the IRSA have resulted in death. This means that ninety-three percent of those diagnosed are still living, a few into their fifties and sixties. The most frequently reported causes of death (one-quarter of deaths) are variations of "sudden death" or "unexplained death," with no apparent underlying cause such as an acute injury or infection. The factors most strongly associated with an increased risk of sudden unexplained death in RS are uncontrolled seizures, swallowing difficulties and lack of mobility. Physical and occupational therapies, nutritional status, or living arrangements made no difference in the incidence of sudden unexplained death. Ongoing studies will help predict which girls are at greatest risk and which girls might benefit most from new medical or educational interventions.

The second leading cause of death is pneumonia. The factors most strongly associated with an increased risk of death by pneumonia are compromised lung function due to scoliosis and difficulty swallowing.

Other causes of death include malnutrition, intestinal perforation or twisted bowel, as well as accidents and illness.

WHAT CAN WE DO TO HELP FIND ANSWERS?

ALTHOUGH SHE MAY BE AT HIGHER RISK for life-threatening events such as pneumonia, choking, and seizures, it is very likely that your daughter will live a long life. However, we are all at risk for accidents of many types and illnesses that are unexpected. A time will come when we will all die. Researchers are ready to listen, to learn, and to share. You can participate in research studies that will help us understand RS. Please consider participating in autopsy research, which can be her lasting legacy and the ultimate gift of help and hope to thousands of families.

I Need Answers

WHERE DO WE GO FROM HERE?

GETTING THE DIAGNOSIS OF RETT SYNDROME is difficult, but there are many people who are willing to help you, beginning with IRSA. Here are a few places to start:

- Join IRSA. You will be subscribed to Rettnet, our online discussion group, and you will receive the Rett Gazette and other materials. Annual conferences and local seminars will bring you the information you need. Support is available at our 1-800-818-RETT crisis hotline. You can be sure that IRSA will fund only the highest quality research and will advocate for increased federal funds in the halls of Congress. As the 2002 Child Neurology Foundation's Advocacy Group of Merit Award winner, IRSA is deeply committed to a three-part mission of research, awareness and family support. We exist to help you.

- Take the time you need to grieve. Feeling depressed and overwhelmed is very natural. Find a grief counselor who is familiar with special needs families.

- Reach out to others who share your Rett journey. IRSA can help you find others in your area.

- Make sure your child's medical team is knowledgeable about Rett syndrome. IRSA can help provide information and can refer you to the nearest specialist.

- Find out what educational services are available for your child. Call the special education department of your local school system.

- Seek out information about financial assistance programs. Call the public health department, social work department of a local children's hospital, your Developmental Disabilities Administration, or local ARC.

- Take care of yourself so that you will be able to better care for your child.

- Don't try to plan for a lifetime in one day.

- Remember that you are not alone.

- Read this book, beginning now.

When we learned that our daughter had RS, we found IRSA and that helped us a lot. We began to share our experiences and we learned a lot from parents who walked the Rett road before. It filled our solitude and gave us support. Our tears turned into a fortress to help our daughter to live better.

"A strong positive mental attitude will create more miracles than any wonder drug."

– PATRICIA NEAL

Atypical Rett Syndrome

"Everybody is individually different."

– SEBASTIAN BACH

THE TERM "ATYPICAL" is sometimes confused with "a typical." However, the opposite is true. The definition for atypical is "not typical." These are individuals who do not completely fulfill the criteria for Classic RS, yet have many of the characteristics and often have a *MECP2* mutation.

About twenty percent of those with the diagnosis of RS have symptoms that are either milder or more severe than classic cases and are considered atypical. Think of it as a continuum of involvement from less severe to very severe with the great majority, those with the Classic form, being in the middle.

Types of atypical RS include:

Congenital Onset RS: developmental delay is noticed shortly after birth and there is no early normal development; or seizures begin before the regression period

Late Onset RS: signs are delayed beyond the typical eighteen-month onset, in some cases to three or four years

Preserved Speech and Hand Skills RS: milder, incomplete symptoms are seen, with age of onset at three to four years

Male RS: boys may not conform to the same symptoms seen in girls. Boys with a *MECP2* mutation most often have a more debilitating condition than girls with an earlier and more severe onset, and do not meet the diagnostic criteria for the diagnosis of RS. However, if a boy happens to have an extra X chromosome (XXY makeup, known as Klinefelter), he may have Classic RS. Still, there are other males with a different kind of *MECP2* mutation who have severe mental retardation and none of the diagnostic criteria for RS.

CONGENITAL ONSET RS

UNLIKE GIRLS WITH CLASSIC RS, girls with Congenital RS may not develop enough skills to really have much to lose in regression. Their development may have slowed down or regressed very early on, and they never develop the ability to sit alone or bear weight, and have little or no purposeful hand skills. They are most often misdiagnosed with cerebral palsy.

It is important to recognize the emerging number of girls (and boys) with mutations in the cyclin-dependent kinase-like 5 gene (*CDKL5*) at Xp22. These children have a severe clinical picture, especially with infantile spasms, and they may resemble those with RS. A test for the CDKL5 mutation is available and should be considered when the clinical picture is very severe and a mutation has not been found in the *MECP2* gene.

We noticed extraordinary delays and had concerns over Olivia right from birth. At three weeks, we took her to the pediatrician to see if all was okay because she never cried to that point. She never moved. She did nurse beautifully. Other than that, she was already choking. Then as time passed, Livvy was not sitting, not babbling or cooing; simply nothing that seemed to be occurring with her twin. As time passed, Livvy didn't sit on her own, never crawled, never pulled to stand, only spoke, "Mama", unable to eat solids or drink without choking. Then, at seven

Atypical Rett Syndrome

months of age we began PT. Over a period of three or four months the therapist noted dramatic decline and regression and wrote a letter to the pediatrician. Then we began neurological consultations directly at ten months of age.

Ellie never really reached major milestones. She doesn't sit, crawl, or walk independently. She has a very hard time eating and has seizures. She has a slight case of scoliosis, wrings, and chews on her hands most of the time. But, Ellie never showed much autistic symptoms and she has always been very social and just loves to interact with people.

We began noticing delays around three-four months. Allison never crawled or walked and had very low muscle tone. She could sit around nine months until about four years. Then, she completely lost the ability to sit on her own. At seven, she has regained a bit of this, but only sitting for a minute or two before losing her balance. She never was able to get to the sitting position on her own. With intense speech therapy she had a vocabulary of thirty-forty words. She now pretty much only says "Mom."

LATE ONSET RS

GIRLS WITH LATE ONSET RS MAY NOT ONLY WALK, but run. They are often misdiagnosed with autism or PDD (Pervasive Developmental Delay) before the diagnosis of Atypical RS is given.

Beatriz can use her hands, and she walks, runs and can communicate. Physically, she has no limits. She eats by herself, and she asks for what she needs. She is in a regular school in a special classroom with four other children who need special care. Her regression was very late, from three to four years old. Now, she is seven and she is very active. She has the MECP2 mutation and does the Rett hand movements, but she can do almost everything that typical children are able to do if she is motivated.

Amy was five years old before she was diagnosed as mentally retarded or autistic. She could count to ten when she was three. She could snap her fingers and ride a tricycle. She could punch her older brother. She did not talk a lot, but had an age-appropriate vocabulary. She leveled off at about age five and a very slow hand wringing and regression began. Her speech became more difficult over the years, slowly decreasing. Today, at thirty-five, she can express herself and ask for things. She can point at objects and name them. She remembers people from her early educational years and will call them by name. She can speak, but she will stall, stutter and stammer sometimes before she gets a word out. At other times, she will let fly with a complete sentence without any effort.

At age four, Maria was only showing little signs and was still speaking five-six word sentences. She had good hand use. Over the past year, she has lost most of her speech and hand functions, but still has many of the wonderful qualities of an atypical child. When she calls out "Mommy and Daddy," it makes our hearts smile. She still bounces with such strength on her trampoline, and our hopes are that her ability to run and jump will never fade.

Rachel was four when diagnosed and the only strong indicator that she had something wrong was her inability to speak. Now at seven, she has emotional outbursts and sleep disturbances, but she has a fairly steady gait, can use her hands and has a very deliberate finger point accompanied by an "ah" to indicate when she wants something. Sporadically, she does say words and likenesses of words and her comprehension always amazes us and her caregivers. She is an average size for her age, and she does not have an abnormal head size. She loves water and can water jog better than I can. She learned how to ride her bike at school last year (with training wheels) and she loves that freedom. Her other big accomplishments are that she can swing and does not need a push to keep going and she can even manage a little ice skating. Her sense of balance is quite good.

Besides Katie's strong physical abilities, both gross and fine motor, she has learned her colors, numbers, letters and her name, just to name a few things. She has learned to use the bathroom, and she shows preference for things, letting me know quickly if I've chosen the wrong thing for her. At four, she began to have seizures, and

Atypical Rett Syndrome

this is when she temporarily lost her hand skills for eating and drinking and playing with toys. She lost her babbling at this time too. When we got the seizures under control, we taught her to use her spoon again, stack toys, drink from a cup, sort objects, push a cart, etc. There are a few things that didn't come back, like the ability to scribble or color, pull a pull-toy, for instance. By six, she was independent once again with her eating, and to this day, we still have her in intense programs to learn her daily living skills, and she continues to maintain the skills that she already had.

PRESERVED SPEECH AND HAND SKILLS RS

GIRLS WITH PRESERVED SPEECH have some verbal language and may even be able to answer questions in phrases. Often, they have better purposeful hand skills and may or may not have higher academic skills.

Katie talks. Most of the time, we understand what she is saying. She does not like to answer direct questions and her answers are sometimes incorrect. We might ask what she had for lunch and she would say "Hardees" and smile. We know she had lunch at school. Katie will break her handwringing to use her hands to play or color.

Molly is three and has always had great eye contact. She is saying about ten new words a month. The words are always appropriate to the situation, but not consistent. She is quite tall and has normal hand and feet growth, but she does have a slight decline in her head size. Molly is almost able to run and she has almost complete use of her hands. She can use a pincer grip but prefers an open grasp. She can help pull her clothes off and pull her pants up and down when she goes potty. Molly is able to grasp but still needs help to actually pull up her pants.

Megan can speak in four to eight-word sentences and she can say anything she wants when she wants to. She is a healthy seven year-old topping the scale at seventy-five pounds. She is very active, and loves to swing and watch "Barney."

MALE RS

Cole, five, has an older sister with RS. Both children have the MECP2 mutation. There was little movement during Cole's pregnancy, and he was in immediate respiratory distress at birth. He was first diagnosed with Failure to Thrive and got a G button and fundoplication at one year. He has no handwringing. He can reach but cannot grasp. He does not have breathholding or hyperventilation, but does have frequent episodes of respiratory distress. He has always had a slow heart rhythm. He suffers from frequent infections and has from three-four hospitalizations each year.

Jaycob has an XXY chromosomal pattern (Klinefelters) and also has the MECP2 mutation. He is nonverbal. He is able to walk, but his gait is stiff and awkward. He does hand-clapping.

Timmy was born with many severe neurological problems. He is now three and still does no more than a newborn. He does not have head control and has many seizures. He uses a G-button. He has very little muscle tone.

BEING IN THE MINORITY OF A RARE DISEASE

PARENTS OFTEN FIND THE DIAGNOSIS OF ATYPICAL RS confusing and bewildering. Having a child with a rare disorder to begin with is tough, but when her symptoms are seen only in a small number of girls, it is hard to find others whose children are similar. Parents of children with Classic RS may envy the atypical child's accomplishments and unwittingly minimize the family's grief or ignore them because their children are higher functioning and they consider these families fortunate.

It is important to remember that pain is not a competitive sport. Children with Atypical RS present their own difficult challenges. Many girls are hyperactive and require constant

Atypical Rett Syndrome

monitoring to keep them safe. Teachers and therapists often do not have enough information about Atypical RS, and throw up their arms in frustration about what kind of programming they need.

When Laina was first diagnosed with Rett, there was very little on Atypical RS. The parents are always confused because we see girls with typical Rett and read the information on Rett and then look at our daughters and shake our heads. Sometimes when I go to Rett groups, I feel like we don't "fit" into the group. Our daily frustrations and problems are much different from families who deal with the typical Rett child.

DIAGNOSTIC CRITERIA FOR ATYPICAL RS

Inclusion criteria
1. meet at least three of six main criteria
2. meet at least five of eleven supportive criteria

Six main criteria
1. absence or reduction of hand skills
2. reduction or loss of babble speech
3. monotonous pattern to hand stereotypies
4. reduction or loss of communication skills
5. deceleration of head growth from first years of life
6. RS disease profile: a regression stage followed by a recovery of interaction contrasting with slow neuromotor regression

Eleven supportive criteria
1. breathing irregularities
2. bloating/air swallowing
3. teeth grinding, harsh-sounding type
4. abnormal locomotion
5. scoliosis/kyphosis
6. lower limb wasting
7. cold, purplish feet, usually growth impaired
8. sleep disturbances including night screaming outbursts
9. laughing/screaming spells
10. diminished response to pain
11. intense eye contact/eye pointing

PROGRAMMING FOR THE ATYPICAL INDIVIDUAL

A WELL-KNOWN SPECIAL educator said, "We have grown heartbreakingly comfortable with the notion that educational success for students with disabilities is more related to the characteristics of the disability itself than to the way that supports are provided to the students." There is a tendency to want to believe that if we know the diagnosis, we will know what to do. If the diagnosis is vague, we continue searching until we get the right one,

Atypical Rett Syndrome

thinking that we will know what to do. However, even for children with very specific labels, it's not the label that helps but rather an understanding of each individual's unique characteristics, the supports necessary, and a belief in success. The RS label should not be used to determine intervention. All individuals with RS are different, and the information found in other chapters of this book should be applied as they relate to the child's individual characteristics. Every child should have a good educational evaluation and assessment of her needs and skills, a good curriculum and related services, and literacy opportunities.

There is no set-in-concrete program for any girl with RS, Classic or Atypical. Suggestions are made for types of therapy and helpful educational approaches but in the end, each child requires her own program tailored to her own strengths and weaknesses. Most therapists and educators are more familiar with girls diagnosed with Classic RS, and may question the diagnosis in a girl who is lower or higher functioning.

Programming for a child with a more severe case of RS may resemble that of a child with cerebral palsy (CP), putting more emphasis on physical therapy and taking into consideration the problems of latency and apraxia with education and communication. Severe physical symptoms may not correlate with severe cognitive deficits, so it is important to also provide a program that is stimulating and not just repetition.

For the higher functioning child, programming may include a modified Applied Behavior Analysis (ABA) approach and activities commonly used with the autistic population.

The fact remains that on both ends of the severity scale and in between, the kind of educational and therapeutic program depends on the child. It calls for creativity and resourcefulness by parents, educators and therapists.

CASE HISTORIES

Emily has an atypical diagnosis and is in the third grade. She receives speech, OT consult and PT. She is currently attending a regular education third grade for morning time, reading (listening comprehension, writing, grammar) science, social studies. She is completing the third grade work in that class with a paraprofessional to help her communicate with a Step by Step switch. We are making no adaptations to the materials except to read things to her. Emily knows some sight words, but I am having a hard time finding out which ones because she is inconsistent and gets bored easily. She completes her math goals in the multiple disability support room. She is working on telling time to the half hour and the quarter hour and on addition and subtraction. Emily also works on the computer in my room using two-step switch scanning and the Intellitools software.

The programs that have helped Laina have been all designed primarily for children with autism and they just change it a little for Laina. Laina has always been in a classroom with autistic children. She has always been the only child with RS and the lowest functioning in the class, but the autistic kids seem to be the most like her and can be good role models for what she is learning. Applied Behavioral Analysis (ABA) and Discrete Trial Training (DTT) have worked best for Laina. She learns primarily through constant repetition. We use a lot of Picture Exchange Communication Symbols (PECS) and switches for communication and have had successful results from timed potty training.

Hannah has maintained most of her motor skills. She has a very hard time cognitively, mainly with letters and numbers. We are able to have her spell/write her name if we use a hand pressure/grasp around or under her four fingers. She tends to take up the whole sheet of paper if we don't assist her. We give her the pressure on the top of the hand and support under her fingers and she is still able to move her hand on her own to form the letters.

Rachel is in a full inclusion program with a one-to-one aide. Through her Individual Educational Plan (IEP), we laid out goals for toileting, speech and physical activities. In her first year, she learned to ride her bike before

Atypical Rett Syndrome

Christmas, far exceeding the goal of pedaling twenty feet before the end of the school year! This year Rachel has a bit more of a structured program so that she has a familiar routine to follow. She will participate with the class when she can for activities like gym, music, recess, and field trips but will mirror activities which require more cognitive work. So when the class is doing a spelling test, Rachel may go work on the computer to work on "stop and go" or "up and down" type concepts. She also works on dexterity of hand use by threading beads and putting together and taking apart connecting beads. She also has dowels identified by color so that she can thread flowers of the same color onto like dowels. Rachel's speech therapy has moved away from the formation of spoken words to photo matching and an activity board as she has a good point and can more easily indicate her wishes. Her assistant has also made a board of the photos of all of her classmates so that she can help with roll call in the morning. She can collect and distribute papers, but she is only given one at a time for distribution as she may just spontaneously throw them to the floor. When she is showing signs of fatigue or restlessness, there is an activity room where she can go and relax, listen to music or just burn excess energy by bouncing on a rebounder or ball. At school, they use objects she can grasp instead of pictures, e.g., to show us the color blue, she would grab a big blue cup. Also, they make her use words instead of pictures for communication in trying to preserve what she has. She has also gained words. She is also starting to parrot language again.

"Respect for the fragility and importance of an individual life is still the mark of an educated man."

— NORMAN COUSINS

The Nervous System

TO UNDERSTAND RS, it is necessary to understand the nervous system, which is the body's message and information center. The nervous system is made up of three parts, the central nervous system (brain and spinal cord), the peripheral nervous system, and the autonomic nervous system. Each part controls some aspect of our behavior and affects how we experience the world.

"Nothing in life is to be feared. It is only to be understood."

– MARIE CURIE

THE CENTRAL NERVOUS SYSTEM

THE CENTRAL NERVOUS SYSTEM (CNS) begins to form during third week of pregnancy into the three basic regions of the brain: the cerebral hemispheres, the brain stem, and the cerebellum. The cerebral hemispheres are located on top of the brain stem, and the cerebellum lies behind it. The cerebellum is still immature at birth. By the fourth month of pregnancy, the brain, although small, looks structurally much as it does at birth. But very dynamic changes are taking place within the structure of the brain cells.

Nerve cells, called *neurons,* make up the basic structure of the nervous system. Each neuron has a cell body containing a *nucleus,* and material called *cytoplasm.* Each neuron has a single long fiber extending from the cell body, called an *axon,* and many shorter branch-like limbs known as *dendrites.* Axons carry impulses away from the cell body, while dendrites receive impulses from other neurons and carry them to the cell body.

The nerve cells of the mature cerebral hemispheres are arranged in six layers. The number and complexity of these nerve cell layers increase as the brain grows. The nerve cell bodies migrate from the bottom layer toward the top and spread their projections as they move. If these nerve cell bodies do not move at the right time and make normal connections with other neurons, there can be resulting developmental delay or abnormality.

The brain and spinal cord are separated into two different regions. The *gray matter* contains bundles of nerve cell bodies and their dendrites and appears grayish in color. The *white matter* is made up of axons which are covered by an insulating material called *myelin.* This myelin coating is developed mainly after birth and aids the rapid conduction of nerve impulses. The dendrites also increase in number and complexity during the first two years of life.

The *neuronal signal* is passed from one neuron to the next across a space or synapse. The axon of one neuron is almost touching the dendrite or cell body of another neuron but there is a space to be bridged. This bridge is achieved by the release of chemicals called *neurotransmitters.* A neuron can release one or more of these neurotransmitters and different neurons may release different neurotransmitters. Neurotransmitters are stored in packets called vesicles and released into the synaptic space when a neuron is sufficiently excited and an electrical signal called an action potential reaches the axonal terminal.

Neurotransmitters can be *excitatory* (e.g. glutamate) or *inhibitory* (e.g. GABA, glycine) to other neurons or have direct effects on muscles, glands, organs, and blood vessels (e.g.,

The Nervous System

acetylcholine, dopamine, norepinephrine). The effects of the transmitter are mediated by specific receptors at the other end of the synapse in the receiving neuron or cell. A receptor can have different subtypes so that a neurotransmitter such as acetylcholine can have a very different action in different places depending on which subtype of its receptor it binds to. These chemicals are found in packets at the edge of the axon, called the *presynaptic membrane*. When they are stimulated by an electrical impulse, the packets open and release the chemical, which then crosses the synaptic space where it stimulates the receptive neuron at its *postsynaptic receptor*.

The brain and spinal cord make up the central nervous system. All parts of the brain work together to achieve various behaviors but they each have their own special characteristics and functions. The brain can be divided into three basic regions known as the *forebrain*, the *midbrain* and the *hindbrain*.

The hindbrain consists of the upper part of the spinal cord, the brain stem and the cerebellum. It controls the body's vital functions like heart rate and breathing. The midbrain lies above the hindbrain, and it controls some reflex actions and movements. The forebrain consists of the cerebrum and the structures hidden beneath it. It is the largest and most developed part of the human brain.

CEREBRUM

WHEN PEOPLE SEE DRAWINGS OF THE BRAIN, they usually notice the *cerebrum*. It sits at the top of the brain stem and is the source of intellectual activities such as memory, imagination, planning and thinking. The cerebrum is the largest region of the brain, consisting of two parts joined together in the middle by the tough tissue of the *corpus callosum*. Although the cerebrum is split in two halves, its two parts (hemispheres) communicate with each other. The two hemispheres look exactly alike, but they are very different in the functions they control. For example, the left hemisphere controls the ability to form words, while the right hemisphere seems to control many abstract reasoning skills. Both hemispheres are divided into four lobes.

The *frontal lobe* is located in the front (anterior) third of the hemisphere. It participates in voluntary muscle movement and in memory skills. *Broca's area*, located on the left frontal lobe, allows thoughts to be transformed into words. The *occipital lobe* lies in the back (posterior) fourth of each hemisphere. It processes images from the eyes and links this information with images stored in memory, then passes them to the *parietal lobe*. The parietal lobe sits in the middle-upper part of the cerebrum. It integrates sensory stimuli such as vision, auditory, touch, pain, smell, and temperature sensations so that they can be interpreted. The *temporal lobe* occupies the lower-middle area. Its main function is to regulate communication and sensation, while other parts of this lobe integrate memories and sensations of taste, sound, sight, and touch.

In early pregnancy, the surface of the cerebrum is very smooth but as the brain grows, indentations appear. By birth, the surface has become very rugged, with crevices (*sulci*) and bumps (*gyri*). The brain region which lies just underneath the surface of the cerebrum is called the *cerebral cortex*. It is made up mostly of nerve cell bodies, or gray matter. The cortex is gray because the nerves in this area do not have the insulation that makes most other parts of the brain appear white. The folds in the brain increase its surface area and the amount of information that can be processed. Just below the gray matter, nerve fibers, or white matter, are found. The cerebral cortex is the area of the brain which controls motion and thought, and may regulate some effects of the brain stem.

The Nervous System

Other structures which lie deep within the brain and hidden from view control emotions, perceptions, responses, and integrated muscle movement. The *hypothalamus* contains several important centers which control body temperature, thirst, hunger and eating, water balance and sexual function, emotional activity and sleep. The *thalamus* is a clearinghouse for information to and from the spinal cord and the cerebrum. The *hippocampus* sends memories out to the appropriate part of the cerebral hemisphere for storage and retrieval. The *basal ganglia* modulate motion and thought, and regulate the effects of the brain stem. Involuntary movements such as dystonia and chorea are the result of basal ganglia dysfunction. In addition to the basal ganglia, the *labyrinth* in the inner ear and the *cerebellum* are also involved in movements. These parts acting together provide a series of checks and balances for motor activities and balance.

CEREBELLUM

THE *CEREBELLUM* LIES JUST BELOW the cerebral hemispheres and hangs behind the brain stem. It coordinates the action of the voluntary muscles, allowing movements to be smooth and accurate. The cerebellum coordinates learned (rote) movements. When the cerebellum does not work properly, a condition called *ataxia* results in jerky, uncoordinated movements.

BRAIN STEM

THE BRAIN STEM (*MEDULLA, PONS, AND MIDBRAIN*) connects the two hemispheres of the brain to the spinal cord. It contains cranial nerves which control important body functions such as breathing, heart rhythm, swallowing, sleep, bowel and gall bladder motility, circulation, taste, salivation, and sensitivity to pain, vision and hearing, facial expression and eye and tongue movement. Dysfunction of the brain stem can lead to problems in any of these areas.

SPINAL CORD

THE *SPINAL CORD* EXTENDS FROM THE BRAIN STEM to the lower back in a cylindrical structure, which is surrounded by three layers of covering called *dura* and *meninges*. The cervical (neck) area and the lumbar (lower back) area are enlarged to enable the peripheral nerve fibers to leave the spinal cord and go to the arms, legs, and body organs. If the spinal cord is injured, motor and sensory messages are interrupted, which results in loss of sensation and movement.

CEREBROSPINAL FLUID

THE *CEREBROSPINAL FLUID* IS REFERRED TO AS CSF. It is a clear, watery liquid that surrounds and protects the spinal cord and the brain and flows through the four ventricles of the brain. It prevents sudden pressure changes within the brain and is constantly recirculated.

MOTOR SYSTEMS

IN ORDER FOR THOUGHTFUL MOVEMENT TO TAKE PLACE, nerve impulses are carried by the pyramidal tract from the motor cortex to motor neurons in the brain stem or spinal cord. The motor neurons then project out to the muscles via cranial and spinal nerves. This *motor pathway* involves only two sets or neurons (pyramidal tract

The Nervous System

neurons and motor neurons) and so is called the *direct pathway*. Effective motor function, however, requires not only activation of this direct motor pathway, but also the preparation of muscles for activity, coordination of activity within muscles and between muscles, and the integration of sensory and motor activity. This involves several other "indirect" motor pathways and brain structures including the cerebellum, basal ganglia, and *red nucleus*. In RS, there appears to be both a lack of effective activation of the direct pathway as well as less effective sensory-motor integration and coordination.

SENSORY SYSTEMS

SENSORY SYSTEMS PROVIDE INFORMATION on the external environment to the brain. Spinal and cranial nerves carry information from external receptors on modalities such as touch, pain, joint position, muscle tone, as well as the special senses (e.g. vision, hearing, taste, smell, balance) into the central nervous system. Sensory information is processed, used in reflexes, in sensory-motor integration and when it gets to the sensory cortex, reaches our consciousness.

THE AUTONOMIC NERVOUS SYSTEM

THE AUTONOMIC NERVOUS SYSTEM CONTROLS automatic body functions such as heartbeat and respiratory, digestive, endocrine, urinary and reproductive functions. The nerve impulses can begin in either the brain stem or spinal cord and spread toward the organs. In RS, many functions regulated by the autonomic nervous system are improperly controlled, irregular or erratic, such as breathing, sleep, salivation, heart rate, swallowing, bowel motility, and vasomotor control. These problems will be discussed at length in the chapter on day-to-day care.

The autonomic nervous system is important in a classic situation known as the *"fight or flight"* response. When we are frightened, several physiological responses take place at the same time. The heartbeat quickens, blood pressure increases, pupils dilate, bronchioles of the lungs expand, and the function of the digestive system nearly stops as blood is redirected to the brain and muscles, allowing us to react to the situation.

The activities of the heart and lungs are influenced by nerve cells in the brain stem. They form part of the autonomic nervous system which supplies the digestive tract and blood vessels everywhere in the body. The autonomic nervous system is made up of two parts. The *sympathetic nervous system* raises blood pressure and heart rate (pulse) to cope with sudden challenges. When the sympathetic system is stimulated, we become excited, red-faced and alert, ready for "fight or flight." At the same time, the *parasympathetic nervous system* acts like a natural brake to keep the sympathetic system from excessive effects.

THE BRAIN IN RETT SYNDROME

THE BRAIN IN RS HAS BEEN INVESTIGATED by various techniques including imaging studies: CAT, MRI, PET, ultrasound, measurements of cerebral blood flow; neurophysiologic studies: EEG, visual, motor and auditory evoked response; classic neuropathology studies: light and electron microscopy and immunocytochemistry; neurochemical studies: mass spectroscopy, tissue autoradiography, and Western blotting. Function has been studied using neuropsychological evaluations and analysis of home movies. The morphology, chemistry, and function of the Rett brain have been considered in relationship

The Nervous System

to time and to the non-Rett brain. From a combination of all of this information a concept of the brain in Rett syndrome has evolved:

> *The pathologic process in Rett syndrome is a failure of neuronal maturation, involving the structural, chemical, and functional aspects of maturation. In Classic Rett syndrome there are subtle, but nonspecific signs of the disorder at birth, which become more recognizable as the child reaches time periods of critical brain development. Some brain regions seem to be selectively involved.*

Neuronal Maturation

THE PERIPHERAL, CENTRAL, AND AUTONOMIC nervous systems are all derived from neural stem cells. These cells, regulated by specific sets of genes, undergo processes of differentiation into specific cell types, migration to designated brain regions, and maturation into the types of neurons that are required for their position and function in the nervous system. A neuron matures in its structure by developing a *cytoskeleton*, an *axon*, and *dendrites* with branches. Functional maturation of each neuron is attained through synaptic contact of axons and dendrites with those of other neurons. This synaptic contact is essential for the normal continuity of development and function.

In RS, there is evidence that some neurons in many brain regions do not mature completely. There is a deficiency of proteins associated with a mature cytoskeleton; there are a reduced number of dendritic branches; the sites for synaptic contact (*spines*) are reduced; the neurons are small and there is an abnormality, possibly an immaturity, of cellular neurochemistry. This population of immature neurons results in a small brain with a profound functional deficit that reflects neuronal immaturity.

The following paragraphs enumerate some specific observations about neuronal immaturity of the Rett brain in general and within the functional domains of the nervous system.

The Rett brain is 30 percent smaller than normal (for age and height) and it does not decrease in volume with time. In RS, there is no identifiable ongoing pathologic process similar to those usually associated with a severe generalized neurological disorder. These include malformations of brain development, storage diseases, demyelinating diseases, inflammatory or neoplastic processes, and degenerative diseases.

There is increased neuronal cell packing density. That is, the cell bodies of neurons are closer together than they are in a non-Rett brain. *Neurons* (brain cells) are reduced in size and there is reduced branching of their processes, called dendrites.

The gray matter of the cortex is made up of columns of neurons with their processes. These minicolumns are reduced in size in RS.

The number of synapses (connections between neurons) in RS is approximately one-half the normal number.

ABNORMALITIES AND CLINICAL SYMPTOMS IN RS

ABNORMALITIES IN MULTIPLE AREAS OF THE BRAIN may account for the following clinical symptoms:

Frontal lobe: The cerebral blood flow is reduced and resembles that of a seven week old infant. Dendrites of pyramidal neurons are reduced. This brain region is involved in mood and emotion.

Caudate nucleus: This is smaller than normal. It is involved in movement.

The Nervous System

Temporal lobe *(limbic system):* There are reduced numbers of dendrites in some gyri of the temporal lobe. It is involved in memory, learning, emotion, and behavior.

Cerebellum: This part of the brain is small, but it is less reduced in size than the cerebrum. With age there is some nonspecific cerebellar atrophy. The cerebellum is involved in equilibrium, balance, fine motor control, and motor memory.

Hippocampus: There is a reduced neuronal size and an increase in neuronal packing density. This is necessary for information processing.

Substantia nigra: This exhibits a reduction of neuromelanin in selected neurons. It is involved in regulation of movement.

Medulla *(Brain stem):* There is evidence of a chemical and functional immaturity in the brain stem involving the autonomic nervous system and affecting sleep, salivation, breathing, heart rate, swallowing, bowel motility, blood circulation in hands and feet, and sensitivity to pain.

Neurotransmitter systems: Many neurotransmitter systems show alterations from normal; 1) dopamine which is necessary in parts of the brain required for movement and critical thinking; 2) acetylcholine which is necessary for memory, cognition, and movement control; 3) glutamate which is necessary for brain plasticity and excitatory communication. Abnormalities of glutamate can be associated with seizures and cell death; 4) substance P which is required for pain recognition and modulation of brain stem function, and; 5) serotonin which is essential in early brain development and in the function of many autonomic control centers.

Olfactory system: This system normally continues to mature throughout life. Studies of the olfactory receptor epithelium in RS have identified a delay of neuronal maturation.

Genetics: The *MECP2* gene is one of the genes involved in the process of neuronal maturation. It is mutated in most cases of RS, and in Classic RS (in which there is random X-inactivation) one-half of the neurons contain a mutated *MECP2* gene and one half of the neurons contain a normal *MECP2* gene. The neurons with a *MECP2* mutation do not completely mature and there is evidence that the neurons with the non-mutated gene are also developmentally affected by the population of abnormal immature neurons. The Rett brain is the complex product of this process of incomplete neuronal maturation and this is the process that must now be defined so that therapies can be devised. Read more in the genetics and research chapters.

"Our nervous system isn't just a fiction, it is a part of our physical body and our soul exists in space and inside us."

– BORIS PASTERNAK

Genetics

THIS CHAPTER GIVES some very basic information about DNA, genes, genetics, and inherited characteristics to help you sort through some of the later information on research. For those of you wishing to delve more fully into this topic, we recommend "DNA from the Beginning" at www.dnaftb.org/dnaftb as an excellent starting point.

Many people feel intimidated when they start to learn or, for some of you, re-familiarize yourselves with these scientific processes. While the "advanced" level courses can get pretty complex, the basics are straightforward and easier to understand than rules of English. That is because the "rules" of biology have far fewer exceptions than the "rules" of English. Take simple spelling, for example: How do you explain to a new learner of English that "C-O-W", "N-O-W" and "CH-O-W" sound different from "S-N-O-W", which sounds like "R-O-W"??? If, as a speaker of English you can work with those "rules," then the biology part will be a breeze.

"Biology has at least fifty more interesting years."

– JAMES D. WATSON

Understanding the basic rules of biology and genetics will help you to appreciate the many advances that are being made in research. These very rules are what scientists rely upon to understand how RS causes differences in the ordinarily very predicable behavior of DNA, genes, chromosomes and cells.

DEOXYRIBONUCLEIC ACID (DNA)

DNA IS THE ORGANIC SUBSTANCE that determines the individual and unique characteristics of all living things, from apples to zebras, and everything in between. That uniqueness is determined by the arrangement of four building blocks called bases. The bases have names: Adenine, Guanine, Cytosine and Thymine, or A, G, C, and T for short. The bases fit together in a certain way, and only in that way similar to the way a specific key fits a specific lock. In all living organisms found to date, the DNA bases bond together. You can think of the shape of DNA as a ladder. The bases form the rungs of a ladder and the sides of the ladder are just sugar and phosphate bonds which are twisted into the famous double helix shape that resides in every cell of every living thing. The only way the rungs will stay together is AT/TA base pairs and GC/CG base pairs, just like you cannot make puzzle pieces that aren't supposed to fit properly stick together well.

DNA is found in all nucleated cells. In humans, the DNA molecule is three billion base pairs long, and that long stretch of information is exactly the same in each of the thirty trillion cells active in a person's body at any given time. This long stretch of information is the instructions which tell the body to keep making you, your enzymes and proteins, your hair color, your ability to gain or lose weight. All of it is influenced by the instructions contained in your DNA. Those instructions are called your genome. If the three billion base pairs of information of your genome were printed out in standard size type on regular sized paper, you would have a book more than seven feet thick. That's how much information it takes to make you be you.

Genetics

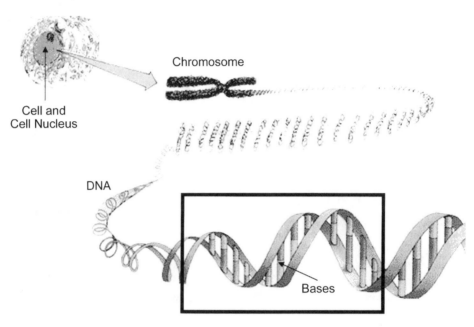

Illustration: Dr. John Butler

DNA in the Cell

It is scientific doctrine that no two people share the exact arrangement (whether you have an AT rung above a TA rung next to three sets of GC rungs, etc) of their DNA molecule, except, perhaps, identical twins. But it is also scientific dogma that the arrangement of DNA is exactly the same in every person in the world for 99.9% of the bases. How can both of these statements be true? The answer is in the numbers. What is left over from 99.9%? That little one-tenth of one percent of three billion base pairs is three million! So there are three million places in each person's DNA that allow for differences, while the other 99.9% is conservative for all human beings.

Overall, biology is a very conservative process. Each person must have the codes for proteins and enzymes that function properly or there will be significant consequences, but there is room for variability as well. There are traits that distinguish us visibly (phenotypic variation) such as hair, eye, and skin color, hair texture, height, and weight, and other traits that genetically distinguish us (genotypic variation), like ABO blood type, Rh factors, and organ transplant antibodies. It is the three million sites that allow this variability tucked between the 29,970,000,000 other bases, in little chunks here and there along the DNA ladder that allows both the statements to be true.

GENES AND CHROMOSOMES

THE CELLS OF HUMAN BEINGS CARRY THEIR DNA instructions in a set of 23 pairs of chromosomes, half of which came from the mother's egg and the other half from the father's sperm. The chromosomes are different sizes and shapes, but they are all made of DNA, packaged with some histone and non-histone proteins (biological "glue") in a particular way in each of the 46 chromosomes that make up the 23 pairs, like a tidy tool set in a busy machine shop, each there in the right place to be used when needed. Take the

Genetics

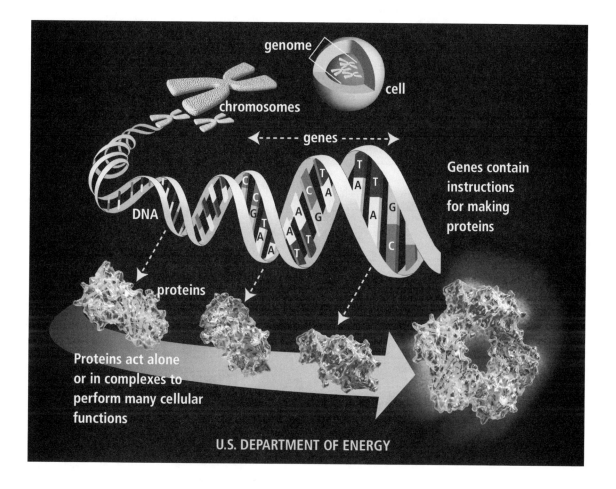

stretch of DNA which carries the instructions for the protein hemoglobin, necessary to bring oxygen to the blood, as an example. Before birth, there is a fetal hemoglobin that supplies oxygen to the baby in the womb. Once baby is "on deck," the type of hemoglobin needed is different. Fetal hemoglobin turns off and a transitional hemoglobin turns on. As the baby acclimates to life on earth, a mature form of hemoglobin is needed and the transitional form turns off while the mature form activates. Each form of hemoglobin is coded for by a different stretch along the three billion base pairs of the of DNA genome. Each stretch of DNA that codes for a different trait is what is called a *gene*.

Each and every nucleated cell in the body contains all 46 chromosomes, in their paired sets of 23, with the exception of the egg and sperm, which are special. They have gone through a particular kind of cell division that lets them wind up with only one copy of each chromosome in each cell, rather than the paired set contained in all the rest of the body cells. This is so that when egg and sperm meet and join together to make a baby, they don't increase the number of chromosomes in the child. (You want to end up with 23 + 23 = 46). Each child, therefore, inherits one copy of each chromosome, and therefore, one copy of each gene, from each parent. The reason your kids resemble you but aren't your, or their sibling's, identical "clone" is because of the way the 23 pairs are "dealt" to each child being made. Each has her own unique "hand" of 46 chromosomes. Remember, each chromosome carries lots and lots of genes, so each is responsible for many different traits!

Genetics

Genetically speaking, making a baby is just like playing cards, only the deck is a little different from the four of a kind deck that makes up our standard 52 card set for playing Poker or Go Fish. For this game, you and your child's other parent have a special deck of cards, each with pairs of cards from numbers 1-22 with the Mom having two queens and the Dad having a King and a Queen as their 23rd pair in their decks, for a total deck of 46 cards needed to play (see illustration). In the great card game of life, each parent must give one of each pair of every "hand" that is played (every time you make a child), but which one of each pair can be different each time you play a "hand."

X AND Y CHROMOSOMES

THE SPECIAL PAIR OF CHROMOSOMES that determine gender are called X and Y. To get a girl, the sperm and the egg both carried the X chromosome (so that girls have two XXs). For a boy, the sperm carried a Y and the egg an X (so that boys have an XY genotype). X chromosomes are very different from Y chromosomes. They are big and contain thousands of genes. Y chromosomes are about one-fourth the size of X chromosomes.

The Great Card Game of LIFE

Mom's Hand		Dad's Hand			Baby	
1♥	1♦	1♥	1♣		1♦	1♣
2♦	2♦	2♦	2♠		2♦	2♦
3♥	3♠	3♠	3♠		3♠	3♥
4♣	4♦	4♣	4♠		4♦	4♠
5♥	5♠	5♥	5♠	One card from each parent =	5♠	5♠
6♣	6♦	6♥	6♥		6♣	6♥
7♠	7♣	7♥	7♦		7♠	7♦
8♥	8♦	8♦	8♦		8♥	8♦
9♠	9♦	9♠	9♣		9♠	9♣
10♣	10♣	10♥	10♥		10♣	10♥
11♠	11♦	11♦	11♣		11♠	11♣
12♠	12♠	12♠	12♥		12♠	12♥
13♦	13♣	13♦	13♣		13♦	13♣
14♦	14♦	14♠	14♥		14♦	14♠
15♣	15♦	15♠	15♥		15♣	15♥
16♠	16♣	16♣	16♥		16♣	16♥
17♥	17♥	17♣	17♣		17♥	17♣
18♦	18♠	18♣	18♦		18♦	18♦
19♠	19♣	19♦	19♥		19♣	19♦
20♥	20♥	20♦	20♣		20♥	20♣
21♠	21♦	21♠	21♥		21♦	21♥
22♣	22♦	22♠	22♦		22♦	22♦
Q♠	Q♥	Q♦	K♣		Q♥	Q♦

It's a Girl!!!!

Genetics

X-INACTIVATION AND SEVERITY

SO THAT FEMALES DON'T END UP WITH TWO "ACTIVE" COPIES of all those genes on the X, one gets shut down in each cell. Extra chromosomes can cause just as many difficulties as missing information, as in the case of Down syndrome, where an extra chromosome 21 causes multiple medical and cognitive problems. Nature has figured out a way to keep females from having too much information from their double dose of X chromosomes. Shortly after fertilization of the egg with the sperm, while there are still just a thousand or so cells, each cell "decides" to turn off one copy of the X. In most cases, this is a random event. For females, each with two copies of the X chromosome in every cell, this means that in one cell the X from Mom might be turned off or inactivated, while in the next cell the X from Dad might turned off. As each of these cells continue to divide and give rise to new cells, only the activated X in that cell line is used by the next generation of cells. They don't turn on or activate the other copy again.

The fur color of cats gives an excellent example of how X-inactivation occurs to change the patterns we can see. For cats, fur color is coded by several genes on the X chromosome. Only female cats can be tortoiseshell or calico cats, because only females have two X chromosomes (male tri-color cats are the result of a genetic misfire and have an XXY genotype, so they are sterile, see below). The splotches of three different fur colors in a tortoiseshell or a calico occur because the different cells of the cat have randomly turned off either the X inherited from the father cat or the X inherited from the mother cat. But since luck determines which will be turned off in any particular cell, tortoiseshell or calico cats have the "luck" to have a line of cells each arising from one of the three separate colors available. Since males have only one X chromosome, it is active in *all* of their cells, so their coat color is evenly distributed. Either one color or solid sets of stripes, but not the mottled or splotchy patches seen in tortoiseshell or calico cats.

The phenomenon of X-inactivation has been known for a long time. The process happens in early embryonic development and is considered a random event. If, however, one of the X chromosomes contains a gene that has a mutation or change which interferes with the normal function or division of cells with that X active, these cells are selected against during development. As a result, tissues may be made up mostly if cells in which

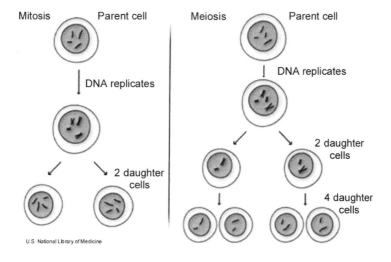

U.S. National Library of Medicine

Genetics

one X chromosome is preferentially inactivated. This is called *skewing* of the X inactivation pattern, About ten percent of women have non-random (skewed) X inactivation.

These are terms used to describe X-chromosome inactivation patterns in females carrying mutations in genes on the X-chromosome. If a woman is carrying an X-linked recessive mutation, then she usually does not have symptoms of the disease. The exception to this happens if she happened to have inactivated the normal copy of the gene in most of the cells in her body, i.e. *unfortunate inactivation*. The opposite event is *fortunate inactivation* and generally is noted in X-linked dominant disorders where a carrier of a mutation is expected to have symptoms but does not. In the case of fortunate inactivation, they have fortuitously inactivated the X-chromosome carrying the mutation and left the normal copy to function.

DOMINANT AND RECESSIVE TRAITS

THE X AND Y CHROMOSOMES ARE REFERRED TO as *sex chromosomes*. All other chromosomes are called *autosomes*. *Dominant traits* are those that show symptoms when just one of a chromosome set has a change or a mutation in a particular gene. *Recessive traits* need both genes on a pair of chromosomes for symptoms to be seen. For dominant diseases, only one parent carries the mutation, and we can generally see it because it affects the parent's development just like the child's. For recessive diseases, the parents are silent carriers because just one normal copy of the gene is enough to get by without symptoms.

For disorders caused by genes on the X chromosome, it gets more complicated. Dominant and recessive are determined by whether a woman who carries a mutation in the gene (on one copy of the X) has symptoms (dominant) or not (recessive). A key feature of the two is that X-linked recessive disorders tend to lead to more males being affected than females, while X-linked dominant disorders are seen more often in girls.

X-LINKED DOMINANT DISORDERS

X-LINKED DOMINANT DISORDERS ARE PRETTY RARE. RS is among the more common of the "rare disorders," with a frequency of between 1/10,000 to 1/25,000 female births per year worldwide. In other X-linked dominant disorders, the mutation is lethal in males. In some of these disorders, severely affected male fetuses have been seen as miscarriages. The thought is that the product of the gene is absolutely required for early development, so that if a male has only the faulty copy, he cannot develop normally and is miscarried. Girls will have some cells with an active normal copy and some cells with an active mutant copy (because they have two Xs).

THE RETT GENE: *MECP2*

FOR YEARS, THERE WAS A LONG DEBATE about whether or not RS was a genetic disorder. This was resolved in 1999 when the gene causing RS was identified. Thanks in large measure to the rare families with more than one case of RS, the cause for the disorder has been traced to mutations in a gene called "*methyl CpG binding protein 2*," commonly called *MECP2*.

Genetics

FINDING THE GENE

THERE HAVE BEEN MANY IMPORTANT BREAKTHROUGHS in our understanding of RS since it was first identified as a unique disorder of common origin. Most would agree, however, that the most pivotal finding was the discovery of the genetic basis of RS in 1999 by Dr. Ruthie Amir working in the laboratory of Dr. Huda Zoghbi at Baylor College of Medicine in collaboration with Dr. Uta Francke at Stanford University. It is impossible to overstate the importance of finding the genetic needle in the haystack of more than three billion pairs of information that makes up a person's entire genetic make-up.

Imagine looking at the night sky full of stars, knowing that at least one of them could begin to tell you the secrets of the universe, but not knowing which one to start with, and realizing that you might have to look at each and every one independently before you find the right one. This is the situation that RS researchers found themselves in during the mid-1990s.

It had become increasingly clear that RS was, indeed, *genetic* in origin. Clues from consistency in some of the clinical observations like hand wringing, decelerated head growth, and developmental onset, and the fact that it was seen almost exclusively in females all pointed to some sort of genetic involvement rather than being caused by a "bug" or "germ." But the *mode of transmission* remained elusive. It just didn't behave like a "good gene should" in terms of being passed from parents to their children. Instead, it seemed to "pop up" spontaneously in families with no previous history of any similar conditions in generations before or after except in a very few cases.

It was precisely these very few cases that gave scientists the opportunity to narrow the galaxy and select the stars upon which to turn their gaze. Because of a few families where RS was seen in more than one family member, with active collaboration from these families, scientists could use the *Mendelian Laws of Inheritance* to start parsing their way through the billions of pairs of information that make up the human genome. And, because RS was clearly linked to being female, the obvious place to start was the X chromosome.

A small number of scientists had already made long-term commitments to understanding RS, investing more than a decade of time and effort in research on the biology of the disorder. Based on all that was known, the research strategy was to make a list of about two hundred genes from the most likely region of the X chromosome, clone them out and then systematically look for candidate genes that *could* be involved while crossing off those whose function made their roles unlikely culprits. Cloning and characterizing two hundred genes is an enormous task, and all were hoping for an earlier, rather than later win. The chromosome region was narrowed greatly through the work of Dr. Carolyn Schanen, who studied the Woodcock family. The Woodcocks had four affected family members, and it was the first time that RS was observed to affect two generations of the same family.

In various laboratory studies, samples from the few cases of familial (inherited) RS and in twenty-four percent of the cases of sporadic RS revealed evidence of differences in one tiny area of the gene they were exploring on the long arm of the X chromosome (Xq28). Subsequent research would show numerous differences beyond the early finding, but even this preliminary result was enough to know it. It was not a fluke. The gene, called *MECP2*, had been found.

It's hard to describe the impact that discovery had on the families living with RS on October 4, 1999. Phones rang off hooks, people cried as they laughed, hugged, danced and cried some more. Because, as every scientist believes, if you know what causes it, and you can figure out how it's supposed to work, then, sooner or later, you can figure out how to correct it. Finding the gene lit the way for all the biomedical research that was,

Genetics

and is, to follow. It permits a reality check, and provides a testable framework that can be repeated and manipulated until the unknown becomes known. The bedrock of knowledge lets you climb the next mountain of discovery.

THE NEXT STEPS

KNOWING THE GENETIC CAUSE CATAPULTED RS to the next stage of research. First, a test was developed that allowed expansion of diagnosis for those who had been waiting, sometimes for years, to know the cause of their child's impairment. More than eighty percent of those tested were shown to have a mutation in the *MECP2* gene, and multiple sites within the gene were found early on to be altered in different patients. We now know that there are more than two hundred mutations identified in *MECP2*, and even more are likely to be identified as the sensitivity of the mutation testing improves and includes more of the DNA comprising the gene. Finding this much variability in *MECP2* mutations began to explain some of the differences in severity and expression seen among those with RS. More research breakthroughs occurred in understanding severity when researchers began checking the "activation status" of the mutated X chromosome within different cell lines, and it was found that *X-inactivation* played an important role in determining the impact of having a mutation leading to RS would have.

Most of us were hoping that the cause for RS would be a single gene trait because science has been able to successfully treat several single gene disorders effectively for years. One example of this is the disorder Phenylketonuria (PKU), where children born with a mutation blocking the ability to detoxify phenylalanine (a necessary amino acid and naturally occurring substance in many foods) suffer neurological damage as the substance builds up in their systems. Several decades ago it was found that this outcome could be avoided if the child's diet was monitored to avoid foods with phenylalanine, and that the deficiency could be identified at birth by a simple blood test now given to all newborns. Although it is a single gene, *MECP2* turned out to be much more challenging.

I prayed that the gene for Rett Syndrome would be a simple one that would lend itself to being fixed and fixing the problems. MECP2 was not the answer to my prayers. It is complex. It acts indirectly through other genes.

HOW *MECP2* WORKS

ALTHOUGH COMPLEX, *MECP2* STILL HAS TO FOLLOW the rules of biology. It is up to scientists to figure out how *MECP2* plays the game given how they know how the overall system works. These very rules are what scientists rely upon in order to understand how RS causes differences in the ordinarily very predicable behavior of DNA, genes, chromosomes, and cells.

Scientists believe that the protein made by the *MECP2* gene, known as MeCP2, may be directly influencing as many as four hundred other proteins. Each of these is controlled by another gene and is a key component for the normal function of nerve cells. The MeCP2 protein is involved in turning off (or "silencing") several of these other gene products at certain times during development, preventing them from making proteins when they are not needed. Researchers have not yet determined all the genes/proteins that are targeted by the MeCP2 protein, but we already know that several of them, such as Brain Derived Neurotrophic Factor (BDNF), are important for the normal function of the

Genetics

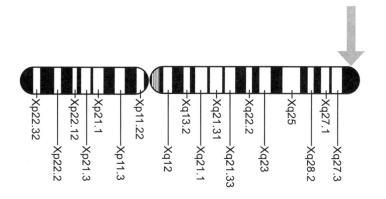

*The MECP2 gene is
located on the long (q)
arm of chromosome X
at band 28.*

central nervous system. BDNF is also implicated in conditions like autism, where genetic bases are suspected but not yet identified.

Research has shown us that the role MeCP2 plays is especially critical as nerve cells begin to mature. This may be the reason that those with RS appear without symptoms for many months or even longer before difficulties arise.

MUTATIONS

A MUTATION IS SIMPLY A CHANGE IN THE DNA SEQUENCE of base pairs from the original sequence. Mutations occur in all of us as we are created from the twenty-three chromosomes inherited from each of our parents. These tiny little changes where a base-pair or two don't line up properly during the early cell divisions leading to us are part of the miracle of genetic rearrangement that helps to make each person unique. Most genetic changes wind up someplace in the DNA where there is no biological impact. But sometimes the mutation will occur in a functional gene and cause problems.

The RS gene is comprised of a segment of that three billion base pair long book of information that is only 75,865 base pairs. There are four active parts of the gene, called *exons* spaced out by three inactive parts of the gene, called *introns*. The active exons are responsible for making the coded messenger RNA which in turn translates the message to create the protein MeCP2. When there is a change somewhere in the active parts of the 75,865 base pairs that is *MECP2*, the instructions for the protein get changed, and it is those changes that disrupt the protein's ability to properly do its job of shutting off certain genes, especially during development, so that other genes can be expressed. The two main parts of machinery running the gene are the *Transcriptional Repression Domain* (TRD) which tells the gene to turn off, and the *Methyl Binding Domain* (MBD) which directs the coding sequence for where the protein is to "sit" on the gene it is repressing.

From a geneticist's perspective, the mutations that cause RS are especially interesting because there are many places that the disruptions across the gene occur which can each give rise to RS—or not! *MECP2* mutations are seen occasionally in people with other disorders, such as autism, but without those defining RS clinical characteristics. Figuring out the relationship between where the mutation is in the *MECP2* gene and the clinical outcome is a fundamental research issue for scientists who seek to understand genotype/phenotype interactions. Thus far, the relationship between the type of mutation a person has and the type of symptoms she expresses has been elusive in RS.

Genetics

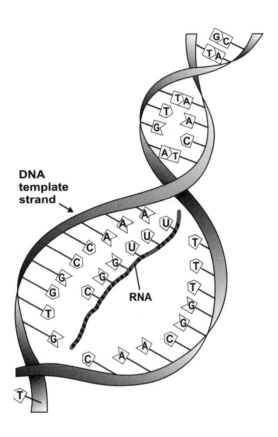

DNA template strand

RNA

Work on genotype/phenotype correlations is progressing (see the chapter on research). We now know, for example, that different parts of the gene are more prone than others to be the site of a particular mutation type, and certain mutation types are more likely than others. For example, there is a clustering of mutations that cause an amino acid change in the protein to occur (called *missense mutations*) that happens more frequently at one end of the transcriptional repression domain (TRD) than in other places; we also know that another clustering of *nonsense mutations* (changes that cause the protein to end prematurely) and *frameshift mutations* (changes that either add or delete bases resulting in a shift in the instructions that make the protein) are found beyond the MBD, and that deletions that tend to occur at one end of the gene are usually bigger than deletions occurring elsewhere and account for about 10% of all mutations seen in RS. But, even though they are clustering in the same region, it is unusual to see two identical deletions within those examined for mutations. By understanding all these differences in the type and placement of the many *MECP2* mutations seen in RS, we can learn to differentiate subtle differences in clinical expressions. We believe that this will ultimately give us the tools to develop treatments able to address each situation with specific answers.

For several years it was a mystery that only eighty percent of those identified with RS had observable *MECP2* mutations; in twenty percent of those tested, the reports came back negative, leaving parents in an uncomfortable limbo. In fact, that twenty percent is why RS continues to be a clinically diagnosed disorder today, rather than one that just rests on a genetic test. And, just to keep you informed on "genetics-speak", the initials RS are the proper way to address RS until it becomes a genetically diagnosed (rather than clinically diagnosed) disorder. When that day comes, we will change the initials to the gene: RTT. That will be a happy day, because it will mean that all who are tested will have a definitive answer about their condition and all nagging doubts can be removed. But for now, we are still learning about the different things that can happen to change the *MECP2* gene, and we are chipping away at that twenty percent. To date, most scientists would agree that those still falling in the "non-discovered genetic cause" limbo is about five to seven percent, with about eight percent more now accounted for by newer, more sensitive testing methods. Recently, for example, it was discovered that besides the different ways that bits can be missing or changed within different parts of the gene, *MECP2* can have large chunks missing that are outside the screening target of traditional testing. In 2005, scientists began to use

Genetics

a new a method for quickly and reliably surveying outside the coding regions of the gene to determine the relative number of copies of each *MECP2* exon*. This method is called Multiplex Ligation-dependent Probe Amplification (MLPA), and it reveals large deletions not seen by the previous method, so that more people can have a genetically defined answer to the cause of RS. Most scientists believe that, ultimately, as the tools of mutation detection become more and more honed, we will be able to find the genetic underpinnings for all of those clinically diagnosed with RS as well as re-classify those who have been misdiagnosed.

What kind of testing should I have done first? There is always safety in numbers. Go with the standard testing first because you are likely to fall in the eighty-seven to ninety percent category and will have to search no further. If you do fall into the gray zone, then MLPA testing is commercially available. If MLPA results are negative, there is wholesale sequencing (see footnote) which can be done by some "boutique" labs.

INHERITANCE

BECAUSE RS IS THOUGHT TO BE A *SPONTANEOUS* (new) mutation ninety-nine percent of the time, it is usually *not inherited*. The genetics of RS are complicated because it's not just one mutation in the stretch of DNA that codes for *MECP2*. Instead there are many places in the DNA that can get disrupted in many different ways. Many of these disruptions result in RS, but many of them do not, and we have not yet arrived at the level of understanding that lets us predict what the differences are in the different outcomes. We will get to that level of knowledge. Scientists are still working out which mutations lead to RS and which do not, and how the different mutations impact the outcome of the disorder. But we do know that, because most of the mutations are spontaneous events impacting the gene in one egg or sperm, most families would not expect to have any recurrences, male or female.

What is the risk of having another child with RS? There are only a small number of family recurrences, and these are mostly sisters or twins. Parents can be tested to make sure they are not carrying a germline mutation. Beyond that, the chances for having another child with Rett syndrome are exceptionally low. *If you have a daughter with RS and no other affected relatives, the chance of having another child with RS is less than one percent for your family (you and your children).* In families with more than one child with RS, the situation is different and would need to be addressed through a professional genetic counselor.

Who should be tested? Both parents can be tested for germline mutations (see Mosaicism below) before they decide to have another child. If a mother has a germline mutation, then her daughters who may seem to be unaffected may also wish to be tested when they reach reproductive age as they, too, may be silent or asymptomatic carriers. Finally, prenatal testing of any babies conceived where RS has already occurred in the family is also an option.

---

* Commercially available screening tests only survey small "best-bet" bits of the gene since DNA sequencing the whole almost 76,000 base pairs is still a technically demanding task beyond the capacities of most commercial labs. While technologies allowing high-throughput sequencing of kilobases of DNA may evolve soon, sensitive screening methods of appropriate areas of a gene of interest will likely remain the testing method of choice for many years, especially as molecular "chips" capable of screening for many disorders at once with just a tiny drop of blood (or cheek cells) are now coming into play.

Genetics

When it is inherited instead of spontaneous, does RS pass through the mother or father? We have to be very careful about how we interpret the family trees when we are looking at a disorder with a high number of new errors in the gene. Recurrences in families may not result from passage of the same faulty copy of the gene from one generation to the next, but may be the chance occurrence of two new errors in the same family. But for close relatives, like sisters, it is more likely that they inherited the same faulty copy from one of their parents who is carrying it silently. We believe that for affected sisters, it may come from either parent, through germline mosaicism in the father or either germline mosaicism or fortunate X-inactivation in the mother. We have identified a few families where RS occurred in two generations and was transmitted through a mother who carried the faulty RS gene silently through fortunate X-chromosome inactivation. We do not believe that a male can inherit a faulty copy of the gene and carry it silently.

Mary has five siblings. I would certainly encourage you to have more children. Not only will it be good for you, but your daughter will be truly blessed as well. Mary's greatest advocates are her sisters and brothers. They'll be her future caregivers (whether it's in a supervisory role or directly). Having other children helped us to appreciate and understand Mary so much more, just like Mary has taught us to appreciate and understand the other children.

Remember, *more than ninety-nine percent of the time, RS occurs because of a new mutation rather than a trait that is passed down from one generation to the next*. This means that the gene was normal in all the cells in the parent, except the particular egg or sperm that went on to make that particular child. We know that mutations occur more frequently in sperm than in eggs, probably because there are a lot more cell divisions taking place to make sperm with more chance for error. Females have all the eggs they are going to have by the time they are born. So if the mutation in the RS gene is occurring more frequently in sperm and the gene is on the X chromosome, we will see more affected girls than boys.

MOSAICISM

WHY DON'T WE SEE MORE CASES IN ONE FAMILY? If having a mutation in the gene means that the child will have RS, then we are not likely to see it run in families, since women with RS don't usually have children. In only one case do we know of a woman with RS who had a daughter with RS. She had a fifty percent chance that the X chromosome in that egg would be the one with the mutation, so a fifty percent chance that if she had a daughter, she would also have RS.

To understand the familial recurrences, there is a phenomenon called *mosaicism* that needs to be explained. Generally, cells go about their business of dividing up the chromosomes into their paired sets and passing them on to daughter cells faithfully without any incident. But occasionally, something happens to disrupt the usual. Gonadal or germline mosaicism is one of the unusual disruptions that happens when a mutation in a gene occurs in a cell in the developing baby, rather than either the parental egg or the sperm. Depending on exactly when during the baby's development the mutation occurs, it could end up in a lot of the tissues in the body or just a few. A person who had this happen in the RS gene during development may be asymptomatic, because the mutation occurred *after* the brain tissue cells had already differentiated. He or she may, however, make eggs or sperm

Genetics

carrying the faulty copy of the gene and thus transmit the disorder more than once. This is the way RS is inherited in about one percent of the cases, and people can be tested to see if they are *germline carriers* before they conceive another child. Germline mosaicism has also been seen in some autosomal dominant and X-linked dominant disorders and can occur in males and females.

MALES WITH RETT SYNDROME

THERE HAVE BEEN A FEW SPORADIC CASES of males with RS-like symptoms reported, and these are being more fully investigated now that we have the genetic cause identified, but there are far fewer males reported with Rett-like symptoms than females. Why is this the case?

Males carrying a mutation in the *MECP2* gene that would cause RS in a female have a severe congenital brain disorder, called encephalopathy. Although appearing normal at birth, they fail to develop and die from respiratory arrest early in life. The clinical picture is very different and these males would not be diagnosed with RS. Most of the affected boys known were born into families with one or more female with RS.

For males to look like classic RS, they have to be mosaics like females are who have random X inactivation. The RS males may have two X chromosomes (e.g. 47, XXY) with one carrying a *MECP2* mutation and random X inactivation. Alternatively, they may have acquired the *MECP2* mutation in early embryonic life so that only a proportion of the cells in their bodies are mutant. Both of these scenarios are rare events but have been observed.

Finally, *MECP2* mutations occur more frequently in sperm cells than egg cells. Therefore, more females are affected because the sperm carrying the mutated *MECP2* could only result in a girl, since males need an X from Mom and a Y from Dad to determine their gender.

CDKL5: A RETT-LIKE PICTURE

IN THE LAST FEW YEARS mutations in a gene called cyclin-dependent kinase-like 5 (CDKL5) have been found in a group of individuals who have a Rett-like clinical picture. Almost all of these individuals have had severe early onset seizures (especially infantile spasms) as part of their clinical picture. At present, it remains unknown what proportion of Rett syndrome patients with no *MECP2* mutation will turn out to have a CDKL5 mutation, but it is likely to be low. CDKL5 mutation testing is not routinely available at the moment through diagnostic laboratories. If you think your child should have this, you should discuss this further with your pediatrician, neurologist or geneticist.

THE FUTURE OF GENETIC RESEARCH

NEARLY EVERY DAY, WE HEAR OF BREAKTHROUGHS in understanding diseases and conditions that were once thought untreatable and incurable. Technological advances in science and the determination of dedicated researchers will no doubt lend their talents to our greater understanding of RS and hopefully, to treatments and cures in our loved ones' lifetimes. Many approaches, including gene therapy, stem cell interventions,

Genetics

cloning and other high-tech biomedical advances, are not trivial. Although these break-throughs are exciting and full of promise, there is a dark side to that promise that must be understood and conquered before some of these treatments are usable on our loved ones. A "magic pill" without devastating side effects could take several decades or more to realize. Biological systems are exquisitely synchronized and highly complex. You can't alter one part without a cascade of events occurring in both the short and long haul. It would be unfair and wrong not to tell you this. Hope is good; false hope can be as damaging as no hope at all.

We know that the road to the discovery of the Rett gene was a long one, fraught with many winding turns. Yet, we also know that the pace of science has accelerated beyond our wildest dreams. Many never expected to actually identify the genetic culprit behind RS. The scientific community has been astounded by the onslaught of new information about RS in just the last five years. And while we know that the cure for RS may not come as quickly as we all ache for, treatments are within our closer reach. We look forward to the promise of what tomorrow's science and technology community can offer.

"If the human brain were so simple that we could understand it, we would be so simple that we couldn't."

– EMERSON M. PUGH

The Parent-Physician Partnership

FINDING A PHYSICIAN

WHEN YOU ARE LOOKING for a physician to consult or to direct your child's care, it helps to have some criteria in mind. Of course, you want a doctor who is competent and knowledgeable. You also want him/her to be warm and caring, someone with whom you can feel comfortable and talk openly. S/he should be gentle with your child and interact with her and be willing to partner with you in finding the best resources to assure that she gets optimum care. S/he should share your philosophy about experimental research and clinical trials. The pediatrician and the developmental pediatrician or neurologist can play a big role in the life of a family affected by RS, so it is important to make sure this person is someone you are comfortable dealing with.

When I walk through the neurologist's door, I have my jumbo binder with all of the latest updates on RS. He always smiles and says, "Let's hear what's going on!"

PEDIATRICIAN OR ADULT PHYSICIAN?

AS YOUR DAUGHTER reaches adulthood, you may choose to continue her care under the pediatrician or seek an adult primary care physician. There are advantages to both. The pediatrician has likely followed her care for some time and is familiar with the health issues RS presents. However, the adult primary care physician may be more familiar with conditions that apply less to a girl with RS and more to an adult. Your insurance may require that she see an adult physician.

If your family sees a family practitioner or general practice physician, you may want to include your daughter in his care. The distinct advantage is that you never have to switch physicians when your daughter matures. As these physicians typically see the entire family, they tend to be sensitive to the needs of all family members concerning RS.

"Too often we underestimate the power of a touch, a smile, a kind word, a listening ear, an honest compliment, or the smallest act of caring, all of which have the potential to turn a life around."

– DR. LEO BUSCAGLIA

I talked to Carol's most important doctor, her child neurologist, before jumping into the adult primary care arena. He was able to suggest some doctors with whom he had a personal relationship, and this gave me some insight. Now, Carol has an adult primary care doctor who readily admits knowing zero about RS. He treats Carol, not the RS. Personally, I like that honesty. He also is a good advocate for Carol's specialists to allow her to remain under the Children's Hospital umbrella, because they've followed Carol for more than twenty-seven years. The two groups communicate through written records and it seems to work well.

The Parent-Physician Partnership

> *We take our adult daughter to our family physician. When there is an emergency, we go to the local hospital's ER, where our family physician is also on staff.*
>
> *Vanesa still goes to her pediatrician and still sees the original orthopedic group, but pretty much has "branched out" to "regular" doctors. In my personal opinion, as she gets older, it is more important to get the best doctors for her symptoms than worry about their expertise on her RS. Besides, I can quickly get them up to speed.*

SPECIALISTS

YOUR CHILD MAY CONTINUE TO SEE her regular pediatrician for routine care, but she may also need the expertise of a specialist, such as:

Developmental Pediatrician—for developmental and behavioral consultation and care

Pediatric Neurologist—if she has seizures

Pediatric Orthopedist—if she has scoliosis, or problems with her feet or hips

Pediatric Gastroenterologist (GI)—if she has reflux, constipation, feeding and gas issues

Pediatric Pulmonologist—if she has severe breathing issues

Pediatric Cardiologist—if she has Prolonged Q-T Syndrome

Pediatric Physiatrist/Physical Medicine and Rehabilitation Physician—for evaluation and care of spasticity and mobility issues.

It is best to find specialists who are familiar with RS. When you call for an appointment, ask if the doctor has other patients with RS on his caseload. IRSA can provide you with a list of specialists in your area who have been recommended by other Rett families. If you live in a more rural area and do not have access to doctors who know a lot about RS, just make sure the doctors you choose are willing to learn. You can do a lot to provide them with good resources, including research updates from the IRSA *Rett Gazette*, local seminars and the annual IRSA conference. The electronic newsletter, *IRSAlert*, provides a very good synopsis of new medical and therapeutic literature. You can also participate in studies at the clinical research centers on Rett. Look in the Help section of this book for contact numbers.

GETTING THE INFORMATION YOU NEED

AFTER THE DIAGNOSIS

AFTER YOU HAVE RECEIVED THE DIAGNOSIS, you will probably want to seek more information and help. When things "sink in," you may find that you have many questions. It may require a more extended conference with the physician, which should be arranged at a convenient time for both you and the physician. Make a follow-up appointment to get the reassurance you need that you have the best information, not only on the diagnosis, but on your child's future care and treatment. There is no question that cannot or should not be asked if it is of concern to you.

WHAT TO EXPECT

YOUR CHILD'S DOCTOR WILL PROBABLY NOT BE ABLE TO TELL you how much she will be able to do in the long run. There are a number of factors that will determine the severity of RS, including her type and location of mutation, X-inactivation rate, and the types of therapy she will get, medications she may take, her home environment, success of her school program and other influences, such as her general health.

The Parent-Physician Partnership

WHAT TO ASK

YOU WANT TO FIND SPECIALISTS who can support you in the long run. It should be an open relationship with lots of room for questions, and lots of respect for your own feelings and directions for care. Most physicians will welcome the opportunity to answer questions. If your physician discourages questions, he or she is probably not the best one to have on your daughter's case. Here are some questions you might ask:

- Is s/he open to learning the latest about RS?
- Does s/he listen to your concerns without making you feel neurotic or overprotective?
- What is her/his philosophy about experimental research? Does this match yours? If clinical treatment trials become available, will he help you participate?
- What is her/his protocol for medications? Is he aggressive about treating seizures? Willing to try diets?
- Can s/he recommend activities which will help encourage your child's development? Make a referral to an early intervention program?
- Is s/he willing to help you acquire equipment through insurance by filling out forms or writing letters?
- Is s/he willing to refer you to other local families?
- Is s/he open to holistic approaches?
- Does s/he talk to your child? Touch her?

For diagnostic tests

What will the test tell us?

Why is this information important?

Will it let me know what to expect?

Will it alter treatment?

Will it lead to a gain or loss of services?

Is there any other way to get this information?

Are there any risks?

How much time will it take to get results?

What is the cost, and will insurance cover it?

For medications

How does it work?

How effective is it?

What are the likely/possible side effects?

Which could be irreversible?

Does the drug need monitoring with lab tests?

How long will she have to take it?

Is there any reason not to use a generic drug?

Should it be taken with food?

Does it interact with any other medications?

The Parent-Physician Partnership

For surgeries

What are the chances for improvement?

What is the risk of death or permanent damage?

What is the risk of not having surgery?

What can be gained or lost by waiting?

What is the risk of anesthesia?

Is there anything else we could try first?

How do you do this procedure?

Is the staff equipped to work with children?

Am I allowed to stay with her?

How often have you done this procedure and what is your success rate?

For alternative interventions

What is the cost of treatment?

What are the risks?

What impact will this have on the rest of the family?

How will I know if it works?

How will I know when to stop?

Does it interact with anything else we are doing?

Your child's physicians, and her neurologist in particular, can play a large and important role in the life of your family. If you are not comfortable or not satisfied that you are getting the right respect and support or that she is not getting the best medical care, don't hesitate to change doctors. You pay the bill.

INFORMATION YOU NEED FROM A TO Z

KNOWLEDGE IS POWER. The more you know, the more you can advocate for your child. Here are the basics in a nutshell:

Aerophagia: A consequence of hyperventilation or difficulty swallowing is aerophagia, or air swallowing. This can result in a very distended abdomen, which is not painful but can reduce space for breathing and eating.

Allergies: Record any adverse reactions to medications.

Audiological evaluation: Every child with delayed speech or loss of speech should have her hearing evaluated by a licensed audiologist. Sometimes this can be completed in a sound-proof booth (visual reinforcement audiometry or VRA) or sometimes a brainstem evoked response test (BAER, ABR) is needed. This can be completed on a child of any age or developmental level. Otoacoustic emissions (OAE) is a screening test and not a replacement for VRA or ABR. This does not have to be repeated unless there is a change such as chronic ear infections or decreased responsiveness to sound.

Bone density: Children with impaired mobility can develop osteopenia (decreased bone density) but this appears to be true for girls with RS even when compared to other disabled children. It did not seem to be related to diet or medications. Osteopenia is a risk factor for osteoporosis and unexpected (pathologic) fractures.

The Parent-Physician Partnership

Bruxism: Bruxism (tooth grinding) happens during daytime, waking hours. A dental appliance is not usually recommended because of the choking hazard. A pediatric dentist is important, as s/he understands children with developmental disorders. A dental check-up is also important when unlocalized pain is suspected.

Clinical diagnosis: Record the age at which your daughter received her clinical diagnosis of RS. The typical age of recognition is between eighteen months to three years, but the clinical diagnosis may be considered tentative until a child is between three and five years of age. Certain rare, slowly progressive degenerative disorders can mimic the appearance of RS. Girls with RS do not continue to lose skills after the initial regression period; girls with degenerative disorders will continue the course of loss.

Constipation: An almost universal problem for children with neurologic impairments. Pediatricians generally have plans for dealing with constipation, but dietary changes are usually the first intervention. More fluid and fiber intake is the best starting point.

Developmental status: An assessment of general function, looking at mobility, communication, feeding, and sleeping is important on a yearly or as needed basis.

EEG: Electroencephalogram; a test to measure and record the electrical activity generated by the brain. EEG patterns seen frequently in RS include generalized slowing, rhythmic slow activity (theta activity), and focal and generalized spikes and sharp waves.

EKG: Electrocardiogram; abnormalities on EKG in girls with RS have been proposed as a possible cause of sudden, unexpected death. There is a higher incidence of "prolonged Q-T interval" in girls with RS than expected. This means that the electrical impulse takes longer to get through the heart than usual, which is a potentially dangerous complication. Baseline EKGs should be obtained in all girls with RS and then periodically (every few years) if the first one is normal. Abnormal studies require referral to a pediatric cardiologist.

Family functioning: If your family is not receiving adequate extended family and/or community support, then you will not have the stamina or well-being to keep on providing care for your children. Parent job stability, parental relationship, health insurance, mental health, and school performance of siblings are all important factors.

Head circumference: Early brain growth is reflected by increases in head circumference. The deceleration of head growth is one of the diagnostic criteria in RS. In later years, some head circumference increase is from skin and underlying tissue. Seeing a decline in head circumference in the first two years of life could be one of the first signs of RS. The term "acquired microcephaly" refers to head circumference, which was initially in the normal range, which is now below the second percentile (smaller than ninety-eight out of one hundred girls the same age).

Health maintenance: Routine well-child visits are just as important for the girl with RS as for any other child. Immunizations are important and not contraindicated by the diagnosis of RS. Discuss the latest recommendations with your child's primary care physician (PCP). Your PCP may be able to help you advocate for your daughter's needs.

Hyperventilation/apnea: Girls with RS have a breathing rhythm disorder, which may be the result of underdeveloped brainstem function. Hyperventilation may be associated with apnea (prolonged pause between breaths). This does not occur during sleep and is not the cause of sudden, unexpected death.

Impacted bowel: known as fecal impaction; blockage of the bowel. This is a serious situation and needs to be treated with colonic lavage (washing out the intestines) or even manual removal of the stool under sedation or anesthesia.

The Parent-Physician Partnership

Medications: Girls with RS may be on medications for seizures, constipation, reflux, or more typical childhood conditions. Keep a list of them, doses and dose changes, and dates.

Molecular diagnosis: Molecular diagnosis (a positive gene test) is present in the majority of girls with clinical RS. If you have molecular confirmation in a girl who meets the clinical criteria, then you do not have to wait any longer to know that this is the right medical diagnosis for your daughter.

Neurologic exam: The neurologic exam is expected to change over time and progressive motor impairment occurs in the majority of girls. A brief assessment of muscle bulk, tone, coordination, and reflexes can be done in a well-child visit. Documentation can help track changes over time.

Ophthalmologic evaluation: Every child who has developmental regression that involves more than language skills should have an exam by an ophthalmologist, preferably a pediatric ophthalmologist (subspecialist) who can assess the health and condition of the visual system. Disorders that can mimic RS, like Batten's Disease, may have abnormal eye findings. This does not have to be repeated unless there is a change in the child's clinical condition, e.g., the appearance of a crossed-eye condition or concern about visual acuity.

Oral-motor function: Most, maybe all girls with RS develop difficulty with chewing and swallowing. If your daughter is losing weight or not gaining enough for her height, her oral motor function should be assessed. Generally, speech and language clinicians are the most expert at assessing feeding and a "swallow study" (an X-ray movie called videofluoroscopy) can be ordered to look at this. Coughing or choking during feeding or drinking is something you should bring to your doctor's attention. The majority of girls may also have problems related to moving food through the esophagus and stomach.

Range of motion: When a girl has RS there can be the tendency of a school or physician to "back off" on physical or occupational therapy. One of the dangers in this "hands off" approach is that girls may develop contractures (fixed and limited movement of the joints). Decreased range of motion interferes both with function and care. This can be considered both a medical and educational need.

School program: Is your child in school? Is she getting appropriate support services? Emphasis should be placed on the fact that this is not a degenerative disorder and maintenance and even progress can be expected.

Scoliosis: Scoliosis, or curvature of the spine, is the most serious orthopedic problem in girls with RS. The initial recognition of this is generally between six and ten years, but rapid progression of the curve generally doesn't occur until after ten years. This can be easily checked every year at the well-child visit and more frequently if a curve is detected. The reason to keep a curvature from progressing is more than cosmetic. Scoliosis can interfere with walking, positioning, eating and breathing. A pediatric orthopedist is qualified to assess and treat this problem.

Seizures: The majority of girls with RS will have a clinical seizure sometime during their lifetime. These seizures may be major motor seizures ("grand mal") or complex partial seizures (spells that may have complex movements and may be associated with partial consciousness); seizures may be relatively easy to control with medications or may be difficult to control. Sometimes, brief, repetitive behaviors may resemble seizures but actually may just be non-seizure related movements. These would not need to be treated, but this is best decided with a pediatric neurologist.

The Parent-Physician Partnership

Tanner stages: Children with neurologic impairment may develop precocious puberty, defined by sexual characteristics (breasts, hair) appearing before eight years of age. Watching for breast bud development can alert the pediatrician to the likelihood that menstrual periods might follow in a couple of years. This is ample time to discuss possible medical interventions for menses.

Therapy: Has your child been dropped from therapy because of lack of progress? School or hospital based therapists have an important role to play in working on self-feeding, maintenance of skills, and prevention of orthopedic problems.

Weight-for-height percentile: Many girls with RS develop physical growth failure for weight and length. Your doctor can compare your daughter's weight to her height (usually on the back of standard growth charts) to see if she is too thin for her height. Evaluation of feeding, caloric intake and oral-motor function can be requested if her weight for height is declining. Growth failure is not thought to be related to increased involuntary movements.

KEEPING RECORDS

YOUR CHILD WILL MOST LIKELY SEE MORE THAN ONE specialist, so it is important to keep her records in good order. Her primary care physician will have to coordinate, read, interpret and analyze the information from all of the specialists.

You can help prevent fragmentation of care by keeping your own notebook. In one section, list the names, addresses, and phone numbers for all of your child's specialists, including teachers and therapists. Another section should contain a chronological list of appointments your child has had. In the next section, make a list of the medications she takes and their dosages, along with the names of the doctors who prescribed them. The next section should be a list of any surgeries or treatments and their dates. This information will be very valuable to show the physician who sees your child for the first time. And it's helpful to you as well. Having so many specialists and appointments, it's sometimes hard to remember.

KEEPING A GOOD DOCTOR

HERE ARE SOME POINTERS to help you keep the specialist of your choice:

- If you have asked for a return phone call, make sure to stay off the phone so s/he can reach you.
- Make regular appointments and keep them.
- If you have to cancel an appointment, try to do it twenty-four hours in advance.
- Try to arrive on time. Arrive early if it is your first appointment.
- Make sure you supply the correct insurance and billing information.
- Bring all medical records, including growth data to the visit. If other records are requested during the visit, be sure to take or send them.
- Write down your questions so that you do not forget something in the rush of the visit.
- Ask for clarification of anything you do not understand.
- Reserve your right to question: question tests, meds, referrals, etc. And if you do not like the answer from a referral, ask for another opinion.
- Pay your bills on time.

The Parent-Physician Partnership

EDUCATING THE DOCTOR

THE NEWER GENERATION OF PHYSICIANS SHOULD BE AWARE of RS; it is discussed in medical school these days. But since RS occurs only once in 15,000 female births, many pediatricians will never have a child with RS in their practice. Therefore, your child's regular pediatrician or even the emergency room physician may not have experience with RS. You can do a lot to stimulate interest and encourage the doctor's education about RS. Keep a supply of IRSA's "What is Rett Syndrome" cards in the car glove box or in your purse. This way, you'll be ready in an emergency. Ask your physician to subscribe to the *Rett Gazette*, and provide him or her with a brochure to keep in your child's chart. Inform the doctor of new developments and treatments, and encourage him or her to visit IRSA at www.rettsyndrome.org. Most physicians want to learn but have a limited amount of time, so your updates will be appreciated.

When my granddaughter was little and I took her to a doctor who didn't know about RS, I took the RS Handbook along with me. I also took the address of where he could order one. That way, the next time they had a patient with RS, they would know enough about it.

New families, please get the support that you need. Listen to your heart. Educate the doctors, young nursing students and medical residents that you meet. They are our future.

PROBLEMS AND EMERGENCIES

WHEN PROBLEMS ARISE

YOU WON'T ALWAYS AGREE WITH THE DOCTOR'S OPINION, and you might not always appreciate how s/he or someone on the staff handles a particular situation. Always remember that you are the one paying the bill, and your daughter is the one who deserves the best quality of care. Don't hesitate to point out your concerns, but always try to take a respectful approach. A good doctor will appreciate any constructive criticism.

Understand that not every professional you'll meet is top caliber. Most are, but many aren't. When you meet one who isn't, don't accept his/her attitude about your daughter if you don't agree. Your instincts will guide you. Listen to your gut. You are the expert about what is normal or not for your child. You are the expert. You are, you are, you are!

Sometimes I think our daughters become human pincushions at the hands of the medical professionals. Some lessons are learned the hard way. Here is what I have learned: Lesson #1: Always tell a nurse who is about to draw blood that your daughter is a "hard poke." They will use a thinner, less painful needle, and will almost always call in someone who is their pro poker. Lesson #2: Never be shy about asking the junior nurse who has poked your daughter for the third time trying to find a vein, and is now moving the needle around under the skin in an effort to locate the phantom vein as your daughter is screaming, to stop and get someone else to draw blood. At a time like that, who cares if feelings are hurt. Note: Do this before you pass out.

Don't let someone tell you that nothing is wrong with your child if you know in your gut that something is wrong. Don't be afraid to insist that something more be done. Don't take chances.

I don't let doctors tell me that nothing is wrong with Kayla anymore, especially her pediatrician. He knows that I get alarmed when something is really wrong. He knows I am not just a frantic mom and he listens to what I say. That means more to me than anything. Just don't blow me off like I know nothing.

The Parent-Physician Partnership

Remember that you get more done by working with the medical community than you will if you establish an adversarial relationship with the physician or his office personnel. This is not always easy when you have a screaming child who needs attention. Here are some ways you can head off confrontation.

Note: The use of "doctor" refers to any primary care or subspecialty professional, physician, nurse or physician assistant. The "reasons" given here are a possible explanation for the observed behavior, not necessarily the only or true reasons.

Problem: Doctor does not know anything about RS.

Reason: There is too much information for one person to know.

Solution: Offer IRSA website, brochure or article. Articles published in medical journals are usually appreciated; those from Parade Magazine are less well received.

Problem: Doctor says, "Let's wait and see" but you don't know why.

Reason: They may want to see whether more staring spells occur before an EEG.

Solution: Ask, "What are you looking for? Can I help record some information for you?"

Problem: Doctor offends you.

Reason: Discrepancy between expectations or cultures of doctor and patient.

Solution: If you need the continued help of this person, tell them, "When you say that, it makes me feel _____." It might make you feel like this is your fault or that your efforts are discounted. If you say nothing, this situation will be replayed again and again. If you bring this to his/her attention, you might be able to repair this relationship.

Problem: Doctor does not speak to your child.

Reason: Many doctors are uncomfortable or unfamiliar with nonverbal patients.

Solution: "Renee likes it when people say 'hello' to her." This lets the doctor know that you expect him/her to talk to your daughter and that she is the important person in this situation.

Problem: Doctor minimizes your ability to understand.

Reason: Sometimes doctors forget what people who speak English and not medicine understand.

Solution: "I think I could understand this better if you could use everyday words." Or "Could you draw me a picture of that?" This shows your interest in learning but also tells the doctor that they are not communicating effectively.

Remember, doctors practice medicine. They don't and can't know everything. We, as parents, need to follow our intuitions and "guts" as to what is best for our daughters.

One often hears the saying that "what goes around comes around." As a professional in the social service field, I know the world of disabilities is very small; if we cut too many ties, they will come back to haunt us. Anger is so much a part of living with disability. It is tempting to blow people away, particularly health professionals who can't "fix" our child or solve our most pressing needs. I've done it myself and I regret it. I remember the dad who boldly exclaimed to some parents that "I decked my Doc" (physically knocked him down). Health and education providers and families must be allies, not adversaries. We need each other. Parents know their children better

The Parent-Physician Partnership

than anyone else; they are the experts. Providers have skills and experience that families truly need and desire. Resilient families exhibit a desire to collaborate in the best interests of the child. They work together.

Back in the early seventies when Angie's RS started to present itself, I placed a lot of faith on the medical community to help me figure out what was wrong with her. I didn't rock any boats or rattle any cages, except maybe my own. It was not in my nature or my upbringing to pound on doors and demand something be done. Worse than that, it would have been abhorrent for me to do so. We had no notion of something being a result of her RS, because we were told she was an enigma. I had quite a learning curve ahead of me. But as one of the old "war horses," I want to encourage you that you can still be "nice" but at the same time be "firm." When a doctor says he or she has no answers, keep pushing for a referral to someone who does. Or tell him he's your last hope. Or say you appreciate his ability to "blow this off" but you and your daughter have to live with it every day. Or say, "That's not an acceptable answer." Or say, "Doctor, if this were your child, you would be as frantic as I am." Bottom line: It's not about your discomfort, your embarrassment, or shyness. It's about your daughter's comfort, health and safety. You are her voice. Advocate for her until they'll do anything you suggest. When your daughter is suffering, it is more than okay to become obsessed. I have learned that when Angie is suffering, I'm suffering, and it is stupid to keep that to myself. Don't get me wrong. Being "nice" does pay off. But you can be "nice and firm" and make people feel good about helping your daughter at the same time.

WHEN TO GO TO THE EMERGENCY ROOM

YOUR CHILD'S SCHOOL OR ADULT PROGRAM probably has guidelines for when to transport to the Emergency Room is necessary. You can notify your local fire rescue emergency team that you have a disabled child, so they will have this information on file. You can also have the nearest hospital keep her records in its computer system with a list of her physicians and a copy of your guardianship papers, if appropriate.

At home, you will have to make this decision. If your doctor's office is open, you may want to call the doctor first to explain her condition and ask whether to take her in. If it is a life-threatening situation, do not hesitate to go to the ER. These situations include:

- when your child has a high fever
- when your child is having difficulty breathing
- when a seizure has lasted more than ten minutes
- when your child is unresponsive
- when you think she is in severe pain
- when her stomach is distended and hard and does not go down
- when a limb is swollen or red

FOR THE PHYSICIAN

GIVING THE BAD NEWS

WHEN GIVING THE DIAGNOSIS of a chronic neurologic condition such as RS, it is important to take a number of things into consideration. "Above all, do no harm" pertains not only to actions, but also to what you say. What you say and how you say it can make a huge difference in a family's ability to adjust and cope with the diagnosis. It is never an easy job, but these suggestions may make it easier.

1. The delivery of bad news is best accomplished when there is ample time to give not only the news, but also to just listen.

The Parent-Physician Partnership

2. What you are about to tell parents will have an enormous impact on their family for the rest of their lives. The time invested in families at the outset may greatly influence their need for time in the future.

3. Reassure parents that there is nothing they did or did not do to make this happen.

4. Deliver this news in person. If you have positive mutation testing, call the day before you are able to meet with the family and say you have "preliminary results from the lab and would like to talk with them." Do not give these results on the phone.

5. Provide a comfortable environment in which to deliver the news. Privacy is an important component of this environment as it allows the family to react to the news according to their needs.

6. Parents should be told together, if possible. Other important family members can be included in subsequent discussions, but the initial discussion is best held with just the parents.

7. Timing is everything; if the family is not able to receive the news at the present time, it is much better to reschedule than to "forge ahead." It is usually necessary to provide several sessions to allow time for all the information you need to get across and for questions to be answered appropriately.

8. Follow the parents' lead to decide how much and what information to share. Their questions will tell you what is most important to them that day. Other things can wait. Don't assume that a family isn't "ready" for some answers. If they've had the courage to ask a hard question, they deserve the best answer you can give them.

9. Begin by pointing out the child's strengths, whether physical or emotional. There is much to be said for recognizing the child as a whole individual, capable of giving and receiving love, joy, and happiness in spite of her handicaps.

10. It is not so much what you say as how you say it. Be aware of nonverbal clues and be careful to communicate what you wish with verbal and nonverbal clues. Parents may remember only part of what you said, but they will remember how you said it forever.

11. Be sure that you communicate a sense of calm, caring composure.

12. Be honest and straightforward without being brutal. The future changes every day. Be realistic, but don't predict gloom.

13. Avoid jargon when possible and if you use "terms," be sure to define them.

14. Offer to answer questions, and be willing to wait through the silence when parents are too numb to ask. It may take some time before they even know what questions to ask.

15. Be aware that the first visit may not be the best time to give the worst news. The parents' ability to absorb the whole picture may be hindered by the emotional stress they are experiencing. Arrange a subsequent meeting for more expansive discussion and for questions.

16. Do not judge the reaction of the family, but try to use it to identify areas where there might be opportunities to help the family or individual members.

17. Just as you should not remove hope, do not argue with denial. As part of the grieving process, denial allows time for emotional adjustment, which is necessary to carry on from day to day. Denial sometimes manifests as "cure shopping" and should not elicit anger on the part of the physician. A compassionate truthful answer is usually more helpful in putting an end to the shopping than is an angry declaration. "Cure-shopping" gives parents a sense of satisfaction when they feel they must be doing something for their

The Parent-Physician Partnership

child instead of "giving up" and accepting the inevitable. Denial does not usually linger; time has its own way of bringing reality into clearer view.

18. Acknowledge the parents' lost dreams for the child they wished for and reassure them that in time, they will make new dreams.

19. Acknowledge the parents' feelings; they will go through shock, denial, grief, anger, and frustration. Assure them that you know it is a difficult time but that you will be there to help them.

20. Always listen to the parents. They may not know the medical jargon, but they know their child. Consider parents to be observant, perceptive, intelligent historians until proven otherwise. Never underestimate the power of their love and dedication.

21. When the child is present, it is important to touch the child, to recognize and acknowledge her. Parents will sense your care and know you value the child. This can make a meaningful difference in the confidence and trust parents feel.

22. If you don't know the answer to their questions, don't be afraid to say so. Some outcomes cannot be predicted. They will develop greater trust if they know you are honest when there are no answers.

23. Never fail to offer referral to sources of information and support groups. It is very important for the family to recognize that they are not alone. Parents should not go home empty-handed. Write down support contact numbers; this gives them links to others who will support them. It gives them some place to start.

24. Tell the family that "this is not easy," "you are doing a good job," and acknowledge their efforts and their feelings as well as the fact that they get tired and discouraged just like anyone else. Let them know they don't always have to be "special," too.

25. Before they leave, ask parents to repeat back what you have told them. This clears up any miscommunication and reinforces your message.

26. Communicate your willingness to be there for them when they have questions in the future or need continued support.

My daughter's doctor told us that she would amount to nothing! I cried and cried until I met my Rett friends who told me to accept who she is and go forward. One mother said "you can't fix her because she isn't broken." What great advice. There have been moments where I have screamed at God and at the world. Then I look into Sarah's eyes. They are so blue. Blue that I didn't even know existed. She giggles and giggles for hours and we wonder what is so funny. She looks at the ceiling as if the angels are watching and playing with her. It gives us great comfort at tough moments.

When he made the diagnosis, Carol's neurologist said, "Is Carol any different today than she was yesterday? Do you love her any less? Can you predict the future? If you can answer NO to all the questions, take her home, let her be a little girl FIRST, love her, never miss a chance for a new adventure, and trust your gut!" His words were simplistic, but eye-opening. I learned to never lose sight of CAROL. RS is NOT who Carol is, it's just how she makes her way through this life. I never forget to celebrate the magic of Carol.

When we saw the doctor for the first time, he told us he was going to test for Rett syndrome, but was fairly certain she did not have it. He said, "It is a very serious disorder," and warned us not to go on the Internet. Of course, it was the first place we went. He was shocked when the test came back positive for Rett. Despite his warning, we found a lot of good information and support at the IRSA website. I don't know what we would have done without it.

The Parent-Physician Partnership

RETT SYNDROME CARE GUIDELINES FOR HEALTH PROVIDERS

Place this form in your child's record.

Aerophagia: Air swallowing can be significant and can interfere with eating and full respiratory effort. Rarely, medical decompression is required.

Allergies: No specific risk related to RS.

Audiologic evaluation: All children with delayed speech or loss of speech should have audiometric assessment. Either VRA or BAER is acceptable. OAE is not an acceptable replacement.

Bone density: Osteopenia may not be prevented even with adequate calcium intake, which is still important. Girls with RS are at risk for pathologic fractures.

Bruxism: Tooth grinding can be severe but does not occur during sleep. Involving a pediatric dentist is important, but children will not grind into the pulp of the tooth.

Clinical diagnosis: The child should fulfill all necessary criteria and should not have exclusion criteria.

Constipation: Treat vigorously and actively with an eye towards prevention at the time of diagnosis. Dietary fiber may be adequate, but check daily free water intake, which may be low. Usual methods of treatment are appropriate (Miralax, mineral oil, enulose, stimulants, and enemas only as needed).

Developmental status: Baseline functional assessment of mobility, communication, feeding and sleeping should be recorded, and changes noted over time.

EKG: Prolonged corrected QT intervals have been reported in girls with RS and may be life threatening. Baseline EKG should be obtained and then repeated at intervals; appropriate interval is not known, but every three years has been suggested.

Family functioning: Check on parental mood and employment, on support of extended family, and on respite care or other community services. Siblings have special needs in this situation; mood disorders or externalizing behaviors can be seen. Check on health insurance/Medicaid; some families bear financial burdens that may be covered by other sources.

Head circumference: Deceleration of head circumference growth is one of the necessary criteria for a diagnosis of RS. Most but not all girls with RS develop an acquired microcephaly with HC below the second percentile for age.

Health maintenance: All of the usual concerns are important. Immunizations are not contraindicated by the diagnosis of RS. Consult the latest *AAP Redbook* for the most recent changes.

Hyperventilation/apnea: Breathing disorder occurs only in the daytime and may be related to brainstem dysfunction. By itself, it is not a health concern, but should be noted as a physical finding.

Medications: Make a list, as always. Until more is known, avoid medications that could increase constipation or affect cardiac conduction.

Molecular diagnosis: The test for the *MECP2* mutation is available through several labs in the country. Not all insurance companies cover this. A negative test does not rule out the clinical diagnosis, but a positive test is confirmatory. Locations of labs are found at www.rettsyndrome.org.

Neurologic exam: Progressive motor impairment is seen over time and may begin with increasing spasticity at the ankles. Brief assessment of cranial nerves, muscle bulk, tone, and coordination can be done as part of the routine physical exam.

The Parent-Physician Partnership

Ophthalmologic evaluation: All children with developmental regression that involves more than language and social skills (as in autism) should have a dilated eye exam by a pediatric ophthalmologist to rule out neurodegenerative conditions such as neuronal ceroid lipofuscinosis (Batten's disease).

Oral motor function: Oropharyngeal dysphagia is common in RS. Girls may have or develop difficulty with chewing, tongue movement, and swallowing, which may impair adequate nutrition or contribute to respiratory symptoms (aspiration, coughing, or choking during feeds).

Range of motion: Contractures develop over time as girls generally have upper extremities flexed and pronated and lower extremities extended, with decreasing ankle dorsiflexion. Check for full passive range of motion. Reduction in PT/OT over time can lead to lack of awareness of this complication.

School program: Children with RS are entitled to an appropriate public education from three to twenty-one years of age. You may need to advocate for the child's needs and emphasize that this is not a degenerative disorder and that maintenance and progress in some areas can be achieved.

Scoliosis: The initial signs of scoliosis generally appear towards the end of the first decade, with possible rapid progression in the second decade. Frequency is variable from study to study but is common enough to warrant regular clinical evaluation.

Seizures: The majority of girls with RS will have clinical seizures. An initial EEG is generally done during the regression phase and may be abnormal with or without clinical seizures. Seizures can be major motor, complex partial, atonic, or myoclonic and may be relatively easy to control or highly complex and refractory.

Tanner staging: Precocious puberty can develop in neurologically impaired children. Recognizing the development of breast buds gives you time to prepare the family for menses.

Therapy: OT and PT are extremely important to maintain physical and functional abilities. Speech should focus on alternative/augmentative modes of communication using eye gaze or switch operated devices; facilitated communication should be discouraged because of clearly designed experimental data that does not support its continued use. Music therapy and hippotherapy are also very helpful.

Weight-for-height: Poor weight gain is a common complication of RS. As one easily obtainable measure of nutritional status, weight-for-height percentile should be recorded at each visit. Growth failure is not thought to be related to increased involuntary movements.

*"Love cures people—both the ones who give it
and the ones who receive it."*

— DR. KARL MENNINGER

Family Issues

2

SECTION TWO

Welcome to Rettland
Family Voices
Care for the Caregiver

Family Issues

Family Voices

Welcome to Rettland

Care for the Caregiver

Welcome to Rettland

THE CLUB YOU NEVER WANTED TO JOIN

IN *THE ROAD LESS TRAVELED*, author M. Scott Peck summed up his book in three simple opening words: "Life is difficult." He was talking about ordinary life, not the extraordinary life of special needs children and their parents. We've heard others refer to their child's stage of development as the Terrible Twos, the Frantic Fours or the Sassy Sixes. Some folks compare raising teenagers to nailing Jell-O to a tree. For most folks, these are temporary challenges as their children grow up and leave home. But Rett syndrome is forever, and the challenges are immense. If it takes a village to raise a typical child, it certainly takes many villages to raise a child with RS.

Families know that from the first time the words "Rett syndrome" are spoken in relation to their child, life is never the same again. Of course, life is harder in some ways and easier in others, but it is definitely different from the ordinary, and full of new challenges.

"Life is not about how fast you run, or how high you climb, but how well you bounce."

– ALANIS MORRISETTE

The initiation to this Club is nearly unbearable: the terror of learning about the diagnosis, the shock of understanding what it means, the sadness of having to tell others about it and the deep, aching pain of facing lost dreams for the perfect child for whom we always longed. It is hard, and the dues are high. We alternately pray to God and shout at God. We cry alone and we cry together. We search for answers, beg for a cure, try everything we can to "fix" our daughter. We try to "fix" the school system. We try to "fix" all of the stares, all of the intrusions on our little dream family. We desperately need to fix it all. But when it all won't fix, we find that we just have to fix ourselves. It takes some time to get adjusted to life in Rettland, but eventually, we find the strength to cope and we learn that these very difficulties call forth our greatest courage and wisdom, helping us to grow mentally and spiritually in ways we never imagined.

We don't choose to join The Rettland Club. It chooses us. Some people feel that they get the job because of their ability to handle difficulty. Others feel that it was by random selection, not by who we are or what we can do but by one great big lottery in the game of life where bad things happen to good people every day. Whichever way we got here, we are here to stay.

It seems like an uphill struggle at first. We don't find any books at the library, and hardly anyone ever heard of RS. The language about the disorder is very complicated and hard for us to understand. We read what we can find and wonder how this all applies to our sweet little girl as we struggle to make sense of it all.

Rettland is very different from anything we have ever experienced. We really don't want to read too far ahead in the literature, because we think that if we just spend enough intense time doing therapies, we could reverse it all. We really just want the magic pill or therapy so we can resume our lives and follow the dreams we had set our sights on when she was born.

Welcome to Rettland

But we hang in there and face things one at a time, relying on others who belong to The Club and some dedicated professionals to help us get through the hard times. In time, we realize that in spite of our struggles, we really learn a lot in Rettland. We make some really good friends, and learn some things about ourselves along the way. In fact, we find ourselves stronger, wiser, more thankful, a little less judgmental, and a lot more spiritual. We learn to see our daughter's strengths and find ourselves bathed in the light of her innocence and surrounded by the warmth of her love. We find times to laugh when others can't even find a smile. We learn patience for her many needs and appreciation for her many small gifts. We move from anger to using that energy constructively, providing better programs for her, learning about Rett syndrome, and helping others. We move from frustration at the lack of a cure to finding ways to support research that will bring it about. We find out how to minimize the bad and maximize the good, and we find the very best of ourselves in the process.

Sometimes we still envy our friends who weren't chosen for The Club, but when we look more carefully to see how they take things for granted, it's really not so bad here. We still have trying times, and still shed tears now and then, but sometimes they are tears of joy. Our outlook is much brighter.

This chapter may make for difficult reading if you are facing a new diagnosis. Those of us who have been there understand your pain, because we also feel your pain. But if you can look ahead just far enough to see that it won't always hurt this way, you can make it, one day at a time. I give you my most sincere promise that in one year, when you read this book again, you will realize just how far you have come and how much of this is true. Your daughter has not been changed by the diagnosis; it is you who have changed. Time and love will help you adjust to your loss and make new hopes and dreams. Your child is still the sweet, innocent child you loved yesterday, and you will love her today and tomorrow until forever. Your love will lead the way.

Rett syndrome may be a heartbreaking disorder, but these are promising times in Rettland. In addition to mouse models of RS with exciting world-class research and the dedication of some of the world's most devoted minds, new technological breakthroughs continue with increasing speed. New methods of augmentative communication and adapted equipment, experimental drug trials, new medications for seizures, constipation and anxiety and other symptoms, and a whole new army of researchers entering the battle for the first time since it was discovered that the *MECP2* gene mutation also occurs in other brain disorders. All of these things give us hope for a better tomorrow.

Give it some time. While it seems like a cliché, the passage of time does help the healing process. It may seem very difficult to accept at first but as time passes, the grief process moves us from panic, fear, helplessness, disappointment, anger and bewilderment to acceptance. In the beginning it is hard to understand, but with time and experience, we learn profound lessons of love. We find that we can survive, and even thrive. You will make new dreams, and you will find the true meaning of unconditional love.

D-Day

DIAGNOSIS DAY IS PAINFUL UNDER THE BEST of circumstances. Most people keep the date and the spoken words close to their hearts for a long time. We may have had suspicions that things weren't quite right, but when the doctor confirms those feelings with a definite truth, the emotional impact is great. The loss of hopes and dreams for the perfect child we longed for seem no less than the pain of losing this child to death, and so we grieve. We experience emotional swings that range from denial to rage.

Welcome to Rettland

Getting the diagnosis of Rett syndrome was bittersweet. We were sad to learn that she had something that seemed so devastating, but it was such a relief to have a final answer, to step off that tumultuous trail of hunting and pecking. It meant we had a name to the face of what was wrong with Kendall. We could answer questions from concerned people. We had a support group. We had something to Google on the Internet. A diagnosis meant answers. It meant the end to the "unknown."

At first I collapsed and surrendered all hope. I should die; my child should die; my husband should die. I considered suicide. But the human spirit would not permit that. I called IRSA and learned that our life was not over, that we could have a wonderful life, just by a different path.

When parents have waited years for a diagnosis, or when the information they have been relying on is misinformation, finding the diagnosis can actually be a relief.

Hearing the words Rett syndrome was a relief. To hear she wasn't going to die allowed me my first deep breath in nine years. I could finally stop being afraid of what the next doctor would tell us. I could finally see a life for us, although much different than the one I had planned. To know that Carol would remain a part of my life made my heart sing.

We were both relieved and scared at the same time. For us, the diagnosis was good and yet it did not change the fact that we have always known that Stephanie is a gift and a treasure. Not everything applies to each girl. They are so unique, and keeping that in mind has kept us grounded.

SO MANY EMOTIONS

Denial   **Anger**

Frustration

Bewilderment

Fear

Bargaining with God   Sadness

Guilt   Grief   **Acceptance**

If you are feeling out of sorts, emotional, irrational, don't think you're going crazy or that you're unbalanced, or even that you are an awful mother. Be kind to yourself because there is probably a very good reason why you are feeling that way.

The fact that your daughter has RS will conjure out of your core every feeling you've ever had, only in heightened form. You'll laugh, cry, rage at unseen demons, negotiate, marvel at small victories (hers and yours), and emerge a person made of tougher stuff than when you went in. I used to be such a major wimp. Now, watch out. Nobody gets between my little girl and Mamma Bear.

THE TEARS COME FIRST

CRYING IS A VERY NATURAL RESPONSE TO THE PAIN of getting the diagnosis of RS. It can be helpful to just let it all out. Keeping the pain inside hurts much more. You won't cry forever, but when you need to cry, go ahead.

Welcome to Rettland

I went through about a month of crying every night when I went to sleep thinking this couldn't possibly be happening to me. Not having a healthy child happened to other people, not me.

One thing I've learned is that if you give into your sadness and have a good cry, the sadness passes a lot faster than if you try and fight it. I actually used to wear waterproof mascara when Mere was first diagnosed so no one would see how much I was crying!

Sometimes I would cry so hard that I would have a panic attack and be unable to breathe. All of the emotions of being sad, terrified, angry, and confused all at one time almost sent me over the edge.

I truly thought of suicide and taking my precious daughter with me. Fortunately, the worst medication in the house was Modan (an older stool softener I had used during pregnancy). Suicide by diarrhea was just too horrible to contemplate! I felt like some of my friends, coworkers, and even family members were saying/acting like having a disabled child was worse than death, and death would be a blessing for her.

I emptied my pain into agonizing silent screams since there was no sound inside of me to come out. Manic projects couldn't lift me. I felt in a haze, in a horrible dream.

SHOCK

AFTER THE TEARS, THE MOST IMMEDIATE REACTION to the diagnosis is shock. The news seems overwhelming and unbelievable. The depth of the news may not sink in right away.

When we were given the news that Kennedy had been diagnosed with RS, I was shocked and very mad that God did this to us. The first couple of months were the toughest.

I was shocked. I thought this couldn't be happening to us; this could not be true. But the more I read, the more I knew that Tia could have RS.

NUMBNESS

FOLLOWING SHOCK, WE BECOME NUMB. This is nature's way of giving us time to withdraw and find ways to cope, adjust, and handle the news. We need this kind of psychic anesthesia to adjust to this painful experience and to survive. Numbness helps us temporarily wall off the flood of grief.

I just felt empty. I didn't want to think about it anymore. I just wanted to run away somewhere so I didn't have to deal with it. My brain was just paralyzed.

FEAR

FEAR CREEPS IN WHEN WE DO NOT UNDERSTAND how we will be able to handle things, or what our child will be like. We lose control of something very important, the future. Learning as much as you can about RS will help still the fear. Knowledge is power. When you can't get over the fear, ask yourself what would be the worst thing that could happen, and then decide how you would deal with it.

I put myself into a deep never-ending hole and tortured myself with racing thoughts of doom, what-ifs, maybes, and shoulds. There was no way out. Fear gripped me.

Welcome to Rettland

The "me" I knew before was in control, focused, and driven. Strangely enough, I think I still appeared that way on the surface most of the time, but lurking below was a deep-seated, overwhelming feeling of sadness. Generally I had only a dull awareness of it but the suddenness with which it would break through and the ferocity with which it would take hold was scary.

GRIEF

GRIEF IS A NATURAL RESPONSE TO OUR INTENSE LOSS. While it hurts more than anything we may have ever experienced, grief has the power to heal us. We have to allow it to surface and move through it, for this is the only way out of grief. Trying to push it away only leads to other problems. Grief runs in cycles and may return when we think we are doing well, such as during holidays or birthdays. We're better prepared when we realize that this is inevitable. Grieve the loss naturally. Sharing feelings is a good way to resolve the grief. Write it down. Put it in a poem, or talk to loved ones and friends. Here are some suggestions for how to work through your grief:

- Set aside a specific time every day to let yourself feel the grief completely.
- Share your grief with someone you trust.
- Allow yourself to let things go for awhile, to be less organized or productive.
- Find a quiet special place to feel the grief.
- Avoid outside noise during this time; let yourself feel the grief.
- Play relaxation audiotapes or CDs to help you relax and unwind.

I started to grieve. My dreams for her future were gone. It was almost like she had died. I didn't want to be different from other families. This wasn't fair.

All I could find in the bookshops was literature on grief arising from death. I had had grandparents die but that was as close as I'd come to grief arising from death. I knew though that this was a quite different form of grief. Indeed, it seemed to me that grief arising from death would be far easier to handle than the day-to-day challenges I was facing in caring for our daughter, as well as trying to cope with the turmoil of emotions going on inside of me.

I went back thru my own stages of grief to what I call my death of a dream. My favorite place to cry was outside late at night when Jen would finally go off to sleep. I remember the deep anger at God and the people who said I must have sin in my life for Him to punish me like this, and also at those who said "she will be healed if you just have enough faith." I also remember the joy when I finally realized what a gift she is and how it was okay to be angry at God because he still loved me thru the anger. Healing takes time.

GUILT

WE WONDER WHAT WE COULD HAVE DONE to cause the problem. Was it carelessness during pregnancy? The drugs we did in college? Was it punishment from God for earlier misdeeds? Feelings of guilt just promote more pain. The truth is that we are totally blameless when it comes to Rett syndrome. There is nothing you did or didn't do that would have made a difference. We all carry mutations that occur spontaneously when the three billion pairs of information that make us who we are, are first combined. Once every ten to fifteen thousand times, some of those expected mutations wind up in the

Welcome to Rettland

stretch of DNA that codes for MeCP2. It is random and if there are any environmental influences and/or genetic predispositions, they are so subtle that there is no way to pre- or post-detect them. Neither you nor your husband had any control over this, just as you had no control over your child's fingerprint patterns or a hair cowlick that won't sit down.

I thought it was because of something I did while pregnant, or from one time she fell in her walker. I also blamed it on the doctor for not taking her the day before she was born when I was in nuisance labor. Then I blamed the nurse who saw her blood sugar was down and did not call the doctor for an hour. But then, they found a defect in her gene. I was relieved because I could stop blaming it on everything else.

So many thoughts raced through me. Was it my fault? Was it his fault? Was it that time I fell? Was it the lead paint in the old house we were renovating? God, why have you forsaken me? I hate you. Why my family? Haven't you already given us enough?

The other side of guilt is feeling like you can never do enough for your child. At some point, we have to admit that it is impossible to do everything with perfection. We do the best we can with what we have. There will be crossroads along the way when we have to make choices: types of therapy, kinds of programming, when to medicate, how much, whether to do surgery or not, when to seek alternative placement, whether to and when to take a vacation alone … the list is endless. There will always be some guilt in every decision we make. It is just impossible to always provide what is right for everyone.

There are never enough hours in the day to do what we have to do, much less what we want to do. We try to divide attention as equally as possible, but it really is hard. We take turns with the children, but Susie always requires more. We just do the best we can. Some days we accomplish more than others.

ANGER

THE STRONGEST REACTION TO A NEW DIAGNOSIS is profound anger. It can also be the most difficult of all emotions to handle. We don't understand why it happens and especially, why it happened to us. Unfortunately, there are no good answers to these questions.

Some days, we're angry at everyone for everything, when we're actually angry about RS. People stare, people don't help, and everything we do seems difficult. It makes us mad! It's OK to be angry about it, but it's not OK to let anger take control. Anger can consume us. It is non-productive and just weighs us down terribly. Anger should be aimed not at her, but at her disability. We are all angry about what RS has done to our girls and to our lives, but hostility and aggression are cumbersome. Get rid of emotions that won't help. Hostility and aggression make a very heavy load.

If you need to vent your anger, do something about it. Find constructive ways to deal with your anger so that it doesn't cripple you. Take a walk, ride a bike, shoot hoops, write it down, talk about it. Accept that some people are ignorant and will stare. When you find yourself getting angry, ask yourself if the anger will change things. Then look for something that can be changed, change it and move on. Anger is natural, but getting stuck in anger is destructive.

It took months to actually get "used" to the fact of her having RS. Until that time, I would be very sad at one moment and then very angry the next. I was mad at the whole world.

She taught me that anger and frustration are futile. They are very real, but when we give power to them, we take power away from the best part of ourselves.

Welcome to Rettland

CHRONIC SORROW

WE MOVE IN AND OUT OF MANY EMOTIONS IN THE CYCLE of feelings that lead to acceptance. There will always be some sadness about RS—this is known as chronic sorrow. We may feel that we have adjusted well until a milestone our child should attain faces us—going to kindergarten, having a Sweet 16 celebration, or attending another child's birthday party. We may fall back into one stage for a short time, but then we pick up where we left off. All of these emotions are important and necessary for acceptance.

When you feel wistful about your friends' kids playing soccer, winning the spelling bee, or being cheerleaders, remember that having a child with RS is not the worst thing that can happen to you. Some of those "perfect" kids will get into drugs or alcohol, get pregnant, shoplift, be insolent, quit school … and bring a lifetime full heartache to their parents. For this, parents may take great guilt and blame. You are about as blameless as anyone can be about your child's RS.

I think I will always have an ache in my heart for that part of our lives that has been lost forever. The worst is when a girlfriend will be talking to me and she'll be complaining about something one of her kids is doing … the same sort of thing that in the past would bug me. But now, I envy that complaint. I would cherish the thought of Kendall and Hayden fighting over a toy. I would love to hear Kendall smart off to me. I want to tell my friend to be happy that she has kids who do those normal things that kids do.

I think once I finally learned that the grief would come in cycles, I handled things much better. It doesn't sneak up on me and whack me over the head anymore. I have learned to truly enjoy the good times and I have built up endurance for the bad times. I now know that eventually, her little angel smile will be back and things will be good for a while again.

I think adjustment is a constant battle. It took about a year for us to finally stop crying every time we saw a child her age doing something age-appropriate. There were times when I thought I had accepted it, only to be hit over the head with a sudden surge of grief.

WHAT DO I DO NOW?

TALK WITH OTHERS

FINDING OTHERS WHO SHARE YOUR SITUATION and understand your feelings can be tremendously helpful. Other parents of girls with RS know what you are going through.

Join the IRSA Rettnet or a chat group and keep in touch with others in the know. Get involved with your local disability community through IRSA, the ARC, Parent to Parent groups or school advisory teams. Attend IRSA's annual conference.

An acquaintance with a disabled child gave me "permission" to love this child with all her damage and I could finally express the love that was bursting in my heart for her.

Talking to people and seeing other girls helped. The turning point for me was my first IRSA conference. When I came back from that, I felt like I could handle anything.

There are some who when faced with an obstacle like this might just choose to give up, but we know our daughters are counting on us, so we trudge on. One day I woke up and realized that I wasn't just trudging anymore. The spring was back in my stride and my burden was getting less and less. So many people have helped make this burden lighter to carry and I believe it all started with other families like ours.

Welcome to Rettland

WHY ME?

IT IS NATURAL TO WONDER WHY this has happened. After all, no one deserves the pain and sadness of RS. In his book, *Why Bad Things Happen to Good People*, Rabbi Harold Kushner explains that he wrote this book for people "who have been hurt by life," to help them find a faith that can help them get through their troubles rather than making things worse. Sometimes bad things just happen for no particular reason. Kushner makes the point that "Why did this happen to my life?" is the wrong question to focus on, and that "What am I going to do with the life I have now?" is a more positive approach.

When Katie was first diagnosed, I thought "Why, God, are you doing this to me? What horrible thing have I done to deserve this?" Finally, the words of other parents sunk in and I realized that I wasn't being punished by God. God had been preparing me my whole life for Katie and I didn't get her until He thought I was ready. I think about our family situation and realized that Katie could not have ended up with a family better equipped to help her through life.

THE "WHAT IF" SYNDROME

WE ALL WONDER HOW THINGS might have been different, but dwelling on the what-ifs is non-productive and only makes us feel worse in the long run.

I went through the "what if" period. I grieved for the "normal" life milestones Carol would miss, but that didn't last very long. I figured that if I let Carol's disabilities weigh us down, we were gonna miss a lot of what life had to offer. Then, I realized that I couldn't change how the world viewed Carol, but I could change how Carol approached the world. Once I got that clear in my head, we never looked back.

I very seldom go down the "what if" road. Sarah doesn't know anything else, and if she isn't aware of what she's missing, then neither should I. I often focus on the good things about her condition. She is always happy! God has blessed her with a great sense of humor and adventure. She loves to laugh, and she's so lovable. I see Sarah as a living, breathing example of God's grace and goodness in our lives.

I don't recall ever wishing that Desire' was "normal." The question is if she didn't have RS would she be such a joy? I don't know the answer to that but the guess that I have is no. Desire' is who she is because she is disabled … just like any other experience in life, having Rett has shaped who she is. Her personality would be completely different if she were typical … she would not be the same child and our lives would be less because of it.

TELLING OTHERS

GIVING THE NEWS TO RELATIVES OR FRIENDS CAN BE HARD. Don't feel pressured to do this until you are ready. It's OK to tell them you're not up to discussing it yet. When you have to repeat the news over and over, it does two things: 1) it reminds you of the deep loss, and 2) it reminds you that like it or not, RS is here to stay. But telling others can be therapeutic, too. You can share your feelings, and hopefully, you will be able to get comfort and support from loved ones who want to help. Not everyone will react the way you want them to; many people feel awkward and just don't know how to respond. This does not mean they do not care.

When people find out that I have a daughter who is disabled, their first reaction is to say, "I'm so sorry." I appreciate that, but I have learned she doesn't cloud my life with worry any more than my other two daughters. The goals and objectives that I have for her are not the same, but the joy I find when she reaches one of her goals is just as sweet.

Welcome to Rettland

You keep your hopes to yourself--so much to yourself that you hardly let yourself know you are thinking them. And then, when they crumble, the effect appears all out of proportion, because no one, not even yourself, knew you'd even dared to hope for something different anyway.

FROM GRIEF TO GROWTH

WHILE ADJUSTING TO LIFE IN RETTLAND IS PAINFUL, we do grow from the process. Our character takes on new dimension with a broader perspective on life. We gain strength to adjust and accept while the love in our hearts grows deeper to give and receive unconditional love. In life, the things that hurt the most often become an impetus for growth.

The most important thing out of all of this is that she taught me everything I know about willpower. Willpower. The strength of our own will. The ability within ourselves to do what is right for us, with the volition to keep going. Wow! My little girl gave to me an education that no college or university could offer. She taught me that life is to be enjoyed regardless of the circumstance. She taught me the true meaning of love and devotion. She led me to a spiritual path and she joins me on this spiritual journey. She challenged me to rethink everything I once felt was "right."

ACCEPTANCE

FOR THE LUCKY ONES, ACCEPTANCE COMES IN TIME. Acceptance of the diagnosis does not mean giving up hope. It is learning to live with the reality of today, never letting go of the hope for a better tomorrow. It takes time and patience and a lot of personal growth to reach acceptance. Acceptance is loving your child just the way she is, with no "shoulds" attached. It is coming to the peaceful resolution that even if your child is never "fixed," she is still valuable, lovable, and a cherished part of your family and the world. Acceptance comes slowly, and often it comes when you are not looking for it. Your child wins you over with her unconditional love, and you learn to return it. You come to love her just the way she is, without painful notions of what you once wished her to be.

The pain of RS lessens as you make new friends in the Rett family who understand every moment of your life. They come from all walks of life, all parts of the world ... but they speak the same language ... and we all live in the same house.

The "couldas" and the "shouldas" will eat you alive if you allow it. Dale Carnegie said it best ... "You only do TODAY. Yesterday, you can't change. Tomorrow is your chance to try harder."

After a couple of really tough years, I found that the life and laughter that we had as a family before has returned. We still have a "normal" family. It's just a different definition of normal than most families have.

I developed an independent nature—stubbornness, confidence—everything I needed to survive this hard and glorious road. At the time, it seemed as though I was in darkness—not much light could be seen, and hope was hard to hang onto. It was kind of like a darkroom where pictures develop. Outside, all you can see is the negative, no color. But it is inside the darkroom that change takes place! It was like I was in the darkroom developing all I needed to be Jessica's mom. I don't have all the answers, faith, or courage for every moment. But I have what I need right now. Along with learning as I go, I think I handle people better now.

Pain is inevitable; misery is optional.

Welcome to Rettland

WHICH PATH TO TAKE

THERE IS NO RIGHT WAY AND NO WRONG WAY in Rettland, just different ways to get to the same place. In fact, sometimes we're not even headed for the same place! We may have different goals and dreams. We all have different expectations and diverse resources. Parents make their choices according to their own agenda, situation, preference and philosophy. Choose the path that fits.

There may be roadblocks in our path from time to time. It may seem that as soon as one problem is solved, another quickly takes its place. It's sort of like the potholes that you just have to steer around. You might get caught in one or two, but you just have to hold on to the steering wheel and do your best to pull out. Some days, Rettland may seem like an obstacle course on which everything seems insurmountable. Just don't try to overcome too many hurdles at once or you'll find yourself flat on the ground.

You are now traveling an unexpected road, and it may be fraught with potholes and turns that take you in presently unknown directions. Along this road you will encounter more wonderful individuals who travel with you. You will also encounter people who will get in your way, block the way to helping your daughter live a full and meaningful life. You will learn how to avoid, go around, or even go through these roadblocks—for your own sanity, and for the love of your angel.

Try not to dwell on decisions that are well down the road. One day at a time in Rettland is enough. Remember, when you finally make it through to the first milepost, you can rest with confidence that you are the best expert on your child and your own resources, and you make the best decisions about her. Any professional worth his salt will tell you that parents are the original experts. Take that to heart and believe in yourself. Then, keep on going …

We all cope in different ways and at different speeds. But you will move on. I'm not saying it won't hurt sometimes, or that it gets easy. But you will find strength to deal with it. Trust me. You will.

I felt I would never smile or laugh again. How could I when my child was so hurt? I didn't "deserve" to laugh or be happy ever again. But I was told that someday we will laugh, feel joy, and stop hating God. Now, I sometimes feel that one of the reasons I am on this earth is to care for this beautiful, innocent, loving young woman who needs me so much.

RULES FOR THE RETT ROAD

START YOUR ENGINE

BEFORE YOU GET STARTED, you may need to focus on the best way to get there. Pay attention to the road markers along the way. They are reminders and warning signs. As you move along, look for these signs and the deeper meaning they may have for your life.

FIND THE BEST SPECIALISTS

LOCATE GOOD MEDICAL SUPPORT NEARBY to carry you through the ordinary day-to-day health problems. If the doctors are not knowledgeable about RS, make sure they are willing to learn. Know where the Rett specialists are for evaluations and for consultations when times of crisis arise. While doctors are unable to cure RS today,

Welcome to Rettland

they can help you provide the best care that will allow your daughter to stay healthy and comfortable and to reach her greatest potential with a full and meaningful life.

I took the RS brochure to our pediatrician for her file. He didn't know much about RS at first, but he is learning with us. We enrolled her in the program at Baylor. They answered every question we had.

YIELD

ACCEPT THAT THERE ARE THINGS YOU CAN CHANGE and those you cannot. Don't waste precious energy for things which cannot be changed. You can change many things … your house, your hair, your job, and a million other things. You cannot change the fact that your child has RS. You cannot change yesterday. You can only make the best of today and look with hope toward a better tomorrow. Sometimes it helps to embrace the Serenity Prayer: "God grant me the serenity to accept the things I cannot change, courage to change the things I can, and wisdom to know the difference."

Concentrate on changing what you can. You can provide good doctors, teachers, therapists, and equipment. You can develop a circle of support with other families who have been there. You can read, teach others, and support research that will bring about the cure. And you can definitely change your outlook. Friends and family will take their cues from how you see things, and the more positive, the better.

The single most important thing we can do for our daughters emotionally is to be happy with them and to be happy ourselves and not make them an object of something we would like to change.

You are at the most difficult spot in the Rett road right now, so hang in there. It will get better. There will come a point where the losses stop. It is just individual for every girl. It's so hard to wait and worry, but things will level out. One day you will wake up and realize that she didn't lose anything yesterday … or the day before that … or the day before … and a great burden will lift. I understand the feelings of powerlessness, because I still have days like that. But that feeling will also come to be less frequent and not so strong. True, you can't make it better, but you will be able to make it manageable.

PACK LIGHTLY

CARRY AS LITTLE BAGGAGE AS POSSIBLE. Concentrate on the things that are important.

Sometimes we just get plain negative. But my Cassie is such a gem; I can't imagine her any other way. If I tried, she just wouldn't be the sweet, funny, giggly girl I know. This is who I know, the smell of her skin, her breath, her hair, her soft little feet. I rub them and kiss them and hold her tight. She closes her eyes slowly to tell me she is tired, or giggles when I find her out of her sleeping bag, kneeling and yelling for me. She pouts and makes crocodile tears when she is sad or hurting. It makes me smile and warms my heart. I could wish for more, but when and if those moments come, I will rejoice. We know and learn so much as we all go, and those blessings we cherish.

DANGEROUS CURVES AHEAD

DON'T EXPECT THINGS TO ALWAYS GO SMOOTHLY. They seldom do. But you can deal with most anything if you are prepared. You can't see around the curves so you may not see them up ahead, but know that they are there. Keep your eye on the road, your foot ready at the brake, and your heart on the journey.

Welcome to Rettland

The analogy of a roller coaster might be overworked and trite, but it is so perfect. For a while things go down-hill and you don't think you can stand another minute of it, and then the car starts heading back up and life is good again. The ups and downs might not always be so steep, but the track doesn't flatten completely and we can know that things will fluctuate. That's about the only given with Rett syndrome!

CONSULT THE MAP

WHEN YOU'RE IN UNKNOWN TERRITORY, it's wise to see what has already been mapped. Look in the library for books by and about families who have made this journey. Call IRSA to join a network of local families so that you can share your concerns and get good ideas that already work. Your child's doctor is a good source of information. Keep asking him/her to explain things until you understand.

The first thing I wanted to do is get involved. I wanted to know all there was to know about Rett syndrome, and I felt comforted by the fact that it was a new disorder because all the people who knew about it were also new and were so easily accessible to me.

ASK FOR DIRECTIONS

WHEN YOU DON'T KNOW WHERE YOU ARE or, worse still, where you are going, don't be afraid to ask for directions. Ask the experts, those with experience and training, or ask other parents who have been there. When you have a question you can't answer, give us a call at IRSA. We exist to help you. If we can't answer your question, we'll find someone who can. And remember, there is no such thing as a stupid question.

We spent a fair bit of time looking on the Internet for information. We found the IRSA web site very helpful and got the most hope from the Handbook. It was so hard to read at first; the stories would make you laugh and cry at the same time, but in the end, they gave us hope!

DRIVE GENTLY

IT'S EASY TO BE RESENTFUL OF OTHERS who have found themselves on the easier route, the one you wanted. They can't appreciate your difficulties because they're on the interstate, where the driving is easy. But, remember that even you didn't have so much compassion and understanding until you found yourself facing RS square in the face. Your sensitivity came with the territory. Take some time to tell your friends about your RS road, but don't expect them to understand as well as you do. They can't. Your wisdom came from experience.

I think that we all need to think back to what we were like before Rett syndrome hit our lives. I remember being sympathetic and caring, but I didn't "know" what it was like, day in and day out, to have to care for someone with such acute needs. And I don't expect others to, either. How can they know? You have to live it to know it.

DETOUR AHEAD

BE PREPARED FOR DETOURS. Always have a backup plan for when the ride is not as smooth as you would like. Take along a survival bag with food, wipes, diapers, music, and whatever else works at the time. You may be going over the river and through the woods to grandmother's house, but feel like you packed for a whole troop of Girl Scouts. But being prepared sure makes things easier when you need something to bring your daughter comfort.

Welcome to Rettland

On the other hand, it's not so easy to plan for the emotional curves that loom ahead. If you remember that detours are inevitable, they won't be so disrupting. When the detour is new and unfamiliar, try to picture yourself soon back on course. In Canada, a detour is called a "temporary runaround." Try to see it that way … a temporary runaround. You may have to settle for changes in your daughter's school program while you work out a better plan. You may have to try several seizure medications before you find the right one. Just stick with it. You'll get there. And when you do, it will be another notch on the list of things you've accomplished that you never thought you could.

I could feel I was coping quite well and then, almost out of nowhere, it would break through. I remember when a girl-friend rang one day and asked how things were going. I rattled on about what doctors we were seeing with Georgia and what little improvements I had noticed. Then she said to me "And how are you?" Well, that was too much! I just broke down, sobbing on the phone for no apparent reason and long distance at that. It must have cost her a fortune.

ROAD UNDER CONSTRUCTION

SOMETIMES IT SEEMS LIKE WE'RE ALWAYS BREAKING GROUND, having to explain things over and over again. You will wish people would just leave you alone. Some days, you'll feel like you can take on the world, and other days, you want the world to just go away. You need those days to shut everything off and rest for awhile. Be gentle with yourself. When you've had some quiet time, you'll be refreshed and ready to start again. You don't always have to answer those questions immediately. Think ahead of some short, quick answers that will fill the moment, but don't feel obligated to relive your hurt with anyone who asks. In time, you'll be ready.

When people ask questions, it gives me a chance to talk about Rett syndrome and sometimes make a friend. A few times, the person has just walked away. Children usually ask how old she is and whether she will be able to talk someday. When young children ask what happened to her, I say, "Oh, that's just the way Suzanne is." I don't want to say anything that might make them think that they could suddenly have RS. I also tell them that she can't talk to them but that she would love to have them talk to her.

SOMETIMES YOU'RE A PASSENGER

MOST OF US HAVE JOBS THAT CALL UPON US for a variety of skills and we have to keep changing hats. At work, I'm counselor, researcher, clerk, secretary, writer, advocate, and lobbyist. When I'm at home I'm wife and mother and I have a number of even more important jobs, so I change hats frequently there too. When I visit my grand-kids, I'm Gummy and I put on still another hat. In each of these roles, I try to wear one hat at a time. But when it comes to being Stacie's mom, it's takes a closet full of hats and too many of them are hard hats. I often have to wear several at once … like teacher, therapist, psychologist, nutritionist, advocate, technology specialist, nurse. Having so many hats on is not only heavy on my head, but it's an expensive wardrobe to maintain.

Although I'd like to wear only one hat at a time, it's very hard to do. Now and then, I have to pass some of my hats around. Some time ago, I took inventory of my hat collection and decided some of them just had to go. I sent the teacher hat to school along with the therapist hat. There, they have specially trained experts who wear the hats well. I look to them for advice, but leave the actual teaching and therapy for school hours. This leaves me more time for wearing my favorite, the love hat, which is definitely the most attractive and most useful one of all.

Welcome to Rettland

At the beginning, I spent nearly every hour of the day either doing therapy or driving to therapy. We were both cranky and exhausted. Then I remembered that things in moderation work better. So I made more time for fun stuff and less time for her "workouts." We are both happy now!

REDUCE SPEED

RETTLAND OFTEN SEEMS LIKE THE INDIANAPOLIS 500. It's part of the world as we know it, the RETT RACE. Try not to speed to solve every problem you think might come up in a lifetime. Learn all you can about RS so you will be prepared for what may come, but remember also that the worst of it may never happen. Your best defense is to be prepared, even for what will not happen.

Your child may not have seizures, and may not need scoliosis surgery. It's best to be prepared with good information, but don't accelerate your worries with problems that may not arise. If they do occur, there may be new treatments, or the problem may be mild. When you find yourself getting anxious about how you will handle the future, think about the many challenges you have overcome already and didn't know you could. If you slow down, you minimize the curves and take them with ease. Don't try to do too much. You'll run out of gas a lot faster.

We are not supposed to deal with all of this information at once. We have to let a little bit of it seep into our conscious mind each day. The thing I most want to stress is that even though you have received a very hard blow, your precious child is still the same darling daughter to whom you gave birth. She still loves you the same way you loved her at first. And she always will, no matter what. She is just going to do things a little differently than what you had planned. Her love is unconditional and lasting. She will forgive all of your mistakes. None of us like Rett syndrome, but all of us love our daughters beyond description. It is this love that keeps all of us going.

When we first looked on the Internet and saw all of the symptoms of RS, we were terrified. I was even afraid to see other older girls with RS. But when we did, it was a good experience. The girls were all so different, and all so sweet. Now I know that Laurie may not have the worst-case scenario and I have stopped worrying. Even if she does, I will be able to handle it like the other families do.

SEEK ROADSIDE ASSISTANCE

YOU WILL FIND MANY PEOPLE WILLING TO HELP YOU with your child if you are willing to ask. And that's the key. Family, friends, teachers, and therapists want to do what they can to help now and then, but you must be willing to ask. Let them help. It opens the beauty of your child to them and makes them better people. Don't insist they do it your way unless it's absolutely necessary. Let them know that you are comfortable with their own ways. And don't expect them to be perfect! Your child may welcome the time with someone new more than you enjoy the time alone! Your daughter will survive just as well in the hands of friends if they use a different feeding technique and she will not get arrested by the fashion police if she wears stripes and plaid while you're away. Learn to ask for and accept help.

In the beginning, I could not have made it through if not for family, friends, and most definitely faith! Each helped me work through all the emotions. The other key for me was actually "Doing Something" from researching Rett, finding services and therapies, going to doctors, etc. I just had to feel like I was doing something.

Welcome to Rettland

ENJOY THE RIDE

LOOK ON THE LIGHT SIDE. Laugh along the way. It makes the trip shorter and much more enjoyable. Your sense of humor will see you through some hard times.

Rett has given us our share of rainy days, but it restored our sense of humor. Maybe it's comic relief. You just can't be sad all the time. We don't get upset about what we used to, and we laugh at what we used to think were problems.

GET A TUNE-UP

NO ONE CAN PROVIDE LIMITLESS CARE for another human being without paying a price. Families often say that caregivers are hard to find, and/or that they can't afford them.

Remember that you will never be good for anyone else if you are not good to yourself first. Do whatever it takes. Change your spark plugs and recharge your battery often. Let people help you. If you can't make it to the next rest stop, jump off at the nearest exit and do something just for yourself. It doesn't have to be expensive or time-consuming. Just make sure you do it. You'll have better mileage for the long trip.

Getting out of the house once a week works wonders. Even a couple of hours away leave me feeling better. I try to not even think about RS at these times.

TAKE SHORT TRIPS

WHEN YOU'RE FIRST STARTING OUT, DON'T TRY TO COVER too much ground all at once. In itself, RS can be overwhelming. Trying to figure it all out and plan for the rest of your daughter's life can be immobilizing. So many things change in education, therapy, and even RS itself. When the time arrives, your plans may already be out of date. Don't neglect the future, but concentrate on the short term. Before you know it, you're adjusting.

You get busy fighting for her and her rights, protecting her, and learning what makes her tick and what ticks her off. Then one day you realize that you and your daughter have a wonderful bond and you have the right to laugh and enjoy your lives the best you can. Get the most out of it.

DRIVE DEFENSIVELY

SURROUND YOURSELF WITH POSITIVE PEOPLE and look out for others who do not share your philosophy or your dream for her. Find people who believe in your daughter and who recognize her strengths. More than anything, she needs friends who value her just the way she is. Her world will be brighter and yours a lot easier.

One's approach to other people is so important in how they view our children. Ashley has always been accepted by our friends and family and I feel so fortunate for that. But sometimes people forget to say hello or forget to say goodbye and I know that it is important to Ashley, so I help them remember. We have a cousin who is a great fun-loving gal but I realized that she thought Ashley really was not there. Then Jan started spending some time at our house and Ashley started laughing at her jokes and Jan got to know her better. Now they are buddies and Jan realizes that Ashley really is there, that it is just difficult for her to show how much sometimes. For me, it is a goal and a challenge that by the time they leave, others will fall in love with her.

Welcome to Rettland

PASS WITH CAUTION

IT'S EASY TO RUSH INTO TREATMENTS that might sound promising. We're all eager for the cure. Check out new or unusual therapies or treatments with experts in the field to help evaluate new directions. See if other families have experience that could help.

At first, we hoped there was some medicine or treatment that would take Rett syndrome away or at least make it better, and quickly. We looked into all kinds of alternate therapies but in the end, none really had a track record with RS. I don't want to experiment with her.

BE FRIENDLY IN TRAFFIC

HAVE PATIENCE WITH THOSE WHO NEVER HEARD of Rett syndrome. Take a positive approach and try to understand that those who stare do so not to be unkind but because they are curious. There are some insensitive people in our world, but they really are few and far between. For each person who is unkind, there are dozens of people who are doubly kind. Some people feel guilty that their children are normal and just don't know what to say. Surround yourself with "up" attitudes, and there's no way to go but up.

I used to watch parents of children with disabilities in awe, fascinated by their ability to cope, by their resilience and by their ability to get on with life notwithstanding. Now I feel proud that maybe someone else is watching me in the same way.

I smile, make eye contact, and when appropriate, introduce myself and Darleen. When someone is just being rude, I go on my way and ignore it the best I can.

BACKSEAT DRIVERS

SOMETIMES YOU HAVE TO LISTEN TO BACKSEAT DRIVERS who want to tell you how and what to do with your daughter, even though they have never been to Rettland. You may have to listen to their answers for everything when you know they don't really have a clue what's going on. Just try to remember that they are only trying to help in their own ways. Then, hold on to the confidence that you know your daughter best, and you make the best decisions when it comes to her well-being. And if you have to say so, say so!

My mother-in-law insisted that Kelsey didn't need a feeding tube. We had to show her the nutritionist's report saying she was malnourished. Once Kelsey started to put on weight and had more energy, she agreed with us.

THE JOURNEY, NOT THE DESTINATION

AVOID ASKING "ARE WE THERE YET?" I don't think we're ever "there." We can always find more ways to grow and learn, more ways to appreciate the delicate beauty of our precious daughters. It works a lot better when we concentrate less on reaching the destination and more on observing the wonderful scenery we find along the road. If we spend too much time worrying about tomorrow, we miss the beauty of today. Most people don't understand this concept until they have met a similar challenge. It makes us put everything in perspective and weigh everything according to different standards. Each of us would gladly give up all of our worldly possessions to have our daughters talk with

Welcome to Rettland

us, run with us, things that most folks take for granted every single day. It opens us to the precious intangibles in life that couldn't be measured on any scale.

All you can do is learn to accept it and make the very best of it. Your life doesn't have to be miserable. I know that sometimes it is, but there is happiness after RS. I can't really tell you how to find it, but I know it's there. I've seen it, felt it. It has touched me. I personally think it might live under my daughter's bed. You just gotta find it.

Eventually, I think I have learned to try to find the bright side in all of this. When I sent out my Christmas letter this year, I told everyone that RS is not something I would have chosen to be affected by, but that it has enriched my life in ways that I had never thought of before. When I updated our friends and family members on the children, I found that Tori's paragraph of accomplishments was just as long and hard fought as my older daughter's.

GLANCE IN THE REARVIEW MIRROR

WHEN YOU FIND IT HARD TO LOOK UP, LOOK BACK AT where you have already been and what you and others have already done. Look around you at what has taken place, including some things you may have once thought impossible. Keep it all in perspective.

Our family does not give Rett power to anything in Britt's life. It is a situation that we deal with in a very positive manner every single day. We have experienced the terror and pain in not knowing what was happening, knowing what was happening, accepting what Rett is and does. At the same time it has never, ever held us back.

CHECK THE WARRANTY

THERE ARE NO GUARANTEES IN LIFE. Even in "normal" families, situations arise that are out of our control–situations like other illnesses, drug dependence, financial woes, strained family relationships. No family is immune to pain. Remember that life hands out its share of problems to all of us. Others' problems may not be so visible, but they are there and they hurt. Check out the good things. One of the absolute guarantees of RS is that there is a rich, rewarding "other side" of the pain–the joy of pure and unconditional love and the ability to recognize what matters and what does not.

Wrap your angel in a world of love and support. Learn all you can about Rett syndrome, but don't expect it all to happen to your girl. She will be her own unique self. She will sparkle, as all angels do. She will challenge you as you never knew you could be challenged. You will grow to be her strongest advocate, her most ardent supporter, and best caretaker. You will learn how special it is to be the parent of an angel.

ROAD RAGE

SOMETIMES WE JUST HAVE TO PUT UP WITH insensitive people. Children who point do so naturally just out of curiosity, but adults who stare may be hard to excuse. Don't automatically assume that the stares are negative. Always take into consideration that the stares may be friendly—from another special parent or someone who admires your interaction with your child, recognizing how well you cope with someone with so many obvious special needs. It may be a professional who is just "observing," or someone who thinks your child is beautiful. Most people who stare are just curious and don't realize they are staring. Sometimes you might stare back. Another time you might stop and politely explain about your daughter. Every now and then you just have to let loose and tell the staring person he's rude. But when you feel the staring is intrusive, there are many ways to cope.

Welcome to Rettland

There will be a few very special people who will be drawn to your daughter. Most won't understand her and will be too self-conscious to ask questions. But the more exposure she has to people of all ages, the more chance those special people will have to get to know her. She will not mess around with superficial friendships. When someone is drawn to her, it will be someone whose life she will influence in a huge way. There are those who are meant to meet her, even in passing, and souls she is meant to touch.

To this day, there are still those I wish would make more effort to be a part of Angie's life. It can still be painful when she is slighted. But there are those unexpected jewels who have made the effort over the years: those who come to her and sing her songs, who meet her once and write poems about her, who show her pictures and tell her their secrets. There are the university student caregivers who are now doctors and nurses, who invite her to their weddings and their grooms ask Angie to dance. There is my niece who is one of her caregivers, who takes her out to dinner with a group of her peers while they sip margueritas and bat their eyes at the waiters.

As the mother of an adult with RS, my response to other people's reactions has changed so much throughout the years. I remember when it used to get me very upset, crying, even not wanting to go out with Renee. That one didn't last long. Then it was anger towards the gawkers. I would stare back, give dirty looks. That one still pops up from time to time, but they never make me cry anymore. If I did find myself crying at this stage of Renee's life, it would be for those naive, ignorant people who are really the ones with the disability. I went through a stage where I tried to be informative, even handing out little cards I typed up. But I found that once a brief explanation was given, the curiosity was gone. I allow people to be curious. After all, who isn't? But I certainly can tell the difference. The way I handle it most of the time now is to speak loud enough to Renee about that gawker by saying something like "Renee, do you owe that lady money?" or "Renee, someone is here to see you." Things like that usually turn their heads quickly.

Kids are just plain curious. I let them look at Renee and watch her. I think it is helpful for children who are not exposed to others with disabilities to learn some by watching, and ultimately asking their mom or dad. Unfortunately, it seems that the adults are the main culprits in this awful situation that we all deal with. For all of you that are still in the first stage where you are emotionally torn by these reactions, rise above it. You have been chosen to do a job that those people would never be capable of doing. Don't give them the opportunity to hurt your feelings. Just know in your mind that although they have a strange way of showing it, the people who make us mad or upset us over their ignorance are usually envious of you for doing the job you are doing and they also know, deep down, that they could not do it.

This may sound corny but my recommendation is to actually practice ahead of time some good responses to these situations. Even role-play them with someone if you can. I am one of those people who always think of that really zinger reply about thirty minutes afterward, so I am left fuming and stewing about what I should have or could have said. Practicing ahead of time helps you bring out those really good responses when you may not otherwise be able to.

Some people use humor, sarcasm, a good put down ... whatever works for you. Even patience and education can work sometimes. Invite a good friend over, pop open a nice bottle of wine and have your friend help you brainstorm some good responses to have handy. This can actually be very therapeutic and fun (I just don't recommend you use any of the replies created after more than three glasses of wine).

Coping with stares has been an evolving process. It hurt brutally when Ellie was a toddler, especially before she was diagnosed with RS, because even I stared sometimes just wondering what happened! However, Ellie is seven now and coping with stares is much easier, especially if Ellie's happy. Sometimes I help Ellie say hello with her communicator. One particularly effective reaction to stares is to ask, "Are you in The Club?" If the staring person looks bewildered I explain that I saw her looking at my daughter and thought maybe she had a loved

Welcome to Rettland

one with a disability. That has quite often opened the conversation to discuss RS. And several times I've been answered "Yes, I'm in The Club ... my daughter/son has disabilities." Getting Ellie to smile at someone or make eye contact is tremendously effective—she can melt a heart at fifty paces.

Stares when she is crying in pain or unhappiness is a little different. I've been known to look at a staring person and say "Rett syndrome. It's tough."

When I see people staring, I remind myself how long I stared and cried and wondered about Jean. I am in a place of acceptance now, but it was a journey, so I try to have compassion for those who have not received the gift I have, to see beyond the outer. I usually will say something like, "Her name is Jean and she loves to use the computer." This startles them out of the dazed look and helps them to connect with her, and mentioning the computer helps them to know they are looking at a feeling, thinking person.

I decided to smile at those who stare at our daughter. Most often, people will return the smile. A smile makes others feel comfortable and has even opened up others to say "hello" to our daughter. It's a much kinder and civilized way of handling the curiosity of children and adults.

HAZARDOUS ROADS

SOME DAYS ARE BETTER THAN OTHERS IN RETTLAND. No matter how accepting we are or how strong we feel, there will be times when our sad feelings just get the best of us. A trip to the pediatrician with "typical" children all around or another child's birthday party is a reminder of the milestones we may never see. Being excluded from an activity because she can't perform or not getting an invitation because she doesn't "fit in" with the group are hurtful, even if they weren't meant to be that way. Others often don't know what to do or say, and it is up to us to show them.

In the beginning, I would get teary eyed and sometimes cry that my baby wasn't able to do the same things that kids her age were able to do. I would ask a lot of "why" questions of God, and pray that she would get better. I also didn't want to put myself in the position to be around other kids at all.

What really hurts is some of our "friends" who know about her difficulties and exclude her from activities. We went to a party, and no one thought of even asking if she wanted to bob for apples, paint a pumpkin, or pin the nose on the witch.

It is upsetting to see her not be able to join in and occasionally, only my other daughter gets invited. But recently we have found a lot more friends who try to accommodate Charlie in everything. The only way we could explain to the other children why Charlie couldn't play was by telling them "her legs don't work" and they seem to understand that.

At first, birthday parties were very difficult. I would often end up in the bathroom to shed a tear. Now, I try not to compare our daughter with the other children, and I get her involved in the activities. Many times, the other children enjoy helping her. I know Danielle enjoys participating in the games.

SIGNPOSTS

LABELS CAN BE USEFUL FOR MANY THINGS, and the situations and purposes for which they are used can vary significantly. They are often necessary, especially when it comes to getting appropriate services and funding. At the same time, some labels can be used to deny services, and limit expectations and opportunities. Sometimes we have to be a bit creative, using more than one label in different situations to get what is needed.

Welcome to Rettland

Often, it is not what the label *says*, but what it *gets* that is important. Requirements and classifications for services vary from state to state. Keep informed on what these are so you can act wisely.

Don't let labels define you or your child, but learn to use labels to get what your child needs. For instance, "malnutrition" or "failure to thrive" does not mean you are a bad mother or that your child is not happy. It means that your child is unable to take in or metabolize food correctly to gain weight. Use this label to get insurance to pay for a g-tube or food supplements. If you think program services are more appropriate under the label "mental retardation," use it. If services under an "autism" program seem more appropriate, use the fact that Rett syndrome is still listed as an autistic spectrum disorder. If your daughter needs a nap at school every day, use a "health impaired" label. This label also addresses other health problems, such as seizures, breathing, and even attendance. "Communication impaired" covers speech therapy and augmentative devices. "Orthopedically impaired" provides for physical and occupational therapies and adaptive equipment. Use the labels to get what your daughter needs.

It is easy to be discouraged from treating her like an intelligent person, because there is so much we have to assume because she cannot tell us, or write or sign like other kids. But I decided somewhere along the way that I was going to assume the best, not the worst.

GETTING THERE IN ONE PIECE

WE ALL START ON THIS JOURNEY AT A PLACE CALLED LOSS. We may find ourselves in locations like Shock and Denial, where we feel numb head to toe. Further along the road, we may arrive at Fear, Guilt, Anger, and Depression, and we may get stuck for a while. Those who have made the trip before us know that after a time, we will make our way to higher places, Understanding and Acceptance, and we will be able to move on. But we need to remember that we all move at different speeds and every stage of the journey is necessary and natural as part of the healing process. We may get to one place only to bounce back to an earlier one time and again.

It may be hard to see at the start, but every painful moment leads us to greater growth. Those who have already traveled this way tell us that after a stay in Rettland, we learn that the soul is without rainbows if the heart is without tears. We discover that what takes the most work brings the most joy, and what we appreciate most is what does not come easily.

We are all different people from our experience with RS, yet we are the same. We learn about priorities and the very simple, most important things in life. In the process, we find ourselves stronger in the broken places and more resilient. We learn patience, wisdom, courage, and strength. In the classroom of life, we find that our daughters are not the students. They are the teachers, for they face the real tests and give the real lessons. Our daughters are far braver, far stronger, and far more patient than we are. And we now know that when God measures a person, He puts a tape around the heart, not the head. Their beautiful, searching, penetrating eyes dance with glee, sing with laughing abandon, and speak to us with their own endearing language of love. These eyes sometimes flash with anger, flood with tears of frustration, and widen with fascination and wonder. They perk up with enthusiasm and fall downcast with disappointment. These eyes express in silence what language cannot, reaching out to capture warm places in our hearts. Our journey with them is jeweled with priceless treasures if we stop to look along the way.

Welcome to Rettland

I feel that dealing with Sara's disability made me let go of that striving to attain the perfect life, perfect mother, perfect nurse, and perfect family. It helped me accept imperfection and find value where others might not. I have learned more that is truly important in life from Sara and having Sara than any book or college degree could teach.

Our girls want to be loved, respected, acknowledged, and recognized for who they are and what they accomplish in life. It is not what we had in mind for her, but then if she had had a choice, it might not have been what she chose either. To all the young families with a new diagnosis: believe in yourself, your gut feelings and your daughter. It is your life and it does not have to be a disaster for the next many years. Treat your daughter as you would any child. You have nothing to lose, but much to gain.

We all have to come to terms with our situations because in the end that is what it is; another situation in our lives. That doesn't discount the situation's impact or importance; however, Rett syndrome does not need to take our life and life essence. We experience the emotional turmoil and the joy, the frustration and the peace. Our dreams are dashed and we find hope. With every single thing we experience, both good and bad, we find something more within us to keep us going, to be the best we can for our children.

Carol is bright and engaged cognitively. She's socially engaged and enjoys our adventures. Successes in the academic area are few and honestly, I don't expect a lot in that area. I accepted, many years ago the "Rett Package." I know the course Carol's life is taking and accept it. When I look at Carol, I see "her" perfection. She doesn't know about war and the ugliness of our world. She only knows about how much the people around her care and love her. Every bird that sits on her window ledge brings her joy. She will always think the Christmas Light Parade at Disneyland happens just because she's there. She will always laugh at my hats and noises. And, she will always know that everyone in her life better treat her right or her mom is coming after them. A can of whipped cream is almost better than George Strait. I love her and she loves me and that's what is important. What I do care about is simple ... having fun with Carol and making her life as meaningful as possible for the time we have together. I don't try to "fix" Rett. I choose to work around it.

She taught me that one hug really can make all the difference. She taught me that singing was the heart's joy and we sing together every single day. She taught me that the eyes can truly say so much more than words will ever. She taught me.

When we had Amanda, we never knew right away that she was teaching us and helping us to face the challenges that life would bring us in the years to come. She taught us that love was stronger than any other emotion, and that with love we could overcome anything. She taught us to have hope and faith no matter what life brings our way. She taught us that life wasn't always going to turn out the way we want it, but we could make it better and even joyful regardless of any situation. The angel in our life taught us a lot but mostly she's taught us that life is a learning experience.

Just remember, you will have good days and bad days, you will adjust the dreams you have for your child but will be in awe at each and every accomplishment. I won't ever say it's easy but the entire experience will change you and probably other family members forever. You will learn much about compassion, strength, and patience. You will learn not to take little things for granted. The sky will become bluer and brighter than it has ever looked before and you will notice the smallest things and see the beauty in them.

The difference between stumbling blocks and stepping stones is in how you use them. No matter what your belief system is, this saying holds true. Simply, we can use our stones to build walls or to lay down a path. Rome wasn't built in a day, but I'm sure it started with

Welcome to Rettland

some stepping stones. If you can clear that path as we travel down it, you have made a road. Others who follow in our footsteps are free to build shelters that will preserve the endeavor. Many times we get lost in how hard the passage is, or how far we have yet to travel. Sometimes our load on the journey gets heavy and we need to sit down and take a rest. It's OK to admit to needing a break; you are doing important work. If we bring people along with us on the journey, they can pick up the slack once in a while. Turn around in your footsteps and see how far you have come. You may have just set down more stepping stones than you remember. Go ahead and count them. Each of those little stones is a blessing, nothing less than an everyday miracle.

BEFORE I WAS A SPECIAL PARENT

By Kathy Hunter

Before I was a special parent ...
I thought RETT SYNDROME was something you got from
Watching too many reruns *of Gone with the Wind*
That is, after you recovered from Scarlett Fever

Before I was a special parent ...
PT meant part time
OT meant overtime
BRACES were something you wore on your teeth.
And a WIDE GAIT was attached to my fence

Before I was a special parent ...
I actually had a savings account
I didn't know that I should have invested heavily
In paper towels, Attends, Velcro and applesauce

Before I was a special parent ...
RIGIDITY was my anal-retentive boss
SELF-INJURIOIUS BEHAVIOR was what I did on a night at the casino
MOOD SWINGS came only with PMS
And VALIUM was used by high-strung socialites

Before I was a special parent ...
I thought BUTTONS went on your blouse, not your belly
GENES were labeled Levi or Guess
And MUTATIONS were confined to the Incredible Hulk

Before I was a special parent ...
I thought the IRSA was the IRS Association
HANDWRINGING was what you did after an audit
SEIZURE was what they did when you failed
And RESIDENTIAL PLACEMENT was a jail term

Welcome to Rettland

Before I was a special parent …
STATUS was something you earned, not dreaded
And when you got it, MOBILITY was usually upward
A FINE MOTOR ACTIVITY was taking the Chevy thru the car wash
And a GROSS MOTOR MOVEMENT was the universal one-finger salute

Before I was a special parent …
VACANT SPELLS were related to real estate
SPASTICITY was a good Jerry Lewis movie
The IDEA was just a bright little thought
And GUILT came from something I did, not from something I didn't do

Before I was a special parent …
BALANCE referred to my checkbook
CIRCULATION was about my hometown newspaper
HYPERVENTILATION was limited to Rover's greeting
And CURVATURE was very sexy

Before I was a special parent …
COMMUNICATION was about saying all the right things
IEP was pronounced IPE
INCLUSION meant tax added
And IMPACTION was a speedway crash

Before I was a special parent …
My other children were called kids, Not SIBLINGS
They played together, not INTERACTED
And my husband's three most important words before drifting off to sleep were
I Love You instead of DID SHE POOP?

Before I was a special parent …
I thought shoes with VELCRO were for lazy people
ADAPT meant telling someone to get over it already
And ASPIRATION meant ambition.

BUT ALSO

Before I was a special parent …

I didn't know that SORROW never leaves you where it found you

I didn't know that such unbridled JOY could come from heartbreak

I didn't know that my child would be my TEACHER

I didn't know the meaning of UNCONDITIONAL LOVE

I didn't realize that the little stuff is really THE BIG STUFF

Welcome to Rettland

I didn't know how well someone could COMMUNICATE without words

I didn't know that milestones are not as important as SMILESTONES

I didn't know that my child would TOUCH the world not from what she has done, but from what she cannot do

I didn't know the POWER of her powerlessness.

I didn't know that I had so much to LEARN.

"Learn to get in touch with the silence within yourself and know that everything in life has a purpose."

– ELISABETH KUBLER ROSS

Family Voices

FAMILY TIES

FAMILIES COME IN ALL SHAPES and sizes these days. With the high rate of divorce, single and blended families have become as common as the traditional two-parent home. Many grandparents are raising their grandchildren as their own when the parents either can't or won't. And some children enter the family through adoption. In most families today, both parents must work outside the home to make ends meet, so they must either rely on other family members or caregivers to help out. While today's families may look different from the past, they are still the glue that keeps us connected and gives us the love and security we need to thrive.

GETTING THE DIAGNOSIS

WHEN A CHILD WITH RS becomes a part of the family, there may be a number of adjustments. After welcoming their "healthy" child home from the hospital, the succeeding months may bring great anguish to parents, who have begun to slowly realize that the child is not developing as expected. The stress of dealing with finding a specialist, making an appointment and the agonizing weeks to months of waiting for the appointment to arrive makes it a difficult time. Parents are able to keep their composure by denying that anything serious could be wrong. But when the doctor confirms their fear that things are not as they should be, their emotions may begin to spin out of control. They are sometimes unable to face even relatives and friends with what seems like the painful truth that their child will always be different.

"Let us make one point; that we meet each other with a smile when it is difficult to smile. Smile at each other; make time for each other in your family."

– MOTHER TERESA

In this new world of disabilities, families find themselves inundated with new information, confusing language, acronyms they never heard before, a long line of specialists, and a bewildering maze of education laws and insurance regulations. Brothers and sisters may feel bewildered by their parents' confusion and sadness, and may feel left out of discussions about their sister. They may feel that their own needs are being neglected. And, of course, they may feel guilty for all of their negative emotions.

Other family members may just not know what to say or how to act. If they have had experience, they will understand that the best thing they can do is to pledge their support and love.

Families are like mobiles. Each member is connected and dependent on the others, and what happens to one has an impact on all the others. It becomes a challenge to keep balance and equilibrium so that everyone gets a fair share of time and attention, and is able to express

Family Voices

their feelings equally. Most families find strength in various places—information gathering, the support and encouragement of others, meditation, a healthy lifestyle, taking care of themselves, and calling on their higher power for inner calm to restore balance in troubled times. They build resilience by talking, sharing, and communicating with one another.

While it is true that the direction of their lives may have changed due to the diagnosis, it is so important for parents to realize that their child has not changed. She is still the little girl they loved yesterday, the little girl who they will love forever. They will face some tough challenges, but their love for her will lead them to make the right decisions for her future and for the rest of the family.

BREAKING THE NEWS TO OTHERS

GIVING THE NEWS TO FRIENDS AND RELATIVES can be hard at times, depending on their sensitivity and maturity. They can be a great sense of strength and support, or they can leave you feeling guilty and hurt. Well-intentioned people sometimes just do not know how to react. Some people find it hard to accept handicaps in others and can be rejecting. Others who were once close may create emotional distance because they don't know what to say or do. It may help to tell them how hard it was for you to accept the handicap at first and to tell them you understand that they may feel uncomfortable. Let them know how much their understanding and support means.

In time, you may find that the interests you once shared with other couples are no longer there, and your friendships may shift to other families who share your situation. There is much to be gained from kinship with other families with special needs children, sharing joys and sorrows in new relationships that will last a lifetime.

IRSA has great license plate holders and bumper stickers to break the ice: "I Love Someone with Rett Syndrome" and "Care Today … Cure Tomorrow" are great "notices" about RS. There are also refrigerator magnets, business-size cards to hand out, fliers, and brochures you can order from the web site.

The friends I once had seem to not call me as much, come around, or include me in their lives. This is very hard! I am not really mad at them, just more hurt.

When Joanne was first diagnosed, we decided to be open and up front about our situation. We called our families together and told them all at the same time. We all had a good cry and felt that they were there for us. In truth, our families have really left us feeling confused more often than not and we've often found it hard to deal with their reactions. There are too many expectations and feelings tied into all of that.

One of the pivotal times in our lives was shortly after our daughter was diagnosed. We had decided to tell everyone about our situation, including families, friends, our staffs, and our students. We found the response overwhelming. We spoke with our families as a group and our friends individually, and then we each took the time to speak to our staffs. We were not surprised to have the entire room crying along with us. From that day forward, we knew that we had people behind us no matter what.

WHEN PEOPLE ASK

YOU WILL PROBABLY MEET PEOPLE in the grocery store line or at the mall who can't help noticing your daughter, and they may be inquisitive. If they ask about her and the time is right for you, just explain it in your own words.

Family Voices

The amount of detail I go into varies depending on who I am talking to. I usually tell people about the motor planning problems it causes and the varying degrees in which it affects these girls. It gives me a chance to "brag" about Tori's accomplishments and to tell people what a little fighter she is.

Unfortunately the first response often is "Oh, what a shame." I usually say, "No, it's not really a shame, she just has a different lifestyle and she's very happy." Then I tell them to go to the Internet for more information because it's very interesting reading.

I always appreciate people talking to Angie. When they ask questions of her, I just smile and say, "She can't talk, but she understands you." I think people feel awkward, not knowing what to say. I felt that way in my pre-Angie days. I agree it's hard in most situations to give explanations of RS, especially while standing in line somewhere. I don't like to get into discussions about RS in front of Angie, because I think it must be embarrassing for her. I think most people want to be kind. At times, it is hard to come up with an appropriate response until much later, when it is too late.

We usually tell them she has RS, a neurological disorder that robs her of most of everything but her spirit. Then I tell them God sent us an angel with a broken wing and we have to take good care of her, love her, and make her smile.

We begin by saying it's a neurological disorder that affects her ability to have purposeful use of her hands and low muscle tone, which is why she doesn't walk or crawl. We then continue by letting people know that she is delightful in her own ways, her smiles, her big brown eyes, and her sweet voice. If the person is satisfied with that, we let them know she is not lacking in personality and she is as sweet as they come and leave it there. But if there is genuine interest, we let them know some statistics, and that some girls walk, some are potty trained, and some have limited verbal abilities, all things we hope Ellie will have someday.

I explain that the apraxia can really be the most frustrating thing for Joanne, as that delay in body response often leads people to think that she doesn't know what is going on or that she can't do something. I encourage people to treat her like any other four year-old child but to be patient and to give her time to respond. I will also explain that we don't rely on her to speak for communication, as there is some frustration for her there, too, and then will go on to explain in brief how we use pictures to communicate.

AN OPEN LETTER TO FAMILY AND FRIENDS

IT MUST BE HARD FOR YOU TO UNDERSTAND what we are going through since our daughter was diagnosed with RS. Sometimes her behavior can be very upsetting, as she screams for hours. Once alert and attentive, she now often looks away and avoids our gaze. She no longer shows interest in toys she once loved. Our lives have become complicated with a future for which we were not prepared. Raising this child is the greatest challenge we will probably ever face. We have gone through the same stages of grief that one would experience at the death of a loved one.

All of our resources, emotional, physical and financial, have been at times taxed beyond measure. However, we know that with love and patience, we can overcome the challenge and provide the best possible for our beloved child and for our family. We try to take it one day at a time. Some days are good and some bad. On the good days, we appreciate the beautiful way she has touched our lives with her precious innocence and taught us the true meaning of love. On the bad days, we need your help.

Our lives will never be the same again, but in so many ways we are enriched. I am sure there are times when you don't know how to respond to our situation. Your support

Family Voices

and loving care can make such a difference in the way we are able to cope. You probably don't know just how much the little things mean. These suggestions may be helpful:

1. Don't be afraid to ask about our daughter. We have spent many hours with specialists to learn about her condition. It helps to know that you are interested.

2. Respect our decisions about her care. We have listened carefully to the recommendations of many doctors and therapists, and have based our decisions on what we feel to be the best for her.

3. Treat our daughter as a part of the family. Include her in the other children's activities. She may not be able to do everything that the others do, but it is important that she does take part. Nothing hurts more than having your child overlooked because she is different.

4. Teach your children about her. Explain her condition in terms they can understand. Tell them it is OK to ask questions. Ten questions are better than one stare. When your children see that you treat her first as a child, they will respond in the same way.

5. Don't forget to say hello. Although she cannot talk, she does love to be spoken to. It may take her a moment to respond, but she will. Good things come to those who wait.

6. Please understand that family gatherings, particularly birthday parties, can be very difficult at times. No matter how accepting we are, we still agonize about the milestones our daughter will not achieve. With time, the pain will ease. Try to be sensitive.

7. Ask if you can help once in a while, but don't be surprised if we don't accept your offer at first. It is hard to let others help when society has taught us that as special parents we have to do everything "special." Keep asking until we let you help. It isn't that we don't need the help; it's just that we don't want to burden you if your offer is not sincere.

8. Offer to care for our daughter sometime so that we can get away together. Remember that everything we do and everywhere we go is much more complicated than the ordinary. There is no such thing as sleeping in on Sunday morning, or any morning for that matter.

9. Offer to feed our daughter at the next family gathering. It does not take a special technique that you do not have, nor will she eat better for us. It will be a good break for her and for us.

10. Don't leave our daughter out when you buy little gifts for the children. If the gift is something she cannot chew or a toy she cannot play with, find something that she can be happy with.

11. Don't tell us that we were specially "chosen" for this child. We are ordinary people who are striving against sometimes extraordinary circumstances to provide a "normal" family life. We were not singled out for the job. It just happened at our house. It could just as easily happen at yours, and you would carry on as we have, like ordinary loving parents who care.

12. Don't underestimate the power of your caring. Everything you do to try to understand will help more than you will ever know.

My friend sent me this powerful message and for the first time, I felt empowered and smiled: "I am so sorry to hear about Vivi. I don't know anything about RS so I don't know what reassuring words I can say except that Vivi is a spunky, strong-willed, intelligent child. Right now she is like a flower seed. She has everything within

Family Voices

her to be all that the universe has designed her to be. Your love, your care, and discipline is her sun, her water, her earth. Vivi holds the promise, and you hold the possibility. Rett syndrome is a life challenge; RS is not Vivi."

REACHING OUT, LOOKING IN

THE SAINTS COME MARCHIN' IN

WE HAVE NORMAL RESOURCES, and our kids have exceptional needs. Most people don't know what it is like to "live the RS life." They are willing to help, but don't know where to begin. But they are not mind readers; it is up to us to tell them how they can help. And then, accept it!

LITTLE THINGS DO MEAN A LOT

HAVING A CHILD WITH RS teaches you that the little things in life really are the big things. We learn to enjoy the simplest pleasures and celebrate small victories, especially when they relate to our children. So, we appreciate every ounce of help we get. The struggles we face with a disabled child are so emotionally taxing that the simplest card or phone call can give us enough energy to be able to face the day.

MOTHERS

MOTHERS ARE THE USUAL CARETAKERS IN OUR SOCIETY, and typically, they are nurturing and protective. All too often, they take care of everyone else in the family, leaving little or no time for themselves. The job of caring for a child with handicaps is a twenty-four hour a day, seven day a week labor of love. The needs of special children do not get less as they get older; often, they are greater. While it may seem impossible, it is so important for mothers to take care of themselves first. Taking time away from caring for their child is just as important for their survival as eating and breathing. Even twenty minutes away reading, jogging, chatting with a friend, or napping can be magical. Moms really have to work at achieving balance in their lives and at keeping their sanity. We deserve to have lives of our own, and we will only have this if we are willing to step forth and claim it by doing those things we know we must, beginning with taking care of ourselves.

In most families, one parent becomes the "designated expert," and typically it is the mother who takes on this role. This may leave the father feeling abandoned, not only when it comes to information on his child, but also in his relationship with his partner. If decision-making is not shared, lines of communication about their child may become strained.

FATHERS

FATHERS ARE OFTEN MORE PHYSICAL in their interaction with their children. While Mom holds the child close, Dad carries her on his shoulders or tosses her in the air. They also react differently to having a child with special needs.

We all adjust to the diagnosis in different ways and on our own time-lines. Fathers sometimes take a little longer in the process because they are off to work and not always as involved in the daily care of their daughter and so are not confronted with the reality

Family Voices

of their many special needs. Sometimes, fathers find more ways to escape facing the situation than mothers—staying late at work or making other excuses to be away from home. Sometimes, they are not as interested in talking about the situation, but this doesn't mean they aren't thinking about it. Men are natural born "fixers," and many times they are intensely internalizing how they can fix this unfixable situation. Fathers don't generally express their pain like mothers do; society says it's not cool to cry. They don't talk to their male friends about it any more than they talk about relationships during the ball game. The loss of control over the situation can be maddening. But they love just as deeply and they grieve just as much.

And, of course, there are many fathers who absorb information like a sponge, take RS on with a vengeance, and get into the fathering role with gusto, becoming their child's best advocate and friend.

YES, IT'S PERSONAL ... AND MUCH MORE

By Ed Flaherty

An editor told me early in my career as a journalist not to take the job home or let home into the job. Don't take it personally, kid, the editor said. It's just a story. But this story is personal, as personal as it gets, and I think you should know that.

Jessica was born on my birthday, and my father's birthday. The third generation of Gabordi kids to celebrate that July day. She is the fourth of our five children. Her birth and early development were normal. She is olive-skinned with dark, Italian features. Absolutely gorgeous.

By about her sixth month, we began to notice small things, the kinds of things only parents would see and worry about. She was a little quieter than the others had been, a little slow to crawl, that kind of thing. Our doctor told us we were worrying too much. Everything would be fine.

About the time she was a year old, I taught Jessica to play patty cake. She was getting good at it. She was making sounds as if she was ready to talk. I know I heard her say daddy once. She has never said another word.

Jessica cannot walk or talk. She cannot feed herself or use a bathroom on her own. She has no control over arm movements. Head development has slowed in proportion to the rest of her body. Mental retardation is assumed. She has lost many of the skills she learned before her first birthday.

We spent sixteen months trying doctor after doctor, moving from hospital to hospital, traveling hundreds of miles and spending tens of thousands of dollars to get a diagnosis. Finally, we learned Jessica has a rare developmental disorder called RS.

The doctor who diagnosed Jessica with RS, she described Jessica's disorder as "the worst-case scenario." My wife and I were sitting on the floor of her office, holding hands, surrounded by medical professionals, a sociologist and a psychologist when she told us that our lives had just changed forever.

That was a decade ago. And she was right.

Rett children experience rapid regression of learned skills beginning about their first birthday. They learn skills, then lose them. Like patty-cake and being able to call for her daddy. It primarily affects girls. New research suggests it can also affect

Family Voices

boys. Jessica would learn something, and lose it. Learn it again, and lose it. Over and over.

We lived about four hours from Pittsburgh. On the way home, I had a dream for the first of God only knows how many times. I was kneeling before God as He stood before a light switch, flicking it off and on, off and on. I was pleading with him to leave the light on. I woke up crying, covered in sweat. That part has never happened again.

None of this makes Jessica your problem. The last thing I want for her is to become a special-interest case, demanding special rights, embroiled in some political argument. I have a good job and health benefits. Even so, we struggle to keep up with Jessica's needs.

She is my wife's full-time job, a labor of incredible love. But we didn't dream that we would lose Jessica's Community Alternatives Program benefits in moving from an economically depressed state like West Virginia to highly developed North Carolina. I worry about services she has lost, therapy she no longer gets, missed opportunities and lost skills. Every time I see an unnecessary road project–one of which could probably fund the entire shortfall in CAP spending in the state–or other waste, I get angry. Then I get over it, and move on.

I understand. Before Jessica, children like her were invisible to me, too. I know that was because I didn't want to see them, didn't understand them. That is one of the many things Jessica changed about me.

Dressing Jessica can sometimes take me thirty minutes or longer. My wife, Donna, has it down to a few minutes. Feeding her can take an hour or longer, and that cannot be rushed. A girl with RS has about a ninety-five percent chance of surviving to age twenty-five, with one of the biggest risks related to difficulty swallowing, according to experts. Life expectancy for people with RS is not fully established, since it is a relatively new diagnosis.

We have resisted having feeding tubes placed in her. We have opposed unnecessary and redundant testing and turned down offers to have her considered for "studies" by medical research institutes. We select doctors who share our view she is a child, not a case. We want as much about her life as can be to be normal.

Life with Jessica is hard. But it is also a dream come true. She is like living with an angel, a person whose smile makes life worth living. She is worth everything.

I used to wonder, sometimes in silence, especially when I was alone with Jessica, other times aloud, why God chose us as Jessica's parents. We have learned much about what is important in life from Jessica. She strengthened our faith and bound our family together. That is not always the case: divorce rates are high among families with children with disabilities. Her challenges tested our own marriage, then drew us even closer.

Her eight year-old brother prays daily that his sister will walk and talk some day. That is at the top of every wish list he has ever written. She is the inspiration and love of her sisters' lives. Her oldest brother is about to enter medical school because Jessica inspired him to want to help other people.

The system our state has set up is forcing families to consider splitting up in order to provide care for children like Jessica. They know we won't do that, that we won't institutionalize our children, so services these children need sometimes are not provided. A generation ago, we would not have had an option. Jessica would have been

Family Voices

placed in a state institution, a more costly, less effective and, certainly, less loving, method of caring for our children.

Parents of children like Jessica have started filing court suits across the nation against states that take this tactic, and they are winning. But it shouldn't have to come to that. The immorality of depriving such children or forcing families to give them up is even more obvious than the legal issues.

The prospect of my child living in an institution is my greatest fear, even more so than her death. My own daily prayer is that God takes Jessica first so that she will never face that prospect. That may seem hard, but Jessica should be with our family, and so should all children, whenever possible.

So it is not sympathy that we seek, only what is right and fair, for our child and the thousands like her across the state.

Like you, I feel like the prevailing topic between me and close friends/family is "Jessica and her Diagnosis." Most of them offer up the typical "it will all work out for the best," "you'll all adopt new dreams and go on to be happy." On the one hand, it's therapeutic for me, but on the other hand, I feel suffocated by the diagnosis, like there's no escaping it.

I no longer wonder why my child is disabled. I've decided it is because I can speak out, that I'm in a position to bring these children to public attention. So I am.

I am adding my voice, speaking out for my child and the others like her who make up society's weakest and most voiceless. Maybe that's the why—the answer to the unanswerable question. Maybe that's what God had intended.

Personal? Oh, yes, it's real personal.

My husband was staying away, becoming a workaholic, distracting himself so that his head wouldn't dance with the questions and pain. He internalized that he now had to carry the full financial burden.

My daughter Jillian's birth would be better described as a surgical emergency than a natural, beautiful moment. Although by all indications she emerged from the traumatic experience no worse for the wear, I wasn't convinced. Some part of my brain believed that she must have suffered some sort of damage. I spent the first six months of her life staring at her, not in the way a father gazes lovingly into his baby's eyes, but in the way a doctor intently studies an X-ray or a biopsy slide. I worried about every twitch and sound she made, believing I was seeing the first manifestations of her damaged brain. For a while my concern eased as she began reaching some early milestones. But when she hadn't taken a step or spoken a word by eighteen months, it was clear that something was wrong, and once again I became fixated on her "problem," and resolved to find the "answer." After a bout of seizures, a blood test confirmed a MECP2 mutation. Ironically, the thing I had fixated on for years (the delivery) turned out to have absolutely nothing to do with her problems. It was a shock to learn that the truth was actually worse than my greatest fears. But after the diagnosis an interesting thing happened. I no longer looked at her in order to try to "figure her out." She wasn't a collection of symptoms waiting to be diagnosed, she was just a beautiful little girl who happened to have RS. And little by little, I began to focus less on her limitations, and more on her. I realized that she has just as much (if not more) to offer than any "normal" kid. Jillian has taught me so many things I never would have known. She has taught me the meaning of unconditional love. She has taught me that absolute joy can be found in a sly smile or even a loving slap on the face. She has taught me that there are indeed perfectly pure people in the world, people who don't have the ability to express a false emotion. When I look at Jillian, I know that I'm seeing exactly how she feels. If she's smiling, I know that she feels complete happiness

Family Voices

in every fiber of her body. And I now know that my primary job in life is to keep that smile on her face as much as humanly possible.

Courtney, thirteen, is one of four and it has never been easy in our house. In the early days when she was the only child, I had a very hard time of it. I was under constant feelings of guilt that I caused her to be like she was. My fault, no one else's. When she started regressing around at about two years, I think I did too. I started not coming home, being a jerk. I finally came around, grew up and am very glad I did. I try very hard to be as big a part of Courtney's life as Mom. I wash her, feed her, and play with her, do all the school stuff, everything. Mind you it's not easy, especially with four young ones around to demand more and more time. Mom and I try to give each of our kids as much equal time as we possibly can. Courtney has taught us things we could only have learned from someone like her. Her absolute love and devotion to us has made us as strong a family unit as we could possibly expect.

In our house it gets better day by day. It has been really hard, both for me and my husband. When Louise is having a bad day, he will also have a bad day. He says that he loves her so much and his heart is broken. Therefore, it´s easier for him to cope with his emotions by taking a walk or sitting at the computer. I have no doubt that he loves her, but it is hard when he turns his back on her. He tells me that he just needs more time to learn how to cope with it and accept it.

I try to stay busy because it's when I have time to reflect on Kate's condition that it gets to me. Yeah, sometimes I cry. But only in the shower. That way I can use the old "shampoo in the eyes" excuse if anyone notices a little redness. (As I lose more and more of my hair however, eventually they'll catch on). I consider myself extremely fortunate to have a wife who is far from "broken." We try to tag-team Kate and give the other a breather.

When Savannah first started regressing, I told my husband that I thought something was wrong. He told me I was crazy, that she was perfect. When she lost her vocabulary, he distanced himself from her. As she lost her hand skills, he suggested to me that we could not properly take care of her and maybe she would need to live with someone who could. When she was diagnosed with RS, he could barely even look at her. Savannah was always his precious little Daddy's girl, and it tore him up to imagine spending the rest of his life watching RS rob him of his princess. He now says that it was a process of grieving. When he first heard the gloomy details of what RS will do, he didn't want to admit that it could happen to Savannah, or to him. He didn't think he could watch it happen. I gave him the time he needed to come to terms with the diagnosis. I would say that he did, in fact, have an epiphany. I never saw him cry before she was diagnosed, and I gave him the support he needed to figure out how he was going to deal with his emotions. I didn't force him. He would watch her sometimes, but it was usually from a distance. One day I came home and found him rocking her in his arms and crying. He apologized to her for being "gone." He has been a wonderful, loving, caring and supportive father to her since. That was over a year ago. It took him a few months to learn how to deal with it, but he did learn. They are once again inseparable.

I first met Crystal nearly twenty-three years ago when she was almost three years old. While she didn't have a diagnosis at that time, she clearly had some serious stuff going on. She was a beautiful and lively little girl closely attached to her mother, who I was falling in love with. Crystal was not just part of the package, but was a welcome part. I realize that coming in as a stepfather gives me a different position than biological dads. I don't have the potential guilt of cause, nor did I know her before the disorder kicked in. There was no true denial of the diagnosis, except that I couldn't fix it. Crystal was Crystal and I accepted her from the start. The disability, on the other hand, was not understood and I believed I could fix it. I put a lot of energy in that direction and slowly realized that my energies were being directed into helping make life better for her. I was coming to grips with the fact that I couldn't fix it, at least in the short and simple way. That wasn't and still isn't easy to swallow but accepting Crystal has always been. My wife's energies towards RS are hers and while they've been intense at times, she's never neglected the rest of life's obligations. She's not let the disease stop her from being a wonderful mother

Family Voices

to her other child and a wonderful wife. RS has forced us into a different life than we might not have chosen other-wise, but it has been a part of a growing process where the positive has grossly outweighed the negative. While there has been great sadness, missed experiences and adventures ... what an experience and adventure RS has dealt us. I'd have to say that Crystal's condition has been an anchor with all the connotations anchors have to offer ... both positive and negative.

SPECIAL PARENTS

HELPFUL HINTS FOR PARENTS

- Recognize your place as your child's most powerful teachers.
- Listen carefully and provide straight answers.
- See each child's individual value and uniqueness.
- Limit caregiving responsibilities; use respite care and support services.
- Accept your daughter's disability, but also recognize your other children's abilities.
- Plan special time alone.
- Welcome others to the home.
- Give abundant praise to siblings and their sister.
- Be honest about their accomplishments.
- Involve siblings in decisions that may affect them.
- Recognize times of special stress:
  - birth of another child
  - sister with RS goes to school
  - friends reject the sister
  - friends ask questions about the sister
  - RS sister becomes critically ill
  - family keeps secrets about the child
  - parents divorce
  - parents die
  - siblings marry
- Provide a normal family life.
- Don't expect siblings to act like adults if they are still children.

Your daughter will take up more than her "fair share" of your time and energy. This does not mean you will not have time to give to other children. That time will be there. You may have to work a little harder at it than the average family.

COUPLES: A PARTNERSHIP OF CARE

THE EVERYDAY STRESSES OF RAISING A CHILD with special needs can be overwhelming, often leaving us tired, tense, discouraged, and frustrated. In the two-parent family, it can be a seesaw; one parent may be "up" when the other is "down" or strong when the other is weak. While this can be good, tension and resentment can mount when one parent feels he or she is shouldering more than his or her share of responsibility or most of the emotional burden. The other parent may seem angry to cover up feelings of helplessness or dependency, and distance builds. Just as ordinary couples have to work

Family Voices

at their relationship, parents of kids with special needs need to make their relationship a priority. As the old saying goes with any crisis, "It can make you or break you."

Sometimes one parent feels the other is over involved in the child's care. With so many care, school, and family issues, there never seems enough time to get everything done. Nurturing the marital relationship gets pushed to the bottom of the priority list, and feelings of resentment, confusion, and anger often arise. Schedules are changed and favorite activities go by the wayside. Intimacy is often reduced, and the main topic of discussion is almost always the child.

Partners may grieve the loss in different ways. Mothers are usually more outspoken, while fathers often go inward with their pain. No one form of grief is more acceptable than another. It is sometimes hard to understand each other, but it is of great importance to respect each other's individual way of handling very difficult emotions. If your partner does not show his grief in the same way, it does not mean he is not hurting.

It is common for one parent to become wrapped up in the child and for the other parent to retreat. Both are handling it the best way they know how. The parent who is wrapped up doesn't understand the partner's distance and feels a lack of support. The parent who is retreating doesn't understand why the other parent is so deeply involved to the exclusion of what may seem like all else. At times a partner may feel he lost his child to RS and then the other parent as well.

Spend more time talking openly with one another about your feelings to avoid a lot of unnecessary pain. Choose a good time to discuss your daughter's needs with your partner. Avoid making it the first or only topic of conversation after work or when you are both tired.

Your child needs you, but you also need each other, even more now. The couples who seem to manage the best are those who know how to give it their best and still make time for each other. Remember that your child is a very important part of your life, but not all of your life. You need to develop outside interests to achieve balance, because RS can sure tip it over the edge at times. It can test your faith, exhaust your mental and physical energies, and wear thin your patience. But you can deal with the day-to-day challenges of RS if you share the load.

We started seeing a psychologist and this helped so much in order to be able to learn to deal with the disability and the reactions of our family and friends, and to learn to prioritize and to take care of ourselves as well.

Talk with your partner about your situation, knowing that men and women differ in how and when they communicate. Couples can get into patterns of holding their feelings in, sometimes to protect their partner from the pain, sometimes to avoid the pain.

We can't assume that our partner understands how we feel. One partner may need to talk about it and the other may want to run away from it. Don't expect your partner to read your mind. Anger builds when one partner feels unheard or misunderstood.

Take time to be open and to make your feelings known. Make time to talk to each other. We all have busy lives. You may have to schedule times on a regular basis as talk time. Remember that you can't keep a clean house by sweeping the daily dirt under the rug. Take care of things before the pile builds up. This happens in every marriage, but when you have children with extraordinary needs, the problem is so much greater.

My marital relationship has been stronger because of our shared love and belief in Crystal. We've watched helplessly as she has suffered and we've cried together, but, we've also celebrated her victories together. I think that Crystal has given so much to those who have allowed her into their lives, and my wife and I get to share

Family Voices

in that gift. But, I want to be clear here: Crystal and those who love her suffer with her disability and while she's a true wonder, what I'd give that she could be without RS.

Even though I try to ignore what I cannot control and concentrate on the positives of day-to-day living, I believe we have to express what we're feeling every once in a while in order to continue to heal and cope. No answers or cure will come if we all just sit around in total acceptance. We must be angry and refuse to compromise in order to find answers and make progress, but to keep sane and happy, we do have to mellow out and accept RS for what it is.

HELPFUL HINTS FOR COUPLES

- Communicate your needs to your partner. Say what is important to you.
- Listen to your partner. Use your ears twice as much as your mouth.
- Take turns with caregiving, so there are no fixed rules about who does what all the time.
- Be willing to "trade times" with everyday household jobs or getting up at night.
- Share "down" time equally. Take time to let go and relax.
- Plan a weekly "date" and keep it no matter what.
- Taking time off is part of doing a competent job of parenting. It may be the most important thing you do for your child.
- Understand that gender plays a role in parenting.

SINGLE PARENTS

BEING A PARENT IS HARD IN AND OF ITSELF, and we all know that being a parent of a child with special needs is harder. Being a single parent of a child with special needs is probably about the hardest thing many people have had to do. This job, difficult enough for two people under the best of circumstances, can be not only emotionally draining but physically and financially overwhelming when tackled alone. Single parents face holding down a job, making important decisions, juggling schedules, balancing the checkbook, and keeping the house clean, not to mention dividing attention between the other children in the house. Add the weight of caring for the child's special needs–lifting, bathing, feeding and much more, and having to leave work when she is sick, and you have a parent who feels an undue amount of stress and fatigue. In this situation, it is important to call on all available resources.

Meredith's biological father retreated, and disappeared. We're divorced and he hasn't seen her for three years. He said many of the same things I've heard from other fathers: "My heart is breaking." I told her father that it wasn't about him, it was about our daughter and how she feels. I have found that most of the people who have a hard time coping with their special daughters are personalizing it way too much. My advice is to refocus on what she needs, and get over it. She needs you because you're all she has. She has no one else to be strong for her, no one else to advocate for her. It's OK to take a walk to try and clear the cobwebs, but come back soon and stay in there swinging. That's how you love your special child. If you ask what she can give you, or how it's affecting you, that's the wrong question. Ask what you can give her and how you can help.

HELPFUL HINTS FOR SINGLE PARENTS

- Take care of yourself.
- Look to your spiritual side.

Family Voices

- Network with other parents of special needs children. Pick their knowledge bank and apply it to your own living situation. Then get to be good friends.
- Find another single parent and form a child care co-op. You will need a break.
- Be honest with your employer. Explain your situation. If you need to take time off, make the time up. Work through lunches, use vacation time, and negotiate your options.
- Be realistic … burning a rope from both ends will only get you burnt hands. It's perfectly OK to skip mopping the floor or missing a diaper change, but don't miss the big things.
- If you can't fix it today, file it away for tomorrow.
- If you've got family or friends willing to help … ASK for it and take it when it is offered.
- If money is a problem, clip coupons, take advantage of rebates, live within your means and save what you can.
- Cook on the weekends for the whole week, freeze and depend on the microwave.
- Find out what community services are available. ASK for help!
- Appeal to local service clubs, Medicaid or insurance to get equipment to save your back. Invest in a lightweight wheelchair, car or van lift, bath chair, stair lift.
- Remember that there are no right answers, just solutions that work for you. Do your best.
- If you have any energy left, join a club for single parents.

After the divorce, I felt tremendous guilt for leaving my daughter. I see her often but only for a few days at a time, so it's not the same as being the daddy at home. I ache knowing that my wife's present husband, who's a good man and who really cares about my daughter, is more involved in her life than I am. All my involvement locally and state-wide in disability issues helps me feel that I'm a good father, but when I'm honest with myself, I know better. No amount of involvement in a cause makes up for the fact that I'm a part time daddy. Being a single dad, unless you have the day-to-day responsibility of raising her, is not worthy of praise. Do not let us off the hook on this. Too many dads are looking to be absolved for not being there. We deserve no forgiveness. The single moms (and dads) who are taking daily care of their kids deserve nothing but praise.

As I became a single parent rather suddenly, it was rather difficult at first. However, once I got focused, I found that I could concentrate better on the problems and the issues of raising my daughter. Respite help gave me a few hours here and there to recharge, and I was able to have the energy to get by. There is life after divorce. My suggestion to those who are in a situation of suddenly being single is to quickly get over the embarrassment of asking for help. We are super moms at times, but we cannot always fly alone. Reach out and contact the community. Take good care of yourself. Find a good doctor who you can trust. Do something for yourself, and don't let anyone make you feel bad for it.

Shelley's biological father wanted her in an institution quite early on. It's true that she was a handful, but he never gave her a chance. He could hardly look at her. And I would not give her up or give up on her. We divorced when she was three years old. He tried to be a dad to her older brother, but her brother resented the way he ignored Shelley when he came to pick him up. He never picked Shelley up to go with him. Never. She is now forty years old. She does not know him. I remarried when she was about six years old and have a darling man who accepted her from the get-go.

Have at least one person who knows as much as possible about your angel, and who knows and loves her with enough confidence to take her and give you some time to yourself. It is wonderful to have that little bit of alone time without any worries.

Family Voices

One of the biggest challenges is trying to date and have a social life. It's hard to find someone you trust to take care of your child. Then, you feel guilty when you're gone even when you're trying to find someone who is willing and able to knowingly sign up for this roller coaster ride.

FAMILY DECISIONS

MOST FAMILIES WITH A CHILD WITH RS go on to have other children and are glad they did. Not only does the sibling bring them much joy and satisfaction, he or she becomes a great pal and natural advocate for the child with RS. Having another child also brings the magnificent bonus of future grandchildren.

Our second daughter, Becky, was born three months after our first daughter's diagnosis with RS. She has been the very healthiest thing that could have happened to our family. Sometimes I get too caught up in therapy and recording seizures and worrying over Angela's health, and then our Becky reminds me to see the world through fresh eyes, to laugh, to take time just to play. She shoulders some of the worry all parents pour out over their kids so Angela doesn't have to shoulder that alone ... she plays with Angela and laughs with her and gangs up with her in tickle fights against Daddy ... she wipes her chin ... she helps Angela understand that the world can't revolve only around her alone ... she has given Angela the opportunity to learn that it's OK to tell when some-one hurts you (a lesson I so badly want Angela to know for her own personal safety) ... she makes me step back from the sorrow I sometimes feel over Angela's losses, to see the miracle of life, and to remember that Angela is a perfect miracle too. She has taught me that I am a good mother, that the reason Angela doesn't follow "the rules" is not because I don't understand "the rules" or because of something I did wrong, but simply because Angela's rule book is all her own. And deep in my heart, I really needed someone to show me that.

Be forewarned: I never was more physically exhausted than during those months of having a newborn and a toddler to carry, feeding one by spoon and one by breast (at the same time) for hours a day, and when neither one slept through the night, but that part passed. In ways it was like having twins because so many needs were the same, but the differences in size and interests compounded the problem. Life is so much easier now. The needs and abilities are different, but the interests are much more similar. I am so proud of both my girls. We love both of them more than anything.

BROTHERS AND SISTERS

ALL CHILDREN REQUIRE ATTENTION, and all families experience occa-sional problems among siblings. Brothers and sisters of girls with RS experience a number of their own special concerns. The impact of growing up with a sister with RS has far-reaching consequences. Families have to readjust their expectations and increase their focus on the child with special needs. Brothers and sisters can get overlooked or overindulged. Typical kids feel loving and protective toward their sisters, but they can also feel angry and embarrassed. They may actually feel guilty that their sister is handicapped and they are not. Most siblings bear strong feelings of responsibility, whether it is self-imposed or expected by their parents. Even though it can't be avoided, they may resent what they feel are dou-ble standards when they have to do chores and their sister does not. They may fear for the future and whether they will be asked to be their sister's custodian.

Sometimes siblings misbehave or act out to get attention because negative attention is better than no attention. They may become the "class clown" to avoid dealing with their own sad emotions and feelings of lack of attention. These children become obvious immediately. Other siblings are not as noticeable. They seem to feel they have to do everything right to compensate and to get their own share of attention–they become the overachievers. Both

Family Voices

the child who acts out and the child who is so good he grows up too soon may have life-long problems if the problems are not recognized and dealt with.

We learn from brothers and sisters that their experiences are a mixture of many emotions, and they have the same basic needs: openness, sensitivity, guidance from someone who can understand them, and freedom to vent their feelings, both good and bad. They want parents to recognize that they are needed as much as their sister needs them. They need time and attention. While many issues surface, most brothers and sisters worry less than their parents about the outcome of growing up in a family that is different. Most of them seem to exceed all of our expectations in the way they are able to accept and adjust in time.

Each year at our annual IRSA conference, we invite a panel of siblings to discuss what it's like. Parents sit on the edge of their chairs as they listen to stories and feelings that are recollected and shared. We all want to be good parents. We don't want any of our children to suffer, yet we're so often pulled in so many different directions that it's impossible to provide what everyone needs.

My sister, Joanne, is thirty-five. I can only tell you what a privilege it was to grow up with her. Jo taught my other sister and me so much throughout our childhood. We learned from a young age to appreciate special needs families around us. When other children said that they were sorry about Jo, we would always answer, "Why? We are lucky to have a person like Jo in our life." Our Mum and Dad did their best to make sure we had lots of family outings together and we always had people around us helping. I am sure it was hard for them at the beginning. Now my younger sister is a teacher and I am an early childhood teacher. I am also involved with adults and children with special needs. I have two children, five and six. They love their Aunty Jo to bits. They are so at ease with her and they love to help her whenever they are capable. I would say to parents concerned about the siblings; remember to always keep them in the picture. Let them find ways to build their relationships with the RS angels. My children are learning that they too will always have a special relationship with Jo that they will never have with anyone else. How lucky is that!

COMMUNICATION IS THE KEY

IT IS IMPORTANT TO COMMUNICATE FREQUENTLY and openly about your daughter, whether the children ask or not. It is easy to assume that they know what is going on, but sometimes they don't know how or what to ask. They may sense that the subject is painful and difficult for you. Let them know it is OK to ask questions, and include them in some decisions. What and how you tell them about RS will depend on their age.

We got our diagnosis when Jamie was six and Laura was almost four. We explained to Jamie that God makes each of us unique and different. We have special gifts and talents and we use each of those differently. We told her God chose us as parents for Laura because he knew we could be good parents for Laura. He made Jamie the way she is because he knew she would be a good sister for Laura. We also told her there are many different people in the world and we see so few of them living where we do. We told her that she will someday see a huge variety of people with different color skin, with and without limbs and those who need much more help than her sister. We said that she would also understand someday that it takes special people to love and care for other special people. She understood this and would later bring Laura to school every year as a show-and-tell type adventure.

We explain it to our son in terms of the functional problems as they arise, e.g., "Katie can't walk … we need to do PT to help her legs get strong and maybe she might walk when she is older." Or "Katie won't be able to talk but there are other ways to hear what she wants to say." We feel that the main thing is not to hide anything from him.

Family Voices

I think kids often cope with these things better than adults. He is very loving and protective of her and knows that she is different from other children her age. When he is older, we'll explain RS to him.

My son is now 17, and doing great, but I have been thinking about all the years I worried about how RS would impact on him. He seems to have not only survived, but thrived. I have been thinking about a conversation we had many years ago.

"Mum?"
Without looking up I answered. "Yes, Erik."
"Do you love Annie more than you love me?"
That got my full attention!
"The correct answer would be that I love you both, just differently."
"But what is the real answer?"
I took a deep breath and said, "Yes, I love Annie more than anyone." I immediately regretted my honesty.
Erik simply said, "I thought so."
I looked him in the eyes as I said, "I also have some pretty awful feelings about Annie that I never have about anyone else."
"Me too!" Erik was certainly emphatic about that!
"But you, I just love. I don't ever have those bad feelings about you, just lots and lots and lots of love."
He just hugged me and went off to play. Over the years I have worried that I said the worst possible thing, but Erik and I have occasionally revisited this basic idea. He and I later agreed we never hate Annie or have bad feelings about her, but we both abhor RS. I have explained that parents have an all-consuming love for their newborns. It gives them the strength to do all they need to do for their babies. I explained that over the years my love for him had changed, it had in fact become a healthier and far more enjoyable love. It is unlike my love for Annie, which is stuck in the newborn phase of complete absorption, in part because she is completely dependent on me and her father.
Recently Erik came into Annie's room while I was changing a remarkably unpleasant diaper. He said nothing, just stood there. Finally I asked if he needed me. He shook his head no and said, "I'm glad you love Annie more than me, Mum. She needs it."
"Erik, I regret ever having said that to you. I am very sorry you remember my saying that."
"Mum, if you had answered any other way I would not have believed you. Besides I don't want it."
"Want what?"
"I don't want you living your whole life for me. It would be too much pressure."
Boy, did he give me something to think about.

When Hayden was four years old, I began taking him to a family psychologist, just to make sure he was handling everything OK. Turns out he'd been harboring major guilt, thinking he had caused Kendall's "sickness" because he didn't like her when she was born. Once we realized what was going on in his little head, and it was addressed

Family Voices

and snuffed out, things got a lot better for him. Today, Hayden is seven years old and we are back in counseling. There is something called "survivor's guilt" that many siblings of disabled children go through. While Hayden is never unkind to Kendall, I find that he is way more affectionate toward his other sister, Jordyn. He goes out of his way to play with her, help her with things. He'll carry Jordyn up and down the stairs when necessary, but won't do that for Kendall (who weighs the same amount!). He'll get Jordyn out of her crib each morning and put her on the couch next to him so they can snuggle and watch TV. I don't see him doing these things with Kendall and it breaks my heart. I asked him recently why he treated Kendall differently, why he seemed to show Jordyn more attention and love. He said it was because Kendall is disabled, a statement that blew me away. I think that the eighteen months we spent in agony with Kendall, discovering something was wrong with her, trying to get a diagnosis, all the tests, hospital stays, therapy and treatments, all the sacrifices we made as a family have taken a toll on Hayden. And that was so long ago. I feel as though we've really adjusted, finally found our peace after the storm. Apparently, Hayden hasn't. Meanwhile, my younger daughter does not seem to be plagued with these feelings of detachment. She is very nurturing towards Kendall.

EXPLAINING TO OTHER KIDS

YOUR CHILDREN WILL INEVITABLY BE ASKED QUESTIONS about their sister, and it is good to give them some ideas for what to say when the time comes. If your daughter with RS is in a regular classroom, it is also good to visit her class with some explanation for the other students. IRSA has handouts for all ages and this is a great place to start.

There will always be inquisitive people. Explain that curiosity is a natural reaction. Most people simply want to understand something they are not familiar with. Work together on a response that a sibling can use that is easy for him to explain and easy for others to understand. When he encounters someone negative, tell him that sometimes, other people are as handicapped as his sister, only by their attitudes.

Kids are curious and will usually ask someone else what is wrong with Brycelyn, so her sister, Kaci, and her friends get the question quite often. Kaci is the most comfortable with saying that her sister has RS, and she leaves it at that. They will either take that answer or they will then ask if she can talk. Talking seems to be the biggest issues with kids. Kaci then tells them that she talks with her eyes. We always have "yes" and "no" cards with us and if one of her team mates or friends press it, she will "put on a show" and answer questions. Once the kids get used to having her around, they will come up and talk to her and tell her how pretty she looks or how they like her cool clothes.

I generally find myself answering questions from children. I stay very simple, throwing in a few terms and I speak loudly enough for all the starers to hear. They will say, "Why doesn't Jacky walk, or talk, or why do her hands move like that?" I start by saying, "That is the way she was made. She doesn't speak anymore with her mouth; she now uses her eyes and her heart. She gets sad, happy and mad just like you. She requires help from her friends and family and she loves to be helped by her friends." Usually they giggle and understand a little. Parents usually apologize for the questions and I respond by telling them that I love talking about my daughter. She is the joy of our family.

As her classmates got older, they understood better. We would ask the class to raise their hands if they liked pizza! Every hand went up. We said, "Well, that's Laura's favorite food." "How about swimming?" Again, hands went up. "Laura loves to swim." The list went on. What once was taboo because of fear of the unknown was now Laura with her funny smile and giggles. The kids would then crowd around her and want to be the one to sit and read to her first.

We did an experiment with the class. They had to express their thoughts. Someone spoke the thought. Then we said, "Since Laura doesn't speak, you may not. Tell me another way." Then they would try to use their hands to

Family Voices

make word pictures … again, Laura can't use her hands. They didn't know what else to do. So, we talked about the eye gaze and picture boards. The kids had a huge education that day.

For children, we usually say her brain just hasn't told her feet or mouth what to do so she can walk and talk like we do.

When children ask, "What's wrong with her?" I use that common explanation, "Sara's brain has a hurt or sickness which made her not able to talk or walk like you can. Sara can see and hear, and she knows what you say, even if she doesn't act like she does. She loves to watch little children play and talk to her."

FINDING TIME FOR SIBLINGS

YOUR DAUGHTER WILL PROBABLY REQUIRE MORE TIME and attention than the other children, but don't forget that they still need you, too. While it is not always easy or possible, it helps to give as much individual attention to each of the children as possible. Acknowledge their feelings of being slighted at times, and let them know that all of their feelings are real. Try to schedule in some "alone" time with each child. Remember that your other children need you as much as your special child, just in different ways. Reassure them that the reason you spend more time with their sister is not because you love her more, but because she has so many needs.

We told Amy's siblings that Amy just danced to the tune of a different drummer. That was all we knew at the time. Over the years, we demonstrated to our "normal" children that you don't have to be perfect to be loved, that we are all different in our own way. We told them a long time ago that it was okay to get mad at her when she was naughty, just like anyone else, that we all got tired of the mess she made. But, let anyone else give her a sidelong glance and you'd have a "drop dead at forty paces look" that was truly effective, especially from her younger sister. The siblings have turned out to be very compassionate and family-oriented young adults.

If your child is willing, it may help him to learn how to be more comfortable sharing feelings in a sibling support group. There, he can benefit from talking with other children in the same situation. He will learn that his guilt, worries, and need for attention are completely normal. On the other hand, if he feels that this is just one more way his family is different, it may be wise to put it off until another time when he is more receptive.

WHAT INFLUENCES A CHILD'S OUTLOOK

- birth order of the sister with RS
- age of the well child in relation to his sister with RS
- whether you are a single parent family
- family resources
- family closeness
- family size
- how the family views the handicap
- whether or not one or both parents work outside the home
- the family's religious views
- whether the child is institutionalized or in special classes
- the severity of the handicapping condition
- whether or not the healthy child is of the same or different gender

Family Voices

DEALING WITH EMOTIONS

YOUR OTHER CHILD MAY FEEL DIFFERENT from his friends. He may deal with embarrassment by becoming the center of attention as the class troublemaker. He may pretend that he is not embarrassed, or try to escape it by concentrating on outside interests as a distraction. He may overcompensate by trying to be the best student or the best athlete at school. In most cases, however, kids pick up their cues from parents, and their attitudes generally reflect parental attitudes. So, if you can handle embarrassment, he will probably learn to handle it too.

I think that in spite of all the adverse tribulations the normal siblings go through, that these same siblings often become extremely caring, loving, giving, bright, and introspective adults. Living daily with a handicapped person seems to give others around them insight that some adults never attain. I think our other children gain far more than they lose by living with a RS sister. They are shown a love that they can learn from and share with their own families one day.

GUILT IS INEVITABLE

HE MAY FEEL GUILTY about a number of competing emotions—anger, jealousy, sadness, frustration, fear, and hostility. He might feel guilty because his sister has the disability instead of him. He can walk and talk and enjoy activities his sister cannot participate in. He may feel shame if he would rather not be so involved in caring for his sister. He might feel some guilt when money is spent on him that could be used for equipment for his sister. He might want to downplay his own intelligence or good looks, thinking that it would make his sister feel bad to be compared. The negative aspects of guilt are low self-esteem, hostility, difficulty with relationships, and a desire to deny himself things which he deserves. On the other hand, there are many positive aspects: he may be a good child as thanks for the gift of health. He may be obedient, sensitive, helpful to others in need, and expressive with others. For these reasons, many brothers and sisters are drawn to helping professions, such as teaching, therapy or nursing.

As I watch my second "typical" daughter, I see a depth of character beyond "typical" that can only come from living in her special situation. I have seen this in other Rett siblings too; a level of insight and understanding that is uncommonly beautiful. Our kids with Rett have a profound impact on their brothers and sisters, just as they are impacted profoundly by them.

AVOIDING RESENTMENT

THERE ARE MANY WAYS FOR RESENTMENT TO CREEP IN. Parents may be overprotective for the sake of their daughter, not allowing him to do something if she cannot do it, too. Outside activities might be restricted when her brother is needed to help with his sister. She may require lots of time and attention. There may not be enough time to go around so that he does not get much time alone. He may have to sacrifice some things so that money, time, and energy can be spent on his sister. He might feel that her needs come first, and he may resent the fact that he has chores and she does not. He may feel that her presence and her needs dominate everything in the household. He may feel undue pressure to perform with higher expectations for success to compensate for the heartache of what his sister cannot do. He might feel that you love her more because you do more for her. He may resent the fact that he is scolded more because he is more capable.

Family Voices

The negative aspects of resentment are anger, frustration, rebellion and withdrawal. At the same time, if he is given a lot of reassurance, he will learn how to deal positively with resentment, and he will find that he is able to vent his feelings and still be a good person.

Your non-RS children are going to have a little less free time, things, social events etc. because of their sister. Children being what they are, there will be times they will resent her for depriving them of their fun and pleasure. They will get over it. We think Laura is better off for having brothers and they are better/more tolerant for having her as a sister. There is someone in this world that will be there for Laura when we are gone.

Emily has learned that things like not winning a game, or getting a date, or a part in a play aren't really the end of the world. Abby has helped her sort out what is really important in life. Lots of teenagers have trouble setting priorities. I think having Abby has helped Emily in a lot of ways.

THE EFFECT ON SELF-IMAGE

BROTHERS AND SISTERS MAY QUESTION their own intellectual abilities, feeling that others may say they are "smart" only in comparison to their sister. They may feel unworthy of their own accomplishments, whether they are acknowledged or ignored. A sister may secretly wonder if she also has RS without knowing it, since she and her sister came from the same parents or she may worry that she will someday have a child with RS. A brother may unconsciously be waiting for something bad to happen to him, as it did to his sister. Negative self-images can lead to unhappy relationships, destructive lifestyles, and lack of confidence. On the positive side, the majority of brothers and sisters are well-adjusted, happy, productive, and caring. It is important to be honest and fair in evaluating brothers and sisters, being careful not to overstate or understate their abilities. This builds trust and eliminates confusion. Brothers and sisters need to know that every compliment and every criticism they hear about themselves is true and honest.

WHO CAN I BLAME?

LIKE THEIR PARENTS, A BROTHER AND SISTER MUST sometimes wonder why "bad things happen to good people." He may wonder if getting a sister with RS is some kind of punishment. He may blame himself for getting a healthy body instead of his sister. He may pass the blame around from himself to his parents to God and back for him. Usually, he is actually not mad at his parents, but at the situation. Experiences are out of his control, and they hurt. He hates the feelings, but usually feels that his parents did what they had to do. A child may feel neglected even if in reality he is not. Getting short-changed from time to time is inevitable in any family. But when we have a child with RS, parents may find themselves guilty of benign neglect. We thank goodness he can take care of himself, leaving him to fend for himself. This isn't always bad. We just need to learn to reverse it sometimes and neglect the child with RS in harmless ways to give him the support he needs. When they look back, some brothers and sisters tell us they feel their sister received more attention, but knew it had to be that way. Some were jealous of the attention she got, and others felt that they did not lack attention at all. Happily, their thinking matures in time as they are able to put things in perspective.

I'd give anything if there was one certain thing I could point my finger at and say, "That's what caused it." But in doing so, I feel like I'd have to point my finger at God. And I can't do that. I feel like everything happens for a reason. I don't always understand the reason why. I don't think I ever will on this one, except maybe that it has helped me to slow down, not to take so much for granted and to become closer with God himself.

Family Voices

ADJUSTING

A SIBLING'S ADJUSTMENT MAY DEPEND ON HIS AGE when his RS sister came to the family. If she was born first, he may feel that "this is the way it's always been." If he is older and watched her regression, he may feel the pain of loss. Or he may deny his sister's limits or the severity of her sister's condition and its effects on the family. He may wish that it wasn't there and pretend that it will go away. Again, he will take cues from the attitudes of his parents. If he is like most brothers and sisters of girls with RS, he will find extra strength and sensitivity and, in the end, develop a deeper, more meaningful understanding of life.

There are some things that Melinda can do that I am certain a "normal" child couldn't. Melinda has a way of reading people that comes naturally to her. She also has a way of communicating without using words or gestures. Sometimes it is nice just to be able to give her a hug when I'm feeling down. Not many fourteen year old kids whom I have come in contact with are willing to give their big sis a hug without shame.

LITTLE GROWN-UPS

ONE OF THE ISSUES THAT SOMETIMES COMES UP is missing out on childhood. Brothers and sisters often must assume adult-like roles without the maturity or experience they need to handle them. A sibling may feel that he missed his place in the family, because his sister will always be the youngest child. He may accept extra responsibility and avoid making waves because everyone is already so upset, but excessive responsibilities may cause him to miss out on opportunities and friendships. If you must require your other child to include his sister with RS, let him choose the activity. Also, he may feel anxious as his parents grow older and can't do as much for his sister. It will help everyone involved if you include others in your daughter's circle of friends who will help care for her best interests when you no longer can. When children are growing up, they always have to do some things they don't like. There is no doubt that having a sister with RS brings added responsibility. Luckily, it also brings great enrichment and helps brothers and sisters feel needed and important.

EXPLAINING THINGS

SOME QUESTIONS ARE NOT EASILY ANSWERED, but try to be sincere and honest. Let him know that his thoughts and feelings are important, and that emotions and tears are OK. He needs accurate information in a way he will understand. Try to listen carefully to the kind of questions he asks and tell him what he needs to know, taking into consideration his age and level of understanding. Start at the beginning and take your time. Explain your own feelings. Have an open attitude. He will soon learn to trust and confide in you. He needs your attention, special time all alone with you. He needs to know all about his sister now and what the future may hold.

FUTURE WORRIES

SERIOUS CONCERNS ABOUT LONG-TERM CARE can arise when parents are no longer able to provide it. Young children can worry that they, too, will be "sent away." Adult siblings are often in a delicate balance between responsibilities to themselves, their spouses and children, parents, other siblings, and the sister with RS. Parents should plan ahead to reduce the burden of worry. Programs such as guardianship, conservatorship, and

Family Voices

estate planning are aimed at allowing the woman with RS to live as independently as possible without undue hardship on her siblings. Brothers and sisters can be excellent advocates, making sure that all of her needs are met and appropriate services are provided.

WHEN HOME IS AWAY FROM HOME

CHOOSING A RESIDENTIAL PLACEMENT is a very difficult decision. It is important to reassure the sibling that the sister is not going away because she is "bad." Let him know that you love her just the same, but are looking for a place for her to get the kind of treatments she needs to be the best that she can be.

SIBLINGS SPROUT

SOMETIMES, NO MATTER WHAT YOU SAY OR DO, it just takes time and maturity for siblings to see the broader picture. Brothers and sisters usually grow up to make us very proud. Expect some good stuff. Rettland may not always be a rose garden, but it's definitely a place where beautiful things grow. There are many good qualities that come from having a sister with RS, like maturity, patience, awareness and acceptance, tolerance and compassion. There is a heightened sensitivity to prejudice and its consequences and a better sense of values to be gained. Brothers and sisters learn to set priorities based on qualities of goodness toward helping others, appreciation and respect for good health. From their special relationships with their sisters, they learn the most important lessons in life.

We all wish something had been different in our lives. I wish I had a sister or two and not two useless brothers. My older daughter wishes she was an only child. My husband wishes he didn't have his sister. My dad wishes he had been the oldest of his five sibs and not the baby. My niece who is an only child wishes she wasn't. What I am getting at is that it won't matter whether our kids have a disabled sister. They will always wish it had been different.

HELPFUL HINTS FOR BROTHERS AND SISTERS

- Be yourself. Your parents love you for who you are.
- You don't have to be perfect to make up for what you sister cannot do.
- Explain your sister to your friends. They can only be fearful of what they do not understand.
- It's OK for you to be embarrassed or angry sometimes. Tell your parents how you feel.
- When you're having a hard time, write your feelings down.
- Find another special sibling to talk with. Share your feelings.

SPECIAL PEOPLE

GRANDPARENTS AS GUARDIANS

GRANDPARENTS WHO HAVE ASSUMED THE ROLE of full-time caregivers need the same help and support as younger parents. They may find "re-parenting" difficult as things have changed since they did it the first time with their non-disabled children. Often, they are given this role abruptly and without much preparation. At a time when they may have been looking forward to retirement and traveling the world,

Family Voices

they are instead caring for a child with many special needs. There may be conflict with the child's parents about her education or medical care. There may be financial hardships as they spend the money they saved for retirement on the care of this grandchild they love so much. It is so important for grandparent caregivers to access respite programs which are available.

GRANDPARENTS AND RELATIVES

JUST AS YOU NEVER EXPECTED TO PARENT A CHILD with special needs, your parents never expected to be placed in this different role. Their hurt is double; they ache for their child and for their grandchild. They may go through the same stages of grief you experience. What is supposed to be a joyous time turns to one of great concern. Grandparents lose the typical grandparent-grandchild relationship, and may not feel equipped to handle the child's special needs. Grandparents anticipate the perfect grandchild, and they experience lost dreams too. They may be afraid to express their emotions for fear of upsetting the parents and making things worse. They may be emotional at first, but usually adjust and become helpful and supportive. Just as you need understanding, they need a sympathetic ear. Try to understand how they must feel.

The feelings are very much the same as those of the parents, with two big differences. First, a child of my child is twice my child. I hurt twice, once for my daughter and again for my granddaughter. Not just emotional hurt, but physical hurt too, deep heartbreaking hurt. Like any parents, my husband and I worked diligently to provide our daughter with advantages we never had. When she married, she held these same hopes and desires for her family. I hurt when I see my daughter thin and overtired, knowing she is being robbed of the carefree years of youth. I hurt when strangers "treat her funny" because her four year-old is in diapers and drinks from a bottle, while physically she looks totally normal. I hurt when I see my daughter struggle with well-meaning doctors, therapists, and even equipment manufacturers who fail to trust a mother's instinct as to what is best for her child. I hurt when I see my daughter go through the stages of denial, then the "Why me?" then the frustration, bitterness, and finally acceptance. I feel pride when she faces each day with optimism, patience, and a smile. I feel guilty that I live so many miles away and can't be of much help. I feel frustrated that I can't take Megan home with me because of the seizures, sleeplessness, and constipation. I feel sad when I see my grandsons running, playing, growing, learning, and exploring life with such wonder and delight. I grieve that I will never bake cookies with Megan. We will never shop till we drop, sing songs, share secrets, ride bikes, or buy prom dresses, nor will she marry. The list goes on and on. Secondly, a grandmother is once-removed from the situation as far as offering guidance, opinions, and suggestions. She must bite her tongue many times because, after all, the decisions concerning this child are not hers to make. Parents are already bombarded from many directions with well-intentioned advice.

ACCEPTING THE SITUATION

IT MAY BE HARD FOR GRANDPARENTS to face the facts. They may want to think the doctor made a mistake or that it is not so serious. This is their own denial, and it is a necessary part of the grief process. They are not with you day in and day out, so they don't see the problem as you do. Give them some information to read and some time to take it all in.

WHEN GRANDPARENTS DON'T HELP

THIS ATTITUDE USUALLY COMES FROM NOT KNOWING what to do or how to do it. They may be afraid they will do something wrong or harmful. Help them

Family Voices

develop confidence. They don't know what you need unless you tell them. They may see you doing everything perfectly, and assume you don't want any interference. Do ask them for help, letting them know how much it means.

TIME HEALS

EVERY PERSON IS DIFFERENT AND THERE IS NO FORMULA for growth or acceptance. Chances are, though, that they will be touched in the same way you have been.

Many good things have come from our hurt. We are closer to God, for Megan is like an angel sent for a little while to teach us, strengthen us, and set our priorities straight. With her chubby little cheeks, black eyes, and long curly hair, she has taught us perseverance, and that you can still have a smile when all else has gone wrong. She has taught us patience and humility. She has taught us to listen more closely with our hearts to others less insulated from life's problems and hurts. She is a constant reminder that all persons need love and praise. Megan can no longer crawl, walk, talk, or feed herself, but her face lights up when we praise her or hold her close! Is the hurt lessening? No, but acceptance is just around the corner. God's plan is perfect, and one day He will take Megan home where she will walk and talk, and play. Even though the tears are just below the surface, I don't question God's plan or feel bitter anymore.

HELPFUL HINTS FOR GRANDPARENTS AND RELATIVES

- Listen with love. Try to be nonjudgmental and sincere.
- Give us time to adjust. We need time to work things out.
- Respect our choices. You may have a different opinion, but we need mutual strength and support.
- Respect our schedules. We're more overwhelmed than ever.
- Be available. The most precious gift you can give is your time.
- Balance your time and attention among all of the children and grandchildren.
- Don't leave our daughter out. Include her in conversation, games, and fun.
- Love her. She is first a child. Recognize her strengths.

TALE OF TRIUMPH

I have a different perspective, because our daughter is adopted. I don't think RS rules our life, but it definitely changes our life. My family's life may have been changed by choice, but don't we make choices every day? We may make a choice to have another baby, or we may make choice to change jobs. Those choices then change the path of our lives. Sometimes it may be good, and other times it may cause us to struggle. Kristas was one of our best decisions, but sometimes I wonder how it might be without her. However, I also wonder how it might be without my two year-old son … a whole lot easier, I'm sure. But I would not trade either of them for the world. Yes, at times I get frustrated or tired or whatever, but the little smile I get from any one of my kids makes it all worthwhile.

"A family is a group of people who make an irrational commitment to each other's well-being to the point of making each other crazy."

– URIE BRONFENBRENNER

Care for the Caregiver

MY COPE RUNNETH OVER

IT IS SO IMPORTANT to place this chapter near the front of the book and not leave it for the end, just as it is important to put ourselves first in the care pyramid, at the foundation. Some of this information is presented with different words and examples. It is important enough to read twice. Taking care of all of someone else's needs for a lifetime is a task. It is probably the greatest responsibility you have ever had. No

"Love is doing small things with great love."

– MOTHER TERESA

matter how much you love her, no matter how strong you are, no matter how good an attitude you may have, it is a task. All too often, we find ourselves at the bottom of the priority list. Just as the stewardess advises us on a flight, we need to put on our own oxygen masks before helping our children. This is lifesaving stuff we're talking about. It is nearly impossible to provide everything that is needed for someone else when our own basic needs are not met.

There is no getting away from the all-out demands of the role of caregiver. While other family members can fend for themselves now and then, our daughters with RS count on us for every aspect of daily living. We didn't get any job preparation for this role. The hours are long and the vacations too few and far between to make up for the energy drain. We must schedule doctors' visits, therapy appointments and IEP meetings while providing enrichment and stimulation for our special daughters, making sure not to overlook the needs of the other children. It's not always easy to just dial up a babysitter or find a substitute. And there are many deep emotions to balance at the same time. Love is the easy part. Sometimes it's hard to see beyond the sadness and pain. Finding the strength to meet these everyday challenges can overwhelm us at times.

As parents of special needs children, we face many challenges mentally, spiritually, emotionally, and physically. We know that out of sight is never out of mind. It takes strength and energy to pursue the diagnosis, make an appropriate treatment plan, and find others who will support it in addition to all of the many physical aspects of direct caregiving. Emotionally, we must cope with lost dreams for our beloved child, silent stares from an insensitive public and screaming spells that might last for hours, lost sleep we can't recover, and relatives and friends who do not always support us. We face financial challenges we never would have thought possible. It's a brave new world in this club we never wanted to join.

But having joined the club, we soon find that knowing that we're not alone is a big step toward coping. We may look to family for support or to professional counseling, community groups or religion, but may still feel isolated and misunderstood. We often find that other families, those who live in our skin, provide the best cushion for the devastating emotions that accompany the diagnosis of RS.

All parents take on the role of caregiver, but the special parent role is a more demanding one. The difference is that in the typical situation, the need for so much attention diminishes after the first couple of years of a child's life. In RS, the need lasts a lifetime and that's a very long time.

Care for the Caregiver

The very basics of care giving include what we do every day: feed, bathe, shampoo, put on deodorant, brush teeth, style hair, toilet, diaper, dress, and give medicine. We may have to lift and carry her, help her walk, put on braces, reposition her for comfort frequently, or change a bib for drool. We might have to program and reprogram a communication device. We most definitely must know how to operate a VCR and have ESP for when it's ready to rewind or replace. We have to learn to find the right professionals, schedule appointments and therapies, search for the right school and provide special equipment. In time, we learn how to bargain for a shorter route with the bus driver, negotiate to increase therapy on the IEP when they're trying to convince us that less is more, listen to the advice and opinions of family members and friends who know a little but say a lot, convince the insurance company that she really is handicapped (we're not making this stuff up), and keep our wits in public places when she screams, throws up or has a seizure.

It's no wonder we get tired. Taking care of all of someone else's needs for a lifetime is a task. No matter how much we love her, no matter how strong we are, no matter how good an attitude we may have, it is a task. It's a labor of love for sure, but it can be a lot of work. Most of us do what we can to provide for others' needs first, because there is little time for everything. The other kids need time and attention and there is not enough of either for all. So we divide it up as best we can and leave ourselves what is left over, usually nothing. Then, while we're not looking, we may become resentful and tired. All too often, we find ourselves at the bottom of the care list. And then we find that our cope runneth over. We may become exhausted, discouraged, and depressed. Too much caregiving can lead to exhaustion, depression and resentment. If you always fill the glasses of everyone around you first, when it finally is your turn, the pitcher is empty. Make sure to refill your own glass often. You need strength to pass the pitcher.

We need to take a really hard look at how we're doing things and the effect it has on us. We learn that to be really good caregivers, we must first take good care of ourselves. The passage of time helps us better understand that we can't take the disability away and our possibilities of changing it are limited. We can't erase it, so we have to face it. It is important to do all that we can, but at the same time to recognize that we can't do it all. We can, however, find ways to maximize what we do and minimize the challenge. While we can't take away the RS, we can make important changes that will make a difference like better therapies, new communication methods, or environmental modifications. We can find ways to manage the stress of caregiving, beginning with being good to ourselves. Here are some ways to do just that.

HOW TO SURVIVE AND THRIVE

GIVE YOURSELF TIME

THE FIRST STEP IN CARING FOR OURSELVES is to understand that we all live with a mix of many emotions. We need to give ourselves time to work through them. When we find ourselves particularly sad, we can remember to look at our daughters and see that they are happy most of the time. While she struggles with the limits of what she can do, the pain really is ours, not hers.

The frustrations of Rett are so insidious at times … you think you're going along smoothly and handling it when all of a sudden it hits you like a brick wall. "My daughter has RS!" And some of the initial shock and pain resurfaces and leaves you with that knot in the pit of your stomach. I suspect that most of us all have this knot in our stomachs, the lump in

Care for the Caregiver

our throats and the pain in our hearts. No matter the specifics, we are all connected. So that is where our strength lies.

HELP YOUR CHILD, BUT DON'T HARM YOURSELF

TOO MUCH HELPING CAN BE BAD FOR YOUR HEALTH. When your life is organized totally around the needs of others, you are always compromising and this leads to distress. It is very important to learn to take care of your own needs. You don't have to stop being helpful altogether. Caring and nurturing are very important traits. Just make sure that taking care of others doesn't interfere with taking care of yourself.

EXPECT SOME DIFFICULTIES

WE SEEM TO GET DIFFICULTIES IN GREATER SHARE than most. If we keep telling ourselves how unfair it is, we will only become bitter. Of course, it is unfair, very unfair, but what in life is fair? Life gives us a full deck of cards; we get some good hands and some bad ones. Some are easier than others, but we have no choice but to play them all. Play as best you can with the hand you have. It is not the load that breaks us down, but the way we carry it. Remember that no matter how hard you may try, there may be some days that just get you down. It's part of the territory.

YOUR FEELINGS ARE NORMAL

IT IS NATURAL FOR CAREGIVERS TO FEEL SAD, discouraged or frustrated from time to time. Ignoring these feelings won't make them go away; it may even make them more intense. It is important to recognize your feelings. Then, do what you can to feel better. If you are sad, seek an activity that lifts your spirits, such as listening to music, gardening, or watching a funny movie. If you feel discouraged, remember that it won't always be this hard. If you are fearful, think about the worst thing that could happen and make a plan for how to handle it. If you are angry, do something physical to defuse. Take a walk, punch a pillow. Then focus your anger on RS, not your child. If you feel guilty, realize that you can only do what you can do. A lot of RS is out of your control. Then give yourself credit for what you have already done, probably quite a lot.

TALK ABOUT IT

TALK ABOUT HOW YOU FEEL. Things that we try to keep inside always come out later, after they have gone painfully inward. Find someone who will listen. The more we talk, the less we hurt. Other special parents are a wonderful resource, because they can lend support, encouragement, and practical help. Most of all, they can identify with our joys and sorrows. If you have a computer, join the RettNet, where sorrow is divided and joy is doubled.

It was hard at times just having to talk about it, but when I would open up, it seemed to help. Family and friends helped in so many ways. It helped just knowing they were there when I wanted to talk.

BE GENTLE WITH YOURSELF

SOME DAYS, WE FEEL LIKE WE CAN TAKE ON THE WORLD and other days, we want to disappear from the world. It's part of normal adjustment to a diffi-

Care for the Caregiver

cult situation. Life has its ups and downs. When you're having a down day, try to remember that you won't stay down forever. And the best thing is that the good days will be so much better.

SET LIMITS

IF YOUR CHILD HAS BEEN RECENTLY DIAGNOSED, this may not be your year to run for PTA president or to be Soccer Mom. As you adjust to the diagnosis and the new demands of the RS challenge, you will be able to take these roles on again. Set some limits and let others know what they are.

BE REALISTIC

SET REALISTIC GOALS AND EXPECTATIONS FOR YOURSELF. Don't expect to be a perfect housekeeper or entertainer. Divide housekeeping responsibilities and recruit other family members to share holiday routines.

AVOID DIFFICULT PEOPLE

SURROUND YOURSELF WITH PEOPLE WHO ARE ACCEPTING and helpful. Avoid those who are judgmental or intrusive. They only bring you down.

INVEST WISELY

TO SEE HOW YOUR INVESTMENTS BALANCE, fold a piece of paper in half. On one side, list the things you do for others. On the other side, list what you do for yourself. Do your lists balance or even come close to it? If not, it's time to start getting some equilibrium.

LEARN TO ASK FOR HELP

DON'T HESITATE TO ASK SOMEONE ELSE TO HELP. Basically, you have two choices. You can GIVE IN and get help, or you will reach the point where you GIVE OUT and then GIVE UP. It happens all too often in families who have taken first-rate care of their daughters and neglected themselves. They wake up one day and say, "I can't do this one day longer." It's better to get help than try to do it alone. Get help when you first need it rather than waiting for a crisis to build. Where can you find help?

- family members
- teachers
- friends, neighbors, or church members
- doctors, nurses, and other health professionals
- support groups
- parents of other children with special needs

You probably think you shouldn't have to ask for help, especially when it is your spouse. Do it anyway. Asking for help is a skill we need to cultivate, because it doesn't come naturally. Those who find ways to cope the best, learn to ask for help. This is not always easy for many reasons.

It was so hard to finally make the calls to ask for help. My family was pretty overwhelmed and uneducated on how to help us, so I had to look for outside help. Today, I continue to constantly ask for help. There are so many

Care for the Caregiver

great programs out there to help the disabled and their families, but so many don't know how or where to ask. I am constantly searching the internet and on the phone. This is my full-time job.

I think that sometimes we moms just do it all without thinking, like we would our babies or our "typical" children, and we forget to ask for help, or our husbands feel like maybe they wouldn't do it right if they did step in.

When we have needed help we have not found it easiest to ask our families. We have chosen to deal with this and to accept that they have to learn to deal with this situation in their way. We have also chosen to do whatever possible to help our child. We have written letters to many service groups and charities and we have received different types of assistance from different organizations.

Asking for help is admitting to yourself that you cannot do everything it takes to raise your child with RS by yourself. For a mother and father, it feels like failure at first but after a few times, you realize that asking for help is the best thing for you and your child. Asking for help may be one of the things that keeps you sane through the difficult times.

In the beginning it was harder to ask our family for help, but we learned to ask after realizing that we will always do what is best for Samantha.

PRACTICE INCOMPETENCE

PEOPLE NEVER WANT TO HELP when they think they can't do it as well as you or when they know you expect perfection. Be willing to settle for less once in awhile when you need a break. Your daughter can be dressed in stripes and polka dots and the fashion police won't arrest you. She can even have a different feeding or sleep schedule now and then and she'll survive.

LEARN TO LET GO

SOMETIMES WE WANT TO SHELTER OUR KIDS FOREVER. We think others couldn't possibly care for her as we do. Perhaps they can't ever love her as we do, but they can help and care for her. It takes some work to find the right caregiver, but it can be done. Start out with little getaways until you develop confidence.

TAKE IT EASY

TRY NOT TO DWELL ON DECISIONS that are well in the future. One decision at a time is enough. Trying to figure it all out and plan for the rest of our child's life will paralyze us. Many of the things we worry about may never come to pass: she may never have seizures or breathing problems. There may be good treatments for some of the other effects of RS in the very near future. And we're lucky to be led by a team of scientists dedicated to finding the cure for RS. Learn to live one day at a time. Today is a gift ... that's why we call it the present.

VARIETY IS THE SPICE OF LIFE

REMEMBER THAT YOUR CHILD IS A VERY IMPORTANT PART of your life, but not all of it. Develop interests outside your special parent role. Studies have shown that burnout doesn't come from our frantic schedules; it comes from doing too much of the same kind of stuff. Get away from the routine. Find a healthy outlet. Do something physical if you can. And going to the library looking for RS stuff or going to a RS meeting definitely do not count!

Care for the Caregiver

I have a very supportive husband who helps me coordinate the kids' schedules so I can catch up on scrapbooking, napping, shopping, whatever I want. The best relief I've found is to go get an hour massage. All worries, stress, life, are gone for a wonderful hour. And I feel great and ready to go afterward. I can tell when life is getting crazy because I start getting a lot of massages.

JUST DO IT

MAKE SOME TIME EVERY DAY TO DO SOMETHING for yourself, even if it is just for a few minutes. Do some deep breathing, take a short walk, jog around the backyard in the dark, call a friend, soak in the tub, read the comics. If you collapse from exhaustion or simply have a nervous breakdown, your child with Rett has no one else who will help her with the same vigor and determination and love as you do. We owe it to our children to give ourselves a regular break to avoid getting to that point. It is also important to remember that you are entitled to a life, to other interests, to fulfill your dreams, and so are your other children. Achieving this does not mean you are neglecting your child in some way; in fact you are serving her best by being content yourself and giving her a contented atmosphere to live in. This requires that you give yourself and your other kid's time instead of being totally consumed with the practicalities of caring for your child.

We try to have a respite worker come once a week so that we can go out. Often, it's just for coffee, sometimes supper or a movie. Occasionally, we actually do something special. We also let our friends know that we have the respite worker on the same night each week so they are able to plan to be free that night as well.

GET AWAY ALONE

WE NEED SOME TIME TOGETHER for the 3 Rs, Regrouping, Respite, and Rejuvenation. Many parents say they can't get away because 1) caregivers are hard to find and 2) they can't afford it anyway. But let's face it, can we afford not to get away? After all, we will pay one way or the other, either now or later. If we pay now, we may sacrifice some material things to afford time away. If we pay later, we may sacrifice a marriage or our sanity. So, we're faced with the choice to pay the babysitter now, or pay the divorce lawyer or the shrink later. It doesn't have to cost a lot. Time away can be an afternoon or an evening a week. It doesn't have to be elaborate or expensive. On those days when we really can't arrange to go away, we can plan for a nighttime movie date in front of the TV or a game of Scrabble—something far removed from caregiving. You need to nurture and foster your relationship with one another if you plan to be together for the long haul. If you are a single parent, the same applies. Don't consider it a luxury; consider it a necessity and budget for it. Do without something else, not time alone together. There may be many things you need, but you need yourself first. Then you need each other.

One of the first decisions we made in the first few weeks of getting Kendall's diagnosis was that we needed to really take special care of our marriage. We knew the statistics of failed marriages in relation to having a special needs child. We were determined not to be a statistic! We implemented "date night," which takes place every Wednesday night. We have a high school girl come over to watch the children. She feeds them dinner, plays with them, and gets them into bed. That is a night off for us! It's been over two years and we never miss a date night. I highly recommend this to all couples out there.

We went to an agency to find a qualified relief worker and ended up hiring a university student who was in her second year of physical therapy. It was a fantastic job for her as she learned so many things about working with

Care for the Caregiver

disabled kids and it allowed us to go out and feel that our child was in safe hands. We asked her to come every weekend, either Friday or Saturday evening, and for the longest time we'd just go to a coffee shop and talk about the whole situation. It gave us some time out, some time as a couple, a weekly night out (whether we wanted it or not!), and eventually we started to talk about other things, to do other things. In time, we started to feel like normal people for a few hours each week again.

ACCEPT WHAT YOU CANNOT CHANGE

THERE ARE MANY THINGS IN LIFE WHICH WE CAN CHANGE: where we live or work, how we dress, or who we choose for friends. We cannot change the fact that our daughters have RS. We can, however, change many aspects of our lives and hers that will make life easier. Often, it is helpful to marshal the energy which might be spent grieving into making things better. It may not be easy at times, but in those times of struggle you will find a stronger sense of who you are, and you will find that doing something positive helps your outlook.

KEEP IN TOUCH

FIND TIME TO TALK AND PLAY WITH YOUR SPOUSE or significant other. Your child is a very big part of your life. She can bring you closer together, but the many demands on your time can pull you apart. Find time for each other, even if it is just a short time. Make it a priority. Our daughters need us, but we need each other just as much and maybe more.

TOSS THE GUILT

HAVING A HANDICAPPED CHILD IS THE ONLY SITUATION when we feel guilty not because of what we did, but because of what we didn't do. We often feel that we can never do enough. There are never enough hours in the day to get it all done, to be fair to everyone, to give as much as is needed. We may say we can't live with regret if we didn't give it every chance, try every strategy, therapy, or medicine known to man. These are admirable goals, but impossible ones. We are only human. We can only do our very best. Recognize this as soon as you can. It's impossible to get away from the guilt. In your own eyes, you may feel that you can never do enough. Stop trying to do the impossible. If your child is cranky and you take her to McDonald's with the other kids, she takes away from their right to the all American dinner out. So you're guilty. If you leave her home and take the other kids, you've left the poor disabled child at home. So you're guilty again. Guilty no matter what. Accept that and toss the guilt out the window. When she's in good spirits, take her. When she's cranky, leave her at home where she will probably be happier anyway. Everyone wins once in a while. Do the best that you can do.

LEARN TO SAY NO

LEARN HOW TO SET BOUNDARIES. Realize that you can say "no" once in a while and still be a good parent. Let others take responsibility for refreshments for the baseball team now and then. Since you can't do it all, do what is the most important. Set limits on what you have to do and what you really want to do. We don't always have to be the ones in charge of Little League or the car pool. Try saying, "It's my year to say "no." When asked to run for PTA office, say, "This year, I'm only running for my life." Don't take on more than you can realistically do. Keep the demands in balance.

Care for the Caregiver

FORGIVE AND FORGET

TAKING CARE OF OURSELVES MEANS taking care of our hearts, too. Have patience with those who stare. Usually they stare not to be unkind, but because they are curious. They may not understand, but they can't understand if they haven't lived our lives. Don't expect them to. For each person who is unkind, there are dozens of people who are doubly kind. Remember that. Don't expect everyone to understand how you feel. Most have not walked in your shoes and they can't possibly identify with your many emotions. They can't begin to know how much work it is to raise a child with special needs. Try to remember that you may not have had as much insight before you became a special needs parent yourself.

MAKE YOUR HERO A SANDWICH

SOCIETY TELLS US THAT SINCE WE HAVE SPECIAL KIDS, we're special parents and most of us take that to heart. We think that everything we do has to be heroic, and, after all, the world keeps reminding us what saints we are. How many times have you been told how patient and heroic you are? We have to give ourselves permission to be human, to have the same ordinary gripes, and make the same everyday mistakes as the rest of the world. Give yourself a break. You can be sad, mad, fed up, and unspecial. At times you may care as much as Mother Teresa and you can try as hard as Superman, but you don't have to always be special. We are not helpful to anyone around us if we are tired, emotionally drained, sleep deprived and without a social outlet.

In the early years, my mother always praised me for all that I did for Renee and told me I was like Superwoman. This actually made me feel like I had to keep up with my title. Before she passed away, she told me that I needed to ask for help and realized that I'm not Superwoman anymore. I started to take baby steps to ask for help. I hated to admit I couldn't do it all myself and to this day I still, at times, feel like I have to prove to myself that I can do it all. Fact of the matter is ... I can't!

TRUST YOUR INSTINCTS

AS YOUR CHILD'S PARENT, YOU KNOW HER BETTER than anyone. You are the best expert. So when the days come that are filled with frustration and unexpected responsibilities, remember to believe in yourself and your ability to make the best decisions on her behalf. Trust your own judgments and opinions.

KEEP YOUR SENSE OF HUMOR

THROUGHOUT IT ALL, WE NEED TO NEVER LOSE our precious sense of humor. Laughter is internal jogging. Laugh at each other, but also laugh at yourself. Laughter is exercise you need to survive. To others who don't walk in our shoes, what we are able to laugh at may seem warped. It's all part of learning about what's important and what's not.

FIND YOUR OWN STRESS BUSTERS

IT MAY BE DIFFERENT WAYS ON DIFFERENT DAYS. Look at what gives you peace and comfort and then find a way to make it happen.

Depending on the nature of the stress, there are lots of alternatives. A lot of the time I take walks alone in the beautiful outdoors and I often pound the ground and send my stress through my feet right into the earth. It feels

Care for the Caregiver

so good! I also love to go work out with weights at the gym. Because I write for a local paper, I often write when I am stressed … it fuels the creativity and gets it done, then I am not stressing on the deadline.

I think we should do stuff that puts us in control over things; it makes the world less overwhelming. Working in the garden can definitely replace stress with a great kind of exhaustion, and I can bring bounty to my home with it. And yes, sometimes I even hang out with my husband and watch a movie.

When I start feeling really stressed out, I know it's time to turn to others for help. I do not have family in the area and my mother-in-law cannot lift McKenna, so I had to look for other resources. First, my husband and I went through the budget and made some adjustments so that we can have a woman clean our house every other week. I love coming home to a spanking clean house! Well worth the money if you ask me!

Sometimes, I end up finding something in the house that really needs to be done and just start it. Then my mind is off the bad stuff and really into what I'm doing. Some days, I volunteer at a local food pantry/kitchen. You will find that you don't have it that bad after you see what others are going through. And it really feels good to help others, even if it's sweeping their floors.

Something completely UNrett seems to be rejuvenating. There is so much with RS that is outside our control that sometimes just digging in where we do have some control can be a real stress reliever. So in addition to the physical benefits of exercise, there's some mental benefit of knowing we have control over that aspect of our lives during that moment. Cleaning can give that same feeling of putting something under our control again. Hobbies, if one can work out the time factor, could do the same.

Any time I snatch for myself always brings me back to Jess a happier, healthier, and more refreshed mom. If I am weary, weepy, grouchy, and bitter, you can bet the best of vibrations are not flowing into my household, and of what benefit would that be to anyone? I am so adamant about taking advantage of caregivers if you have them, because I regularly do not have that leisure. I love to do everything and anything with Jess … I just love being her mom. But in order to be the mom she needs, I can't be a martyr and pretend I wouldn't love some help.

ATTITUDE IS EVERYTHING

SITUATIONS MAY BE OUT OF OUR CONTROL, but we choose our attitudes. It's not what happens to us, but what we do with what happens to us that counts. We can't change RS, or how others will act. We can only change ourselves.

CELEBRATE LIFE

RECOGNIZE THAT WHILE IT PROBABLY IS THE BIGGEST ISSUE at your house, RS is not the only issue. Find some time to notice the good things that are happening all around. They help us recognize that on the balance, life is good. We have many things to be thankful for. We have all learned a new definition for heartache, but we've also learned the most important and profoundly simple lessons in life. We've been to places we'd rather not visit on this journey, had situations we'd surely trade. But there is always a lot to be thankful for, if you take the time to look. In the end, we've learned that family, health and well being, making a difference, are all that really count.

HAVE FAITH IN YOURSELF

DON'T THINK THAT YOU HAVE TO KNOW HOW to do everything perfectly or the way that others suggest might be right. You ARE the best expert on your child. Listen to your own heart.

Care for the Caregiver

TAKE TIME FOR YOURSELF

WHEN YOU GET RETT LAG, REACH FOR THE OXYGEN. A twenty-minute power nap does wonders. Meditate, stare out the window or go for a walk when you can. When you've had some quiet time, you'll be refreshed and ready to start again.

DO SOMETHING DIFFERENT

DEVELOP INTERESTS OUTSIDE YOUR SPECIAL PARENT ROLE so that you avoid burnout. Find a healthy outlet that has nothing to do with your child's condition. Do something physical if you can. The following rules apply: Do it. Do it today. Do it with gusto. Do it without guilt.

FIND A SUPPORT GROUP

TRY TO FIND A LOCAL SUPPORT GROUP for families of children with special needs. It does not have to be specific to RS. This gives you a chance to share feelings honestly without having to be strong for family or friends. Other group members know how you feel because they have also experienced a lot of the feelings you have. Even if you are generally shy with strangers, you will find yourself among friends very quickly. If you don't want to talk, listening can be therapeutic. You will learn that you are not alone.

GET PROFESSIONAL HELP

HOW DO YOU KNOW if you need professional help? Pay attention to these danger signals:

- using excessive amounts of alcohol or medications like sleeping pills
- loss of appetite or eating too much
- depression, loss of hope, feelings of alienation
- thoughts of suicide
- losing control physically or emotionally
- treating your child roughly or neglecting her

If you experience any of these symptoms, you may need to consider professional counseling. Knowing that you need help is the first step toward feeling better.

Ask your doctor to recommend a counselor, or contact your local hospital, mental health department, or the yellow pages to find a psychologist, social worker, counselor, or other mental health professional.

FIND RESPITE

THE SHORT DEFINITION FOR RESPITE is *relief*. Getting away from the routine of caregiving is an essential part of good caregiving. This story is a good illustration:

A lecturer, when explaining stress management to an audience, raised a glass of water and asked, "how heavy is this glass of water?" Answers called out ranged from 20g to 500g. The lecturer replied, "The absolute weight doesn't matter. It depends on how long you try to hold it. If I hold it for a minute, that's not a problem. If I hold it for an hour, I'll have an ache in my right arm. If I hold it for a day, you'll have to call an ambulance. In each case, it's the same weight, but the longer I hold it, the heavier it becomes." He continued, "And that's the way it is with stress management. If we carry our burdens all the time, sooner or later,

Care for the Caregiver

as the burden becomes increasingly heavy, we won't be able to carry on. As with the glass of water, you have to put it down for a while and rest before holding it again. When we're refreshed, we can carry on with the burden."

Being overwhelmed with the many needs of their child and other responsibilities, parents are often unaware of what kind of support even exists. It is important to know what you qualify for and how to get it.

Respite services vary depending on where you live and the age of your child. You may have to go through an agency, or you may be allowed to select your own respite worker.

- Check with your state Department of Mental Retardation or Department of Developmental Disabilities to see if there is state funding for care.
- Check with your local ARC. Some offer programs such as Family Share that will match you up with another family that has been trained and is willing to share caring for your child.
- Contact your child's social worker, the local Developmental Disabilities Administration or Regional Center and inquire if there is a respite budget that will allow you to pay caregivers.
- Some senior centers have intergenerational programs made up of seniors who love to provide "grandparenting."
- Churches often have youth groups or members who are willing to come in and help with child care.
- Check with the local high school to see if it has a list of babysitters.

The best part of having someone help is you get back some of your independence. You can have the aide help you physically take your daughter anywhere. I brought our aide to the state family picnic. I even brought her daughter to play with my son and the rest of kids. We had a blast. I was able to socialize and know that Sarah was well cared for.

LOCATE A LOVING CAREGIVER

AS YOUR CHILD GETS OLDER, YOU MAY FIND THE NEED to hire a daily caregiver. If your daughter has no day program, you may need the caregiver to allow you to continue working. If her care is complicated by your bad back, or if she has become too heavy to lift continually, a regular caregiver can provide relief. Or, you may need the caregiver to provide for your daughter so that you can travel or take vacations.

Bureaucrats seem to make sure that funding information is hard to locate, but it's there somewhere. Be aware that finding the funding for a caregiver is only the first step. All too often, parents have the funding but can't find anyone to fill the job. Due to low pay and benefits versus high expectations for performance, it is not unusual for frequent turnover in the field. Workers may have less education or, take the job as a temporary situation while they learn the English language.

While it may take some time, it is well worth the effort to find someone you trust, who can come into your home so you can get out of it when you need to. It may take some effort, but whether it is going to the grocery store or a weekend at the lodge, respite is a very valuable component of your child's total well-being.

Giving up a child to someone else's care is difficult even for families with typical children. When the child can't talk or express her disapproval of the arrangement or how she

Care for the Caregiver

is being treated, it complicates things greatly. No matter what age your offspring may be, she is still your child. Finding someone to help care for her the way you do may be a challenge, but you can come close. It will take some creativity and resourcefulness. The important thing is to establish respite time on a regular basis so that you can count on it.

> *I had a home health aide and it was great to have an "extra set of hands" with Sarah. She did everything, from bathing Sarah, playing games with her, singing to her, walking her around the mall with me, and even helped with small household chores like laundry. Today, Sarah's level of care has changed so she requires nurses. It has to do with having a feeding pump, meds, suctioning, and a nebulizer. Aides are not allowed to do any of those.*

- Private insurance or Medicaid will sometimes provide for a home health aide or nurse, depending on the level of care, amount of hours needed, what your insurance policy specifies. Your child's doctor will need to write a Letter of Medical Necessity. Be prepared to be turned down the first time. Keep at it.
- Keep in contact with state agencies. Things can change. Something unavailable now may be available in the future. Most states have web sites with phone numbers to call.
- Ask your child's social worker or DDA office about funding for a caregiver. Programs generally allow seven to ten dollars per hour for care.
- Ask neighbors and friends if they know someone who might be interested.
- Ask your daughter's teachers and therapists if they are interested, or if they can recommend someone.
- Place an ad in your local newspaper, the church bulletin, or a local college bulletin board. Include as much information as you can in the ad so you don't have to screen too many unqualified people.

  Loving caregiver for (young) (older) girl with RS in our home. Must be dependable, gentle, enthusiastic, and creative. Great job for college student majoring in nursing, special ed, or therapy. Will train (Experience required) (Experience helpful but not required). West Chicago, Rosemont section, 123-4567, $_ an hour to start.

- Go through an agency. The value to doing it this way is that the applicant is pre-screened and may be trained and supervised.
  - Is the agency licensed, accredited, or Medicaid approved?
  - Is it for profit or nonprofit?
  - Does it train staff? How?
  - What is the job description?
  - Are aides licensed or certified? By whom?
  - What are the formal training requirements?
  - Who supervises?
  - Are there work hour restrictions?
  - Is attendance monitored?
  - Who is the client contact person?
  - What are the agency fees? Are there subsidies? A sliding scale?
- Ask the applicant why she is applying for the job. Is it just for a salary, or does she have some special interest in caring for others (such as a disabled family member)?
- Check references carefully. If the applicant has embellished her qualifications or lied on her application, cross her off the list immediately and move on.

Care for the Caregiver

- Do a criminal background check.
- If you have even subtle reservations about the applicant, go with your gut. You have the ultimate choice.
- Don't minimize the demands of the job. Prepare a checklist of things she will be required to do.
- You may choose to stay at home while the caregiver is there until you become confident with her care. Use this time to do other things around the house, or just relax.
- It will probably be easier to get someone to come in for several hours at a time rather than an hour a day. If the caregiver has to ride the public bus, she may invest more than an hour in travel.
- Consider supplementing her salary, according to her qualifications and how helpful she becomes. If you can subsidize one dollar an hour, it may make the job more attractive. Don't do this to start out with. Tell her you will consider it.
- Start out with an agreed-upon trial period. Trust and relationships take time to develop.
- Relief will probably not be achieved immediately. It takes time for the caregiver to get to know your child and her routine.
- Make a *Taking Care of ME* book about your child with photos of familiar activities, routines and a list of how you like things done. Include the following:
  - emergency numbers
  - likes and dislikes
  - tips for emotional comfort
  - tips for handling challenging behaviors
  - routines
  - positioning, exercises, use of equipment, monitoring ambulation
  - safety considerations
  - method of communication and any use of technology
  - sleep patterns and bedtime routine
  - feeding, diet and fluid intake
  - bathing and personal hygiene
  - medication administration
  - seizure protocols
  - gastrointestinal concerns

RECIPE FOR STRESS

By Claudia Weisz

Take an unlimited amount of obligations, and fit them into a limited amount of time. Combine with any number of things over which you have no control. Add a sedentary lifestyle and several hands full of junk food and mix well. Add a family member who needs constant attention and care. Refuse all offers of help. Add several hours of sitting in hospitals and doctors' offices, several hours of nighttime caregiving, a handful of unexplained screaming spells, a dash of explaining to others why she is crying. Be sure

Care for the Caregiver

to mix in a container where no one understands and stir with a spoon of solid tension. Add self-pity to taste. Serve with loneliness and isolation. Variations of this basic recipe can be created from the following optional ingredients:

Some sort of medication can add flavor to your stress recipe. Telephones add to the mix, (especially flavorful if your phone number is very close to that of a local real estate office with rental and sale signs all over town, or better yet, a teenager.) Just as a little sugar and spice added to vinegar makes a delectable sauce, certain ingredients added to your recipe for stress balance its flavor.

The first thing to remember in any recipe is the importance of weighing the ingredients. Weigh upsetting events on a scale of one to ten. Get support. Even great chefs have their assistants. Reach out for help. Give support. Again, watch quantities.

Animals can add to stress or relieve it. Stroking a pet can lower blood pressure; damaged furniture or carpeting may raise it. Add some squabbling siblings (these are nice served with a sprig of anger). A demanding or complaining spouse or boss is best served drawn and quartered or filleted. (Avoid marinating, especially in wine). Malfunctioning office machines are most effective if served with a deadline. A vomiting dog is most effective combined with a light colored, deep pile carpet, preferably new). A constantly meowing cat adds a nice touch, especially one with fleas. Any pet will do, as long as it needs constant feeding, and letting in and out.

Share yourself, but don't give it all away. Eliminate unnecessary ingredients. Often the finest sauces are those with the least ingredients. Simplicity can be elegant. Do you really need the pet, or should you keep the pet and get rid of the carpeting?

Take stock of your ingredients. Make a list of the things which upset you. Are you really upset at the dog or at the kids who said they'd take care of him? Do you have "isolation" mislabeled as "privacy?"

All recipes are easily altered. If you are too heavy-handed with any one ingredient the result will lack balance. Remember, you are the chef!

BENDING AND LIFTING

IT IS IMPORTANT TO LEARN HOW TO LIFT CORRECTLY so that you place the least amount of strain on your body, particularly your back. With so many important caregiving tasks, preserving your own health and well being is a must.

It is a good idea to attend one of your daughter's PT sessions to get suggestions for the best ways to care for her with the least lifting possible. Your school district may even allow you to have special PT sessions for training purposes. Ask your school administrator or request it in her IEP. While good lifting techniques can prevent injuries, they will also make transfers safer and easier. A training session should include: transferring in and out of your car, in and out of the tub or shower, in and out of a sitting to stand position, placing the wheelchair in and out of the car, and any other situations which pull on your back. When lifting, widen the base of your stance and bend your legs while keeping your back straight.

When transferring from bed to chair, lean your daughter forward into your shoulder. A sliding board is an inexpensive piece of equipment which can be used for safe trans-

Care for the Caregiver

fers. If your daughter is able to learn to assist you, practice often so she can gain strength to help.

There are a number of mechanical devices when lifting becomes too difficult. Ramps, platform lifts, stairway lifts, and elevators increase accessibility and decrease back strain. Bathtub and bedside lifts can be invaluable.

When changing diapers, it is better to roll the girl on her side to place the diaper under her rather than to lift her hips. It may not seem like a lot of strain to lift her, but over time, lifting the wrong way can be harmful.

The PT showed me how to lift Sarah with my legs and not my back. I get to Sarah's level and cradle her like a baby. It is so important to carry as close as possible to your body instead of extending your arms. For me it has been a life-saver. There are tight spots that sometimes I have to lift under her arms to move and then to carry, I go back to the cradle method.

The hardest time of lifting Sammi is when I have to put her in the car. It seems to be easier if I put her on the right side of the car in back. I put my left arm behind her back and lift her legs with my right. She can't help at all with this, so it is all on my back. When I get her out of the car, I turn her legs to the outside, stand upright and have her to "slide" on out of the car while I'm holding her hands.

We have a ceiling track lift now that is used mainly by the nurses who come in to bathe and do respite with our daughter. My husband and I do two-man lifts and this has been fine for us.

We installed a type of barrier-free lift. My husband designed an aluminum track that is bolted into the ceiling and rafters that goes from her bed to the bathtub. We purchased an electric wench to run along the track. We use a body net that attaches to it and then we can lift her up and down with only one person. It is very helpful. I can lift her into the bathtub or wheelchair by myself.

Bending too often can also stress the back, particularly when bathing, dressing and changing. If she is smaller, a changing table can be used. When older, an electric hospital bed that can be lowered for standing transfers and raised for diapering and dressing is helpful. Some parents are very creative making adjustments to regular beds and other equipment to accommodate the need to bend less.

To help the problem bending over on the bed, we have ordered a shorter height box spring and frame. Angela's bed is about six inches lower than a regular bed. When she sits on the end, her feet can touch the floor. The lower bed height is enough that I can kneel next to the bed to change Angela.

We put the bathtub up on a platform and cut out underneath the platform so the person bathing Kayleigh can place their feet under the tub and they do not have to lean very much when washing her. This has made an incredible difference. She also has a tilt wheelchair and we had the tilt altered so it tilts a little more down and forward when we want Kayleigh to do a standing transfer. This makes it easier for her to come to a standing position with assistance and again, less stress on our backs.

LIFTING TO PREVENT BACK INJURIES
General Principles of Lifting
- the force is against you
- lift from the waist
- add upper body weight
- watch your weight
- warm up before lifting

Care for the Caregiver

Causes of Back Injuries
- lifting from the waist, and twisting
- lifting overhead or away from you
- heavy, repetitive lifting
- awkward position
- unbalanced load
- sitting/standing in one position too long

Steps to Prevent Back Injuries
- test the objects weight first
- get help
- balance your stance
- squat down, hug the load
- lift gradually, using the legs
- change direction using feet, not waist
- reverse guidelines to lower the load
- exercise, weight, rest, and warm-up

Safe Lifting for Your Child
- Protect yourself
- Use proper equipment

"You give but little when you give of your possessions.
It is when you give of yourself that you truly give."

– KAHLIL GIBRAN

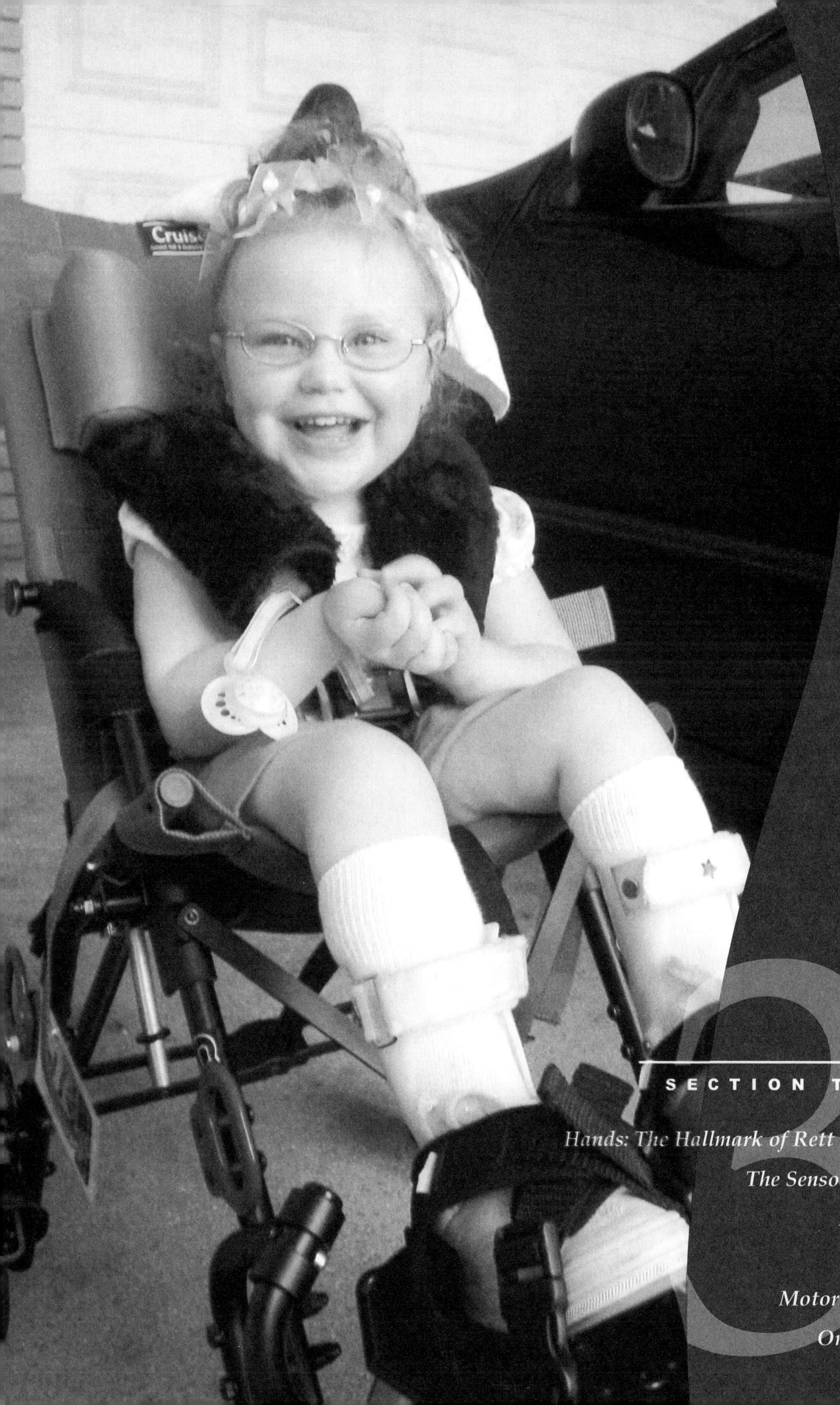

Common Problems

3

SECTION THREE

Hands: The Hallmark of Rett Syndrome

The Sensory System

Behaviors

Seizures

Motor Problems

Orthopedics

Common Problems

Behaviors

The Sensory System

Hands:
The
Hallmark
of
Rett
Syndrome

Seizures

Orthopedics

Motor Problems

Hands: The Hallmark of Rett Syndrome

HAND FUNCTION

LOSS OF PURPOSEFUL HAND USE

WHILE THE STEREOTYPED hand movements in RS are the most noticeable aspect of the disorder, they are not the first symptom to appear. Loss of purposeful *hand use* begins first, and is often a subtle loss over time. The child has less interest in manipulating objects, and begins to drop toys or lose grasp of the cup or morsel of food before it gets to the mouth.

"Her hands are instruments of her heart, not her head."

– BARBRO LINDBERG

REPETITIVE MOVEMENTS

REPETITIVE HAND MOVEMENTS THEN FOLLOW. These movements are almost constant while the individual is awake. These stereotyped movements can change over time.

HANDS AND THE DIAGNOSIS OF RS

HAND MOVEMENTS ARE ALSO SEEN IN OTHER DISORDERS. In making the diagnosis of RS, what she does with her hands is not as important as what she does not do with her hands compared with what she once could do. The combination of normal hand use followed by loss of purposeful hand use must be present for the diagnosis of RS to be confirmed.

DEGREE OF SKILL LOSS

THE DEGREE OF LOSS OF HAND SKILLS WILL VARY with the age when her regression began. This is more difficult to show when the onset is early, because as an infant, she has not yet developed a repertoire of hand skills. When home movies of infants who are later diagnosed with RS are viewed, it is evident that even before regression, some girls show subtle signs that hand use is not entirely normal in infancy. She may lose most or all of her hand and finger skills, yet she may be able to regain some skills after the regression period.

As an infant, she may develop a normal pincer grasp, allowing her to pick up small objects with the thumb and forefinger. This ability gradually diminishes to a palmar grasp, where the palm and fingers are used in a raking motion. Sometimes her grasp is lost entirely and a striking movement is used instead. Often, as an infant, she can hold a cup or other object, but gradually, she loses the ability to keep her grip on the object. It is as difficult for her to keep holding an object as it is to grasp it to begin with, so it is common for a girl with RS to succeed in picking something up, only to lose her grip and drop it soon after. Hand and mouth movements are often synchronized and when she opens her mouth, she may drop the spoon or piece of food. She may be able to hold the cup for a drink, and then drop it in mid-air.

Amy has extreme difficulty picking up things. She will look hard at what she wants, rock and hyperventilate and sometimes, but not often, the hand will come flying out and swipe at it.

Hands: The Hallmark of Rett Syndrome

Samantha used to drop her cup. We laminated a big red circle made of red construction paper and had her "aim" for the circle for about two years. One day, I realized that she was no longer dropping her cup on the floor! Now when she picks it up to take a drink, she'll place it back on the table. She will still drop it and sometimes it will land on the table on its side, but nothing like it used to be.

TYPES OF HAND MOVEMENTS

CHARACTERISTIC HAND MOVEMENTS CHANGE OVER TIME, but usually begin with non-specific waving or odd postures of the hands. Often, the next movement seen is hand mouthing or clapping, followed by mid-line hand washing, hand wringing, or hand rubbing and squeezing. Some girls hold their hands apart, rolling or manipulating the fingers or twisting the hair or grabbing at their clothes. Some girls bite or lick their hands or hold them in distinctive postures. The hand movements are repeated over and over again the same way. Each hand follows its own distinct pattern of movement. The speed or rhythm of hand movements can sometimes be useful in "reading" her mood—excitement, anger or happiness.

HAND MOVEMENTS CHANGE WITH AGE

AS SHE GETS OLDER, THE HAND MOVEMENTS ARE SLOWER and less intense, but they still remain. An older girl may sit with her hands folded in a tight grip that is hard to break open, tapping or strumming her fingers. Joint contractures may prevent her from bringing her hands together at midline. Increased spasticity may make grasping more difficult but allow her to increase her grip. Girls who remain mobile tend to have more intense and active hand movements.

Malia put her hands in her mouth for all different reasons. When she was upset, she would do it one way, bored another way, happy another way. It was kind of a barometer on how she felt. Once you got to know her, you could read her moods.

Cierney twists and clasps her fingers real tight. She's pretty much always busy with one and sometimes both hands working on twirling her hair. She shakes her hands when she's really happy and excited.

Jenn mouthed her hands constantly for a long time. She would insert one hand into her mouth and within two seconds replace it with the other, and then two seconds later she'd switch again. About age 4-5 it was not only periodic, but different in form. She would just pat her mouth with her right hand while her left hand patted her chest. Both hands moved quickly. Then as she got older, they slowed down. And now she very gently pats them as before or pats her hands together in her lap.

There are moments, and they occur more and more over the years, that Amy is calm and interested in activities, holding her hands in her lap. That is a hopeful development.

PERFORMANCE AND HAND SKILLS

IN ADDITION TO STEREOTYPED HAND MOVEMENTS, the girl with RS has a significant degree of apraxia, which interferes with her ability to perform intentional motor movements with her hands. She has the desire and will to move her hands, but cannot make them do what she wants them to do.

She may also have hand tremors, which make using her hands even more difficult. Spasticity and uneven muscle tone can also affect the hands. In some girls, the thumbs are pulled

Hands: The Hallmark of Rett Syndrome

in across the palm and it is very difficult to bring them back out. This can make difficult grasping absolutely impossible.

She often acts as though she perceives sensory input from her hands differently. She may resist hand-over-hand assistance and may dislike having her hands touched. Due to her apraxia, ataxia and stereotyped movements, it is often difficult for an observer to determine the intentions of her uncoordinated movements, which appear to be random. The stereotyped hand movements increase when she is stressed or bored.

SHE CAN'T STOP MOVEMENTS

IT IS IMPORTANT TO RECOGNIZE that she is not causing the repetitive hand movements to happen. They are happening to her. They are not due to self-stimulation. Even in situations where she wants to, she is usually unable to break up these movements on her own. They may be subdued, but the hand movements are continuous during waking. They increase in intensity when she is under stress, whether positive (happiness, eagerness) or negative (discomfort, anger).

REDUCING HAND MOVEMENTS

WHILE IT IS IMPOSSIBLE TO STOP THE HAND MOVEMENTS, it is possible to reduce them by distraction (using the hands in an activity), restraining or holding the non-dominant hand to increase use of the dominant hand, and using various splints to immobilize the hands and/or elbows. Tolerance for inhibiting her hand movements differs from one girl to another, but many girls seemed to be relieved when the splints are put on.

During therapy she does better with choice-making and hitting switches if her right hand is lightly held down so that the dominant left hand can be used. There is no way she could use a computer but she does have a lot of success with a BigMac switch and similar type switches.

In our earlier days with her, before splinting, we wrapped her non-dominant hand and loosely tied it to the wheelchair arm rest.

Kendall's first splints were made from noodle connectors. You know those things you use in pools? Her PT cut them in half length-wise and attached Velcro strips to the top and bottom. These can be made to any length. What was great about these splints was that she still had range-of-motion, but she just couldn't get her hands to her mouth.

If we control Selena's right hand, the left generally is able to control itself. We keep a hand puppet on her right hand. It helps her keep her hands down; she doesn't like her vision blocked and they are big enough to get in the way. It cushions the blow when she really gets going to get those hands up there. And, they are a conversation starter—it gives people something concrete to talk to her about. The kids in her class love them and like to "help" her play with them.

It's amazing how much more outward and focused she is when her hands are not interfering. We use weights to keep her right hand down (ankle or wrist weights that wrap around and secure with a Velcro strap). We've also used roller blade wrist guards (remove the piece that is on the palm side) either on her hand or wrapped around her elbow to keep it extended.

Hannah would scratch the backs of her hands until they bled. We gave her a set of various car keys/key chains/ toys to hold. If she has something to play with in her hands, she is less likely to wring them or put them in her mouth.

Hands: The Hallmark of Rett Syndrome

SKIN BREAKDOWN

SKIN BREAKDOWN AND INFECTION can be a significant problem in the girl who puts her hands in her mouth routinely, or whose hand movements are aggressive. Creative therapists and parents have come up with a number of good solutions—holding one hand, distracting her, massaging her hands, providing stimulating hand activities, or putting gloves, wristbands or tube socks on her hands.

Rachel constantly has her hands in her mouth, and this causes skin breakdown and swelling of her fingers. Some of her fingers are twice the size they should be. Arm splints keep her hands out of her mouth but allow her to wring them. The plastic comes in some really nice colors—Rachel's are a pretty purple.

We discovered an over-the-counter lotion which is non-toxic, but supposed to form a barrier on the skin to protect it from harmful irritants and help heal damaged skin. It is sold in our local drug stores, usually located near the pharmacy. It very simple to use; just clean and dry hands and apply the lotion. It dries invisible, does not wash off, and last for at least four hours. I have been applying it three or four times per day, and have been able to reduce bracing to only when I am feeding her. Her hands have nearly healed completely and her fingernails are growing back. The product is called Gloves in a Bottle (www.glovesinabottle.com).

REDUCING STEREOTYPED HAND MOVEMENTS

SHE DOES NOT HAVE CONSCIOUS CONTROL over her hand movements, so it is impossible for her to stop them at will. The role of her compulsive hand motion is not entirely understood. It could be a need for extra stimulation to make up for something the brain is lacking, a different or strange sensation in the hands which is relieved by the movements, or the product of a need for motion that does not have a normal outlet. Studies have shown that when the hand movements are blocked completely, the feet often take up the movements, or she will rock. Sometimes, when the hand movements are blocked for a time, they return with double intensity.

The more alert she is, the more she will do the hand movements. She takes things in her mouth, but in my opinion it is not to gain information on the objects. She cannot help herself; it is involuntary behavior, and nothing can stop her.

It is hard to say whether we should or should not discourage these movements when we do not fully understand them. However, when the hand movements are inhibited, many girls are more social and interact more with the environment while they decrease hand to mouth movements and hand wringing behavior. Splinting the hands may allow for greater concentration and more functional use of her hands.

Anca actually seems relieved at times to have the wringing and hand-to-mouth behavior stopped. We take her elbow braces off after a while if she becomes fussy. We then put them back on and it calms her tremendously.

Angie seems greatly relieved to have her arm splints on. When she has a screaming spell, she hits herself in the mouth and bites hard on her fingers. As long as she can still get her hands together, she is not stressed about the splints.

We finally found arm splints that are wonderful. They are inflatable and zip up the arm. You can make them as "full" or as "soft" as needed. We find that Taylor seems to enjoy having one arm at a time splinted for about thirty minutes each in the morning and afternoon. We use them for concentration purposes.

Hands: The Hallmark of Rett Syndrome

Before using a method to reduce the hand movements, consider and respect her own needs. Does she use these movements to express anger or excitement, happiness or sadness? Will she have a way to express these feelings without using her hand movements? What is her reaction to having the hand movements restrained? Some girls are irritable, while others seem relieved to have their hands splinted. If the hand movements create a type of sensory input needed by girls with RS, hand splints may provide this input or alter the need for it in some way.

For some girls who are frustrated by arm splints, hand splints can be used. In some cases, a combination of the two techniques used simultaneously or in sequence may be more beneficial. Hand splints may be used to keep the hands open. The thumb is held in an abducted position (away from the body) while the wrist is kept in a neutral or extended position. This allows her to make better use of her hands, or helps to keep the hands from reaching the mouth, avoiding injury. Inhibiting the hand-to-mouth behavior allows more appropriate visual input, which encourages increased eye contact and interaction. Reaching and grasping may be easier. Sometimes, the splints have an overall calming effect.

Alyssa's movements are more intense when there is something on her mind and she is trying to get you to figure it out. When we see her doing it more frequently, we try to see what might be going on that is causing it, and sometimes just putting the splints on for a little bit gives her a breather and a big sigh of relief! Sometimes I think that she doesn't like doing the movement either, but doesn't know how to stop it.

Splints should not be viewed as restraints, but as an aid to treatment. They work most effectively to reduce hand movements in those girls who have mid-line hand movements. Her orthopedic specialist and occupational therapist should be consulted to determine the kind of splints which would be most helpful.

With the splints, she still hand mouths but it is much "lighter" and there are longer periods when she actually puts her hands down, especially when eating. We find that we have to put splints on her when doing P.T. exercises so she will sit for longer periods and actually bear weight on them.

I notice a calming effect when Brittany wears her elbow splints for 15-20 minute increments. This eliminates biting and self abuse and allows her to use her hands and concentrate.

USING SPLINTS

SOMETIMES, THE ABOVE METHODS DO NOT WORK well enough, and the next step is to devise arm/hand/elbow splints for her to wear periodically during the day. Home made arm splints can be made with rolled up magazines, potato chip or orange juice cans or soft pliable plastic. One parent successfully used a leather golf wrist brace with velcro closure. When these are ineffective, specially fitted splints can be made by your child's OT or with a prescription from her orthopedic doctor. You can purchase readymade splints in various sizes and materials.

Splinting may allow more functional use of the hands. Splints are very effective in keeping hands out of the mouth, and allowing attention to shift outward to the people and surroundings, giving the person better purposeful hand use. Some splints hold the elbow stiff and allow no movement, while others block flexion past a certain point but allow elbow extension. It is important for any device to be carefully evaluated by her therapist for fit and functional use, and to be sure she is comfortable. A list of manufacturers is included in the Equipment and Ideas chapter.

Hands: The Hallmark of Rett Syndrome

Sarah's arm splints have helped her gain better eye contact, as she tends to lean down as she brings her hands to her mouth. She was always looking down. Now she will look straight ahead most of the time with them on. And with some PT, she has gained the ability to turn her head to the side to look over her shoulder. So it has helped to teach her to communicate and concentrate. It has also helped her oral motor function as she doesn't have a heap of fingers in her mouth to deal with, so she gets sounds out better, eats a lot better and is easier to feed. Over all, I feel it has helped her physically. She's not bent over and her arms are not held tightly all day.

We have started splinting Jessica's left elbow so she can't get her hand to her mouth. It had got to the point where her left thumb was constantly in her mouth and it seemed to be overriding everything else. When she was tired/angry/upset she would bite it really hard leaving huge welts, and the skin was starting to break down and form hard calluses. She was no longer playing with her toys as much as we knew she could, and feeding her was a nightmare!

Initially we weren't too sure about splinting her elbow. But now, we are so glad we are doing it. It has made a huge difference, she seems much happier—now she can play with her toys again! We had noticed she wasn't her usual smiley self but hadn't connected it to her hand mouthing. The skin on her hand is starting to soften again and the sores have healed.

With the splint, she is still able to bring her hands together and tap/wring them, and the splint has a slight bend so she has some movement. We have found that we only need to splint the left elbow. She will bite the right only when she is upset or angry and occasionally rest the thumb in her mouth but nothing like she did with the left.

The splinting really only seemed to distress Corieen; she seems to need the motion. As time has gone on, she is able to separate her hands by herself sometimes to swipe at a toy or a switch, or to use her computer. When she is unable to separate by herself we will stabilize one hand, encourage her to use the other, and then let her go back to the wringing again. At school she is assisted as necessary like this so she can go back to the wringing in between making choices on her computer. It seems the more she wants to do something, the more she is able to separate her hands and use the left one purposefully.

HOMEMADE SPLINTS

The very first splints that Rachel had were Playtex baby bottles, the kind where you insert a liner into it. Her pre-k teacher lined them with terry cloth to keep them from sliding down. They were long enough that Rachel could not bend her elbows but she still could wring her hands together at midline.

We have recently found that the arm immobilizer that Haley is wearing for her broken arm is a wonderful tool for when she is working on the computer. She can still wring her hands, but she can't get both hands in her mouth and does much better at the computer.

Jacky's splints are handmade—large ("fancy") terry washcloths, stuffed with pieces of rubber or bubble wrap, etc. We wrap a tennis elbow strap around the terrycloth that is wrapped around her elbow and secure it with Velcro.

Nikyla's grandma makes her splints in several different colors with different appliqués sewn on. They are made with washable, cotton fabric and to prevent the bending they have plastic stays in them. They are nicely lined and do not leave marks on the skin.

An elbow splint really helped Jess focus on her toys. Her therapist made her splint out of some neoprene (wetsuit material) and Velcro with a piece of plastic stiffener sewn into it.

We used frozen concentrate orange juice cans, then added a sock with the toe cut out to help keep it in place. Later, we went to homemade splints and now we have splints that are hinged, so that she can bend her arm

Hands: The Hallmark of Rett Syndrome

but not enough to put to her mouth. She seems to be able to focus better when her hands are away from her mouth. This seems to help her cope with things we can't figure out or "fix."

TYPES OF SPLINTS

FULL HAND SPLINTS EXTEND FROM IMMEDIATELY BELOW the wrist to immediately above the finger tips on the palm side of the hand, with the thumb protruding in a comfortable position to the side and the fingers slightly bowed inward toward the thumbs. Half hand splints are molded in the same way as the full hand splints, but extend from below the wrist to the middle finger joints. Elbow splints extend from the forearm, around and just above the elbow, maintaining a comfortable bowed position.

Custom splints are made from various kinds of plastic which are thin, smooth and rigid, but moldable when heated, such as Theraplast or Polyform. The splints are fitted to the child's contours. They should have a washable soft foam liner that does not absorb odors or bacteria. Elbow splints should allow for twenty to thirty degrees of elbow flexion. Both ends should be flared to prevent pressure sores. The straps should be adjustable to allow the arm to extend, but prevent it from flexing toward the face. Hand splints should leave the pads of the index and thumb exposed so that she will get the necessary sensory feedback when the splints are worn.

ONE SPLINT OR TWO?

IT'S BEST TO SEE HER REACTION AND TOLERANCE for the splints. Some girls enjoy having both hands, arms or elbows splinted, while others prefer one at a time. When trying to encourage more purposeful hand use, it is best to splint the non-dominant hand, leaving the other hand free for her to use.

THUMB SPLINTS

SPASTICITY AND UNEVEN MUSCLE TONE can also affect the hands. In some girls, the thumbs are pulled in across the palms and it is very difficult for them to bring them back out. This can make difficult grasping absolutely impossible. Uneven tone can also pull the wrist off to one side.

There are also soft thumb abductor splints which are made out of a dense cell foam and Velcro. They don't prevent hand wringing or mouthing but can be used to increase function and reduce the chance of deformities. They do this by gently pulling the thumb out and away from the palm of the hand, which places it in a better position for grasping objects.

OTHER TREATMENTS

PROVIDING AN ENVIRONMENT THAT IS NOT TOO STRESSFUL or demanding and the use of vibrators and gentle hand massage can be helpful. It is important to remember that it is probably not wise to limit the hand movements completely unless they are interfering in some way – for instance, greatly limiting her functional hand use or causing sores on her hands or mouth. Moderation is best.

We have discovered a very simple way to keep Angie's hands still. We put a hot water bottle filled 2/3 with very warm water (with the extra air squeezed out) either on her lap or on the table in front of her. She loves the feel of it and will let her hands rest on it relaxed and still for 15 to 20 minutes. She likes to squeeze it.

Hands: The Hallmark of Rett Syndrome

We've had good luck putting long white athletic socks on one and sometimes both hands. I think Chelsea still has the movement in her hands without feeling constricted by gloves, and she doesn't put her hand in her mouth at all when the sock is on.

I find Sarah is more willing to try things if her extremities are warm. She tends to have cold hands and feet most of the time, so I try hard to keep her warm and cozy if trying to do something requiring her to respond.

Roselyn puts her hands to her mouth constantly. When she was younger we did use elbow splints, but she got very frustrated. For years now I have made little bags of terry toweling with elastic that just slip over her hand.

When Dani started mouthing her hands at age two we started giving her a pacifier or gummy bears sewn into polyester organza, with a long tail so she couldn't swallow. We also used a special hands-free baby bottle and she learned to hold the nipple, attached to a long flexible tube, in her mouth for long periods of time.

INCREASING HAND SKILLS

THE USE OF A SPLINT ON THE NON-DOMINANT HAND may increase her ability to concentrate, and to use the dominant hand in functional activities. Adapting materials so that she can more easily succeed provides good reinforcement. Encourage her to use her hands by using activities or rewards that are attractive to her.

Velcro is a life saver. I use it so that Briana can hold things: spoon, dolls, new adaptive paintbrushes, and even sippy cups. It helps her maintain her grip, and has even helped her get better at grabbing and holding onto items she wants. She has been reaching more, and retrieving items she wants both at school and at home with less frustration.

I made a designer grip glove—a Velcro catcher's mitt of sorts. Briana and I play catch with one of those fuzzy balls and have a blast. Now I just have to teach her to throw forward. She makes me fetch for the most part, but it's so much fun, and according to her P.T., great reflex training.

Be sure that her goals for hand use are realistic. It may take a long time for her to gain skills. It is not practical to think that she will ever have completely normal hand use. But with hand-over-hand assistance, adapted equipment, time and patience, she can learn some functional skills that will give her great pride and satisfaction, and which will make a meaningful difference in her life.

Karina has to practice a specific movement over and over to have it "installed" in her system. That may take years. For example, she has a lift for going upstairs. It has a tiny button for on/off, and she has been able to handle that for three years. During all this time, I practiced with her to teach her to use the big yellow button for going up and down. She has to push it sideways and keep it there, and as soon as she releases her grip, the lift stops. You can understand how difficult it is for a girl to hold a firm grip. For three years I held her hand on the button, pushing it together. Last week she did it on her own for the first time. She is only capable of going downstairs, pushing left to right, which is easier for a left-handed girl than pushing right to left. But she sailed down the stairs all by herself, big smile, making four or five stops, but pushing the button again. How proud we were.

Voluntary hand use is increased when she is relaxed and strongly motivated in non-demanding, interesting or pleasurable activity, such as eating. Some girls can finger feed, while others can use a spoon or fork with assistance to scoop the food. Often, she is motivated to use her hands during music therapy. When the music therapist sits close and an

Hands: The Hallmark of Rett Syndrome

instrument is easily within her reach, she is interested and strongly motivated to strike the instrument, even though her actions may be jerky and uncoordinated.

Hand use can definitely be relearned. Before Meg's regression, she could use her hands for anything. She was feeding herself, coloring, turning pages in a book, manipulating objects, climbing, all the things a two-year old should do. Then, she wouldn't use her hands for anything. Now at 5, she will hold your hand when she needs help stepping up on a step and even holds a hand rail independently to climb stairs. We just stand behind her and hold her free hand. The key is that she needs to be highly motivated.

Eye-hand coordination is usually poor because looking (input) and reaching (output) are difficult to coordinate at the same time. Often, she has to look first, look away, and then reach without looking. If she is very motivated and anxious to touch an object, she may have to "gear up" her body for action, but there is always a delayed response. If standing, she will begin to rock back and forth or lean forward. If sitting, she may begin rocking, hyperventilate, grind her teeth or make facial grimaces. Her hand movements may increase in intensity and she may tense her body, sometimes staring closely at the object, sometimes staring off. This can last for a few minutes. Then, she may suddenly lunge at the object without looking at it. She may succeed in picking up the object, but all too often she results in knocking it to the floor instead.

Kim can feed herself using a fork with a built-up handle that has been molded to her grip, provided we spear the food first. She can pick up the fork and put the food into her mouth, but then the fork falls. I sit on her left side, and make a warm cradle of the palm of my left hand, and she rests her left hand, which is holding the fork, in it. I follow her movement up to her mouth and down to the table, and have been finding that Kim can retain her grip on the fork for the duration of the meal.

Karina began using her hands again at about 5 years. She has slowly progressed all these years. She eats with a fork now and can pick up the food with it herself. She tries two times: if she fails to get something on her fork then she uses her hands. Then she places the fork next to her plate (or throws it), always in my direction. She takes the fork again to eat, etc. She does the same with the cup.

CHEAP AND EASY TOOLS

Adapted crayons:

- 3/4 × 3/4 × 1/2 PVC plumbing T. One for each color crayon
- 1 inch wide duct tape
- 1 inch wide Velcro ribbon. "Soft" side in 8 inch lengths, "Picky" side in 1-1/2 inch lengths
- "fat" crayons

These are very easy to do. It is simply a 3/4 × 3/4 × 1/2 PVC plumbing T. Take a piece of the "soft side" of Velcro ribbon, thread it though the top of the T. Use the smaller "picky" side to attach the ends. It now has a large handle with an adjustable strap. Place the crayon, (you may need to shorten it) into the 1/2 opening. Use the duct tape to secure it. Now you have a renewable adapted crayon. Real easy.

Easy & Cheap Adapted Utensil Grip:

3/4 inch wide × 5 inches long "soft" side Velcro ribbon
3/4 inch wide × 1-1/2 inch long "picky" side Velcro ribbon
3/4 inch wide × 9 inches long elastic

Hands: The Hallmark of Rett Syndrome

Take the elastic and the small piece of "picky" Velcro. Match up the sides and one end (picky side up). Sew together in a zig-zag stitch on all sides. On the reverse side, on the opposite end, match up the "soft" longer piece of Velcro in zig-zag stitch. Sew just the bottom and sides. Leave the inside end open. This is where you insert the spoon or fork. Now that you have it sewn, take the ends and meet them up. The "picky" end should overlap the "soft." You now have a lightweight adjustable utensil holder for those who can't maintain a grip.

All God's kids got a place in the choir
Some sing low, some sing higher
Some sing out on the telephone wire
And some just clap their hands …

– GOSPEL SONG

The Sensory System

INSIDE OUT, UPSIDE DOWN AND BACKWARD

OUR SENSES PROVIDE US with the information we need to function in the world. We perceive sights, sounds, smells, tastes, temperatures, pressure, pain, our own body position, movement of our body parts, and movement of our body through space. Because we can receive a lot of input from our different senses at any one time, it is a huge task for the nervous system to sort out, determine what to react to and what to ignore, and how to react and when, as well as the strength of our reactions.

Many girls with RS are reported to be less in tune with their senses as babies and more inactive than their brothers and sisters. Some seem uninterested in the world around them. Others have strong reactions to particular sights or sounds. In infancy, these responses are not seen as a dramatic sign that something is wrong. But when a girl enters the regression phase of RS, there is no mistaking it. It becomes obvious to everyone that her world has turned upside down, inside out, and backward. Something is wrong. She may cry inconsolably and act frightened at sights and sounds that were not a problem in the months before. She may become hysterical at any change in her environment. She may reject being handled, not wanting to be touched. Favorite foods may be rejected. She may look away and refuse to make eye contact.

> *"Seeing, hearing and feeling are miracles, and each part and tag of me is a miracle."*
>
> – WALT WHITMAN

All of this is terribly confusing for parents. We wonder what in the world is happening. It seems that everything that worked before fails. Our child is miserable, and we are equally upset. It is one of the most bewildering aspects of RS, knowing that something is wrong and not knowing where to turn. All too often, we feel that in her misery, she has rejected us too.

While it is a stressful time for parents, it is an even more difficult time for her. She knows that something is wrong. During the regression period, she is terribly confused by the sensory input she receives. She cannot make sense of things that look, sound, taste, smell, and feel differently than they did a short time ago. Sounds that may seem normal to you may all of a sudden be painfully loud to her. The distance from the high chair to the floor may seem like she's looking down from the rooftop. Sensory chaos is all around her. She may go from hyperactive to unresponsive for days. Her world does not make sense.

During this time, it is most helpful to recognize that she is not rejecting you; she's rejecting the chaos. Understanding this and providing structure and security to her world will reduce her anxiety and yours, as well. When she begins to lose skills, our first inclination is to rush out and buy every book on therapies we can find in an attempt to head off the impending disaster. We want to bombard her with stimulation from every corner, rocking, stroking, singing, even spinning her to stimulate those senses which seem to be refusing or amplifying input.

The Sensory System

It goes against our theories about the need for brain stimulation and early intervention, but during the regression period in RS, providing too much stimulation is probably not the most helpful thing to do at this time. It's better to provide emotional security and soothing comfort so that she can adjust to the sensory calamity. When her sensory impressions have been moderated, she'll be in a more responsive mood for therapies that can really help.

You need to first make a connection with her and let her know that you love her and that she can trust you. Just from observing my daughter, RS must be very frightening and frustrating. I would suggest you just love and play with her and get her to react to you. The formal stuff will come in time. In general, girls with Rett love people. Just be a special person for her, and follow her lead.

In time, she gets better. Either she learns how to sort out and handle these sensory highs and lows or her sensory impressions normalize to some degree. Even so, she will always have some difficulty perceiving, interpreting and integrating sensory stimuli, and this may cause her to become distressed or panicked. One parent said her daughter can tune out a train running through the family room at times, but she always bolts straight up in bed from a sound sleep at the first light touch of her doorknob.

Sometimes using two senses at once can be overwhelming, so she unconsciously chooses to concentrate by "looking" over "listening," or chooses to "smell" before she "tastes."

Situations affect Amy in scary ways, like crossing from a light floor color to a dark floor color. She doesn't look particularly scared but can't do it on her own; she needs a slight nudge to tell her it is OK.

Her teachers found that she was very upset when changing activities if they didn't give her any warning that this was happening. So now they tell her and show her photos of the new activity well before changing and this has helped enormously.

Terra is absorbing all the information we are feeding her, but it is all scattered in her brain. Her brain has no files to put this information into, so it becomes useless to her. We are going to put files into Terra's brain by teaching her through each of her senses. One example: making microwave oatmeal. Terra will begin the process of making her own breakfast by learning first through touch. She can feel the texture of the oatmeal and the texture of the water. When it's together, she feels the texture changes. As it cooks, she can see and smell the difference in the oatmeal. The sound of the microwave stopping tells her ears that something has just happened. Completing the oatmeal with milk and water, hand over hand, she sees another change and smells it too. Finally, her taste buds tell her that something good has just happened from this process. It will take a long time but eventually, she will be able to file this under breakfast in her brain. Then, she will be able to sort out some of the academics involved because it will all make sense to her.

THE FIVE SENSES

SIGHT

MOST GIRLS WITH RS HAVE NORMAL VISION with the exception of near and far sight, which can be corrected with glasses, and crossed eyes, which can be corrected by patching and surgery. Often, a girl will look at an object she wants to pick up, and then glance away before she reaches for it. She may look from the corner of her eye or use a side-glance instead of looking straight on. When approaching something new

The Sensory System

and unfamiliar, she often looks quickly, glances away, and looks again several times before she finally settles on the object of her attention. Then, she often leans forward to visually inspect the object carefully. Some parents describe their daughter's vision as "either or," shifting quickly from things close to far away, but not taking in what is between the two. Sometimes she cannot visually follow an object except in short jerky movements, while at other times she can follow smoothly.

It seems Lisa can't process what she sees and look at it the same time. She will see something she really likes, and then look away for awhile, then back at it. It always seemed very strange to us when Lisa first started walking. We still had to hold on to her hand. She closed her eyes most of the time we were walking on the sidewalk, but she always knew when we came back to the curb, and would step down without prompting.

Before Katri began to lose her hand grasping, she would always look at her food on the tray and look away before she took the food and put it to her mouth. At the time, my wife and I thought that she wouldn't use the utensils because she wasn't concentrating and looking at what she was doing. Now I think she was focusing on the task, but to do so she has to look away.

When something interferes with Kim's view of an object, she will adjust her gaze to improve that view. It happens so frequently. Either she looks away, or she turns her head, and when ready, she will look directly at the object in question. I think that it is a genuine attempt to improve a situation that has gone bad.

Objects with a distinct figure-ground effect with sharp contrasts or clear outlines (white door on a painted wall) seem to catch her attention more quickly. The combination of lights and motion, such as mirrors, glitter or candles, is also attractive. Many parents report that their daughters are drawn to eyes, whether in person, on a doll, or a photograph. These preferences are seen in infant development. As a girl gains experience, she may learn to discriminate in more sophisticated ways than using sensory impressions.

Karina used to close her eyes the moment anyone came in her line of vision. That was also during the regression period and lasted about two years.

During regression, Kim would not look anyone in the eye. If we came too close, she would shut her eyes rather than look at ours. I didn't understand, but now think it may be related to seeing in bits, and there may have been something unpleasant about looking at our eyes.

It's as if looking at the object would be painful, so instead she will risk soulful glances, quickly, quietly, fearful that if they were to hit their target the object would disappear.

Dani has often not been able to look right at an object she really wants to pick up. Even when she's finger painting, she doesn't look at the canvas until it's finished.

Visually, Leah may both be defensive to some visual information and have difficulty coordinating her eyes together to know where she is in space. This can add to her fearfulness of moving on uneven surfaces.

Depth perception is altered, and the girl with RS who is able to walk often hesitates when she must go up or down. Going up steps is difficult enough, but going down steps is often impossible. This is because she perceives the distance from one step to another as much higher or lower than reality, and she fears falling. It is the same when she changes level, grade, or texture.

The Sensory System

Another sensory disturbance is alteration of orientation in space, the inability to judge the body's position as upright or tilted forward or backward. This will be discussed further in the Therapeutic Approaches chapter.

Meghan will have problems with changes in the floor or ground. She is not always looking down, so many times she misses them. But, every now and then in unfamiliar territory, she will come across a change she doesn't know how to negotiate. We try to help her by telling her verbally, "it is a step" or "it is not a step." Sometimes, she just needs to look at it for a minute and then she will go over it. It can be just paint on a parking lot.

It really helps Becky if there are no steps and if the difference between the kitchen floor and the carpeted floor is as even as possible. It also helps if the colors are similar so she doesn't feel as if she will "fall off" from one room to another.

SOUND

HEARING IS NORMAL IN RS, EXCEPT FOR MILD PROBLEMS that may result from recurrent middle ear infections. The young girl with RS may have a larger incidence of these infections and fluid in the middle ear, which could lead to hearing problems later. She uses sounds to associate various elements of her environment. While she can concentrate on visual images by continuing to look at them, sound images are here and gone. For her to concentrate, they must be repeated. Sights and sounds are very important in making sense of her surroundings.

Noisy surroundings are very uncomfortable for some girls and they become very agitated and irritable. Others may react by laughing, or even going to sleep to shut the noise out. Unexpected, loud, shrill, or high-pitched sounds may frighten or confuse her. She may have a preference for a particular kind of music or rhythm.

When Stephanie was two years old, the sound of running water from the water faucet, a vacuum cleaner, or lots of people making the same sounds such as cheering, clapping, or singing would make her tremble. Now that she is almost four years old, she loves to be hugged and cuddled, likes running water to be falling on her head, still hates the vacuum cleaner, but thinks people clapping are cheering her on.

At times she almost seems angry until the noise is resolved. When she was younger, crowd noise seemed to affect her more than now. Her teacher at school has noticed and voiced that she is "sensitive" to a lot of "noise stimuli," except music.

Amy gets overstimulated by children crying. She gets very tense. She will sometimes escape to her room or she will start yelling her own version of Rett-rap or she will have a seizure. It's too much stimuli coming her way at one time and she can't handle it.

Briana is especially sensitive to other children who scream and cry. She has never had a seizure, but the loud noises of another student screaming make her become agitated and tremulous. When a new student came into her class this past fall and would spend the better part of each day screaming and crying, Briana became a ball of frustration. Her skills fell short of her usual productivity, and her emotions were all knotted up. When she arrived home from school, it took me close to an hour each day to get her to relax and be comfortable. I started having trouble getting her ready for school in the mornings, as she protested wanting to be there. She covered her ears before she even got on the bus, and her little fists would be clenched. The trouble stopped only when the other child was removed from the class during her crying fits.

The Sensory System

TOUCH

MANY GIRLS ARE SENSITIVE ABOUT THEIR FACES. They don't like having their faces washed or teeth brushed and hate being splashed by wind, rain or snow. They often rub their eyes or scratch their faces. They may look at food for a long time on the spoon before they take it to their mouths. They prefer food at room temperature rather than hot or cold, and texture is frequently more important than taste and smell. They swallow solids more readily than liquids.

When addressing problems with tactile sensitivity, it's best to remember that all touch is not perceived equally. Light touch is often more difficult to tolerate than deep pressure. Likewise, a girl may be able to touch her own face without becoming distressed but becomes upset when someone else touches if for her. This is because touch originating from the self is less powerful than touch arising from somewhere else.

She also hated being touched. I remember her sitting on my lap with my arms around her but not touching. Still, when she noticed my arms, she would push me away.

Leah appears to be both insensitive to some types of touch and hypersensitive to others. A good sense of touch is important to emotional development, hand skills, and attention. Leah would use her hands more if she were more aware of them. She is defensive to light touch stimulation and has some lack of registration. She has a problem differentiating protective versus discriminative information. Protective touch gives withdrawal or defense, while discriminative touch provides the brain with precise information on size, shape and texture of objects and environment. The ability to separate whether touch is harmful or not is essential for tool use, attention, many aspects of social and emotional development, and tolerance of self-care activities including grooming and eating. Leah constantly mouths objects to give her more information. The mouth has the largest touch representation area in the body.

In my experience, it is very useful to stimulate her sense of body and hands by massage, tickling, stroking gently, all sort of body games including the rough ones. Karina has come a long way in accepting others to touch her and in touching objects herself. It did come very slowly and gradually.

TASTE

GIRLS WITH RS SEEM TO HAVE NORMAL TASTE SENSES. Just like other children, they have likes and dislikes.

I always thought it was strange that McKenna would grab the lemon slice out of my iced tea when she was a year old and suck on it. McKenna has always been able to pack away a ton of food, but she also eats almost anything. She sucks on lemons, eats dill pickles, loves all of her veggies, and even eats the baby food meats! She can be picky though ... she will only eat hamburgers from McDonald's. She likes chicken sticks from Burger King, but won't touch McDonald's nuggets. She will eat the canned macaroni and cheese but not the "good stuff" like Kraft! She will eat rice with veggies but won't touch rice pudding! Go figure! She will drink anything, milk, juice, pop, even coffee. I wonder if she has taste buds.

SMELL

THE SENSE OF SMELL IN RS SEEMS TO BE NORMAL.

Shanda can smell food a mile away! She gets lots of enjoyment out of eating new foods.

The Sensory System

AROUSAL AND CALM

THE NERVOUS SYSTEM MODERATES OUR LEVEL OF AROUSAL. When everything is working right, we are able to remain awake and alert, provided that we have had enough sleep without becoming upset or hyperactive. Many younger girls with RS seem to get over-excited easily and end up screaming and crying in situations that involve too much sensory input. On the other hand, many girls fall asleep frequently during the day-time. It may be that their quality of sleep is poor and they are simply tired, or it may be the effects of medication. Or, it could be a problem with sensory modulation, which is regulated in part by the level of serotonin. Following are some exercises to either rev her up or settle her down.

Calming Sensations
- Slow, rhythmic, back-and-forth movement. Most calming when eyes are righted with the horizon.
- deep pressure or steady compression
- slow stretch (avoid using with children who have low muscle tone)
- wrapping tightly in a blanket
- firm stroking over large areas
- warm temperatures
- simple shapes with rounded contours
- unchanging visual stimuli
- subtle or subdued patterns with pastel colors
- gentle, singsong rhythms
- simple melodies and low tones
- dim light
- weighted vest or blanket

Arousing Sensations
- Activities that involve rapid, jerky movements that involve a change in direction. The most arousing are movements that are unpredictable.
- hanging upside down (inverting the head)
- swinging on suspended equipment
- spinning around (watch for autonomic reactions such as increased perspiration, nausea, flushed or pale skin, hiccups. These signal overarousal!)
- light touch
- cold temperatures
- bright colors or lights
- red and yellow shades of color
- black-on-white or white-on-black patterns
- loud music with rapid tempos
- all odors

The Sensory System

- rough textures
- objects with irregular shapes and angular edges
- touch to the face

PAIN

ALTHOUGH IT MAY VARY, most girls have a high sensitivity to pain and difficulty expressing their pain in conventional ways. They may tense up and freeze instead of crying out loud. There may be a delay in feeling pain. Often, "external pain," such as a bump on the head or a shot, does not seem to hurt as much as "internal pain," like a stomachache or gas. Some parents report that their daughters feel pain differently in various parts of the body. A fall on the front of the head may seem to cause great pain, while a fall on the back of the head may not cause any reaction at all. Sometimes a child's fracture is not discovered until two days later when swelling sets in. This poses serious problems when trying to identify the source of crying. Is it pain or is it boredom or frustration or anger? The chapter on behavior offers a checklist to help sort it out.

MEETING SENSORY NEEDS

The Benefits
- decreased need to self- injure
- improved attention
- spontaneous expression of new skills and abilities
- improved social skills
- decreased fear and anxiety
- improved communication
- improved ability to handle distractions and interruptions
- improved ability to adjust to changes
- improved ability to experience joy and have more fun
- increased positive interaction with others

Leah used to get sick and throw up any time she was on a swing, but with more experience she got used to it and now enjoys it. We took her to a specialist in Sensory Integration and got exercises that are supposed to help. We did leg and arm rubbing, and pushed in on her shoulder joints, hands on shoulders. We used leg weights, Ace bandage wraps and several other exercises several times a day for a month. This is supposed to provide both physical improvement and better focus and concentration. Once the exercises were done, she became much calmer. She actually said "mo" (for more) since she liked it.

Sensory Integration Therapy has really worked with Katie. She is very aware of her hands and uses them very well. Swinging on a platform swing has brought back her depth perception and equilibrium. We still see occasional problems in this area, but they are quicker to go away. We are also trying the brushing now, on the palms of her hands. She has never been a hand wringer, but she is a fist clencher. She can now relax her hands when asked to and will actually hold her hand out to you when she knows she is going to have them brushed! Katie has always tickled the palms of her hands and the bottoms of her feet. She still does, but not as intensely as she

The Sensory System

used to. We also give Katie a good rubdown twice a day. She loves it! I believe all of this together has made her more coordinated, a better walker and better skilled with her hands.

Corinne loved the exercise ball so much that we bought one for home. Much of this activity is also good for muscle isolation and strengthening. Her PT explained that what she was doing on the exercise ball was something I could also do at home and that it would help to strengthen the back muscles and help to prevent scoliosis. What works best for Corinne is the deep pressure/joint compressions, especially when on her arms and shoulders. I have found that pressure on her shoulders will allow her to move her arms/hands more accurately without me having to guide her so much. This gives me a more accurate understanding of what she is reaching for. It also enables her to push her walker better and not have me push for her.

Initially, it was very difficult for her to withstand and she cried. Now, she has no problems at all with this and she has begun reaching for food objects and accepting hand over hand play. She still grinds her teeth constantly even with the oral stimulation from the gum care brushes. Yet, I personally believe that children can learn and understand so much about the world around them through touch and Sensory Integration can only benefit them.

When Corinne is sitting, standing or standing holding on, we press downward on her shoulders giving her a better awareness of where she is. They call this deep pressure and it seems to have a lasting (albeit short) effect. For some time afterwards she is better able to take her hands apart and to use them functionally. This also helps with her learning to push her walker. She tends to lean back but by pushing downward she "gets" the forward motion. Unfortunately, it disappears too quickly!

Using weights fatigued Amanda. I would not try it again, but other parents feel weighted vests calm their kids. I think it is a burden to Amanda, but before we did it, I felt it might help her walk better and stabilize her tremor. It did not. I would not try weights again. I think it pulls her muscles too much and she structurally cannot support added weight.

I like the idea of wraps and joint compression. I think our kids are loose and cannot support weight sometimes and that this might help. Putting orthotics in Amanda's shoes definitely helped straighten her feet and helped her walk better. It basically took some of the support off her body.

Kim has been doing Feldenkrais functional integration (FI) all this year. There is much pressing on the shoulders while Kim is lying down on her back (eventually she was able to do that, with just small bolsters under knees and ankles, head back resting on folded towels). It is in short rhythmic pulses, and very gentle. If there is any slight resistance, the PT tries another way. The idea is that it is felt through the bones down to the feet. It is also done in the other direction, i.e. from the feet towards the shoulders. It must feel very good, because Kim just loves it.

The way you look at your daughter changes and the therapists are all professionals, so they'll have a lot of positive things to say. So initially, things seem to help. The true test is after you have done a therapy for three to six months, stop and look at her current level of functioning. Measure several areas with concrete toys, environments, tasks, social issues, etc. Then, after six more months, see if she has actually improved or has stopped regressing compared to prior six-month point in time, not from the initial starting point. Anyone can say she improved from the initial point, just from changing the way you look at something.

We did the platform swing in the house, swinging outside, brushing, shaving cream, massaging, and all that stuff. It was fun for us and Amanda, and we needed some fun things to do. She loved the platform swing in the house with a mirror, and she loved to kick balls and balloons on the swing. It was hilarious, some of the sessions, we really got her "cooking." Like all therapies, it seemed to help socially in some ways initially but overall, after two years, she actually walked worse and did not seem less tactile defensive.

The Sensory System

SENSORY INTEGRATION DYSFUNCTION

IN HER BOOK, *Understanding Rett Syndrome*, Barbro Lindberg writes, "Individuals with RS have difficulties taking in, interpreting, and integrating sensory impressions, from the outer world as well as from their own bodies. Not only do the girls have difficulty in sorting, integrating and choosing among the multitude of impressions. They may also have problems in modulating the strength of the sensory impressions they receive." This means that a sound that is in itself not very strong may be perceived as extremely loud, or on the contrary, that something that "ought" to be perceived as strong pain, for instance, or may not be perceived at all.

Integrating all of our sensory perceptions so that we can make sense of our world is called sensory integration. *Sensory Integration Dysfunction* (DSI) is a complex disorder that causes problems in processing sensations which cause a number of difficulties in detecting, registering, modulating, discriminating or integrating sensations properly. Those with DSI process sensation from the environment or from their bodies inaccurately, which results in "sensory seeking" or "sensory avoiding" patterns or "dyspraxia," a motor planning problem which is known to be the most fundamental handicap in RS.

SENSORY-SEEKING BEHAVIOR

SENSORY-SEEKING BEHAVIOR OCCURS WHEN THE NERVOUS system is not able to process sensory input and the child may be under- or over-responsive to sensation. This results in seeking out sensory experiences that are more intense or of longer duration.

Sensory-seeking behaviors may include:

- hyperactivity (attempt to get more movement input)
- running, pacing, jumping, climbing, body crashing
- mouthing, hands to/in mouth
- lack of awareness of touch or pain, or touching others too often or too hard (may seem like aggression)
- enjoying sounds that are too loud, such as TV or radio volume—poor regulation is the inability to adjust sensations and internal body functions to just the right level
- difficulty making transitions from one situation to another—poor regulation
- inability to unwind or calm self—poor self regulation
- unable to coordinate swallowing with breathing (thus unable to do three suck-swallow sequences in a row)
- poor respiratory patterns
- autonomic nervous system shutdown/overload with too much stimulation
- difficulty sleeping
- difficulty waking up
- difficulty having bowel movements
- body crashing, deliberate falling down, lots of climbing
- staring at objects and/or flicking them on fingers to watch

The Sensory System

SENSORY-AVOIDING BEHAVIOR

SENSORY-AVOIDING BEHAVIOR OCCURS when the nervous system feels sensation too deeply, too easily, or too much, making the individual over-responsive. This may cause them to be sensory defensive, a "fight or flight" response to sensation.

Sensory-avoiding behaviors may include:

- overly sensitive to touch, movement, sights, or sounds
- fear of movement and heights
- very cautious about new things or experiences
- uncomfortable in loud or busy environments
- overly sensitive to food smells, "picky eater"
- withdrawal/shutdown/going to sleep
- preferring to be away from everyone
- aggression

Children with DSI are often clumsy and awkward, and they have difficulty with gross and fine motor skills, imitating movements, and problems with balance, movement sequence and coordination due to poor motor planning. Motor planning requires that correct information goes to the brain, is interpreted correctly and receives an appropriate response from the body. Poor "data" (sensory information) into the "computer" (brain) results in "programs" (motor planning). There is no neurological flexibility to respond to change. Rigidity with routine and need for control is a common adaptation.

Sarah is terrified of falling and if she is on a moving dentist chair or going backward on an X-ray table she stiffens, trembles, and wrings her hands tightly. If we walk her too fast, she cannot handle it and has tremors and goes legless on us.

GETTING A SENSORY INTEGRATION EVALUATION

What to Look for in the Evaluator

1. How many years of experience has the evaluator had doing direct sensory integration treatment? *Nothing teaches sensory integration better than doing it and seeing what works and when.*

2. What kind of experience does the evaluator have with the population/disability and system (schools, community mental health, etc.)? *Weigh in what will probably work in the environment providing the intervention and how that population responds.*

3. What type of continuing education does that person have? *The more eclectic you can be, the more tools you can choose from. Some very helpful areas of knowledge are: sensory integration in general, respiration, oral, therapeutic listening, vestibular, immune system, internal regulation, digestive tract, and cranial sacral therapy.*

4. Is the evaluator creative/intuitive? *It takes a lot of intuition combined with factual findings, refined observation skills, and experience to come up with solutions that are specific to the situation. Some solutions have to be very creative.*

5. Is the evaluator skilled at balancing practical versus a valid technique? *For example, evaluators may determine that swinging would be beneficial, but they also need to determine if there is a safe place that is large enough to suspend equipment for the size of the client. They may also need to weigh the expense and determine if the system will pay for the equipment.*

The Sensory System

6. What is the evaluator's interaction style? *Are you included in problem solving and solution finding? Is there respect for the loved one as a fellow human being? Individuals often relax and cooperate better if they sense acceptance. Does the evaluator give consideration to your loved one's likes/dislikes?*

What to Look for During the Evaluation

1. The evaluator should determine the areas of greatest concern and what would make life easier for the individual and the service provider. Referring problems might include:
   a. refuses tooth brushing
   b. self-injurious behavior
   c. screams loudly and frequently

2. A good sensory history is critical! The evaluator needs to know not only the "behavior," but also frequency, intensity, circumstances, and how long it has been occurring. A sensory history form is filled out by the caregivers before arriving. The therapist then goes over it with them during the evaluation to be sure that they understand it and gather the aforementioned data. It is very helpful if the caregiver communicates ahead of time regarding the aspects of the syndrome the individual demonstrates.

3. People familiar with the person evaluated must be there. They will know the individual in ways the evaluator cannot discern. The direct caregivers will give critical information as to whether a recommendation will work. They often help adapt a concept to get it to work.

4. A pertinent medical history and medications taken are needed to determine what is strictly a sensory integration issue, or a medical or behavioral issue and how they interplay.

5. This is an adventure of finding puzzle pieces. The first four items listed above reviewed with the caregiver will give many of the puzzle pieces.

6. While there are no standardized tests that measure sensory integration dysfunction in individuals who are very involved, there are inventories that can provide a great deal of helpful information. The Sensory Profile (SP) is a caregiver checklist that rates specific areas of sensory processing as being "typical, "probable difference" or "definite difference" from the general population. The test examines behaviors across a wide variety of settings and situations and, depending on which version is used, the test is appropriate for those ages infant through adult. The Sensory Integration Inventory (SII) is another checklist that can reveal useful information. There are other sensory tests out there as well but, like the SP and the SII, all of them require someone who is knowledgeable in the area of SI to interpret the results and make treatment recommendations.

7. Key components needing intervention are identified from the previous six noted items.

8. Actual interventions are then tried to see what works, is liked by the individual, and gets cooperation. There must be enough equipment/supplies available at the test site to be able to try many types of interventions.

Recommendations

1. Interventions are tried, discussed with caretakers, and then taught. It is critical to also consider the environment, other people affected, dependability of providers and issues of the individual (unable to tolerate the music, will not go inside the mouth, etc.).

2. The interventions that are most effective are very specific to the individual and surrounding circumstances.

The Sensory System

3. Written instructions are provided before they leave. Standard techniques are already in a handout form.

Summary

For a sensory diet to be effective, it must be specific to the individual. The evaluator needs good puzzle-solving and pulling-the-picture-together skills. Recommendations must be affordable and workable within the setting in which they are to be done.

TREATING SENSORY INTEGRATION DYSFUNCTION

SENSORY INTEGRATION THERAPY (SIT) incorporates the fields of neuropsychology, neurology, physiology, child development, and psychology. Occupational and physical therapists use this treatment to help organize the nervous system to process and better integrate sensory input. Using sensory and motor activities, often in the form of play, the therapy focuses primarily on three basic senses: tactile (touch), vestibular (sense of movement), and proprioceptive (body position) to better understand how the child perceives sensation and how that affects attention, emotions, motor skills or learning. Treatment usually takes place in a large, sensory-enriched (fun) room and involves lots of movement, such as swinging, spinning, and also tactile, visual, auditory, and taste activities.

Some common terms used in the treatment of sensory processing problems include:

Proprioceptive input is unconscious information from the muscles and joints about position, weight or pressure, stretch, movement, and changes of position in space.

Vestibular input is unconscious information from the inner ear about equilibrium (state of balance), gravity, movement, and changes of position in space.

Kinesthesia is the unconscious awareness of body parts in relation to movement. The brain combines all the information from outside the body (through vision, hearing, touch, taste, and smell) with information from inside the body (from the inner ear and the muscles and joints) to form a conscious, overall awareness of one's body in all activities.

SENSORY INTEGRATION TECHNIQUES

DEEP PRESSURE TO THE MUSCLES CAUSES SPECIFIC touch receptors to fire. This has a calming as well as organizing affect on the nervous system (think massage and hugs).

Leg and Arm Rubbing is a technique used to fire the tactile receptors of the extremities and can be either calming or arousing depending on how it's done. It can also be used as a means of desensitization for girls who have difficulty integrating touch sensation.

Joint Compression refers to any activity or technique that quickly compresses the bones on either side of a joint. In SIT, joint compression is typically applied at the shoulders, elbows wrists, hips, knees, and ankles. Quick compression of a joint causes the surrounding proprioceptors to fire. The brain thinks that the joint is in trouble and signals the surrounding muscles to contract so that the joint can be stabilized. This is used to help improve low tone and to provide the girl with a better awareness of where her body is in space.

Brushing is a technique in which a specific type of surgical scrub brush is used over specified areas of the body. The brushing protocol is typically followed by joint compression and is used to calm and integrate the nervous system. It is most useful in helping girls who have difficulty with tactile hypersensitivity. Often when therapists refer to "brushing"

The Sensory System

they are referring to the Wilbarger Protocol. This is a regimen done with a special technique on a specified schedule.

Weights in SIT are used to activate the proprioceptors that in turn can provide the girl with an increased sense of calm and a greater awareness of where her body is in space. They can take the form of wrist and ankle weights, shoe pockets (weights that can be attached to the top of the shoes), weighted vests, and weighted blankets. Weights can also be added to external devices such as spoons for added sensory input and to decrease the tremors that come with ataxia.

Wraps also provide information to the proprioceptive system through deep pressure. As a result, they can have the same calming effect as weights and are a useful alternative when weights can't be tolerated. Wraps can range anywhere from swaddling with a blanket to Spandex clothes and neoprene vests.

We have used brushing on Amanda and have seen results in tactile awareness. It is just a soft brushing with a surgical brush and massaging after with a terry towel or just your hands. We use a loofa sponge in the tub at bath time, and we go over the whole body, some area with giggles and some areas with resistance. Amanda's right hand is pretty good but when we put texture on the left hand, it's pulled away. Little by little, it's getting better. Hand usage and awareness is what we are after, and it's tough, but we see her carry her book bag and purse, and pick out groceries at the store. Sometimes they make it to the cart and sometimes not. We eat a lot of funny toast, because Amanda gets the bread at the store, and what a grip! We dare not put it back because she's always watching us!

We use a brushing program, with firm strokes and joint compression every two hours. This is good not only for tactile hypersensitivity (not liking touch), but also for proprioceptive input (sensory feedback) that the body obviously does not get on its own. Firm pressure and joint compression integrates this natural sensory mechanism.

We did brushing and compression but it was time consuming; by the time I was finished with one session, I felt it was time to start all over again. We did it under the guidance of a therapist and it was very rigid. We did every two hours for a week or so and then on to every three hours for a few more weeks and so on, until we were up to only a few times a day. I think it was worth it. We saw results in only a few weeks. We continued doing the technique for a couple of years and on occasion we go back and do it if she is not feeling well. It really relaxes her tremendously.

SENSORY INTEGRATION ACTIVITIES

HERE ARE SOME IDEAS for things you can do at home:

Sensory Box

Get one of those plastic sandboxes. They usually come out in the spring at places like Kmart or Wal-Mart. Fill with millet, or short grain rice. Now you have a "sensory sand box" that, if eaten, is no big deal.

Feely Box

Put a variety of sensory items in one box. Use things that are fun to feel, like makeup brushes, surgical sponge brushes, shaving cream, stamps, paint, adapted crayons, maple syrup (it makes great shiny pictures mixed with a drop of food coloring), carpet, wallpaper and fabric swatches, corrugated cardboard, "fun noodles" (cornstarch packing peanuts that stick together with water), Play-doh, Goop.

Movement Activities

Activities that activate the proprioceptive or vestibular system can include swinging, rocking in a chair or on a rocking horse, sledding down a hill, playing on a Slip-N-Slide, riding

The Sensory System

behind a bicycle, and climbing through a pile of pillows. For those girls who are more mobile, jumping on a trampoline can be lots of fun as well as beneficial.

Shaving Cream Play

Squirt some shaving cream on a tray or table, roll up her sleeves and let her play. This is a great tactile activity that can also be done in the bathtub for easier cleanup. A variation on this could include finger painting or using pudding for those who like to sample their artwork.

Joint Compression

Ask your child's physical therapist to show you and explain how it works. Many school therapists will not get involved with teaching you how, but a private therapist or someone whom your child sees in the hospital more than likely will. It's very easy to do and it really works at helping the child focus and use muscles.

Brain Gym

This has to do with integration of both sides of the brain and crossing over midline. You can order a teachers edition of the book Brain Gym by Paul E. Dennison, Ph.D. and Gail E. Dennison, Edu-Kinesthetics, Inc., P.O. Box 3395, Ventura, CA 93006-3395 USA, 888-388-9898.

VESTIBULAR SYSTEM

THE VESTIBULAR SYSTEM IS PART of the larger "sensory system" and is responsible for registering either movement or the perception of movement, in the brain. Once movement is registered, the body responds by making postural adjustments. The vestibular system is responsible for a girl's ability to balance and to move in a coordinated manner. The vestibular system lets her identify movement, whether her body or something near her is moving. It makes it possible for her to lift her foot just high enough to climb a step or to bring a cookie to her mouth without missing.

While problems with vestibular function can cause incoordination and poor balance, it can also affect a girl's desire to move. Sometimes girls with RS have vestibular systems that either under-register or over-register vestibular input. When they under-register, the girl may feel "driven" to seek out additional movement. When this happens, the girl may spend lots of time rocking back and forth. She may want to swing for long periods of time or be constantly "on the go." She requires a greater amount of movement in order to feel "right."

Girls who over-register vestibular input have the opposite problem. For them, a little vestibular input goes a long way. These girls are generally fearful of movement and tend to over-react. They get carsick easily, cry when placed on a therapy ball, and thoroughly dislike being spun around.

VESTIBULAR STIMULATION

VESTIBULAR STIMULATION GENERALLY REFERS TO the therapeutic use of movement. Its purpose is to help a girl organize her vestibular system so that she can make coordinated and appropriate responses to movement. Vestibular input can be powerful, however, and too much can result in a spectrum of autonomic reactions ranging from a few hiccups to vomiting and feeling horrible for hours. While it seems some girls can spin in circles endlessly and suffer no ill effects, others can be made absolutely miserable with very little movement. While rocking back and forth in a chair is both beneficial and

The Sensory System

enjoyable, spinning on suspended equipment should probably not be attempted without consulting a therapist.

PROPRIOCEPTION

PROPRIOCEPTION IS THE KNOWLEDGE of where our body is in space. It originates in the muscle spindles and joint capsules. Proprioception is the sense that allows us to correctly know where our arms and legs are at any given time without having to look. It makes it possible for us to lift our foot just high enough to climb a step or to bring a cookie to the mouth without missing. Deep pressure and weight bearing stimulate these proprioceptors and are responsible for giving us a physical sense of self.

Problems with proprioception can result in movements that are poorly coordinated. It can also leave a girl without a clear sense of where her body ends and the rest of the world begins. Like vestibular input, proprioception can either be under-registered or over-registered in the brain. When a girl under-registers proprioceptive input she will seek to feel "right" by stimulating the receptors in her nervous system. She might do this by grinding her teeth or needing to be wrapped up or held tightly in order to calm down. A girl who over-registers proprioceptive input might become upset by hugs or refuse to sleep under her blankets.

TREATING PROPRIOCEPTIVE PROBLEMS

MANY GIRLS WITH RS RECEIVE LITTLE PROPRIOCEPTIVE INPUT due to their impaired mobility. Many also under-register what little input they do receive. These girls often benefit from the use of a weighted vest, a weighted blanket, weighted "shoe pockets," spandex clothing, or vests made of neoprene.

Weighted Vests

The weighted vest is one method of providing deep pressure, and it is used to help calm and relax the child so that sensory stimuli can be processed. The vest also gives the child unconscious information from the muscles and joints. It is especially helpful for children who are easily distracted, hyperactive, or lacking in concentration. There is limited research in this area of therapy, but many therapists feel that the use of a weighted vest is beneficial in promoting awareness of body position, coordination, balance, eye/hand coordination, spatial perception and hearing and speaking skills. When figuring the amount of weight to put in the vest, the general recommendation is five percent of the girl's body weight. It's also important to note that weighted vests shouldn't be worn for long periods of time without a break as a "rebound effect" can occur.

Neoprene Vests/Wraps

These are vests made out of the same material as wet suits. They're stretchy, fit snugly, and can have the calming affect of weighted vests without the added weight. Clothing made out of Spandex can have a similar affect on some girls, as can wrapping with an ACE bandage or bundling up in a blanket. It's a bit like wearing a hug.

Weighted Blankets

These are useful for girls who have trouble settling down at night or who have problems with frequent waking. The additional weight provides proprioceptive input that can be calming.

The Sensory System

I like the idea of wraps and joint compression. I think our kids are loose and cannot support weight sometimes and that this might help. Putting orthotics in Amanda's shoes definitely helped straighten her feet and helped her walk better. It basically took some of the support off her body.

Brittany has a weighted vest and I have seen some positive results as far as calming her by increasing the proprioception. The one for my daughter is constructed with all the weights around the bottom. I am going to make a new one disbursing the weight evenly throughout. The OT recommends that you start with no more weight than five percent of the child's total weight, gradually increasing as tolerated to as much as twenty-five percent of her body weight without imposing undue restriction on her mobility. Physical conditions should be discussed with her doctor and her OT. The vest should not be left on more than ten to fifteen minutes.

I made Amanda's weighted vest by taking a jeans jacket, cutting off the sleeves, and sewing inside pockets around the bottom for weights. I went to the hardware store and bought different sized big washers. I made the internal pockets seal with Velcro on one side so I could change the weights. I talked to a couple of therapists before I did this.

"Our five senses are incomplete without the sixth—a sense of humor."

– ANONYMOUS

Behaviors

AIN'T MISBEHAVIN'

WHETHER IT IS PERFORMANCE or mood, when it comes to typical behavior in RS, the one thing that is consistent is inconsistency. We all have moods, influenced by internal forces (headache, constipation, fatigue) and external influences (weather, activity). In RS, moods sometimes change abruptly and it is nearly impossible to figure out why. One of the most difficult aspects of these mood and behavior swings is not knowing how to return her to calm when she is anxious, or to happiness when she is sad. And then there are the times when she awakens in the night laughing uproariously for hours, impossible to quiet in the dark, wee hours.

It is easy to call this misbehavior, but a closer look tells us that much of it is out of her control. However, at other times, her behavior is a powerful form of communication.

> *"Feelings are real and legitimate; children behave and misbehave, for a reason, even if adults cannot figure it out."*
>
> – ANONYMOUS

When I feed Jocelyn, sometimes she won't open her mouth. If I try to "force" even gently, she resists (and wins every time), but if I pull the spoon away and say "OK, whenever you are ready," she'll usually open up readily. Sometimes, she won't open until I test her hot cereal first and make sure that it's not too hot! I think letting her know she has some control over a situation helps.

She will let you know when she is not happy. It will start with frowning, then follow with squeaky moans if you don't listen to the facial expressions. That is how she talks, with expressions, and her big beautiful big brown eyes can say a million words.

Leah occasionally has crying spells, and she is difficult to console. She has two types of crying. The first is "upset crying," which can be from having her feelings hurt, being hungry, or wanting to go the bathroom. The second type is when she is really hurt or something is really bothering her. There is a different tone, cadence and temper to the crying and we can easily tell the difference when things are really wrong. I think crying is one way she communicates, but sometimes she loses control of it.

REGRESSION

MANY GIRLS WITH RS GO THROUGH A PERIOD of social withdrawal and difficult behavior during the regression period, which can be one of the most trying aspects of the disorder. While it may seem like bad behavior, it is most likely the result of her confusion. She may be irritable and sleepless, cry for long periods of time and resist your attempts to hold her. She may become very upset if things in her surroundings are changed and she may turn her eyes away to avoid eye contact.

Behaviors

It is a difficult time for her as she adjusts to many changes. Her bewilderment is understandable. She has lost her ability to use words and to make sense of the world around her. Her body does not move as freely as it used to. She has lost the security and control she was just beginning to master.

During this difficult time, it is hard to know just what she needs. The security that comes from structure and routine, and the comfort that flows from love and understanding are very helpful. She needs to experience success in spite of her handicaps. She needs understanding and patience. It helps parents to remember that this period will pass.

Mya cried for about two years. I know in my heart that it was her frustration over what was happening to her little body. Her regression was very slow and therefore, I know she knew exactly what was going on. She is now six and for the most part, she is a happy little girl. She still has her days, but nothing like it used to be. It will pass. It takes time, but it does pass.

I can tell you the screaming/crying spells don't last forever. The main thing, I think, is not to let it drive you crazy. My husband said he just had to put Sherry down and get away from her a little. Nothing he did seemed to help and it was horribly frustrating for him.

I remember that we tried a lot of things to soothe Katie back then, but usually what worked for her was to just get her back to our home, to her room, where everything felt safe again to her.

Kendall could literally be ecstatic over being at school playing, and be a wreck in the car on the way home. Places and people she had loved made her cry and go ballistic. We could be playing one minute, and throwing a tantrum the next. These episodes had really hit their peak at two-and-a half years old, and thankfully, had pretty much disappeared by three-and-a-half. We sometimes had an occasional outburst, but nothing like that second year!

Jess would cry in terror and what seemed like excruciating pain. Screaming! We would all cry. It was so awful for many months as I remember, soon after our diagnosis. I still think it was just pain and activity in her brain trying to deal with the regression. Jess soon "accepted" it and pulled through.

When Haley entered what we now call "the bad years," we found two things that had a miraculous ability to calm her when she was upset: swinging and listening to music. The combination was so effective we installed swings indoors in both of the homes we have lived in.

At one time, I tried very hard to make her feel safe and loved. We spent a lot of time cuddling and rocking and singing. I did not push her into anything that bothered her. By two years, she started to come out of it, and notice more. Food and music have always been the great motivators.

As she comes out of the regression stage and learns to cope with this new unpredictability, she gradually makes better eye contact, and regains emotional balance and interest in people and her surroundings. In fact, many parents call their daughter a "social butterfly" in middle childhood.

BE PREPARED

CHANGES IN THE ENVIRONMENT CAN OFTEN TRIGGER outbursts, especially during the regression period. This often makes getting away from home difficult, even if it is just a trip to the grocery store. It helps to always tell her in advance where you are going and what you will be doing. For some girls, this extends to even moving from one position to another or to another room in the house. Tell your daughter calmly how you will move her body and where you are going. Reassure her that she will be fine.

Behaviors

Start out with short trips to the store and gradually increase your time out. Make sure to take a "survival kit" with snacks and a drink. This is a good time to use the Walkman, or take along her security blanket or other cherished object.

For doctor and dentist visits, tell her why you are going and what to expect before you go. Tell her what procedures will be done and assure her that you will stay with her and make sure she is as comfortable as possible. If it will be a noisy environment that she can't tolerate, let her know that you understand this is difficult for her. Reassure her that she will soon be back in her comfortable environment at home.

Stefanie gets very upset and starts yelling and eventually has a total "meltdown." As you can imagine, a flipped out, eighty-five pound ten-year-old and a cart full of groceries does not make for happy times, not to mention her sister and brother who seize the moment to pull a few stunts of their own. We have just learned to respect Stefanie's limitations in these areas and try not to take her into a place that will provoke a "meltdown," kind of like you learn not to wear perfume around someone who has asthma.

AFTER REGRESSION

AS SHE GETS OLDER, SHE MAY CONTINUE on a much more even emotional level than at an earlier age. In general, the crying spells from earlier years fade with time, and the girl with RS becomes happier and more content. This is due in part to chemical changes that take place as the girl with RS gets older. The majority of girls do get better in time but sometimes, there is a return to the earlier crying, much the same as in earlier years, but now louder. Crying, screaming and whining can accompany sleeplessness. Self-injurious behaviors such as face slapping, face hitting and hand biting may occur. Parents report that their daughter hasn't cried for years, which makes it even more puzzling. Schools are concerned that something serious is going on, and parents are convinced of it.

This crying is almost always related to discomfort and pain due to physical causes. It can be thoroughly frustrating, but it is critical to do the detective work to figure out what is wrong.

She was about eight and started having screaming bouts and biting her arms. We knew she had reflux, but didn't realize that it could cause damage to the esophagus. After a three day hospital stay, we found out that she had classic stomach ulcers, esophageal ulcers, stomach migraines, and impaction. No more reflux, teeth grinding, arm biting, screaming, and clearly, no more pain. It has been several years, and she's still all smiles.

When I ask Lauren on her talker where it hurts, she lets me know her stomach hurts, head doesn't, and it's her upper stomach that hurts. When she eats late in the day, she takes a couple of bites, then breathes deeply and pushes away.

The thing that took us the longest to figure out, involved shortened heel cords as a cause for her feet and calves cramping several times a day. The foot problems may be caused by Angie curling her toes when she walks in an effort to hold on to the floor with her feet. When lifting her out of the shower where she stands, her little flat feet act like suction cups, and I hear a sound similar to pulling a suction cup off a window. Also, long periods of sitting, letting the feet drop, will shorten the heel cord over time. She now wears Ankle Foot Orthoses (AFOs) and has very few cramps anymore.

CRYING

CRYING HAS A PURPOSE. IT SIGNALS anger, sadness, frustration or pain. Babies learn shortly after birth that crying brings a response, and mothers learn quickly

Behaviors

to distinguish the kind of cry they hear. Crying is the only form of communication that babies can use to indicate their discomfort, hunger or thirst. Because girls with RS have difficulty communicating any other way, crying becomes a logical choice. We try to read her many forms of body language and understand her expressive eyes, but we don't always consider her crying as a form of communication. But if she is uncomfortable from sitting in one position for too long, hungry or angry, crying seems a logical choice when nothing else works to get the message across. Parents have described it this way:

• She acts as if she is in acute pain.
• Sometimes she cries as if her heart is breaking.
• She cries as if she wants desperately to say something.
• She cries bitterly, sobbing at times.
• Sometimes it appears to be a tantrum.
• She is inconsolable, with giant, sad tears.
• Sometimes she is crying one moment and laughing the next.
• She cries when she is somewhere she doesn't want to be or doing something she doesn't want to do.

Never underestimate her ability to understand. Talk to her and tell her you know she is doing the best that she can. Figure out some sort of communication system so that she can indicate whether she is sad or mad, or whether she hurts. It could be gazing at or touching symbols, pictures, "yes" or "no" cards, or even blinking.

When Angie was particularly upset one night, I told her I was going to place my hands on her body and she should blink her eyes when I touched her where the pain was. She became very quiet and still. I touched her head, asking, "Does your head ache?" Nothing. I touched her ears, "Do your ears ache?" Huge blink. I asked again, "Angie, do you have an earache?" Huge blink. Then I assured her I would take her to the doctor first thing in the morning. I put heat by her ears in the form of a rice-filled sock heated in the microwave, and gave her Tylenol and with that assurance, she was quiet the rest of the night. The next morning, the doctor confirmed that both ears were infected.

Becky Sue has had those crying spells off and on for many years. We go through the list to see what it might be; toes in shoes wrong, sticker somewhere, not enough sleep, too much sleep, medication, or premenstrual symptoms. I always talk to Becky and ask her what's wrong and how can I make it better? Sometimes just the talking and hugs soothe her, sometimes not.

Some people suggest that girls cry just to be crying or that it is "brain derived." Common sense tells us that no one cries for fun. If she is crying, you'd better believe something is wrong. Maybe it is physical; maybe it's emotional. Maybe she's trying desperately to tell you something and crying is her only way of communicating. Chances are, it isn't entirely under her control. Paying careful attention to her non speech cues about her needs may alleviate some of the distress. Don't assume she is crying just because she has RS. The first priority is to make sure nothing is physically wrong. Here is a list of things to have her doctor rule out, in top to bottom order of how frequently they cause pain and/or screaming spells:

• Is it heartburn or reflux? Does she burp or regurgitate? Cry after eating?
• Is she constipated or impacted? Has she had a regular BM?
• Does she have a urinary tract infection? Does she have strong or scant urine?

Behaviors

- Does she have a toothache? Does she refuse food, sweets, or cold?
- Could it be a headache? Does she squint her eyes or hit her head?
- Could it be a sore throat? Does she refuse to swallow?
- Could it be an ear infection? Does she pull at her ear?
- Does she have low blood sugar? Need several small meals a day?
- Does she have cramps? Is it time for her period?
- Is she limping or favoring one part of her body?
- Does she cry when she is moved?
- Does she have vaginal discharge?
- Does she wiggle and squirm like she itches?
- Is her brace too tight? Does she have red marks?
- Does she have leg or foot cramps?
- Does she have allergies?
- Could she have gallstones?
- Could there be an ovarian cyst?

TRY THIS

CAREGIVERS STOP AT NOTHING in trying to get to the bottom of what is making her cry. Sometimes they are able to help. Their suggestions include the following:

- give her food or drink
- change wet clothes
- treat constipation
- massage her arms, hands, legs
- remove her from a crowded situation
- put her in a quiet room or a dark room
- change her routine or return to an expected routine
- avoid excessive cold or heat
- avoid becoming emotional or upset in front of her
- take her to the toilet
- play her favorite music or video
- adjust her seating
- cuddle her
- distract her
- take her for a car ride
- put her in a warm tub
- rub her tummy
- stroke her forehead
- wrap her in a warm blanket
- talk to her soothingly
- use a weighted blanket to comfort her
- use a communication system

Behaviors

We found that Angie actually needed to snack between meals because she seemed to have blood sugar drops every two hours. Even though she ate like a horse, I suspect she did not absorb all the nutrients she was taking in. Giving her cheese and other high protein snacks helped, but even applesauce helped a little.

SCREAMING

THE DISTINCTION BETWEEN CRYING AND SCREAMING is intensity and volume. While crying is often used to indicate pain or sadness, screaming is often used to get your attention, to let you know that something is either wrong or unacceptable.

Alexis did scream and carry on for over a year. We finally put her on a schedule, which included meal times, TV times, potty time, book time, playtime, you name it. We did these things every single day in the same routine and it paid off. The screaming stopped, Alexis became a much happier child to be around, and she learned along the way.

TRUST YOUR INSTINCTS

By Claudia Weisz

There are a few things you can do to figure out why your daughter is crying. For example, if she starts to scream just before dinner every night, you could try feeding her a half hour earlier, or giving a light snack after school. That's an easy one. But let's say she's been screaming whenever you want to take her for a walk. You get her coat on and she starts. Because you don't want to tug her around the block screaming, you take the coat off and don't go. She stops. What are the possibilities? She could simply not like going for a walk, and is telling you so. Or she could have pain, or perhaps her shoes don't fit properly, or her braces are tight, or perhaps her toes curl under or other foot deformities are becoming painful to her. To figure this out, you need to see how she walks the rest of the day, and in other situations.

If she's in a wheelchair and reacts that way, maybe it hurts to breathe cold air, or perhaps she doesn't like the extreme cold or heat. Maybe the neighbor's big dog scares her. To determine if something is serious, you need to keep track of the frequency, duration, and intensity of the crying or screaming spells. Occasionally, you will misjudge the seriousness of the need, or perhaps never figure out her problem. Failing to recognize a serious problem prolongs the discomfort and can overwhelm you with guilt. Don't let it get you down.

It's inevitable to step in puddles of guilt from time to time, but the danger comes when we decide to lie down and soak it up. Just step through, empty your boots if you need to, and keep walking. In other situations, especially "out of the blue" ones, you must use all your senses eyes, ears, touch and smell, and a lot of intuition. You can learn to interpret your child's cries.

Look to see the expression on her face. Check her eyes for fear or anger. Are there tears? Look at her schedule. Are you late with her lunch or snack? If she uses the toilet, does she appear uncomfortable during urination or elimination? When was her last bowel movement? Is she chafed in areas that seldom see the light of day, and are seldom dry? That could make anyone cranky.

Behaviors

Feel her forehead for fever, feel her tummy to see if it's distended. If you keep a food/mood chart, you'll perhaps make a connection if there is a food that repeatedly disagrees with her. Or, perhaps she's been swallowing air, which is common in our kids. Run your fingers around her waistband. Are her clothes binding? Does she wear a belt or jeans that are cute, but miserable to wear when her abdomen expands from air swallowing? Feel her hands and feet. Is she cold? Hot? Feel her limbs for hardness, (cramping?) and compare left with right. Check her shoes for pebbles or bits of cereal…you never know! Check her hair clips and rubber bands. Tight pony tails can give a headache, and sometimes a hair clip can pull hair quite painfully. Is a label from her shirt scratching the back of her neck?

Do you smell vomit on her pillow in the morning? This could signify a reflux problem, causing a burning sensation in her esophagus. Is she passing gas, but having difficulty eliminating? Does her breath smell unpleasant, perhaps from infected tonsils, strep throat, stomach trouble or bad teeth? Is there a distinctive odor you can describe to her physician?

Listen to the intensity of her cry. Is it an irritating, constant whine, or an ear-piercing, heart-stopping scream? Does it start suddenly or slowly build? How long does it last and how does it stop? With or without your help? How often does it occur? Same time every day? All day once a month? Three times a week? How long does it last? What helps? Tylenol? Antacid? Laxative? Enema? Massage? Music?

You're the expert. If she has a normally sunny disposition and suddenly begins to have screaming spells, your task is to determine why. You are likely to be the person best acquainted with any changes in her life, as well as her normal disposition. We must remember just because these girls have RS does not make them immune to all the other discomforts common to mankind.

There is a reason it disturbs us so to hear our children cry. It's been built into us, motivates us, and ends with us madly searching for answers. There is a danger in assuming that because these girls can't talk, we can't find out what's wrong. Don't believe it. We are their advocates, their connection with the rest of the world. Their cries are supposed to produce stress in us so we can come to their rescue. It's one of the basics of human nature.

COMMON PHYSICAL CAUSES FOR CRYING AND SCREAMING

FOLLOWING ARE THE MOST FREQUENT PHYSICAL CAUSES for crying and screaming. All of them have treatments that are quick and easy.

Gastroesophageal Reflux: This occurs when stomach acid backs up into the esophagus. It is extremely painful. It can be treated with prescription anti-acid medications. Over-the-counter preparations seldom are strong enough. Read more about this in the chapter on Nutrition and Feeding.

Constipation or Impaction: It is possible to be constipated and have diarrhea at the same time. Impaction occurs when stool is lodged and cannot move. It is very painful. Read more in the chapter on Day to Day Care.

Dystonia: Alteration in muscle tone causes painful muscle cramps or spasms, close to the midline of the body (neck, shoulders, hips). In RS, dystonia often involves the legs or feet. Medications are helpful. See the chapter on Day to Day Care.

Behaviors

Urinary Tract Infection: Since stool can enter the urethra from a soiled diaper, or having her hands in the area, urinary tract infections are easy to get. Look for strong odors or dark urine. Antibiotics do the trick. See the chapter on Day to Day Care.

Vaginal Infection: Wet diapers make a perfect environment for germs to enter the vagina, even in very young children. There may or may not be obvious discharge. Look for squirming or pulling at her vagina. Your doctor can prescribe medication to take orally. See the chapter on Day to Day Care.

In addition to the above, in all ages but especially in older girls, we have found an alarming number of cases of *gall bladder disease*. It is important to recognize this condition because it is a treatable cause of pain and distress. The exact cause of gallbladder disease in RS is not known. Most gallstones in adults are silent and do not cause symptoms. A wide variety of "dyspeptic" symptoms (fat intolerance, flatulence, bloating, heartburn, nausea, and vomiting, have been attributed to gallstones, but none represents true biliary pain associated with gallstones. Gallstone attacks occur when gallstones obstruct the biliary tract, resulting in distention (swelling) of the gallbladder and biliary ducts. Pain in the upper abdomen, sometimes moving to the shoulder, occurs suddenly, is severe, and lasts for one to three hours. The pain is not colicky (increasing and decreasing rapidly in intensity). The pain slowly disappears over thirty to ninety minutes and leaves a vague ache. The attack can occur anytime and is not related to meals, fatty or otherwise. Nausea, vomiting, paleness, and sweating may accompany an attack. While gallstones may cause acute pain, other forms of gallbladder, pancreatic, or liver disease may result in persistent pain, vomiting, or fever.

If your child has symptoms and seems to be in unexplained pain or distress, you should ask your doctor to consider gallbladder problems. To make a diagnosis, your child's doctor will order an abdominal ultrasound, the most specific test to detect gallstones. In addition, your child's doctor may order blood tests to look for signs of infection and liver or pancreatic disease. Other tests such as a computerized tomography (CT) scan or endoscopy may be performed to evaluate potential complications of gallbladder disease.

Until recently, the most common treatment for symptomatic gallstones was a surgical procedure called cholecystectomy, which required a large abdominal incision to remove the gallbladder. Today, laparoscopic cholecystectomy is more commonly performed and requires only a tiny incision. All children with gallstones are considered for surgical treatment, even if asymptomatic, because the natural outcome of gallstones in this age group is unknown.

In addition to gallstones, a condition known as *biliary dyskinesia* has been reported. In this condition, the gallbladder does not empty as it should. It will not be detected on ultrasound, but requires a special radioactive dye test to confirm.

If your child has gall bladder disease, be sure to report it to IRSA. We are funding an important systematic review of cases for the medical literature to make physicians aware of the problem in RS.

COPING WITH CRYING AND SCREAMING

NOTHING IS WORSE THAN HAVING A MISERABLE CHILD when you can't figure out the mystery of the misery. It seems like the "cry button" is stuck in the "on" position and there is no way to turn it off. In fact, it is difficult for her to stop. It can drive you to distraction trying to figure out what is wrong and trying to make it better.

Behaviors

Sometimes, trying to soothe her only makes the crying escalate. When you've tried every-thing from both lists, try to remember the following:

- She doesn't want to be this way.
- She is doing the very best she can do.
- It will be over before long and she will be her sweet self again.

Jocelyn often times goes through "bad days" when she cries or screams. Most of the time though, it will tend to only be a short bout, part of the day, or often solved by a change in activity. I found often that when it's time to leave, she begins to cry, but as I ignore it and continue to put her in the car and turn the music on, she begins to calm herself again and is fine. Other times I feel that it's truly an emotional frustration that causes the tears. These times, after I've determined that it's nothing I can "fix," I let her know that I'll give her some "space" to work it out herself. Again, she seems to get over it better on her own. I try to think of my own bad days. Some-times I don't want everyone trying to make it better either, but would rather be left alone.

EARLY AUTISTIC TENDENCIES

KIDS WITH RS WHO WALK ARE MORE OFTEN AUTISTIC-LIKE dur-ing regression, more highly spirited, irritable, have difficulty concentrating and sleeping, are unable to cope with change, and are easily distracted by noise or activity. They use a lot of energy just figuring out how to move. Those who do not walk are more often described as happy, content, quiet, and observant. This may be because they do not have the problem of concentrating on movement.

FRUSTRATION

GETTING TO THE BOTTOM OF THE PROBLEM BEHAVIOR takes time, patience and a lot of support. In spite of all of these things, answers are sometimes elu-sive. It can be upsetting to the most resourceful parents.

When I was a little girl, I knew my mother was magic. She could fix anything. There was no knot she couldn't untangle, even those I had tried to fix myself and just tied even tighter. She could make me feel better with a kiss and a BandAid. She gave me her special quilt and "skip tea" for the flu and I got better. I looked forward to being a magic mother myself someday. I wish I could have my mom's magic. But my kisses and hugs just don't fix what-ever is wrong. My little one has been howling for nearly four hours straight this morning. My heart can't stand this. It's that way most mornings here lately, some days never letting up till bedtime, and has been a relatively steady factor in our lives for over two years now. At the beginning we called 911 countless times in case this could be her appendix or a twisted bowel. We've talked with specialists all over the country and they all just scratch their heads. She's had batteries of tests that came out clean and tried a few meds that messed up her system. The closest to an answer any doc can give is intestinal gas, but even that is guessing. We're praying with all our might that weaning her off the ketogenic diet will allow her system to rest (the suggestion of several specialists). In the meantime, she's pretty miserable, my little sweetie. I wish I could be magic like my mom. At least I am expert at untying strings ... but that doesn't seem as magic right now as it did when I was five.

MOOD SWINGS

THE PENDULUM CAN SWING quite dramatically in a short period of time. In RS, moods can fluctuate to extremes within the space of an hour when nothing else in the

Behaviors

environment has changed. The girl with RS may be laughing one moment and screaming the next, without explanation. One parent described her daughter as a "tornado waiting to land." Attention and performance can also vary considerably within a short period of time.

We have noticed these patterns all of Amy's life. We call it "earth to Amy" days. When she is locked out, she is locked out. Other times, she will be very responsive, verbal, walk, and be in tune. These are the days when she initiates conversation, smiles, laughs appropriately, and gets the joke. These moods follow no rhyme or reason.

Shanda has days when everything she tries to do goes great, and other days when she can't do anything right. On the "off" days we just read her favorite books and watch movies. On her "on" days, she is a bubbling fountain of joy!

She will be lying on the floor as quiet as a mouse and then she will burst out in this hysterical laughter that just puts everyone in a good mood. These are my best times with her. She can be so "iffy" at times. We never know whether or not she will "allow" us to play with her. We respect her space and leave her alone, but when she begins laughing like that, we take it as an invitation!

What's funny, or aggravating, about all of this is that her mood swings are so violent sometimes. Just the other day, she went from hysterically laughing to screaming at the top of her lungs so loud she sets off the glass break sensors on our security system.

NIGHT TERRORS

SLEEP OR NIGHT TERRORS ARE MOST OFTEN SEEN in typically developing toddlers, usually around age two. They occur when the child goes into deep sleep very quickly. Often these episodes begin with a scream and an abrupt awakening, and are followed by disorientation. They are different from routine nightmares. Night terrors are considered a sleep disorder, much like sleep-walking. Stress can increase the likelihood of sleep terrors.

Kristas scared us one time when we found her in her window sill banging on the window. We tried some sleep medications, but they didn't help much. She eventually outgrew the sleep terrors.

When she was a toddler she frequently woke up with nighttime terrors/tantrums and it was very difficult and emotionally draining for both of us, because they would last for hours. But we came across something that has been a lifesaver and has been extremely beneficial to our Rosie. It's called a Kelliquilt, a twenty-five pound, weighted blanket. We wrapped Rosie in it like a cocoon during those times and the deep pressure calmed her down and also protected her. It has been the best purchase we ever made. We still use it now when she is very anxious and her engine is too revved up and needs to come back to neutral.

FACIAL MOVEMENTS

OTHER BODY MOVEMENTS AND BEHAVIORS CAN BE SEEN. Facial grimaces, such as stretching, twisting movements of the lower jaw, lips and tongue, are common in the younger girl. She may chew or bite her lips or blow bubbles. Sometimes these grimaces get worse when her hand movements are interrupted. These movements are thought to be involuntary, something she cannot control.

Behaviors

TOOTH GRINDING

BRUXISM, OR TOOTH GRINDING, can be an annoying problem. It is described as a "creaking" sound, like uncorking a wine bottle. Some parents have reported success using jaw massage to relieve the grinding. Others have had orthodontic appliances made by the dentist with varying rates of success. Some feel that anxiety medication helps. Another tactic is to give her a soft towel or object to chew on in place of the grinding. The bad thing about tooth grinding is that it can drive you crazy. The good thing about tooth grinding is that it always almost goes away when the permanent teeth come in.

One thing that helps Carly is a plastic, rubbery "chewy." She wears it around her neck and can pop it into her mouth when she wants. It doesn't look like a baby teether. We have to be careful with her having things around her neck, so she never wears it in bed.

Ashley, nine, used to grind her teeth constantly. She almost ground them flush with her gums. But she doesn't grind her teeth anymore, only if she is feeling bad. Then I know she doesn't feel well.

Nadya is a tooth grinder. Someone suggested giving a magnesium supplement. I give her a calcium supplement that contains 250mg magnesium per dose. This has stopped her tooth grinding completely and when I forget to give it to her the grinding returns.

Miranda tends to teeth grind when her usual repetitive motion is restricted. If we hold her hands and she can't clap/wring them, she will then kick her feet. If she's not in a position where that works, she then grinds her teeth.

Ashley will grind her teeth when she is uncomfortable. Other times, we are not certain what the problem is, but it is my gut feeling that something is "off" with her, disturbing her normal balance of things. She has a soft mouth guard.

Dani's speech therapist showed us how to massage the inside of Dani's cheek. I could feel how tense the muscles were, and it relaxed her. Now we give her a pacifier to chew on and she rarely grinds her teeth.

Sherry pretty much outgrew the constant, severe teeth-grinding and now only does it occasionally. We can sometimes get her to relax her jaw by rubbing very gently in little circles around where the jawbone connects and near the temples, that whole area. She likes that a lot.

We made a "chewing necklace" from aquarium tubing with an infant teether. Angela wears it around her neck and can put it in her mouth when she wants to chew or grind. It even looks "cool" like some of the jewelry her friends wear.

ROCKING

SOME CHILDREN ROCK THEMSELVES, either as self-stimulation or to communicate. Sometimes they rock when their hands are kept apart or the stereotyped hand movements are interrupted. It can make feeding a challenge, trying to feed a moving target.

We simply tell Rachel to "stop rocking" or "hold still" when we are about to give her a bite. Believe it or not, with practice she listens to us about seventy-five percent of the time. I think the food reward for her is strong enough that she knows that, in order to get the food, she has to sit still for a few seconds.

Behaviors

Katie sometimes rocks "just for fun." It is not overly extreme, just enough to topple over if she is free-sitting on the floor or mat. She smiles and laughs a lot and seems to be having a good time. At other times, she rocks to relieve gas or when she needs to have a BM. This rocking is much more exaggerated, and usually her body stiffens. She bangs her head pretty hard too, and clenches her teeth with facial grimaces; this is always a sign to put her on the toilet.

Ashley rocked around the age of two, but it did stop. Once we got Ashley on a program of one-on-one stimulation involving lots of activities for fine motor, gross motor, etc., the rocking stopped.

Carol was a "rocker and slammer" early on. I enrolled her into a program that was developed for autism and sensory integration. Once Carol learned how her environment felt in relationship to her body, many of her self-stimulating behaviors stopped.

Stacey is now twenty-one and she used to rock at about age two. In fact, she rocked so hard on her hands and knees that she literally shook her crib apart. It stopped around the age of three or four.

NOISE IN PUBLIC

GOING OUT IN PUBLIC is not always easy, especially during the early years when crying is often a dilemma. Noise is sometimes a problem that draws unwanted attention from others. Taking along a drink and a survival bag of munchies is imperative, even if you are off to the restaurant. A headset with her favorite music is also a huge help.

Ashley is getting to be so noisy when we go out in public. We usually just deal with it but we don't even attempt to go to a sit-down restaurant. As a family we only go to noisy places and places where you can get your food fast, and we try to go to places that aren't busy.

We go to restaurants where there is handicapped parking close by. One of us goes in to get a table, while the other remains in the car with Stacie. Whoever goes in, brings a menu to the car, then returns to the table with everyone's order. We don't bring Stacie in the restaurant until the food is served. She takes her seat and eyes her meal with delight. She's so busy eating, there is no room for noise, and we're all happy.

We take Carly out to eat and we know she is messy and sometimes loud. Lately, she needs to see what is going on in the kitchen. So, we park her there (with one of us watching) and make sure she is not in the way. Also, we tip extra well because the waiter/waitress has to work extra hard for us (before and after the meal).

TANTRUMS

GIRLS WITH RS ARE NO DIFFERENT FROM OTHER CHILDREN when it comes to wanting their own way. It is more understandable since they have so many obstacles to daily living. Without speech, they often have to rely on our intuition to guess what they want. It can be embarrassing and stressful when out in public. Just ask the mother of any typical preschooler.

Shanda usually tantrums when the teacher is working with another child and this is for gaining attention. When she tantrums during lunch, music class, and other noisy times of the day, they take her out in the hall, so she is using tantrums to escape from a situation she doesn't like.

With every new behavior, I always ask myself, "Is this going to be cute for a teenager?" Throwing food, stealing food, screaming, playing in her diaper, spitting … the list goes on. Put a behavior plan in place at home and at

Behaviors

school. Ask a professional for help. It's too important for the child's self-esteem. To ignore and avoid a behavior feeds the behavior. That child's world becomes so narrow and it sets her apart from the world, not to mention what it does to you and the other family members.

Sara goes through screaming spells when she has had enough and wants to go. We get a lot of stares from people and it used to really upset me. Now, we try to avoid going out at times when we know she is going to be tired and we don't try to take her if we know she won't enjoy what we are doing. That was the hard part because we want her to be involved with the family, but we have come to realize we are just torturing her and ourselves.

FUNCTIONAL BEHAVIOR ASSESSMENT

IT'S A GOOD IDEA TO KEEP DATA on when the behavior appears and what has happened just previous to the outburst. This may give an indication as to whether it is caused by pain, emotion, or a need to communicate.

Functional Behavior Assessment is a method used to determine what the child is trying to communicate with her behavior. Every time the child has a tantrum, you should look carefully at the antecedent of the behavior (what takes place prior to the negative behavior). This includes not only what she was doing, but also, what everyone around her was doing. Notice the environment, time of day, and what was expected of her. Then, briefly describe the tantrum, followed by a description of what action was taken by adults and peers when the tantrum occurred. After a number of recordings, everyone involved in the child's care should review the recorded information to form a hypothesis about what the child is accomplishing with the behavior.

The negative behavior may have several different functions. Most commonly, it is gaining attention, escaping from a task or situation, or getting something the child wants. Once the function of the behavior has been identified, you can use Positive Behavior Support (PBS) to support her positive response and she can be taught another behavior (such as activating a switch or doing some kind of vocalizing that is not a tantrum) to accomplish the same function. This method is an effective way to get at the root cause of the behavior and eliminate it.

My daughter took to knocking over water glasses at the dinner table. In response, my husband started removing everything within her reach and even removed her from the table. She started refusing to take anything he fed her and knocking the fork from his hand, making a mess and getting him frustrated, and then shutting her eyes and ignoring dinner altogether. It started making family meal time very stressful. We tried getting her to drink from the cup, but she just wanted to tip it out. To make a long story short, she wanted the ice, and that is how we found out she likes to chew on ice chips. She had been trying to reach into our glasses to get the ice! She wasn't intending to be bad or make a mess, just trying to get us to understand her desire for ice. Now, she gets a cup of ice chips at the dinner table along with her water glass and all is peaceful.

CHALLENGING BEHAVIORS

CHALLENGING BEHAVIOR IS ANY BEHAVIOR which is difficult to manage, disruptive, or harmful. It can be hard to determine why the behavior began and how to change it. In general, we know that behaviors have a specific function. Sometimes, she may engage in this behavior simply out of habit or as a tension reliever, much the way a young child might suck her thumb. Other behaviors may be her way of sending important

Behaviors

messages. Until we discover the meaning of her behavior, we may not be able to change it. More importantly, until we know why she is doing the behavior, she will not get the response she seeks. Hand or wrist biting can mean more than being frustrated. It can mean, "I hurt and need to belch," or "I need attention," "I am constipated," or "This is too hard for me." To determine why she is engaging in the behavior, consider these factors about her:

- her physical state, including illness, seizures, and neurological status
- the situation in which the behavior occurs
- a knowledge of her usual concerns

Many typical toddlers go through a brief phase of biting, hitting, or spitting because it gets attention. As they develop language, they find more effective ways of getting attention and having their needs met. Girls with RS do not develop language and it may take a long time, even with an intensive, highly structured teaching program, to teach them acceptable ways of responding.

Stefanie occasionally hits or pulls hair and she gets a "time out" at her desk or in the corner, while the rest of the class is doing something cool. It is effective if it's done consistently. Stefanie definitely knows that these behaviors are not acceptable, but does them anyway to get a reaction. I have explained to her that just because she has RS does not mean she can get away with bad behavior. I know she understands from the look in her eyes, but sometimes she is just a little stinker.

Briana went through a biting phase. It was her way of telling people they were overstepping their boundaries with her. Another student had pulled Briana's hair, so she bit him. I didn't condone her biting, though I was very happy that she had defended herself.

Studies have shown that if you can teach a new behavior that accomplishes the same task as the old, undesirable one, the child will leave the old behavior behind and use the new one. So if hitting is her way of saying hello, try to replace the behavior. As soon as someone approaches for a greeting, gently put your hand on her hand. Say a cheery "Hi" for her and have the friend make eye contact, touch her hand gently and warmly, and say "Hi" in return. In this way, you have taught her how to greet people appropriately. You may have to set up situations in which she can greet someone perhaps dozens of times each day, continued over several weeks. Another major factor in changing the behavior is learning to change our own response to it, which can actually reinforce the negative behavior.

Amanda used to bite. We let her bite pillows or have a doll she could bite., but generally, she wanted to bite other people. The best way we distinguished behaviors was to give her alternative behaviors and this takes much time. Eventually, we have taught Amanda to say "you me" for "you meanie," or "I'm mad." It took about a year, with lots of practice and animation to show her. Then one day she just said it in a rage, and is still able to when she is mad.

It is easier to change the environment than to change the behavior. People who work with her should be tuned into her needs, and be able to read her signals. These can be very subtle and easily overlooked. It is important for everyone to remember that her behaviors are challenging for her, as well. It is not her, but the disorder that drives the behaviors. Structuring her environment to decrease her anxiety level does not mean letting her get

Behaviors

away with whatever she wants to do. It means that expectations should be within her ability. She should have frequent pauses and many pleasant interactions. If you use a positive approach, seeing her as capable, she will develop self-confidence. Keep a positive attitude and treat her with sensitivity and respect, seeing her first and the disability second. You may be surprised at how well she responds.

It is important to bring people in her life into a "circle of support." This can include parents, relatives and friends, as well as school or community professionals and anyone who is committed to effecting a change. In this supportive environment, you can share different perspectives and ideas for helping her in various aspects of her life. The "circle" can also be a very comforting resource for her and those with whom she relates. The "circle" may even improve strained relationships.

Jenna would pinch and claw at our faces until she fell asleep. For about a year and a half, my husband and I had scratches on our faces almost daily. Nothing we tried decreased the behavior. We tried time-outs, pressing our teeth into her arm and shaking our heads and saying "no." Jenna is four and a half now and rarely bites or pinches. Most bites now are little nibbles to get your attention. Sometimes she even giggles because she knows she is being bad. I am almost certain all her behaviors were caused by sensory issues and the frustration of not being able to communicate.

POSITIVE REINFORCEMENT

SOME KIDS WANT ATTENTION, even if it is negative attention. While it may be hard at the time, ignoring the negative behavior can work. Instead of telling her "no" and drawing focus on the bad act, wait until she is not doing it, and then praise her highly. Give her attention for the behavior you expect.

When Ashley would bite, we tried sternly telling her "no" and sometimes reacting adversely when surprised. It stopped when we ignored the behavior. She would also bite one of her arms. She had a teacher's aide who this really bothered and every time she was around Ashley, she reacted adversely to this. I began noticing that when Ashley was around the aide, she would hold her arm right up to her and bite, looking at her the entire time. This shocked me. I asked her not to react to Ashley doing this, and finally she stopped doing this altogether.

AGGRESSION

IT IS NATURAL TO FEEL ANGRY WHEN AGGRESSIVE BEHAVIORS are aimed at you. Using your circle of support is helpful, and using respite to get time away here and there gives you time to recoup.

Jessica bangs her head when she is mad, and if you are holding her, she will head butt you if she can. She has really hurt me before and herself as well. Also she will kick and if she hits her shin, she will just keep on kicking or whatever it is, such as hitting her elbow or smacking something with the back of her hand. She doesn't seem to mind that kind of pain ... But let me get a brush to brush her hair and she tries to run!

Kim used to take very deliberate aim at my nose and hit it hard with her forehead. Having no means of communication in those days, she did all she was able to do. However, I did not understand. I think some things that might help other girls are holding her close and reassuring her, playing some music with a strong rhythm and melody, but not too loud, and perhaps rocking gently with it. If this helps, it might be worth trying some form of communication system if you don't already have one. Even for her to answer "yes" or "no" questions you would ask her, to help relieve her frustration at not being able to make the actions she wants to make.

Behaviors

Her new method is a very loud, and I do mean loud, scream followed by slapping motions. Anyone in the way will get a good pop. Mom gets one from time to time. I don't discourage this behavior as it is one of the few ways for her to let people know that they have stepped in a bit too closely. I'm trying to teach her a better method of showing her disapproval. A nice scream in the ear doesn't hurt too terribly.

SELF-INJURIOUS BEHAVIORS

SOME GIRLS WITH RS INJURE THEMSELVES. Most often, this takes the form of biting or hitting themselves. Some medications have been found effective in treating these episodes, probably due to their sedative effect. Seroquil and Revia have been found effective. It is important, however, to rule out any physical cause or source of pain or frustration first. Experts feel that girls who injure themselves may do so because they have a high threshold for pain. Girls with RS often have high circulating levels of B-endorphins, one of the body's natural painkillers which is chemically related to opiates, like heroin or morphine. It is possible that endorphin levels are elevated because of the self-injury. No one is certain which comes first.

After much deliberation and anxiety, we put Stefanie on Tranxene because she was very agitated and getting worse. It seemed like any little thing set her off. Sometimes it was that she was not feeling well and we weren't picking up on it. Other times it was due to general frustration, and other times we just didn't know what the trigger was. She was yelling, hitting herself in the head constantly and had significantly thinned out her waist length hair from the ears forward. We were at our wits end, and more importantly, Stefanie was obviously not happy. I read somewhere that drugs in the valium family can become habit forming, but if the choice is a miserable child who hits herself in the head and is so incredibly miserable that she screams all the time, or the habit-forming drugs, I go for the drugs.

At about age seven or eight, she began self-injurious behaviors. She will pull hair, pinch, and scratch herself or others but will also bite herself. It seems if she can't get someone else she will get herself and this behavior is severe. We find that isolating her in a safe area so she can't hurt anyone else works best. I have a short hallway that I can block at both ends with a gate. It allows her to calm down and then we let her out as soon as she's better. She does understand she needs "nice touches" to get out.

Another strategy that helps, especially if you are out, is to put oven mitts on her hands so she can't hurt you or herself. We tape them on at the top and remove them as soon as she calms down. It works well.

While at times a girl may appear to have an increased tolerance to pain, sometimes her pain threshold is less than normal. Little things like a scratchy clothing tag or a wrinkle in a sock may seem terribly irritating and cause her to bite her hand. Surely sensation is distorted, but it seems selective.

We have instructed caregivers to assume that something gentle like a range of motion exercise is causing a painful response if she reacts negatively, such as biting her hands. Then we back off until she can tolerate some more exercise. We don't want to deprive her of part of her therapy time, but don't want her to feel that we are hurting her.

Maria slapped her chin, then across her cheek repeatedly. When she was upset, she would punch herself in the jaw. Because we had no insurance, no diagnosis, and no intervention, we got creative. We made her first arm brace for her out of a potato chip can! My husband cut the metal ends off, cut it lengthways down the side, lined it with foam padding and Velcroed it around her elbow so she couldn't bend her arm to hit herself. I always had to laugh

Behaviors

when she wore it at the grocery store. They always wanted to charge me for the Pringles, and stared at me dumbfounded when I handed it to them! If nothing else, it made a good conversation piece!

No matter what you do, even changing her diaper, Brit begins to hit herself in the chin and eye, cheek, and temple area. Her arm splints have been on more than off, and I try to put them on before changing her, etc. I purchased water wings to use in the bathtub. She bites herself very hard when mad or agitated. We saw a whirlwind of these behaviors for a period of five months about a year ago, and then one day they were gone.

Stephanie slaps her body, usually her thighs, when she is angry, frustrated, or tired. She also pulls other people's hair occasionally and says "Ow." This is usually to see the reaction from the other person. When she was younger, around age two, she used to pinch herself and anyone who got in range, too.

We do not have a lot of problems with this anymore except for scratching the moment you remove Angela's clothes and occasional rocking which results in head banging but can be controlled. When she was going through the regressive period at two, she pulled her hair out constantly. We had to keep a bonnet on her at all times. She even pulled out her eyelashes. She was so miserable at this time, crying inconsolably and vomiting if touched. Even after these symptoms stopped, the hair pulling continued for about another year.

SUGGESTIONS FOR CHALLENGING BEHAVIORS

- Look for a quiet time to interact. Positive times reinforce caring relationships.
- Believe in her ability and desire to "be good."
- Provide adequate support and respite time for caregivers.
- Try to determine if she is bored and provide more stimulating activities.
- Allow her to participate in choice-making to give her some control.
- Go beyond letting her watch what is going on. Include her in normal experiences of daily living.
- Physical restraint should be a last resort. Make it as brief as possible but long enough to provide safety.
- In severe cases, medications might be helpful. There is no one drug that works best for everyone.
- The use of "aversives," such as squirting her face with cold water to interrupt the behavior, are not recommended. They are damaging to her self-concept and self-esteem, and are too easily abused.
- Explore various communication methods.

HOW TO HELP WITH CHALLENGING BEHAVIORS

- Spend time in a comfortable environment. Get to know her.
- Ask her for permission to help her.
- Remember that all behavior is a form of communication.
- Recognize that difficult behaviors often arise from unmet needs.
  - loneliness
  - boredom
  - powerlessness
  - insecurity
  - not feeling valuable

Behaviors

- ○ lack of ability to communicate
- ○ untreated pain
- Develop a support plan for her.
- Develop a support plan for her supporters.
- Don't underestimate her potential.
- Help her to develop relationships with people who care.
- Help her to develop a positive identity.
- Help her make a contribution. She needs to be needed.
- Give choices instead of ultimatums.
- Help her to have fun.
- Talk with her primary health care physician.
- Help her live a healthy lifestyle.

MEDICATIONS

SOME PARENTS REPORT THAT THE USE of various medications are effective in reducing screaming spells when they arise from anxiety. These include Revia, Buspar, Ativan, Seroquel, Prozac, Celexa, Nortriptylene and Zoloft, to name a few. Check with your child's physician to see if medication will be helpful, and which medication is best. Some anticonvulsants, such as Tegretol or Depakote, are helpful in mood control. Don't hesitate to ask for referral to a specialist such as a developmental pediatrician, pediatric neurologist, or child psychiatrist. Try each drug one at a time and monitor its effectiveness. It can take several weeks for a concentration of the drug to build up in the body, several weeks to see if it works, more time to adjust the dosage, and still more time to take her off the drug to see if it has been helpful. Be patient.

Heather took Revia for self-injurious behavior and aggression. Her condition worsened and she became more aggressive. We did not keep her on it for more than a period of a week though. It scared us and we took it away under the doctor's approval. Be prepared for anything, as different girls respond differently to medicines.

Revia does work for her, but it took a good two, almost three, weeks to see results. We basically started it for the extreme fussiness and lack of sleep. I never linked her hand movements to this, but since she started a year ago, her movements have gone from a hard hit to the face, even sometimes biting her hands, to a gentle flicking and definitely a more calmer hand movement. Now she only wears splints when at school or when we are out and about.

Heather's self-injurious behavior did decrease and we use the arm bands even less now than before. We don't have to use them now for more than a few hours at a time, maybe twice a month. It is great. We use Tylenol when she gets fussy and that is it.

When our daughter turned five I started to see a change. Slowly she became quieter and not so aggressive. The biting stopped. For some girls this will take longer. Even at age eight she did not want to sit quietly through church. She could not handle large crowds, etc. Now at sixteen, she can handle large crowds, sit quietly in a assembly, etc. We still deal with the medical aspects, but other aspects have changed such as alertness, accepting new situations, socialization, etc. Time will hopefully be on your side too.

Yard by yard ... life is hard. Inch by inch ... life's a cinch.

– ANONYMOUS

Seizures

FOR MOST PEOPLE, seizures are a frightening thought. They can be simply described as a kind of sudden static, or bolt of electricity in the brain. Watching a seizure for the first time can be alarming, but learning what happens during a seizure reduces our anxiety and helps us learn how to react with calm and understanding. Your daughter with RS may never have a seizure in her life, or she may have seizures that are well controlled with medication. Knowledge is your best ally.

Epilepsy is a broad term that is used to describe recurring seizures or the potential for recurrence of seizures. Seizures are called by various names including fits, spells, convulsions, and attacks. A seizure is a sign of a disorder and in and of itself is not an illness or a disorder. You can not "catch" epilepsy. It does not cause mental retardation, is not a mental illness, and is not anyone's fault.

"In our lives there is bound to be some pain, surely as there are storms and falling rain; just believe that the one who holds the storms will bring the sun."

— ANONYMOUS

THE CAUSE

WHILE MUTATIONS IN THE *MECP2* gene are found in ninety-five percent of girls with Classic RS, how these mutations cause RS is not known. We do not understand why some children with RS have seizures while others do not. However, since RS involves the nervous system, it is not surprising that seizures occur. If seizures do occur, the onset tends to be between two and ten years of age. However, bear in mind that seizures are often over-reported in RS. Only fifty-percent of those with RS truly have epileptic seizures. Other "seizures" are a consequence of motor dysfunction (stiffening, rigidity, tremors), autonomic dysfunction (cold, blue extremities, facial flushing, pupil dilatation or enlargement), awake breathing abnormalities (breath-holding, hyperventilation, blank staring), gastrointestinal disturbances (acid reflux), or other behaviors seen in girls with RS. These non-epileptic episodes would not be expected to be responsive to antiepileptic drugs (AEDs).

A VISIT TO THE NEUROLOGIST

IF YOU SUSPECT THAT YOUR DAUGHTER is having seizure activity, it is wise to consult with a doctor who specializes in the treatment of seizures. It will put your mind at ease and it will assure that she gets a thorough evaluation of her seizure status. Check with other families in your area for the name of a qualified child neurologist. If your daughter does have seizures, you will be in frequent contact with him or her, so it is important that you are satisfied with his or her knowledge and experience, approachability, and

Seizures

willingness to consider you as partners in your daughter's care. Seizure control is an evolutionary process and it is peculiar to each different individual. What works for another child may not work for yours, and what once worked for your child may not always work.

SEIZURES HAPPEN

EVERY BRAIN CELL IS AN ELECTROCHEMICAL UNIT that generates a very small electrical current. The brain sends out electrical signals through our nerves. The brain receives signals along the nerves from all parts of the body. Normally, this electrical activity is well regulated and organized. Sometimes there is sudden excessive or erratic electrical activity. When this happens, it may result in a seizure. The electrical disturbance that accompanies this seizure may arise from any part of the brain. The kind or type of seizure may indicate the area in the brain where the electrical disturbance arises.

IS IT A SEIZURE?

A CLINICAL SEIZURE RESULTS from the excessive, synchronous discharge of brain cells (neurons), which brings about a change in movement or behavior. If no change is seen in behavior or movement, it is not considered a clinical seizure. Rarely, a seizure discharge may be recorded during an EEG (electroencephalogram, the recording of ongoing brain activity) without any obvious clinical change in a person. More frequently, random EEG abnormal discharges are recorded in many girls. These are not seizures and in themselves do not require antiseizure medication.

In RS, it can be difficult to determine whether she is having a clinical seizure or autonomic responses that look like a seizure. Often, seizurelike behaviors are seen, but seizure activity is not seen on the EEG during these events. Girls with RS have vacant spells that resemble absence seizures, but are not. Often there are jerky movements and eye rolling that are associated with seizures, but in RS they are involuntary movements that are not seizures.

NON-EPILEPTIC EVENTS IN RS

THE FOLLOWING EVENTS MAY LOOK LIKE TYPICAL seizure behavior, but in RS, they are often *not* seizure related:

- Motor events
  - twitching
  - jerking
  - head turning
  - falling
  - trembling
  - staring/vacant spells
- Other Events
  - dilated pupils
  - laughing/screaming episodes
  - breathing: apnea and hyperventilation
  - nighttime awakenings

Seizures

Jessica gets the shakes when she first wakes up in the mornings or after a daytime nap. It is like she is really scared and surprised by any movements. She does not walk and so when we pick her up we give her big cuddles (she hangs onto us so tightly) and reassure her until she collects herself. If we sit her on the floor, she grabs hold of whatever she can to stabilize herself and has a look of fear on her face. We have put it down to her poor balance and think that while lying down she feels secure and comfortable but when brought upright into sitting her balance reactions are "confused." It takes her anywhere between five and fifteen minutes to stop shaking. We have also noticed that if she is afraid by a gross motor activity that may push her a bit hard she will get the shakes; when this happens, we just back off and let her recover. We have discussed it with doctors, who don't believe it is seizure-related.

Management of Non-Epileptic Events

- Recognize any potentially treatable medical or surgical disorders.
- Consider the use of atypical neuroleptic drugs such as Risperdal or Seroquel.
- Consider the use of anti-anxiety medications such as Buspar or Diazepam.
- Consider the use of antidepressants (SSRIs, tricyclics).

DIAGNOSING A SEIZURE

THE DIAGNOSIS OF EPILEPSY (SEIZURES) IS MADE on the basis of the parent's description of seizures, physical and neurological examinations, and the electroencephalogram (EEG) findings. An EEG is a test to measure and record the electrical activity generated by the brain. It does not measure intelligence. Small electrodes are placed over the scalp and held in place with tape or a special paste. Your daughter will experience no pain or discomfort during an EEG recording, but she must remain still during placement of the electrodes. Therefore, she may become upset and cry. In some situations, she may need medication to make her drowsy in order to record her brain activity during sleep.

The EEG will show changes that may indicate an abnormality in one or many areas of the brain, localize the specific area of the brain that is involved, help determine the type of seizure, and reveal the kind of medication that can best control the type of seizure.

In individuals who do not have epilepsy, the EEG recordings resemble squiggly lines with waves that are similar in height. In most people with seizures, abnormalities are seen as little bursts of electrical activity, called "sharp waves" or "spikes," that interrupt normal rhythm.

The EEG records only the electrical activity present at the time the EEG is being recorded. Therefore, a seizure will not be recorded unless she has a seizure during the recording. However, if she has had a recent seizure, the EEG tracing may show changes that are helpful to the physician in determining appropriate treatment. An EEG measures waves on the surface and outer layers of the brain only. If the EEG does not show seizure activity during what you think may be a seizure, it doesn't mean that seizures are not occurring. It could be that they are taking place deep within the brain and cannot be measured by conventional means.

The neurologist will determine if an EEG is necessary. The EEG should be recorded in both the awake and sleep states since the abnormal activity may be seen in either or both. With medication, the seizures will probably decrease in frequency or be completely controlled. This does not mean the EEG will necessarily be normal.

The EEG looks different when she is awake and asleep, and some abnormalities may only be seen when she is drowsy or sleeping. Some children have a normal waking EEG and a very abnormal sleep EEG.

Seizures

Routine repetition at periodic intervals is not necessary, but repeating the EEG may be necessary if seizures change in character, severity or frequency. Children with RS frequently have abnormal EEG patterns. This abnormal pattern may include activity called *epileptiform abnormalities* that may be recorded in persons who have seizures. The information supplied by the EEG may help define the specific seizure type. The physician can then choose the most appropriate anticonvulsant drugs. However, a normal EEG does not rule out the diagnosis of epilepsy or mean that seizures have not occurred. On the other hand, if there is no history of a seizure, an abnormal EEG does not make the diagnosis of epilepsy.

THE EEG IN RETT SYNDROME

WHILE THE EEG IS USUALLY ABNORMAL IN RS, there is no diagnostic pattern. EEG patterns frequently seen in RS include generalized slowing, rhythmic slow activity (reported as "theta" activity), and focal and generalized spikes and sharp waves.

READING THE EEG

THE EEG CAN PICK UP "ARTIFACTS," such as muscle twitches and eye blinks that are not coming from the brain. It is not abnormal to see these on an EEG. The abnormalities that are important include spikes, slowing, and evidence of seizures. They may be either focal (localized to a specific area of the brain) or generalized (seen all over the brain).

Spikes are abnormal discharges from brain cells. The abnormal discharges may involve many brain cells and may result in an EEG seizure discharge and seizure. When spikes are seen in a specific area of the brain, it may indicate where the seizure began. Multifocal spikes give an indication that there are many abnormal areas of the brain.

Slowing of the EEG is determined when it is compared to the normal rhythm of the EEG, which varies with the age of the child and whether she is awake, drowsy, or asleep. Generalized slowing is often seen in children with chronic brain dysfunction.

Evidence of seizures refers to the association of specific abnormalities on the EEG with specific seizure types.

AMBULATORY EEG

IN SOME CASES, IT IS NECESSARY TO OBTAIN a twenty-four hour EEG to see if the behavior correlates with EEG seizure discharge. This is usually performed with a small tape cassette worn with a belt around the waist that is attached to small electrodes placed on the scalp. The cassette can record an EEG for twenty-four hours without changing the tape. When the person who is observing the child feels that she is having a seizure, the adult pushes a button, which records a mark on the tape. The physician then compares the EEG tracings with what was observed to see if the reported events are actual seizures.

VIDEO EEG

THE BEST WAY TO ANALYZE POSSIBLE SEIZURE ACTIVITY is to both see and record the events. Video EEG monitoring uses a camera to record movements and behavior while the EEG is also recording. The physician is then able to compare all of the child's behaviors to see which, if any, are epileptic seizures. These may require treatment to prevent recurrent seizures.

Seizures

GENERAL EEG FINDINGS BY STAGE

Stage I

normal or minimal background slowing

Stage II

background slowing
rhythmic theta
rare epileptiform discharges
epileptiform discharges may occur before the onset of clinical seizures

Stage III

more background slowing
abundant epileptiform discharges, mostly during sleep
loss of developmental features

Stage IV

continuous epileptiform activity OR
lack of epileptiform discharges and faster background activity

TYPES OF SEIZURES IN RS

EPISODIC ELECTRICAL EVENTS CAN OCCUR in different parts of the brain. The type of seizures they produce will differ depending on what area of the brain is affected and the direction and speed as the event spreads. Each type of seizure may require a different medication. Girls and women with RS may experience generalized and partial seizures, but there is not one specific type of seizure seen in RS. Your child may have only one type of seizure or she may have more than one type. It is important to remember that some children with RS never have seizures. Most seizure disorders respond well to medication.

GENERALIZED SEIZURES

TONIC/CLONIC SEIZURES: These seizures have been called "grand mal" and are now referred to as generalized tonic/clonic seizures. When the EEG is recorded during a generalized seizure, the seizure activity seems to start all over the brain all at once. Since the whole brain is involved, the seizure may involve all muscles and motor functions with loss of consciousness. Generalized seizures can be "large" and convulsive, with muscle movements such as jerking or stiffening, or "small" and nonconvulsive with alteration of consciousness but no jerking movements. If she loses consciousness, she may fall and may then have rhythmic jerking of all extremities or stiffening followed by rhythmic jerking. The tonic phase is when stiffening occurs. Since all the muscles are contracted, the chest muscles also contract, and breathing may become difficult. She may cry out because of air rushing out of her lungs, but she is not in pain. Lack of oxygen causes a bluish tinge around the lips and face. Saliva may cause a gurgling sound in the throat. The jaw becomes tightly clenched. The clonic phase then begins with rhythmic jerking and tightly clenched fists. The arms, legs and head may flex and then relax. This usually lasts no more than a few minutes. When she regains consciousness, she may be sleepy for one or two hours afterward. After rest, she should be able to go back to her usual activities.

Absence Seizures: This type of seizure, which has been called "petit mal," starts suddenly. It is characterized by brief staring spells without a preceding warning. There may be

Seizures

head-bobbing or eye blinking. Absence seizures generally last just a few seconds and end as abruptly as they began. Afterward, she returns to her usual activity without a period of confusion or sleepiness. Absence seizures can be confused with complex partial seizures because they both involve staring. It is important to differentiate the type of seizure to determine the type of medication that will work best.

Myoclonic Seizures: Formerly called minor motor seizures, these events consist of abrupt jerks of muscle groups and involve brief, sudden, twitchlike movements of one or more extremities. They may take many forms. A foot may kick out, a hand may fly forward. Myoclonic seizures may arise from deep structures in the brain stem that control tone and posture, causing an abrupt increase in a muscle group that brings about a sudden movement of that part of the body. However, myoclonic jerks are not always seizures. When falling asleep, most healthy individuals experience a sudden jerk and awaken with a startle. This is a normal sleep phenomenon.

Akinetic/Atonic Seizures: This type of seizure is as sudden as a myoclonic seizure. However, it is characterized by a sudden loss of tone or posture. If standing, the child may suddenly become limp and drop to the floor. If sitting, one may simply see loss of tone with the head falling forward or backward. These seizures are brief. The child returns to her usual activity immediately afterward. These seizures may also be referred to as "drop attacks."

PARTIAL SEIZURES

THE SEIZURE IS CALLED PARTIAL when at the beginning of the seizure the electrical disturbance is limited to one part of the brain. The electrical disturbance may spread to involve the whole brain. If this occurs, the seizure has become secondarily generalized.

Simple Partial Seizure: These seizures may involve movement with rhythmic jerking of one extremity of one side of the face or body, or they may involve the senses, with a particular tingling, burning or abnormal sensation in any part of the body. There is no alteration of consciousness.

Complex Partial Seizure: During this type of seizure there is some alteration of consciousness. The child is unable to make meaningful responses or her usual responses. The seizures may be characterized by confusion, loss of alertness, and staring episodes, either alone or combined with automatic behavior such as picking at the clothes, smacking the lips, or random nonpurposeful movements of the arms or legs.

RECOGNIZING A SEIZURE

IT IS SOMETIMES DIFFICULT TO TELL THE DIFFERENCE between autonomic responses associated with RS and seizure activity. Some breath-holding episodes, cyanotic spells (turning blue), jerky tremors, inattention, and eye-rolling movements ordinarily associated with seizures are not seizures in RS. You should observe the sequence of events that occur. For example:

- Is breath-holding followed by jerky movements or vice versa?
- Observe the movements. Are they rhythmic or random?
- How long does the episode last?
- Does she sleep afterward?
- Observe her eyes. Does she stare vacantly or have eye rolling? Eye deviation?
- Does her head drop?

Report these observations to your child's physician.

Seizures

All of these events have been observed during breath-holding episodes as well as during seizures. During a breath-holding spell, the child does not breathe, turns blue (cyanotic) or white (pallid) and may lose consciousness. Sometimes, breath-holding spells result in a seizure. Breath-holding spells are not seizures by themselves and are not serious.

It may be necessary to obtain an EEG with video monitoring of the breathing or movement pattern to establish whether or not the events are seizures and need to be treated. This is very important to establish, because in addition to their beneficial effects, all AEDs have potential side effects.

In Ashley's case, severe breathing episodes and seizures do have some similar characteristics, but generally are quite different. Her eyes are a big clue to seizures. Her eyes will freeze, and have been known to roll upward, or in one direction only. In breathing episodes, her eyes are free to move around. Ashley's face becomes quite flushed during seizures. There is more movement in her arms during seizures. There is a tightening during breathing episodes, but not as much movement as there is in seizures. Ashley appears frightened or stressed during seizures. I do not notice this during severe breathing episodes. Also, her lips will often turn blue in a seizure but not in a breathing episode. She has had severe apnea where her lips will turn blue, but these episodes do not resemble a seizure.

Karina has this sort of shaking her body, grimacing her face and stiffening and jerking her arms and legs. It lasts one or two minutes, and then she relaxes again. She tends to bend over forward when she is walking, and sideways when she is sitting. It happens frequently, many times a day, but some days more than others. She started this when she was about eight years old. It is not epilepsy. She has that too, and it definitely is different.

We took video of a student during her "seizures" and the neurologist said most of what we were seeing was "involuntary motions" dealing with a breathing problem. This girl looks like a falling tree when she has these involuntary movements. Her seizures are a little different.

If too much comes at Dani too fast or if we leave the TV on with no lights and the light from the TV blinks, she will have a seizure. She is sensitive to loud noises too.

Brit has had seizures since four months, but they have never been evoked by sound, visual or tactile stimuli. I remember this because we could take her anywhere and we would play games and scare her like "boo" and hide around a corner and she would giggle. Now, however, ripping a paper towel off in front of her has given a seizure, along with a glimmer of sunlight on a therapist's watchband, even a cough or sneeze. Closing the car door is hard to do quietly. Going over the bumps in the sidewalk triggers a seizure as well. She began this hypersensitivity at age five and a half.

WHAT TO DO WHEN A SEIZURE OCCURS

IT MAY BE HARD TO STAY CALM during your child's seizure, particularly the first time. Most parents get to be pros at it over time. Once a seizure has begun, there is actually little you can do to stop it. You do not need to do CPR. There is nothing you can do to stop the stiffness or start the breathing. Mouth-to-mouth resuscitation will not work because her chest will not expand. You can gently support her.

During the seizure

- Do not put anything in her mouth.
- Do not restrain her.
- Do not call an ambulance unless the seizure continues for more than five to ten minutes.

Seizures

- Do try to put her on her side.
- Do put something soft under her head.
- Do loosen tight clothing around her neck.
- Do remove sharp objects from the immediate area.

After the seizure

As the seizure stops, she will usually let out a sigh and go into a deep sleep, known as the "post-ictal" period. This period may vary depending on the length of the seizure, but it usually lasts from ten minutes to a couple of hours. If she wants to sleep long, it is OK. Sleep is a healthy way for her brain to recover from the overexertion.

- Do stay with her until she is awake and alert.
- Do be comforting and reassuring.
- Do allow her to return to activities if she is all right.

WHEN TO CALL FOR HELP

IF THE CLONIC (JERKING) PHASE OF THE SEIZURE lasts more than five to ten minutes, it is advisable to call an ambulance. Check with your child's own neurologist to determine how long you should wait.

MEDICATIONS

EEG ABNORMALITIES ARE COMMON IN RS. The goal is to treat the seizure disorder, not the EEG. If your child has an abnormal EEG but does not have a history of seizure like activity, she does not necessarily need to take anticonvulsant medication. Even some individuals who have no neurological problems and never have seizures may show abnormalities on the EEG at some time. In research studies of RS, nearly all girls with RS showed an abnormal EEG, while only from one-third to one-half of them had epileptic seizures.

If she does have seizures, many different AEDs are used for specific seizure types. There is not a specific medication for the treatment of seizures in RS. A pediatric neurologist needs to know what type(s) of seizure a child is having before prescribing medication. The primary objective of drug therapy is to control the seizures with the least possible drug side effects. Fortunately, AEDs are generally safe and severe side effects are rare or very infrequent. All side effects should be reported to your physician. Any change in behavior, including slowing (oversedation), hyperactivity, lack of coordination, or other behaviors of concern to you are appropriate to bring to the physician's attention.

Either we don't medicate and Jenn has lots of seizures and is "out of it" most of the time, or we medicate and her seizures are minimized but the trade-off is the side effects and her not being "with it" some of the time. Nothing's perfect and I can't expect the impossible. I know there's an adjustment phase with new medications as the body needs time to learn how to work with them.

There are many drugs to prevent and treat seizures, but it is not entirely clear how or why they work. We do know how these drugs are absorbed and metabolized, and we know about their side effects. Some drugs are more effective than others for different seizure types.

Seizures

Once the seizure type has been identified, the choice of drugs is made on the basis of the drug's effectiveness, cost, the child's age, and other drugs she may be already taking and any drug allergies or sensitivities.

The objective of AED therapy is to use the lowest dose of drug with the least number of side effects to achieve the best seizure control. Sometimes higher doses are necessary, and more than one drug may have to be used to achieve seizure control. It is important to remember that all drugs, including aspirin, have side effects along with their beneficial effects. Side effects may occur during the first few days on the drug until the body adjusts. Some drugs may require dose adjustment or discontinuation if the side effects are unpleasant.

The **Benzodiazepines** (Valium, Klonopin, Tranxene, Versed, and Ativan) are grouped together as a class of AEDs: The benzodiazepines potentiate the neuroinhibitory effect of the GABA neurotransmitter. Valium (diazepam), Ativan (lorazepam), and Versed (midazolam), are used to treat status epilepticus (discussed later). Klonopin, Tranxene, Valium and Ativan are also used in long-term treatment of seizures. The drugs in this class are useful for absence seizures, but are most effectively used to treat myoclonic and atonic seizures. Since each of these drugs can cause drowsiness, irritability and hyperactivity, they are usually chosen as "add-on" drugs when other drugs do not bring the seizures under control by themselves. The body can develop tolerance for drugs of this type, so the dose may need to be increased to maintain a therapeutic effect. Diastat or properly formulated generic Valium may be used per rectum by parents to interrupt prolonged seizures (ten minutes) or serial seizures. The use of rectal diazepam (Diastat) has proven to be safe when used properly and has helped reduce the number of ER visits. This drug can be given at home by the parents as directed by their child's physician.

Carbamazepine (Tegretol) is used for simple and complex partial seizures and generalized tonic/clonic seizures. It does not interfere negatively with behavior and learning and has no cosmetic side effects. Tegretol should be started at a low dose and increased each week for the first several weeks until the appropriate therapeutic blood level is reached. Side effects include drowsiness, dizziness, blurred vision, lethargy, nausea/vomiting, lack of coordination, decreased white blood count, and decreased platelets. One good side effect of Tegretol is elevation of mood. Tegretol may make atypical absence worse.

Ethosuximide (Zarontin) is used for akinetic/atonic seizures and is most valuable in treating generalized absence seizures. It has no effect on partial seizures. Side effects include drowsiness, dizziness, GI upset, headache, hiccough, hyperactivity, and nausea/vomiting. Zarontin can cause allergic reactions, but these complications are very rare. In most cases, it is safe, well tolerated, and effective.

Gabapentin (Neurontin) is a well-tolerated "add on" medication for partial complex and generalized tonic/clonic seizures. It does not interfere with other medications, so it is helpful for those girls taking multiple drugs. It has a short duration of action necessitating multiple daily doses. The most common side effects are sedation, fatigue, dizziness, ataxia, nystagmus, headache, nausea, and weight gain.

Lamogitrine (Lamictal) is used for the treatment of partial and generalized seizures as a primary drug or as an "add on" drug, used in combination with other drugs. It should be used cautiously with Depakote/Depakene because of a possible likelihood of hypersensitivity reaction (skin rash). It is useful for patients who cannot control their seizures adequately with current medication or who experience unacceptable side effects. Side effects include skin rash, dizziness, headache, double vision and unsteadiness.

Seizures

Interactions with other antiepileptic drugs may alter its duration of action. From available studies it has been concluded that oxcarbazepine and lamotrigine do not affect cognitive function in healthy volunteers or in adults with newly diagnosed epilepsy.

Levetirarcetam (Keppra) is approved by the Food and Drug Administration as adjunctive treatment of partial seizures in adults. Effectiveness in generalized seizures has been reported. It has been successfully used in children. Side effects include somnolence and dizziness. Behavior problems are reported and may necessitate discontinuation.

Oxcarbazepine (Trileptal) is chemically related to carbamazepine. Oxcarbazepine is approved for the treatment of partial seizures in adults and children aged 4 years and older. Side effects associated with this antiepileptic drug include somnolence and ataxia. More severe side effects such as liver dysfunctions seen with carbamazepine are not reported for oxcarbazepine.

Phenytoin (Dilantin) is used for tonic/clonic and simple and complex partial seizures. This drug can cause allergic reactions, so if a skin rash develops after the first two to three weeks, the child should be seen by the physician immediately. Dilantin may cause mood changes and lethargy. Overgrowth of the gums reportedly occurs in about half of the children who have therapeutic blood levels. When taken over a long period of time, Dilantin can cause the development of coarse facial features and more extensive growth of body hair. Side effects include tremor, anemia, loss of coordination, double vision, nausea/vomiting, confusion, and slurred speech.

Phenobarbital (Luminal) is used for tonic/clonic and simple and complex partial seizures. Phenobarbital is ineffective for absence seizures. Since it is metabolized slowly, it is usually given only once per day. Allergic reactions are possible, so the child should be observed carefully for skin rashes. The most important adverse side effects are in behavior and learning. Other side effects include drowsiness, lethargy, and hyperactivity, which can result in changes in behavior and learning.

Primidone (Mysoline) is used for tonic/clonic and simple and partial complex seizures. It is metabolized by the body into phenobarbital. The child should be carefully observed as the drug can cause hyperactivity and behavior problems. To avoid sedative effects and personality changes, Mysoline must be started at a low dose and increased very slowly over several weeks. Side effects include drowsiness, appetite loss, irritability, nausea/vomiting, dizziness, and loss of coordination.

Tiagabine (Gabatril) appears to be an effective antiepileptic drug for partial seizures but may exacerbate certain types of generalized seizures. Its use is limited by short duration of action, decreased rate of absorption when given with food, and lower levels in the evening than in the morning. Side effects include generalized weakness, cognitive disturbances, and depression.

Topiramate (Topamax) is used for partial or partial complex seizures and generalized seizures. It may also be useful for difficult-to-control generalized seizures (atonic) and infantile spasms. When Topamax is combined with Dilantin, the dose of Dilantin may need to be increased. If Dilantin or Tegretol is added or withdrawn, the dose of Topamax may need adjustment. Side effects include lethargy, agitation, headaches, drowsiness, lack of coordination, nervousness, dizziness, and arm/leg tingling. At higher doses, loss of appetite and weight loss can be seen. Side effects include confusion, psychomotor slowing, and difficulty with concentration. It is important to observe closely for the risk of kidney stones and maintain adequate hydration. Oligohidrosis (decreased sweating),

Seizures

infrequently resulting in hospitalization, has been reported in association with Topamax use. Decreased sweating and an elevation in body temperature above normal characterized these cases. Some of the cases were reported after exposure to elevated environmental temperatures. The majority of the reports have been in children. Patients, especially pediatric patients, treated with Topamax should be monitored closely for evidence of decreased sweating and increased body temperature, especially in hot weather. Caution should be used when Topamax is prescribed with other drugs that predispose patients to heat-related disorders; these drugs include, but are not limited to, other carbonic anhydrase inhibitors and drugs with anticholinergic activity.

Valproic acid (Depakene) and **Divalproex Sodium** (Depakote) are used for tonic/clonic, absence and myoclonic, and simple and complex partial seizures. These two drugs seem to work better after the child has taken them for a couple of weeks. When either of these drugs is stopped, it continues to work for several weeks. Each of these are very safe drugs, but should be used with caution in children under the age of two, and preferably alone. Side effects include nausea/vomiting, indigestion, sedation, dizziness, hair loss, tremor, lack of coordination, weight loss and/or gain, and changes in liver function.

Zonisamide (Zonegran) has been used for the treatment of a broad spectrum of seizure types including generalized seizures (tonic/clonic, absence, infantile spasms and myoclonic seizures) and all partial seizures. Side effects include somnolence, cognitive problems, and anhydrosis (lack of sweating).

Seizure medication should never be stopped abruptly. Your child should continue with her medication even if she has not had a seizure for quite a while. She may continue to be at risk for having seizures. She will not become dependent on the drug; anticonvulsant medications are not addicting. If she can keep control of the seizures for a number of years, she may be able to be taken off these medications without recurrent seizures. But stopping the drug must always be done slowly and with a doctor's careful supervision.

Over time, we built Jenn up to dosages of 800 mg Tegretol, 200 mg Phenobarbital, and 20cc Zarontin in one day just to control the seizure activity. Now, Jenn needs only 5cc of Tegretol per day.

GENERIC OR BRAND NAME

ABSORPTION RATES OF ANTICONVULSANT MEDICATIONS may vary with different manufacturers and there may also be some difference in their metabolism. This may cause varying blood levels, which may either allow seizures to occur or lead to toxicity. Using brand name drugs instead of the cheaper generic forms helps avoid these problems. And, always stick to the brand made by the same manufacturer.

VITAMINS AND CALCIUM

THE ADDITION OF VITAMINS TO A BALANCED DIET is of no value in the treatment of seizures. There is concern that AEDs may effect calcium metabolism and bone mineralization. This is not proven for RS. Supplementation with oral calcium should be done under the supervision of a physician.

MEASURING DRUG LEVELS

THE TERM "DRUG LEVEL" REFERS to the amount of medication in the blood. Drug levels are usually measured two to three weeks after a new drug is started or the dose changed. The amount of drug in the blood will indicate if she is in a therapeutic range and

Seizures

make sure her dose is not toxic. If there is toxicity, especially when she is on more than one drug, the blood test can help determine which drug should be decreased. In general, if the child seems to be doing well, blood levels are repeated once or twice a year.

OTHER TREATMENTS

KETOGENIC DIET

SPECIAL DIETS MAY BE RECOMMENDED by your daughter's physician as a last resort when anticonvulsants have proven ineffective. The ketogenic diet, one of the oldest treatments for epilepsy, is one which is very high in fat. The diet provides the minimal amount of protein necessary for growth and virtually no carbohydrates. Most of the calories consumed come from fat, using butter or cream. It is a very restrictive diet and can be difficult to begin and maintain. The diet simulates the effects of prolonged starvation by causing the body to burn fat rather than carbohydrate as its main energy source. The ketone bodies, which are the result of this fat metabolism, are utilized as an energy source by the brain. Why this results in improved seizure control is unknown.

The diet begins with several days of fasting. *The ketogenic diet must never be attempted except under strict medical supervision* and by a team which can provide support for the family during the difficult period of adjustment after the diet is initiated. The diet can be dangerous if not done properly. Food on the diet is strictly limited and not always appealing. A typical meal might consist of a small amount of meat, fish, poultry or cheese, a serving of fruit, an additional serving of fat such as butter or mayonnaise and a serving of heavy whipping cream. While some say the family ends up eating in the closet and the diet is too restrictive, others say the effort is worth it when seizures are under control for the first time. The diet should be given a four to six week trial with ketosis well maintained. If seizure frequency is significantly reduced, the diet can be maintained and an attempt try to reduce and stop AEDs made.

Katie has been on the ketogenic diet for almost two years now with wonderful results. However, when she gets sick, she can sometimes have breakthrough seizures.

Potential side effects include reduction in bone mass, kidney stones and thinning of the hair. Increases in plasma lipids have been reported, but their significance is not clear.

Sugar-free supplements of multivitamins and calcium need to be provided. Medicines such as antibiotics and daily used substances like toothpaste must be monitored for carbohydrate/sugar intake.

The majority of children with few seizures will achieve seizure control with one medication. When the first medication fails to control the seizures, a second medication is added. The ketogenic diet should be considered only for children who have more than two seizures per week despite treatment with at least two different anticonvulsant medications. The diet may also be used when the frequency of seizures, despite medications, interferes with the child's daily function, or when serious adverse side effects result from medications.

The decision about whether to use the ketogenic diet should be made by informed parents and their physician. The diet is not a cure-all, nor is it intended for everyone with epilepsy.

A form of diet less disruptive to family eating is the MCT diet, in which a special oil is added and she can eat most foods. Still, at least sixty percent of calories must come from fats and carbohydrates must be limited.

Seizures

Meghan had amazing success on the diet. Her seizures were cured from it—no meds, normal diet now. It wasn't easy but it was worth it. Meg didn't seem to mind it too much. She wasn't happy to give up McDonald's nuggets, but she did OK. It can be very tough for a child who is able to feed herself, but I think sometimes as a parent you have to look at the big picture and realize the two years of restrictions and unhappiness are worth it in the long run if you get a cure. You will know in a couple months if it will work.

We did the ketogenic diet for two and a half years. It gave Angela a ninety-five percent improvement in seizure control. Angela developed a rare side effect on the diet that forced her to discontinue. But were it not for that, I'd have her back on the diet in a heartbeat. It isn't easy, it is stressful, it's a huge commitment, but for all that, it is very worth the benefits we saw. We got to have our girl "back" for a whole year and it was probably the happiest time in our lives.

VAGUS NERVE STIMULATOR

THE VAGUS NERVE STIMULATOR (VNS) is a device that is implanted under the skin of the chest with wires that wrap around the left vagus nerve in the neck. It is used to control seizures that are unresponsive to traditional anticonvulsant medications. The VNS sends electrical signals that are applied to the vagus nerve in the neck for transmission to the brain. The vagus nerve is one of the primary communication lines from the major organs of the body to the brain. When parents, caregivers, or teachers sense that a seizure is imminent, they pass a magnet over the VNS generator in the chest, which activates a painless electrical stimulation, thus interrupting the seizure. The most common side effects include hoarseness, a prickling feeling on the skin, shortness of breath, and increased coughing. These side effects diminish over time. As with any surgery, there is a risk of infection. Benefits include reduction in seizures and reduction in AEDs.

Julianna's VNS was turned on and she didn't appear to feel a thing. When the neurologist stimulated her for the second time and tried the magnet on her, she didn't even flinch. I can't even tell when it is going off.

Desire had no trouble at all with the surgery and went home the same day. They waited two weeks after surgery to turn it on. The only negative side effect was mild coughing when we used the magnet, but that stopped after the first two weeks. The other side effects were increased energy, increased focus, and the return of her personality. It was pretty awesome. When we had the implant done, Desire was averaging between fifty to seventy small seizures a day and a seizure requiring Diastat every other day. After all of the adjustments, she has now been seizure-free for two weeks.

The VNS is helping Alexis. It is not a quick fix and it takes some time for it to work. I do see a difference in the amount of seizures a day; they are much less than before the implant. Alexis still has one or two through the night. I would tell anyone considering the VNS that it is a personal choice for family and your daughters. For us, it has been a roller coaster ride so far. It takes a great deal out of us caring for her, but it is more the seizures causing the care and the problems, not the VNS. The better side is less seizures and no drugs, so that is a good thing.

STATUS EPILEPTICUS

A SEIZURE THAT LASTS A VERY LONG TIME (thirty minutes or more) is referred to as *status epilepticus* (SE). "Convulsive status epilepticus" refers to tonic/clonic seizures, and "nonconvulsive status epilepticus" refers to an episode of absence spells, staring spells, or periods of confusion that last for more than a half hour. In most children who have SE, the cause is not known. The most common cause of convulsive status in a person who already has seizures is a blood drug level which is too low to control seizures.

Seizures

Status epilepticus may occur from missed doses, interaction with another drug that has interfered with the drug's effectiveness, or substitution of a generic drug that is not well absorbed in the bloodstream.

Very prolonged SE can cause brain damage. However, it may not be the seizures themselves, but the underlying cause of the seizures, such as infection, trauma, or tumors that may cause brain damage. Most children with SE recover without significant new deficits.

When convulsive SE occurs, it is important to bring the seizures to an end as quickly as possible. Most likely, this will take place in the emergency room of the hospital. Here, she will be observed, blood will be drawn, and oxygen will be given if needed. She will probably get an IV (intravenous line) to supply fluids and to give AEDs into the vein if it becomes necessary. This is the fastest way to get medicine to the brain where it is needed. A number of medications may be used, but Ativan and Valium, which are quick-acting AEDs, are usually given first. Their effectiveness may wear off quickly and another seizure may occur. An additional drug such as phosphenytoin (IV Dilantin) is then given, which is slower to start acting but lasts longer.

Most of the time, the SE can be controlled within a half hour to an hour of arrival at the hospital. In prolonged cases, it may be necessary to give large doses of medication or general anesthesia, which usually stops the seizures. While these episodes are frightening to watch, most children recover well and do not have lasting damage, even from prolonged seizures.

When nonconvulsive SE occurs, it is more difficult to detect because it does not involve body movements. The child may seem detached or just "not herself." The only way to know if nonconvulsive status is happening is to do an EEG, which will show constant spike-wave abnormalities. It is treated with AEDs given into the vein, and the child then returns to her normal state.

FINAL THOUGHTS

THE GOALS OF TREATING SEIZURES include:

1. To identify epileptic seizures and to distinguish them from non-epileptic behaviors.
2. To prevent further seizures, especially prolonged or frequently recurring seizures, in order that the individual can enjoy the best quality of life, and do all that she is capable of without untoward side effects from the treatment, particularly oversedation, adverse behavior, or cognitive dysfunction, and motor impairments.
3. Use the most effective treatment with the least side effects and expense.
4. Maintain her seizure free for a period of time sufficient (often two-three years) to be able to discontinue (slowly) the treatment and have her remain seizure free.
5. To improve not only the quality of life the girl with RS but also that of her family.

"I exist as I am, and that is enough."

– WALT WHITMAN

Motor Problems

MOVEMENT IN RETT SYNDROME

THE STEREOTYPED HAND movements seen in RS include the characteristic washing, wringing, mouthing, rubbing, clapping and/or tapping which are almost constant while awake. These movements are neurological and are not under the girl's control. She can no longer stop the hand movements at will than she can stop breathing at will.

Other movements are learned and can become automatic, like lifting her arm to put on her shirt and stepping up a curb. We all do these things without consciously thinking about them.

Still other motor movements are those which derive from emotional involvement with the task—whether it is a wish, need, discomfort, necessity, or compulsion. These movements arise from emotional excitement and are not consciously controlled by her. She may not be able to perform when given directions, but performs automatically because of her strong motivation. You may ask her to pick up the glass and she cannot. Yet, if she is very thirsty, she may be able to suddenly pick up the glass skillfully and drink it without spilling a drop. She is as surprised as you are, and if you ask her to repeat the action, she is unable to do so. This can happen with speech, when out of the blue she blurts an appropriate word, never to repeat it again. Again, she acted without thinking.

> *"Challenges are gifts that force us to search for a new center of gravity. Don't fight them. Just find a different way to stand."*
>
> – OPRAH WINFREY

RANGE OF MOTOR ABILITY

THERE IS A WIDE RANGE OF MOTOR ABILITY SEEN IN RS. Some girls will never learn to walk while others can continue to walk for decades. Some girls have almost no hand skills while others can perform some purposeful use. The severity of motor symptoms is determined by the genetic mutation and the time of regression as well as the child's general health and stamina.

MOTOR PROBLEMS

APRAXIA

MOTOR APRAXIA IS THE INABILITY to plan and carry out a motor response; it is the inability to coordinate thought and movement. Motor apraxia is perhaps the most fundamental handicap seen in RS as it involves all body movement, including speech and eye gaze. While the girl with RS does not necessarily lose the ability to move her body, she

Motor Problems

loses the ability to tell her body how and when to move. She may have a desire and a will to perform a specific movement, but is incapable of carrying it through.

Leah has under-registration of input and difficulty preparing muscles to initiate an action. This may be contributing to her lack of task initiation. She does have a drive for information to the muscles and joints and it is expressed as teeth grinding. Leah may be doing this to help increase her postural stability.

While apraxia refers to the *inability* to coordinate thought and movement, dyspraxia is less severe, referring to *difficulty* coordinating thought and movement. Both terms are applied in describing RS.

Motor apraxia/dyspraxia makes it difficult for a girl to perform purposeful movement. She may want very much to reach for an object or climb into a chair, and yet it may take her quite a while to organize the action. In some cases, it may be impossible for her to plan and carry out even seemingly simple movements. When she is able to reach out, for example, she may overreach or underreach. She may push against something too hard or not hard enough. The apraxia is more evident when she is in unfamiliar situations and becomes even more difficult when she is asked to follow directions. The more she has to think about what to do, the more difficulty she has in performing. She may see something she wants across the room, desire to move toward the object, and end up turning in circles instead. She may want to take a toy from the shelf, but end up knocking it onto the floor.

Apraxia is impossible to overcome, but possible to minimize by understanding and putting her movements into perspective. Much of what seems to be aimless or unintentional movement may actually be purposeful action gone wrong. She may stare at an object intently, hyperventilate, rock back and forth and wring her hands, all in getting "geared up" to move. Often, she looks at the object, and then looks away before she reaches or moves. When she does move, she may not be successful in doing what she wanted at all, or she may move in the wrong way. It is most frustrating for both parent and child, but paying careful attention to her body signals is beneficial in helping her to be successful. Look for consistent behaviors and try to interpret her signals. In rare situations, she can momentarily overcome the apraxia, particularly when she is emotionally motivated. This happens when she moves automatically, without thinking about how to move. Examples of this are scratching an itch, reaching out to grab a cookie, or blurting out a word in joy or distress. To help minimize the apraxia, look for activities with emotional incentives that will reward her with success, so that she can "do" before she has to "think."

Lauren took me to her favorite toy, which was partially hidden on a lower shelf and she really wanted to get it out. She stood there holding my hand and moving her other arm and hand back and forth while looking at the toy. Finally I told her, "You need to bend over to get it" and she immediately did so. With a little physical help and three to four reminders to bend, she got her toy. Often I find I must remind her of each movement she needs to take. Otherwise, she's totally stuck.

Sherry can scratch an itch, or reach out and push my arm away when I'm doing something she doesn't like. The other day she was having a leg cramp in the bath and I wouldn't have known it except that she pinched me pretty hard to get my attention! But when it comes to conscious actions, like when she's staring at an object intently like she wants it, she seems to be unable to translate that desire into action.

Apraxia involves almost all movements and behaviors of those with RS. It does not affect intelligence. In fact, it hides intelligence, because it makes it difficult for us to determine what

Motor Problems

she knows when she cannot use gestures such as pointing or signing to indicate her understanding. Even if she is given extra time to complete a task, the apraxia may prevent her from acting or indicating that she understands.

I believe Amanda does well with behavioral training because she is apraxic, and apraxic children do better when the focus is one on one in environments that are very rewarding and repetitive. We spend as much time with Amanda as we can, but it is difficult after so many years to keep up this pace.

BALANCE

BESIDES AN UNBALANCED GAIT, SHE HAS DIFFICULTY with upper body weight bearing. Her protective responses (putting out her arms to catch herself in a fall) are usually poor. Backward protective response reactions are often delayed or absent.

As you learn to read her body signals and her own private language of movement, reward her with praise for her intentions. Explain that you know how hard it is for her to succeed, and praise her for each little step toward the goal. Assume that she understands what you have to say, acknowledging at the same time that she may be incapable of complete success. Use of augmentative communication devices and switches can greatly enhance her ability to communicate and succeed. Seize the moment by providing activities that are motivating.

SPATIAL DISORIENTATION

SPATIAL DISORIENTATION OCCURS when she cannot correctly perceive the "upright" position of her body. In order for her to feel that she is upright, she leans forward, backward, or to the side. There is less interference with walking if she leans forward, but this may eventually affect her posture and lead to kyphosis. It can lead to loss of ambulation due to an inability to shift weight forward to initiate steps.

The treatment that has been utilized is an over-correction procedure, taking her into the spaces that frighten her. She should be physically and emotionally supported through this procedure. Start with her lying horizontally on her side, back or stomach for up to thirty minutes and progress to partially upright on a wedge, ball, or the therapist's lap. Continue to advance by placing her feet on the floor while leaning into the corrected direction.

ATAXIA

ATAXIA, A DISRUPTION OF BALANCE, is often the earliest motor problem seen in RS. It leads the joints to become temporarily fixed or locked into a position of stability. This reduces the girl's mobility in changing from one position to another. Due to ataxia, the legs are often far apart both standing and sitting, and weight shift from one leg to another is difficult. Moving her may cause extreme distress at fear of falling, but movements she makes on her own are not upsetting. Her righting reactions (ability to return to upright when placed off balance) and equilibrium responses may be slowed and ineffective. Movements in RS are often described as jerky truncal ataxia, the shaky movements that occur when she tries to keep her balance.

Weighted vests and belts are used to decrease ataxia. Segmental rolling is used, rolling her over where there is a twisting between her shoulders and hips. This activity helps to stabilize balance. The therapy ball and floor activities can also be used to stimulate the balance system. Repetitive practice of various activities which promote weight shift and rotation in functional movement skills are helpful.

Motor Problems

TREMORS

JERKY TREMORS ARE OFTEN SEEN IN RS. They often resemble a seizure, but are not. They can occur when the child awakens from sleep or when she is excited or frightened. They also occur when she goes off balance. They can involve the trunk or the extremities.

One of Jessica's biggest problems in the last few years has been her tremors. It is a combination of breathing erratically, shaking all over and jerking in spasms, some of which go from one arm to the other and across the chest at once, like an electrical shock, just pulsing, zap, zap, zap. When it is bad like this it interferes with eating, daily activity, and of course, sleep. Sometimes it's on and off for most of her day. We found through our neurologist and a couple of twenty-four-hour video EEGs that this is not classified as a "seizure" even though it looks like a seizure. She is confused and upset. There is nothing we can do except "holding therapy," which works some of the time. I hold her from the front with both arms around her and just try to stabilize her shaking. We talk about relaxing and breathing easy. Sometimes laughing spells tie into it, especially at night. It all goes together. Just an overload of brain signals.

MUSCLE TONE

HYPOTONIA

IN A HEALTHY NERVOUS SYSTEM, the muscles are sent messages instructing them to either tighten or relax to a certain degree. This allows us to move freely while at the same time maintaining an upright position against gravity. Hypotonia is decreased or "floppy" muscle tone and is the result of a neurological problem, not a lack of exercise. It is difficult for the hypotonic child to move efficiently as she is generally weak and has poor endurance.

HYPERTONIA

SOMETIMES, MUSCLES ARE TOO TIGHT, or hypertonic. These muscles are difficult to stretch or elongate and this makes movement difficult. Hypertonic muscles are frequently referred to as being spastic and in severe cases can lead to contractures. If the muscles are too "floppy" or too tight, movement can be difficult and abnormal movement patterns emerge. These can be very difficult to correct once they are established.

In many cases, girls with RS start out hypotonic but later become hypertonic during their school years. It is not uncommon to have mixed tone in which some muscles are too tight while some are too loose. This results in structural problems such as scoliosis, which occurs when muscles on one side of the trunk pull harder than the muscles on the other side.

SPASTICITY

SPASTICITY IS MUSCLE TONE that is abnormally high and results in muscle tightness that can make normal movements difficult. Spasticity is not usually seen until the school years. It may only be a slight increase in muscle tone which leads to toe-walking, or may be a more severe increase in muscle tone involving the whole body affecting even respiration and swallowing, and leading to scoliosis, or curvature of the spine. It may also lead to contractures, irreversible shortening of muscle fibers that causes decreased joint mobility.

Severe contractures, particularly in the ankle and elbow joints, can develop in spite of regular weekly home and school therapy.

Motor Problems

RIGIDITY

RIGIDITY OCCURS WHEN THE MUSCLE BECOMES STIFF CONTINUOUSLY.
Treatment for muscle spasticity and rigidity involves activities which reduce muscle tone and can provide temporary help for rotation, weight shift and weight bearing. Both gentle heat and therapeutic massage can also be useful in helping to relax tight muscles. When using heat, however, it's important to be cautious as many of the girls have impaired sensation and burns can accidentally occur.

Muscle relaxants are sometimes used to control spasticity and rigidity. These include diazepam (Valium) and baclofen (Lioresal). Botulinim toxin (Botox) injections can be used to stop muscle spasms. It takes about a week to ten days for the Botox to take effect, and the treatment lasts from a few weeks to a few months.

Stephanie has had four Botox treatments over the last two years. Her hamstrings and adductors (inside thigh muscles) were very tight. When she stood, her knees were bent and turned inward. She was in extreme pain when trying to stand, transition, and it was so sad. After Botox, she stands straight up, walks two hundred feet plus in her walker (she is not normally ambulatory by herself), and is so much more happy ... she can move! Just make sure you have a very experienced, qualified doctor who is doing the procedure. It is painless. We are given Emla cream to put all over her legs an hour before the procedure to numb the area, and Steph never says a peep. The whole procedure lasts about a minute or even less.

We have had Edie's heel cords and hamstrings injected with Botox and also did the casting. Unfortunately, we didn't have much success. She did become much more flexible, but it only lasted for a couple of weeks. In my opinion, it wasn't worth what we went through for that limited amount of time. We were diligent with stretching and increased PT, but it just didn't work for us.

Baclofen can be given orally or intrathecally (directly into the spine). Oral and intrathecal baclofen can have potential side effects. Some side effects include dizziness, drowsiness, headaches, nausea, and weakness. When given intrathecally, there are fewer side effects, but this method does require a minor surgical invasive procedure. Oral Baclofen is usually tried first. If there is too much sedation or other side effects, the Baclofen pump is tried.

The Baclofen pump delivers the medication directly into the spinal fluid through a catheter (a small, flexible tube) and a pump. The pump is a round metal disc, about one inch thick and three inches in diameter. It is surgically placed under the skin of the abdomen near the waistline. The pump stores and releases prescribed amounts of medication through the catheter. Using an external programmer, adjustments can be made to the dose, rate and timing of the medication. Patients must return to their doctor's office for pump refills and medication adjustments, typically every two to three months. The pump is taken out and replaced at the end of the battery's life span (which is usually five to seven years).

DYSTONIA

DYSTONIA IS AN ALTERATION IN MUSCLE TONE which causes cramps or spasms of muscles close to the midline of the body (neck, shoulders, hips), but in RS it is also seen in the legs and feet. It can be very painful, and often goes unnoticed until the cramps are witnessed. Treatment commonly consists of using medications, such as Klonipin/Clonazepam, which is very effective. Dystonia can range from mild to very severe and debilitating.

Motor Problems

Jamie had severe dystonia when she was eleven. It started out as a slight leaning and progressed to an arching in her back. I was very concerned about it causing her scoliosis to worsen. Jamie went from walking independently to not being able to stand. Then she lost crawling and sitting and within six months, she could no longer even swallow properly and just laid on the floor in a backward arching position and pleading with me with her eyes to help. This was extremely difficult for me to even bear to watch my child go through! I really began to believe that she was dying, losing so many skills in such a short amount of time. We tried a number of drugs that didn't help, and finally tried Klonipin/Clonazepam and it began to work. She did regain walking independently for about two years.

MOTOR MILESTONES

CRAWLING

MOST INFANTS WITH RS DO NOT ACHIEVE a traditional reciprocal crawl (when the left hand and arm move forward, the right leg comes forward, and vice versa). This is due to the difficulty girls have with the kind of motor coordination that is required for crawling. Most girls have different crawling patterns, such as "scooting," "rolling" or "bunny hopping," which do not require coordinated use of the hands. Most girls begin these movements later than usual. Girls who graduate to walking usually discontinue crawling, which is actually more difficult.

SITTING

MOST GIRLS ARE ABLE TO ACHIEVE INDEPENDENT SITTING, but low muscle tone may interfere with her ability to sit without support. At a later age, the development of severe scoliosis can pose problems with balance when sitting.

WALKING

IT IS DIFFICULT TO PREDICT WHICH GIRLS will walk and which will not. In general, those with the poorest muscle tone have more difficulty walking. However, girls have been known to walk for the first time as late as sixteen years of age. So don't give up easily! Weight-bearing exercises, physical therapy with range of motion exercises and practice walking should be done regularly. With proper motivation, support, and encouragement, some girls with RS are able to continue to walk independently for decades.

Most girls do not run and almost all have difficulty going up and (especially) down stairs. Their gait is awkward and clumsy, usually with the legs wide apart and stiff. Balance is difficult.

In addition to their motor handicaps, girls with RS have apraxia, sensory and perceptual problems, difficulties shifting from one movement to another and lack of coordination. These combine to make walking a difficult task. As they get older, other problems such as scoliosis, increased muscle tone, and decreased tactile perception (feeling) in their cold, swollen feet make walking difficult.

Megan never walked as a baby, but she did pull up in her bed. Shortly after she accomplished that, the regression started and she never walked. She also never crawled. She gets around on the floor by rolling and scooting on her back. She does love to be on her feet and I have assumed she is too old to learn to walk. But there is a spark inside me motivating me to continue trying to get her to walk. When she stands, she doesn't seem to understand how to pick up her feet to take steps most of the time. Then at times she has actually taken more than one or two steps with support.

Motor Problems

KEEPING HER UPRIGHT

IT IS OF SIGNIFICANT IMPORTANCE TO HER continued health to keep her on her feet and walking as long as possible, even for a short time every day. Once walking is lost, a number of problems can worsen, such as scoliosis, osteoporosis, and problems with breathing and digestion. To maintain her body in a standing position, she has to use her hypotonic trunk muscles. Being in a standing position lets her take deeper breaths and bearing weight helps maintain bone density.

SUPPORTED WALKING

MANY GIRLS CAN WALK WITH SUPPORT, either by partially holding her or using a walker. It is good to "practice" walking, even if she does not become independent.

You may find that if she is an independent walker, she may actually walk better with less assistance. When both hands are held, some girls tend to depend on someone else, leaning instead of walking straight. So, sometimes it is better to use a hand on the shoulder to steady her or to hold only one hand if possible.

WALKERS

WALKERS COME IN VARIOUS TYPES AND SIZES according to her needs. Some have seats to "catch" her when she needs to sit down. Others do not have a seat, but rely on her to hold the handles to stay upright. This may be difficult, as it may call for her to maintain grasp for longer than she is capable. If this is the case, creative genius can usually come up with a way to secure her hands to the handles with gloves, mittens, elastic bandage tape or Velcro.

Kayla used to only walk with push toys but she refused to walk alone. One day, her teacher held a broom up and made Kayla hold on to it and walk while she held the top. When Kayla felt safe, she let go of the broom and just started walking holding the broom straight up in the air. After that I thought she might be attached to a broom for life but after about a week, she lost the broom and walked alone.

Allison learned to walk at six years after significant intense physical therapy in the home. I turned one of our bedrooms into a "gym" for her PT, and installed a homemade ladder of one inch dowels that Allie would use to learn her crossing pattern. With her hands on the rungs we would move left hand, right foot, right hand, left foot, and so on. Mom would take the hands and I the feet, or vice versa. We made a game out of it, several times a day. Allie actually enjoyed it once she got used to the game. I don't remember how long it actually took, but in a few months Allie was walking if someone held her hand. She now walks all over the house on her own.

TRANSITIONAL MOVEMENTS

TRANSITIONAL SKILLS ARE THOSE MOVEMENTS which allow us to change position, such as rolling, getting to sit, pulling to stand, etc. Sitting and standing when placed are skills which are kept longer. Strong extensor muscle activity in legs and back, spinal rigidity, lack of upper extremity weight bearing, a disturbance in spatial orientation, and inability to grade movement are factors that contribute to loss of transitional skills.

Transitions are as important as walking. Girls who have retained the ability to walk should have an opportunity to practice transitions daily. Girls who are unable to perform transitions by themselves should be led through the motions with verbal and physical

Motor Problems

help. This will help maintain mobility and reduce the amount of lifting required by the caretaker. Again, apraxia rears its ugly head, as learning transitional movements is a major motor planning feat.

With the girl seated on a therapy ball, the therapist attempts to elicit righting and equilibrium responses. During this activity, the therapist controls the speed, direction, duration, and delivery of the movement to encourage active responses into flexion and rotation. The activity must be carefully geared to the child's level of tolerance. Range of motion, strength and tolerance for these postures are developed.

The therapist should practice functional transition activities while giving verbal direction with reassurance and physical assistance. Getting a child onto all fours is possible even with a girl who has a strong objection to being prone, if she is reassured that the therapist will protect her face in case the hand wringing interferes with her ability to maintain weight bearing on her hands.

When a girl fears falling forward, leaning forward to stand up can be very difficult. When the therapist pushes her forward, she reinforces her pushing backward. To help alleviate this problem, the child can be seated on a bench, which is then tipped back forcing equilibrium reactions to get hip flexion. The child should be assisted to stay flexed as the bench returns to the upright position. This helps her tolerate the forward movement that she fears due to her spatial disorientation. When her tolerance is increased, she will then actively shift forward to pull to standing.

"I cannot do everything, but I can still do something.
I will not refuse to do the something I can do."

– HELEN KELLER

Orthopedics

MUSCLE CONTROL AND COORDINATION

THE ABILITY TO GROW STRAIGHT
and tall and to walk normally depends upon normal
muscle balance, tone, and coordination. We often do
not think that muscles are important in how the body
grows and develops, but they are. It is really the control of those muscles which is critical. This control is
determined by that amazing biologic computer, the
nervous system. RS may affect the development and
function of the back and arms because of defects in
muscle control and coordination.

*"Don't
give up.
Don't
lose hope.
Don't
sell out."*

– CHRISTOPHER REEVE

DEFORMITIES

EVERY GIRL WITH RS IS DIFFERENT;
you know this from experience. This means that a doctor cannot predict with certainty
what will happen to a particular child. However, he can give some patterns and examples
and maybe give an approximate guess as to what might happen in the future.

Because of the abnormal muscle coordination, some muscles are overactive and pull
certain joints out of balance. This happens most commonly about the ankle and hip. In
the ankle, excessive pull of muscles which push down may cause the foot to be pointing
straight down or down and in. If this does not interfere with balance or cause calluses, it
may be left alone. Often it does, so there are numerous ways to treat it.

The most common deformities seen in RS involve the spine. Scoliosis involves a twisting and side-bending of the spine. Kyphosis involves a forward arching or lean of the spine.
These problems develop in as many as one-half of girls with RS. If mild, they cause no problem. Bracing may help in some patients to keep the curves from getting worse, but we are
still not sure how successful this is. At any rate, all girls with RS should be checked for spinal
curvature during the yearly physical.

AMBULATION

AMBULATION OR WALKING IS A SKILL which also requires a certain level
of coordination. Most children with RS are able to walk, but some never gain this ability
and some lose it. Walking helps to keep bones strong and the muscles, heart, and lungs
in shape. It is good to encourage walking in those who have the ability, but virtually
impossible to teach if the coordination is not present. It is a good idea to motivate girls to
walk regularly and do as much as they can for themselves. Walking is a marker or a sign
in this sense: persons who are not able to walk will have to be checked more thoroughly
for spinal curvature, hip dislocation, and fractures.

OSTEOPOROSIS

OSTEOPOROSIS IS VERY COMMON IN RS, and should be monitored by an
endocrinologist often as the girl grows. This condition should be suspected mainly in

Orthopedics

children who do not stand by themselves or who have had a fracture. Bone density is affected by medication and children on some anticonvulsants or who are nonambulatory are at increased risk. Diagnosis of osteoporosis is made by a DEXA scan, an X-ray method to measure bone mineral density.

It is still unclear if calcium supplements alone will combat osteoporosis in RS. If a child is getting a normal amount of calcium in the diet, it is clear that supplements are not necessary.

Medications such as Fosamax may be helpful in the majority of cases. In those with very severe osteoporosis, Pamidronate may be used. IV infusion is done in a one to three day hospital stay (depending on the hospital), and is repeated every few months over a period of several years. This treatment helps the calcium stay inside the bones and puts a coating over the bones to make them stronger. In addition, oral calcium supplements are needed to keep calcium in the bloodstream. All of this must be monitored by an endocrinologist. The treatment improves bone density, although it does not return to normal. The fracture rate should decrease. The treatment will probably not decrease the risk for scoliosis, because the scoliosis is due to the neurologic disorder, not to bone fragility.

Our daughter has just finished her seventh treatment with Pamidronate. We have seen great improvement and no more broken bones. I would recommend this option if it is recommended.

Our daughter could not sit for longer than a half hour due to her osteoporosis, and now she is very comfortable for long periods. She told us by using her picture symbols that she needed to lie down and rest her back. She also told us she was in back and bottom pain. Once she had rested on her side she told us she felt better and the pain was gone.

Christina has gone for Pamidronate infusions every three months for a year and a half now. She tolerates it well and there has been significant improvement in her bone density after a year of treatments.

FRACTURES

IN SPITE OF NORMAL INTESTINAL ABSORPTION OF CALCIUM and Vitamin D, girls with RS have low bone mineral content and decreased bone density (osteoporosis). Fractures can occur quite easily with minimal trauma. Weight-bearing and standing exercises help the bones maintain density and strength. Calcium intake should be encouraged. Because of her abnormal response to pain, it may be impossible to know that a fracture has occurred until there is swelling, bruising, or limping.

Michelle fractured her wrist one time; it took us a week to figure out where the pain was coming from. We would have never found the problem had she not had the bruising at the fracture site.

A while back we had a hand and wrist X-ray done on Lauren for bone age. They also found a healed wrist fracture. Lauren does walk and has had a variety of falls over the years. She tends to be quite a stoic about pain, breathing hard, and getting quiet when in the same situation her brother would have been crying for a long time. We had no idea when it happened.

Sammi had a bone scan yesterday and it showed a fracture of her tibia near the ankle in the growth plate. He said there were five levels of breaks and this was level one, the least. She will have a walking cast for six to eight weeks.

We went for Amelia's annual checkup and everything went well until X-ray time. The X-rays showed extreme bone loss in Amelia's feet and pelvis. I was shocked because I had no idea.

Orthopedics

TREATMENT FOR ORTHOPEDIC PROBLEMS

PHYSICAL AND OCCUPATIONAL THERAPIES

A THERAPIST CAN HELP A PARENT realize the most of a girl's abilities. Such a professional can help parents to understand what is reasonable to expect from a child or adult. They can help to maximize independence. Also, a therapist is often the most knowledgeable about use of adaptive equipment which may help each person, and whether it fits and is used appropriately. A therapist is also trained to monitor for deformities and can help to tell if contractures, curvatures of the spine, or dislocations are happening. They are very helpful in regaining function after surgery. It is also important to understand, though, that each child has limits of achievement which are determined by her underlying neurological situation. As much as all professionals want girls to achieve a high level of function, it is also important to respect what is possible and not expend time and resources on goals which cannot be met at the expense of other aspects of school and family life. This type of understanding may require time and input from the parents, pediatrician, orthopedist or neurologist, and therapist.

BRACING

BRACES ARE OFTEN REFERRED TO IN THE MEDICAL FIELD as *orthoses*. They are preventive devices. They provide support if there is weakness, or prevent deformity. They do this by stretching or counteracting muscles which are acting abnormally. Unfortunately, they can never correct a deformity beyond the point to which it has developed. Any attempt to do this would cause pain or pressure sores. If a deformity is too great, it may not be possible to brace.

Some parts of the body are more easily braced than others for practical reasons. The knee and hip are almost impossible to brace. The spine, foot or ankle, and the hand are the most appropriate areas to brace. Bracing for spinal deformity can make it easier to sit and, in some cases, can prevent curves from worsening. Some curves will worsen anyway, so the use of braces in RS should be an individualized, try-and-see approach. Braces for the foot and ankle may help children to keep the foot flat and therefore stand or walk better. Any child wearing a brace, especially for the first time, should have the skin checked frequently to make sure no pressure problems are developing. Any time a brace is used, it should add to a child's overall function and well-being, not detract from it. A parent is in the best position to see this and should let the doctor know if it is making things worse.

We used a brace for the period of time when Rosemary seemed to be experiencing growth spurts. She has never been ambulatory. We then reduced to brace wearing only at night, and tried to compensate with PT exercises and side-lying positions to keep her flexible and counteract the curve. Did it help? Who knows? She is at about 38 degrees now and has been stable for a while, but we are no longer able to be as vigorous with the positioning and PT due to osteoporotic fracture risk. I felt the brace kept our Rosemary too removed from human touch, among other things.

BOTOX

BOTOX, OR BOTULINUM TOXIN, IS A MUSCLE RELAXANT purified from bacteria. It can "turn off" a muscle for period of about three months. It is given by injection. Different means are possible to numb the skin before it is given. It has several

Orthopedics

possible uses in RS: to counteract a newly developing contracture (not an established one), to delay surgery in a young child, to assist in rehabilitation or stretching, and to predict the effects of muscle-lengthening surgery. It does not seem to be able to prevent hip dislocations or correct stiff, established deformities. It has no known permanent side effects, but one to five percent of patients may develop temporary aching, temporary increase in weakness, or an allergy. It can be used more than once; the effect wears off each time after the three months or so is over. It is very expensive medication, so often specific approval is needed from the insurance company for its use.

My daughter Lyndie, fourteen, had eleven Botox injections in her paraspinal muscles. For us, it was almost more of a hassle getting the pre-op tests done (going here, there, and everywhere for ECG, blood work, physical, and then faxing results to the orthopedist) than the actual procedure itself. Once all that was squared away, the procedure was done in an operating room under general anesthesia. For Lyndie, it was really and truly no big deal. It took about forty-five minutes from start to finish, followed by about another forty-five minutes in recovery, and then discharge and home. Lyndie had a great day at home the same day, and was off to school the very next day without any side effects or pain. She really didn't skip a beat. Unfortunately, the Botox only lasted about four-and-a-half months. It greatly helped increase the flexibility of her spine, and enabled her brace to actually reduce some of her spinal curve. The most important thing is that Lyndie seemed to feel better when her back was more relaxed.

CHIROPRACTIC CARE

CHIROPRACTORS MANIPULATE THE VERTEBRAE of the spine and the joints and muscles of the body. This manipulation is felt to improve the flow of nerve impulses to the brain, which increases the body's ability to solve its health problems. Some of the techniques of massage and physical therapy used by chiropractors today are similar to those used by physical therapists.

ORTHOPEDIC SURGERY

ORTHOPEDIC SURGERY IS ALSO DIRECTED AT IMPROVING the person's overall function. Usually the decision whether to perform surgery requires input from the parent (who sees the person daily and in multiple environments) as well as the therapist and surgeon.

Foot and ankle deformities are corrected if they are impairing walking or standing and can't be treated by brace alone. Tendons can be lengthened and bones realigned or reshaped if necessary. Fusion of bones is sometimes done if there is no other way to preserve the alignment and shape. These are usually successful with a minimum of long-term complications.

Spine deformities can be successfully corrected, if it is decided that the deformity is causing pain or impairing the person's ability to sit comfortably, interact with the environment, or possibly distort the chest cavity. The spine is corrected using long rods which are shaped to the normal posture of a spine. They hold the spine in place and allow it to fuse in this straight position. Sometimes there are two parts to the surgery, with an operation in the front to free up the spine and promote fusion, as well as rods placed in the back. This surgery often requires five to seven days in the hospital. The risk to the spinal cord is fortunately only a few percent. Girls with RS often require several months to regain their comfort, energy, and personality. In the end, most families felt the surgery is worthwhile if the problem was severe. It is often helpful to talk to other families, therapists and physicians before making the decision. What is right for one person may not be right for another.

Orthopedics

THE FEET

THE FEET ARE OFTEN COLD, BLUISH-RED AND SMALL, due to inadequate circulation. Other foot problems in RS result from muscle imbalance. The most common is equinus, a downward pointing of the foot. This is due to tight or overactive heel cords. She may have valgus, when her heels are together and the toes apart, forming a V. Or she may have varus, when the toes point toward each other, making an A shape as she walks on the outside of her feet, but this is not as common. She may have pronation, walking on flat feet with her ankles appearing to collapse inwardly.

Lisa has swollen feet due to her limited mobility and weight. Lisa does walk, but she walks slowly and certainly doesn't get the kind of exercise a typical teenager would. She also walks very flat-footed, and so doesn't have that heel-toe motion that would help push fluids back up into her legs. Her feet have always been cold, so she doesn't have great blood return from her feet back to her heart, so fluids are pooling a bit in her feet. To counteract all of this, Lisa walks regularly throughout the day. She never sits with her feet down for prolonged periods, and we elevate her feet during the day. We also put higher socks on Lisa up to her knees so that her feet and ankles get gentle pressure and compression.

WALKING

THE GIRL WITH RS WALKS ON THE BALLS OF THE FEET rather than with the foot flat as normal. This may or may not hinder balance. In some cases it improves balance. If severe. It may also make shoe fitting more difficult. In the child who does not walk, contractures may interfere with supported standing in a prone stander.

ANKLE FOOT ORTHOSES (AFOs)

IF THE MUSCLES TO THE HEEL CORD ARE OVERACTIVE but not truly tight, a plastic ankle foot orthosis (AFO) brace may help hold the foot flat. Short leg braces and splints are often used along with physical therapy to maintain range of motion and to minimize involuntary movements that interfere with functioning. They also prevent contractures, which occur when muscles consistently have increased tone, keeping muscles in a shortened position which can severely limit movement. The brace maintains a specific muscle group in the desired position, which permits optimal use of the joint. If the heel cord is tight and the foot cannot be brought to a flat position, serial casts or heel cord release surgery may be necessary.

The brace consists of a custom-fitted molded plastic splint worn inside the shoe, which extends behind the calf. Decreasing the extension of muscles at the ankle may also help decrease muscle tone in the hips, allowing for sitting in a more stable position. This change of ankle position allows the child to stand with the foot flat, which improves her stability and support. Correction of her abnormal foot posture may also affect the position of her hips and knees when she stands, thus helping her to walk better. Braces and splints are custom-made and need to be changed as the child grows.

SERIAL CASTING

SERIAL CASTING IS SOMETIMES DONE TO REDUCE ankle contractures. The child's feet are fitted with a series of short leg casts which hold the foot in place over several weeks' time. The casts are removed, the feet stretched, and then the casts are

Orthopedics

reapplied and again removed. The constant stretch of the cast allows tight joints and tendons to relax over time.

The first casting is set with the foot in a neutral (ninety degree) position if this is possible. If not, the foot is taken to the end of the range and stretched just a little further. The subsequent castings will angle or stretch the foot upward a few degrees each time to achieve the desired outcome, a loose heel cord. Each casting may last from four days to two weeks at a time depending on the recommendation of your therapist, orthotist, podiatrist, or orthopedist.

Serial casting changes the structure of lengthening muscles. If a prolonged stretch is applied to a muscle and tendon, it will stretch a little. Then when it is stretched from the new position, further improvement will occur. It also works because the brain receives the constant feedback of a stretched heel cord and she learns the feeling of walking on corrected feet. The hope is that after the cast is finally removed, the effect may last three to six months, which is long enough for her to benefit from walking or therapeutic activities. If it is successful, you may begin the whole process over again and enjoy the continued benefits.

The positive side of this treatment is that the casts are temporary, the procedure is not surgical, and it leaves the heel cord intact. Casting is also cheaper and safer than surgery. On the downside, serial casting is not a remedy and will not work in every situation, especially if the tendon is very tight. Talk to your doctor or physical therapist. Because of the impaired circulation in her feet and legs, great care must be taken to prevent pressure sores under the casts. Extra padding and frequent cast changes will help.

SURGERY

FOOT SURGERY CAN BE USEFUL when severe joint deformities or contractures have developed. A surgical procedure can increase the range of motion through releasing, lengthening, or transferring affected muscles. When the heel cord is tight, the child walks on her toes. Heel cord lengthening at the ankle may assist walking by giving her a more flat-footed gait. The heel cord is cut in a way that can be lengthened and allowed to heal in a cast. There are many ways to do this. A hamstring release, lengthening, or muscle transfer around the knee may also promote better walking.

Careful evaluation should precede surgery, which always has risks and benefits. While surgery may increase mobility and help avoid painful osteoarthritis (joint inflammation), there may be complications or the surgical intervention may be less than successful. Discuss the risks and benefits with your child's physician.

She will be discharged either the same day or up to a few days later, depending on how she has done. The feet should be elevated for two days and checked for swelling. She may bear weight according to her own tolerance after one or two weeks. The cast stays on for six to eight weeks. Extra care must be taken to prevent pressure sores. A brace is then fitted to prevent the contracture from recurring. This periodic immobility should not decrease her ability to walk if she is encouraged to walk within one to two weeks after surgery in her casts.

SHOES

SOMETIMES ORTHOTICS MAKE THE FITTING OF SHOES more difficult, since they add width to the dimension of the foot without adding length. Things are even harder if the foot is wide to begin with. Here are some suggestions: An articulated (hinged) orthotic is the widest of all. If you are using this, see if your child really needs this

Orthopedics

feature. Use a low-cut shoe, not a high top. Simple canvas shoes are better than the thick, fancy athletic shoes. Velcro straps are easier to put on than laces. As a last resort, you can order custom made shoes.

THE HIPS

IN THE HIP, SOMETIMES THE ADDUCTOR OR FLEXOR muscles pull very tightly. This can make it hard to walk straight or even to rest the hip in a straight position. A hip dislocation may follow over time. If tightness in these muscles is noted, a physician should follow it over time to make sure there is no dislocation developing.

Hip dislocations are usually painful if they are left untreated over time. This is true even if the person does not walk. Therefore, as soon as an early dislocation is discovered, it is best to recommend surgery so the problem can be corrected with as little surgery as possible. Surgical measures include lengthening of the muscle and coverings of the joint, and in later stages, cutting and reshaping the misshapen bones. A cast or brace is needed to hold the hip in place for four to six weeks in most cases.

HIP INSTABILITY

THE HIP IS A BALL-AND-SOCKET JOINT. It must be in perfect alignment to last throughout life without arthritis. In some girls and women, due to abnormal muscle pull with growth, the ball is very gradually pulled out of the socket. If this is partial, it is termed subluxation; if it is total, dislocation. This may cause pain later in life. Hip dislocation may occur from persistent increased hip adduction (movement toward midline of the thigh), particularly in the child who does not walk. Release of the hip adductor muscles and (sometimes) removal of the nerve which supplies them can be helpful.

When she is sitting, Renee leans to the left. While bearing weight, she won't put her right foot down. When I try to straighten her, she fights it and seems very uncomfortable. She has increased spasticity, which in turn has pulled her hip out slightly and she is relieving the pressure by putting her weight on the opposite side.

PREVENTING PROBLEMS

PROPER POSITIONING IN A WHEELCHAIR OR BED CAN HELP if the hip adductors are tight. Stretching and bracing or even muscle lengthening to maintain the hips' ability to abduct, or spread apart, may be helpful, but is unproven. For all practical purposes, awareness and early detection are the key.

TREATMENT

EARLY SUBLUXATION CAN BE TREATED by muscle lengthening, a relatively simple procedure. If treated, surgical realignment of the bone, or osteotomy, may be necessary later.

THE BACK

KYPHOSIS

KYPHOSIS IS SPINAL CURVATURE AS SEEN FROM THE SIDE, often termed "hunchback." A small degree of kyphosis (up to 45 degrees) is normal, present in

Orthopedics

everyone as part of the normal spine contour. While kyphosis is often seen in RS, it does not usually progress to a serious degree. Kyphosis is not as medically serious as scoliosis. It does not harm the lungs, but it may cause discomfort if severe. It may impair socialization by preventing her from being able to hold her head up and look around.

TREATMENT

KYPHOSIS IS TREATED BY A BRACE similar to that used for scoliosis. This may be indicated if the curve is greater than 50-70 degrees in a growing child. Again, this is not as common as scoliosis in children with RS. In curves of 80-90 degrees with discomfort, surgery may be indicated.

Exercises cannot prevent or treat scoliosis or kyphosis. However, she can exercise in the brace. Stretching to decrease hip adduction contractures and hip, knee and ankle contractures may be beneficial. This should be done slowly, over thirty to sixty seconds each stretch, without sudden force.

One study which looked at intervention strategies of over one hundred girls with RS concluded that although physical therapy appeared to be more effective than bracing, none of the various noninvasive methods including physical therapy, bracing, casting, and combinations of these appeared to halt the progressive course of scoliosis. Physical therapy can help to maintain the flexibility of the curve so that greater correction can be achieved with less risk of overstretching the spinal cord.

Surgical intervention appeared to be the most effective means to reduce and arrest spinal curvature. It is possible that bracing is less effective due to decreased muscle tone and balance which result from long term use. Therefore, it may be worthwhile to combine an aggressive physical therapy program with use of a brace during periods of inactivity.

This study also revealed that girls who had higher motor function had a lower incidence rate of both scoliosis and surgical intervention. While it appears that noninvasive interventions do not alter the ultimate course of scoliosis, the clear relationship seen between gross motor skills and scoliosis call for an aggressive, ongoing physical therapy program. This program should start at an early age and should be aimed at building, maintaining, and retaining gross motor skills.

SCOLIOSIS

SCOLIOSIS IS SEEN OFTEN IN RS. Three-fourths of all girls with RS in three large studies had scoliosis, although some curves remain minor. Why this occurs is one of the mysteries of RS, hopefully to be better understood by research. Scoliosis occurs when the spinal vertebrae rotate from a nearly straight column shape to a shape like a spiral staircase. On X-ray, it appears as a side-to-side curve.

The bony part of the spine by itself, is flexible rather than rigid. The spine has dozens of small muscles on both sides. They must be well coordinated in order to hold the spine straight. Scoliosis in general can be from abnormal muscle tone or balance. The muscle pulls differently on one side of the spine than the other, causing the spine to bend. This abnormal muscle pull probably occurs in response to lack of coordinated signals from the brain. Differing muscle pull on two sides may cause scoliosis in RS.

DETECTING THE CURVE

A CURVE USUALLY BECOMES NOTICEABLE between nine and twelve years of age if one is to develop. A few girls have developed curves in early childhood

Orthopedics

although they have not worsened rapidly at that age. Scoliosis should be checked for visually on all girls with RS at any age. This can often be done without X-ray.

Before scoliosis is diagnosed, it can be screened for by observing the shape of the back. If the child is able to stand, it can be done while she bends forward. If not, she should be checked while seated, looking down from above. Normally, the ribs and muscles are the same shape on both sides of the middle of the back. If on one side they stand out much more, an X-ray should be done.

When Nichole sits, she leans to the left. When we're getting her dressed, she leans to the left and forward. When she's in the car with a regular seat belt, she can hardly be seen because the left side of her body is almost touching the seat. One leg is also wider and more muscular than the other. To see her stand, you would think one leg looked shorter than the other, but when they measure, they are the same.

X-Rays

X-RAYS SHOULD BE DONE when a child has an abnormal examination as just described. If a curve is found, follow-up X-rays should be done every year in young girls. With slowly progressive curves, they should be repeated every six months during rapid growth or progression.

Check Progression of the Curve

PROGRESSION MEANS INCREASE OF THE CURVATURE. This is extremely variable. In some girls, it rapidly increases while in others it does not. This is why all minor curves are not treated from the start. However, the bigger the curve and the closer the child is to the adolescent growth spurt, the more likely the curve is to progress.

The Effects of Scoliosis

SCOLIOSIS CAN CAUSE AN ALTERATION of sitting balance, which may lead to practical problems with seating. It can also cause compression of the lungs by the twisting of the chest. This becomes significant in curves over about seventy degrees. It is important to prevent this.

Prevention and Treatment

UNFORTUNATELY, WE DO NOT KNOW how to prevent scoliosis altogether, but it can be treated once it starts. For small curves in growing girls, braces are used. In large curves in older girls near the teen years, surgery is used. Physical therapists, orthopedic surgeons and chiropractors don't all agree on how to prevent and treat scoliosis, so it can be confusing. Response to treatment varies with each child. Some girls have early signs of scoliosis in spite of aggressive therapy while others may have minimal curves even as adolescents, even without intensive therapy.

We have been using an NMES (neuromuscular electrical stimulation system) machine with Jen. Her orthopedist suggested it be used with the physical therapist and it seemed to help relax the muscles in Jen's back.

A brace should be used when a curve is over twenty to twenty-five degrees and the child is still growing. It is not effective if the curve is much over forty-five degrees. The brace is a molded, padded and plastic "jacket" designed to apply gentle pressure in the proper areas to straighten the spine. It is worn under clothing. It does not hurt, although

Orthopedics

it can cause pressure sores if it is started too fast or if the child outgrows it. The brace should be worn for eighteen to twenty-three hours per day, depending on the doctor's orders. Braces should be checked and changed as necessary and should not interfere with mobility if they have been correctly fit. Ask for an adjustment if there appear to be problems with fit.

She will need to wear seamless undershirts under the brace, which helps to avoid creases that can irritate. These may come with the brace. If not, they can be purchased through department store catalogs or a hospital supply pharmacy.

The goal of using a brace is to slow the increase of the curve, not to make it straighten permanently. In most cases, the curve will continue to increase, but hopefully, at a slower rate. Thus, the child may have an acceptable curve at the end of growth (less than 40 to 50 degrees). It is usually recommended to postpone surgery until she is nearly finished growing, if possible. In some cases, the brace does not work or the curve may be too big already, and surgery should be considered.

The big argument in favor of braces seems to be buying time. On the other hand, anytime you restrict movement, you automatically restrict the stress the bones require to develop and maintain integrity. When Crystal had her surgery, her surgeon stated that it was refreshing and reassuring to do the surgery on a girl who hadn't been braced. He said he could see that the bones were in good condition and had the stamina to hold the rods.

Kelsey's curve had gone from twenty to thirty degrees in a year and we decided to brace her. Bracing did not work for us. Her curve continued to grow, and quickly. In fact, we only braced her for about six months and she went from 30 to 43 degrees. We knew it was time for surgery.

These little RS girls put up with so much and in the long run demonstrate a virtue of resiliency. It may take a bit of adjusting, but they do adapt so well. I remember Jenn got so used to her body jacket that she was fearful at first without it! Kids adapt well. It's us parents who go through hell worrying about them!

SCOLIOSIS SURGERY

SCOLIOSIS SURGERY WILL MAKE HER STRAIGHTER, and will markedly decrease her seating difficulty. It may allow her to use a hand which was previously used for supporting herself. Surgery will also prevent the lung compression which may occur with more severe curves. If she is in a wheelchair, it will probably need to be adjusted before she leaves the hospital … she will be taller!

Lyndie's curve had almost reached 60 degrees and was fairly flexible (a huge C curve to the right thoraco-lumbar region). Lyndie had two titanium rods inserted and did really well. Her surgery was done on a Wednesday morning, and she was discharged the next Monday, five days later. We are very thankful we had Lyndie's curve surgically corrected. She is like a new kid since she no longer has back pain, and she is walking and feeling better than she has in years.

Jodi's spinal curvature had increased to forty-five degrees and it was interfering with her breathing, coughing ability, and her digestive system. Her spinal surgery was a complete success. At her follow-up visit, we learned that she is now two inches taller and has gained six pounds. The curve was reduced to seventeen degrees.

Laura amazed everyone with the ease with which she flew through the surgery and recovery. She tolerated the pain with minimal medication and her vital signs remained strong. The doctor surprised us four days after surgery by saying she could be dismissed that day. She was dismissed on Day 6, only because my husband and I felt a little unsure of ourselves in caring for her at that point.

Orthopedics

At thirteen, Ashley had two curves greater than fifty degrees, lumbar and thoracic and her organs were compromised. She had one respiratory infection after another. Seating was becoming a problem. We chose the surgery. Recovery was slow but good. It's amazing the difference it made. She sits straight and the respiratory infections decreased. It was the best decision we made for her. The best advice I can give to parents is to work with physical therapy before surgery and work on transfers for afterward, and keep those bowels moving. Do not let them get constipated secondary to surgery and pain meds. We had great success.

PROS AND CONS OF SURGERY

The drawback of the surgery has been her inability to rotate her spine, which had allowed her to roll over in bed with ease before the surgery. Now, in spite of the fact she can walk, she needs to be turned in bed at night. On the plus side, she is healthy and never had a critical moment in her life, no pneumonia, and her heart and lungs are not compromised by a curved spine. She prefers to hold on to someone's hand when walking, but if there is something she wants to do, such as sitting down, she will let go and walk over to her chair.

Scoliosis surgery is very serious, but if it is needed, it will prevent permanent damage to lungs and heart from crowding and is best done while the patient is strong enough to withstand the surgery. I know it is scary, and I hope Heather never has to go through anything like it again, but I am glad she had it when she did. The surgery was a complete success, with correction to 12 degrees. Heather gained weight after her surgery and also began menstruating, which is common after surgery. For her, it was a good thing.

WHAT TO ASK THE SURGEON

DECIDING WHETHER TO DO THE SURGERY IS PROBABLY a very tough decision. The more you know about what will happen, the more prepared and comfortable you will be with your decision. Ask which surgical technique will be used and how it is done. Ask what may be involved in postoperative care, (length of time in bed, when and if post-op brace is fitted, and when weight bearing can be re-established). Ask for suggestions on techniques to feed her, take her to the toilet, and bathe her after the surgery. If the surgeon is not familiar with RS, provide literature on the topic. Talk to other parents who have been through it. It is probably best if someone can stay with her in the hospital for her comfort and security and to be able to better interpret her nonverbal messages. Make sure to plan for the postoperative period when she comes back home and your own energy level is low. See if you can get help with lifting, bathing, and general nursing.

THE PROCEDURE

THE SPINE IS STRAIGHTENED USING STAINLESS STEEL or titanium rods. A bone graft is placed along this entire area to cause it to fuse solidly so that no further curvature will occur. The rods usually become partially covered with bone and can be left in the body forever. They do not cause problems unless the patient is very thin.

CORRECTION OF THE CURVE

THE CORRECTION VARIES WITH THE SIZE OF THE CURVE, age of the child, and stiffness of the spine. Usually, at least forty to sixty percent of correction can be achieved. Anything in this range is acceptable, as long as the sitting balance is good. The goal is mainly to prevent worsening. Straightening the curve too much carries a risk of over stretching the spinal cord. Therefore, the surgeon does not always try to straighten the curve completely. The surgeon does not need to do this as long as the back looks straight and balanced from an external perspective.

Orthopedics

ANESTHESIA

ANESTHESIA IS NOT A PROBLEM because seizures can be controlled under anesthetic. However, the period after surgery may bring problems. Therefore, the seizure disorder should be as well controlled as possible before surgery. Blood tests for levels of seizure medications should be within the desired range before surgery. In addition, appropriate medicines should be given to her immediately after the operation. It is also important for her to be as well nourished as possible before surgery.

RECOVERY

SHE WILL BE DROWSY ON THE FIRST DAY AFTER SURGERY, but will feel better by the third or fourth day when she is also eating well. A blood transfusion may be necessary, but this can come from the patient herself by pre-donation or from a relative if desired. The hospital stay is usually six to ten days.

Potential complications include infection (1-2% risk), which usually becomes evident within the first two weeks and may require cleansing out of the infection. Rod displacement occurs in up to five percent and may require surgical repositioning. Nerve damage is the most serious risk, but also the least common, occurring in less than one per five hundred patients. This could range from numbness to weakness of one or both legs. If it does happen, it may be partially or fully reversible. Pseudoarthrosis, or failure of the bone to fuse at one level, occurs in about one percent of cases, and may require bone graft.

They put a post-surgical brace on Angie and carefully let her dangle her legs over the side of the bed. Three nurses, a therapist, my closest friend, and a deacon from our church were there too. The medical people said she would be light-headed and shouldn't stand yet. Angie grabbed my hands and stood up and took off out of that hospital room (with me hanging on) and right down the hall. She was hot to get out of there! At that time we thought we were observing a miracle.

Bearing weight depends on the quality of the bone and its ability to support the rods. Usually, this is adequate to allow standing within four to six days. In some cases, a brace or cast may be necessary, and it is applied at this time. Usually, the energy level is back to normal by six to eight weeks. It is best for the child to avoid any impact activities or forcible bending for six months.

GETTING READY FOR SURGERY

THE HOSPITAL USUALLY HAS A HANDBOOK FOR PARENTS. It is a good idea to ask for one before admittance, so you can get oriented to the hospital routines and policies.

Be sure to visit the floor and room(s) where your child will be spending the next week. Take note of the bulletin board and other ways that you can decorate the room to make it fun for her. Check for sleeping arrangements for you or whoever may be staying with your daughter.

It is a good idea to speak with another family whose daughter has had this surgery as well; preferably a family who has a child similar to yours.

Here are some suggestions for things you can do in advance of the surgery:

- Make sure the school is clearly told that surgery is to take place and given the date. Send it in writing by registered mail. Your daughter is entitled to school services in the hospital

Orthopedics

or while recovering at home. At the hospital, the social worker can send the school a letter requesting home schooling for four to six weeks.

- Prepare your daughter as best as possible. Read Going to the Hospital books to her. Reassure her that you are going to be there for her, that she is going to get her "ouchie" [or whatever term you use] fixed.

- If your daughter has special feeding instructions or feeding rates for tube feedings, get them in writing from the responsible doctor ahead of time.

- Check with social services at the hospital for reduced long-term parking fees and help with meals for you or whomever if needed.

- Stock up on instant microwavable meals and snacks.

- Arrange for respite to assist you after the surgery. You will need it.

- Talk to the anesthesiologist well in advance and provide information about the irregular breathing patterns and oxygen saturation levels of girls with RS. The anesthesiologist can consult with one of the Rett centers to better understand the disorder before the surgery ever gets started.

- If your daughter's surgery is in the morning, you may have to come to the hospital the day before to register and do the "workup." Plan on spending the whole morning or afternoon in the hospital. Bring diapers, food, tape recorder, books, etc. If surgery is booked for the afternoon, you can come that morning. Either way, the hospital staff will call you and tell you when to come. They will give you instructions about when your child should stop eating and drinking before surgery. Be sure to ask about when to give medications.

- Your daughter must not eat or drink on surgery day from midnight on. If surgery is in the afternoon, she can have clear liquids until four hours before surgery.

- When you come to the hospital for the preparation appointment, you must first go to admissions office. Hospital staff makes sure your information is correct in the computer. Be sure you bring your daughter's immunization record, list of medications, and insurance cards. Also bring the name and phone number of your child's pediatrician.

- After that you will go to the surgery admitting department. Your daughter's vital signs will be taken along with a history. She may need to provide a urine sample (and may need a catheter). Here you can ask to speak to the anesthesiologist assigned to her case.

- Then you will be sent to the blood room where the lab technician will draw blood to match blood types for transfusions. If you want to use your family's blood for the operation, donations should be received a week before the surgery.

- If the operation is the same day, you'll go back to the surgery admitting department or to the surgery waiting room. If it is the next day, you can go home now!

WHAT TO TAKE TO THE HOSPITAL

For Your Child

DO NOT UNDERESTIMATE THE STRESS that your daughter will experience. Try to make her room as familiar as possible. Here are some things to take:

- earphones and tape recorder, portable DVD player
- favorite audio and videotapes
- favorite books
- toothbrush

Orthopedics

- AFO's for walking
- brush and comb
- augmentative communication device/s
- push pins for the bulletin board
- decorations for her room, such as tinsel with stars
- Clothes to bring her home will have to fit over her spinal jacket or brace if she gets one. If she has a g-button, have them cut a window in the brace in the right area so you can still access the button.
- extension cord; essential for the portable DVD player or VCR

For Parents

It will be a stressful time for you as well. Sometimes sitting and waiting is more tiring than exercise. Take some things along for your own comfort, such as:

- bottled water
- notebook and pen
- phone numbers of friends
- IRSA's phone number (1-800-818-RETT)
- cell phone and charger (cell phones are not allowed inside the hospital except in certain areas)
- mirror
- tissues
- snacks (you may not get away to get meals some days!)
- mug and tea bags (the nurses' station can heat water for you)
- Rett Syndrome brochures
- laptop computer
- reading material

For Hospital Staff

Take plenty of Rett syndrome information and brochures with you to the hospital before and after the surgery, so all staff involved will have a clear understanding of your daughter's condition. They will appreciate this.

THE SURGERY EXPERIENCE

On the Day of Surgery

THE HOSPITAL STAFF WILL TELL YOU when to come to the hospital on the day of surgery. If your daughter has long hair, French braids are best. Her hair will get very matted with all the lying down.

First you go to the admitting office, just like before. They will send you to surgery admitting again. But this time, after all your questions and checking your daughter's vital signs, you will be asked to change her into the hospital gown and wait in the pre-surgery room. If the surgery time is soon, this is a good idea. If there are a couple of hours, you can wander around. They will give you a beeper and you can give them your cell phone number.

Orthopedics

When it's time for surgery, you will all be escorted to the surgery admitting room. Here you get a booth with a bed and a TV. A nurse may give your daughter an oral medicine to relax her. You may stay with her until they wheel her off to surgery. She should be very relaxed and may even fall asleep. You can ask the staff to wait until you are comfortable with your daughter's state before they take her to surgery. While you are waiting for your daughter to fall asleep, the doctor usually comes to visit with you and answer any questions. The anesthesiologist will come to explain his/her part of the procedure. A surgical nurse may come also.

After they take your daughter to the operating room, you will go to the surgery waiting room. There is a phone where you can call the operating room to see how the surgery is going. When the long surgery is over, the surgeon will come to tell you how it went. You can go to intensive care to see your child. There is one nurse assigned to two patients there. You may choose to go home to rest while she is on the skilled care floor, or you may decide to stay with her at all times.

The Day after Surgery: Day One

The day of surgery is known as day zero. The first day after surgery is day one and so forth.

When your child is stable, they will move her to an orthopedic room. A nurse and a nursing assistant will be assigned to her. Be sure to use the charts provided here from the beginning because there are an overwhelming number of people who come in to talk with you, especially if your child is young or cannot speak. Remember, you are part of the team who care for your child. In fact, you actually manage your child's case.

The first day your child will be groggy, have a sore throat from the breathing tube during surgery and her face will look swollen because the surgery was performed with her lying face down. The nurses' station has all kinds of goodies and one of them is a glycerin sponge on a stick. Theses are great for moistening her mouth and she may suck on it for water. Go slowly in feeding her, even water. The anesthesia can cause nausea.

There are also little envelopes of Vaseline for her lips. She will also have a catheter in, as well as a drain from the wound. These plus the IV drip and pulse line make for a lot of lines to watch out for! If you get a really attentive nurse or assistant, your child will be turned every time her vital signs are taken. Some time in the middle of the night, the respiratory therapist will show up.

The doctors like to visit first thing in the morning; usually between six and seven. The surgeon will come, or a resident who helped with the surgery. The anesthesiologist will also come. You will also see someone from the pain management team. This is where the charts come in handy to keep track of all that they tell you, and who says what.

Your daughter will sleep most of the day. To keep her from getting bed sores, the nurses/aides should turn her every couple of hours. They will teach you how to do it too.

The first night is surreal with people coming and going, machines beeping, children crying and you worrying about your child. Sleeping pills help a lot.

Day Two

Your daughter will sleep most of this day, too. It is basically a repeat of day one. But this day, you may get a visit from the physical therapist with instructions on how to do transfers and how to handle your child after surgery. Like everyone else, therapists are busy, but don't let them stop serving you until you are comfortable with taking care of your child.

Orthopedics

Stay on top of things. When the machine beeps, call the nurse's station. If her diaper needs to be changed, or she needs pain medication, call the nurse's station. They are very busy, but someone will eventually come.

The catheter will probably come out day two or day three. When it does, you can double diaper her so you do not have to move her as often for that. Put a larger or regular size diaper on the outside with a smaller diaper used as a liner. Fold the diaper down in the back so that it does not touch her incision, as there is a chance of infection.

Day Three Through Discharge

The days blur together, but keep on using whatever method you like to keep track of people, medications, etc. Your child will probably be in the hospital about a week.

Don't forget that she may understand everything you say. Be careful how you talk in front of her.

Discharge Day

The day has finally arrived! You are anxious to be back in familiar surroundings where you are really in charge! Your daughter is also! Do not underestimate the stress she feels from being in the hospital along with the pain from the operation.

Don't be in a hurry. Be sure you talk with every one you need to. Find out when you can bathe her, how long she can be up, walking, standing, how to transition her, carry her, etc. Find out about the medications: how long she should be on the medications you get at the pharmacy. Ask the doctor to call the medication in to your home pharmacy. It will save time waiting for the very busy hospital pharmacy. You'll go home sooner.

Be sure you have the equipment you need: a bath chair, a hospital bed, a reclining wheelchair. (The PT should have instructed you in the use of the chair.) Don't forget the services you need when you get home: a prescription for PT from the surgeon, including what he wants them to do; A Range of Motion (ROM) plan from the PT; and if possible, a nurse to come two or three times to look at the wound.

Continue the medication chart at home to keep track of when you give what medicine. You can go to the records office in the hospital and request that the records of the surgery be sent to her pediatrician. This is a very good idea.

You will get discharge instructions which are helpful. Read them before you leave the hospital. Ask questions.

The PT can help you take your child to the car, and show you how to transfer her.

Post Surgery

You will go home with medication. Be sure to give it as instructed. Check for side effects on the accompanying handout. Ask the doctor how long pain may last: two weeks? Three weeks? This is especially helpful if your child doesn't speak and can't communicate where it hurts.

Be aware that complications could develop: low iron or anemia from not eating, constipation, upset stomach including vomiting from the antibiotics, yeast rash from the antibiotics, weird reactions from all the drugs, and even withdrawal from the pain medicine. The pain team from the hospital is available at all times for questions, so don't hesitate to call them even after you are home.

Keep the wound clean and dry, even if you have to cover it at the bottom (ask the nurse).

Orthopedics

CHARTS AND FORMS

DAILY CONVERSATIONS

NURSE: _____   DATE: _____

ASSISTANT: _____

CHARGE NURSE: _____

_____

TIME: NAME:

_____

TIME: NAME:

_____

TIME: NAME:

_____

TIME: NAME:

Orthopedics

DAILY CONVERSATIONS

NURSE: _____ DATE: _____

ASSISTANT: _____

CHARGE NURSE: _____

_____

TIME: NAME:

_____

TIME: NAME:

_____

TIME: NAME:

_____

TIME: NAME:

Orthopedics

DOCTOR'S VISITS
SURGEON

NAME: _____ DAY/TIME: _____
QUESTIONS:

COMMENTS:

NAME: _____ DAY/TIME: _____
QUESTIONS:

COMMENTS:

NAME: _____ DAY/TIME: _____
QUESTIONS:

COMMENTS:

Orthopedics

DOCTOR'S VISITS
SPECIALIST

NAME: _____   DAY/TIME: _____
QUESTIONS:

COMMENTS:

NAME: _____   DAY/TIME: _____
QUESTIONS:

COMMENTS:

NAME: _____   DAY/TIME: _____
QUESTIONS:

COMMENTS:

Orthopedics

DOCTOR'S VISITS
SPECIALIST

NAME: _____   DAY/TIME: _____
QUESTIONS:

COMMENTS:

NAME: _____   DAY/TIME: _____
QUESTIONS:

COMMENTS:

NAME: _____   DAY/TIME: _____
QUESTIONS:

COMMENTS:

Orthopedics

DOCTOR'S VISITS
PAIN MANAGEMENT

NAME: _____   DAY/TIME: _____
QUESTIONS:

COMMENTS:

NAME: _____   DAY/TIME: _____
QUESTIONS:

COMMENTS:

NAME: _____   DAY/TIME: _____
QUESTIONS:

COMMENTS:

Orthopedics

DOCTOR'S VISITS
PHYSICAL THERAPIST

NAME: _____   DAY/TIME: _____
QUESTIONS:

COMMENTS:

NAME: _____   DAY/TIME: _____
QUESTIONS:

COMMENTS:

NAME: _____   DAY/TIME: _____
QUESTIONS:

COMMENTS:

Orthopedics

DAY & TIME	DRINK	FOOD	BM	URINE
DAY ONE				
DAY TWO				
DAY THREE				
DAY FOUR				
DAY FIVE				
DAY SIX				
DAY SEVEN				
DAY EIGHT				
DAY NINE				

Orthopedics

DAY ONE					
NURSE: (day) _____ (night) _____					
ASSISTANT: (day) _____ (night) _____					
MEDICATIONS: _____					
_____					
_____					

TIME: ▶ MEDS: ▼					

LIQUIDS:

BM: (time)

Orthopedics

DAY TWO

NURSE: (day) _____ (night) _____

ASSISTANT: (day) _____ (night) _____

MEDICATIONS: _____
_____
_____

TIME: ▶ MEDS: ▼					

LIQUIDS:

FOOD:

BM: (time)

Orthopedics

DAY THREE
NURSE: (day) _____ (night) _____
ASSISTANT: (day) _____ (night) _____
MEDICATIONS: _____
_____
_____

TIME: ▶ MEDS: ▼					

LIQUIDS:

FOOD:

BM: (time)

Orthopedics

DAY FOUR

NURSE: (day) _____ (night) _____

ASSISTANT: (day) _____ (night) _____

MEDICATIONS: _____

_____

_____

TIME: ▶					
MEDS: ▼					

LIQUIDS:

FOOD:

BM: (time)

Orthopedics

DAY FIVE

NURSE: (day) _____ (night) _____

ASSISTANT: (day) _____ (night) _____

MEDICATIONS: _____
_____
_____

TIME: ▶ MEDS: ▼					

LIQUIDS:

FOOD:

BM: (time)

Orthopedics

DAY SIX

NURSE: (day) _____ (night) _____

ASSISTANT: (day) _____ (night) _____

MEDICATIONS: _____

_____

_____

TIME: ▶ MEDS: ▼					

LIQUIDS:

FOOD:

BM: (time)

Orthopedics

DAY SEVEN
NURSE: (day) _____ (night) _____
ASSISTANT: (day) _____ (night) _____
MEDICATIONS: _____
_____
_____

TIME: ▶ MEDS: ▼					

LIQUIDS:

FOOD:

BM: (time)

Orthopedics

MEDICATIONS AT HOME					
MEDICINE (What for)					
DAY/TIME GIVEN					
DAY/TIME GIVEN					
DAY/TIME GIVEN					
DAY/TIME GIVEN					
DAY/TIME GIVEN					
DAY/TIME GIVEN					
DAY/TIME GIVEN					
DAY/TIME GIVEN					
DAY/TIME GIVEN					
DAY/TIME GIVEN					
DAY/TIME GIVEN					

"Not everything that is faced can be changed,
but nothing can be changed until it is faced."

– JAMES A. BALDWIN

4

Care and
Management

Nutrition
and
Feeding

Day-to-Day Care

Day-to-Day Care

THIS CHAPTER WILL DESCRIBE some of the common problems of girls with RS and how to treat them. It is important to remember that each girl is different, and your child may never have some of the situations presented here. The chapter will also explore ways to make your child more comfortable and how to maximize resources and select products for her care.

"Success is the sum of small efforts, repeated day in and day out."

– ROBERT J. COLLIER

GASTROINTESTINAL PROBLEMS

GASTROINTESTINAL PROBLEMS occur frequently in girls with RS. Bowel habits are one of the most common issues that parents want to discuss with their daughter's physician. Bowel habits usually are described in terms of stool frequency, consistency, and size. Children generally have bowel movements between three times daily and three times weekly. The amount of time required for digested food to pass from the mouth to the anus in children is approximately forty-eight hours. The stool should be soft, but formed in consistency. The average weight of stool output is approximately two to two and a half ounces daily. Despite these generalities, bowel habits vary widely among children.

CONSTIPATION

CHRONIC CONSTIPATION IS ONE OF THE MOST COMMON gastrointestinal problems, experienced by more than eighty-five percent of girls with RS at one time in their lives. Most have at one time had difficult-to-pass, large, hard, and dry bowel movements, which occur every three or more days. Constipation occurs often in RS due to a number of factors which include: lack of physical activity, poor muscle tone, diet, drugs (especially anticonvulsants), inadequate fluid intake, scoliosis, and pain and discomfort associated with elimination.

Constipation in RS usually means either undue difficulty with defecation or abnormal stool retention. The large bowel has a variety of functions, the most obvious being the containment of food residue prior to evacuation. The movement of food residue through the large bowel is a function of two centers of neural control, the *central* (brain) nervous system and the *enteric* (intestinal) nervous system (ENS); the muscles of the pelvis, known as the *levator ani* and the *coccygeal muscles*; and two muscles intrinsic to the large bowel, the *internal* and *external sphincters*. Two types of motility patterns occur within the intestinal tract: *haustral shuttling* (to and fro movement within a small segment of the intestinal tract) and *massive peristalsis* (movement from the top to the bottom of the intestinal tract). The urge to defecate frequently occurs after ingestion of a meal because food stimulates hormones within the gastrointestinal tract which, in turn, stimulate the ENS. Research studies to better understand the abnormalities of large bowel function in girls with RS have not been performed.

Day-to-Day Care

Constipation can cause severe discomfort, pain, and even bleeding due to small anal tears. Some girls express their discomfort by increased anxiety, hand biting and even seizures. Constipation in RS can appear at any age, as early as the first or second year of life or it may be delayed until her early teens. The good news is that appropriate management leads to improvement and in many cases complete normalization of bowel movements. Some girls may pass small, hard stools at infrequent intervals; they may strain to expel stool; and, on occasion, painful defecation and bleeding occur because of anal fissures (tears). If chronic stool retention is present, there may be severe abdominal pain, vomiting, and *fecal impaction*. When your physician performs a rectal examination, he or she may feel a large amount of hard stool within a dilated (stretched) rectal vault. Once the rectum and large bowel become chronically dilated because of persistent fecal impaction, bowel movements are difficult unless treatment is initiated and maintained consistently until the bowel resumes its normal elasticity.

How Constipation Begins

WHEN FOOD LEAVES THE STOMACH, IT MOVES through the *intestine* (bowel) until it is passed as stool. First it passes through the *small bowel*, then the *colon* (large intestine) and finally through the *sigmoid* (final portion of the large intestine) and out of the body through the *rectum*. The intestine is made up of an elastic tube with muscle fibers that produce churning movements, which make the contents move along until they are passed. In RS, it appears that nothing is wrong with the muscle and nervous components of the large intestine, rectum, and anus. Reflexes that produce bowel movements are normal. There appear to be no anatomic problems, such as a blockage, or organic condition, such as diseased bowel. This type of constipation is called *functional*.

We do not understand why, but the girl with RS has a tendency for stool to travel slowly through her bowels and for bowel movements to be infrequent. This leads to a large accumulation of stool at the sigmoid and rectum. Normally, the accumulation of stool at the rectum triggers the need for a bowel movement, which results in emptying of the rectum. However, when the rectum is enlarged by a large volume of stool for a long period of time, the urge to have the BM is lost. When this happens over time, it makes it much more difficult for her to recognize when she needs to have a bowel movement. The prolonged distention of the rectum and the sigmoid from large amounts of stool will cause loss of muscle tone. Consequently, the bowel becomes large and "baggy." This makes it even more difficult to for her to pass the stool.

The large intestine and the sigmoid can absorb a lot of water from the stool, so the longer the stool stays in the intestine, the drier it becomes. This causes bowel movements to become less frequent, larger, and harder, becoming more uncomfortable and painful. She may then begin to associate bowel movements with discomfort and pain, and begin withholding stool. The vicious cycle has begun.

If constipation is left untreated, it can lead to *fecal impaction* (blockage of the bowel). This is a serious situation and needs to be treated with *colonic lavage* (washing out the intestines) or even manual removal of the stool under sedation or anesthesia.

Diet

THE DIET PARTICULARLY INFLUENCES BOWEL HABITS. Dietary roughage adds bulk to stools and makes them softer and easier to pass. Dietary roughage includes foods such as bran muffins, oat cereals, raw fruits and vegetables, and popcorn.

Day-to-Day Care

Children ages 7 to 18 years should consume three to five servings of vegetables and two to four servings of fruits daily. A serving size approximates one cup of raw or one half cup of cooked vegetables and fruits. Commercially available fiber substitutes can be found in pharmacy stores. Fiber products are safe to use because they are not absorbed from the intestinal tract. A heaping teaspoon of powdered vegetable fiber per day usually is sufficient, but three or four times that much is safe to use. However, many children do not like the taste or texture of these fiber products. In addition, the use of these products may be more difficult in girls with RS due to their chewing and swallowing problems.

Fiber

Fiber is an effective laxative that can be used over a long period of time. It absorbs water and prevents the stool from becoming dry and hard, even if it stays in the colon for a long time. There are several ways of doing this. First, encourage her to eat green vegetables and fruits every day. Second, use unrefined flour in all baked products. Whole grain bread or dark breads are better than white bread and whole wheat or bran muffins are better than muffins made with white flour. It is very important to remember that fiber can only be effective if it is given with adequate fluid. When you increase fiber, you must increase fluids accordingly.

Some dry cereals or other sources of fiber may be difficult for girls with RS to chew. To make it easier to chew and swallow, fiber can be added to or mixed with foods, and cooked without losing its effectiveness. The amount of fiber cereal given during the day can be divided into two or three portions and given with milk, juice, fruits, or included in other foods.

Fiber Supplements

Fiber supplements are often recommended for adults, but are often ineffective in children because they usually don't like them. There are many products which can be bought over the counter which are fiber derivatives or similar bulk forming agents. These include methyl cellulose (Citrucel and Maltsupex), or psyllium (Metamucil, Fiberall). Most of these supplements come in a powder form which can be mixed in any liquid. In general, girls two to six years of age need between one-fourth and one-third of the recommended adult dose, from six to twelve years, one-third to one-half of the dose, and over twelve years, the usual adult dose. It is important to introduce the fiber gradually since at first some temporary bloating, gassiness, and discomfort may occur. These symptoms usually disappear. Caution should be used when gastrostomy feedings are in use, as fiber supplements can clog the tube. Prune juice is a source of fiber which has an excellent laxative effect and be used daily or every other day.

Foods High in Fiber

- Whole grains, breads and cereals are high in fiber. Use hot cereals including oatmeal, and cereals with seeds, bran and nuts. High fiber cereals in amounts of one half ounce to one ounce a day in girls from two to six years of age, one to two ounces a day in girls between six and twelve years of age, and two to three ounces in children over age twelve supplies most or all of the dietary fiber requirement.
- Raw fruits and vegetables are better than processed ones. Leave skins on when possible and serve dried fruit, or fresh prunes, pears, peaches, and apricots.
- Dried peas, beans, seeds, nuts, and popcorn. (Use these cautiously if she chews poorly.)
- Use unprocessed bran in foods or liquids throughout the day. Gradually increase the amount given.

Day-to-Day Care

Fluids

Adequate water intake is important. The large bowel is efficient in conserving water for the body by absorbing it from the stool. If the body does not get enough water, the stool becomes drier and more difficult to pass. If you give fiber without adequate fluids, it increases bulk without lubrication, which means a painful trip down the *alimentary canal*. Some liquids, such as milk can be constipating when consumed in excess. However, limiting milk intake may be detrimental to the development of the bones, particularly in RS, where there is risk for *osteopenia* (bone mineral loss) and fractures.

Any fluid is helpful; milk, juice, flavored drinks, soups or plain water. Fresh fruits, vegetables and some cooked foods contain fair amounts of water. A minimum of two glasses of fluid a day is recommended for girls less than two years of age, three to four glasses for those two to five years, four to six glasses for those five to ten years of age and six to eight glasses in girls greater than ten years of age.

Frequency of Elimination

What she eliminates is relative to what and how much she eats, so this can vary. She should be able to pass a stool without pain or distress. Many people think that once a week is "normal for her," but once a week is not normal for anyone! If she is not having a bowel movement after adequate fluids and fiber and requires frequent laxative use, the physician should be consulted. She should not go longer than three days without a bowel movement.

Preventing Constipation

The best way to manage constipation is to prevent it or avoid the vicious cycle described above. Chronic constipation can be a source of serious discomfort and irritability, so it is important to treat it aggressively. She should empty her intestine and rectum completely and regularly with each bowel movement so that they regain their normal size and tone. Daily exercise and occupational and physical therapies may help the problem. Develop a bowel program that stresses the following:

- Increase fluid intake.
- Modify diet with high fiber intake.
- Distribute fiber throughout the day.
- Provide "laxative" vegetables: pears, prunes, apricots, squash.
- Limit "constipating" foods: apple juice, white rice, cooked carrots.
- Give unprocessed bran (1 serving = 1 tablespoon). Make sure to give it with increased fluids.
- For those girls who are able to sit on the toilet, sitting once a day at a specific time, especially after the largest meal of the day, may sometimes be useful in achieving regularity.
- Miralax is a laxative which has been very successful. It is a colorless, odorless, tasteless powder that is mixed with water or juice. It is available with a prescription.

Treatment for Constipation

Treatment for constipation should be initiated early at the first hint of symptoms and should be maintained consistently to have a sustained effect. Girls with RS usually have significant *rectal inertia* (stool remains in the rectum), which is probably related to neurological dysfunction in ways that we do not yet understand. Simple stool softeners, "natural products," and

Day-to-Day Care

dietary fibers usually are not sufficient enough to sustain good rectal motility. Parents should beware of the herbal products used to treat constipation. Some products have additives that may lead to unwanted side effects. Good choices for treating constipation are polyethylene glycol-electrolyte solutions (PEG-ES) such as Miralax and Milk of Magnesia.

The strategy for the use of these medications depends on the clinical status of the girl. PEG-ES is a gentle laxative, is very safe, is not absorbed, and WILL produce results within two to three days depending on the dose used. However, the PEG-ES must be mixed in an adequate amount of fluid (water, juice, milk) to be effective. Consequently, it may be necessary for her to drink larger volumes of fluid than can be readily accomplished because of her swallowing difficulties. In addition, parents must obtain a prescription for the use of PEG-ES. Milk of Magnesia is a more potent stimulant and does not require as large a volume to be administered. However, if Milk of Magnesia is used for protracted periods at high doses, your physician may need to monitor periodically the level of magnesium in her blood. In some instances, both drugs may be used together to establish and maintain good bowel habits in girls who have stubborn constipation. Other laxative preparations, such as senna extracts and lactulose, are available but are less effective. Occasionally, bisacodyl (Ducolax) suppositories may be necessary on a more regular basis for some girls who have profound *rectal dysmotility* (slow movement).

Mineral oil can be used to help her achieve regularity, which may take from weeks to months. Check with her physician for the starting dose. Not enough mineral oil may be ineffective, and too much mineral oil will cause a significant amount of leakage into her underwear or diaper. After four to eight weeks of regular daily or every other day soft bowel movements, the dose of mineral oil can be gradually decreased by about one-third every two weeks and hopefully discontinued completely. It is not recommended for frequent or chronic use due to the irritating effect it has on the colon.

Mineral oil is safe as long as your child doesn't have a problem with choking or aspirating food that passes accidentally into the lungs. The oil is very difficult to remove from the lungs and can cause serious complications. However, it can be used for prolonged periods of time without causing nutritional problems or creating any habit or dependency.

Enemas are good for clean-out procedures and occasional problems, but are not advised to be used routinely. Their constant use may interfere with rectal muscle control, leaving her dependent on them to move her bowels. If enemas are required more than once or twice a month, it is likely that other changes need to be made in the diet or the dose of mineral oil.

Occasionally, Angie will go two days without a bowel movement, and is obviously uncomfortable. We keep a chart of "the action" on the bathroom wall. When we suspect she needs an enema, we ask her if she wants one. She will reply "yes" (by holding her eyes closed) almost eighty percent of the time. When she doesn't close her eyes, we wait for a few hours or until the next day before asking her again. Usually she has gone by then.

We use Fruit-eze. It's a thick jelly-like paste, made of dates, raisins, prunes, and prune juice that you put in oatmeal or on toast or however she will eat it. It comes in a five pound jar and costs about $30. We go through one jar about every ten months. For a two ounce sample, call 1-888-734-8527.

Massage

Certain massage techniques, when done on a routine basis, can be helpful. They are used as part of the comprehensive treatment regimen, not to replace it. Check with her doctor to see if massage is recommended.

Day-to-Day Care

The following two massage techniques are recommended in *Pediatric Massage for the Child with Special Needs* for an effective constipation massage routine:

Water Wheel

Put one hand in the middle of her abdomen, below the rib cage. Slide your hand down toward the groin area. Then, repeat with the other hand in paddling movements. Continue alternating hands, making sure that one hand is always in contact with the stomach.

Sun-Moon

In this exercise, both hands move in a clockwise direction. This is very important as it follows the natural movement through the intestines. Your left hand is the "sun." Move it in a continuous clockwise circle. Then, visualize a clock face on her stomach. When your left hand gets to 6 o'clock, your right hand (the "moon") will move in a semicircle from your left (9 o'clock) to your right (5 o'clock). Lift your right hand over your left to return to the 9 o'clock position. Repeat in a continuous motion.

For the relief of constipation, these two exercises can be done together in the following sequence:

Water Wheel six times. Push knees together into tummy and hold (no longer than five seconds in children with special needs because it can interfere with breathing).

Sun-Moon six times. Push knees together into tummy and hold (again, no longer than five seconds). Gently bounce legs. Repeat three times.

> *I tried many other things to help but none really helped much but since using this recipe my daughter has been able to have a large soft BM each day without anything else. 3 cups golden flaxseeds, 2 cups sunflower seeds, 1 cup almonds. Grind these up, then mix together and store in an airtight container in the refrigerator (probably good for about two weeks). Use one to two tablespoons once a day in oatmeal or fruit smoothie.*

Clean-out Procedures

If she already has hard, dry bowel movements which she has difficulty passing, and if bowel movements come no more often than every three days, more aggressive measures are called for. The first step is to assure that the rectum, sigmoid, and the *distal portion* (end) of the large bowel are completely cleaned out. Laxatives taken by mouth do not work effectively if there is a large amount of stool in the distal intestine. The best way to get started is by cleaning this portion of the intestine with enemas. Pediatric Fleet enemas can be used in girls up to six years of age. Beyond this age, adult size enemas are necessary. The clean-out should be done with one enema a night for two or three consecutive nights. Fleet enemas are inexpensive, can be bought over the counter and have easy-to-follow instructions.

Once the colon has been cleaned out, the measures which follow will be much more effective. The next step is to soften the stools by increasing the amount of dietary fiber in the diet as described above. This will assure that the stool remains moist and soft for a longer time, making it easier to pass.

Next, it is important to lubricate the intestinal contents so that it is easier for the intestine to move things along. Mineral oil is the best product to use for this purpose. Flavored mineral oil preparations, such as Kondremul and Haley's, are sold over the counter. The dose is usually determined by her weight and adjusted up or down as needed. A dose of one to two teaspoons twice a day in girls less than six years of age, one tablespoon twice a day up to twelve years of age, and one to two tablespoons twice a day in older girls is usually

Day-to-Day Care

effective. These doses are only rough estimates of what is needed, so the dose may need to be increased or decreased by one-third or one-half depending on the results.

Constipation and Diarrhea

It is possible for her to be constipated and have diarrhea intermittently. This happens when newly formed stool passes over the hard stool and "leaks" out. When a child repeatedly resists the urge to defecate, a mass of stool accumulates in the rectum. Fecal material from high in the colon then trickles around the obstruction, and soiling results whenever the external anal sphincter is relaxed.

Impaction

Fecal impaction occurs when the stools become so hard and dry that they cannot pass through the rectum without special measures. Several methods can be used, which include manual removal of stool, special enemas, irrigation with a rectal tube, and giving a special clean-out preparation through a tube inserted into the nose. In very serious cases of fecal impaction, surgery is necessary.

Patience and perseverance are important. Constipation takes a long time to develop, so it may also take a long time to achieve fully satisfactory results. Some improvement will usually be evident by the first or second week of treatment. However, it is very easy to go back into the vicious cycle even after initial improvement if you are not persistent with the treatment. If the frequency of bowel movements starts decreasing in spite of adequate diet, fluids, exercise and fiber and three or four days go by without a bowel movement, it may be necessary to again clean out the colon while continuing the other measures. Constipation is a difficult problem in RS, and may require persistent medications.

The goal of bowel management is to allow the intestine to return to its normal size and tone by regularly emptying all its contents. In this way, she learns that bowel movements need not be difficult or painful. This realization will encourage her to stop withholding, and, as a result, bowel movements will be regular, soft and comfortable. These measures can be helpful to manage most girls who have constipation problems. However, it may be necessary to consult her pediatrician or pediatric gastroenterologist to tailor the treatment to her individual needs. Constipation can be a debilitating and distressful condition, but it is treatable.

Intestinal Gas

Gas pains can be terribly uncomfortable. Keeping her bowel movements regular and avoiding "gassy" foods will help. If she is unable to pass gas regularly, it may be helpful to sit her on the toilet so that she will strain and release some gas. Over-the-counter preparations such as Milk of Magnesia given daily, can also help. Maalox contains simethicone and can also be helpful. Simethicone is a foaming agent that joins gas bubbles in the stomach so that gas is more easily belched away.

Some laxatives work by increasing the amount of gas and fluid in the colon (lactulose-Chronulac), and this may make abdominal distention worse, especially if constipation is not already under control. These should be avoided if there is a history of air swallowing or abdominal distention. Decrease the amount of carbonated beverages and other foods that increase gas formation in the large bowel, such as beans, corn, and broccoli.

Antacids, such as Mylanta II, Maalox II, and Di-Gel, also contain simethicone; however, these medicines have no effect on intestinal gas. Dosage varies depending on the form of

Day-to-Day Care

medication and the patient's age. Digestive enzymes, such as lactase supplements, actually help digest carbohydrates. Activated charcoal tablets (Charcocaps) may provide relief from gas in the colon. Studies have shown that when these tablets are taken before and after a meal, intestinal gas is greatly reduced. The usual dose is two to four tablets taken just before eating and one hour after meals. Beano, a newer over-the-counter digestive aid, contains the sugar-digesting enzyme that the body lacks to digest the sugar in beans and many vegetables. The enzyme comes in liquid form. Three to ten drops are added per serving just before eating to break down the gas-producing sugars. Beano has no effect on gas caused by lactose or fiber.

I give the double-strength Mylanta to Sarah. I think sometimes she has heartburn and swallows air to try and burp as this relieves the discomfort. The Mylanta gives her relief in a matter of minutes. She has the chewables in her bag in case we need them when out.

We have found that Maalox seems to help her more than Mylicon. It seems to give her some kind of relief almost instantly. We give it to her through her g-tube. We were also told you almost can't give too many of the Mylicon drops.

We use Phazyme daily as a preventative to tummy pains. Our pediatrician said that simethicone is one of the safest medicines out there. We use the pill form and hide them in food. Kimberly's fussy tummyaches have almost completely disappeared since we started this daily.

One very proactive nurse suggested something I had never heard of called "stomach migraines." She said that these are seizures of the stomach that feel like a migraine headache. They are controlled with antiseizure medication, so we started Meredith on Tegretol.

Kelsey began taking Primal Defense several months ago for her ongoing problems with painful gas episodes and multiple GI problems. We've had great success with it. You can buy it at your local health food store. Gas is still a problem, but the painful, screaming episodes are no more.

I found a product called Little Tummys, gas relief drops for excessive swallowing of air. It doesn't help her completely but it does enough to make her much more comfortable. She gets really irritated when she has a lot of gas, and I give her a few drops. She's back to her old self in a few minutes.

GASTROESOPHAGEAL REFLUX (GER)

AFTER A MEAL, FOOD AND ACID FROM THE STOMACH surge back up into the esophagus. GER occurs when the muscular part of the lower esophagus that normally prevents food and acid in the stomach from backing up into the esophagus malfunctions. GER can cause vomiting or inflammation of the esophagus, called *esophagitis*, and inhalation of food or liquid into the lungs, called aspiration.

GER is common and, for most people, it does not interfere with health. GER is suspected when there is weight loss, irritability after meals, vomiting after eating, or continued upper airway congestion. Heartburn is a specific symptom of reflux and conservative treatment can begin without further diagnostic studies. However, heartburn cannot be seen, so it is sometimes difficult to detect in girls with RS. Other early symptoms include clusters of coughing, frequently increasing at mealtimes, and increased swallowing. Stomach contents can reflux all the way into the throat or nose (*nasopharyngeal regurgitation*) causing coughing, choking, and difficulty breathing. She may regurgitate at night, and you may notice only nighttime coughing or wheezing. You may find evidence by the presence of fluid or blood

Day-to-Day Care

on her pillow. She may have recurrent pulmonary infections that are brought on by regurgitation with aspiration.

GER can be very painful. Some adults who have this problem mistake it for a heart attack. The most serious consequence of reflux is food being drawn into the lungs, resulting in *aspiration pneumonia* or lung abscess. In addition to causing great distress and discomfort, acid reflux may lead to wheezing or cessation of breathing, poor weight gain, esophagitis, esophageal strictures (narrowing), or changes in the lining of the esophagus that may predispose her to cancer in later life.

Heather began having sporadic episodes of forceful belching, "dry heaves," and gagging for no apparent reason. Her appetite decreased to outright refusal to eat or drink.

Lauren cried for hours, slept very little, vomited blood and yeasty smelling stuff that fermented in her esophagus because it refluxed up and stuck was there. My pediatrician would say "that's interesting," and "she's neurologically irritable." Finally another pediatrician saw her, put things together, and started her on Reglan and an acid reducer. Sleeping improved and screaming almost totally stopped.

Testing for GER

GER can be diagnosed by specific tests. A barium swallow study is not sufficient. The doctor may order an upper gastrointestinal (UGI) series. She is given a drink of barium and a series of subsequent X-rays follow the path of ingestion. If the study is negative for GER, but GER is still suspected, her doctor may request an overnight pH probe study, which is the most definitive test for GER. The doctor also may decide to do an endoscopy to look into the esophagus. Biopsies are taken to confirm the presence of inflammation. If inflammation is found, the doctor may order a gastric emptying scan to determine if delayed emptying of the stomach aggravates acid reflux. *Manometry* is a test that may be used to look for malfunction of the muscle at the end of the esophagus, but this test is not practical in girls with RS.

Treatment for GER

Symptoms may be provoked or aggravated by lying down or bending over after meals, wearing tight-fitting clothes, straining for bowel movements, eating the wrong foods at the wrong time, or exercises such as physical therapy soon after eating. Some medications may make GER worse.

Initial treatment involves an antireflux diet which restricts spicy, acidic, and greasy foods as well as coffee, tea, cola, alcohol, peppermint, and chocolate. The quantity of food eaten at one sitting should be limited. Weight should be kept within the normal range. Elevating the head of the bed six inches for sleeping or resting is very important. Putting blocks under the legs of the bed or a wedge under the mattress is more beneficial than pillow-bolstering. The use of pillows may actually make symptoms worse for some people. Chewing gum or sucking candy may relieve symptoms because the release of a lot of saliva can soothe an irritated esophagus. Beverages can be thickened with commercial thickening products to decrease swallowing and choking difficulties.

Heather is not happy about giving up her spicy foods. She loves Italian dishes! We keep her sitting up in her wheelchair for a minimum of twenty minutes following meals. If she needs to get out of her wheelchair, we maintain an elevated head position. She sleeps in an electric hospital bed for easier positioning.

Day-to-Day Care

Antacid medications such as Maalox or Mylanta may be helpful. Do not initiate antacid use without a doctor's direction, as antacids interfere with the absorption of many other medicines and are to be completely avoided with some medicines. If symptoms persist, drug therapy should be instituted. Drug therapy is aimed at increasing the esophageal sphincter pressure and decreasing gastric acid production. In some cases, it may be desirable to decrease pyloric sphincter pressure, particularly if delayed gastric emptying is present. Acid blockers include drugs such as ranitidine (Zantac) or famotidine (Pepcid). Lansoprazole (Prevacid) or omeprazole (Prilosec) are used when the symptoms are severe.

Propulsid (cissipride), a drug that is not available in the US, increases esophageal and gastric motility. Propulsid should not be used in girls with RS, as it increases the potential for heart wave abnormalities (prolonged Q-T syndrome) which are often found in RS.

To Minimize GER

The following foods strengthen the muscle valve in the lower esophagus and help to prevent acid reflux:

- low-fat, high-protein foods
- low-fat carbohydrates (bread, cereal, pasta, crackers)
- calcium, as in fat-free milk and low-fat yogurt

FOOD SELECTION FOR GER

Group	Recommend	Avoid
Milk or milk products	skim, 1% or 2% low-fat milk; low-fat or fat-free yogurt	whole milk (4%), chocolate milk
Vegetables	all other vegetables	fried or creamy style vegetables, tomatoes
Fruits	apples, berries, melons, bananas, peaches, pears	citrus such as oranges, grapefruit, pineapple
Breads & grains	all those made with low-fat content	any prepared with whole milk or high-fat
Meat, meat substitutes	low-fat meat, chicken, fish, turkey	cold cuts, sausage, bacon, fatty meat, chicken fat/skin
Fat, oils	none or small amounts	all animal or vegetable oils
Sweets & desserts	all items made with no or low fat (less than or equal to 3 g fat/serving)	chocolate, desserts made with oils and/or fats
Beverages	decaffeinated, non-mint herbal tea; juices (except citrus); water	alcohol, coffee (regular or decaffeinated), carbonated or citrus beverages
Soups	fat-free or low-fat based	chicken, beef, milk, or cream-based

Day-to-Day Care

The following foods weaken the muscle valve in the lower esophagus and aggravate acid reflux. Avoid giving her:

- fatty or fried foods
- peppermint and spearmint
- whole milk
- chocolate
- creamed foods or soups
- oils

The following foods irritate an inflamed lower esophagus. These may need to be limited or avoided:

- citrus fruit and juices
- grapefruit, orange
- caffeinated soft drinks
- pineapple
- tomato

Surgery for GER

The aim in most cases is to achieve symptomatic relief with medical therapy while watching for complications. In addition to esophagitis, complications can include ulcers and strictures in the esophagus, aspiration pneumonia and other chronic pulmonary diseases, gastrointestinal bleeding, and failure to thrive. If symptoms persist or complications develop, surgery may be necessary. A surgical procedure called a *fundoplication* may be performed. In this procedure, the opening from the esophagus to the stomach is made smaller, thereby preventing reflux. When a fundoplication is performed for the purpose of treating GER, it does not interfere with taking food by mouth.

Lauren had acid reflux which was so severe that she now has some permanent cellular changes in spots on her esophagus called Barrett's esophagus. *Fundoplication really helped greatly, but some damage was already done. We had her on acid blockers and Reglan since she was five years of age, but during the last few years it wasn't enough.*

H. Pylori Bacteria

HELICOBACTER PYLORI (H. PYLORI) IS A TYPE OF BACTERIA which researchers believe is responsible for the majority of peptic ulcers. It weakens the protective mucous coating of the stomach and duodenum, which allows acid to get through to the sensitive lining beneath. Both the acid and the bacteria irritate the lining and cause a sore, or ulcer.

The most common symptom is abdominal discomfort (a dull, gnawing ache). It usually comes and goes for several days or weeks. Other symptoms are weight loss, poor appetite, bloating, burping, vomiting, and nausea. It is relieved by eating and by the use of antacid medicines. Some people experience only very mild symptoms or none at all. If your daughter has pain accompanied by bloody or black stools, bloody vomit, it could be an indication that there is a perforation (when the ulcer burrows through the stomach or duodenal wall, or when acid or the ulcer breaks a blood vessel). It could also indicate

Day-to-Day Care

obstruction (when the ulcer blocks the path of food trying to leave the stomach). To see whether symptoms are caused by an ulcer, the doctor may do an upper gastrointestinal (GI) series or an endoscopy. H. Pylori is treated with antibiotics.

GASTROINTESTINAL PROCEDURES

CT SCAN: IS OFTEN CALLED A CAT SCAN, which stands for computed axial tomography. This test is a method of body imaging in which a thin X-ray beam rotates around the body. A computer analyzes the data to construct a cross-sectional image, which can be stored, viewed on a monitor, or printed on film. The CT scan allows a three-dimensional model of organs.

Endoscopy: an exam that uses an endoscope, a thin, lighted tube with a tiny camera on the end. The patient is lightly sedated, and the doctor carefully eases the endoscope into the mouth and down the throat to the stomach and duodenum. This allows the doctor to see the lining of the esophagus, stomach, and duodenum. The doctor can use the endoscope to take photos of ulcers or remove a tiny piece of tissue to view under a microscope. This procedure is called a biopsy.

Ph probe: a wire probe with Ph paper is inserted through the throat to near the esophageal sphincter muscle. Acid reflux is measured while she goes about normal activities.

Swallow study: an exam in which the child swallows a chalky liquid called barium under an X-ray so that the process of swallowing and the movement of the food from the mouth to the stomach can be observed. The procedure is videotaped so that it can be studied to see if there are problems with swallowing and how well the airway is protected during swallowing.

Ultrasound: may be called a sonogram. High-frequency sound waves are sent out by the ultrasound machine, and these waves reflect off body structures to create a picture. While lying down, a clear, water-based conducting gel is applied to the skin over the area being examined to help with the transmission of the sound waves. A handheld probe is then moved over the abdomen.

Upper GI series: is an X-ray of the esophagus, stomach, and duodenum. It is necessary to drink barium to make these organs and any abnormalities show up more clearly on the X- ray.

Gastrointestinal Crises

Gastrointestinal problems are important components of many signs and symptoms seen in RS. These can be not only persistent and cause a significant level of discomfort for many girls, but a small number can eventually become life-threatening problems. While the likelihood of these situations is not frequent, it is wise to be educated.

Intestinal volvulus can occur when a loop of bowel twists on itself. This happens sometimes from birth in otherwise normal individuals. When volvulus occurs, there is a sudden blockage of the passage of intestinal contents. This will lead to a rapid distention of the abdomen and backing up of fluid and gas, usually causing vomiting, which can be violent. This will also lead to an inadequate supply of blood to the twisted segment and gangrene (death and tearing) of the intestinal wall, spillage of contents into the abdominal cavity, peritonitis, and infection.

In a condition known as *intussusception*, the bowel may telescope upon itself (like the finger in a glove). This leads to all the signs of intestinal blockage that occur in volvulus,

Day-to-Day Care

but additionally, the lining can slough off, causing bloody stools. Fortunately, these latter complications are rare.

Severe impaction, volvulus, and intussusception can all cause complete intestinal blockage. Signs of intestinal obstruction are:

- sudden appearance or marked worsening of abdominal distention
- vomiting, usually violent and sometimes containing bile (green or yellow)
- sudden onset of severe unremitting pain or discomfort
- decreased passage of stools when constipation was not previously present
- diarrhea and/or bloody stools

CIRCULATION

PERIPHERAL (AWAY FROM THE TRUNK) CIRCULATION appears to be impaired from an early age. The feet are often cold and blue or red, and do not grow as they should. At a later age, the feet become purplish and swollen with skin that looks like it is shrinking. The feet and legs are often several degrees cooler than the rest of the body.

It is important to keep her feet and legs covered well so that they will stay warm and comfortable. Try using layers of socks for optimum warmth. Be cautious when using microwavable or battery-operated socks to avoid burning the feet.

A regular pair of socks, with wool socks on top and then her AFOs has improved her circulation dramatically. You can buy pediatric socks at a ski shop; they are not bulky and they come in nice colors; they are pricey, but worth it. We also check her feet periodically during the day and massage them if needed and we elevate her feet if she's sitting watching TV.

BREATHING

EPISODIC, ABNORMAL BREATHING PATTERNS ARE COMMON in RS. Breathing irregularities may be pronounced, or in some cases may be so subtle that they are not even noticed by parents. These patterns appear to be more exaggerated when the girl with RS is agitated. Irregular breathing patterns often begin at preschool age and may change in character and decrease in frequency in adulthood.

Abnormal breathing patterns may include *hyperventilation, breath holding, apnea,* and *rapid and shallow breathing.* These abnormal breathing patterns may be different in each girl in type, frequency, and intensity.

Breathing is usually abnormal during wakefulness and tends to be normal during sleep. However, because the girls are often awake at night, the breath-holding episodes may be mistaken for sleep apnea.

Breathing becomes more irregular under emotional or physical stress. It appears that these abnormalities result from poor coordination of voluntary control of breathing with the respiratory center of the brain stem.

The abnormal breathing episodes can resemble epileptic seizures, but they are not. Sometimes, what is thought to be a seizure is not, and some seizures may fail to be recognized when she is asleep or even awake. Vacant spells are brief interruptions of awareness that may resemble seizures but are not.

Day-to-Day Care

For the majority of girls, irregular breathing patterns become less noticeable as they get older. The younger girl with RS appears to have more hyperventilation while the older girl has more of a type of breathing known as *Valsalva Manoeuver* explained on page 236.

Although episodes of breath holding produce great anxiety for parents to watch, they are always followed by regular breathing. Observing the irregular breathing can cause great concern, but experts in RS recommend a low-key approach, taking comfort in the fact that girls do become accustomed to the irregular breathing, and regular breathing will soon return. While it may seem like forever, it is important to stay calm and in control. There is a lot of research at present directed at answering these questions.

SHALLOW BREATHING

MOST GIRLS WITH RS HAVE SHALLOW BREATHING. The lack of deep breathing often puts the bottoms of the lungs at high risk for collapse. This is one reason why some girls catch cold very easily and often develop pneumonia. Shallow breathing can be a hindrance after surgery and can lead to fever during recovery. It can also interfere with normal sleep.

HYPERVENTILATION

THE MOST STRIKING BREATHING PATTERNS OFTEN NOTICED by parents are periods of overbreathing with fast, deep breaths. Such *hyperventilations* are often interrupted by cessation of breathing, known as *apnea*. When she overbreathes in this way, she may seem agitated with increased hand movements, dilated pupils, increased heart rate, rocking body movements, and increased muscle tone.

Deep breathing expels more carbon dioxide from the body than usual, so her hyperventilation causes her carbon dioxide level to fall. Carbon dioxide is one of the body's normal waste products carried in the blood. Its purpose is to maintain the acid/alkali balance so that cells can function normally. When her carbon dioxide level falls, cells cannot function normally. Hyperventilation may cause her to feel dizzy and her fingers to tingle.

BREATH HOLDING

DURING PERIODS OF BREATH HOLDING, the individual takes in breath and holds it, at which time breathing is stopped. Oxygen saturation in the blood, normally 97 percent and higher, can be greatly reduced in RS, sometimes as low as 50 percent. This may cause her to feel faint.

AEROPHAGIA

AIR SWALLOWING IS KNOWN AS AEROPHAGIA. Most people swallow small amounts of air routinely when they are under stress or eat rapidly, swallow unchewed food, or chew gum. Any time there is gastrointestinal discomfort such as heartburn, frequent swallowing of air and saliva may bring some relief, resulting in substantial amounts of air in the stomach. Most of the air that is swallowed is either burped and passed out of the mouth or passes into the small bowel. Once air is out of the stomach, it must travel the whole length of the intestines before it is passed as intestinal gas. In most people, this does not cause a problem. However, if the volume of air is very significant, it can cause complications. Many girls with RS swallow an excessive amount of air during

Day-to-Day Care

breath holding, which results in *abdominal distention*. Their tummies become very bloated and hard.

Air swallowing can be difficult to detect. Air can be swallowed inadvertently in significant amounts each time she eats. It can also occur throughout the day in small amounts. Sometimes it is easy to hear air as it is being swallowed. If her upper abdomen is distended shortly after she eats it could be that she is swallowing air. Here are some signs and symptoms associated with air swallowing:

- audible swallowing at any time, including sleep
- severe dysfunction of swallowing, with air swallowing apparent while eating or drinking
- abdominal distention, usually following feedings or episodes of hyperventilation and breath holding
- frequent burping (may be beneficial)
- large amounts of gas passed through the rectum

If a large amount of air stays temporarily in the stomach, it will lead to sudden distention of the upper part of the abdomen. The stomach stretches, creating significant tension. If the girl with RS is unable to burp or pass gas, the bowel wall may become thin over time. This is especially true in individuals who have a poor nutritional status. Extreme distention of the wall of the stomach may lead to rupture. Several cases of *gastric rupture* have been reported in girls with RS. Once the stomach or any part of the intestine is torn, this will lead to-, an acute inflammation and infection of the abdominal cavity. Without immediate attention, *peritonitis* may lead to death. However, severe problems are infrequent, even though gastrointestinal problems are common in RS.

If air is passed into the intestine adequately, gastric distention will be less of a problem. But it can accumulate in the mid intestine, causing distention of the abdomen and uncomfortable cramps. Constipation and medications that slow down the passage of stool can worsen abdominal distention.

What to Do

If you suspect that she is swallowing air, there are a few things you can do. Decrease the length of mealtimes if it appears she is swallowing air while eating. Minimize stress and discomfort. Sit her in an upright position after she eats to help her burp and decrease the amount of gas in the stomach that is passed into the bowel. Keep on top of constipation so that gas does not accumulate in the mid intestine. In some situations, even the frequent use of enemas (not routinely recommended) may be preferred to severe episodes of abdominal distention.

If these measures are not adequate and her abdominal distention is severe, you may need to ask the advice of her physician on more aggressive methods. This might include the placement of a tube through her nose into the stomach (*nasogastric tube*) or the placement of a tube through the abdominal wall into the stomach (*gastrostomy button*). This will help to decompress the bowel and allow the gas to flow out. It will prevent gas from advancing into the intestine. However, once the air is beyond the stomach, the bowel cannot be decompressed with any of these tubes. Some surgical interventions to prevent reflux, such as the Nissen fundoplication, in which the opening from the esophagus to the stomach is closed, may help in GER, preventing heartburn or intermittent vomiting. At the same time, they can also increase the chances of a complication from air swallowing, since she is now unable to burp to get rid of gas.

Day-to-Day Care

The risks and benefits of such surgery should be weighed carefully in each patient prior to making this decision. In rare situations, the placement of a ***colostomy*** (opening the bowel into the abdominal wall) may help in allowing adequate flow of intestinal contents and decrease the complications from inadequate passage of stool.

Early detection as well as consultation with a gastroenterologist is extremely important to avoid progression of the problem and to manage it as early as possible, thus preventing more severe complications.

Apnea

CENTRAL APNEA OCCURS WHEN SHE LETS A BREATH OUT and fails to take another breath, causing a temporary cessation of breathing. This occurs often in girls with RS when they are awake. It usually does not cause serious problems. When she holds her breath, her oxygen levels fall. Sometimes her lips may turn blue and she may even lose consciousness briefly. However, she usually begins breathing again on her own. Apnea would be serious if her oxygen level fell low enough to a level known as *anoxia*. This is typically not seen in RS.

Since most girls breathe normally during sleep, an apnea monitor is not usually necessary. During the daytime, the apnea can occur so often that it would be difficult to keep up with. However, some families choose to use monitors when she sleeps for peace of mind.

The apnea monitor monitors her heart rate and her breathing. Although we don't use it on a nightly basis, whenever she is sick and/or more prone to having seizures, we put the monitor on her and it has alerted us to seizures because her breathing stops and/or changes.

Valsalva Manoeuver

VALSALVA MANOEUVER TAKES PLACE when a girl takes in a long inspiration and tries to force it out while the airway is shut. This causes a sudden change in blood pressure and heart rate.

In RS, irregular breathing occurs primarily when she is awake and does not usually occur during sleep. When she is awake, the periods of abnormal breathing result from probable immaturity of neurons regulating breathing mechanisms. During periods of sleep, the brainstem respiratory center takes over. These changes in body function allow us to breathe regularly and continuously. When abnormal breathing is seen in some girls with RS during sleep it may be from airway obstruction that is caused by mechanical problems in the breathing passages, usually from enlarged tonsils. Mouth breathing, snoring and frequent ear infections may be signals that your daughter has a problem which should be evaluated by an ear, nose, and throat specialist.

These abnormal breathing episodes can be alarming to watch, and may make her somewhat uncomfortable, but they are not felt to cause permanent damage. It is not known why the normal breathing during sleep brings out EEG abnormalities, while abnormal breathing during wakefulness causes the EEG to normalize to what is often seen in RS. Cessation of breathing during sleep is not typically seen in RS. However, if your child stops breathing for short periods of time while asleep, you should talk with her physician. She may need testing to rule out airway obstruction. This is a separate problem from RS, for which there is treatment.

Day-to-Day Care

OXYGEN

IF CHRONIC AND PROLONGED, lack of oxygen can be life threatening. Most girls with RS who hold their breath do not have dangerously reduced oxygen flow. However, when there is chronic oxygen deprivation and the oxygen levels fall more than fifteen times an hour, supplemental oxygen can be beneficial.

Allison was evaluated in a sleep study where it was determined that she had abnormal breathing and periods of apnea while sleeping. She will breathe very shallow for several breaths, then take one or two very deep breaths. She does not have enlarged tonsils or adenoids. She has an oxygen concentrator and is on one half liter while sleeping. She also gets oxygen following seizures when she is at home, especially if she is given medication such as Diastat, which can slow breathing. I do it for my own peace of mind.

Initially when she had seizures that included the apnea, we would administer a rescue breath and immediately put the oxygen on her, monitoring her oxygen saturation levels (O₂ sats). We came to realize after many seizures that included the apnea that she will restart her breathing on her own and she brings her oxygen saturation back up on her own without the supplemental oxygen. With that said, we are not comfortable letting her go too long without restarting her own breathing so we will always be very vigilant and keep the oxygen nearby.

Karen is on supplemental oxygen all the time. She has been since her second severe pneumonia which followed rapidly after her first. She saw a lot of pulmonologists and they feel that her lung damage keeps her from getting enough oxygen.

Melissa was in the hospital for a week to see if anything else might be causing her lack of energy. They gave her all kinds of tests. She had already had her tonsils and adenoids out so that wasn't it. Then they tested her on oxygen to see how much she needed. It finally was decided she needed to be on supplemental oxygen around the clock.

THE VEST

THE VEST SYSTEM IS A MEDICAL DEVICE designed for clearing excess mucus from the lungs. Used widely in homes and hospitals, it consists of an inflatable vest connected by flexible tubes to an air-pulse generator. The generator rapidly inflates and deflates the vest, gently compressing and releasing the chest wall. This technology, called high-frequency chest wall oscillation (HFCWO) loosens, thins, and moves secretions toward central airways so they may be more easily cleared. The Vest system is a product of Advanced Respiratory, Inc., located in St. Paul, Minnesota. For more information about The Vest system, call: 1-866-411-8378 or visit www.thevest.com.

The Vest has been so great for Emily; it has literally saved her life. It can be rented and there is help for the rental costs from the National Airway Clearance Registry. The Vest works so well for patients with low muscle tone who don't have a productive cough, who can "literally suffocate" from all the mucous that the vest dislodges from the lungs.

Rachel seems to tolerate the Vest well. She used it the last two times she was hospitalized. She has been using a nebulizer for years, and we always did chest PT afterwards. The Vest is supposed to be much more effective than the chest PT and will cut our sessions in half since she can wear it while she is receiving her nebulizer treatment.

ENDOTRACHEAL INTUBATION

AT SOME TIME, USUALLY DURING SURGERY, your child may need *endotracheal intubation.* This is a procedure by which a flexible plastic tube is inserted through

Day-to-Day Care

the mouth down into the trachea (the large airway from the mouth to the lungs). The tube serves as an open passage through the upper airway. The purpose of endotracheal intubation is to permit air to pass freely to and from the lungs in order to ventilate the lungs. Endotracheal tubes can be connected to ventilator machines to provide artificial respiration.

POSITIVE AIRWAY PRESSURE MACHINES

THE BILEVEL POSITIVE AIRWAY MACHINE (Bi PAP) is a noninvasive mask type of ventilator which is used to regulate breathing during sleep. It is very expensive and requires a prescription.

She was put in the unit with the thought she would have to be intubated. Instead, they used Bi PAP to keep her airway open, and The Vest for chest PT. It was absolutely awesome. She loved the movement and would just grin from ear to ear when we activated it. It was amazing at how well it worked for her.

Joanne has had several sleep studies done and definitely has centralized apnea. She has slept with oxygen on for several years in order to maintain her oxygen levels and has had a Bi PAP mask for over a year. The Bi PAP has made the hugest difference. Joanne's sleep study results have shown that she can have several hundred centralized apnea moments each night, so several hundred times a night her breath is held and her oxygen levels dip dangerously low. With the assistance of the Bi PAP mask, she now can maintain her oxygen levels, clear out more carbon dioxide, and get a much better sleep. There is also the added benefit of better health, better growth, and overall better quality of life.

The respiratory folks used a new gadget on Karissa called an EZ Pap. All that was required of Karissa was for her to take breaths into a mask, and it created a positive pressure in her lungs to help them fill fully and to help the air get down into the alveoli. To get the mucous out, they used the mask in combination with Xopenex Treatments and chest PT. She did not mind it at all but couldn't always coordinate her breaths to get a good pressure going if she was too tired. The EZ Pap seems ideal for Karissa because she is such a shallow breather.

MEDICATIONS

BUSPAR HAS BEEN USED in carefully selected situations. It is recommended only on an individual basis under close medical supervision. Respiratory and autonomic function should be recorded before and during treatment and if no measurable benefit is seen, the drug should be stopped. The dose must be related to the specific case and situation. At best, this medication may improve breathing rhythm. It cannot be expected to reverse the underlying immaturity of the brain stem in RS. The importance of the limited success with this substance is just that it confirms the suspicions that serotonin deficiency is an important part of the disorder and it helps us to plan more effective therapeutic approaches.

Note: Buspar should not be looked at as a cure-all. Even in situations where it is effective, it must be treated with the same caution as any other drug. Because its use for this problem is new and largely unevaluated, there is no general recommendation. **Naltrexone** (*Revia*) is an opiod antagonist that was tried in girls with RS and found to have beneficial effects on breathing. In the study, the dosage was 1mg/kg, but can be adjusted by her physician according to her response.

Magnesium citrate or **magnesium orotate** has been used for the treatment of the hyperventilation seen in RS after it was used on a child to treat seizures and her hyperventilation/

Day-to-Day Care

apnea improved. Researchers then tested low-dose magnesium for treatment of the respiratory irregularities in six other children with stage 2-3 RS. They used an initial dose of 4 mg/kg/day divided into three doses, then increased the dose as tolerated to a maximum of 10/mg/kg/day or until diarrhea developed.

The parents recorded numbers of severe hyperventilation/apnea with cyanosis (turning blue) occurring in a thirty-minute period on a daily basis for five days before treatment and after one month of treatment. They found that apnea with cyanosis and hyperventilation decreased.

Magnesium citrate is available over-the-counter as a "sparkling" laxative that costs about one dollar per ten ounce bottle. The concentration is 58.1 mg/ml so for a child who weighs 55 pounds, the maximum daily dose is 1.4 cc (1.4 ml) per dose, three times a day. Start at one teaspoon in the morning and evening. Increase the dose to the point of diarrhea, then drop back one dosage both morning and evening.

PNEUMONIA

PNEUMONIA IS AN INFLAMMATION AND INFECTION of the lungs, which often follows a common cold or the flu. It can range in seriousness from mild to life threatening. In *infectious pneumonia*, bacteria, viruses, fungi, or other organisms attack the lungs, leading to inflammation that makes it hard to breathe. Pneumonia can affect one or both lungs. Infection of both lungs is sometimes popularly referred to as *double pneumonia*. Pneumonia ranks sixth among all disease categories as a cause of death. It is best to do everything you can to prevent pneumonia, but if your child does get sick, recognizing and treating the disease early offers the best chance for a full recovery. Bacteria are the most common cause of pneumonia in adults (*bacterial pneumonia*), while viruses are most often the cause of pneumonia in children (*viral pneumonia*). Lack of normal movement makes the individual with RS more prone to pneumonia. Typical symptoms include cough, fever, and sputum production. The diagnosis of pneumonia is confirmed with a chest X-ray.

Aspiration-induced pneumonia is often called *chemical pneumonia or aspiration pneumonia,* caused when food surges up from the stomach after a meal and causes vomiting into the lungs. When there is risk of aspiration, a g-button is recommended. If her risk is very high, she may need to eliminate eating and drinking by mouth.

TREATMENT

ANTIBIOTICS ARE USED TO TREAT BACTERIAL PNEUMONIA, but antibiotics are not effective in treating viral pneumonia. However, in some cases, the two types of pneumonia are hard to distinguish and antibiotics are prescribed anyway. Sometimes pneumonia can be managed at home, but if your child has low oxygen levels or residual damage to the lungs from previous episodes of pneumonia, she will likely need to be hospitalized. In the hospital, she can receive intravenous antibiotics and oxygen therapy.

It is important to get her to drink plenty of fluids to help loosen secretions and bring up phlegm and to get lots of rest. If she is bedridden with pneumonia, it is really important that she be rolled from side to side often, even during sleeping hours, so that fluid doesn't build up. Repositioning from side to side, getting upright, sitting or standing and

Day-to-Day Care

walking help keep the fluid from building up in the lungs. Periodic chest-clapping is helpful in producing a hearty cough to clear things out. A course of pneumonia usually takes about two weeks, but it may take a long time for her to recuperate and return to her normal energy level. Once pneumonia has occurred, scar tissue builds up in the lungs, making her more susceptible to another episode.

VISION

MOST GIRLS WITH RS HAVE NORMAL TO NEAR NORMAL vision, approximating that of the regular population. Vision can be tested even in infants and young children by a pediatric opthamologist.

STRABISMUS AND AMBLYOPIA

ABNORMAL ALIGNMENT OF THE EYES sometimes occurs. This is called *strabismus*. It may be caused by an abnormality of the eye muscles or in the nerve supplying these muscles. *Esotropia* is the form of strabismus which results in cross-eyes (the eyes turn in). In *exotropia*, the eyes turn out. The strabismus may be noticed in one eye or both, and it may either come and go or be continuous. It may only be noticed when the child is tired. If it is intermittent, esotropia does not usually cause vision loss. If it is caused by farsightedness, wearing glasses can correct it. However, if the esotropia is continuous and is not treated, it can lead to *amblyopia* (commonly known as lazy eye), one of the most common eye disorders in children. The crossed eye 'turns off,' and only the stronger eye is used. Amblyopia is treated by making the child use the weaker eye by covering the strong eye with a patch, sometimes for long periods of time.

Jacky was eight months old when she began wearing glasses, well before we knew anything at all about RS. She crossed both eyes, but after about a year or two, her eyes stabilized and there were no prescription changes. Then last year she began getting her hands up to her face and knocking her glasses off, so the doctor checked her eyes and said she could stop wearing glasses. We just went for her six-month checkup and it has been a year and still no glasses.

Katie crossed her eyes a bit between the ages of two and three. The eye doctor said that eye crossing is a natural developmental thing kids do at a certain developmental age and that kids who are developmentally delayed sometimes just do it later and not to worry unless it goes on for a long time.

Emily started eye-crossing quite a bit when she went through her regression at about age three. I was worried and took her to an eye specialist who did recommend glasses. I was concerned because the lenses were so strong, especially since the doctor said her actual eyesight was fine. I stopped letting her wear them and over the past year it has gotten better by itself. She seems to do it mostly when she is very excited.

Rachel has worn glasses for astigmatism and extreme farsightedness since she was about one year old. She tolerates the glasses well, and a recent eye exam showed she had not grown out of any of the above. One thing I was impressed by was that her fine motor skills improved greatly with the glasses.

THE HEART

THE AUTONOMIC NERVOUS SYSTEM CONTROLS heart rate. Studies have shown that the *atrio-ventricular conduction* (transmitting) system of the heart is

Day-to-Day Care

developmentally immature in RS. Reduced heart rate variability stops the heart from speeding up adequately during periods of excitement, stress, agitation, or exertion and also keeps it from slowing down adequately as it should during periods of rest and calm. Abnormal heart rhythms (*arrhythmias*) are sometimes seen, and these seem to become more pronounced with the advancing stages of Rett syndrome.

In healthy people, the cardiovascular system is under increased *vagal tone* during hyperventilation in an attempt to balance the effects of over breathing on the heart. In girls with RS, the vagal tone is not increased, so the effects persist, causing irregularities. The sympathetic nervous system is on "high" during breath holding in anyone, but in RS regulation of heart rate and blood pressure by vagal tone is very poor. This low vagal tone during breath holding and hyperventilation creates an imbalance, which is known to predispose individuals to cardiac arrhythmias and possibly sudden death. It is felt that these irregularities of the heart may account for the sudden unexplained deaths that occur in RS.

ELECTROCARDIOGRAM (ECG)

SOON AFTER DIAGNOSIS YOUR DAUGHTER SHOULD HAVE an *electrocardiogram* (ECG). If abnormal, then referral to a cardiologist should be considered and further ECGs done per recommendations of the cardiologist. If your daughter has been previously diagnosed with RS but has not had an ECG, an ECG should be done and repeated every two to three years.

LONG Q-T SYNDROME

LONG Q-T SYNDROME (LQTS) IS A RARE INHERITED DISORDER of the heart's "conducting" or "electrical" system. "Q-T" refers to one of the intervals that characterize a normal heartbeat cycle. In people with Long Q-T syndrome, this interval is sometimes longer than usual, which disturbs the heart's rhythm. The disorder may cause attacks of fast heart rhythm, which can be serious. Long Q-T syndrome may explain some rare instances of sudden death in young people where no obvious abnormality is found.

If abnormalities are reported on the electrocardiogram, specifically "long Q-T interval," a cardiologist may be consulted. Nonspecific ECG changes probably do not warrant medications. Other ECG findings such as long Q-T interval may warrant medications depending on the evaluation of the cardiologist. If the Q-T interval is significantly prolonged, the cardiologist may prescribe medications such as beta blockers (propanolol or Inderal). One contraindication for use of propanolol is asthma, but there are other medications that the cardiologist may choose to treat Long Q-T syndrome.

After testing negative two years ago, McKenna recently was found to have a severe case of Long Q-T syndrome. The cardiologist said the first step was to start her on a beta-blocker to slow down the heart. We tried Atenolol. She raised the dosage eight times and it had absolutely no effect on McKenna's heart rate. Then we tried a different beta blocker called Nadolol. She raised the dosage once and that seemed to do the trick.

Long Q-T syndrome causes an abnormality of the heart's *electrical* system. The *mechanical* function of the heart is entirely normal. The electrical problem is due to defects in heart muscle cell structures called ion channels. These electrical defects predispose affected persons to a very fast heart rhythm (*arrhythmia*) called *"Torsade de Pointes"* (TdP) which leads to sudden loss of consciousness (*syncope*) and may cause sudden cardiac death.

Day-to-Day Care

TEMPERATURE REGULATION

GIRLS WITH RS SOMETIMES HAVE DIFFICULTY keeping an even body temperature. They may run a fever with no source of illness. This is not a cause for alarm. They often do not sweat when they are hot, or they sweat in patches instead of all over. They tend to prefer moderation in temperatures, particularly with food.

Heat and humidity are often problems for the girl with RS, and can lead to severe discomfort or can even cause a seizure. For this reason, it is important to provide air-conditioning in extreme heat at home, on the school bus, and at school.

The same concern applies for cold temperatures. Due to her poor circulation, her feet and hands are often cold and bluish. If she is very thin, she does not have much natural insulation. Keep her feet warm with layers of socks, and make sure she has enough warm clothing on. Be sure to keep her covered while on the toilet, as she may chill easily.

Kimberly does not tolerate extreme heat or cold well at all. She basically just wilts in the heat. She will start turning red and will eventually start vomiting. She does not do any outdoor activities during the summer. The only time that she is outside is to go from the house to the car, etc. When she was little, we used to take her to the beach and pool and we realized that she was so miserable that we just stopped taking her. Now when we go to the beach, she stays indoors during the day and we take her out at night. Our school district has air-conditioned, handicapped-accessible buses, but I drive her back and forth to school every day just to make sure that she is cool enough in warmer months and warm enough in cooler months.

SLEEP

SLEEP PROBLEMS ARE RELATIVELY COMMON in girls with RS. They often take a long time to fall asleep and have several interruptions in sleep during the night. As a result, their total sleep time is reduced. They may cry at night, but the majority of girls awaken laughing or "talking." Studies have shown that girls with RS sleep less at night as they get older and more during the daytime. When they do have a "bad" night, they generally increase their sleep the next night to make it up.

Girls with RS often have shallow breathing patterns. When they do not take enough deep breaths, especially when sleeping, they do not take in enough oxygen. This affects lung capacity as well as energy levels during the day, sleep, and overall growth and health. Shallow breathing results in an increase in carbon dioxide. This increase gives them just enough of an energy increase during sleep to continually prevent them from going into a deep sleep. Instead, they "nap," or sleep for a short time without going back to sleep, and never get fully rested.

Sleep problems in RS can be disruptive for the whole family. Both the girl with RS and her family need healthy sleep to be at their best. Some parents use earplugs, a VCR with earphones in her room, or sleep medications. Some try soundproofing her room with a "white noise" machine or a fan. One family even covered the walls with thick cotton batting to muffle her nighttime noises. One study measured the effectiveness of the hormone Melatonin in girls with RS. While Melatonin did reduce the time it took to fall asleep, it did not reduce the night wakenings.

Many girls with RS awaken during the night laughing. These episodes can last from a few minutes to more than an hour. They seem to come and go, but persist in some until middle age or later.

Day-to-Day Care

Here are some suggestions to promote better sleep:

- Have a standard bedtime routine every night. This will give your daughter a "signal" that it is time to relax and get ready for sleep. Try to pick an activity that is not done at any other time of the day. Avoid rough play before bedtime.

- Encourage her to fall asleep independently. If she learns to fall asleep with assistance such as being rocked to sleep, having you in bed with her, having the radio on, or drinking a bottle, she will have difficulty falling asleep under any other circumstances. She becomes dependent on your assistance and can't fall asleep without it. It may seem like a good idea since it works to get her to sleep, but in the long run it can actually worsen sleep problems and can lead to a vicious cycle. When she awakens in the night, she will be unable to go back to sleep without some intervention.

- Going to sleep and waking up should take place about the same time every day, including weekends. Allowing her to sleep at irregular times imbalances her body's natural biological clock. When she goes to sleep later at night and sleeps later in the morning, you are actually feeding into her body's natural tendency to be out of sync with the demands of daily living. She will continue to fall asleep later at night or awaken at night. If she has the opportunity, she may catch up by sleeping during the day. While catch-up sleep may be okay on the weekends, she loses school time when she naps during the week. Children who don't have the opportunity to sleep during the day often adjust by simply getting less total sleep. Reduced or disturbed sleep may result in irritability and daytime fatigue and increases in challenging behaviors such as tantrums and self-injury. So, the way to improve sleep patterns is to regulate the timing of sleep, not to just allow her to sleep at any time of the day.

- Naptimes should occur at the same time and for the same length every day. Most parents want to allow their daughter to get some extra sleep if she did not sleep well the night before. But, letting her sleep at irregular times will only maintain or worsen an existing sleep problem. If she cannot stay awake every day at the same time, allow her to sleep every day at this time. Many girls take cat naps. Try to allow these at the same time every day and attempt to keep her awake at times outside of the regularly scheduled nap times. Keep track of her sleep-wake pattern for a week and see if there are any times in which sleep is likely. If so, try to make those sleep times as consistent as possible by keeping her awake at all other times and allowing her to sleep only at the scheduled nap times.

- If she does not sleep consistently at the same time every day and you want to encourage more regular sleep, begin by making a schedule of sleep-wake times. First, allow her to sleep at those scheduled times and wake her up at the end of the scheduled nap. Second, choose a time interval in the day when you will definitely keep her awake. Continue to allow her to cat nap throughout the rest of the day. As your daughter begins to tolerate the awake time, extend that interval by one-half to one hour. Gradually continue extending the wake interval until she is only sleeping during the scheduled nap times. If she continues to have sleep problems at night, you may want to consider further decreasing the length or frequency of daytime naps.

- Try to minimize the amount and type of intervention you provide during night awakenings. This may be hard because you are missing sleep too while you're trying to figure out why she is awake. You are anxious that she may be awake because of a bad dream,

Day-to-Day Care

a wet diaper, an upset stomach or some other problem which she can't correct. Unfortunately, going to her room and interacting with her during night awakenings may only make the problem worse. She may continue to waken during the night in situations where she has a valid reason for being awake but also in situations where she just wants some company. It is hard to know how to respond to her real needs without contributing to the sleep problem. The best solution is to provide the minimal amount of attention necessary to take care of her needs. Change her diaper or give a drink without a lot of fuss, place her back in bed, and leave the room. If there doesn't seem to be a valid reason for her to be awake, reassure her that everything is all right, and then quietly leave the room. If you do check on her, do it as soon as she begins to cry. If you only go into her room after she has been crying for a period of time, she only learns to cry harder and for longer periods of time to get your attention. The most important thing to remember is that she needs to go back to sleep by herself.

Changing her sleep pattern may not be easy. If you do make a change, you can expect her sleep to worsen before it gets better. Unfortunately, there are no magic cures. If she has had a sleep problem for years, the problem will not change in just a few weeks. Development of good sleep patterns takes time, effort and consistency on your part. Earplugs and prayer help, too!

Here are some suggestions that parents have reported work:

- medications: Benadryl, Atarax, Elavil, Ativan, Tranxene, Melatonin, Trazadone, Clonidine, Remeron
- snack before bed
- warm/cool dark, quiet room
- deep massage
- white noise machine or fan
- waterbed
- car rides
- soft music
- warm socks
- egg crate mattress
- soft blanket
- warm bath before bed
- settle-down time with quiet talk
- warm milk
- warm water bottle on her abdomen
- relaxing audiotapes
- no sweets before bed
- an active day with exercise
- quiet stories before bed
- bowel movement

We use Melatonin for Amber and it seems to help. We still have problem nights sometimes anyway, but not near as much when using the Melatonin. On the nights when she won't sleep and wakes up happy, I usually

Day-to-Day Care

put her in front of the TV with her favorite DVD and go back to sleep. She usually stays up for a few hours and then falls asleep on the floor.

Jean's sleep hinges on being adequately fed. If she wakes up in the night, I know that she will not get back to sleep unless I give her some blended food. So, my formula for a good night's sleep is a good day's food and a top-off if needed in the night.

Kendall can fall asleep anywhere, any time. She goes to bed at 8 pm and sleeps all through the night. We got her a heated mattress pad. I set it on low, add in flannel sheets, and she's as snug as a bug in a rug!

If she wakes up at night I have her sit upright on her bed (without back support). The sitting tires her out and takes her mind away from trying to put herself to sleep. When her head is hanging low, I know she's ready to fall asleep and I put her down.

PAIN

SOME GIRLS WITH RS SEEM TO SHOW A HIGH TOLERANCE for pain. They do not react to a needle stick for blood, for instance. Many have high levels of beta-endorphin, the body's own natural pain killer, so this may explain why. However, response to pain is sometimes inconsistent. A girl may not cry when she bumps her head, but cry loudly when she has gas pains. So, her insensitivity to pain is erratic. It could be that she feels internal pain more deeply than external pain. Or it could be that she has a delay in reacting to pain that is mistaken for tolerance. It is likely that she has some disorganization of pain input and processing. Take care to realize that even though she doesn't react as if she is in pain, it is quite possible that she is. The most common causes of pain are reflux, constipation/impaction, and dystonia. Other causes to investigate include tooth decay, urinary tract infection, earache, vaginal infection, headache, sinus infection, and all of the other ills that affect all of us. This topic is also covered in the chapter on behavior.

DROOLING

EXCESSIVE SALIVA AND DROOLING ARE A COMMON PROBLEM in RS, especially in girls who have difficulty closing their mouths. Therapies aimed at reducing drooling include tapping around the outside of the lips, rubbing ice around the outside of the lips before a meal, and using battery-operated vibrators for extra stimulation. A taste of lemon or vanilla on the lips will stimulate lip closure, as will sucking through a straw. Many girls with RS wear colorful bandanas that are color matched to their clothing to catch the wetness. They are stylish, easy to change often, and washable. When drooling becomes a very serious problem, a medication called Artane can be taken, or a Scopolamine patch can be worn. An ear, nose, and throat specialist can be consulted to see whether surgery will help. The types of surgery done include salivary gland removal, parasympathetic nerve surgery, and salivary duct adjustment and/or re-routing. Some physicians recommend the use of Botox injections of submandibular salivary glands.

What has been helpful is some of the oral work she received from sensory integration therapy to help her be more aware of her tongue, cheeks, palate, etc. They do this by massaging and stretching the insides of the cheek; brushing and applying upward pressure on the palate; brushing and pushing in and backward on the tongue; pressing

Day-to-Day Care

down on molars; stimulating taste receptors on her tongue and cheeks with intense sour, strong mints, spicy foods, and cold Popsicles or sucking with Mr. Freezies. The mouth is such a strong sensory place and also provides a calm and more organized state when it is stimulated and she is more aware of her mouth and placement of tongue. She sucks great from a straw, imitates lots of facial expressions, vocalizes and is able to stick out her tongue when it was hard for her to do before.

Over the years we've had lots of drooling, some from seizures, some from reflux, and some just from the loss of swallowing skills. During seizure activity there's a periodic loss of control in swallowing, and apparently with reflux the body tries to compensate by increasing the production of saliva. With the deterioration of swallowing skills, this can become a constant messy problem. Jenn wears neckerchiefs to fashionably catch the drool.

Some friends of ours who have a daughter with RS are using a Trans-Derm Scop patch on Audrey for drooling. This patch is primarily used for motion sickness, but works for drooling, as it does dry out the mouth. It does have some side effects, but they have encountered none with Audrey.

Vanesa uses Robinul for drooling, starting with a low dose, because of our everlasting concerns with constipation. She takes 1 mg in the am and 1 mg in the afternoon. If she is going out at night, we will give her an extra dose to help minimize her drool while out. We have had no ill effects, but it does seem there are days when she still produces a lot of saliva.

We use Liquid Warhead sour candy when needed and it works really well. You cannot help but swallow.

Hannah was our little faucet! She was on Levsin orally four times daily, with no results. Once we heard about this study on Atropine, she started taking one drop of Opthalmic Atropine (Isopto Atropine 1%) in the morning, and we repeat one drop at bedtime. She no longer has to wear bibs or have her chin wiped on a constant basis. She has not had any side effects from this at all. We cannot say enough positive things about it!

Our friends have used the Atropine (one eye-drop daily) and they can't believe how well it works.

We give Shelley a grape liquid decongestant/antihistamine every morning. This helps her breathe better through her nose, stops the blowing/huffing, and cuts the drooling way back. When someone comes over or we go out, I always give her a dose a half hour or so before. It really makes a difference. We just make sure to give her extra sips of water, as it does dry the mouth out.

I have been doing the "drool therapy" using flavored extracts—orange, pineapple, cherry, etc. The first trick is to look at the alcohol content. If it is 40 percent or more, dilute it by half with water. If it is under 40 percent, use it straight. I take a Q-tip and dip it in the extract, then ask Becky to "open." I run it down both sides of the tongue, and then dip the other side and slide it under her tongue. At first, do it after eating, brushing teeth, drinking and before bed. We started with five to six times a day. Do it for a couple of weeks at least, to get her to go along with the program. You can back off when you see she's not so drooly all the time. If she drools all morning but not in the afternoon, stop the afternoon one and see what happens.

I used to put my finger under her chin and say, "Swallow, Angie." To our utter amazement, she did. It was as if she needed a physical cue.

Carol hasn't drooled or had swallowing/mouth closure issues for years. I wrote the process into her IEP with a verbal cue of "close your mouth, Carol," followed with a gentle upward lift to her chin, followed with "swallow, Carol." Admittedly, it took a lot of patience and constant reminding, but it worked.

PUBERTY

IN HEALTHY GIRLS AS WELL AS GIRLS WITH RS, puberty begins around the age of eight when the pituitary gland begins to secrete hormones. These hormones

Day-to-Day Care

travel through the bloodstream to the ovaries, where they trigger growth and change. The first observable change is breast budding. One breast may start growing before the other, and they may grow at different rates so they may appear unequal in size at first. Eventually, they will be the same size. Next, she develops pubic hair and, later underarm hair. She goes through a growth spurt and her hips and breasts become more rounded.

THE GYNECOLOGIST

THE NEED FOR A WOMAN with RS to see a gynecologist is the same as any other woman. Most maturing girls should have a physical every year after the age of eighteen, unless they are taking birth control pills, the use of which requires an examination regardless of age. She should see the gynecologist if a vaginal infection is suspected. The examiner should be gentle and patient, and the parent should stay with her, giving reassurance and comfort. A gynecological exam can be less distressing if she is lying on her side.

MENSTRUATION

MENSTRUATION (MENARCHE) USUALLY BEGINS about two years after the breasts begin to bud. It is considered "normal" if a girl begins her period after nine years and before sixteen years. Most healthy girls begin menstruating around the age of thirteen. This is usually the case in RS, but menstruation is delayed in some cases when the girl is very thin. Before hormonal changes can begin, she must reach a critical body weight of around 106 pounds, which some girls with RS may never achieve. She must also have the right amount of body fat and body water for menstruation to begin. In spite of this, many girls with RS begin their menstrual cycles at the expected time. Others may begin their period earlier or later than usual. Some girls have noticeable pubic hair earlier than what is typical. The first few years after menstruation begins, it is normal for her cycle to be irregular. She may skip a period now and then.

During the last two weeks of the menstrual cycle, she may retain water, which causes swelling not only in the abdomen but sometimes in the hands, feet, and breasts. The increased level of hormones also affects the gastrointestinal tract, causing the GI tract to empty more slowly and produce gas. Because stool and gas are moving more slowly through the intestines, constipation and bloating may be more noticeable during the two weeks before her periods. Each month when the period begins, the hormone levels drop and diarrhea sometimes becomes a problem. To avoid premenstrual bloating, avoid gas-producing foods and add bulk fiber to the diet.

HYGIENE

THE EFFECT OF INCREASED ESTROGEN in her system is a thin, whitish, mucus-like discharge. This causes no discomfort and should not have an odor or cause itching, redness, or lesions on the skin.

Menstrual flow is odorless until it comes in contact with air and bacteria. Bathing and the use of disposable wipes are helpful. Sanitary napkins can be used in the panties or can be inserted in the diaper for extra protection.

VAGINAL INFECTIONS

A VAGINAL INFECTION WILL USUALLY HAVE AN ODOR. It may be very white, thick, and cottage cheese-like, or yellowish or greenish in color. It may cause

Day-to-Day Care

itching and may produce redness. Yeast infections will usually cause a bright red diaper rash with itching. If she has any of these symptoms, her doctor should be contacted.

Vaginal irritation is common in girls over three years for a number of reasons. Inadequate bathing, wiping from back to front or washing too vigorously may cause problems. Sitting on the ground without protection and high-sugar diets may also contribute to difficulties, as well as wearing clothing that is too tight and does not let air circulate. Pinworms and anal scratching are other sources of vaginal irritation. To avoid these problems, change her diaper frequently, give warm baths, and use bland lotions or ointments to protect the skin.

PERSONAL HYGIENE PRODUCTS

THE PRODUCT USED FOR HER PERIOD may depend on her mobility. Sanitary napkins may be inserted in her underwear or in her diaper. Some people just rely on the diaper. Slim tampons for teens can be used, and are most easily inserted when she is lying on her side, legs drawn up. Be sure to insert the tampon completely into the vagina, as it will be uncomfortable if it is only partly inserted. If tampons are used, it is important to change them often. As with anyone who uses tampons, it is important to recognize the signs of *toxic shock syndrome* (TSS), which occurs most often in women younger than thirty. TSS is a rare but potentially dangerous disorder caused by bacteria which find a breeding ground in the absorbent nature of the tampon and moisture of the vagina. Sudden fever of 102 degrees or more, vomiting or diarrhea, dizziness, and rash are the symptoms to watch for. A physician should be consulted immediately.

Stacie puts her hands in her pants. This was a problem when she began having her period and we decided to try a slim tampon. I calmly explained each step as I inserted the tampon. This has been very successful, avoiding mess and odor, and she seems comfortable. I would not send her to school with a tampon, because I wouldn't want anyone else to change it. But it makes a good alternative when we we're out.

MENSTRUAL CRAMPS

IF SHE SEEMS UNCOMFORTABLE, over-the-counter preparations for menstrual pain such as Haltran or Motrin may be adequate. If these do not work effectively enough, her physician can prescribe a stronger medication to give relief. A hot water bottle on the tummy may help.

PREMENSTRUAL SYNDROME (PMS)

PMS IS A PREDICTABLE PATTERN of physical and emotional changes that occur just before menstruation. Most women experience these changes from a mild to moderate degree. The symptoms can develop any time after the midpoint of the menstrual cycle, and usually end soon after the period starts each month. PMS may cause bloating, breast tenderness, weight gain, fluid retention, fatigue, nausea, vomiting, diarrhea, constipation, headaches, skin problems, or respiratory problems. It may also cause emotional changes that include depression, irritability, anxiety, tension, mood swings, difficulty concentrating, or lethargy. If your daughter has a period, you may notice some of these changes taking place. It helps to remember that these changes are predictable and short-lived. Seizures can become worse prior to the onset of periods.

Day-to-Day Care

The birth control pill will reduce her menstrual flow. Other methods to eliminate her period altogether include shots of Depo-Provera and surgeries known as *endometrial ablation and hysterectomy.*

CONTRACEPTIVES

NEWER LOW-DOSE ORAL CONTRACEPTIVES are more effective and have fewer risks. There are dozens of brands on the market today. Your daughter's physician should be consulted about the risks and benefits and the type of pill that is best for her. Possible side effects, which are usually minor, include nausea, breast tenderness, fluid retention, depression, and nervousness. A sense of fullness may be felt in the breasts or pelvis. Weight gain may occur, but in RS, that is usually a plus! Some beneficial side effects include lighter menstrual flow and fewer cramps, regular and predictable periods, and decreased likelihood to develop breast lumps, iron-deficiency anemia, ovarian cysts, endometrial or ovarian cancer, or rheumatoid arthritis. Birth control pills are usually taken for three continuous weeks and during the fourth week, no pill or an inactive pill is taken. The menstrual flow will then begin. If no menstrual flow is desired, the active pill is continued without interruption.

It is not harmful to her to take the pill without a break, and it will help you with hygiene problems by stopping menstruation. While she will not have a regular period, she may have some spotting.

Angela takes a birth control pill called LoEstrin. Its particular value is that it reduces and in some women completely eliminates the monthly period. She has no more severe PMS, no cramps, and very light periods that never last for more than two days.

Ashley was placed on birth control pills because of her heavy flow. I can honestly say that her periods are not a problem. I know that before she got on the pills she had cramps, but I do not believe that she has them now, at least not to any large degree. I automatically give Ashley Tylenol the first three days of her period just to alleviate any possible side effects.

Heather didn't have her first period until age eighteen, probably because of low weight. When she started, it was with a vengeance in a cycle of flowing ten days, stopping for ten days. Heather was started on Ortho-Novum and continues to this day. Her periods are generally one to two days of flow and the predictability is nice. If she is cranky, we don't have to wonder if it's PMS!

Depo-Provera, given by injection, is a long-acting form of progesterone, which is an ovarian hormone produced in small amounts during the second half of the menstrual cycle. Because it does not contain estrogen, it does not produce many of the side effects of birth control pills. Depo-Provera suppresses ovulation without completely suppressing production of estrogen, the other normal ovarian hormone. Depo-Provera produces changes in the *endometrium* (lining of the uterus) so that menstruation is less likely to occur. The first shot is given immediately after a menstrual period and every three months thereafter.

A frequent side effect of Depo-Provera is irregular bleeding. After being on "the shot" for six or seven months, most women stop having periods altogether. Some studies have reported weight gain on the medication. Some women have had continued spotting and have discontinued the medication for that reason. Ovulation sometimes does not resume for a year or two after the medication has been discontinued. The American Academy of Pediatrics Committee on Drugs found "no conclusive evidence that Depo-Provera is

Day-to-Day Care

harmful to humans "but it acknowledges that there is controversy about the potential undesirable long-term effects of its use."

Stacie had a terrible time with Depo-Provera. It took a couple of rounds of shots before we figured it out. She became very aggressive and irritable. And when we did figure it out, we had to wait months to get it out of her system. I've heard of other girls who had the same problem, but also some girls who do just fine on Depo-Provera, so it's hard to say how any individual will react.

Becky Sue began Depo-Provera injections about three years ago. She weighed ninety-five pounds at the time. Within six months she had gained thirty pounds and remains stable at one hundred twenty-five pounds. Also, she has acne on her forehead, which can be a side effect of the shots. She receives her shots every twelve weeks and we know she is due by the eleventh week, as she will have mood swings, crying and/or laughing.

Beth began her period last year. We tried the Depo-Provera injection throughout the fall and early winter. Beth was extremely depressed. We opted to stop the injection and her smile and wonderfully happy demeanor has returned.

We tried the Depo-Provera shot and unfortunately for Courtney, it was a horrible experience. We thought we had gone back in time to our earlier phases of Rett. The poor girl's screams were nearly constant, and she could not sleep. The shot did not totally wear off until approximately five to six months went by and we swore we would never consider it again.

ENDOMETRIAL ABLATION

ENDOMETRIAL ABLATION IS A LASER PROCEDURE which is done on an outpatient basis, and is usually performed on women who have an abnormally high degree of bleeding. From one to three months before the procedure, the patient is given a drug to thin the uterus so that the laser can penetrate the endometrium. Under general anesthesia, the laser is introduced through the vagina to vaporize the endometrium. The laser has a small camera which projects the image on a screen, and the surgeon follows this image. The procedure requires no incision. Two out of three women have a permanent cessation of bleeding following the surgery. The endometrial ablation has advantages. It does not require hospitalization overnight, there is less pain because it is not an invasive surgery, and it requires less recovery time. Because the endometrium is a tough membrane, however, when done in younger women it may grow back, causing the period to return and making it necessary to repeat the surgery.

HYSTERECTOMY

HYSTERECTOMY (REMOVAL OF THE UTERUS) is the most permanent and certain way to end her period. It requires surgery and removes the possibility of pregnancy and menstrual periods, and eliminates the potential for uterine cancer. Hysterectomy requires hospitalization for several days and a period of recovery is necessary. Each state has different laws and requirements, and most states have some procedural process to protect her rights. Getting permission can be a lengthy process, but hysterectomy is a final solution to menstrual problems.

The decision to have Megan's uterus removed was the right thing for us. There were many legal obstacles. The most disturbing one was that we would have to have a court-appointed guardian for her and it could not be either me or my husband. The only requirement was the need for a second opinion. We had it done when she was nine years old and she went right back to school after the holidays. After about a week you would have never known she had

Day-to-Day Care

the surgery. The result is one less humiliation for Megan to suffer at school if she were to have an accident, plus peace of mind for us.

Amy's procedure was done before she ever had any periods. She came home that night and slept. We never had to give her pain medication and she never showed signs of PMS throughout the years. It's just a non-issue with us now. It's done. I grieved for weeks before the procedure, but felt a great sense of relief the day it was done. It was just one more step to the admission that Amy would always do the very best she could.

Angie had her uterus removed because of endometriosis, which is not related to RS. All the doctors I consulted felt it imperative to try everything under the sun before doing any surgery. You would have thought I was asking them to put her to sleep forever. She still has her ovaries, but I can see a big change in her overall energy and disposition. Her recovery was uneventful. I wish we had done this years ago.

SEXUAL MATURITY

PARENTS OFTEN WORRY ABOUT THE PROBLEMS created by sexual maturity. Most are uncomfortable with masturbation, which can be seen in young girls as well as mature ones. This kind of stimulation is not abnormal. It is a satisfying and natural part of sexual maturity. It can be embarrassing when it happens at inappropriate times, but it will not hurt your daughter. Learning to control the behavior in public places can usually be accomplished through behavior modification techniques.

POTENTIAL ABUSE

MOST PARENTS SHARE SOME FEAR as we look down the road to when our daughters are no longer in home care. As difficult as it is to confront, protecting her against potential abuse is very important. Keep her away from risky situations, watch for the danger signs of molestation that will be seen in her behavior, and trust your instincts. If your daughter lives in a group home, you can request only female caregivers. It is sad to say, but because girls with RS are essentially defenseless, they can be targets for predators.

DAILY CARE

SKIN CARE

Hand and Mouth Sores

CHILDREN WHO PUT THEIR HANDS IN THEIR MOUTH often get sores on the hands or around the mouth. Keeping the skin dry is the ultimate goal in treatment, but this is often difficult to do. Antibiotic cream should be used if there is infection, along with keeping the hands and mouth as clean as possible. Cold weather can make this a difficult challenge. Arm or elbow splints are effective in keeping the hands away from the mouth and are usually well tolerated.

I made some flannel bibs with snaps at the back to help keep Erica's hands dry. It isn't always possible, but we keep putting her hands under the bib. This way, she wipes her own mouth too!

We put little socks on her hands, but we have to keep changing them so they stay dry. We use A&D Ointment or Neosporin. The doctor recommended Cortaid with A&D Ointment on top of it.

Day-to-Day Care

We bought some of those small knit gloves for children, the ones that look impossibly too small, but stretch a lot. Each night, we rub a good solid moisturizer like Aquaphor into her hands, and then put these gloves on her hands. She never bothered them all night, and it allowed the creams to really soak in. During the day, if her hand-mouthing was really bad, we'd put the gloves on her then. We used extra-large safety pins to attach the gloves to her sleeves so that she couldn't pull them off. We bought about a dozen pairs of these gloves, in all colors. I coordinated her gloves for the day to her outfit. These gloves washed up perfectly and lasted a long time.

Pressure Sores

Pressure sores are caused by the blood supply being cut off to an area for a long period of time. Frequent repositioning is important. When sitting stationary, she should be moved every twenty to thirty minutes, when lying down at least every hour, especially if she is thin and has bony areas. If the pressure isn't relieved and blood supply restored to the area, the tissue dies. It first looks like a pink spot. If normal coloring doesn't return in ten minutes of having pressure relieved you may be heading down the road to a sore. Daily whirlpool baths, using an air mattress, and gel packs to cushion the area work well.

Diaper Rash

Try Triple Paste. A dermatologist recommended this for Danni. It is a miracle cream. It is over-the-counter, but we have to order it from the pharmacy. You can get it direct from the company at www.sumlab.com or 1-800-533-SKIN. It is specifically for diaper rash.

Ask your doctor about prescribing some Nystatin powder. I have also used the cream, but when Kelsey had her surgery they used the powder and so now I ask them to prescribe that.

The doctor told me to buy Bag Balm, a product for cow udders. It comes in a green tin and you can buy it in some drugstores. Sometimes you have to ask the pharmacist. You can also find it at some pet supply stores or farm supply stores. I put it on her bottom and it took care of it right away. I thought it was a miracle.

We have used Corona ointment, which the pharmacist recommended. It has been my best friend for this kind of stuff.

We have mixed Maalox into Desitin. It was a great help as the Maalox reduces the acid.

I find that Balmex works much better than all the other diaper creams including A&D, which I have tried when things are raw. Balmex seems to heal better.

My friend told me to take regular old Vaseline, but rather than apply it to the child' bottom, take an old spatula and apply a coating of Vaseline to the inside of the diaper (in the crotch area). I was desperate, so I tried it. By the next day, I could see a significant improvement in the skin on her bottom. This made a believer out of me.

Carol, having never had any kind of a diaper rash, developed a red fire rash from an antibiotic after having been hospitalized. Try Clotrimazole over-the-counter for vaginal use. I used it just like Desitin. Excellent results!

We use Calmoseptine, sold in the pharmacy over the counter. It does wonders on a diaper rash and it seemed to relieve any discomfort that she was having right away.

We do a baking soda soak, pat dry, air dry, then put on an ointment about four times a day.

Aquaphor cream works wonders and is like Vaseline, so it doesn't stain or hurt if it gets in the mouth.

We give Kimberly lots of yogurt. This puts the "good" bacteria back in.

Day-to-Day Care

If the rash is a yeast infection from taking an antibiotic, a good regimen is to apply a dab of Lotrimin mixed with a dab of cortisone cream to the entire area after each diaper change, making sure to change her very often so the area stays as dry and unsoiled as possible. If there's a way you can let her little bottom air out without her having too many accidents, that would also be helpful.

Hair Removal

When your daughter gets older, you may choose to shave her underarms and legs with a regular or bikini type razor, which is more narrow and easier to use with girls/women who are very small. Another option is to use commercial preparations or to use a mustache trimmer. Shaved underarms and legs add to her well-groomed appearance.

I shave Stacie's underarms and legs while she is in the tub or sitting on the toilet. It takes only a couple of minutes and makes such a difference in her hygiene. She loves those smooth legs!

Taylor is very hairy. I have always been apprehensive about shaving her legs. We did the nasty-messy Nair thing but Taylor is constantly in motion so it really wasn't a success. I bought a new product called Nair Sugar-Waxing Roll on System. You heat the entire container in the microwave for fifteen seconds, then roll it on a small area, apply the strip to the area, and pull it off. It was amazingly easy and non-messy. The stuff smells great. Any residue rinses off simply with water. Taylor has a high tolerance for pain and she whined a bit, but that was it.

DENTAL CARE

KEEPING HER TEETH CLEAN is very important to avoid cavities and pain that can interfere with eating. Tooth grinding can wear the teeth down considerably and over a long period of time, this may cause pain as the roots are closer to the surface. The first visit to a dentist, preferably a specialist in dentistry for children, should be done after the appearance of all twenty primary teeth, around the age of three. If the dental staff is patient and skilled, they will be able to care for her teeth with the least anxiety.

Tooth decay is often caused by excess sugar consumption of all types including drinks, chocolate milk, tea, and juices or milk, especially when given at night in the bottle. Cavities develop when food debris collects, leaving an accumulation of thick yellow plaque. Proper brushing is essential to remove it. It is best to brush while she is lying down, so you can see while brushing. There is no need for toothpaste in the beginning, and only a small amount of toothpaste is necessary when it is used. This is especially important because toothpaste is not made to be swallowed, and she may not be able to spit it out. Swallowing a small amount of toothpaste is okay, but low fluoride toothpaste is best, such as the kind that is made for baby's first teeth. Plain or salted water or mouthwash can be used to wet the toothbrush. Regular fluoride treatments are a must. The toothbrush should have soft bristles and should be the right size for her mouth. Toothbrushes come in a variety of styles including musical ones that can make the job easier. Electric toothbrushes with a small head are effective. If she resists using a toothbrush, a damp washcloth is a good substitute.

Plaque buildup and bad breath can be treated with Chlorhexidine, a prescription mouth rinse. It can be applied by dipping the toothbrush in and then brushing around or soaking a piece of gauze and rubbing the teeth.

Often, it is not tooth brushing, but proper positioning and keeping the mouth open that is the main problem. For some girls, the stimulation of a toothbrush triggers a bite reflex and it can be very difficult for her to let go. To keep her mouth open, try taking a few tongue depressors and stacking them together. Wrap the stack in gauze to provide

Day-to-Day Care

some padding, and cover the whole thing with adhesive tape to make it somewhat water-proof. Place the stack of tongue depressors between the molars on one side of her mouth while you brush the other. She will be free to chew on the tongue depressors and you will be free to brush. Try to experiment with different ways to find out how she is most comfortable and relaxed, and what position allows you to best see what you are doing.

Too much fluoride can cause mottling (white/brown discoloration spots) on permanent teeth, even though they are very decay resistant. This is something to consider for anyone wondering about the addition of fluoride (in the water, pills, or toothpaste). Tooth decay may be a bigger problem for our kids than slight discoloration of the teeth. Remember, too, that this discoloration only occurs with excessive amounts of fluoride, not the amounts found in toothpaste or in public fluoridation.

If the toothbrush fails, Oral B makes a "finger glove" for brushing teeth. It can be used without water.

We started out using the flavored toothpaste with a small infant's toothbrush. It was the taste of the toothpaste that first got her to open her mouth. We have now moved onto a mild, mint-flavored children's toothpaste, which she wasn't keen on at first but we stuck with it and generally she is happy to have her teeth brushed. When I do it, I hold her bottom jaw in my hand and at times do have to place a bit of pressure to keep her mouth open.

We began by doing some simple massage around the mouth and cheeks and then worked on a routine with a NUK brush. This is less stimulating and easier for many kids to handle. We would roll it along the tongue, press down on her teeth, rub it on her lips, etc. Over time, we were able to use a regular toothbrush and now Joanne is just fine with a spin brush.

Our pediatric dentist taught us to brush Brit's teeth by putting her in a virtual headlock. It isn't as bad as it seems. While she's sitting in her chair watching TV, we go behind her and wrap her head with one arm (we give her a verbal prompt to let her know it is coming) to hold her still and brush her teeth with the other hand. It takes a couple of times to get the hang of it, but it is more like brushing your own teeth because you're behind her, not in front of her.

At first, I would get the electric toothbrush out and just turn it on and hold it on less sensitive parts of her body, tummy, and hands. We worked up to the outside of her face. I kind of did a face massage with it for a few minutes each day, and eventually worked my way into her mouth. She took a long time to get used to it. Now, though, she really likes to brush her teeth, and holds the brush with us.

Try using a thin washcloth after each meal. Buy the cheap washcloths and wet one down and with your finger, wipe each tooth. We have always stayed on top of her teeth but these kids really need complete X-rays of every tooth and regular cleaning from the dentist. Some of Shelley's teeth looked fine until they X-rayed and they were shocked to see how fast her teeth went bad. You don't want to have to deal with root canals, so stay on top of it. These girls cannot have false teeth as they get older and they need to really chew their food as well.

My absolute favorite solution to the brushing problem is the Collis Curve toothbrush. It is easy, quick and pain/vibration-free. We use the Collis in the morning and the Sonicare (child size) at night.

Orajel makes a "training toothpaste" called Orajel Toddler. There's no fluoride in it so it's safe to swallow if that's an issue at your house.

We used the handle of a wooden spoon to keep Rachael's mouth open for tooth-brushing. I soaked the handle in vanilla extract, and rinsed it with an antibacterial mouthwash after use. Another mom told me she found a vanilla-scented nylon doggy chew bone worked well after whittling one end down a little. I let Rachael chomp

Day-to-Day Care

on the left side while I brushed on the right, and vice versa. Rachael seemed to enjoy chomping on the spoon handle. She now cooperates very well with brushing.

We have been using the Dentrust toothbrush and it is really great! I don't get bitten anymore when I brush Sherry's teeth and I don't have to hold her mouth open with my fingers. This toothbrush brushes all three surfaces of the teeth in one pass because it's got three brushing surfaces and you run it along the teeth as though it is a train and the teeth are tracks. You can get it at the grocery store for around $3 or so. I have seen similar toothbrushes in catalogs for people with disabilities but they are more expensive and are basically the same thing.

We use lemon-glycerin swabs to moisten and clean her mouth. Heather seemed to really appreciate the moisture they provided and the taste as well. These swabs come in several flavors and can be obtained at any medical supply place. They really help the comfort level of anyone in the hospital or having any kind of mouth or dental work.

Our dentist told us to let our daughter chew on a toothbrush even when it isn't tooth-brushing time. Just the chewing and saliva created by it will help to clean the teeth.

Finding a Dentist

Try any of the fifty-six dental schools in the US, or call the American Dental Association at 800-621-8099 www.ada.org, or go to www.specialdentist.com. By entering your zip code, you can find the closest dentist who treats special needs patients.

Orthodontics

Crystal's dentist, who also specializes in handicapped children, told me that he did not recommend braces because just trying to do the monthly tightening, keeping her mouth very clean, and the pain associated with normal brace wear is usually not worth it unless her teeth were so bad that she really needed them. I have had braces and I have to agree it is no picnic.

It no longer occurs to me that her teeth are not as perfect as I wanted them to be. After all, Anne Stuart is not what I expected her to be in the beginning and I have learned to accept that, too. Just hang in there and let nature takes it course. It's a process we all have to deal with and with our girls, it is just tougher to realize we really don't have control about these things. Just try to take it one tooth at a time!

TOILET TEACHING

GIRLS WITH RS UNDERSTAND WHAT THE TOILET IS FOR. Their handicap is in not being able to communicate their needs. It may take some trial and error, some time training and careful observation of her nonverbal signs, but it is possible for her to be toilet trained. You may need to make some adaptations, such as a seat reducer so she can sit on a standard toilet or a specially fitted seat support. A footstool is important to give her some stability and to keep her feet from getting uncomfortable dangling. Sitting her on the toilet may also help her pass uncomfortable gas. Be sure to keep her covered up so she doesn't chill when she sits for more than a couple of minutes.

Even if you don't get 100 percent success, using the toilet is such a huge benefit to all. It may not be a time-saver, especially at first, but her pride in this accomplishment is huge.

We started Angela on the potty at around age two during the times we knew she had to go, usually at bath time. We did that for about a year; she didn't have an interest. Later, we started giving her chances after each meal as well. This was when she achieved bowel control, which has been nearly 100 percent for over two years, unless

Day-to-Day Care

she is sick. From there, we added scheduled trips between meals for chances to urinate and try to make sure she has a BIGmack to alert us to the need when she is at home. It's been a slow process, nothing "overnight" like her little sister, once she made up her mind. But the self-esteem of being able to control this aspect of her life has been just wonderful, and the private time we have together is special to us both.

Katie has been walking herself to the bathroom when she has to have a BM for a few years now. It was hard at first to get the school to recognize what she wanted, but we finally got there. As for urine, finally, in this last year, we noticed that she was starting to urinate when she would sit on the toilet, so we did a "rapid potty training." It was not as fast as we'd hoped, but now for the most part, she is dry when we take her into the bathroom. It's not 100 percent and even though she will walk herself in for BM's, we still have to remember to get her there for urine. But she is getting there! She is dry more now than she was before, and we are noticing that she is taking herself in sometimes for the urine as well. For us, it has been a matter of consistency with all who work with her, and having these people recognize her signs. Sometimes she's so subtle she might just stand by the bathroom door, and some of her therapists didn't recognize this sign.

We use a strict time schedule and also follow natural times she might have to go, after meals, upon waking, even naps, and then every few hours. This cues her to use the toilet at those times and to hold until the next toileting time. I have the toilet on Mary's IntroTalker, but also take her when she gets a panicky look on her face that she needs to go.

We began to work on toileting when Jocelyn was four. It took a long time but the option was to continue diapers, so what did we have to lose! Don't give up, keep your expectations high, and don't be afraid to take risks. We often brought Jocelyn "out" without a diaper long before she was mostly "trained." I found that she also did not like to have accidents and would try to hold it, but I think putting panties on her was a show of confidence that I believed she could do it. Sometimes she did have accidents, and then I told her that I thought she did her best and I'd try better to "listen" to her messages. We continued to work together; I believe that success was as dependent on my understanding as her bladder control and it was a team effort in success and failures. She started the fourth grade in panties and still wears them. She does wear Pull Ups at night, but usually they are dry.

We leave a Cheap Talk device with "I want to go to the bathroom" in convenient places. Leah will use it when it suits her. Given a choice and a chance to communicate, she will use the toilet. When we are on top of things, she will stay dry the whole day. There are times she is working so hard to hold it in that she will urinate right before I get her on the toilet.

I hung a musical crib toy on the cupboard near the toilet, and when Angie would go (I stayed to hear her tinkle) I pulled the string and praised her. The music and action of the toy was a terrific reward. She caught on immediately and always tries to hold it for us.

We started training Katie at 2 years 8 months and in some ways she was trained sooner than our son. From the day we started, I have not had to change a dirty diaper. She's very regular and even if she's not, she can indicate by straining noises that she needs to go. If we are out during her "usual time," she will hold on to it for up to two hours until we come back home. On one occasion recently, I felt she needed to go while we were out, and I held her on a toilet and it worked instantly. I was thrilled. We put her on the potty at least every two hours and she always produces something and beams with delight when we praise her for it.

TOILETING HELPFUL HINTS

SCHOOL STAFF SHOULD BE ADVISED not to leave the girl with RS on the toilet too long. She may become cold and uncomfortable and may show aversive behavior.

- Have the toilet ready before you get her there.
- Make sure she is seated comfortably with proper support for her back and feet.

Day-to-Day Care

- Use a seat belt if necessary.
- Give extra fluids and put her on the toilet at regular intervals.
- Give her a lots of praise and a reward that she will look forward to when she is successful. Food always works!
- When she begins to gain success, gradually increase the intervals between toileting.

  For bowel training:

- Put her on the toilet when you notice her strain.
- Put her on the toilet after meals, especially after dinner.

BATHING

IF SHE DOES NOT SIT WITHOUT SUPPORT, IT MAY BE HARD to get her in and out of the tub and keep her stable and safe while you wash her. There are a number of waterproof bath chairs available, ranging from mesh sling-back styles to rigid plastic benches and chairs. A hand-held shower hose can be very useful in the tub, especially for hair washing. Waterproof wheelchairs are available for use in roll-in showers. A mesh table that hooks into the back of a roll-in shower provides a safe way to bathe without undue bending by the caregiver.

SEATING AND POSITIONING

PROPER SEATING AND POSITIONING ARE VERY IMPORTANT for her comfort, and also allow her to participate and use her body in the best way she can. Seating should include a solid seat and solid back to ensure upright, level pelvic alignment. Lateral support can be added if necessary to keep her from slumping or leaning to one side. She should be well-seated in the high chair, car seat, stroller, at the table and in her wheelchair, wherever she sits. Comfort, balance, and safety must be taken into consideration when choosing seating equipment or positioning.

An evaluation should be done by a team of qualified professionals including physical or occupational therapists, an orthopedist or rehabilitative medicine physician, a rehabilitation technology supplier, and parents. If she is in school, her classroom teachers may want to join the team. Together, they should consider a number of issues beginning with her home, school, and community environments and the type of seating and positioning she needs to function at her optimum level. Different seats and backs should be combined to simulate different positioning options. A pressure mapping system should be used to identify areas which might be conducive to pressure sores, which can occur when she sits in one position for long periods and cannot shift her weight to relieve the pressure. Cushions should be provided for any areas that might cause a problem. She may need additional supports depending on her ability to sit and hold her head independently.

Seating and positioning strategies should take into consideration her use of technology, such as computers or communication devices. She should be able to have full access to these in a comfortable seating position that enhances her use of technology.

If the equipment is not customized, you may be able to try it out at home before purchasing it. Equipment can cost from hundreds to thousands of dollars. Most health insurance

Day-to-Day Care

companies or Medicaid will cover most or at least a portion of the cost if the equipment is ordered by the physician and justified by the evaluation team. If health insurance is inadequate, equipment dealers may be able to give you a list of resources, such as local service clubs, which might help with the cost.

"Any idiot can face a crisis—it's day to day living that wears you out."

– ANTON CHEKHOV

Nutrition and Feeding

THE NUTRITIONAL CHALLENGE

MOST GIRLS WITH RS present a challenge when it comes to providing enough nutrition. Even those with healthy appetites are usually quite thin and short, and many meet the definition for *protein-energy malnutrition*. Malnutrition results when dietary intake is insufficient to meet the body's energy needs, and it has many causes. Studies have shown that many girls with RS have lower energy (dietary) intake than healthy girls the same size or age. The result of insufficient dietary intake is thinness, loss of muscle mass, and decreased resistance to infection. Nutrition and feeding are very important to improve their quality of life and make other therapies possible.

Every girl has her own unique food likes and dislikes. While she may have different tastes and nutritional needs, she shares a number of characteristics with the typical girl with RS. She has a good appetite, enjoys food, and has strong food preferences. She can eat a wide range of foods but may need longer time at meals. She has limited self-feeding skills. She does not need a special diet, but may have problems chewing, swallowing, and eating different food textures. Constipation is a common problem in part due to delayed movement of food through the intestinal tract.

"Nutrition represents one of the most important aspects of treatment in RS. It is the cornerstone by which all other forms of therapies are made possible."

– MARYLYNNE RICE ASARO, R.D.

Adequate intake of food does not guarantee good nutrition. The gastrointestinal tract must be able to perform three major functions: the controlled movement of food from the mouth to the anus, the digestion of food, and the absorption of nutrients.

The girl with RS may have problems sucking, chewing, or swallowing. She has poor tongue mobility, which makes it difficult for her to take in and move food around her mouth. Food does not clear the esophagus as it should. When she swallows, solids and liquids pass from the pharynx into the esophagus, stomach, and intestine. The churning movements (*peristaltic waves*) needed to propel food through the intestinal tract may be reduced, and there may be delayed emptying of the stomach. All of these factors add up to the potential for nutritional problems.

Many of the characteristics of RS add to problems with feeding and nutrition, and different stages may present unique challenges. Following is a list of the clinical features commonly seen in RS and the effects which they have on the girl's nutritional status.

ABNORMAL BREATHING

ONE STUDY SHOWED an association between poor nutritional status and breathing disturbances, suggesting that hyperventilation and hypoventilation interfere with

Nutrition and Feeding

Symptom	Result
Failure to thrive	Stage 1: Lack of weight gain
Growth failure	Stage 2: Weight loss
	Stage 3: Poor linear growth (height); weight stabilization
	Stage 4: Weight Loss; linear growth arrest
Decreased Energy/Nutrient Intakes	Poor linear growth
Loss of Hand Use	Loss of self feeding skills; increased caretaker time; increased feeding time
Impaired chewing and Swallowing	Increased risk of aspiration
Increased Salivation	Increased risk for dehydration; increased fluid needs
Seizures	Drug/nutrient interaction; altered vitamin/mineral needs; ketogenic diet for seizure control
Scoliosis	Distorted gastrointestinal anatomy

breathing. However, hyperventilation does not increase total daily energy expenditure (burning calories).

APPETITE

WEIGHT GAIN IS POOR in more than 85 percent of girls with RS, although most parents believe their daughters have average to enormous appetites. Parents often describe their daughter's intake of food as surprisingly large considering her age and size. An early theory suggested that girls with RS may burn more energy while engaged in their constant stereotypic hand movements. However, studies have now shown that even though girls with RS spend a lot of time in motion with their repetitive hand movements, they actually burn less energy, have lower energy intake and sleeping metabolic rates than their age-matched peers, and may use their body's energy less efficiently because they are undernourished. These factors provide an imbalance over the long run which contributes to the growth failure so common in RS. Many girls actually meet the criteria for moderate to severe malnutrition. Girls with RS require more energy than other girls their age to reverse their poor weight gain and growth arrest.

When Jane decides she is not going to eat, she will take only two or three bites of food and then say, "All done." She means what she says, and no amount of coaxing can get her to eat more. When she does this we have resorted to using 10 cc syringes and she will take about three cans of Boost, plus water, plus her meds.

Never is Angie's eye contact better than when one of us is eating something. She looks at the food, then us. The food, then us. If she really wants to get her point across, it's always about food.

Nutrition and Feeding

| NUTRITIONAL REHABILITATION |

PLANNING A FEEDING PROGRAM

AN ASSESSMENT OF HER NUTRITIONAL STATUS WILL HELP to determine if it is necessary to supplement or change her current feeding program. An assessment usually includes height and weight measurements, but also may include body skinfold measurements and a record or recall of her actual food and beverage consumption. Her feeding plan should be aimed at improving nutrition, promoting weight gain and linear growth, developing and enhancing feeding skills, reducing feeding time, and minimizing constipation.

For girls with little appetite and serious feeding difficulties, any problem on the list below should be evaluated promptly by her health care professional. Interventions in her dietary care plan should be considered. A period of alternative feeding strategies may be necessary until her nutritional status improves.

- ability to keep the lips closed on food
- defective chewing, defective swallowing
- choking; involuntary or obstructing movements
- vomiting or regurgitation; excessive secretions
- poor appetite; and dependence in feeding

The options for nutritional rehabilitation depend upon the degree of malnutrition, the degree of chewing and swallowing difficulties, the risk of aspiration, and your preference. Regular meals can be supplemented with extra snacks or meals. When this approach is inadequate to meet her nutritional needs or if she has significant swallowing problems and risk of aspiration, other methods of feeding are often necessary. *Nasogastric* (NG) tube feedings may be recommended. With this method, a tube is passed through the nose and esophagus into the stomach so that food is taken directly to the stomach. NG tubes generally are recommended as a temporary measure. Or, your physician may recommend a *gastrostomy button* (G-button), a device which may require a surgical procedure under general anesthesia to create an opening through the skin into the stomach. The "button," which resembles a mushroom on a stalk, is placed in this opening (*stoma*), giving a direct route for feeding to the stomach.

Vitamins

Vitamins and minerals are essential for her health as they contribute to growth and development. A healthy girl who eats well will receive a good amount of nutrients in her diet and does not need vitamin and mineral supplements. However, if she has allergies, is tube fed with a homemade blenderized formula, or is extremely underweight, vitamins and minerals may be helpful. Giving too many supplements can be dangerous. Always consult with her doctor before giving vitamin and mineral supplements.

All vitamins and minerals are important for children, but they do not increase weight. Only dietary energy from carbohydrate or fat will increase weight. Key vitamins and minerals include folate, vitamin D, calcium, iron, and zinc.

Amounts should be based on weight, dietary intake, exposure to sunlight, and drugs. Excessive dietary intake of vitamins and minerals can be just as harmful as insufficient dietary intake.

Nutrition and Feeding

Carnitine Deficiency

Carnitine is a natural substance that is necessary for energy metabolism. It is produced in the body and is found in the diet, particularly in red meats and dairy products. Carnitine transports fats into the mitochondria, the cellular furnace where these fats are converted into an energy source.

Carnitine is important because the heart and skeletal muscle tissue rely on the utilization of fat as their major source of energy. Without carnitine, the use of fatty acids as an energy source for all tissues is reduced.

Carnitine deficiency can be due to a decreased natural synthesis of carnitine in the body, or an altered transport of carnitine across the muscle cellular membrane, where carnitine is known to be active. If the diet lacks carnitine or the body over utilizes or loses carnitine, deficiency can result. Young children with neurological disorders who take multiple anticonvulsant drugs are at the highest risk for carnitine deficiency. The use of valproate (Depakote) may be associated with carnitine deficiency.

The symptoms of carnitine deficiency are muscle weakness, lethargy, hypotonia, *encephalopathy* (altered mental status), neurologic disturbances, and impaired growth and development.

Examination of muscle tissue is the most accurate way to measure carnitine. However, blood level determinations are preferred since they are not invasive.

Amanda's carnitine levels were fine. But since we had read about carnitine deficiencies and Depakote, we decided to try it anyway. On carnitine, she definitely had more energy and needed less sleep. Without the carnitine, she slept four to five more hours a day.

Levocarnitine, the synthetic form of carnitine, is the only treatment approved by the Food and Drug Administration for the treatment of carnitine deficiency. The brand name is L-Carnitor, and it must be given by prescription. Your doctor may suggest carnitine supplements, which can be purchased at health food stores under various brand names. However, the regulatory requirements for health food supplements are not equal to those of prescription drug products. Insist on a prescription.

Nicole's overall disposition and mood have improved and she seems to be less fussy. Her appetite has increased and she has gained two pounds. Her bowel movements come almost every day and are less hard than before. We saw increased alertness, better attention span, more initiation on her part with her peers and teachers. Her teachers also would testify to these changes.

The use of carnitine may result in mild gastrointestinal complaints such as nausea and vomiting, abdominal cramps, and diarrhea. These symptoms usually disappear when the dose is decreased. A "fishy" body odor may occur, but also disappears when the dose is reduced.

FLUIDS AND DEHYDRATION

WATER IS ESSENTIAL FOR LIFE. THE INDIVIDUAL WITH RS may have difficulty sucking and swallowing fluids, which puts her at risk for dehydration and

Nutrition and Feeding

constipation. Drooling may add to her fluid loss. The following fluid requirements may be helpful:

Age in Years	Weight in Pounds	Cups of Fluid
1-3	29	3-4
4-6	44	3-4
7-10	62	10
11-14	101	10-12

Meeting fluid requirements can be a real challenge. You have to be creative and persistent. Here are some helpful tips:

- Distribute fluid intake evenly throughout the day.
- Request her school to give fluids in a minimum amount daily.
- Thicken fluids to make drinking easier (with pureed fruit, instant oat cereal, unprocessed bran, dehydrated infant foods, or a commercial product).
- Use a variety of foods which count as fluid when they become liquid at room temperature (Popsicles, ice cream, Jell-O).
- Slushies or other "icy" drinks are a good source of fluid.
- Include lots of vegetables and fruits in her diet. They contain the highest amounts of water of all solid foods.
- Decrease natural loss of water by putting a humidifier in her bedroom or keeping her indoors when it is very hot.
- Avoid highly sweetened fruit juices as they can actually increase her need for fluids.

Rebecca found drinking a challenge. She couldn't hold the cup and had trouble closing her lips. Our technique was to hold a cloth under her chin to give support to her lower jaw, and to catch the drips. We used a tilted or cut-out cup so we could see how far to tip it.

We taught Jocelyn to use a straw by giving her juice boxes. You can squeeze the box gently and force the juice up through the little straw. Once it gets started she can almost continue the sucking action just by swallowing the juice in her mouth. Kind of like priming the pump. Once she gets going, it's close to an automatic action and she doesn't have to think too much about what she is doing.

We get water in Allie using a spray bottle, spraying little bits of water into her mouth. She loves it and never spits it out, provided we don't overdo it. We also bought a cheap snow cone machine and give her crushed ice (some times with juice) to keep her hydrated.

We have some cups which have a hole in the middle of the cup so that the child can grab it. There is a larger size cup available. We found ours at K-Mart.

I attach aquarium tubing to a plastic water bottle (Thermos with a short flip-up spout). The bottle can rest in a bag on the belt of Dani's wheelchair and she can still drink from the long tube without assistance from anyone.

We went to a beauty supply store and bought a bottle used for applying hair color or perms with a pointed tip, very pliable and "squeeze sensitive." We cut a comfortable length of fish tubing to run from the very bottom to

Nutrition and Feeding

several inches above the tip. We snipped the point of the bottle to fit the tubing snugly and threaded it through. This takes very little pressure to send the liquid upward. It is also clear, which facilitates allowing only enough liquid into her mouth as is comfortable or to get her sucking.

Crystal uses a sports bottle. It must be an airtight bottle. At first we had to squeeze it a little to get the "juices" going. Since she closed her mouth around the straw, when she swallowed, a siphon would automatically be started. She caught on and the process is easily initiated by her except on "down days." On those days, we sometimes need to help her get started. The sports bottle is nearly spill-proof and age-appropriate. She reaches out for it.

We use a squeezable plastic glass with a straw in it. As she drinks, we slowly squeeze the glass so that the fluid goes up the straw and she can drink freely, but has to suck to get it out. Then we gradually squeeze less fluid until she gets the hang of it, and has to suck on her own.

We use a Pat Saunders drinking straw, which has a one-way valve. After removing the lips from the straw, it stays almost full. There is also a clip on the side of the straw to hook onto the side of small glasses or cups. The clip prevents the straw from falling out of the cup. Only clear liquids can pass through the valve.

Asha uses a Playtex Sippy Cup and a drink bottle that has a straw and push-down lid. I attached elastic to it and hang it around her neck so she can retrieve it if she lets go.

We purchase straws from a local restaurant that are very slim. This works wonderfully for Stephanie, as she would also hold the liquid in her mouth and then lose it. We also leave the straw in her mouth only for a short time, removing it before she is done.

It is important to be sure she is getting ample fluid. If you see the following signs, call her doctor immediately. Dehydration can be serious:

- decreased amount of urine (check number and wetness of diapers)
- dry lips
- sunken eyes, dark circles under the eyes
- dry skin (press on skin to see if skin bounces back)
- extra thirst
- headache, fatigue, dizziness
- weight loss

INCREASING WEIGHT

INCREASING HER ENERGY INTAKE will increase her weight, but this alone does not replenish her muscle mass completely. When she gains weight, body fat is increased, but muscle wasting persists for a period of time. Repletion of muscle mass occurs gradually in some girls, but requires attention to the diet and physical activity. We know that good muscle mass, strength, and function require, in part, a well-balanced diet sufficient in protein, minerals, and vitamins. Physical activity such as walking is important to maintain muscle tone and strength. A recent study showed that a physical fitness program using a specially designed treadmill and executed on a daily basis is capable of improving functional ability of girls with RS.

Nutrition and Feeding

HOW TO INCREASE WEIGHT AND LINEAR GROWTH

INCREASING HER DIETARY ENERGY INTAKE WILL INCREASE her weight and linear growth and improve her alertness and interaction. A high fat and high-carbohydrate diet has been shown to improve weight gain. A high-fat diet may be prescribed to achieve better seizure control. You can increase energy by adding margarine, butter, cream sauces, and syrups to vegetables, fruits, and cereal. A mid-morning, mid-afternoon, and bedtime snack can be given in addition to three regular meals. Carnation Instant Breakfast, milkshakes, and Ensure or Pediasure are high-energy supplements which can be given between meals in liquid form. Small frequent meals during the day with added carbohydrates and/or fats help increase weight and also may decrease irritability and agitation.

Our daughter takes Scandishake, which is a high calorie supplement, 600 calories in eight ounces. It comes as a vanilla, chocolate, or strawberry powder that you mix with milk or a lactose-free product. It actually tastes good. Since Kate started taking it, she has gained five pounds. She had not gained in three years.

Christina drinks Deliver which has more calories, vitamin D, and MCT oil. It's very thick and tastes great!

Choosing Foods

The following foods are high in fat and energy content. Each time you serve a meal or snack, ask how you can sneak in some more energy. Try adding extra of the following:

Avocado	Processed Cheese	Half and Half	Sausage
Fried Foods	Processed Meats	Ham	Cream
Gravy	Chips	Sour Cream	Cream Cheese
Salad Dressing	Hot Dogs	Steak	Whipped Cream
Cottage Cheese	Instant Breakfast	Custard	
Ice Cream	Whole Milk/Yogurt	Nuts	
Mayonnaise	Oils	Bacon	
Fish Packed in Oil	Peanut Butter	Butter/Margarine	
French Fries	Banana	Cheese/Spread	

Low-Fat Foods

Nutritious foods are often low in fat. You can increase their fat content by doing the following:

Fruit: top with whipped cream, yogurt, or nuts

Pasta, bread, potatoes and vegetables: use liquid squirt butter or margarine or add gravy

Vegetables: fry or sauté, including potatoes or bread crumbs; top with cheese

Dairy products: add Instant Breakfast, flavorings, Ovaltine or nonfat dry milk, ice cream, milkshakes, eggnog

Crackers or bread: spread peanut butter or cream cheese

Nutrition and Feeding

Other Ways to Gain

Increase energy intake:

- Increase the number of meals daily
- Increase amount of food at each meal
- Provide high energy liquid supplements
- Give high-energy snacks
- Increase fat and sugar content of foods
- Limit mealtime fluids
- Limit high-fiber foods (which are filling)

Increase fat and carbohydrates:

- Fry foods
- Add oil, gravy, butter to foods
- Use syrups and table sugar
- Increase intake of fruits and juices
- Add fat to carbohydrate foods

FEEDING PROBLEMS

PROBLEMS RELATED TO FEEDING AND NUTRITIONAL NEEDS are frequent concerns, as girls with RS seldom develop mature patterns of chewing and oral motor function. Swallowing may be difficult, especially with liquids. It may be difficult for her to bite hard enough at the right time to eat a sandwich. Abnormal tongue movements, low or high tongue tone, scoliosis, increasing shoulder girdle tightness, and neurological problems may contribute to feeding difficulties. Many girls develop gastroesophageal reflux (GER), which occurs when acid from the stomach backs up into the esophagus, causing burning, pain, and irritation.

POSITIONING

POSITIONING IS IMPORTANT to enhance swallowing during mealtimes. The closer you can get her in the normal upright position, the better. Her head should not be tilted back. This position is not only uncomfortable, but dangerous as well. Her chin should not be touching her chest—it is very difficult to swallow in this position. She should not eat or drink while lying down—this position increases the chance of inhaling a small amount of food or liquid into the lungs. Her bottom should be firmly seated in the chair to avoid fatigue and her feet should have a proper footrest.

If she feels like she is off balance, not well supported, tipping, or afraid of falling, she will shift her concentration to these sensations and will not be focused on chewing, swallowing and using her hands to eat. Your child's therapist and her physician will help you determine a therapeutic position for feeding.

ASPIRATION

IN SWALLOWING, THE CHILD MUST BE ABLE TO FORM a *bolus* (mass of food) and then coordinate the contraction of her muscles to move the food from

Nutrition and Feeding

the back of the tongue to the pharynx and down the esophagus. The epiglottis folds over the opening of the trachea to prevent food from being inhaled into the lungs. If there is poor coordination of these muscles, there is a risk for aspiration of food into the lungs, known as *aspiration pneumonia*.

Evelyn started raspy breathing every time she ate and drank. We were concerned that she was aspirating and took her for help. The swallow study showed that Evelyn does not swallow immediately, putting her at risk of aspiration. They are telling me she should not eat anything.

Sarah has silent aspiration, so she can't take anything by mouth. She now gets five bolus feedings during the day including water and Gatorade along with a nine-hour feeding overnight.

CHEWING

PROBLEMS WITH CHEWING AND SWALLOWING are common in girls with RS. These problems may begin early in life. The cues that trigger normal chewing of solids or semi-solid foods seem to be lost. Many girls with RS have abnormal movements such as tongue thrusting and waves of involuntary tongue movements that get in the way of effective chewing. When younger, the oral motor tone of her cheeks, lips, and tongue is abnormally low, but as she gets older the tone increases to abnormally high. These changes in tone and tongue movements interfere with chewing.

When Rae was two, we noticed that she had poor chewing, although it never stopped her from eating. But she did have problems eating certain foods—peanut butter or mushy foods. The therapists suggested stimulating her mouth with a Nuk trainer. It's like a toothbrush, but with "nubs" instead of bristles. It also stopped the grinding a little. We do not give her things with which she absolutely cannot deal, but we do give her foods to make her chew, to help strengthen the tone in her mouth.

Gina has trouble chewing different textures. Food must be put in her mouth on either the left or right sides of her back teeth in order for her to be able to chew it. Her therapist says she has trouble lateralizing her tongue to maintain proper chewing. She has difficulty with many foods. For the most part, her meals go in the food processor.

When my daughter was having pneumonias all the time, they suspected that she was aspirating liquids. We could hear the croupy sound when she drank liquids.

A careful evaluation of chewing and swallowing should be obtained to determine the best intervention strategy. Correct positioning will decrease rigidity and may be all that is necessary to minimize the problem. Frequently, the use of *thermal stimulation* (ice slush or Popsicles) helps the girl who "forgets" the food is still in her mouth. This technique heightens the sensory awareness in her tongue and cheeks and allows her to better chew and swallow. If she hyperventilates during eating, caution should be taken to make sure she has swallowed before offering her another bite. One sip of liquid should be given at a time to avoid swallows that could cause choking or aspiration.

SWALLOWING

THE CUES THAT TRIGGER THE SWALLOWING OF LIQUIDS, particularly thin liquids like water or juices, often are impaired in the girl with RS. Swallowing requires coordinated muscle contractions to move the food or liquid from the back of the tongue to the pharynx and then down the esophagus. It is necessary to close the mouth

Nutrition and Feeding

to swallow, which can be difficult for the girl with RS. Thin liquids and large pieces of food are more difficult to swallow. To make it easier, food can be mashed, chopped, or pureed and thin liquids can be thickened with commercial thickening agents or household cooking items such as tapioca, cornstarch, and flour, if appropriate.

To swallow effectively, food must be organized into a bolus (clump). Thin liquids are more difficult to swallow than solids or thickened liquids. Also, raw carrots are difficult to swallow because the pieces tend to scatter in the mouth and don't clump together. So, what might appear to be a "touch" thing may really be a "swallowing" thing.

Girls with RS often have difficulty chewing and swallowing, with difficulty closing the mouth during swallowing. If problems are suspected, a *video fluoroscopy study* during swallowing is recommended. Sometimes, switching to foods that are chopped, mashed or pureed and easier to swallow will take care of minor problems. However, if the swallowing study indicates that she is prone to aspiration, a feeding tube (G-tube) may be considered. This will avoid aspiration and pneumonia.

Laney has a delayed swallow. She lets the food puddle in the back of her throat and if it is not cleared with a drink or another bite of food, a little goes in her sinus cavity.

Swallowing Assessment

A video fluoroscopic study, or swallowing function study, can be performed during swallowing if *oral-pharyngeal dysfunction* (swallowing) is suspected. Minor problems can be handled by changing the diet to include foods that are easier to swallow or blenderizing foods to a pureed consistency. If there are serious swallowing problems, a gastrostomy button often is recommended to avoid problems of aspiration or pneumonia and to decrease the long and difficult process of oral food intake.

Clare had no problems with the video fluoroscopy, although she wasn't awfully keen on the taste of the barium, which was mixed with her favorite breakfast cereal. We found the video fluoroscopy very helpful in explaining many of Clare's difficulties in eating and drinking. Until we saw the video fluoroscopy we did not know, for example, that the reason for her delay in swallowing was due to her acquired habit of "tongue blocking" to prevent aspiration.

We first did a swallow study for Alexis at age two. She could not swallow thin liquids. At the time, we did not even suspect anything was wrong. I took a small cooler with foods she normally ate with us to the swallow study. Do the feeding yourself with a speech therapist present. If you have fed her your way and the advice that no food at all is the way, go with it.

Oral Motor Therapy

Oral motor therapy is usually provided by a pediatric occupational, physical or speech therapist who has had special training. An assessment is done to look at patterns of the lips, tongue, jaw, and cheeks for eating, drinking, facial expression, and speech, and to see if any of these patterns interfere with lip closure, mouth opening, and forming a seal around a feeding utensil (bottle, straw, cup, spoon, etc.).

My daughter had oral motor therapy to help her with her biting, grinding, drooling, eating, and swallowing difficulties. The same kind of therapy helped relax her jaw and reduce the discomfort of Temporal Mandibular Joint Disorder (TMJ).

Nutrition and Feeding

Oral motor activities should begin with the use of a dry towel first, and progress to a wet towel. If she resists the towel, the hands can be used. Stroke the face muscles from ears to mouth, and then from eyes to mouth, following the edge of the nose. Then, stroke from the center of the top lip to the right side of the mouth and repeat on the other side. Stimulate the teeth and gums in a circular motion from the center of the mouth toward the back and then toward the center.

Some other oral motor activities include:

- using a weighted vest to produce calm
- pulling thickened liquid from a straw
- using iced or chilled foods for a wake up effect on the tongue
- using strong flavors: spicy, sour and salty foods to increase tongue activity
- using a NUK massage brush for tongue activities
- using an Infa-Dent baby toothbrush to massage the tongue and cheeks
- doing bite-chew activities with different foods

We used a combination of sensorimotor techniques and tedious stepwise sensitization; e.g., in learning to eat grapes she started with 1. grape peeled and sliced and placed in the side of the mouth; 2. grape peeled and halved and placed in the side of the mouth; 3. grape halved and placed in the side of the mouth; 4. small whole grape in the side of the mouth; 5. regular size whole grape with skin placed in side of the mouth; and 6. regular size grape placed on tongue. The last one was the hard one and just took time and persistence. We didn't even know we were doing oral motor therapy.

Electrical Stimulation Therapy (E-Stim)

One approach to the treatment of swallowing disorders is the use of electrical stimulation applied to the surface of the front of the neck. The electrodes are about the same size as a 9-volt battery.

Ashley went from aspirating liquids to being able to safely swallow again. The stimulation didn't seem to bother her and she didn't cry at all or try to take it off. After fifteen one-hour sessions, she was able to safely drink again.

We had a great experience with E-stim. They called it vital stim therapy, but I assume it's the same. Rachel had just turned two when we started, and the therapy took place three times a week for about a month. The therapy feels like someone grabbing your neck. Rachel tolerated it very well. We did a pre- and post-therapy swallow study, which was disappointing, because it didn't show much difference. However, we really noticed that she was able to "feel" her food more. There was less gagging, more awareness of her oral cavity. It made a big difference in feeding and drinking. We plan to repeat this therapy if and when we notice a decline in her swallowing. If nothing else, I feel it has maintained what she has, slowed her regression and improved her awareness.

Thickening Foods and Drinks

Thickening foods and drinks can be important to your child's feeding plan. Thickened liquids move more slowly than thin liquids, allowing more time for swallowing. They are also not as scary to a child with poor swallowing skills. Thickening foods increases their texture and encourages a wider range of foods. They also help reduce reflux because the weight and thickness of the food make it easier to keep down.

Nutrition and Feeding

Here are some ways to thicken:

- Start out with a pureed fruit or vegetable and gradually add juice to thin it.
- Add dried infant cereal to drinks or foods.
- Add yogurt, instant pudding mix, or soft tofu to thicken liquids.
- Add sour cream, mayonnaise, or mashed potato flakes to thicken foods.
- Add bread crumbs to soups.
- Add applesauce, mashed banana, oatmeal, or cream of wheat to small bits of fruit, mashed potatoes, and refried beans.

Commercial thickeners can also be used. A list of these can be found in the Where to Go for Help chapter.

G-TUBES AND BUTTONS

NASOGASTRIC TUBE (NG TUBE)

THE NASOGASTRIC (NG) TUBE IS A SOFT TUBE which passes through the nose and down into the stomach. One advantage is that surgery is not required to place the tube. It can be used for up to several months to provide additional nutrition, and the child can still eat by mouth. The tube can be kept in place for several days. However, the tube can be uncomfortable, causing gagging or irritation of the nose, throat or esophagus and sometimes it can interfere with breathing. For these reasons, it is used as a short-term solution.

GASTROSTOMY (G-BUTTON)

IF SHE CANNOT SUCK, SWALLOW, OR CHEW well enough to get enough nourishment for normal weight gain and growth, or if she has recurrent bouts of aspiration pneumonia, when food surges up from the stomach after a meal and causes vomiting into the lungs, a gastrostomy should be considered.

A small opening is made surgically in the abdominal and stomach walls, and a small, plastic, pliable device (the button) is placed through the opening into the stomach. This is minor surgery, but generally requires anesthesia. She is fed either blenderized feedings or commercially prepared formulas through the button. Before she leaves the hospital, you will be taught how to care for the button. A one-way valve prevents stomach contents from leaking out of the stomach. For feedings, the plug is removed and tubing is inserted. Another procedure for creating an opening for a tube feeding into the stomach is called a *percutaneous endoscopic gastrostomy tube* or PEG. This procedure may not require general anesthesia and can generally be done with local anesthesia and intravenous sedation. If she is at risk for aspiration, a fundoplication may be done as well. The surgeon makes the opening from the esophagus into the stomach smaller, which prevents regurgitation (vomiting) and acid reflux.

By the age of three, Britt was so thin she was "wasting," or using her muscles for energy because she had no body fat and was taking in so few calories. Her weight percentile fell off of the chart as she grew taller. Each meal or snack became a torture session for me. I didn't realize it at the time, but there is nothing worse in this world than not being in a position to help your own child. I would feed her for forty-five minutes or so and she would eat

Nutrition and Feeding

a handful of Lucky Charms. I felt helpless. My husband couldn't spend hours each day helping me feed her. Britt had very little energy, was very withdrawn and didn't smile much.

Facing the Decision

The idea of using alternative feeding methods is often upsetting for parents. It is hard to consider letting go of traditional feeding methods for a way that seems "unnatural." Some parents feel that they have failed or look at it as yet another skill that she will have to lose. These are all normal reactions. However, the best way to cope with change is knowledge and information. One big consolation is that afterward, families are always glad they made the decision. The most often repeated comment is, "Wish we had done it sooner." The child gets the nutrition she needs and is more alert, healthier, and more comfortable. There is no more second guessing about how much medication was swallowed. Adequate fluids are easy to provide. To top off the list, parents no longer have to spend hours each day struggling to get her to eat.

I put off the G-tube for three years. We would puree her meals and spend about an hour at every meal feeding her and another couple hours every day getting fluids in her. Sometimes she would bring it all up and we would have to start over. Meals were very stressful. After two bouts of pneumonia and a swallow study that said she aspirated on all consistencies, I knew it was time. My only regret is that we didn't do it sooner.

I was sure I could get enough food and fluid into her to keep her healthy and "force" her to gain weight. Admitting I had failed was one of the hardest things I have done since we entered Rettland. That said, the G-tube has been the single most positive thing we have done for her. Going for the G-tube is not a failure. It is a positive step toward providing all the best that we can for our girls.

Our daughter's swallow study showed that she was micro-aspirating with pretty much every swallow. Oral motor therapy hadn't been enough and she needed to have a G-tube placed. As devastating to us as the recommendation was at the time, her G-tube has been an absolute godsend on a lot of fronts and we are so glad she has it now. Rest assured that it isn't the "end of the world" like we thought it would be.

Danni was ten when she got her G-tube. I had to get over myself and realize that this wasn't about me or my ability to feed Danni or keep her from being hungry, but it was all about Danni and her nutritional needs. We have never regretted this decision. We have never looked back, either. She is much happier, healthier, and more alert.

Shelby constantly sputtered on any liquid we gave her, and the result was that she was lethargic and weak. She also never chewed, and I calculated that we were spending approximately five to six hours a day just trying to get nutrients in her. Major frustration for both child and caregiver. She also was starting to aspirate. Finally, we never knew if she was getting all her medicine, because it always seemed like half of it would come rolling down her chin. Or, she would pocket it in her cheek somewhere like a squirrel, and it would come out later. Shelby has had her gastrostomy button for fifteen months now, and it has literally saved her life.

Unless there are reasons such as the risk of aspiration of food into the lungs, girls with gastrostomy buttons can continue to eat food by mouth. Gastrostomy feedings may be necessary for life if chewing and swallowing function are poor and cannot support adequate dietary intake for normal weight and height gains. However, if supplemental feedings are no longer needed, the gastrostomy button can be removed. Neither the button nor the hole is permanent, but a scar will remain. Even if the button is not used for feedings, it is

Nutrition and Feeding

often used to "vent" air from the stomach when air swallowing and bloating are a concern. The button also serves as a "safety valve" for medications and fluids when she absolutely refuses to drink by mouth.

The J-Tube

A *jejunostomy tube* (J-tube) is also placed through the abdominal wall, but it goes to the *jejunum* (the beginning of the small intestine). It bypasses the stomach, thus helping to prevent reflux of feedings from the stomach. If the doctor allows it, the child can still eat by mouth. The tube is cared for in the same way, but it has one drawback: it requires a continuous drip feeding. This means the child must be connected to a feeding pump most of the time.

The G-J Tube

If the child already has a G-tube, the G-J tube uses the same stoma. This tube has an additional line which extends to the top of the small intestine (jejunum). Medications are delivered via the G-tube port, and formula, juice and water are fed via the J-tube port.

The first eight years following placement of Jenn's G-tube were the healthiest years she has ever had. Her G-J tube was placed after a near-fatal bout of pneumonia caused by a severe increase in her reflux issues, causing reflux-induced aspiration pneumonia. It's not without its faults or hassles, but it was the best solution for Jenn given the set of circumstances at the time.

Placement Procedures

Most gastrostomy procedures require hospitalization. The abdominal wall is cut and a tube is placed and secured. A canal is made from the abdominal skin to the stomach, which is called a stoma. Special feeding tubes are placed into the stoma at the time of feeding, and then removed.

Following surgery, a catheter tube is usually used, and when the site has healed, it is replaced with a different type of tube. The tube extends twelve to fifteen inches from the skin and stays in all the time. Attention needs to be paid to the tube so that it doesn't slip down into the stomach too far. At the end of the tube is a clamp or plug. For feedings, the clamp is loosened and a syringe is attached to the tube.

A *button tube* lies flat to the skin, without any tubing. For feedings, the flap (port) is opened and a special adaptor feeding tube (extension) is put in. Advantages of the button are that it is less obvious and because it is flat, it is less likely to be moved or pulled out by the child or by activity. The button is placed after the surgery site is healed.

One surgery which does not require hospitalization is called a *percutaneous endoscopic gastrostomy (PEG)*. It is done as an outpatient procedure. Local anesthesia is used to numb the area and the tube is placed with a special scope.

It was a relatively short procedure, only about forty-five minutes, and her hospital stay was only two days. Britt was dehydrated when she got out of the surgery and it seemed to set her back for a day or two. She now had a hole in her stomach. It's one of those things that just is not natural, yet there it was. For the first few weeks she had a long tube hanging out of her stomach and it was awkward. We had to put a lot of netting around it to keep it close to her stomach so she wouldn't pull it out. But within weeks, they switched her to a

Nutrition and Feeding

Mic-Key, which is just a little button that sits flush against her stomach. We gave her the formula by "bolus" (put the formula straight into her button) three times a day. Once you get the hang of it, it's no big deal. It becomes second nature.

Sammi stayed at the hospital for a couple of hours and then went home. She did just fine. The home health care nurse came out to show us how to hook her up and then came back a couple of other times to see how things were going. Make sure the doctor writes a note for the home health care nurse.

Feeding Schedule

When she first begins, your child may need a feeding every two to five hours all day and night. As she adjusts to the tube, you can adjust her schedule to as close to normal as possible, allowing for three "meals" a day and "snacks" in between.

Types of Feedings

Formulas may be given as a continuous drip, an intermittent bolus feeding, or a combination of the two techniques. Continuous drip feedings, as the name implies, are given by continuous drip over a ten to twelve hour period or more. Bolus feedings consist of several ounces of formula given over a ten to twenty minute period with several feeds a day. Drip feedings are used when the child cannot tolerate much formula in the stomach all at once. The child's tube is attached to a longer tube and then attached to a drip feeding bag and drip regulation system (often called a kangaroo pump). The pump system is set to deliver a certain amount of drips per hour. Some children are given a combination of both types of feedings, using bolus feeds during the day and drip feedings at night.

The total amount of formula given and the rate of administration varies on the basis of energy needs and the tolerance level of your child. A combination of these techniques allows greater flexibility in feeding and can be adjusted to fit the family schedule.

How to Feed

In the beginning, it may seem like there aren't enough hands to coordinate holding the child and all the equipment. Soon, you will do it all with ease. Be sure that your hands and the equipment are clean. Pour formula into the syringe and let it flow into the tube. You will notice that the higher you hold the tube, the faster it will flow. Your child may gag or vomit if the feeding is given too fast. She may get the hiccups if the feeding is too fast, too hot, or too cold. Lower the syringe to slow down the flow.

Giving Medications

One distinct advantage of tube feedings is giving medications successfully. First, check with the pharmacist to see if the formula and the medication will work well together and won't change the nutritional value or clog the tube. All medications given through the tube should be flushed with 10 to 15 cc of water to clear the tube.

Ask for medications in liquid form if possible. Ask if tablets can be crushed and given through the tube. Crushing them causes the medication to act quicker than if the drug were swallowed whole. However, some medications cannot work properly if crushed.

If your child takes more than one medication, it is important to check with the doctor or pharmacist about drug interactions.

Nutrition and Feeding

Formulas

Commercially prepared, nutritionally complete formulas are designed specifically for young girls and adolescents. Home-prepared formulas are acceptable substitutes. However, you should consult your physician and dietitian for assistance in the preparation of blenderized formula to ensure that your child receives adequate energy, protein, vitamins, and minerals. Supplemental vitamins are not needed if she is taking a commercially prepared formula.

The cost of tube feeding will vary depending on the quantity of formula used. The costs include formula, syringes, and, if formula is given by continuous drip, bags, tubing, and a pump. Many insurance companies or Medicaid will cover the cost of all or a portion of these supplies. Check with your physician's office. Sometimes a letter of necessity is helpful in getting these costs covered by the insurance company. The letter should state that the formula is life sustaining due to lack of weight gain and malnutrition due to reflux and inability to chew and swallow properly due to neurologic impairment.

Adjusting to the G-Button

If the formula is given too rapidly, nausea, vomiting, bloating, abdominal cramping and diarrhea may occur. Constipation may be encountered, not as a result of the formula but due to the increased volume. This problem can be remedied by giving additional free water, formula with fiber, or using a bowel stimulant such as Milk of Magnesia, Miralax, lactulose, or a senna preparation. Problems associated with the button include tissue buildup, or granulation, around the gastrostomy button, a blocked tube, and leaking around the button. These problems are easily remedied. Rarely, infection or an allergic response occurs and may necessitate removal of the button. It is important to check the balloon for the amount of water needed to keep it in place.

We found there is an adjustment phase after a G-button is placed. Jenn had sporadic vomiting the first couple of months after the surgery. But once we settled on an appropriate schedule and her body adjusted and we learned not to move her immediately after a feeding or allow her to bend forward after a feeding, the vomiting subsided. Finding a feeding schedule tailored to Jenn's nutritional needs, yet allowing time for water feedings as well without overloading her was a challenge initially. But once set, it runs smoothly. And it's easily adaptable if we get off schedule. With the timed feedings, giving water, toileting, and medicine, we live by the clock!

It became liberating once I realized that if she's not on the pump for a night, it's not a disaster. So if we travel for only a night or two, we don't bother with the pump and just bolus her meds and feed her by mouth. If we go somewhere for an extended period, we bring the pump and apparatus. It's not that bad to tote with you. We rig the bag of formula with an S hook on an old microphone stand when we're in hotels. If we have a sitter that can't hook her up and we know we're getting home late, we don't set it up. But probably 95 percent of the time, her pump is set up in the evening.

Kayleigh had not gained any weight in three years. The gastroenterologist told us that nutritional supplements were needed and possibly a G-button. We were upset. I thought I could fatten my girl. I am a farmer's wife and I had fattened the rest of us. So I came home ready to cook up a storm and fatten my girl. For two years with the help of specialists and nutritionists we tried, but Kayleigh only got worse. So, she had G-button surgery, and today she has a Mic-key button. She is seventy pounds, not thirty-eight pounds. She is on the growth chart! She is using her hands. She is stronger and she is advancing in skills, and she has a better quality of life.

Nutrition and Feeding

She was failing to thrive before surgery. She bounces back from seizures better today. She still eats foods she likes, but she gets her supplement at night.

Skin Irritations

Sometimes, skin irritations develop from leakage, tape irritation, pulling on the tube, or infection. Signs of infection include any unusual redness, drainage, swelling, or warmth at the stoma site. Report this to the doctor immediately.

- Try to keep the skin around the stoma dry and clean, but too much cleaning can irritate the skin.
- Changing the tape may help. Use silk adhesive, paper, or plastic tape.
- Leotards or Onesies can be worn under clothing to keep the child from pulling.
- Commercial products are available. Ask your doctor about Critic Aid, Proshield Plus, and Stomahesive Protection.

Granulation tissue may form around the freshly healing stoma. This appears as red skin which bleeds easily. The doctor can "burn" the extra tissue off with silver nitrate in his office, or you can use it at home with a prescription. However, silver nitrate can be painful and it doesn't prevent new growth. Coating the area around the granulation tissue with Vaseline prior to treatment with the silver nitrate helps to avoid burning healthy skin. Maalox applied to the skin around the stoma works well to keep it dry and helps to ward off granulation tissue.

The most effective treatment for Angela was zinc oxide cream; Sween's Critic Aid Skin Paste was what we used to get things under control. Since then, we have used a less powerful zinc oxide cream called Calmoseptine; its ingredients are not very different from zinc oxide-based diaper creams.

Some people use prescription Kenalog cream to prevent growth. You do want to use it sparingly; one side effect can be little black hairs that grow around the stoma. Not exactly feminine.

Lots of families swear by diluted eucalyptus oil, swabbing it around the site daily.

Typical Results of Tube Feeding

The results of supplemental oral or G-button feedings are positive. Girls who have been supplemented with adequate amounts of formula gain weight and grow taller. Parents and teachers also report improvements in attention span, eye gaze, disposition and stamina.

I can tell you from my own experience that this procedure was the best thing I ever did for my daughter. Her quality of life improved in every aspect; she had more strength, endurance, alertness, better eye contact, and best of all, she gained weight. It was a global improvement.

Last year at this time she was about thirty pounds and looked like she was starving. Today she is beautiful, round-cheeked, forty-four pounds, and much healthier. For us, the G-button was the only way to go, and we have not regretted it for one moment. Shelby actually grins from ear to ear when she sees me coming toward her with the feeding stuff. She knows that she can be satisfied without that awful struggle.

Jamie has had her Mic-key button now for almost five years and swims every day in the summertime, sometimes for hours. She has never had one single problem with her button. She rarely uses hers for eating anymore

Nutrition and Feeding

ut we have kept it just in case she needs it for extra nourishment or fluids, but she mostly just uses it for vitamins and medications.

The results have been amazing. Until only recently, Jenny had no illnesses at all, no bronchitis, pneumonia, not even a cold. The G-button has made caretaking much easier for us and her teachers at school. Her vomiting is greatly reduced, but still occurs on occasion.

Keep a Spare

Be sure to keep a spare button with you for emergencies. Not all hospitals and doctor's offices carry the right size or style you need.

GROWING OLDER

UNLESS AGGRESSIVE NUTRITIONAL REHABILITATION is undertaken, she may always be thin. However, she may gain too much weight if overfed through her gastrostomy button. Even without the button, she may become obese after her teen years if she overeats because she no longer has the extra energy requirements for growth.

Ashley weighs one hundred twenty pounds at age twenty-five. Measuring only fifty-four inches in height, Ashley is approximately twenty pounds overweight. Although she walks about a mile each day, the weight has not come off easily.

Shelley was such a tiny thing; for years she was underweight, but then in her thirties, she slowed down and started to gain weight. She went from her normal eighty pounds to over one hundred ten pounds, too heavy for her.

"LOVE: A word properly applied to our delight in particular kinds of food; sometimes metaphorically spoken of the favorite objects of all our appetites."

– HENRY FIELDING

Therapeutic Avenues

5

SECTION FIVE

Communication
Education and Learning
Therapeutic Approaches

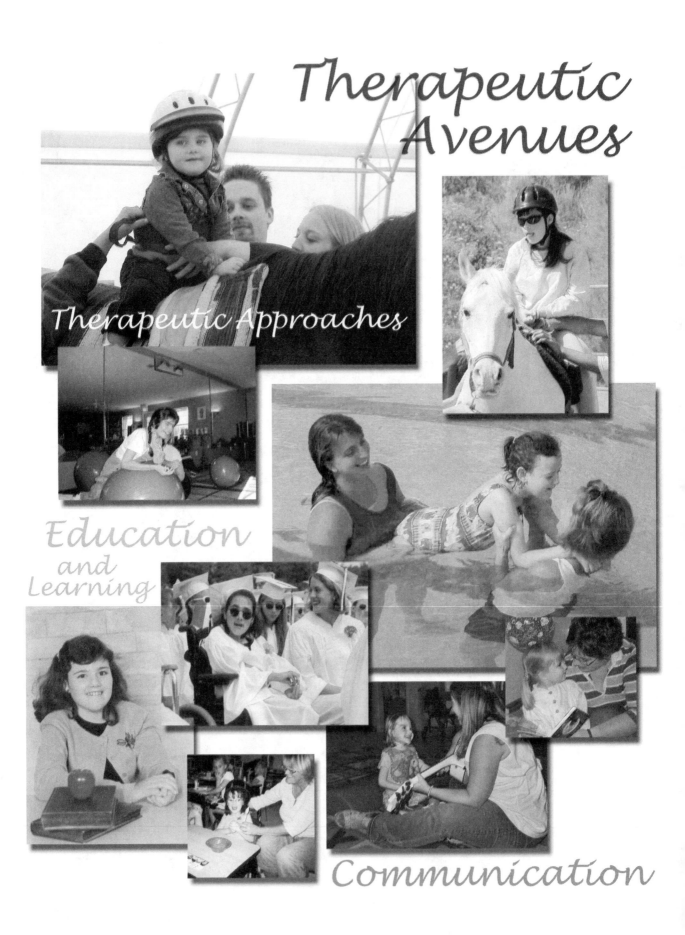

Therapeutic Avenues

Therapeutic Approaches

Education
and
Learning

Communication

Communication

LANGUAGE WITHOUT SPEECH

GIRLS WITH RS show a strong desire to communicate despite their lack of expressive language and loss of functional hand use. This is evident by their eye gaze, facial expression, and body gestures.

We know that most children with RS have greater *receptive* language (what they hear and understand) than *expressive* language (spoken language). Parents consistently report that their daughters understand far more than they are able to communicate. They see their girls laugh appropriately at jokes or things which happen to other family members. They see her eyes briefly turn toward something being discussed or a movement in response to a question.

Many children with RS seem to have the mental ability to speak. Researchers have indicated that the speech areas of the brain appear to be intact. However, it seems that those with RS lack the motor control or nervous system connections to be able to do so. We know that many children blurt out a word or two under stress or excitement and never repeat it, and we know that some higher-functioning girls can speak in phrases or sentences. So we know that language is "in there." Our challenge is to get it out.

When it comes to communication, we are as handicapped as our girls are. We struggle to find ways to understand what they know, and to interpret their needs and wants. Others are handicapped, too. People often don't know how to react to those who are nonverbal, so they talk "at" them instead of "to" them. The abilities of girls with RS are so often misunderstood. It is so important to give every child a means of communication, to stimulate her receptive language in order to enrich her life, develop a base for emerging communication, and develop academic concepts.

"Not being able to talk is not the same as not having anything to say."

— ROSEMARY CROSSLEY

At times someone will ask a question about what Sherry likes or thinks. Much more often now I say, "Well, let's ask her" rather than answering for her, even if I think I know the answer. Also, I am making a point of talking directly to Sherry when in a group in such a way that people can be "educated" about her ability to respond, and see firsthand how she does this. Now a lot of people are feeling much more comfortable interacting with her, and they get very tickled when they see the responses.

Girls with RS vary widely in their communication methods and abilities. Some girls retain speech to varying degrees. This speech may pop out when least expected or when her need or emotional level is so strong it seems as if an electrical connection suddenly is made, then lost again. Some girls use eye gaze to communicate while others may be able to use their hands to point or give a picture to another person. Some can produce sentences through typing with a pointer or by touching a series of pictures on a communication device.

Communication

Body language is an important element of communication, though it is sometimes subtle and difficult for other observers to interpret. Sorting through all of the possibilities for methods of communication may seem mind boggling at first for families, educational staff and even speech-language therapists.

I talk to her, just as if she would understand everything. I tell her everything that will be happening, in great detail. I explain things to her about the wind blowing today or the sun hiding behind clouds and that makes it cooler. Many times she will "talk" back to me with sounds or her eyes. I always listen to every utterance she makes.

The girl with RS often appears to know what she wants to say, but cannot plan out the movements needed to say it, due to verbal apraxia. In addition, she may have underlying oral motor problems that affect speech, as well as chewing and swallowing difficulties. Her ability to communicate in sign language, gestures, and other body language is hindered by her lack of purposeful hand use and her motor apraxia. Though she knows what she wants to do, it may be difficult for her to use computers, switches and other devices because they require too much eye-hand coordination. Even her eye gaze is affected by apraxia, so that eye pointing can be difficult. Understandably, this can be very frustrating for her, so motivation is very important. If she believes she can get what she wants without communicating, she probably won't work up the effort, because it is so very difficult for her. She will take the easier approach and just wait for others to provide what she wants or needs. Communication is a very basic human need, and the lack of it can lead to complacency, frustration, social withdrawal, or severe behavior problems.

I know this is a tremendous oversimplification, but sometimes it seems that communication with Sherry is like trying to talk on a cell phone with someone in bad weather, heavy traffic, and unfavorable terrain all at the same time. I listen hard and try to figure out the garbled transmission, through the "fuzz" and interference. Which is the communication and which is the interference?

IMPORTANT CONSIDERATIONS

EVERY CHILD IS DIFFERENT

ALL CHILDREN HAVE THEIR OWN STRENGTHS and weaknesses. No method of communication will work for every child. The challenge is to find some method or adaptation for the child to have active participation and a feeling of control and choice in every activity.

VISION

IT'S A GOOD IDEA TO HAVE THE CHILD'S VISION TESTED if there is any question of how much she can see. Vision problems are not part of the clinical picture of RS, but are seen widely in the general population. If she has any visual difficulties, pictures, or symbols may need to be larger in size. Black and white symbols on colored backgrounds are easiest to see. It could help to have different colors represent different categories; e.g. feelings/light blue, foods/green. Yellow and red are the most salient colors for students with visual impairments. In general, increasing the figure ground contrast will help the student understand the pictures better; and if vision is very poor, representational objects would be preferred (not miniature objects, but representational objects; e.g. for computer activity, a mouse could represent the computer).

Communication

DISTRACTIONS

WHEN WORKING ON COMMUNICATION SKILLS, try to keep the room as free of distractions as possible. This is important not only for the child, but also for the listener. Communication is hard enough as it is without distraction. And remember, girls with RS often do best with one modality at a time.

Amanda is very noise sensitive, nervous of other children, and cannot focus or concentrate with other kids present, so her therapy is 1:1 in an isolated room.

It is important, however, once skills have been established, to work on communication in a more typical environment like a classroom (at home this would be when siblings are present, with the TV on, etc.). This time could gradually be increased as she grows more competent in her communication.

BELIEVING IN HER

IT IS SO HARD TO FEEL THAT YOUR CHILD UNDERSTANDS and be unable to find others who will support her. Both in and out of school, the people who work with your child are such an important ingredient in her success. Believing in her ability to learn is basic. Frustration is part of the territory in RS, and sometimes, others can leave us so disheartened. Find people who believe in your child. They are more valuable than any brand new school building or piece of adaptive equipment.

THE GIFT OF COMMUNICATION

By Bonnie Keck

What a pleasure it is to be able to share something that is near and dear to one's heart. We gladly tell others about individuals or events in our lives, and the feelings they trigger deep inside us. Relaying our needs and personal reflections is just a way of life for most of us—something we basically take for granted. However, for a few individuals, like my sixteen-year-old daughter Lyndie, sharing her thoughts and feelings with others is not such an easy task. In fact, it requires a monumental effort.

Communication is obviously a two-way street. It requires a sender and a receiver for every transferred piece of information. For Lyndie, it has been the sending that RS has negatively impacted so greatly. Lyndie speaks only six or seven words, and her hands are neurologically stimulated to wring together almost incessantly, thus making gesturing very difficult. For many, it would seem that no speech and no hand usage preclude learning the skill of communication. Many folks (sadly, some of whom work in professional careers) are tempted to take that one step further, and thereby assume that these inabilities equate to little intelligence.

It is at this point that the receiver comes into the picture. As Lyndie's mom, I have become adept over the years at reading her eyes. There has been much expressed through those eyes, but of course, I could only retrieve the most primitive messages, such as "I am hungry" or "I am tired." Often she would elicit a smile to mean "yes," but that was not always reliable. Then at the age of three, Lyndie was enrolled in an

Communication

early intervention program where a speech therapist began to work with her. Although she was one of the lowest functioning children in the class, this speech therapist dared to take a chance that perhaps Lyndie could be taught to stop her hand wringing just long enough to choose what she wanted when given the choice between two objects. The risk was rewarded, as Lyndie learned to release her right hand to choose a desired object. From there, she progressed to choosing between pictures of objects, then pictures of objects with labels, and, finally, by the age of seven, between cards with labels only. Indeed, this child who was once thought to be "unteachable" had learned to read.

Communication opens the door to every individual's world, with or without disability. For Lyndie, it has not only provided an outlet for exchanging information for socialization, but it has also opened a huge door for her academically. Through Lyndie's minimal communication system of choosing, her receivers in the classroom have also become believers in her cognitive abilities. Slowly she has shown them that she is capable of absorbing and learning academic material, and through homework and tests modified to her system of communication, has succeeded in passing eighth grade regular education classes.

The ultimate goal of communication, which seldom requires consideration in the lives of most people, is for people to independently relate their inner thoughts to another. At present, Lyndie is working on learning a computerized eye gaze system that will allow her to spell out her own thoughts without being given preconceived choices someone else has decided to offer her. We don't know if she will be able to master this system; we know she will not succeed if we do not give her the opportunity. Through Lyndie's improved behavior over the years, we can assume that her ability to get her point across to others has made a huge difference in the quality of her life. It is our deep hope that someday she will be able to share with us the invaluable hidden treasure of all her inner thoughts and dreams.

EYES THAT TALK

GIRLS WITH RS SEEM TO HAVE SUCH EXPRESSIVE EYES that often speak for them. One child said of his sister, "She can't talk, but she has really loud eyes!"

WHERE TO BEGIN

FOR ALL OF US, COMMUNICATION OCCURS IN MANY WAYS, and you will find that different strategies work best in different situations. By combining methods you will find that she becomes a more effective communicator. It is very important to start with items or actions that are very meaningful and motivating to her, and gradually increase their number.

Begin by finding a good speech therapist and augmentative communication specialist to be on your team. A good therapist is not necessarily one who knows everything about RS, but one who is eager to learn about it and what may help. The therapist is someone who will see the girl as an individual and will not need to put her into a cookie cutter box of what may or may not work for her. She will be someone you are comfortable with, and one who says she doesn't know when she doesn't know. You can educate therapists about

Communication

> ## THE LANGUAGE OF LOVE
>
> Jennie talks quite well. Listed below are some of her favorite looks, such as:
>
> "Get out of my space," when she is watching her favorite video.
>
> "You think I am gonna eat that!" when she doesn't want to eat her meal and the lips are locked tight.
>
> "That is what I want for dinner," when she sees the cake I baked for the church social.
>
> "I hurt … please find what is happening to me" or the harder one, "Why am I hurting?" more probing and quieter.
>
> "It is okay. I know you gave me that shot for my own good and all is forgiven" to the eyes of the good looking doctor.
>
> "I can't believe you really left me."
>
> And then there is the look and smile that many of our friends and family have come to love. It says, "Ain't I somethin' and I love you, too."
>
> The laugh and giggle and even a look that says "You really don't have to act so silly just to entertain me, but I love you for it."
>
> But the one that can stop my heart is the one that says "I love you, too."

RS, but it is next to impossible to educate them about how to be kind or how to keep an open mind.

You can ask the school district for an *augmentative communication evaluation* at the school district's cost if the team determines it is necessary to meet the child's needs (and in RS this is a certainty). States vary in how they provide this service. Some have evaluators at a regional or county level on whom the school district can call. The special education supervisor should either know this or be willing to find it out. In other states, it is possible that the district may need to contract with a specialist through a specialized hospital or private practice. Ideally, this person should be available for follow-up when necessary.

In looking at what motivates the child, it can help to look at a number of different types of communication functions including expressing wants and needs (requesting, choice-making), commenting, social exchange, and participation in group activities

There are a number of ways of teaching communication strategies, depending on what she can do and how she does it. The first step is to take time to observe the strategies she is already using. They may be subtle and not very effective, but all children find ways to communicate. Does she fuss or smack her lips when she is hungry, rub her eyes when sleepy, lay her head down to show boredom? To show you what she wants, she may move toward it, or gaze at it with her eyes. She may reach out and touch or "swat" at it or stare at it with her eyes to draw your attention toward it. She has very expressive eyes, and she may talk with them. Her ability to eye point increases with age. She may increase her overall level of activity or hand stereotypies to express herself.

By acknowledging and putting words and actions to those messages, even if they don't seem to be directed toward anyone or really purposeful, you can show her you know she is telling you something, and her actions will become more purposeful.

Communication

I found that she is a very complex young woman and that she has lots of things to communicate, but only a few ways in which to do this. Her vocalizations, cries, screams, and tears can mean different things in different situations. She may make the same sound to go to the bathroom, get someone's attention, show us that she does not want to leave the hockey game, or stop an activity altogether. I try to ask her what she's trying to say by giving her different choices and trying to narrow it down. She will usually stop "vocalizing" when I have hit the right choice.

Ideally, parents, teachers, therapists, and caregivers can get together to work out common goals and a plan for action. The plan needs to have small steps and instructions that are practical and specific so that everyone can incorporate them into the daily routine. A consistent approach is vital. When planning a communication program, consider expectations for each setting carefully. Communication programs must start with an assessment of her own interests, along with what and how she is already successfully communicating. You need to build on her successes, not replace them with other methods. For example, if she takes your hand and drags you to the garage door at home when she wants a ride, she will probably not be motivated to point to "car" on a communication device elsewhere in the house.

Lyndsay has a backpack that her aide carries with her everywhere, with all of her folders (Wants and Needs, Academics, Social, Holidays and Themes), which include laminated pictures with Velcro. They pull out the appropriate ones that apply to the activity that they are doing and put them on a board for Lyndsay to choose from.

Jess has a Chat Book. The first page explains that "I cannot talk but I would love you to have a chat with me." It then introduces Jess and her family with photos.

MOTIVATION

IT IS IMPORTANT FOR HER TO BE MOTIVATED to participate in the activity. Making it fun and using reinforcers that are meaningful to her are helpful.

Food doesn't motivate Carly. Her motivations are more of the ability to do things. For example, if she walks in her walker she gets to go where she wants: the library, the cafeteria, or to help the janitor (a favorite activity).

Angela wasn't much interested until we used a BIGmack programmed to say "Turn the page, please" and we hit pay dirt! She loves books ... a perfect match! We wouldn't turn the page until she was ready and requested.

BODY LANGUAGE

IN MANY RESPECTS, WE SHARE HER HANDICAP. We may find it more difficult to understand her than for her to understand us! When we speak to her, we can change our pitch or tone of voice to aid our expression. But we may not know how to interpret her behavior, emotional expressions, body language, and facial expressions.

Whenever Jenn puts her hand on our faces, we call those "Jenny's kisses." If I ask for a kiss she can respond so sweetly by placing her hand on my face. It is one of the most delightful, exhilarating experiences ever!

Sherry makes a fist, slightly held up, similar to the sign language symbol "yes." She must have picked this up from other kids at school who were using sign language, because we never taught it to her or suggested it. We simply saw that she was doing it as a definite gesture and discovered she was using it for "yes."

Stacie can shake her head for "no" when she is very motivated, and particularly when she has had enough to eat or drink. It happens spontaneously, and she actually surprises herself!

Communication

DEVELOPING CHOICE-MAKING SKILLS

THE OPPORTUNITY TO MAKE ACTIVE CHOICES can mean the difference between becoming a passive or active participant within her world. If she is not given enough opportunity to interact as independently as possible, she may just sit back and watch the world go by, depending completely on others to decide for her. If she has a reasonable means to communicate, she will be reinforced by the communication itself and will be more willing to keep on trying.

Following are some ways to assist her in choice-making:

- It is important for her to look at you to confirm her choice, since she will often look back and forth to check out the pictures a few times before settling on one.

- Make sure the choices involve objects, people, or activities that are motivating and desirable to her, and that are available when the choice is made. Determine the method of making the choice that requires the least effort and time on her part. You want her energy to go into communicating, not improving her motor skills. Always give her plenty of time to respond, and be aware that she may need to gear her body up with other movements to get started.

- When beginning, offer her only two choices at a time. As her clarity and skills improve you can increase the number of choices to as many as she can handle at a time, usually three to four. Make sure to show her you understood her choice by naming it and providing it immediately. For example, "Oh, you want the music. Here it is!" Each successful communication will lead to more motivation to communicate again.

- You can start by offering her only choices of things you expect her to want. If her choice-making seems random, you can try pairing something she really likes with something neutral, such as a Barney tape with a pair of pants. Remember, she gets what she chooses, so she will learn quickly to choose her favorite.

- Determine whether she can recognize pictures, and how realistic they need to be, starting with familiar photos as most concrete, and moving to line drawings as most abstract. If pictures are difficult for her, use real objects, miniatures, or parts of objects, such as a rope to signify her swing. You can then pair the picture with the object and eventually fade out use of the object.

- She may require some extra cues at first. For example, you can hold or point to the choice on the left while naming it, then do the same with the one on the right. You can cue visually by shining a flashlight on each picture or moving your finger toward it to help her eyes track and to draw her attention. You can use auditory signals such as tapping each picture or snapping your fingers to remind her to look. Physical cues include hand-over-hand assistance to help her touch a desired choice, nudging her elbow toward a choice, or gently touching her face to help her turn toward a choice.

- You may be able to fade out cues, then need to increase them again when introducing new concepts. Having pictures available during ongoing activities may help to introduce her to them before she must make active choices.

- If she will not make a choice, try changing to something else which may be more motivating. If you are pretty sure she wants one of the choices, try making it clear that she must communicate first. For example, "First show me which you want, then you can have the Coke or the cookie." Remember that if she is not used to making choices, it can

Communication

be very tiring for her at first. She may also wonder why you suddenly cannot anticipate her needs. She may also take the choices a step further than you expect.

AUGMENTATIVE AND ALTERNATIVE COMMUNICATION

MOST GIRLS WILL BENEFIT FROM *augmentative* and *alternative communication* (AAC), which is a modality to assist people with communicating who have little or no verbal speech. Everyone uses AAC through written language, body language and facial expression. These avenues may be difficult for the girl with RS, so she may need to use eye gaze, head pointing, communication boards, switches, and voice output communication devices.

AAC helps to promote both receptive and expressive language. It also helps improve self-esteem, which aids learning. Using a multisensory approach to language provides a richer experience and allows the child to learn through visual and auditory means. AAC increases motivation and participation, and encourages interaction with her peers. It also promotes social skills as she learns to take turns. And, it provides a basis for emerging literacy.

Methods for AAC could be divided into four levels of technological complexity. *"No tech"* methods would include signing, using pictures and objects without voice output, facial and body language, and eye gaze. *"Low tech"* methods would include devices with voice output, but only one choice or one page recorded on them. *"Mid tech"* devices are capable of using a number of pages/overlays with a larger vocabulary that can be stored; they are not computerized. *"High tech"* devices are like computers, allowing for the greatest number of options.

SUCCESS WITH AAC

REMEMBER THAT RECEPTIVE LANGUAGE comes before expressive language (language must go in before it can come out). Increase attention by using visual supports or exaggerated gestures, tapping an object or cueing with a flashlight. Use motivating toys and the child's own interests to develop fun games. Language is not learned by imitation alone, but by a wide assortment of experiences that provide many repetitions of concepts and words. Use a broad variety of functions, such as comments, requests, jokes, teasing, and protesting, in conventional and conversational language. Avoid asking too many questions, but when a question is asked, make sure to provide a concrete way for the child to respond (symbols or pictures). Expect delayed processing time and try to minimize distraction. AAC use is learned over time. Giving a student pictures, etc., as a means of using them in and of itself will not ensure success. What will ensure success is finding a few good modalities for access and practice, practice, practice in functional contexts.

USING EYE GAZE

IF YOU WANT HER TO BE MOTIVATED to use eye gazing, the choices provided for her in the beginning should be meaningful to her. Color and letter identification can get boring, especially if repetitious. If her choice results in an outcome, it will be more motivating.

Start with one highly motivating choice and have her look at just that item. Use varying places in space, mostly left and right. This ensures that the student can localize the

Communication

object and that eye gaze is appropriate. When you start with two items, just like in PECS, the student may be happy with either one, so you don't truly know if a choice has been made. When you do get to two choices and she picks one, you will know from her reaction if it is wrong. Still give it to her, but indicate that you know she doesn't like it by saying, "Oh, you didn't want the Froot Loop. OK, let's try again." She will soon find out how much fun it is to have some control with her choices.

If you are using photos, use realistic ones for eye gaze. Cut all around the main item, removing the background unless it is essential. This decreases the distraction factor.

Eye gaze symbols really can be a "language," so kids need to be immersed in them whenever possible. You should have seen how our house looked when Angela was little. Early American Preschool might be the decorating theme! Just be sure to always have the symbols labeled with words for a smooth transition to words later.

We found that when Lauren had the choices of "hi" and "bye" she would typically point to "bye" when she wanted to leave a situation, and she would point only to "hi" with her best friend, hoping she would stay.

There is a hierarchy, even in eye gaze of a) tangible objects; b) realistic photos; and c) representational symbols. If need be, you might try stepping back to objects to teach eye gaze. When she has gotten to where she will hold a clear gaze, then you move up to photographs of the same things and, after that, symbols of them. But also keep in mind that some kids will perseverate on photos and may need to move on to symbols fairly rapidly. My daughter really enjoys studying the detail of photos or detailed drawings, so we find that simple symbols that get the point across quickly let her focus on the choices rather than be distracted by pictures.

A trick we use to help my daughter when she is distracted is to hold all the choices together with no spaces, just to focus her attention, and then move them apart. She will continue to track the one she chooses. You can mount them with Velcro to the ends of tongue depressors or, if you need greater distances between symbols, a footlong ruler, and fan them apart with your hand.

We ask our daughter to confirm her choices by looking us in the eye as confirmation after she has made her selection. Since any eye gaze is exhausting when she is not feeling good (heavy motor demands), we don't ask this second step of her then.

Eye gaze or eye pointing can be a very good way to communicate, but is sometimes difficult for the girl with RS. It may help to space things far apart or to place them in an up-and-down plane instead of side to side. There are a variety of ways to hold or place pictures or objects for eye gaze. Positioning of both the girl and the objects or pictures is important. Make sure she is positioned for maximum stability of her trunk and head so that her gaze can be accurate. Observe the direction she watches the best, down on a table, on a slanting board, up at eye level, mostly to the left, etc., and use this information for placement. If possible, teach her to look around at all the items until she sees what she wants, stares at it, then looks at your face to make it clear she has made a choice.

There are a variety of homemade and commercially made holders for eye gaze pictures or objects. An E-tran is a large clear plexiglass board with a hole in the center or made in an open three sided shape for the other person to watch through. Items are attached around the outside, usually by using Velcro. A similar but more easily portable holder can be homemade out of PVC pipe and Velcro. It can be placed on a table or held, and tilted in the best direction. An eye gaze vest is another option, worn by the receiving person, with the possibility of having Velcro or pockets on the front to contain items. Commercially available eye

Communication

gaze frames are available from Enabling Devices, Crestwood Communication Inc., and through the Wisconsin Assistive Technology Initiative Web Site. In addition, you can also use an inexpensive clear photo frame found at stores like Wal-Mart, or the clear cover of a disposable baking pan.

Kaitlynne will answer with her eyes. With her meals, we hold two different kinds of food, tell her which each kind is, and she will look at what she wants to eat. Anytime we have not asked, all her food ended up all over us and herself.

Lyndsay communicates well with her eye gaze. We give her a selection of four to six pictures depending on the situation. Her vocabulary has increased tremendously, as her cognitive development grows. We started out using eye gaze and touch. We soon realized Lyndsay could move much quicker just using her eyes. She was getting very frustrated waiting for her own hands.

Eye Blinks

PARENTS ARE VERY CREATIVE in finding ways to use their daughter's most available movement for communication. In addition, there are some new computer systems which use a camera to track eye blinks to control programs. There are a few switches that use eye blinks to control a switch activated item. A few girls have been successful in operating these systems. One manufacturer of a formal eye gaze computer reported that they tried the system with more than twenty-five girls with RS, and it hadn't been a fit for any of them.

I used to sit Angie on my knees facing me, and wink at her. She seemed to like to see it and would watch intently. Then I asked her to blink back at me, and when she did, I would give her a good bouncy "horsey ride," saying "Good blinking!" She loved the bouncing, so although she couldn't wink with just one eye, she could do it with both.

One day my husband just asked Sherry if she could blink once for "yes," and twice for "no," and she immediately blinked. She's gotten better and better at the one blink for "yes," although she doesn't do the "two blinks for no." Just having a reasonably dependable "yes" response has allowed her to have at least some control over her life and to make some choices.

Using Yes/No

PARENTS HAVE DISCOVERED MANY CREATIVE WAYS to make "yes/no" work for their daughters. They also suggest a third option of "maybe" or "I don't know" because sometimes the answer is not "yes" or "no." Make sure your questions are clear and concrete at first. Sometimes it helps to tell her both possibilities first, for example, "Do you want to stay home or go in the car?," then ask each separately to allow her to answer, and be ready to honor her choice. Generally it is best to keep the "yes" and "no" consistently in the same positions, rather than switching them, though some parents have found switching helpful in clarifying answers.

You may want to start with a large Yes symbol on green and a large No symbol on red. Put them far apart (we put them on her wheelchair tray) about a foot apart. We always put "yes" on the left and "no" on the right. When they are far apart there is no mistaking which one she chooses and now that she knows which side they are on, she makes choices much more quickly. A really easy way to communicate when she is on the go!

Communication

We took a five by eight three-ring binder and put a green piece of construction paper with "yes" and a smiley face on it, and a red piece with "no" written across it and a sad face. She does really well with eye pointing her choices.

Lauren used a "yes/no" necklace, which was simply a narrow, elongated piece of cardboard covered with clear contact paper and hung on a string with symbols and the words "yes/no" on one side and "hi/bye" on the other side. We held the necklace for her and steadied her hand to point.

Angela uses "yes/no" cards and is very consistent with them if the question is simple. When she had her scoliosis surgery, she was too weak and confined to effectively point, so we purchased two Mylar balloons and used a Magic marker to write on them so they would approximate her cards. We tied one on each side of the bottom of her hospital bed and she could make choices by looking at the appropriate balloon.

When we use the "yes/no" cards, I let her know I just want to make sure I understand her answer, switch the positions of the cards to make sure her answers are consistent and repeat the question. I have found that when the answer is "no," it takes her longer to respond. Be patient! I let Maria know that if she refuses to answer me, I take it as a "no" until she answers. So if I'm trying to determine whether or not she wants something, if she doesn't answer, she gets nothing. It has prompted her to respond rather than ignore me.

I took a paper plate, and cut out the center circle. I wrote "yes" in green marker on one, and "no" in red marker on the other one. I show them to Maria, telling her which one is which, and ask my question. She uses an eye gaze at the appropriate response.

One thing I often do for a check is to reverse the question. "Do you want your bath now?" can reverse to "Would you rather have it later?" I always let her know that it is her receiving that I am checking, not her ability to answer!

Lapel pins work, too. Stick "yes" on your right shoulder and "no" on your left shoulder. The caregiver can easily determine which one she is looking at.

FLASH CARDS

USING FLASH CARDS CAN BE EFFECTIVE because they are big and have the words printed with the picture, too.

We use several different types of cards with Alexis offering her choices between two items. We play games with the cards, and make it fun. Alexis can recognize her name in print, the color yellow and she can pick and choose certain videos and foods. She nods her head "yes" when she is done.

PICTURE EXCHANGE COMMUNICATION SYSTEM (PECS)

PECS IS A COMMUNICATION SYSTEM which has been used successfully with children who have a wide range of communicative, cognitive, and physical difficulties. It begins with teaching a student to exchange a picture of a desired item with another person, who immediately honors the request. It is important to note that what is on the picture being exchanged is not relevant at this point in time. What is relevant is that something is given and something is received in a token exchange system. Verbal prompts are not used, in order to build immediate initiation and to avoid dependency on prompting. The system is then used to teach initiation of communication at a distance, and then to teach discrimination of symbols, finally putting them all together in simple sentences. Eventually, the student is taught to comment and answer direct questions.

Communication

This system can be adapted for girls who have difficulty holding a regular picture by gluing the picture on cardboard or on foam board, or by putting felt on the back of the pictures.

- **Phase I**—Teaches students to initiate communication right from the start by exchanging a single picture for a highly desired item. It does not matter what is on the picture at this time.
- **Phase II**—Teaches students to be persistent communicators, to actively seek out their pictures, and to travel to someone to make a request. For girls who are not ambulatory this can be done by having them access a single hit voice output device that says "Come here please, I have something to tell you," (to get a partner to come to them from a distance).
- **Phase III**—Teaches students to discriminate pictures and to select the picture that represents the item they want.
- **Phase IV**—Teaches students to use sentence structure to make a request in the form of "I want ____."
- **Phase V**—Teaches students to respond to the question, "What do you want?"
- **Phase VI**—Teaches students to comment about things in their environment both spontaneously and in response to a question.
- **Expanding Vocabulary**—Teaches students to use attributes such as colors, shapes and sizes within their requests.

PECS needs to be done often. Teachers typically begin using it once a day, and once a routine is established, they build in other times during the day. If this system is being used, it is very important that the parent be trained in it as well and use it at home for maximum benefit. However, requesting is only one small part of communication and PECS should be combined with other methods of communication. PECS may not be effective with every child.

*Several years ago we worked very, very hard with my daughter on PECS, and I feel we did it properly (went to trainings, got the instruction book). Sadly, I must report that Kelsey never did as well with this as we had hoped. Then, we switched over to SECS, a Symbolic Exchange Communication System. With this we would use little 3-D items which matched whatever **item it** was we were trying to teach, such as a little toilet (from a doll house set) to indicate toilet, a little 3-D tape player (from Barbie accessories) to indicate her tape player, a little TV magnet to indicate our TV. Try as we might (and we worked really hard on this), we only had very limited success with it. Whenever we would "test" her, her responses were always little more than 50 percent, which again is no better than guessing. So I can't say with any certainty that this was an effective method for our daughter.*

Lyndie illustrates what cutting edge communication researchers are beginning to discover about lots of non-verbal kids. Many get bogged down in visual detail. The old recommendation to move from object to photo to line drawing to symbol has been seriously questioned because too many of our kids get stuck studying the details of photos and line drawings. The other problem is that this means learning unneeded picture "languages" on the road to symbols, which slows the kids down. The new recommendation, which I certainly advocate from our personal experience, is to move straight to the symbols. You may need to pair them with objects initially, but that is really only during a very short time while the child develops the concept that symbols can stand for something.

Communication

FACILITATED COMMUNICATION (FC)

THE DEAL CLINIC RUN BY ROSEMARY CROSSLEY in Australia trains people with a variety of disabilities to use *facilitated communication*. They have defined it as: "to facilitate is to make easier. In facilitated communication, the task of using a communication aid is made easier for a person with severe communication impairment. The degree of facilitation needed varies from person to person, ranging from an encouraging hand on the student's shoulder to boost confidence, to full support and shaping of a student's hand to enable isolation and extension of the index finger for pointing." The goal is to allow communication to flow as easily as possible, but also to gradually decrease support when able, so that the individual is doing more on her own. Facilitation also can be used to support other body parts, such as the head when a head pointer is used. It is very important to let the person being facilitated clearly control the direction and end point of the movement, to decrease facilitator interference as much as possible. Facilitated Communication has been surrounded by a great deal of controversy, with suggestions that facilitators are unwittingly guiding the student or making choices for her.

It is important when this method is used to be sure that the girl, and not the facilitator, is making choices.

Information on Facilitated Communication can be found on the Web at: www.soeweb. syr.edu.

Angela uses FC to speak with her family and teachers. She uses a combination of methods to communicate, such as "yes/no" cards, a language board, and a keyboard. Although she uses the language board and the" yes/no" cards with her family and at school, Angela doesn't type for everyone. Typing isn't easy for Angela since it requires concentration and a steady hand. To type, she isolates one finger and rests her hand on another person's hand or arm. The facilitator doesn't guide Angela's hand to different letters, but merely helps to steady the hand by providing resistance.

Lauren uses FC in a variety of ways. One "no tech" method that's successful, especially for doing schoolwork when we need new words, is an erasable board. I help her first by placing her finger on each word as I read them, then use FC to let her choose the answer she wants.

COMMUNICATION BOARDS

COMMUNICATION BOARDS CAN BE A VERY FUNCTIONAL and portable way to provide access to choices. They can be made out of anything from a manila folder covered with contact paper to a foam board with a Velcro strip along its length to a large piece of cardboard on the front of your refrigerator. They can hold objects Velcroed on or placed in pockets, pictures, words, or any combination. They can be set up so that she can take pictures off and hand them to a receiver, or point with her finger or even her nose, a head pointer or light. They can be stationed anywhere in a classroom and geared to specific activities in that area, placed on a lapboard to go with her, or placed in strategic locations around your house. She can point to them by herself or with someone steadying her arm or head.

Generally, communication boards should be used expressively. A goal is to get her to initiate use of the board without always just responding to questions. A board can also be used to show academic knowledge, holding colors, letters, or words for her to identify when named. Remember that pointing to named pictures or academic information can be a good

Communication

teaching tactic, but it may quickly become boring for your daughter. She has a great need to express herself, and that should be the main purpose of the boards. Remember to place social language, information about favorite people, etc. on boards whenever possible. When boards are made for specific activities, they should contain conversational words such as "Wow," "Cool," "Uh Oh," or "My turn."

We have one set of picture cards at home, and one at school. School uses a lapboard with Velcro on the board and on the cards. At home we use a desk easel. Rachel makes choices from two or three items: food, toys or activities. It's been great.

She uses her boards most successfully when they are hung on walls as the walking seems to help her with her motor planning for pointing. She initiates communication on her own by walking to the boards herself or coming up to an adult and looking them straight in the eye until someone takes her there. Many times she points independently but often needs a physical prompt under her arm. She's even able to use a menu board which tells us which board she wants to use. We are currently offering vibration to her arms and hands and she will reach for it, apply vibration and then push it away. She likes it so much that we will add that as an option on her boards. It's been a thrill to watch her communication grow. She's a happier girl!

It takes Leah a long time to even become interested much less become good at new skills. We had been exposing her to communication boards for over a year before she began using one on her own. It took probably eighteen months for her to use it routinely and now she is showing constant improvements. Likewise with computers, at first she ignored them, then became a little interested, and then finally began to interact with them. I believe it is important to be patient and keep working with our girls. The seeds we plant may take longer to sprout than we are used to, but the ground is still fertile.

CALENDAR BOARDS

CALENDAR BOARDS OR BOXES ARE SIMILAR to communication boards, but are generally used receptively. They contain pictures or objects which show the activities of the day. One might start with circle time, include therapies which occur that day (maybe a picture of the therapist), lunch, art, bus, etc. Her teacher can use a piece of cardboard with a Velcro strip, and each morning Velcro pictures or words depicting the schedule on the board. This can be discussed with her at the beginning of the day and before each change of activity. When an activity is finished, its picture or name can be placed in an envelope at the end of the board. Calendar boxes can be lined up in a row, with each holding an object which is taken out during the activity and picture symbolizing an activity. Then, when the activity is completed and the object is returned, the box is closed. Daily calendars can be extremely helpful with girls who are upset by changes and transition, since they can anticipate what comes next. They can also help teach sequencing skills.

I must say our favorite assistive "tech" of all time is a nine by twelve inch dry-erase board. We have one in every room of the house, backpack, car, everywhere. It is portable, unbreakable, no batteries to wear out, and no symbols to fumble to find. Because Angela does read, we can write out choices as words or phrases in the corners. Sometimes I'll read the options so I can explain what I mean, as they are often specific in meaning to the context of the conversation; of course, I don't read them for her if it's a study activity. I put strips of Velcro on the back to hold super-frequent choices (more, all done ...) so we don't lose our creativity, rather than letting her make up her own response, but the dry-erase board does provide a lot of flexibility and spontaneity in what choices we can offer.

Communication

HEAD POINTERS

A HEAD POINTER ALLOWS A GIRL TO COMMUNICATE using head movements and can include a light attached to a visor or headband or an actual pointer connected to head straps made to fit firmly on her forehead or chin and angled so that she can touch pictures, words, letters, or a communication device as accurately as possible. A physical head pointer has the advantage of use for purposes in addition to communication. It can be used to type on a regular or adapted keyboard, and it can be used to draw and/or write if the girl has enough head control. When using a laser light pointer, care must be taken to keep the beam out of others' eyes, as it may be harmful. It is also important to make sure the laser or pointer is lined up with her eye gaze or the result can be very confusing. Some small flashlights and lasers also heat up, and care must be taken to protect the skin.

A pointer can be very effective for a girl who has relatively accurate head movement, but little hand use. It may be much quicker and easier than gearing up a hand and arm for a controlled movement. Make sure when using a pointer that the communication device is not held too close for her to see it accurately. If you are using a physical head pointer, it can help to angle the communication system (device, pictures, etc) so that the back is about five to seven inches off of the table (or place it on a slant board). Commercially made head pointers are available through Sammons Preston and Flaghouse.

My husband bought a little laser pointer which looks like a penlight. He made a hole with a hot skewer in the front of a cheap rigid plastic sun visor we already had, inserted a rubber band through the hole, and attached the laser pointer to the front of the visor by hooking the rubber band loops around each end of the pointer. He also made holes in the back of the visor to put elastic through, so the visor would fit snugly. Then he used a small pinch-clip (like the kind that attaches a pad of paper to a clipboard, but very small) to the pointer to hold the button "on" and voila! The whole process took about half an hour. Sherry loves the pointer.

CHOOSING VOCABULARY

CHOOSING VOCABULARY IS IMPORTANT. It may help to make a schedule of daily activities, such as eating, tooth brushing, dressing, group activities, free time, television. Determine possibilities for choice-making within each activity--for example, choosing which article of clothing to take off next at night. Remember to include fun actions and social comments, not just objects. Many people start with "yes" and "no" for the first choices. For some girls this works well, but for others, use of more concrete choices is better. Think of typical toddlers and their first words. "No" comes pretty early, but it follows other social words and requests.

Choosing appropriate vocabulary can sometimes seem more difficult than choosing a communication method. She will not be interested in using the device or method unless it contains vocabulary which is motivating and functional for her, and it must be easier for her than other methods of communication. Stay away from using only words like "lunch," "bathroom" and "music." Make sure that anything available for her to choose can be acquired immediately, at least initially. As she becomes more familiar with using her vocabulary it is okay to have these pictures available, and if she chooses this picture, you can tell her that she needs to wait until later, just as you would with a child who is verbal. For example, placing "bus" on her device, which is only available at the end of the day, is useless at any other time. However, if going for a short walk is an option throughout the day, it might be more

Communication

useful. It is best to start with specific activities, especially if the number of messages is limited. Sometimes simple talkers or communication boards can be set up in several places around the classroom or house, to be available for different activities. There is no reason she must be limited to having only a single talker available.

Pictures can be photos, magazine cutouts, flash cards, or labels from favorite foods or music. In addition, there are computer programs such as Boardmaker, which can be used to generate pictures or icons. These days you can also scan in pictures to print off your computer. In addition, an enormous number of images are available online by going to the Google search page on the Web and clicking on images before conducting a search. It may be worth your while to purchase a small laminator to preserve the pictures you make. This will increase picture life and in the long run save you a lot of work.

Often teachers and therapists limit the number of choices based on how many pictures can be grouped together for a girl to make a choice. Just because she can deal with only two or three pictures at a time during an activity does not mean it's the maximum she should have on her communication system. It is important to note however, that provision of multiple pictures at any given time is not always the most beneficial way to present pictures to any given girl, and care should be taken to determine the maximum amount of pictures she can choose from in a functional period of time.

When using the pictures is motivating, she may be able to deal with a larger grouping for expressing herself. Generally, use of a system starts with pictures or icons (symbols) that contain complete messages, for example, "Blow more bubbles" and a picture of the bubbles jar. Later, depending on her coordination and abilities, it may be possible to separate out words so that she can build her own sentences. This works well on the more complex computer-like devices. She may also be able to go from screen to screen changing themes herself on these devices. You may have certain messages, such as "yes/no" or "I'm done," which go in the same place on every page or screen. It is important to note that girls will want to have access to vocabulary that contains a number of parts of speech and communication functions, not just nouns. Here are some examples of vocabulary for talkers, communication boards, and eye gaze boards:

> **During therapy time:** "Pick me up," "Swing me around," "Bounce me on the big ball," "Rub my feet."
>
> **For the VCR:** pictures of two choices of tapes, "Put it in the VCR," "Turn it on," "That's my favorite," "I don't like that one."
>
> **What hurts:** place pictures of any parts of the body which tend to hurt her, maybe starting with head, stomach, and feet, then using "yes/no" to get more specific as you touch parts in the area she chooses and ask if each hurts.
>
> **Circle time:** "I'm here!" "Its raining today," "My turn," "Let's sing my favorite song."
>
> **Social:** "Hi, my name's _____, what's yours?" "How's it goin'?", "Come talk to me," "Have a good one, "See ya later," "He's cute."

A good storage system for your pictures is essential to ensure maximum use. Storage systems that have been effective for people include the following:

- Velcroing them on file folders stored in a three-ring binder sorted by categories carrying frequently used pictures in a waist tool apron (found in the tool section of many stores)
- Wearing "yes/no" cards on an attachable key ring

Communication

- Storing cards in a fishing lure or craft box sorted by category
- Placing pictures around the home or school in the places they are most likely to be used: for example, toy pictures near a toy box, food on the fridge, movie choices by the TV).

SWITCHES

SWITCHES ALLOW A GIRL TO ACCESS MANY THINGS she would not otherwise be able to access due to difficulty with hand control and apraxia. They are a means of accessing another item indirectly. They can be used for a number of purposes including learning cause and effect, access to recreation (independent play), access to communication devices, access to a computer, and environmental control. Through the use of cause and effect she learns, sometimes accidentally, that "If I do this, something predictable will happen." At first, use the switch to activate something she already enjoys such as a tape recorder with music she loves or a VCR with her favorite movie. When using the switch is rewarding, she will be more willing to do it. She may need help to steady her hand, and experimenting with switch positioning to maximize success may help. Explore different switches to see which works best, looking at pressure needed for activation, size, pressing versus swatting, etc.

Switches can be used to operate computers and communication devices, both for simple cause and effect programs and for more complex programs that require scanning. This can be a difficult concept, because a girl must follow a light or box as it moves across a line of pictures and be able to press a switch to stop it as soon as it reaches her choice. Some simple communication scanners called clock scanners can contain several pictures, and a switch is hit to move a dial as it moves around the set of pictures. A latch switch can be attached so that one hit of a switch starts the movement and one hit of a switch stops the movement.

There are a number of different kinds of switches available through different companies including Enabling Devices and AbleNet. There are also a large number of recreation items currently available that have been adapted for switch use. Some battery operated items can be adapted through a switch adaptor placed in the battery compartment of the item and then connected to the switch. The company that you get battery adapters from can give you a good idea of whether a toy you have or want may be adaptable with a battery adapter.

Switch Uses

PowerLink by AbleNet is an excellent device to help girls learn to activate any electrical appliance in their home, including lights, radio, TV, blender, mixer, etc. This type of switch gives a girl control over her environment through an alternative means. It encourages independence by allowing her to participate and entertain. The PowerLink can be ordered with a wireless switch (recommended) that is at a good angle for girls with RS. A touch of the switch will activate the electrical item (when it has been plugged into the PowerLink).

Switches can also be used to interact with a computer, and some switches are available that are specifically designed to emulate various functions of a computer mouse. One type of switch functions as a single mouse click and can be used with single switch software or with pre-made PowerPoint presentations. A good example of this is the USB Switch Click. There is also a switch interface available that allows you to use a few switches to emulate different mouse functions such as right AND left click. A regular switch (or two) can also be used with an IntelliKeys keyboard to interface with the IntelliKeys functions.

Communication

An excellent activity that you can easily do with a home computer is to create a Power-Point presentation using pictures from a family event or activity. The pictures can be imported into PowerPoint (most digital cameras should be able to readily provide pictures that can be uploaded into PowerPoint) and you can record your voice (or a sibling's voice) to go along with the pictures and describe what happened. You can then use a USB switch mouse to allow the student to give the presentation herself.

Another use of switches is to provide indirect access to a voice output device. This can be done using a number of switches attached through jacks to mid tech voice output devices such as a Cheap Talk 4 or 8. When she hits one switch, it will activate the icon square to which the switch is connected. Another way to use switches to activate a voice output device is through scanning. This is typically done with the higher tech devices such as the Dynavox system devices. The device can be set to move through the pictures (scanning can be set up a number of different ways), and the student can press her switch to make a choice of pictures. This task requires a lot of motor precision and accurate timing and may be difficult for some girls with RS.

Another thought is to hook up switch operated toys through the BIGmack, as they will respond for the length of the spoken message. It's a contrived way to get a comment in, but if your child always laughs or smiles when the toy works, then it's appropriate for a comment like "I just love it when my little puppy barks and wags his tail! He's so cute!"

Positioning and Switch Placement

Positioning her for maximum hand use and accuracy is important. Her feet should be flat on the floor or on some other supporting surface. A shoebox filled with something heavy can help to do this if her feet do not touch the floor in the chair she typically uses. It is also helpful to have her positioned so that her upper body is at 90 degrees relative to her thighs, and her thighs should be at 90 degrees relative to her shins. To get her to use her hand to activate a switch, place her nondominant hand in her lap or hold it down gently. This will help break up the hand movements that interfere. Try placing her dominant forearm on a table or desk for support and stability needed to activate a switch. She may need instead to have room to "wind up" and use her arm to swat at the switch. You can use any part of her body that works to activate switches, including cheek, chin, foot, knee, or elbow. She may also benefit from having her nondominant hand held gently down, or to have her nondominant hand in a splint. Look for where she has the most functional, consistent and controllable movement.

Beginning Switch Use

To start with her hand, try placing the switch just to the inside (thumb side) of her dominant hand. It should be positioned so that it is as easy as possible to activate. In the beginning, she may press the switch accidentally. Soon she will begin to understand the connection and learn to press it on purpose. If she doesn't attempt to press the switch herself, you can tell her to "press the switch" and wait a few seconds. Then, if needed, help her move her hand onto the switch by gently lifting her arm just under her wrist, telling her again to "press the switch." As she gets better, gently tap under her wrist to "cue" her to move her hand along with your verbal cue. Gradually, as she improves, tap or touch further back on her arm to "cue" her. Your goal is to fade out both the physical and the

Communication

verbal cues so that she is initiating switch use herself. This should not be a problem if you have found a movement she can use voluntarily and a resulting action or activity she really likes. It is important to give her a period of time to initiate the motor movement to hit the switch, and not to continually provide verbal cueing; it is both distracting and annoying. Remember that she will probably become bored quickly unless you change the activity frequently, though many girls have certain favorites that they can repeat infinitely. It may help to stabilize the switch using either Dycem (bought from catalogues) or with drawer adhesive found in the kitchen section of many stores.

VOICE OUTPUT DEVICES

USE OF A VOICE OUTPUT DEVICE or VOCA (more easily referred to as a "talker") is attractive for a number of reasons. It gives her a voice, which changes the way people look at her and what they expect from her. People are more likely to speak to her if they realize she can speak back. It also allows a message to be broadcast across the room, when no one is with her. Voice output devices are considered assistive technology equipment, thus they are covered by education regulations.

A variety of talkers are available, ranging from very simple, with just a few message squares, to very complex, computer-like devices with almost infinite vocabulary available. They can be used by touching the message squares (direct selection), attaching switches for messages, or using a switch for scanning. Each device has advantages and disadvantages including memory time, pressure of touch required, size of message squares, ease of changing pages or message screens, and ease of programming. Size and weight of a device may be important for a girl who is ambulatory, while ease of access may be more important for a girl who uses a wheelchair and has less movement.

Low Tech Devices

Single-hit "talkers" come in various sizes and shapes. They can be used one at a time or more than one can be used in an activity. Pictures or even objects can be Velcroed or taped onto a one-hit VOCA and you can record and change as often as needed. Some communication devices come with jacks set up to plug in multiple regular switches, which can be used in place of single switch talkers. The device is then programmed rather than each switch, but pictures can still be placed on them. Communication devices can be placed at strategic locations at home or in the classroom, so she can indicate bathroom, food, music, or whatever she chooses.

I have purchased talking picture frames from Radio Shack and made them into push button devices. They're small and fold so they can close. You glue a pencil eraser to the tiny push button inside. Then when the frame is closed, you can push on it and the eraser pushes on the button saying the words that you've programmed it to say. I get double sided tape and glue them to the refrigerator for "ba ba" or to the door for "go bye bye" or by the bathroom entrance, for "go potty."

We love the small switches from AbleNet that you can hook together. We have four hooked together and we continuously change them. Her dad will record a silly song on it in the evening for her to discover the next day and get her daily dose of chuckles, or her brothers will secretly record something on it.

Alexis uses the Go Talk, hitting the buttons for her choice. We don't always get what we want, but if she can't hit the button she will certainly look in the direction of what we have asked for.

Communication

At home we found the talker to be helpful in Lauren's communication with her brother. To get her turn she could press the "I want to swing" message when he was swinging, which was much clearer than longingly watching him swing. Having a real voice works! The voice and its potential are motivating to us as well as to Lauren.

Mid Tech Devices

Mid tech devices are those devices that have more than one message option, but are not built like a computer. They typically have digitized (you record) speech and require paper overlays that you make with software like Boardmaker. There are a large number of mid tech devices available for use. The most popular devices are Tech Talks or Cheap Talks that are available with a number of different icon numbers and arrangements. There are also devices available with changeable keyguards to change the number of message options at any given time so that the device can grow with the student. These are available from Enabling Devices and AbleNet.

High Tech Devices

High tech devices are like computers with touchscreens and allow a student to switch between two page options (with messages) by pressing or activating a button that links to the next page (like touching a link on a Web page). They typically use synthesized (computerized) speech with the capability of recording small amounts of natural sounding speech (up to about fifteen minutes). Most of these devices allow you to choose your own messages, how they are displayed, and how many are available at one time. New or improved devices are constantly coming on the market. They are lighter and easier to program, with more options and more flexibility. For our music lovers, you can even record or synthetically program music on devices. The most widely used high tech or "dynamic display" devices are Dynavox System devices (DV-4), Prentke Romich devices (Vanguard II) and the Mercury by Assistive Technology Inc.

Choosing a Device

When choosing a device, try to find a speech-language therapist who is trained in AAC and familiar with a variety of devices, their advantages and disadvantages, and who can train people to use them. It is best to try out several different devices to see her reaction, and ability to activate messages and to explore the complexities of their programming. When doing a trial, allow for plenty of time for her to adjust to and learn the system. The recommended amount of time for a trial is between six to eight weeks. Try to obtain a device which she can use effectively now, but which also provides room to grow as her skills improve. It may take a while for her to realize its usefulness or she may quickly figure it out and use it functionally. It may take a long time before she initiates its use. It is also important to remember that her needs and skills may change over time, and if, after a time, you find that what you had chosen is no longer effective, pursue another option. It is important to remember that a higher technology device isn't always a better option, and that a recommendation for a lower technology option does not necessarily reflect the therapist or specialist's assessment of how intelligent your daughter is.

Ideas for Using Voice Output

It is important to remember that voice output devices can be used for a number of different communication functions including requesting, choice-making, commenting, participating in activities, and interacting socially. You may need to bring this up with your

Communication

speech-language pathologist because it is easy for the therapist to get stuck in the rut of sticking only with the functions of requesting and choice-making.

Some phrases to program:

Yes
No
How are you today?
Did you like your lunch?
Are you ready to listen to a story?
My name is ____.
What's up?
Way to go!
What have you been up to?
What's your name?
Raise your hand if you like the story.
Anything special going on at school today?
Well, it's time for me to go.
See ya later.
Are you ready to listen to the song?
Raise your hand for the one you liked best.

You can leave off the repeating word or line of a song that she knows, so she can sing along when you reach that spot. For example, the button could say "All through the town" so that she can chime in on every verse of Wheels of the Bus. Or it could say "EIEIO" for chiming in with "Old MacDonald," etc. The key is that it makes the singing interactive and it teaches the kids to listen, anticipate, and time their strikes. The same concept works beautifully with repeated lines in storybooks too … and there are oodles of wonderful ones! A nice thing about some repeating lines is that they can be paired with symbols, which is something you want to do at every opportunity.

CLASSROOM IDEAS

Single Switches

- Put in repetitive lines to stories
- Put in repetitive lines in a play scenario
- Put in speaking parts in a play
- Put in items for behavioral alternatives

Step-by-Step Switches (Ablenet)

- Use for story retell
- Use for social conversations
- Use to program lines for others to repeat, i.e. simple finger plays, poems, prayers
- Use for jokes, riddles, give spelling tests to others
- Voice Output Devices (TechTalk by Mayer Johnson, Boardmaker)
- Use for turn-taking in game play
- Make fun comments about stories
- Make sure there are fun comments that are useful
- Develop multiple overlays for many situations

Communication

- Use color coded and white symbols
- Pre-teach what is on the overlay
- Use picture-aided language stimulation; model use of the talker yourself
- Make empty overlay with Velcro to put on symbols
- Keep common symbols in the same location; reduce planning demands

Adapted Play (Focused Learning Solutions)
- Utilize thematically-based playmates
- Offer two choices to keep the play moving
- Let the child lead as much as possible
- Allow for fun and problem-solving
- Big props will allow for more active choice-making
- "Wh" props can be used throughout the day

Adapted Books
- Adaptedstories.com
- Velcro-sensitive books (Focused Learning Solutions)
- Hard copy and computer versions of stories
- Emergent literacy for older students
- Activities to support concepts related to stories
- Adapted reading books and four block reading activities
- Simple writing activities to promote story retell

IntelliKeys
- IntelliTools.com (Activity Exchange)
- Classroom Suite contains three programs
  - Interlopes Studio for Learning
  - IntelliTalkII—talking word processing
  - IntelliMathics
- Overlay Maker allows adaptation of overlays to facilitate hand use and/or eye gaze
- IntelliKeys makes interaction with the computer possible

Suggested activities include:

- Introduce the book the teacher will be reading.
- Ask a peer a question about the story: Was it about bears? What did Goldilocks just eat?
- Ask a peer to read a story with them (peer can help turn pages if needed).
- Lead a game of Simon Says.
- Lead a game of Bingo by being the caller.
- Recite a repetitive line of text (preschool and kindergarten teachers are wonderful resources for repetitive text books such as The Very Busy Spider by Eric Carle).
- Sing a repetitive line in a song.
- Ask peer to turn the pages in a book.

Communication

- Use a sequencer to say the Pledge of Allegiance.
- Use a sequencer to say the day of the week, month and date.
- Use a sequencer to count to ten.
- Use a sequencer to give an oral report about a topic of interest (or a book report).
- Give instructions to other students for a recipe.

Two years ago, Sarah had a crush on a boy from life skills class who regularly came to visit her class. Sarah tried (in vain) to get his attention. I (of course not knowing any of this) recorded things on Sarah's switch every day with the intent to help her start a conversation. So I recorded: "Hi I'm Sarah and today I'm wearing a red sweater." Well, of course you can guess who walked in the class that day. Again he tried to ignore her, but buddy, she was ready! She continuously pushed her switch. He turned around, stuck his tongue out, and told Sarah he already had a girlfriend. Apparently Sarah knew that was not true and laughed as hard as she could!

SEQUENCERS

A SEQUENCER IS A ONE-HIT DEVICE that sequences messages. For example, the first selection says the first part of the message, and the second selection says the second part of the message and so on. One device is made by AbleNet and is called the Step by Step Sequencer. Another device is made by Abilitations and is called the Sequencer. There are also a number of different styles of sequencers available through Enabling Devices. The device can be used to read a repetitive line in a story in group time, say the Pledge of Allegiance, tell what she did last night or what she did at school, tell a joke, count, or recite a recipe. They are an excellent inclusion tool, and excellent for turn-taking in a conversation. An excellent way to use them is to record what she did during the day to tell at home, and to record what she did at home to tell her classmates.

Some examples of how one-hit VOCAs are used at school are: during circle time she can say "I'm here" or she can be the child who asks what the weather is today. She can take messages to another teacher down the hall, going with a friend. She can say "How's it goin'?" to a cute boy. Having verbal output is very rewarding both to a girl and to recipients of the message.

COMPUTERS

FULL-SIZED COMPUTERS ARE A GREAT VEHICLE for learning and play in the classroom, although they are not very portable. While laptops are more portable, their screens are small and their keyboards cannot be moved out of the way if alternative access methods are used. An Intellikeys USB keyboard can be attached to any laptop with a USB port. While touch-sensitive screens are available, they are harder to find and more expensive on laptops. Computer programs and games can be very motivating, especially those with sound and action. Sound cards, external adaptive devices, switches, and software can be easily added to your computer to provide needed input and output methods. You can adapt a keyboard by making a cardboard cover with pieces that stick out underneath to hit the keys you designate, so that she can depress a key by hitting anywhere on the cover.

Some external adaptive devices include:

Touch Window: This is a clear plexiglass cover, attached to a full-sized computer monitor or built into a monitor that responds to light touch. It can also sometimes be removed from the computer screen and used as a large switch for some cause/effect programs. A

Communication

touch screen is highly recommended due to the difficulties using either a keyboard or a mouse. If possible, it is best to purchase a touch screen that has been built into the monitor rather than one you attach to a monitor separately due to calibration issues that frequently occur with one that has been attached externally. It is probably best to contact your computer manufacturer to make sure it is compatible. Mayer-Johnson offers a number of different touchscreen options.

IntelliKeys Keyboard: This is a large, flat alternative keyboard that comes with various alphabet and number overlays which are large and easy to access. Keyguards can also be purchased to place over the varying overlays to provide a more defined space for access. Software is available from the company, including IntelliPics 3, IntelliTalk 3, Intelli-Mathics 3, and Overlay Maker which can easily be used to create your own overlays. These can be used for learning and some communication. Some software from IntelliTools and other companies come with overlays designed for use with it. Both Softouch and Attainment Company produce software that can be bought with overlays for the IntelliKeys keyboard. Keyguards can be purchased for any of the overlays that come with IntelliKeys, and for some other standardized overlays. IntelliTools also has a section on its web site that has pre-made activities made by parents, teachers, and SLPs that can be downloaded for free if you own the keyboard.

Discover Switch: The Discover switch is a way to use scanning setups with a student. Scanning can have a high cognitive load for many girls, and requires precise timing of the switch press to coordinate with the screen.

Switch Activated Mouse, Switch Interfaces: Switch interfaces are generally used more for cause/effect and simpler but fun software. Several companies put out software that can be activated with a switch. A switch can be activated with any part of the body and any switch will work with any of the interfaces. A switch activated mouse or other interface is needed to connect any switch to the computer.

Roller Mouse, Joystick Mouse: There are a number of varieties of mice available that are not traditional. They can function with a track ball (KidTrac) or with a Joystick. Mayer-Johnson carries a couple of different types of alternative mice.

Christina is able to communicate with facial expressions and eye gaze. Our assistive technology team developed a scanning device which allows Christina to, with the help of a light cue and verbal feedback, scan pictures and objects to enable her to make choices. Christina is prompted and with physical assistance hits a vertical blue switch mounted on her tray to move the light. She also uses this switch to interact with adaptive toys and interact with computer software. Each day is different. My approach to therapy has to be flexible due to my dependence on how Christina is feeling that particular day. Her ability to hit her switch varies from day to day. However, I can always get Christina to smile! My frustrations lie within the fact that her responses are so inconsistent and something that I see one day I may not see for another week.

Eye Tech Digital Systems: Along with several other manufacturers, Digital makes an eye gaze setup for a computer which uses a video camera focused on the user's eyes watching for pupil movement and eye blinks. It requires rather precise eye control, but some girls are able to use it.

Headmouse: There are a number of different types of alternative mice available that function through tracking head movements. They typically use a small reflective dot placed

Communication

on the user's forehead that a camera placed on top of the computer picks up and translates to mouse movements. Very stable head movements are still required at this time to emulate the mouse in this fashion. A highly recommended tracker is available from Madentec and is called the Tracker 2000.

New adapted access comes on the market constantly, and adaptations other than those mentioned here may fit a specific girl's needs better, so it is important to explore several possibilities. She may find that different access methods work best for different purposes.

Laura presently has an IntelliKeys that works in conjunction with her laptop computer that she uses at home. It takes a lot of preparation and foresight to prepare the overlays (like a place mat that has pictures or words you must design with a program like Anthelices overlay maker). Each time you change the overlay you must also make a change to the computer program. The Anthelices works with the computer, but not separately. It isn't a portable setup.

I got some very simple, but bright software with good sound that's just cause-effect off AOL. One of them was called Baby Smash and another, even better one, was Baby Power. Both were for Macs, but probably similar stuff is there for IBMs. They were both set up so that a child could touch any key on the keyboard and make something happen. They work with a touch window on or off the computer screen.

MUSIC AS COMMUNICATION

THE GIRL WITH RS IS USUALLY VERY SENSITIVE TO MUSIC, and enjoys the quality of the sound. Music therapy is a very motivating channel for communication. On a receptive level, she enjoys listening. On an interactive level, she can use the music to express her emotions and communicate her knowledge and choices. The therapist will acknowledge her feelings and she gains confidence as she learns that she can participate and succeed. Musical activities also provide opportunities for her to initiate hand movements and improve hand skills. The musical activity must be meaningful and interesting for her to build opportunities. Delayed reactions are common in RS, but when music is used, the delay is considerably reduced. Music therapy can provide ways in which communication can develop and learning can be enhanced.

Goals of Music Therapy include:

- maintain and maximize function
- increase the level of awareness
- increase responsiveness level
- increase communication
- increase purposeful hand use
- elicit vocalization.
- increase focusing, attention and eye contact
- provide opportunities in choice making
- relaxation and calm
- express inner feelings
- pure fun and enjoyment

Read more about music therapy in the Therapeutic Approaches chapter.

Communication

PERSISTENCE

IT MAY TAKE SOME TRIAL AND ERROR to find the right combination of methods or devices, but persistence pays off when she is successful and happy.

It is unbelievable how well Laura did with the Alpha Talker. It is easy to use, has high quality speech and uses anyone's voice. The Alpha Talker can be configured with either four to eight or thirty-two locations. It can be accessed by keyboard, head pointer, or by scanning. It has a lightweight, sleek design and a carrying case is available. It can interface with a computer to save work to disc, and to perform limited computer stuff. It can also be used to load commands to operate environmental controls as well as plug in for a Jelly Bean switch. A remote switch adapter is available to permit up to eight single switches to be connected to the Alpha Talker.

Lyndie makes independent choices of three words on the DynaVox. We also have a letter board programmed into it, to look very similar to the manual board she used for a long time. She wears an adaptive pointer splint to help her point to the letters, and also uses facilitated communication when using this board.

Mary uses an IntroTalker with eight cells containing digital messages. We started out with switches on two, "hungry" and "thirsty," and when she achieved them, moved to "yes" and "no." From there we prioritized her needs. The IntroTalker has become Mary's voice. The switches are so easily activated that movement across the room would set one off. Once, Mary's teacher told her, "Oh, shut up; you're talking too much," which sent Mary into laughter.

Leah uses Cheap Talk, a device with eight buttons covered by pictures, for which we record a "command," "I want to eat," "I want to drink," "I need to go potty," "More." Leah touches the picture and the device says the recorded command. In the morning when I feed her, help her eat, give her a drink, etc. she typically won't use her device since I don't make it necessary. The other morning I started reading the paper and immediately I heard "More," "I want to eat" coming from the Cheap Talk. The week before we got busy and forgot she was still sitting at the table after dinner and sure enough, after a while she used the device. So while I find it difficult to ignore my little darling, sometimes it works.

What I like most about the DynaVox 2C is that it easily changes from level to level so, in other words, you could ask Dani what she wanted for dessert, "ice cream" or "cookies," and if she chooses ice cream, you can have another page linked to that page and the screen would immediately change to give her a choice of say vanilla or chocolate. It's quite impressive but it comes with a big price tag.

Samantha has IntelliTools. I made the Intelli-Keyboard a giant button so when she pushes it, the page will turn on the book or the song will continue.

I was amazed at Lauren's ability to use the DynaVox 2C compared with simpler devices which limited her vocabulary and options too much. In six weeks at an intensive AAC clinic she learned how to link together words to form phrases and could move from screen to screen when asked. We use facilitated communication methods to steady her hand, but everyone who has worked with her feels she is making clear choices about what she wants to say. It's time consuming to program, but school staff can do some for specific topics that come up, and I can do the rest.

Michelle uses the Vanguard Plus with the tracker built in to it. She has very good head control and can use it very well. It can also be used with different switches, so if that works better on some days we can use that option. The Springboard required too much hand use for Michelle, even though she can point, pick up pennies, and feed herself. It just took too much planning and pressure to push the button.

USING WORDS

THE GIRL WITH RS MAY MAKE MOUTH MOVEMENTS and try very hard to talk. At times she may say a correct word in the middle of a string of babble. Most

Communication

often, her words come at random, when she is not concentrating on speaking. She may call out "mama" when she is in distress or feels frightened. She may blurt out an appropriate word when you least expect it, and then be unable to repeat it ever again. This is usually limited to a few words; most girls with RS do not achieve considerable spoken language. Sometimes, in a highly motivating situation, she will utter words or phrases. It is important to remember that this is often due to severe apraxia and may not be cognitive in nature.

Megan, like many girls with RS, does speak occasionally. When she does, it is very clear. A word seems to come from nowhere at odd times when we least expect it. She is fairly consistent with saying "Mama," especially when she is agitated.

Lyndie has also unexpectedly belted out words and sentences over the years, with one of her funniest efforts occurring just a few weeks ago. She was doing her PT at the outpatient pediatric therapy department, and her PT had her riding the "special needs bike" through the hallways. She lost her coordination while holding one of the doors and trying to help Lyndie steer, and accidentally bopped Lyndie right in the head. Lyndie looked up at her and said, "What the heck?!" Her therapist was floored and thought it was great! I thought it was great too, and was very thankful she chose not to curse at her!

Tori had about fifteen to twenty words in her vocabulary before her regression. She never used her language as her sisters did, so I knew something was up. I used to tell people it was like working with a stroke victim. We would look at picture books and I would try to get her to say the names of animals after me. She would scrunch up her face and work her mouth as if she were trying to get it out. More often than not, these sessions would end in tears of frustration. One day, shortly after one of these sessions, we walked outside and the neighbor's dog was there. I said, "Casey, what are you doing here?" and Tori said, clear as a bell, "Casey."

Noi has only uttered one full sentence in her twelve years. We had a cat named Thomas O'Malley, who was very protective of Noi and would guard her when she was getting ready to go into a seizure. When Noi was about seven, I heard her fussing one morning. I went to check on her. Just as I turned the corner, she sat up in bed and yelled, "Stop it kitty cat!" I about had a heart attack. I said, "Did you say stop it, kitty cat?" I don't even know where she got it from, because I had always called him by his name. She looked at me and said, "Yeah!" and she looked down at her feet. Thomas had slipped under the covers and was playing with her feet, probably chewing her toes.

I was putting Amy to bed and I asked her why she didn't sleep upstairs anymore in her old room. I didn't really expect a reply because she's been sleeping downstairs for over five years now. She said, "I can't see the dooorr!" Well, I was shocked. I just moved that room around a little bit to make my sewing easier. I never put the two events together. I thought she just didn't want to negotiate the stairs.

Maggie never had words before she started regressing at fifteen months. Now she is five years old and she can say some words with a lot of prompting. She can say "all done," "yeah," "no," and "mom." Sometimes she says a word out of the blue and we are all amazed.

One time when I was picking Leah up, she said "Ma." Lord knows what she meant, and I reacted by saying "What do you mean 'Ma,' you should be saying 'Daddy.' You're hurting my feelings." She immediately said "MaMa" and started giggling. For a while afterwards she would say "Ma" when she saw me and start laughing.

The last time Gina said something was about five years ago. She was sitting on the toilet and she yelled, "I done." It is funny, when she did say something, it was out of the blue and clear and never to be said again.

Angela is eighteen and still says an occasional word or two. "Mama" is consistent. She says "no," "all wet," "ready" and a few others sporadically. Occasionally she will say someone's name. Sometimes she just comes up

Communication

with a word or phrase out of the blue and we never hear it again. She always speaks more when stressed, particularly when she has a fever.

Sherry says an occasional verbal "yes" or "esssss." It seems to us that she uses whichever of these "yes" responses she can manage to produce at the given moment. The only thing close to a "no" we get is an occasional definite shaking of the head, also hard to distinguish from her frequent "head-swinging" side-to-side.

Although Amanda has some spontaneous words, they are few and far between. To say something when we ask her to is almost impossible, but with the apraxic approach we are getting about thirty sounds/words out of her when we ask, and attempting to imitate even if she doesn't do it right for other sounds and words. It has taken about a year to get this far.

While most girls with RS will not have competent speech, a few girls with mild RS are able to talk. Generally, they had a late onset of Rett symptoms and kept the language they had before regression. Sometimes the speech is repetitive or "parroting." Yet, some girls can use their limited speech to make their wants and needs known. Since we know that spoken language is possible, even if it appears only randomly, we must continue to work diligently at helping girls with RS communicate any way they can.

A Note to Parents

ACCESS TO COMMUNICATION IS IMPORTANT in all areas of the IEP, not just those which are specifically earmarked to be communication. It is important to remember that the SLP isn't the only one responsible for these goals; they are too important to be reserved only for isolation with the SLP. The teacher should follow through, and if this is not happening, parents should express their concern.

Using specific device names are discouraged in the IEP. If a specific device is mentioned, it legally means that device always has to be used for that goal. This is not always appropriate, especially due to the variance in motor ability seen in girls with RS. It also creates a problem if the device breaks and needs repair; technically, the goal can't be worked on at that time. However, the following clause can be used if the student owns the device: "Mercury device will be available to student as provided by parent."

Although the percentage of accuracy is not always in the best interests of a student, it is important in many cases. We want to see progress over time, and we recognize that some days will be better than others. Simply having the opportunity to say "yes" or "no" without any tracking of percentage is not as meaningful. If the percentage is always lower than 50 percent, it might not be the most appropriate goal at the time. One way that goals can be both measurable and factor in inconsistencies is to write a percentage accuracy that will take place on some of the days tried or in some of the trials: "Robin will _____ with 75 percent accuracy on two of three days tried." It is also acceptable to write goals that are "participation" goals, goals "that are tracked simply by the fact that an opportunity was given a certain number of times: "Martha will use a voice output device to greet a peer at least three times per week."

IEP Objectives for Communication

1. Marsha will say "Hi, how ya doin'?" to at least one other student each morning using her single switch communication device (if cueing or other physical assistance is necessary, it should be specified, so that a specific routine is always followed).

2. Sally will, with 75 percent accuracy on three of five days per week (allowing for inconsistent days), use eye gaze to answer yes/no and "none of them" questions about what

Communication

she wants to do next using cards containing icons plus words, which will be placed on her eye gaze frame during choice time.

3. During circle time, Danielle will use a voice output device to say "I'm here," and will introduce one song or book at least three times per week.

4. Given access to an eye gaze frame with four pictures placed one at each corner of the frame (or another way if needed for this student), Mary will choose color to match picture with helper (may be assistant, may be SLP) 65 percent of the time on one of two trials. (re: she will get 65 percent accuracy on half of the times this is tried).

5. Given access to a voice output device, and with a helper steadying her hand at the elbow by gently pressing it to the tabletop (need to specify where and how arm will be steadied for consistency), Lauren will point to three (three and four will most likely give different results for her) icons on the device to describe something she has done or wants to do with 40 percent accuracy on three out of five days per week.

6. Cara will independently hand a picture to another student when given three pictures as choices for what she wants to eat or do next at least once per day with no cueing on three of five days (allowing for the possibility that she will need cueing on two of those days).

7. Given access to a sequencing voice output device, and accessed from a seated position (steadying won't be too helpful if she is standing) with an adult steadying her arm by placing gentle pressure on her wrist onto the table, Lauren will present a short verbal report with a beginning, middle, and end, and at least five phrases, at least two times per quarter.

8. Using eye gaze (with words if needed) or a voice output device, Carol will tell what part of her body hurts with four choices, or how she is feeling (four choices).

9. When asked basic information questions (Are you a girl?) Maggie will use eye pointing to indicate yes or no with 75 percent accuracy in two out of three trials.

10. Given four choices on an eye gaze board, Lara will answer Who and What questions about a story with 80 percent accuracy in three out of four trials.

Annual Goals

Currently, IEPs are written with both annual (yearly) goals and either objectives or benchmarks. Objectives are different components of a goal that can be addressed either separately or concurrently, but one does not need to be achieved before starting another. Benchmarks are a set of goals that are accomplished in a specific order in order to reach the annual goal. They are worked on in a sequence, not concurrently. An IEP can be written using either objectives or benchmarks under the annual goals, or with a combination of the two.

An example of an annual goal written with objectives would be:

Annual Goal: Given access to a mid tech (more than one button) communication device, Lauren will make at least one comment per day ("that was yucky"), and one request per day ("juice please") without verbal or physical cueing during a structured activity.

Objectives:

A) Given access to a mid tech device, Lauren will make at least one comment a day without cueing during a structured activity.

B) Given access to a mid tech device Lauren will make at least one request a day without cueing during a structured activity.

Communication

An example of an annual goal written with benchmarks:

Annual Goal: Katy will use a sequencing voice output device to take three turns in a conversation with a peer without physical or verbal cueing in two out of three trials.

Benchmarks:

By October, Katy will use a sequencing voice output device to take one turn in a conversation with a peer without physical or verbal cueing in one out of three trials.

By December, Katy will use a sequencing voice output device to take one turn in a conversation with a peer without physical or verbal cueing in two out of three trials.

By February, Katy will use a sequencing voice output device to take two turns in a conversation with a peer without physical or verbal cueing in two out of three trials.

By May, Katy will use a sequencing voice output device to take three turns in a conversation with a peer without physical or verbal cueing in two out of three trials.

HOW TO PAY FOR THIS STUFF

MANY DEVICES ARE EXPENSIVE, but you may have insurance coverage that will help. Medicaid pays for high technology devices in almost every state. Insurance may pay for high tech devices depending on your coverage. Devices are typically classified as durable medical equipment. Insurance may pay for a mid tech device (it depends on whether the vendor of the device will put through an insurance request), but will rarely pay for a low tech or no tech device option. Medicaid will currently pay for a new device every five years, and insurance companies vary in how often they will pay for a new device; it typically varies between three and seven years.

Keep in mind that schools are required to fund appropriate devices that are needed to work on IEP goals. Remember that it is an IEP team decision to pursue a device. Successful trials over time, documented by parents, the teacher, and the speech language pathologist or AAC specialist are useful in helping to persuade a school district to purchase a device. The law also says that if a student needs assistive technology equipment to complete homework so that she can benefit from her educational program, the device must be available at home. Communication in all settings including home is necessary in order to learn how to communicate at school, so using her talker can be considered her homework.

With insurance companies, be sure to emphasize the medical, not educational need. Ask for a demonstration before you make a purchase. Most companies will come to you. You can also request an assistive technology evaluation through the school district.

Ask the speech therapist if she can recommend a technology borrowing center where you can keep the device on loan for awhile, even if it has to stay at school.

TYPICAL COSTS AT THIS WRITING
Eye Gaze Communication Options

Clear Clock Communicator: scanning clock communicator made by Enabling Devices, $105

Eye-Talks: clear bendable simple eye gaze frame: available from Enabling Devices, $15

Eye-Talks with Shelves: available from Enabling Devices, $35

Opticommunicator Maxx: Eye Gaze Board from Crestwood Communication Systems, $105

Communication

Low Tech Communication Devices
- BIGMack, Little Mack: Single hit talkers made by Ablenet, $99
- Attainment Personal Talkers: pocket-size communication device, $12 each from Attainment Company
- Step by Step Sequencer w/o Levels (Big or Little) Sequencing Talker by AbleNet, $139
- Step by Step Sequencer with Levels (Big or Little): Sequencing Talker by AbleNet, $159
- Various Sequencers without Levels Made by Enabling Devices, $108-$130

Mid Tech Communication Devices
- iTalk 2: 2 choice communication device by AbleNet, $119
- SuperTalker Progressive Communicator: communication device with changeable overlays from 1-8 choice options, $369
- Cheap Talk (4 or 8 messages), Made by Enabling Devices: Toys for Special Children, $100-$300
- Communication Builders: Progressive Communication Devices that have varying number of overlay options to grow with your child: made by Enabling Devices, $210-$300
- Go Talk 4, 9 or 20: communication devices with carrying message options (4, 9 or 20), available from Attainment Company, $159-$249

High Tech Communication Devices
- Vanguard II: synthesized and digitized speech, computer emulation, and infrared environmental controls; this device uses Minspeak, a complex linguistic coding system that allows users the ability to create a wide variety of novel utterances. Full color display by Prentke Romich, $7,095
- DV-4 (DynaVox): A computerlike device, with touch screen-type activation, which can have almost infinite messages and screens using linking icons to move from screen to screen. It comes with many preprogrammed pages based on research of language use. DynaVox Systems, $7,295 (Recommended due to its sturdiness, usability, and customer service)
- Mercury: runs software such as Speaking Dynamically Pro, Functionally Speaking … dynamic display communication device built into a computer that can also function as a computer in the non-dedicated version (built on a Windows XP platform), by Assistive Technology Inc., $7,892-$8,134.00

Switch Adapted Items
- Battery Device Adapters from AbleNet, $9
- All Turn IT Spinner: adapted spinner for games from AbleNet, $93
- Adapted Swirl Art: adapted for switch use by Enabling Devices, $38
- Various Switch Adapted Toys: including remote control cars, plush toys, musical toys, fans and more: wide selection available from Enabling Devices, prices vary

Environmental Control
- Airlink Cordless Switch, goes with PowerLink by AbleNet, $79
- PowerLink Environmental Control Unit from AbleNet, $182
- TV and VCR Remote: one hit remote from AbleNet, $92

Communication

COMMUNICATION HELPFUL HINTS

- Remember that she has not lost the will to speak and act, just the way to speak and act.
- Be alert to her subtle cues, particularly visual ones and body language.
- Modify signs that are easier, in her repertoire of movement, and suit her needs.
- Pay attention to where her eyes are pointing. She may be trying to tell you something.
- Increase her self-confidence by improving her self-awareness; use mirrors, photos, slides, videos.
- Allow ample time for her to respond, and encourage others to do the same.
- Make the reinforcement fit the message, and find vocabulary which can be used frequently or during specific daily activities.
- Minimize distractions.
- Be sure that she is seated comfortably and positioned correctly for maximum control and movement.
- Some girls cannot communicate when they hurt. When she is well, ask her what was troubling her before.
- If she is uncomfortable or agitated, make a list of likely problems and ask her those, using "yes/no." It's best to include "something else?" on the list.
- Start small, but do not underestimate her language level or potential.
- If she seems bored and does not respond, things may be too simple, not too difficult.
- Make communication fun and build it into her own interests.

Use any method that works, and uses the least time and physical effort to communicate, including:

- Eye pointing or use of a head pointer or light, or even nose pointing
- Use of a pointer attached to any part of her body which works the best
- Use of "yes/no" cards or switches of various sizes and shapes, hand operated, chin operated
- Use of a voice output communication device

REVIEWING THE BASICS

1. Girls with Rett syndrome use a variety of ways to communicate, but they may be very subtle. Parents know a lot them.
2. Make use of every bit of body language.
3. Girls with RS understand much more than they are able to express, though their abilities in this area, as in others, vary greatly. Remember that abilities in one area do not necessarily reflect those in another area.
4. Expressive communication needs to be functional and worth the effort or it won't be used.
5. Many different methods (eyes, gestures, voice output device) can be used to augment each other, so use what works the best, and don't try to replace what is already working with something new or harder.

Communication

6. Make movements for communication methods as easy as possible, so she can concentrate on telling you something, rather than on the movement required.

7. Auditory processing may be delayed, and output further delayed while she processes movements of any body part, even eye gaze.

8. If she seems to be falling asleep, not attending, look at her interest in the subject matter first. She often does not want to repeat something once she has demonstrated that she can do it, and she may be bored or frustrated.

9. Adding in music may really help both receptive and expressive communication.

10. Work toward literacy. Many girls can learn to read at least some words and do simple math. Some seem to be functioning very near their age level in elementary school.

11. Her communication is limited more by what we can provide than by her potential (for example, having a limited vocabulary to choose from).

I. Places to begin
   1. "Yes-no," "I don't know," "None"
   2. Simple choice-making
      - She can easily learn to choose between her favorite videos or music.
      - If you're not sure she is really making a choice, try one thing she really likes and another that is neutral (music or pants).
   3. Eye gaze
      - Eye contact may be very good, with a special quality to that "Rett stare" or may be poorer and more autistic-like.
      - She may not be able to use vision together with auditory or movement.
      - Even eye movements can be difficult, so she may need to dwell on her choice, rather than look at the picture, then her communication partner.
      - Carefully observe the maximum number of choices she can handle, making sure the subject is of interest.
      - Watch for use of eye gaze beyond pictures, to you or the real object, and as cues for her mood, or attention level.
      - Use a flashlight on her head if possible.
      - Parents are beginning to use devices like the Headmouse with a DynaVox or computer (a headmouse would use head movement and would be different from eye gaze).
   4. Hand use
      - Splinting may help.
      - Hold down one hand to increase accuracy with the other hand.
      - Consider presenting voice output device or pictures at a 90 degree angle (like a computer screen) to her.
      - See if she can point in any way and how big the target needs to be.
      - Present pictures or voice output device at a slant (on a 2" thick 3 ring binder).
   5. Schedule boards
      - For organization, not expressive communication.
      - Help with transitions.
      - Can be very simple and use objects or more complex using symbols

Communication

6. Picture Exchange Communication System
   - She hands picture to communication partner and gets what is on it
   - Very concrete and clear
   - Can use eye gaze and adult helping with the exchange, along with other adaptations.
   - Little emphasis on social exchanges and other important communications.

II. Voice Output Communication Devices
1. Switches and simple devices to use for communication: "low tech".
   - Don't abandon successful no tech methods when these are introduced, they are often more efficient for the girls and may allow her to make a greater number of choices than with voice output alone.
   - Girls who are ambulatory seem to do well with switches placed strategically around their home or classroom, NOT JUST ONE.
   - Use a switch on any body part that works, chin switch, etc.
   - Make use of them for greetings, circle time, messages to another classroom and with books.
   - Some come with the ability to program a series of phrases
   - Move on from single switches as quickly as possible, but do not limit her to one single level device with only one theme available.
   - Single level devices can be combined with other more complex, but less portable devices for quick exchanges.
2. Multilevel devices (mid tech)
   - Contain variable number of message number options.
   - Use digital recorded speech (your voice).
   - Need to have pictures or overlays changed by communication partner.
   - Move here as soon as possible, since she may be able to handle only a few pictures at a time, but needs them in a variety of settings.
   - Make them activity specific, not general for the day.
3. Computer-like devices (high tech)
   - Use mostly a synthesized voice, but can record special things on most.
   - Almost infinite vocabulary and possibilities, with no paper overlays.
   - Some girls can handle these devices, which allow for a variety of subjects with a few pictures in each, so don't hold them back due to cognitive expectations.
   - Direct access is best, but it is possible to use other methods of access.
   - May be easier to use than mid tech due to higher degree of variability.
4. Remember the vocabulary
   - What does she want or like the most?
   - What is available to her at that moment? (for example: going home may not be an option)
   - Better to make it specific rather than to only use broad information such as lunch, bathroom, and music.
   - If she can access only one message at a time, put short phrases on each one. If she can access several at a time, start to putting a few words on each, which lets her combine them to make her own phrases.

Communication

• EXAMPLES:
1. During therapy time: 'Pick me up" "Swing me around" "Bounce me on the big ball" "Rub my feet."
2. For the VCR pictures of two choices of tapes, "Put it in the VCR" "Turn it on," "That's my favorite" "I don't like that one."
3. What hurts: Use pictures of any parts of the body which tend to hurt her, maybe starting with head, stomach and feet. You can then use "yes/no" to get more specific as you touch parts in the area she chooses and ask if each hurts.
4. Circle time: "I'm here!" "It's raining today, "My turn," "Let's sing (favorite song)."
5. Social: "Hi my name's _____, what's yours?" "How's it going'?" "Come talk to me" "Have a good one" "See ya later" "He's cute!"
6. Scripted: Tell a joke; Give directions to class; Give a short report
7. More scripts: "Guess what I did on Saturday!" "I went skiing" "I think I saw you there" "What was your favorite run"
8. "Did you see movie, TV show?" "I thought it was scary" "What was your favorite part" "Tell me more"
9. Take messages to other teachers or office and use device to say "I brought you this message" "Thanks a lot" "Have a great day"
10. Use her device with a book, either telling one repeat phrase throughout the book, or telling something brief from each page (reading it).

It is a good feeling when you speak with the teachers, aides and therapists at school and they are blown away by her ability to communicate. It finally makes you feel less alone in knowing how much your daughter truly understands!

"Success is blocked by concentrating on it and planning for it ... Success is shy—it won't come out while you're watching."

– TENNESSEE WILLIAMS

Education and Learning

WE LEARN SOMETHING NEW about RS all the time. It doesn't always happen at the molecular level, nor is it always a startling scientific revelation. But every day we hear something more about the capabilities of girls with RS. Like our girls, we have a lot to learn. Years ago, when we heard of a child who was making progress, we said it certainly couldn't be Rett syndrome. A number of medical articles called RS a form of dementia. One of the first news articles said that girls with RS always die in their teens. Most of the medical literature was worse than bleak. Getting the diagnosis of RS was nothing short of devastating. The diagnosis and the disabilities are. But not the child within. Her little soul and spirit are there just as they were before, probably stronger and fuller than was ever recognized.

Years ago, we called persons with Down syndrome by the terrible term "Mongolian idiots." That's what we believed, and that's what they became, because that's what we expected of them. People used to say that kids with Down syndrome were "such happy children" and that's all that was ever expected of

"There is something much more scarce, something rarer than ability. It is the ability to recognize ability."

— ROBERT HALF

them. There was no trust, no faith, and little hope for what they could learn or do. Parents were told to institutionalize their kids from birth and "get on with life." Somewhere along the way, someone got daring enough to try and to believe that kids with Down syndrome could learn. Now, some years later, we know of course that kids with Down syndrome can learn a lot. That's what we expect of them nowadays. They go to kindergarten and are expected to learn to read, and many of them do. Some even go on to achieve much greater things.

When we're told that our child is disabled, all of the faith and trust and belief we have are at once shattered. We may fight against it with no less fury than a stampede of wild elephants but, ultimately, most of us accept the inevitable. We do away with expectations. We lose touch with our old dreams because they're out of reach. And sometimes those dreams turn into nightmares as we face the challenges in our new existence in the subculture of "the disabled." Sometimes we're so caught up in it that we forget to make new dreams or to even have the faith that they could exist now that the old ones have been forsaken. We dare not make new dreams because it hurt too much when we lost them before. Instead of remaining our "child," she becomes our "disabled child" and everything takes on new meaning with the new label.

When RS first came to the attention of the American medical community, researchers devised a strict list of diagnostic and supportive criteria and a staging system for describing the natural history. One of the items on the list was "severe mental retardation." However, in 1988, an international team called the RS Diagnostic Criteria Work Group, which

Education and Learning

was comprised of the foremost authorities in the field, changed the wording to "apparent severe mental retardation," because there was increasing evidence that dementia, an ongoing process, was not accurate. Although all girls with RS tested in the severely retarded range, there was no professionally accepted way of assessing their true intelligence. This was the very first hint of a new horizon. It was for the first time accepted that mental retardation in RS was presumed in the absence of a good way to disprove it.

About this time, when parents described higher functions in their daughters, most everyone said, "Must not be RS!" Progress?! There was nothing in the literature about progress. "This must be someone who doesn't know anything about RS." The "progressive" in RS didn't mean progress. Because we didn't expect progress, we didn't look for it.

Most everyone described bright eyes and a knowing look, the on-again off-again feeling that they are "in there." Slowly, we realized that parents weren't the only ones who believed. It is not unusual for parents to believe (they call it wishful thinking) that their child understands, but it is remarkable for teachers, doctors, therapists, friends and relatives to all agree. In RS, they all agree that there is more than meets the eye. She understands far more than we can imagine. Just because she can't show it doesn't mean she doesn't know it. Finally, after so many years, the medical community has begun to agree that her most fundamental disability is a physical one, one that can be measured. The problem is that we cannot adequately evaluate her intellectual capabilities.

How is progress measured? Of course, it is easier for the child who can walk to show us that she understands. She can come to the kitchen to show us she is hungry. The child with better preserved hand use can touch the book to tell us she wants a story. But what of the child who can't do either? Does it mean that she understands less? Not necessarily. In fact, keen observers have noted that often it is the girl who has the least mobility who is seems to be taking in the most from her surroundings.

When you visit a roomful of severely disabled kids or adults, it is easy to pick out the girl with RS. Not by looking at her hands, teeth grinding, spinal curvature, or hyperventilation. Those are all good clues. But usually, the girl with RS stands out in the classroom among the others because she often is very observant, watching your every move. She seems to be taking a lot in. Her difficulty is getting something out.

Can girls who have made progress have RS? Think about RS as a ladder with a bottom and a top and a lot of rungs in between. Since we don't know the basic nature or extent of the brain impairment in RS, why can't there be varied levels of ability? We see it all the time in other disabilities. We see it in children who learn more typically. Why shouldn't there be kids with RS who have varied abilities?

Some girls with RS got a bigger "dose" than others and will likely be more severely affected. Some may not make much progress, but some will. It probably has more to do with the "dose" of RS from the beginning. But how do we know? Can other girls do the same if we expect them to? If we believed that they could do it? If we looked for evidence of higher thought? In the absence of evidence to the contrary, what if we assume that they can and will make progress rather than assuming progress does not occur? And if we never tried to teach them, how could they ever learn?

No parent should feel guilty that their child is more severe because they didn't work hard enough. Many parents have spent most of the daylight hours working with their girls to try to get them to demonstrate knowledge. We would all die trying. Some families have patterned their girls for years without dramatic success. But maybe that is the key. What if they can't demonstrate it? Does it mean that we should believe in them any less? Could it be that

Education and Learning

we just haven't devised a way to help them demonstrate their knowledge? Think about the number of times your daughter said something you thought was appropriate or acted as if she understood.

"Typical" children are self-fulfilling prophecies. When we constantly tell them they are bad or stupid, they know no other way to act. When we praise them for the good things they do and recognize their strengths, they live up to our expectations. If we give up at the outset and determine that our girls with RS will never achieve, for sure they will never achieve. Belief and praise won't strengthen muscles or stop seizures, nor can they miraculously conjure up ability that is not there. But belief helps us to recognize strength. Trust helps us to have confidence in our own ability to judge. And as the mothers and fathers of these girls, we are more equipped than anyone to be able to "read" them and to intuitively know when they're with us. We shouldn't be afraid to say so.

Imagine how it opens their world for our girls just to be able to communicate two words, "yes" and "no!" And imagine how much they can tell us about what they know with these two little words, the two most powerful words in existence. Imagine if they can use one purposeful movement to operate a computer and have learned to read. The whole world is accessible to them. We have to continue to find ways to reach our girls and teach them. But most of all we have to believe in them, because all of the modern technology in the world, all the switches and computers, all the bells and whistles, will not work if we do not believe and trust and expect it to happen. We are pioneers on the frontier of this new wave of thought. The new horizon is before us. It's in our reach. All we have to do is believe.

We are now rewriting the natural history of RS with young girls who are diagnosed very early, and who have the benefits of early intervention and inclusive education, a wide range of therapies, hopeful new drugs and an accepting society. The future for girls with RS is full of more promise than ever.

INTELLIGENCE AND ABILITY

INTELLIGENCE IS WHAT IS CALLED A CONSTRUCT, meaning it is a concept to which folks have assigned meaning. Intelligence is typically defined as a very general mental capability that involves the ability to reason, solve problems, comprehend ideas, and learn from experience. Psychologists have devised tests to measure these abilities in people and use the results to rank the people and make decisions about them.

There are various theories of intelligence. One on which a number of intelligence tests are based is called the Horn theory. John Horn developed a theory of intelligence that identified two broad factors of intelligence. One of the factors is called "*crystallized intelligence.*" This is the knowledge an individual has obtained from the culture. In other words, it's what you learn. The other factor he called "*fluid intelligence,*" or one's ability to reason and solve problems. In other words, it's how you learn and think.

Many of the standard tests of intelligence or ability draw their underlying theoretical assumptions from this theory. Because these traditional tests of intelligence and ability require hand use and speech, sometimes the psychologist doing the testing may substitute a different kind of test to get an idea of the child's abilities. These substitute tests may be of receptive vocabulary or the ability to categorize. These should not be considered a test of the broader intellectual ability, but may give you, as well as the educational personnel, some insight into your child's ability.

Education and Learning

There are other theorists who have proposed alternative views of intelligence, however. Howard Gardner, for example, has proposed a theory of *multiple intelligences*. His work has had a profound impact on education. He has identified seven different intelligences. Those intelligences are logical-mathematical, linguistic, musical, spatial, bodily-kinesthetic, interpersonal, and intrapersonal. Rather than a single score, he argues that a person's abilities can best be expressed through a profile. So, someone with RS might have the ability to appreciate musical patterns (musical) and express great empathy in response to another's pain (interpersonal). These abilities are not assessed at all on a traditional test of intelligence or ability but may be avenues to learning.

Regardless of the theory of intelligence to which one adheres, it is clear that humans benefit from opportunities to learn and have new experiences. Even if the girl with RS is limited, intelligence is not static. There are different and, likely infinite, capabilities of the mind to absorb and grow. We just have to find the ways.

"Ability is not only that which can be measured by external achievements— ability is everything that exists within, whether it can be expressed or not."

– BARBRO LINDERG

SOME LEARNING CHARACTERISTICS

COMPREHENSION

THERE ARE SEVERAL IMPORTANT FACTORS to take into consideration when trying to determine how much the girl with RS comprehends. The most important aspect is her delayed responses. It may take her some time to react to what she has been asked. Sometimes we make a request and then move on to make another request before she has had time to act on the first. She doesn't concentrate in a conventional way, so it may appear that she is not listening, distracted or bored. Her lack of eye-hand coordination and apraxia combine to make it difficult for her to give you the correct signals that she understands—whether it is by talking, acting or following directions. Add to this the fact she does one thing at a time.

This is significant for intake and output issues (listen and do), but also important when she is asked to do two things at once, such as walk toward an object and pick it up. For her, listening and reacting or walking and grasping are as confusing as trying to type and do math at the same time. She often uses one sensory channel at a time and becomes absorbed in it, tuning out the other senses to lessen her confusion.

Asking her to follow verbal directions only makes it harder, because she has to think about how to do it. We wish she could follow the Nike philosophy and "Just do it," but she must have emotional motivation first so that she can act without thinking. All of these challenges or disabilities prevent her from fully participating in her world, which allows her to gain the necessary experience to reach her full potential.

When you put it all together, you can understand that it is a difficult problem for her to show us how much she knows. We are left to rely on our interpretation and intuition, which may not always be correct. It is important to take into consideration all of her difficulties along with her own motivation and interests before judging her abilities. It is also helpful to recognize the difference between her "intellectual level" and her "functional level." They are not the same.

Education and Learning

I have noticed over the years that Jocelyn will almost mirror someone's expectation of her. In other words, if someone perceives her as not very aware, she doesn't bother with them. She is very perceptive, and I think she figures, "Why waste my time?" On the other hand, someone who treats her with respect and dignity and who expects that she understands even if she cannot respond (not just faking it because she can tell a mile away!) she will respond appropriately. Many people treat her nicely but do not expect much, more like a sweet child rather than the young adult that she is. I don't think she holds that against them; she understands that might be all they know, but she definitely holds back.

What matters is that I take Lauren from where she is now to as high as she can go in learning about her world. I do, however feel that for too many years I bought into the idea that Lauren could learn very little, and allowed her to be placed in classrooms where she learned almost nothing, except for what we did with her. She was not exposed to normal learning situations. As a result, she has very minimal understanding of many aspects of the world around her. As I have changed in my attitude, asked her what she understands and what she doesn't, and started really exposing her and explaining things to her, I'm amazed at the smiles I get when giving her much more advanced information.

My belief is to expose your child to age-appropriate things but let her lead the way. Always give her credit even if you don't understand her choices. My daughter is very much age-appropriate although she is severely multiply-impaired. She loves everything that a typical thirteen year-old girl does, but I don't know if she cognitively appreciates things on the same level as her friends.

Her interests are scattered, as are her developmental levels. What I appreciate in watching her grow is that she does understand what goes on around her and that she needs the assistance of people to engage her environment. She shuns those who don't tune into her and comes alive for those who make the effort to understand and communicate with her. Is she ever going to write a thesis? Highly doubtful. Can she tell a fun story with choice-making? Absolutely!

Darleen presents as a person who really doesn't comprehend much because she now has less alert eye contact, the kyphosis keeps her head down, she is totally non-vocal, and she is passive with movement. She does, however, understand more than anyone will ever be able to evaluate or know for sure. She is highly sensitive to the feelings of others, and knows instantly if someone accepts her or not. I believe we owe it to our girls to believe they understand everything and err on the up side rather than suggesting they don't.

I've never seen a girl with RS who doesn't think. For all I know, Angie thinks far more profound thoughts than I do. I just know when I read to her, she prefers real pictures to cartoons, certain kinds of music over others, she hates liver, flirts every chance she gets, and when I prepare her for what is happening next by telling her what to expect, (step up, let's wash your face, etc.) she responds by stepping up, raising her face to me. I know that when she whines and we are playing Twenty Questions, if I guess the correct thing her whine converts into a chuckle. She has to whine first, because the chuckle for some reason isn't self-starting and she has to kind of "roll into it." She can also blink her eyes for "yes" when I ask her questions. This is how I know she can understand language.

The most important thing to realize is that she could understand language before I understood her responses. We must give our children the benefit of the doubt. If we are going to be wrong, it is far better to believe the child can understand us so we will talk to her and teach her, than to believe she can't and never even try. Some day, some way, she'll find a way to show us she understands!

FLUCTUATIONS

GIRLS WITH RS HAVE WIDE FLUCTUATIONS in attention, mood, and performance. One day, you may be impressed that she seems to know everything there is to know, and the next day, you can easily be convinced that she knows very little. She

Education and Learning

may be calm and peaceful at breakfast and agitated and irritable at lunch, solemn and detached in the afternoon, and alert and interested at bedtime. She may react to the same music in different ways on different days. She may start out crying and end up laughing. It can be difficult for her, but also for parents, who try everything that should work but feel powerless. Many families report that their daughter is the emotional thermometer of the family. It helps to recognize that these fluctuations are not under her control. Again, they are happening to her. Whether you call them irregular impulses, short circuits, or system overload, something physiological is happening to her. It is not her fault because it happens and it is not your fault because you can't control it.

When Taylor has "good" days, she's happy, energetic, vocal, more open to change, very responsive and her cognitive level is high. When we play learning games on these days, she is usually correct in her responses. When Taylor has what I call "autistic" days, she's lethargic, inattentive, indifferent, and either doesn't participate in the learning games or responds incorrectly.

We have witnessed time and again that Beth, fifteen, makes a dramatic and memorable response when something is very important to her. And even though we think we know her well, we can't always predict what's most meaningful to her in life.

One problem is that sometimes our girls are "with it," and sometimes they are "zoned out." So sometimes people see "evidence" of Sherry's comprehension, and sometimes she is unable to respond. I have explained to Sherry that each time she reaches somebody it is something important, and when she does, sometimes I will turn and whisper in her ear, "You are convincing them, aren't you?" or "You showed them you understand," and we smile over the victory.

CONCENTRATION

GIRLS WITH RS DO NOT ALWAYS CONCENTRATE in a typical way. They may look away and seem detached, or they may seem distracted or as if they are not paying attention. This is confusing, but it is important to accept that "what you see" may not always be "what you get."

Most experts who spend some quality time with RS girls agree; the girl with RS understands far more than she can tell us. Since it is easier for her to take information in than it is to interpret and act on it, she always takes in more than she gives out. She may seem disinterested or unresponsive, when in fact she is concentrating very hard on what is being said. Parents have many stories about how their daughters have shown what they understand. It is through these confirmations, and not through judging their outward appearance or their performance on standardized tests, that we come to understand how clever they really are.

We are proud of her and have always known there is more substance to her than she is given credit for. All you have to do is spend some time with her and you realize she understands and will respond in her own way to everything that is said to her and even to conversations that aren't directed to her.

RESPONSE TIME

RESPONSE TIME IS ALMOST ALWAYS DELAYED. Give her the time she needs to respond. It may be after you have moved on to the next task or left the room.

If Nikyla's teacher waited two minutes on most days, Nikyla would lose interest, walk away, and move on to something else. She hates to be bored. On good days it takes four to five seconds. On bad days, it's a minute or more.

Education and Learning

MEMORY

SOME GIRLS AMAZE US with what they remember.

Jocelyn's first aide in school when she was three became a good friend. Then Joce moved to another school and saw Lynn on occasion, maybe once or twice a year. Lynn moved to Arizona and came back for a visit about ten years after she had worked with Joce. Her once blond hair was now dark brown and she now had braces on her teeth. She did look very different than when she worked with Joce. It took her a while to warm up, but as Lynn was talking to her about things they did when they were together and songs they sung, Jocelyn suddenly put two and two together and remembered. Her smile and giggles made it very clear. It was amazing to see the moment of recognition.

My brother only sees my daughter a half dozen times a year, but as soon as he walks in the door, she beams. I get so jealous. He doesn't have to do or say anything but "hi" and he gets the biggest and best smiles.

Carol remembers more than I do. We recently ran into her biological father for the first time in four years. Carol knew him immediately.

UNDERSTANDING TIME

SOME GIRLS WITH RS DO NOT HAVE A GOOD UNDERSTANDING of time. When she hears the pots and pans rattling, she is ready to eat. She may become very angry or sad if her food is not served immediately. Routines and schedules are helpful in everyday situations. Gradually, she learns that her food will be served in due time. But it can make things more difficult when the routine must be changed, for instance, to eat out. Having handy a few morsels of finger foods, i.e. raisins, grapes, or crackers may save the day. When she approaches the toilet, she urinates. Be ready!

LEVELS OF MOBILITY

THOSE WHO COME IN REGULAR CONTACT WITH RS GIRLS often comment that she is aware, but difficult to reach. Many issues are at play, not to mention how complicated the girls are themselves. They share many common characteristics but may vary widely in motor performance. Her level of mobility does not affect how much she understands, but does affect how she is able to respond.

The girl with higher mobility often began with a preliminary diagnosis of autism. She has a higher activity level and often has more pronounced hyperventilation. She may attempt more purposeful hand movements, but also has more intense hand stereotypies. Her attention span may reach dramatic shifts in a short time and she may be more prone to emotional outbursts. She is more physically active and seems to have a higher psychic tempo overall. Her mobility allows her to demonstrate her needs (she can walk to the faucet for a drink), while at the same time, it causes her frustration (she has to figure out how to get there).

The girl with lesser mobility often began with a preliminary diagnosis of cerebral palsy or global delay. She is less active and her hand stereotypies are calmer. Her psychic tempo is slower and during delayed responses, she often appears to be in deep thought. She does not experience mood swings as dramatically and appears to be more emotionally stable. Her motor coordination is slower and she is better able to regulate incoming sensory stimuli and responses. While her lack of mobility gets in the way of demonstrating her wants and needs, she develops a good eye-gaze response.

Some girls will be a mixture of both groups, or will change groups over time. All in all, the degree of her physical impairment does not correspond with her intellectual ability.

Education and Learning

If she has less mobility, it does not mean she has less comprehension. Because she is able to walk does not suggest that she is smarter. However, different therapeutic approaches may be more or less successful in a given group.

I think some girls are better able to show what they know because they have fewer intrinsic motor problems and/or have learned to use communication tools. Girls who say an appropriate complete sentence once every five years or even once in a lifetime don't become suddenly intelligent for one minute and then slow again. They just have a rare moment when they can express themselves because they do it reflexively. On the other hand, it is nice to know our girls have language even when they don't have speech.

MAKE IT INTERESTING AND FUN

WE ALL LEARN BETTER when the subject and the way it is presented are interesting and the process is fun.

Terra needs learning to be fun or she shuts down. When it's hard or boring, it's almost as if she's asking me why she should learn this. "Where will it get me?" She's a very bright girl; she knows what's best for her. So, in a sense, she is teaching me how to teach her.

THE RIGHT TO AN EDUCATION

ALL KIDS CAN LEARN

WE ARE STILL LEARNING HOW TO TEACH and the most effective ways to teach. It is an ongoing process. What we do know is that all children can learn, and teaching should be based on that child's ability. We need to remember to challenge our kids, not to keep them pacified. Learning is thrilling and exciting and all children should share in this.

We do not know how much children with the most severe disabilities can learn, because, frankly, we have not taught them and we do not have valid ways to measure what they know. There has been an assumption that they could not learn or would not benefit from instruction. In the United States, recent changes in educational policy have mandated that ALL children be educated and the schools demonstrate their progress in the general education curriculum. This mandate opens new possibilities and is changing assumptions about what all children can learn. In other words, perhaps they can learn. Perhaps we just need to teach them. Rather than assume they are so disabled that they cannot learn, what if we assume that the possible level of academic achievement is a result of the supports provided for learning and is not related to the characteristics of RS? You still may wonder if anything is getting through, but it is better to give your daughter something to think about and take the chance that you are not wasting your time, than the reverse. And education, once begun, can go on forever through books, cassettes, videos, etc. ...

Girls with RS learn by looking and listening. They are very responsive to what goes on around them. They understand cause and effect and object permanence. They react to tone of voice and seem to understand verbal messages. They seem to understand the sequence of events when situations are repeated. They are able to make associations between what they see, hear or feel and something else they experience in a given situation. Although most are nonverbal, it is not uncommon for girls with RS to utter a sudden word or phrase when highly motivated. Parents give many convincing examples of how they know and

Education and Learning

understand their world. We now know that at least some girls with RS can recognize colors, shapes, and letters of the alphabet. Yet often those skills are not taught. Even more disheartening, some believe that there is no reason to teach those skills because they will never use them. However, the level of understanding seems to be greater than what traditional tests can demonstrate. Furthermore, contrary to earlier theories, it appears that girls with RS continue to learn following the regression period. Studies are now under way to determine factors which influence learning in RS. We have much to learn and many attitudes to change.

At Amanda's IEP review, the therapists listened when I told them just how much she does understand and what she can do. We are working on reading and are developing a much larger communication system for her. Her IEP reflects her abilities and strengths, and recognizes her potential. Lately I have greeted her at school saying things like, "Guess what we are going to try today?" She giggles and gives me that knowing look.

Because we had already started an educational program for Ashley before we knew about RS, we saw some positive signs that Ashley was comprehending and had the capability to show us she was learning and could progress. Being told that Ashley was profoundly mentally retarded and would not learn was not a concept we accepted. Ashley at twenty-five is still bright looking and alert. From our experience with Ashley, these girls are capable of continuing to learn and understand.

KNOW YOUR RIGHTS

THE INDIVIDUALS WITH DISABILITIES EDUCATION ACT (IDEA) is the United States' special education law. The most recent passage of that law is IDEA 2004. IDEA mandates how school districts and states provide educational services to children with disabilities and provides safeguards to assure that children with disabilities have a free and appropriate education. Before you get started, do your homework. Know the law. Call your state department of education and request copies of all the laws, programs, and school (public and private) listings that you can get. Get a copy of Parents Rights from the school and read it ahead of time. This will outline all of the safeguards and will help you know how to access the services. Fight for what you believe in. As the best experts on their child, parents have enormous power. Don't be intimidated by professionals. You are your child's best advocate and the most important person involved in planning for her.

TESTING METHODS

BEFORE A GIRL WITH RS CAN RECEIVE educational services, she must be assessed to determine what services will help her benefit from instruction. Classic developmental and achievement testing methods require use of the hands or verbal communication, both of which are difficult for the girl with RS. Sadly, methods for assessing their cognitive development and achievement are not adapted to their specific problems, such as delayed responses, sensory confusion, dyspraxia, slow visual and auditory processing, and fluctuations in consistency. These problems pose a risk for underestimating their intelligence and academic achievement. On the basis of these tests alone, it is assumed that girls with RS function very low. However, parents and professionals who work with these girls recall example after example of associations they make, indicating that their level of understanding is higher than test results reveal. Traditional tests tend to reveal more about what they cannot do than what they can do. It is therefore not appropriate to use one test or scale to make assumptions about their cognitive level.

Education and Learning

When she entered public school, her IQ tests showed her to have an IQ of 42. She is now five, and is using eye gaze to identify pictures, colors, and feelings. Her speech therapist is working hard to adapt the tests so that we can more accurately score her IQ. She has happily performed learning tasks when we found the right avenue of communication for her.

Alyssa was tested before we had the Rett diagnosis when she was two. At the time they wanted her to stack blocks and grasp objects. Of course they determined that she had the cognitive level of a three month old. This simply blew me away because at the time our son was three months old and I understood and communicated with Alyssa a heck of lot better than Tommy. It bothered me that they had never met her and ignored both me and her caseworker who told them she can't use her hands, but they just used standardized testing on her and, of course, she didn't do well.

Pre-requisites for a Testing Situation

1. The tester should be someone with whom she is familiar and comfortable.
2. She should be positioned comfortably and a PT or OT should be present to give input. This is helpful because the therapist/s can evaluate while helping the main tester do her job.
3. Testing should be done in a setting that is familiar and comfortable for her. It is most helpful if she can be evaluated in various settings—at school during meaningful activities, and at home one on one with a parent or caregiver.
4. Part of the testing should be informal "behavioral observations," taken in a natural setting, where skills not found on the tests can be observed.
5. Tests that measure receptive language or reading skills should be adapted to her motor needs. While the school may argue that the test is invalid unless delivered in a standardized format, you may argue back that the test is invalid for her to begin with if it is not adapted to her needs.
6. Don't try to do too much at once. If she gets tired, stop and begin again on another day.

Remember that you are always free to disagree with the school's evaluation, and get another evaluation done by a professional of your choice. The school also has to allow you to provide supportive documentation such as medical reports that must be included with her evaluation.

Methods of Adapting Tests (If Testing Is Necessary)

Before testing her receptive language, it is important to determine if she knows the words/pictures used and the concept of "yes/no." By law, tests must be given using the preferred communication method of the student. The test should be given over a number of days so as not to get a "down" day and make a wrong conclusion.

1. Use the Peabody Picture Vocabulary Test (PPVT), in which a child points to named pictures. While the PPVT is not an intelligence test, the resulting scores have been shown to be highly correlated with scores of intelligence tests. This means that for typically developing children, the score they get on the PPVT is similar to the one they might get on a test of intelligence. Because the PPVT can be easily adapted, some believe it to estimate intelligence more accurately. The pictures can be copied, pages cut up, or pictures enlarged, then placed on an eye gaze frame or placed further apart for easier pointing if necessary.

Education and Learning

A recent study of five girls with RS using the Peabody Picture Test showed that all five girls were able to choose from a field of four at a consistent rate (some of the schools claimed they couldn't chose from a field of two). All five girls were able to give the same answer to probe questions at a minimum of 20 percent of the time. While this seems low, just by chance they would do it 6 percent of the time. The girl who performed best on the test was able to give the same answer 42 percent of the time. When Boardmaker symbols were substituted for the Peabody line drawings, all of the girls performed better. This study shows us there is a need for further investigation in this area, and it underscores the need for appropriate assessment methods and instruments for girls with RS. It also points out the need for consistent use of augmentative communication.

However, while the PPVT results are better than other tests because these types of accommodations can be made, there are still a number of problems. As demonstrated by the above study, the line drawings are often not easily interpreted and they may pose motivation issues, for example. Furthermore, if the child has not been taught vocabulary or had typical life experiences that would have offered her opportunity to learn pictures and vocabulary, then the test reflects learning and not intelligence or ability. The caution here is that the PPVT may still underestimate intelligence.

2. Use tests which have parts that can be adapted. You will get a non-standardized score, but it may more accurately reflect her abilities. This may not work in all cases, but may help some.

3. Use a "yes/no" response as the tester points to the pictures asking, "Is this a ____?", using word cards she can touch or look at for "yes/no". This is a higher receptive skill than asking her to point to the ___.

4. Look for and record informal expressions of those developmental and academic skills that are typically assessed using standardized tests. For example, *object permanence* is the ability to understand that things and places continue to exist even when they can no longer be seen. It is a level of development thought to be an important precursor to understanding language. In a standardized test of this ability, the child is seated at a table and watches as a block or other toy is placed under a screen, typically a piece of cloth. The child is then asked to find the block or toy and is expected to look under the screen. There are, of course, many reasons why a child with RS would not be successful with this task and therefore would be scored as not demonstrating object permanence. There are however, many informal ways we can assess object permanence. For example, does she remember that favorite toy or food is kept in a cabinet or pantry? Does she go there or look there when she wants it? How about if you put it in a new out-of-sight location? Does she look for it there? One can devise many informal assessments of skills and knowledge that are assessed with standardized tests. While informal assessment does not change the score, it may open opportunities that would be otherwise denied because of the underestimation of intelligence, cognitive development, and academic achievement.

Her level of motivation, interest in the information, and the structure and repetition of the situation enhance what she demonstrates in a testing situation. She may be disinterested because she is bored or frustrated, not because she does not understand. Her capacity for learning is increased by the number of experiences she has.

IQs are just measurements of the ability to take IQ tests. At some point with the schools, I just refused their stupid assessments. Instead, the assessors wrote down their individual statements of what Molly could do and

Education and Learning

what she needed to do. I long ago refused to participate in the "dig three raisins out of the cup" test, because Molly knew that was really dumb and if she flung the cup just right, she could booger up the wall with raisin squish. Molly was not about taking tests and being smart and quantifying stuff. She was about getting up in the morning and having a good time. She had more spunk and personality than any of the so-called experts who constantly judged her abilities or lack of them. She really taught me that who you are is much more important than what you can do.

At home, we mostly anticipated Yvonne's needs, and she expected and still expects us to know or guess what she wants. But in school, Yvonne would use her communication board, correctly match words to pictures, and correctly punch numbers on a calculator in math class. She often didn't "perform" when it was a test situation, so her scores usually started high, then fell off (boredom), or went negative (deliberate wrong answers, accompanied by a twinkle or laugh at the joke). Communication is still limited and she rejects changes to her communication "system" so the new devices now available don't help her. But she enjoys books geared at teenage to adult readers, biographies, and novels with a plot (we read them to her).

LABELS

THERE IS SOME CONTROVERSY over the labels used to describe the intellectual abilities of girls with RS. While medical journals inevitably describe them with the term "severe mental retardation," many parents and advocates feel that this outdated term is not accurate, limiting their educational opportunities, and giving a negative public image. We do know that apraxia interferes with communicability and that has to impact how someone with RS shows what she understands, but we do not really know the extent of this. Most people feel that girls with RS understand more than they can express, but we still do not know how much. While the scientific evidence collected to date indicates that individuals with RS do have limited cognitive abilities, many parents and educators dispute the extent and range of disability. Traditional tests to measure intelligence are woefully inadequate for RS because they rely on physical responses of speech and gestures, which the child with RS does not have.

New scientific findings about the genetic picture of RS show us that there is a broad scatter of the type and location of mutations, resulting in a wide range of mild to severe clinical presentations. It could be that there is a similar range of cognitive abilities (not necessarily correlated with physical severity) ranging from mild to severe deficits. There may be dramatic differences in learning and cognitive abilities based on X-inactivation of the mutated gene. While those with RS can be remarkably similar in many ways, it is important not to paint with broad strokes what "the" child with RS can do. Mouse studies show that different areas of the brain make different choices in X-inactivation. So a bad brain choice (more inactivation of the non-mutated gene) in regions having to do with motor control does not mean that there was a bad choice in cognitive areas (which could have inactivated the mutated gene). Likewise, a good choice in one area doesn't mean a good choice in all areas. It is important to realize that everyone might be correct in their own observations and interpretations. The parents who say their daughter has higher cognition and the parents who says their daughter is more like a younger child may all be right.

It is important to give every child with RS a chance and assume the best. Until there is more research on this subject, it is important to provide a positive school environment that allows for opportunities to learn, based on each child's strengths and weaknesses. Whether you prefer the term "cognitive impairment," "intellectually disabled" or "learning impaired"

Education and Learning

does not matter. She is not a "learning impaired child." She is always a person first, a "child with RS, an individual with learning impairment."

In Yvonne's early years she carried the label "profoundly retarded" because she scored zero on tests. We preferred to say she was "untreatable" because she didn't have communication skills to respond appropriately. But the teachers assumed she didn't understand and talked about her and discussed their plans in front of her without including her. She was desperately unhappy, and beat her face every day, usually with nosebleeds, so this was treated as a behavioral problem. It was only when we realized this was in fact "communication" that we made progress, and got to the bottom of the issue.

The school district may assign a label to your child in determining her eligibility for special education. The label is done for the purpose of categorizing her main disability so that she is placed in what the district deems appropriate placement or receives appropriate levels of assistance. The kind of label your child receives also determines the amount of funding the school gets for educating your child. Bear in mind that a child with the label "severely or profoundly cognitive impaired" does not necessarily have to be in a classroom that is exclusive to children with the same label. Your child's Individual Educational Plan (IEP) is created for your child's unique needs and the program should reflect this. Labels and placement can be changed when necessary.

The label "mentally retarded" tells educators nothing about how a child learns or what conditions help or interfere with progress. It is a most useless label. It remains an option for her in the future if needed, however, because we do know she needs different supports than the average learner.

In my state, age six is a banner year for determining whether a child's early developmental problems are going to remain with her for a lifetime and make her eligible for funding of lifetime services. Some states have a series of conditions that are considered lifetime developmental problems. Other states just lump it all under a "mentally retarded" classification. You have to do a little homework.

My daughter had a "profoundly mentally disabled" label for many years. That did not keep her from attending a "trainable mentally disabled" classroom with part-time inclusion in regular classes. Placement can be changed as the needs arise. Labels can also be changed. Hers is now "physically impaired."

There is no doubt in my mind that our fifteen year-old daughter is not as smart as all the other kids in her class. She is fully included and has been for ten years. As a family, we are very much at peace with who she is as a person and always see her as an individual/teenager first. We treat her this way, speak to her this way and cherish her completely.

We do have to accept that our girls are mentally disabled. They will always need someone to care for them. We are caught in between a rock and a hard place. We want to give them the best chance at achieving the most they can in their lives. We want them to be as "normal" as their peers. I know Heather has a good life and will make choices in it but she can't run that life. A lot of the older girls didn't get the great advances in education that the younger ones will have. It will make a difference in their lives for the better. We have to keep our heads out of the clouds and our feet on the ground for the future.

I know my daughter has a cognitive disability, which limits her ability to learn in an intellectual way that would be considered age-appropriate. She is still capable of learning but will not ever be able to keep up with her peers on a scholastic basis. Does this bother me? I guess it depends on the day. Some days I can handle her disability better than others. But mostly, her cognitive impairment is just part of who she is. I still love her and I do not

Education and Learning

think she is less of a person. We do not talk down to her. We still treat her as a thirteen year-old and she is still respected in our home as having an opinion. But we know she also has limitations. I accept that wholeheartedly and I love her just the same.

It may be a long time before anyone ever figures out the optimum method for our girls to clearly communicate their thoughts. But it's always amazed me at the many reports of severely affected girls who send clear messages by words or actions that astound their parents. Very few kids will floor everyone by blurting out a word or phrase. Sometimes it will be a hand on the arm and a smile as a response, or a sidelong glance and a raised eyebrow. Maybe it's a chuckle or a sly smile at an appropriate time.

> *"The lights are on, and just because she often pulls down the shades, it doesn't mean there is no one home."*
>
> – CLAUDIA WEISZ

EARLY INTERVENTION, DAY CARE AND PRESCHOOL

EARLY INTERVENTION IS A TERM USED TO DESCRIBE an array of services, programs, or resources available to children birth to three and their families. Early intervention services are different than school-based services because there may be many different agencies or individuals involved in providing the needed services and often, there is a coordinator or coordinating agency that helps families access those services. The law also makes it clear that while it is the state's responsibility to coordinate the services, families may be charged for some services. The other aspect that is different from school-based services is that rather than having an *Individualized Education Program* (IEP) for the child only, the family has an *Individualized Family Service Plan* (IFSP). In other words, it is centered on the family and not just the child. The IFSP contains information about the services necessary to facilitate a child's development and enhance the family's capacity to facilitate the child's development through everyday routines and activities. Through the IFSP process, family members and the various service providers work as a team to plan and implement services that address the family's unique concerns, priorities, and resources.

According to IDEA, the IFSP shall be in writing and contain statements of:

- the child's present levels of physical development, cognitive development, communication development, social or emotional development, and adaptive development;
- the family's resources, priorities, and concerns relating to enhancing the development of the child with a disability;
- the major outcomes to be achieved for the child and the family; the criteria, procedures, and timelines used to determine progress; and whether modifications or revisions of the outcomes or services are necessary;
- specific early intervention services necessary to meet the unique needs of the child and the family, including the frequency, intensity, and the method of delivery;
- the natural environments in which services will be provided, including justification of the extent, if any, to which the services will not be provided in a natural environment;
- the projected dates for initiation of services and their anticipated duration;
- the name of the service provider who will be responsible for implementing the plan and coordinating with other agencies and persons; and
- steps to support the child's transition to preschool or other appropriate services.

Education and Learning

I remember the very first time that I left Kimberly at her preschool when she was two. I think I cried every day for the first two weeks. But, it was so worth it. They were just wonderful. She learned so much and got so much therapy and all of the staff there just loved her so much.

Before a child is three or school aged, a family may be in need of day care. Even though your IFSP service coordinator may be able to assist in locating an appropriate resource, finding quality day care is a challenge for all families. The special needs of girls with RS may make a day care setting reluctant to include her. While you want to "get her in," you really want to "get her in" where she is welcome and appreciated. Is the day care director supportive of having your child there? Reluctance is not a good beginning sign, but don't give up. Other families have reported this unwillingness at the start. If it persists, it's probably best to look elsewhere. Ask about staff turnover. This is a good indicator of the day care atmosphere. If staff are coming and leaving all the time, it is not good for your daughter. She needs consistent care, and frequent staff changes will be disruptive and interfere with the good care she needs. Visit the room where your daughter will be spending the day. Is the staff excited about having her attend? Does the staff interact with children at a child's level? Is the classroom well run? Is it structured and organized? Or are the children just running around out of control? The facility does not have to be brand new and modern. It is not the school site that creates excellence, but the people who work in the setting who make a difference. Look for a setting where the people who will care for her are warm, understanding, willing to adjust, and who believe in her as a positive addition to the program. This is true from day care through high school.

The best day care placements we had for Stefanie were those where the staff loved her devotedly. They weren't special education preschool teachers, just day care staff who loved kids, and had a special place in their hearts for Stefanie.

What we want for our Megan is what we want for our other daughter: safety, health, happiness, a sense of belonging, and all the right tools for her to achieve her utmost potential.

When a child reaches the age of three she will have her first IEP. Sometimes preschool services are provided in your neighborhood school, but school districts may also provide services through community preschools or Head Start programs.

When my daughter first went to preschool, I went with her. The staff was very nice about it. I just told them how hard it was and so I went with her every day and helped in her classroom until I felt good about her teachers and her school. It took me two months! When I saw how happy my daughter looked, I stopped going every day, but I still make some surprise visits. Now, I live for the time that she goes to school. She is happy to see the bus and I am happy to get a break. I used to feel so guilty, but I know now how much that little break helps my daughter and also me. I think she gets bored with me all day. So when she comes back from school, I have more energy and she seems happy to be back.

THE INDIVIDUAL EDUCATION PLAN

WHAT IS THE IEP?

THE IEP IS A WRITTEN PLAN FOR THE SPECIAL EDUCATION and related services specifically designed to meet the unique educational needs of a student with a disability. The IEP is an outline for the child's special education, a commitment in writing

Education and Learning

of the resources the school agrees to provide. It specifies goals, including academic and functional goals, based upon the student's present level of academic achievement and functional performance, which are outlined by those involved in planning and providing services. For students who take alternative assessments aligned to alternative achievement standards (those that are not the same as the standards of the general education curriculum) the IEP must include short-term objectives and benchmarks. The IEP also designates the educational placement or setting, and the related services necessary to reach these goals. It must include the date when services will begin, how long they will last, and the way in which the student's progress will be evaluated. The IEP also must state the extent, if any, the student will not participate with non-disabled peers in the general education classroom.

The IEP is a good tool to identify the student's needs and specify how they will be provided for. It is an opportunity for parents and educators to work together as equal participants. The IEP is revised as the needs of the student change, and is reviewed periodically as an evaluation of the student's progress toward meeting the educational goals and objectives. Finally, the IEP serves as the focal point for clarifying issues and cooperative decision-making by parents, the student and school personnel in the best interest of the student.

IEP meetings are held to develop the program by a committee that includes a school administrator, the student's special education teacher, a general education teacher, the parents, and the student when appropriate. Additional participants in the IEP meeting may include vocational teachers, therapists, guidance counselors, rehabilitation counselors, pupil personnel staff, and others at the discretion of the school and/or parent. You will be notified in writing with a notice that must include the purpose, date, time, and location and a list of who will be in attendance. The meeting must be scheduled at a mutually acceptable time and place. You may bring along an experienced parent or other person as your advocate. You also should come prepared with instructional goals you have for your child.

By law, the IEP must be developed within thirty calendar days after eligibility for special education is determined. The IEP must be completed before actual placement and before the start of special education and related services. Unless requested more frequently, the IEP committee must review all IEPs at least annually.

The IEP should:

- be comprehensive, covering all areas of need, including communication, behavior, socialization, self-help, academics, perceptual-motor and gross-motor skills, vocational skills, and transition services, related services, and needed accommodations in both general (regular and vocational) and special education.
- have goals and if the student will take an alternate assessment, short-term objectives and benchmarks that are stated in measurable, observable behaviors.
- be based on a developmental or functional sequence of skills.
- fit the student's current level of academic achievement and functional performance and expected growth rate.
- be written in language that is easily understood by both parents and professionals.
- be developed as a partnership of parents, the student, and school personnel.

IEP Language

Direct services are specialized instructional services provided directly to the student in the general education classroom, the special education classroom, community, or other appropriate settings.

Education and Learning

Indirect services include consultation services by other service providers (e.g., school psychologist, vocational counselor, guidance counselor) to assist them in developing programs appropriate for the student. The special educator may monitor the student. The general education teacher(s) of all included students should be provided consultation services as needed.

Related services consist of transportation and any other developmental, corrective and other supportive services, such as ordering and setting up equipment. This may include speech therapy, physical and occupational therapy, recreation (including therapeutic recreation), social work services, counseling services (including rehabilitation counseling), and medical services (for diagnostic and evaluation purposes only) as may be required to assist a child with a disability to benefit from education.

Transition services are put in place to plan for the student's gradual transition to post-school programs. Beginning not later than the IEP which is in effect when the student turns sixteen, the IEP must include annual postsecondary goals and needed transitional services. This includes a statement from agencies responsible for services after graduation before the student leaves the school setting.

Assistive technology services are those that help an individual with a disability to select, acquire, or use an assistive technology device. Services include a functional evaluation in the person's customary environment; and the selection, design, fitting, customizing, adapting, applying, maintaining, training, repairing, purchasing, leasing, or otherwise providing for the acquisition of assistive technology devices.

The IEP and Therapies

The purpose of providing therapies in school is so that the student can benefit from instruction. It is important to have her therapies spelled out in the IEP. Teachers and therapists are there to assist her in any area she cannot accomplish alone. If she can't hold a spoon, brush her teeth, use the toilet, or turn pages, occupational therapy would be appropriate. If she needs help with learning to walk or range of motion, physical therapy would be needed. Each of these is necessary to help her get the most of an education. Knowledge and persistence pay off. Sometimes it's all in the way you word it in the IEP. The more creative you can get to make the goal "appropriate" for school, the better your chances of getting the goal approved. If it assists her learning, it should be on the IEP. Conversely, a school district does not have to provide a therapy unless it is provided to help the student benefit from the instruction on the goals of the IEP.

I have found on several occasions that goals are set and then not met. The reasons given are that she refuses or shows no interest. I recently helped another RS mom set up goals for her daughter's IEP. They wanted to cut down her therapy time because she wasn't making the goals. They were not motivating her to do what they wanted. Trying to get her into a four-point stance (hands and knees) was modified to attempt to make her crawl to a toy. Getting her to take steps was modified by putting M&Ms around the room that she could have if she walked there. Make the goals realistic, but give her the incentive to want to do it! Stick to your guns. This mom called me after the IEP meeting, and was excited to report that they ended up giving her more time instead of cutting it! She even got an extra snack time added to Maria's day by writing the goal: Maria will increase fine motor activities with a pincer grasp on small food items for fifteen minutes each day. She gets the direct OT, and the extra calories!

We approached the IEP with a list of things we wanted to see included in her program, but by the time the teacher and the assistant principal were through reviewing their proposed goals, most everything we'd planned to bring up had already been covered. Many of the activities are written to include peer participation as a

Education and Learning

source of motivation. They are looking for ways to incorporate a music therapist, at least for an assessment, but everyone who works with her told us how responsive to music Naomi is. And we didn't have to tell them! Things often take longer than we would like, but the attitude from the top down has been respectful and cooperative, and the classroom environment is wonderfully positive and inclusive.

Stand your ground on the important things and let go of some of the less important stuff. The more items there are on the table, the more bargaining chips you have. Make each thing on your list look as important; this way when it comes time to narrow the list down you get the important stuff while letting go of the least important things. Remember to ask for what you need in the IEP; give it all time to work through the system. If they don't meet the needs of the IEP by the end of a quarter, ask for another meeting and see if there is anything you can do to make those things happen.

Always work with the school, not against them. In the early years, the last thing we want to do is start out on the wrong side of the school door. We have a long way to go and sometimes by waiting, we eventually get what we want.

Extended School Year

One option on the IEP is whether an extended school year (typically over summer) is necessary because a student may lose skills if not in school for a period of time. This is a definite priority.

Making Changes in the IEP

You or the school district may request a change in the IEP at any time. An IEP committee must meet, with prior notice to the parent/legal guardian or surrogate parent. If the revised IEP results in the partial termination of special education and related services, written parental consent must be given before the termination of services. What if we don't agree on the delivery of services? Ask the therapists what they recommend and why. Get as much information as you can before a review meeting. Keep a "Let's see what we can do to help my daughter" attitude. Ask how getting less services helps your daughter. Provide written documentation of her need for therapies. If the excuse is used that she is "not making progress" in therapy, use the argument that in RS, where loss of mobility is likely, "maintaining" is progress.

Sample IEP Education Goals

- Angela will ask a peer to read a story with her using voice output two times per week and will attend to the story for five minutes.
- Given four choices presented in four corners of an eye gaze board, Lilly will answer who and what questions about a story with 80 percent accuracy in four out of five trials.
- When asked to match a safety sign to a sight word (for example, the word "stop" is matched to a picture of a stop sign). Carly will pick the correct sight word (using eye gaze) in 65 percent of trials.
- When asked a yes/no question about the content of a story, Maria will correctly answer in 75 percent of trials on four of five days tried.
- When asked to choose a coin (penny, nickel, dime, or quarter), Lisa will choose correct coin with 80 percent accuracy in two out of three trials.
- When shown a number of objects, and asked "how many," Susie will pick correct number of items from four choices in 80 percent of trials on three out of four days.

Education and Learning

- Becca will choose a book to read with an adult or peer at least two times per week.
- When given a word, April will correctly pick a rhyming word from a set of two, presented at shoulder width and at eye level, with 70 percent accuracy, and will confirm her choice by looking at the communication partner.
- When given a word, Tonia will pick a word that begins with the same sound from a set of four, presented on four corners of an eye gaze board, with 65 percent accuracy on two of three trials.
- When asked if two words sound the same, Deirdra will indicate "yes" or "no" using a communication device, in 60 percent of trials.

IEP Resources

Writing Measurable IEP Goals and Objectives
By Barbara D. Bateman and Cynthia M. Herr
Aligning IEPs to Academic Standards for Students with Moderate and Severe Disabilities
By Ginevra Courtade-Little and Diane M. Browder

Available from The Attainment Company, 1-800-327-4269, www.attainmentcompany. com

PLACEMENT AND LEAST RESTRICTIVE ENVIRONMENT (LRE)

ONCE THE IEP IS DEVELOPED AND THE ANNUAL GOALS have been agreed to, placement must be determined according to these goals. The student must be placed in the *least restrictive environment* (LRE) appropriate for her. IDEA requires education in the least restrictive environment, as much as possible, with peers who do not have disabilities, separating from such peers only when modifications of regular education setting or provision of aids and services do not afford the maximum feasible benefit. The statute compels states and school systems to ensure that to the maximum extent appropriate, children with disabilities, including children in public or private institutions or other care facilities, are educated with children who are not disabled and that special classes, separate schooling, or other removal of children with disabilities from the regular education environment occur only when the nature or severity of the disability is such that education in regular classes with the use of supplementary aids and services cannot be achieved satisfactorily. The federal law applies to all states and the state cannot offer less than the federal law.

Considerations for least restrictive environment include:

- the opportunity, to the maximum extent appropriate, to participate with nondisabled age appropriate students in academic, nonacademic, and extracurricular activities.
- a setting as close as possible to which the student would be assigned if she did not have a disability.
- consideration for the amount of time and the distance she must be transported from her home.
- removal from the regular educational environment only when the nature and severity of the disability is such that education in regular classes with the use of supplementary aids and services cannot be achieved.

Education and Learning

- consideration for any harmful effects the placement may have on the student.
- provision of the quality of services the student requires.
- programs and services as specified in the student's IEP must be appropriate to meet her needs.
- the same type of placement may not be appropriate at every stage of her life. The Admissions and Release Committee (ARD) should decide together what best meets the student's needs at the time, and as a group develop the IEP. Once the IEP is developed, the committee decides where it can be best implemented. Be sure this isn't the other way around. The committee determines placement usually once a year, but more often if needed.

Sometimes the answer is a regular education inclusive classroom. Other times it is a quiet self-contained classroom. Sometimes it is half a day in each. Sometimes it is home schooling. So on and so on …

The options for placement in the public schools (the continuum of services) are listed here, beginning with the least restricted environment:

Option 1: Direct instruction and/or consultative services within regular/vocational education

Option 2: Direct instruction and/or consultative services within regular/vocational education with content instruction in a resource room

Option 3: Direct instruction and/or consultative services within regular/vocational education with content instruction in special education classes

Option 4: Self-contained in a special education classroom with integration as appropriate

Option 5: Self-contained in a special education classroom with no integration in regular public school

Option 6: Separate public day school for students with disabilities

Option 7: Separate private day school for students with disabilities

Option 8: Public and/or private residential facilities

Option 9: Homebound

Option 10: Hospital

CHOOSING AN EDUCATIONAL SETTING

PLACEMENT

YOUR OPTIONS FOR SCHOOL PLACEMENT MAY DEPEND on where you live. The best situation is when you can observe more than one school environment and choose which placement is best suited to your child. Make a list of your options. Check out every setting, beginning with the regular neighborhood school. Look at both the early childhood inclusion program with typical students and the special needs classroom. Then check out the special programs for children with disabilities. All of these programs may not be available in your school district. The district must provide transportation if an out-of-district program is the most appropriate for your child.

Education and Learning

Visit each of these settings with a notebook, both when students are present and when you can talk to the teacher alone. And remember, the appearance of the building is not as important as the attitude of the people who will be working with your child.

Make a list of questions to ask. You will want to know:

- Do they have experience with RS? Children with communication problems?
- How many months a year does the school run?
- Are summer programs available?
- How many days do the children attend class?
- What are school hours?
- What professionals are in the classroom?
- Will she have a personal aide?
- How many children will be in the class?
- Are there opportunities for interaction with children who do not have disabilities?
- What is the ratio of adult to child in the classroom?
- How far is the restroom? Are there provisions for privacy?
- How many hours of therapy would be available for your child?
- How many room transitions must be made each day?
- What kind of therapies will be provided?
- What types of assistive technologies do they use?
- Are communication devices available to the students?
- Does the school have good adaptive equipment?
- Is the equipment in good repair and is it being used by the students and staff?
- What is a typical school day schedule?
- What is the curriculum? Do they have classes in art and music? What about academics?
- Will they take field trips?
- Are parents encouraged to participate?

It is possible that more than one placement would fit her needs. You may want to consider a combination program. For instance, she may benefit from being in the special education classroom twice a week and a "regular" classroom twice a week. Or a half day in each might be an alternative. Similarly, for a younger child, she may do well in the special needs classroom three times a week and the early childhood or preschool classroom twice a week. It is important to take everything into consideration after asking the right questions and discussing the issue with her therapists. Sometimes they can be your best advocates!

Make sure to discuss your child's history, her needs, and potential placement in that order. It is illegal for the school to tell you what it has first and then try to fit your daughter into it. Her needs come first, then placement according to those needs.

The key words to use are *"appropriate"* and *"inappropriate"* when discussing her school program. Always talk in terms of your child's needs and provide written documentation for what helps her and what does not.

Her educational plan must be based on her needs, not the staff needs; what she needs, not what the budget can afford. There is no standard RS teaching approach, just as there

Education and Learning

is no standard CP teaching approach. It must be tailored to her specific needs. If you do disagree with the suggested approach, explain why you think that the program is not appropriate for your daughter's needs. Stay calm and stick to your guns.

Plan to drop in for a short, friendly, informal meeting with the principal, school psychologist, therapists, and nurse before the formal meeting. They won't be able to discuss her placement outside of the formal meeting, but you can get valuable information about the program and insight about the school's philosophy and a feel for the school's atmosphere.

When it comes to therapies, make them apply to her need to be successful in school. If she needs to have physical assistance to move from one place to another during the school day, it can be used to justify the need for physical therapy. If she needs to be able to sit and attend to be able to learn, she may have to work on balance and focus, etc. Phrase things according to what needs to be done in a school setting, long and short term, and then what supports need to be in place to meet those requirements.

Make sure you have some academic requirements set up before you walk in the door, in the form of cognition and academics, self-help, fine motor, gross motor, speech, and socialization goals. Base the requirements on things the school does for kids your daughter's age. That's why it helps to walk around the school. You'll get better ideas.

If this is her first time in school, try to schedule the meeting well ahead of your daughter's third birthday in case you have to go to mediation. Delivery of services must begin within a designated time after everyone agrees on the services. Take good notes, and put all of your requests in writing with a copy to the school's superintendent if you think it is necessary.

At the beginning of each year, I send a letter to Megan's new teachers, aides, and therapists. It explains everything about Megan including her early life, medical stories, our journey and discovery, schooling, and the hopes and dreams we have for her. I get pretty detailed in the school part so they can see what is done at school, what works, and what we expect basically! I give them the IRSA Web site and a lot of handouts.

1:1 ASSISTANCE

A TEACHER'S ASSISTANT OR CLASSROOM AIDE is an important aspect in educating the child with RS. On the IEP, the aide is justified as a method for delivering an accommodation. Since girls with RS have limited functional use of their hands to walk, eat, toilet, and participate in activities, they need this accommodation to help them participate in the classroom environment and take part in classroom activities. Teachers who value their aides and parents as equal partners in their child's team bring great strength to the program. Individual attention from the 1:1 assistant and a team approach go a long way to providing the best for the child, with respect for her strengths and understanding for her unique needs. The teaching assistant should not be solely responsible for the instruction of the student with RS or for making accommodations. These are the responsibility of the teacher, although the teacher's assistant may provide support to the student during the teacher-created lessons.

We have four assistants who do different things with Sami throughout the day. It has worked really well for us. Each assistant will work with about three to four different children each day. I have found that it keeps the assistants "fresh" in that one person doesn't have to deal with one child for the whole day. Each assistant brings something different to Samantha and I feel that it helps her learn to adapt to different people and different situations.

Education and Learning

Sami has her favorite assistant, but she will work for all of them. After a very short while, each assistant learns Sami's moods, strengths and weaknesses.

Lyndie has had a 1:1 aide for the past seven years, and I can tell you the aide is an integral part of our team and the biggest influence of all in Lyndie's educational progress. She is the "wind beneath Lyndie's wings" so to speak. If she doesn't do her job well, Lyndie's IEP program doesn't fly and we all have one miserable student on our hands.

Ashley's aides were more important to her while in school than her teacher. She had a 1:1 aide all through school. The aides would alternate each week, staying with a particular student for the whole week and then switch to another position. When there were four aides, she would have one aide all week for one week a month, and then the routine would begin again. We would make suggestions for goals to her teacher but it was the aides who actually implemented the goals and who knew Ashley and all of her capabilities or weaknesses.

INCLUSION AND LRE

IN THE UNITED STATES, MANY BELIEVE that IDEA requires schools to practice inclusion. The law, however, requires students be educated in the Least Restrictive Environment (LRE), which may or may not mean inclusion. The term inclusion is not included in IDEA or in the regulations. Nevertheless, a rapidly increasing number of girls with RS attend regular classrooms in their own neighborhood schools, from preschool and kindergarten through high school. Through successful parent-teacher collaboration and good school staff support, this has been a very positive trend. Friendships and social relationships are encouraged through this inclusion process, which no doubt increase her exposure and value in the community.

Inclusion with non-disabled peers increases her motivation. Parents report that some girls are able to achieve a greater attention span and develop the ability to sit and to concentrate for longer periods of time, and their negative behaviors are decreased. The other students learn consideration, responsibility, acceptance, and confidence.

Inclusion is not meant only for high-functioning girls. Just as the word implies, inclusion means that it is available to all and everyone is invited. Some girls with the most serious challenges are successfully included in regular programs. Really good schools do a good job with students with all kinds of needs and conversely, not-so-good schools tend to be less than thrilling for many students. There is very little that can be done for a student in a self-contained classroom that can't be done in a regular classroom if all the team players are very creative. When everyone is prepared, the program is well supported, and the child's needs are met, parents report success. Experience is the best teacher.

However, some parents do not choose inclusive settings, preferring instead a more sheltered environment. Additionally, as a new wave in education, all teachers do not readily accept inclusion. Some feel they are unprepared for teaching students with special needs. However, once they have experienced a child with RS in the classroom, many teachers who were reluctant to participate in inclusive settings became their best advocates. The program is only as good as the people who believe in it.

There are no situations that work for everyone. Each family must decide what is best for their daughter. True inclusion takes a lot of commitment, teamwork and cooperation. Poor inclusion can be worse than no inclusion at all.

We all want our children to have friends and to be accepted. The other children and the staff are constantly acknowledging our kids when they see them. It does my heart good! I think we do need to teach children and adults alike that we all have feelings and although we are all very different, we are all very much the same.

Education and Learning

Full inclusion is about anybody and everybody being there. You don't have to have a certain score or cross some line to have it. Just being a person is enough. Sometimes administrators forget or perhaps never thought about it, but special education is a support service, not a place. Girls with RS do not have to earn a place in a regular classroom. They are entitled to it.

From the time she was ten years old, Molly attended regular schools. I don't think anyone really could prove or disprove just how smart she was. For our family, inclusion was the dignity of being as full a player as she could be. It was about having a group of girls to eat lunch with and then go out on the playground with, with adults available if assistance was needed, but not hovering. It was the opportunity to be a part of the real world. It was about where we wanted Molly to be as an adult in the regular world and what she needed to learn about it by being there.

When I dropped Lauren off at school this morning, some girls were on the playground and a few of them were from the first grade class she attends part-time. Immediately, the girls started saying "hi" to Lauren so we stopped to talk. They started talking to her, asking me questions about her and telling me all about how Lauren comes to their class. Then just when I thought it couldn't get any better, a couple of the girls asked if Lauren could sign their yearbook. Things like this just make me so happy and Lauren, too.

Katie is ten and has been included in regular school since kindergarten, along with being in an extended resource room. For us, part-time inclusion has been the best way to go. If Katie is having a Rett day, or is just not herself, she has a place to "escape" with her aide, where she can hang out all day. And no one is mad at her; no one makes her feel bad about it. If anything, the kids in regular class usually come looking for her, or check on her, to make sure she is OK. It's the best feeling to see your child accepted by so many "typical" children, and actually have them get invited to birthdays and play dates!

We were forced to place Ann in segregated self-contained classrooms until she was sixteen. We began fighting at thirteen to have her taken out of this environment because of the staff ratio of 4:1. After a three-year battle, they agreed to neighborhood high school and full inclusion. This school has no other students with the level of disability as Ann. Ann was an instant success, and within six weeks she was nominated for the freshman homecoming court. I began to notice that Ann stood straighter and held her shoulders up proud, and everyone in her life noticed the drastic difference in Ann's self-esteem. Who would your daughter be more interested in communicating with … someone else who had problems communicating? Parents? Teaching staff? Or her typical age peers whom she loves to be with? Which would be more motivating? For Ann, her non-disabled peers brought out far more than adults.

Angela is fully included in a regular first grade class following a year of full inclusion in kindergarten. She is astounding the school staff with her ability to **learn,** *putting to rest any misconceptions about her potential that were assigned to her in the past. I put in many hours behind the scenes adapting materials and preparing picture icons to accompany theme lessons. She has three aides trained to work with her, with 1:1 help by two regulars who rotate on any given day (this way she doesn't have an unfamiliar sub if one of the two regular aides is absent). The special education teacher comes to the classroom to monitor her progress and offer suggestions for adapting materials. This gifted teacher and the friends in class who are so very important to Angela motivate her to work very hard despite her battles with poor health. Despite her poor health, Angela identifies words, abstract calendar concepts, many math concepts appropriate to first grade, is beginning to spell, has excellent story comprehension, and on and on. She is exposed to so many more concepts than she would be in the resource room (where, by the way, she was spending a few hours at the very beginning of the year, a place where she defied the teacher by refusing to work. Period.) and she is allowed to move on to new concepts, which can be a real problem within special education. Academically, this is the best placement for Angela.*

She wasn't in regular classes to learn eighth grade social studies or tenth grade earth science, although she might have. Who really knows? She was there because she was a student in our community and this is where she learned

Education and Learning

how people interact with each other and how to behave and get along. Along the way she occasionally made a friend who truly cared about her and spent time with her because she or he liked her, not because it was his or her job, and he or she was being paid to be with her. I sometimes made the argument that because her needs were so great, she needed the supports of a regular environment even more.

Kayleigh has a better quality of life and a chance to be a flower girl, have birthday parties with buddies from the our neighborhood school, share secrets with her older sister and quick kisses from her brother. Last year a few of the girls in Kayleigh's class at school really "took a shine" to her. Two of them even invited Kayleigh to their birthday parties, a very big first for her. We decided to take the next logical step and have a "kid" birthday party this year for Kayleigh. We invited three of the friends from school, a neighbor girl, and another girl from a neighboring suburb who also has RS. The whole party was a great success. The "typical" friends were fascinated to see another girl with RS and realized that Kayleigh isn't totally unique. Their acceptance of both girls with RS is an incredible boost for our family morale.

Kimberly is in a "special" class and has physical education, library, music and art with fourth and fifth graders. I would not want her placed in "regular" classes all day. I think it would be very stressful on her and at times distracting to the other children in the class. We feel she gets the appropriate amount of therapy, interaction, inclusion, and education "for her" in this class.

We tried a full inclusion approach for Amanda with emphasis on communication for two years. At the end, she was no better off. Her gross motor skills were worse, fine motor skills were the same, communication was a little better when in a quiet isolated environment, noise sensitivities were about the same, and her social emotional ability seemed about the same. This fall, we put her in a school placement for about fifteen hours a week. She also has OT, PT, ST, and some social time. The bottom line is we now take a mixed approach with a lot of protection and she seems OK with this. I do find if we emphasize the social stuff too much, it does not work for skill building. Amanda needs quiet and 1:1 to build skills. But I don't want her isolated all day. Everyone needs a buddy. It was only this year that she seemed to be consistently happy in a classroom situation.

Carly has been included with her class since preschool. Now that she is in sixth grade, we have seen less inclusion, but there was more opportunity in the earlier grades. I think the noise she makes is more disturbing to the adults than to the kids. They take it more in stride. I never had a preschool or kindergarten teacher ask to have her removed because of her more typical noises. My suggestion is to include her for as long as it is possible.

WHEN TO START INCLUSION

IT'S NEVER TOO LATE TO START, but it is best to start early. Kids are much more open and accepting at the elementary level. By the time you reach junior high school, if you don't part your hair on the right side, you're teased. When typical kids go to school with differently-abled kids right from the start, it becomes typical.

Most kids do not see the social stigma that is often attached to kids with disabilities. Once the situation is explained clearly, they regard each other as just kids. However, preparation is the key word for success in an inclusive classroom, for teachers, students and other parents alike.

We have always been very protective of Crystal and at first didn't know if public school was really a "safe" place for her with other children whispering, making fun and all of those mean things that some kids do to those less fortunate. What really helped us to feel comfortable about it was the sensitivity training the teacher did with some of the grades that would be integrated with our kids. The results were wonderful! It gave the kids a chance to meet our kids, ask questions and to understand a little about everyone having some type of "special needs" and that

Education and Learning

they have a lot of the same likes and dislikes that they do. No longer are they afraid of our kids and they now know that it's okay to say "hi" or to play at recess with them.

ADVOCACY STRATEGIES

ENTITLEMENT

THE TWO MOST IMPORTANT PUBLICLY-FUNDED resources available to children and adults with developmental disabilities are special education and (in California), regional centers. There are other public benefit systems, but none are based upon individually determined needs without regard to the family or beneficiary income or assets. Unlike other systems like Social Security, Medi-Cal or Medicaid, Department of Rehabilitation, public transportation or In-Home Supportive Services, access to special education and regional center services and supports are an entitlement—that is, if the individualized plan contains a goal that requires that a service or support is necessary in order to accomplish a goal/outcome. Then, either or both of these service systems may have a responsibility to ensure that the service or support is provided.

INDIVIDUALIZED PLANNING

THE FUNDAMENTAL PROCEDURE TO IDENTIFY and obtain services or supports within either special education or regional center systems requires the development of an individual plan. Development of a meaningful plan for either a child or an adult is the backbone upon which all services/supports stand. A table full of professionals who sit bright-eyed may overwhelm us with our daughter's plan already prepared. Unfortunately, the plan may not be based upon the knowledge or concerns of families, but by what may be either the convenience of delivering services within a classroom environment or the current budget or resource limitations and considerations of a regional center.

When a parent really reads the contents of either their child's IEP or the regional center's IPP, there may be little to be found that is of great practical value. Examples for a child might be the need for toilet training (or has toilet training or self-feeding been in the plan for ten years?). Plans need to include things that really matter for the person and their family: goals that make a person as independent as they are capable of; activities that will make life easier for everyone and allow the person to participate as best they can in the community without embarrassment and with dignity. Has maximizing the person's mobility really been explored? Has she had an in-depth physical and occupational therapy evaluation? Does she have access to a standing table? Is the goal to expand the time that she can carry her own weight? Is she able to make choices? How can music therapy play a significant role to motivate learning and how do you go about getting it? These can be educational goals, but similar goals for adults can be just as important.

Certainly, maintaining skills is critical for individuals with RS. Each regional center is required to have a crisis plan for each client. What is the plan in case the primary caregiver is not available or your girl hasn't slept for a week and the primary caregiver is at wit's end?

THE PLAN IS YOURS

IT IS NOT ABOUT THE SCHOOL DISTRICT or regional center. Objectively look at your current plan and take the time to think out of the box about what would really

Education and Learning

make a difference in the life of your loved one and your family. Go down the list of goals one by one and ask, "Does this really matter?" Then ask, "What is important, what matters to my child and to me and makes a positive difference"; goals should be measurable and they should have timelines. If you have been trying it for five to ten years and it hasn't "taken," it's never been presented properly or it isn't going to happen. Move on. Prepare your own plan. You can do it and you will be proud that you did!

KNOWING THE SYSTEM

NEVER ASSUME THAT ALL THE PROFESSIONALS in your life have a clue about what they are doing or love your child as if she were their own. People working for agencies are restricted by budgets, administrators who tell them what to do, lack of information, lack of resource development, misinformation, and yes, laziness. We meet some of the finest people we will ever know, but we also encounter people we could gratefully do without and cheerfully feed to the alligators.

The best advocates *know the answer to the question before they ask it*. Learn about the system your child is in. They are all different and so are the rules. County, state or federal laws control every public benefit system. All have web sites and brochures. All have regulations that provide greater detail about their law. They even have policies and guidelines. Never assume that what you are being told is absolutely true or entirely complete information. Federal law is more important than and supersedes state law. Special education is federal law, but each state has its own state laws and regulations. Regional centers are controlled by state law, but they now receive federal dollars through Medicaid. That's why some families are not required to pay for their children's services while others, not on the waiver, are being charged. Policies and guidelines mean nothing unless they are consistent with the law. Most important, all decisions made by an agency that receives funding to provide public benefits must have an appeal/fair hearing procedure.

RECORD KEEPING

THE ADVOCATES WHOSE CHILDREN OR ADULTS receive some or the most of what they need are those who have at least a passing knowledge of the agency's legal requirements and keep good records. When there is a good paper trail, your chances of getting what is needed are many times more likely to occur.

Whenever you are talking to anyone with an agency, keep a record of:

- the date of the communication
- the name of the person with whom you are communicating
- the issue you are discussing
- the outcome of the conversation, i.e., "Mary Agency said that she would check out why my daughter, Susan, had not been provided her twice weekly physical therapy during the past three weeks. Mary said she would call me back by August 30, 2005 … "

Mark your calendar when it was agreed that Mary would call you back. When people don't follow through, stall, or won't give you an answer, send them an email or letter that is return receipt. Hand deliver it and have your copy signed that it was received. Always keep copies of everything for yourself. Do not give away originals.

Be polite, but be firm. Clearly express your expectations and any agreements that have been made. Sometimes, when emotions are hard to control, asking a friend to read what

Education and Learning

you have written can help you to know whether what you are saying makes any sense at all and your points are clear.

Follow-Up

Follow-up letters to a meeting are a good way to be sure that your concerns and needs are not ignored and you are all on the same page.

SAMPLE LETTER

Date:

Ron Sincere, CEO
Oh, So Nice Agency
Lovely Lane
For Goodness Sake, CA

Dear Mr. Sincere,

Thank you and Jane Good for meeting with me about my daughter's need for a toilet training program to be included in her IEP (or IPP). It was my understanding that you would check out the resources for this service and get back to me by August 30, 2005 about whether this service will be provided. Regardless of your answer, we will need to schedule an IEP (or IPP) meeting where a goal will need to be written or the service will be formally denied. I think we all believe that being able to toilet as independently as possible is an important goal for my daughter. I will, of course, feel it necessary to appeal a denial. If there are questions or I have misunderstood our agreement, please advise at your earliest convenience. Thank you again for meeting with me. I look forward to hearing from you by August 30, 2005.

Sincerely,

Polly Perfect Parent

MEDIATION AND DUE PROCESS

WHAT IF YOU DON'T AGREE WITH YOUR DAUGHTERS' IEP, placement and/or delivery of services? The first approach is to ask the teachers and therapists what they recommend and why. Ask how getting fewer services or less access to education helps your daughter. Keep in mind that special education services, and attitudes and policies toward inclusion vary greatly from state to state, and even within districts. If the excuse is used that she is "not making progress," gather documentation of progress or provide information about the progression of RS. Get as much information as you can before the IEP meeting. It is always important to be cooperative and collaborative, and to avoid becoming adversarial. Keep a "Let's see what we can do to help my daughter" attitude. Provide

Education and Learning

written documentation of her need for therapies. If all that fails and you still disagree, you don't have to sign the IEP. You have other options. You can ask for mediation or a due process hearing. A school district can also request mediation or a due process hearing. The law states that the school has to keep your daughter in her current program until the dispute is settled.

IDEA requires states and school districts to allow disputes to be settled through a mediation process. Mediation is voluntary and must not be used to deny or delay a family's right to a due process hearing or other future actions, although states or school districts may require that, if parents choose not to use mediation, they meet with someone from an appropriate, neutral dispute resolution center or organization. Each state maintains a list of qualified mediators and the state must pay for the mediation. All discussions with the mediator are confidential and may not be used by the parent or the school district in future legal actions. If the mediation is successful, then a written agreement documents that agreement.

The next option is a due process hearing. There is no specific "rule of thumb" for pursuing due process. But, because it is a long, expensive, and painful process, make sure that:

- you have a competent lawyer (i.e., one who knows special education law) who can explain to you why s/he is confident you have a winnable position.
- you have a competent expert witness (a medical or education professional) who can competently explain why the school's program is "inappropriate."
- you can prove (probably through your expert witness) what is "appropriate."

From the parents' perspective, these things can be very difficult, not only because hiring lawyers and experts is costly, but because it is an emotionally charged time for them (keep in mind that it is not an emotionally charged time for anyone else in the process). So the school personnel, the lawyers, and the hearing officer are not swayed by emotional outbursts. It is hard for parents to understand that while they are having nervous breakdowns, everyone else is just doing their job.

It is important for you to be able to prove what is "appropriate." It may not seem like it is legally relevant, but when you are going to due process, you are asking a hearing officer to "fix" something. So even if you put on the most compelling case, and the hearing officer agrees that the school has dropped the ball entirely, s/he's going to be sitting there thinking, "so what do you want me to do about it?"

While districts have the burden of proof that they have provided a free and appropriate education (FAPE) in the LRE, even if the parents file, parents have to do their own homework in advance. It may take quite a long time and quite some expense to figure out what will work for your child. Keep in mind that you may have up to a year to file due process, so it is possible to refuse to consent to an IEP and wait quite a long time before filing due process. *Do not file your notice of due process until you are ready to go to hearing.* The time frame from filing your notice and the start of the hearing is very quick, and so it is not wise to file for due process and then go about finding a lawyer, an expert, and figuring out what educational program is appropriate for your child. Once you are prepared and ready to go to hearing, then file for due process (you can even use the expedited process at that point).

What increases the chances of victory? Being prepared and having a decent lawyer. Who pays? Parents have to pay for their own lawyer and their own experts. The school pays for the hearing officer, the court reporter, the space for the hearing, and the transcripts. The only way for parents to get their attorneys' fees and costs back is to win at due process, and then

Education and Learning

file another lawsuit in court requesting their fees and costs be paid. What happens if you lose? You're done. You can either consent to the IEP and send your child to school, keep your child home, send her to private school, or move. Unfortunately, sometimes it is easier to just move. The process is so frustrating that some parents who won at due process still moved. This is not so easily accomplished when you have other children who don't want to move.

We originally filed for due process for failing to provide a 1:1 assistant for Morgan to be able to achieve the IEP goals. We included causes of action relating to the disparity in the placement, five days in the school system and only three days in a developmental day center. They wanted us to send her to the school but without an assistant, and it wasn't going to work. She was better off in the developmental day program she was already attending, but they only offered three days there (they didn't have a reason for the disparity). They also didn't want to put her in a classroom at school with "normal" kids. She was going to be in a totally disabled classroom, without explanation as to why. The developmental day program had both normal and disabled kids in the classroom. They refused to move on either issue. So, we sued them. The administrative law judge asked if we would be open to mediation. We were, so we went to mediation and got five days in the developmental day program and a 1:1 assistant. That is a very short summary of the two-month process.

Heather had been in a private school for more than three years. At the time she started this school, she couldn't even hold her head up. It was very intense therapy. When Heather turned six, the school district had the right to bring her into their system if they had a correct classroom to meet her needs. The district said they did and at the time; I had no choice and couldn't prove otherwise. The school year started and it was downhill after that. It was a severe and profound classroom and all Heather would do is cry all day. After six months, I took her back to the private school for an evaluation, which showed that she had regressed in all areas. I started looking into other placement, but I couldn't find any funding that would accommodate it. So I started due process. I went through all the steps and the school did its own evaluation and set up another IEP meeting. I refused to sign the IEP and wrote the letter to get a formal hearing with a lawyer. Someone from the education department sat as the judge. Heather wasn't allowed to attend and I couldn't submit the evaluation from the private school. They had all the appropriate paperwork to show that the district was following the IEP that came from the private school. The district did change a few things, but we lost the case. The IQ test they used indicated that she was the lowest level on the scale and that is what they based their classroom settings on. I learned that anything can be written down on paper to make it look good.

We filed after several requests for a PT evaluation with the school. By law, the school is required to assess if requested by a parent if there is concern. Once I filed for a due process/mediation the school agreed to the assessment and ongoing therapies the same day they were served the hearing date. It's a shame that parents have to push things that far.

Our daughter's school was not agreeing to the terms we were requesting for her IEP. We interviewed a recommended lawyer and considered his fees and his services. We contacted our Regional Center, and it made recommendations and offered to support in minimal ways. This led us on a deeper search. We decided to attempt to go to mediation with our school and represent our daughter. This option was free and allowed us to go to the next step if we needed to. In the end, we were able to present our case, come to an agreement, and win without any fees.

Our due process hearing with our high school district has changed our lives forever. Lindsey had been successfully and fully included through eighth grade when the high school district started giving us a fight, taking us to federal court twice to try and remove Lindsey from school. The second time resulted in the judge ordering a due process hearing. Shock, devastation, and heartbreak best describe the feelings surrounding our defeat. The financial devastation is secondary to the emotional devastation, most of all being the loss of Lindsey's inclusive

Education and Learning

education. Despite the outcome and the indescribable stress that our family has endured, we would make the same choice. We are not only at peace with our decision, but proud of the path that we have chosen and the hard work that went into our case.

We should be out there trying to get the funding, education, and support we need in caring for our daughters. But we need to do it in a way that informs, educates, and wins minds over, not demands and threatens, though there is a time and place for that when all else fails. I don't want my school board to help us because it "has to." I want the board to help because they see and understand the need. Otherwise all that happens is the squeaky wheel gets oiled, but never changed, and the next person in line has to go through all the hassles we did.

THE TEACHING PROGRAM

FOR EVERY GIRL, A GOOD TEACHING PROGRAM begins with a secure emotional environment, which contributes to her potential for learning. When she feels safe, she is more reachable and teachable.

The program should revolve around her own abilities, wants, and needs, taking each of these into account in addition to her stage of RS. For instance, in Stage 2, the regression period, it may be wiser to delay concentration on fine or gross motor development, choosing instead to provide security at a time when she is feeling emotionally unbalanced. When she feels more secure, she will be more capable of using her body.

A NOTE TO THE TEACHER

IT MUST BE DIFFICULT FOR TEACHERS to understand parents. We can be wily creatures! We can be demanding and critical, and even downright cranky sometimes. We can expect too much of you, and we can expect you to have all of the answers. We can insist on having you do it our way when you know that you learned differently in school. We can probably test your limits. We sometimes expect you to spend all day 1:1 with our daughters, even though we know you have many other students. Sometimes we are very sure we have the only right answers. Sometimes we can't have enough of your time or attention. We can be demanding. You can understand that better when you realize that everything we do is born of love for our children. There is no more formal education than by experience. We are the best experts on our child.

We look to you for wisdom, knowledge, and expertise. We trust you with our most precious possessions, our children. We appreciate the time and love it takes to make the best situation for them. Let's work together.

ACCESS TO THE GENERAL EDUCATION CURRICULUM

BECAUSE GIRLS WITH RS have such enormous physical challenges that limit or eliminate conventional forms of communication, they have typically not been provided opportunity to learn the subjects that other children learn in school. Arguments against instruction in academics have focused on the question of "when will they ever use it?" That is a question we all can ask ourselves, however, if we consider when we have used much of what we learned in school. Learning, though, keeps our minds active. An active mind has been shown to stave off Alzheimer's and other forms of dementia in older adults. We have greater self-awareness and self-satisfaction when we learn something. Why would it be any different for someone with RS? Knowledge for the sake of knowledge is a uniquely

Education and Learning

human desire. We should never limit someone's access to that knowledge because of a disability. Instruction in age-appropriate academic material has proven to be stimulating, challenging, and successful for girls with RS. We also now know that receptive language for girls with RS is thought to be much higher than has been routinely accepted. Therefore, exposure to and instruction in academics may result in more getting through than they can express to us.

Some people confuse access to the general education curriculum and inclusion. They are not the same thing. Inclusion and access to the general curriculum overlap certainly; however, one could be placed in a general education classroom and have little to no access to the curriculum. Alternatively, a student could be in a special education classroom and have many opportunities to be engaged in the general education curriculum.

Girls with RS learn by listening and seeing. Therefore, it stands to reason that they will learn more if there is more to hear and see. They need to hear good language models and be in a literacy rich environment. We have to teach skills in context and connect learning to real life experiences, but not solely teach "functional" life skills that they may never be able to achieve. We need to inspire them, find their interests and teach to and with those interests. We have to provide real-life experiences they can connect to learning. If they demonstrate they know something, then move on and stop asking them to prove they know it over and over. Who would not get frustrated and begin, at best, inconsistent responses, but at worst, acting-out behavior, when asked the same question many times over?

From my experience, asking for consistency with a girl with RS is unreasonable. There are good days (when all the connections are working) and there are bad ones. The assumption should be that what she does on her good days is her best, and it's time to move on to the next step. My Darleen did a three-shape form board one time in her entire life. She did it! She understood shapes. She didn't need to do it a dozen times to convince me. She also matched colors no more than two or three times. She knows colors! Very few of our girls are able to be consistent. But we shouldn't punish them because they have a malfunctioning neurological system. And we shouldn't hold them back either. Imagine, wanting to read, but being refused the chance to learn, wanting to know what is normal, but never being allowed to be around normal students. It isn't always what a child can demonstrate, but rather the opportunity given to experience and learn.

School boards have a different ruler of success than we do as parents. School personnel think success means "accomplishing xyz skill two out of three times with 95 percent accuracy." They are geared to write IEPs with this ruler of success in mind. I don't think they consider apraxia, which is the greatest disability that our girls face. What I stress in my daughter's IEP is that her mind has the willingness and the knowledge to accomplish xyz skill, but her body is unable to carry out the commands of the mind. To attempt to measure this two out of three times with 95 percent accuracy is simply ludicrous. We must come up with acceptable means of "measurement."

Kim must have spent a dozen years in various "special school" settings, where special education teachers tried to teach her "living skills." These consisted entirely of motor actions that she was unable to perform because of her severe disability. The terrible boredom of being "taught" to brush your hair, brush your teeth, etc., when the actions just cannot happen is enough to make anyone scream and bang their head? I know I would! Putting RS girls who cannot talk in a class with a bunch of others who cannot talk doesn't make for really interesting discussion. And it doesn't allow them to make friends. How do you make friends if you cannot communicate? What can you possibly do? Learning to read, and hence receive a real education, is giving them a lifelong ability to be interested.

A critical notion here is that if a girl takes part in the general education curriculum, as she should, then the instruction in it should be purposeful. Each lesson should have specific learning objectives specifically designed for her. In many cases, with appropriate accom-

Education and Learning

modations such as use of different materials or forms of presentation, she may be able to participate fully and achieve the lesson objectives. In other instances, while she is exposed to the lesson in all its complexities, there may be specific objectives for her. For example, if a lesson about the solar system is believed to be too difficult, the focus of her instruction may be shapes (e.g. round), counting (nine), sequencing (the order of the planets) or labeling/identifying (sun, earth, moon).

In order for access to the general education curriculum to occur, attitudes need to change and schools (administrators, teachers, and students) must identify themselves as communities of learners. As long as the focus is on disability and deficits, meaningful access will never occur. The school must have trained personnel who are able to make adaptations that provide access to academics and believe academic learning to be important. The adaptations should be designed to address the unique learning characteristics of students with RS. Very often the adaptation made for students with disabilities in a classroom helps all the students in the classroom. All benefit more from the lesson.

Megan is in her standard first grade classroom most of the day. She learns so much from all the kids. She is starting to learn the addition of doubles and phonics. We have gotten the kids involved in Megan's learning. They help put her weights on her wrists and ankles before lunch (they think it's cool to help and Megan thinks it's cool that they are helping!) Megan has a neat first grade teacher who has incorporated a lot of singing in her classroom for Megan and the other kids love it!

Finally, meaningful access does not just happen. It takes planning. There should be opportunities for teachers to meet together, both special education and general education, to share information and plan. While these shared planning opportunities may mean a change of the systems in the school, they do not need to be special meetings. Sometimes these meetings can take place at regularly scheduled grade level meetings, for example. Additionally, sometimes placing more than one student with special needs in the class may help with coordination of personnel and other accommodations. To help with the exchange of information, all of the teaching staff who provide education services to the student with RS should have copies of the student's IEP or, at least, copies of those components of the IEP that are relevant to a particular teacher's responsibility. Everyone should also have current information on RS.

TEACHING CHOICE MAKING

TEACHING CHOICE MAKING IS VERY IMPORTANT. It's important to help us understand preferences, for example.

I finally convinced the therapist that Lyndie truly could make some choices, if she only offered them to her. She finally conceded and wrote down a few choices. She used pictures first; it took her a while to believe that Lyndie had some reading skills. From the first week when she began offering Lyndie a choice of what activity she wanted to do that day, she was like a new person. She very rarely is uncooperative anymore. She now has been given some control over what she is to do for the day.

In academic contexts, choice making is also very important. In these situations it is not a preference but there is a specific answer that we are seeking to get an understanding of what she knows, not what she wants. This is not "yes/no," choice- making but a choice of two possible "yes" responses.

Education and Learning

We made some alphabet shapes out of cardboard and thick sandpaper. Emily loves the feel of this. We also made some letters out of fur fabric. We try to spend twenty minutes at home in the morning before school just feeling and talking about the letters. Emily put the C next to a picture of the cat. We have made some large flash cards with pictures of words beginning with ABC. We made the flash cards big so they are nice and clear and easy to touch. They are laminated so they are durable.

The other day the school told me that they had begun to show Shanda two different flash cards with letters on them and ask her to eye point to a certain one and low and behold she got all twenty-six letters right!

In this type of choice making one of the "choices" should be incorrect. At first the distractors should be every different, such as a card with a letter on it and a card with a totally unrelated picture or even a blank card. Gradually the choices should be more similar, the differences less apparent. It may take a while for a girl to understand the difference in the tasks of indicating preference and providing a "correct" answer, but that understanding is essential for instruction as well as for assessment. Choice making then becomes the method for assessing general knowledge, comprehension of stories, answering math questions, identifying words, letters, numbers, shapes, and so on.

Finally, teaching "yes/no" should be attempted only after some success with the choice making described above. Sometimes we want to start with "yes/no" because it is easiest for us, but it is the most difficult cognitively and developmentally.

The concepts of yes/no were also taught to Kayleigh. We started out with questions like "Do you want more _____?" or "Do you want to stop?" We made sure that the answer was not always going to be "yes." She needed to learn "no". Kayleigh is now answering yes/no recall questions each day. This shows us she remembers yesterday's events and has memory retention.

LITERACY

LITERACY IS A BROAD CONCEPT and does not have a simple definition. Literacy is more than being able to read words. There is numeric literacy and computer literacy, for example. Definitions of literacy can change depending on the culture or home country of an individual. Language, however, is at the root of literacy learning, therefore in order to "be literate," one must have opportunities to hear good language models, communicate with others, have opportunities to solve practical problems, and see and interact with written language and pictures. For typically developing children, many of these things happen informally, incidentally through using spoken language in play, attempts at reading (using pictures) and writing (scribbling). Those opportunities are often limited for children with RS. Children with RS, therefore, need to have specially planned literacy opportunities, models, and interactions as well as good home-school collaboration.

Access to literacy activities is often limited for the girl with RS. At school, IEP goals generally concentrate on therapeutic, behavioral, and basic life skill goals. At home, care of the child's many health and custodial needs may take priority over reading activities. Girls with RS need to see literacy in action, however. There need to be materials available at home, including books on CD, and programs like Intellikeys and Click-It. Parents should get a library card and check out books often. If you can, scan a book into the computer and use switch-activated devices. If there is time, you can make your own books together with your daughter on subjects relevant to the family.

Education and Learning

Any visit to the bookstore or library may make you feel that choosing appropriate books is challenging or overwhelming. Initially, you may choose picture books where you weave the tale as you share the book with your child. The books can also be simple books, focusing on names of objects, letters of the alphabet, numbers, and beginning word sounds. You may even use books with one word. An example of this type of book is Arthur Geisert's *Oink*, and the follow-up book, *Oink, Oink*. When choosing a beginning book to read, choose books that have repetitive, predictable lines and large clear, illustrations. Bill Martin's book, *Brown Bear, Brown Bear What Do You See?* is an example of this type of book. You can even program a BIGmack switch so she can produce the voice output for those repeated lines. After that you can move to stories that are cumulative tales with simple but predictable story lines so she may begin to make predictions about a story. Examples of this kind of book are Wanda Gag's *Millions of Cats* and Don and Audrey Wood's *The Napping House*. Later, include good children's literature such as Maurice Sendak's *Where the Wild Things Are* or Ludwig Bemelmans' *Madeline*.

Children learn about the importance of reading and writing by what they experience at home. They learn that written language has a very important role in communication. Parents teach them the value of print. Let them see you use literacy. Point out words and numbers to your daughters throughout the day. For example, point out street signs, labels on food, and controls on the CD player. Show them the greeting cards you both send and receive. You can also label objects around your house (tape the written label on objects), so they begin to associate the written word with the object. Make these events significant. Let her hear the language of other children and hear the difference between spoken language and written language. Tell her stories. Help her hear good syntax and learn more vocabulary through listening. Listening comprehension is one of the building blocks to reading.

Most girls with RS enjoy reading books together. Use the books that she shows interest in, fun books, and books where you act out the stories. If initially she does not seem interested or is resistant, persevere. Read the books over and over again. Repeated readings help the child enjoy the book, understand the book, and learn the vocabulary. Typical children are often heard to say, "one more time!" when a favorite story is read, and girls with RS are no different.

Literacy is also about interactions with others. Label pictures as you read to them and wait for her to look and respond. After she begins to have some understanding of print, build in comments and questions on the story, not based only on labeling. Ask predictive and evaluative questions, and ask, "what's next?" questions. Give clues, and build working memory and reasoning skills. Build reading skills a little later, when literacy has value and attending is better. Use photos, pictures, or words to develop reciprocity, narrow the range of possible responses, and organize and teach her how to play.

Coordination with school is also important. You need to know what the teachers are trying to accomplish. Ask the teachers what books or poems her class will be reading and studying. If there is not a copy of the book the school can let you borrow, see if you can check one out from the library. If you can read the story or poem several times before the rest of the class does, then she will be more prepared and may be better able to attend as well as respond in class. You can also make sure her communication device is programmed so that she can interact about the book or poem as well.

A formal study of storybook reading by mothers and their daughters with RS revealed an increased frequency of symbolic communication and labeling/commenting in all of the six study participants. The study by David Koppenhaver, Karen Erickson, and Brian Skotko

Education and Learning

showed that storybook reading interactions between mothers and girls with RS can provide a useful context for language and communication learning if support is made available to both mothers and children.

Girls with RS may have considerable difficulties learning to read, but the intervention studies suggest that the problems can be overcome. The following are some recommendations from their research:

- **Read lots of storybooks!** Girls in the study increased their attention, increased pointing to pictures to answer questions or comment, and increased their overall awareness of the stories.

- **Point to the pictures or words as you talk and read about them.** Keep pointing until your daughter or student has directed her attention to what you're talking about. Give her enough time to respond. If her attention is diverted, point it out again. However, don't insist on attention to everything on every page.

- **Always have pictures or picture symbols representing key vocabulary available to encourage your child to comment and ask questions while reading.** Start with just two different pictures/symbols and model how to use them by pointing to them whenever you read or say them.

- **Include a BigMack switch in your storybook readings if possible.** Many children respond more favorably to voice output.

- **Explore holding the child's nondominant hand.** This should increase her ability to use her dominant hand for turning pages and pointing to pictures. If it works, consider making or purchasing a hand splint.

- **Expect participation and wait when you ask a question or provide an opportunity to comment.** Some girls with RS took thirty to forty seconds to respond. Eyes seemed to be the quickest response mode for most—they look at the picture that they intend to point to long before their hand(s) ever follow. If you don't get a response after X seconds (whatever you decide through experience with your child), repeat the question. If you still don't get a response, you can try modeling the response with hand-over-hand interaction with your daughter.

- **The position of the child, the book, the picture symbols, and the BigMack matter!** Some girls could use the symbols if they are lying flat; some needed them velcroed on to a vertical frame. Some girls needed the BigMack switch up high so that they could push it down with a chin or the side of their head. If these devices are not working at first, try another position.

- **Assume competence in your child or student!** No matter what any expert tells you or how often, the kids with severe or multiple disabilities who "make" it are the ones whose parents consistently involve them in family activities, conversations, and experiences.

I'm no expert on early reading programs, but Rebecca could read and had good comprehension. We didn't do anything special. We just read to her a lot as a child and then when she started school she did the regular reading program and homework (simple books). We read them together. She also used to watch TV which often has words written and pronounced at the same time. We taped Sesame Street off the TV and let her watch these. Rebecca could read but never had anyone explain the concepts to her. We didn't think she could understand, so the reading was a huge surprise. She had a good general knowledge but had strange gaps—she didn't know about traffic lights for example, but from her seat in the back of the car she wouldn't have had a good view and of course couldn't ask why we stopped and started.

Education and Learning

ANGELA LEARNS TO READ

Angela learned to read pretty much like any other kid … lots and lots and lots of lap reading with some attention drawn to words, just like you naturally do with kids. Her preschool had the "letter of the week." She's always been fully included in regular classrooms, so her reading programs are the same off-the-shelf ones the other kids use. In kindergarten, they used ReadWell by Marilyn Sprick, which I was very concerned about because it is so heavy on the phonics. I had no idea if she even relates to letter sounds, being nonverbal and all. But she got it! The teachers use a special hand motion to point out the sounds in the words (this looks kind of like a ball bouncing on ocean waves under the letters of enlarged words). When Angela would read words in isolation, her eyes did the same "bouncing ball" motion, so we had to figure she was making the same phonetic connections in her head. In first grade, they used Harcourt, very much a naturalistic reading program that didn't have much phonetic emphasis and I worried over that, since she'd done so well with phonics. But it went beautifully. Her teacher didn't believe that Angela was necessarily limited by the typical Rett delayed response time and expected her to improve her reading rate just like all the other kids … and Angela really rose to the expectation. All the kids had to know the unit sight words and be able to say them within 3 seconds. Angela could pick hers out visually within the three second time limit too! Sure blew me away! The second grade reading program she's in now is literature based, and she acts like a fish happy in its water.

SPECIAL CONCERNS

FATIGUE AT SCHOOL

We used to have a lot of problems with school and the school nurse to accommodate my daughter's nap at school. They felt that when she's asleep "she isn't getting anything out of school, so there is no benefit for her to be here." They even wanted me to sign an "Individualized Health Plan" which specified when to send my daughter home if she has naps exceeding their expectation. I refused to sign such a plan and have had doctors back me up. Since then, I have been very strong on this issue.

In my daughter's IEP, we specified her need to have a nap at school. No one argued with it, and the school even specified in the IEP to have a proper setting and mat for her nap.

ATTENDANCE

We had our doctor write a note about her attendance. We also wrote an addendum to Kimberly's IEP, for her to be allowed to miss as many days as needed due to her having RS. Two years ago, Kimberly missed five weeks of school straight because of pneumonia and a string of illnesses all in a row. Things just happen with our girls!

HOME-SCHOOL COMMUNICATION

KEEPING A NOTEBOOK TO SEND BACK AND FORTH from home to school is a good idea. It keeps the teacher informed if your child is having an "off" day and is a great way to share successes and failures at home. Some parents use a daily form, which is easy to fill out and informative.

Education and Learning

HOME-SCHOOL CHECKLIST

Child's name _____

A.M. NOTE TO THE TEACHER

Sleep: restful ❑   fitful ❑   overslept ❑   under slept ❑
         awake during the night ❑

Breakfast: ate well ❑   ate some ❑   ate little ❑

Disposition today: enthusiastic ❑   attentive ❑   lethargic ❑   tired ❑
                     happy ❑   sad ❑   irritable ❑   agitated ❑   vocal ❑
                     wobbly ❑   sleepy ❑   silly   other _____

Physical discomfort (explain):

Parent comment: (what happened at home last night, upcoming appointments, and news to share, etc?)

Medication adjustments: No ❑   Yes ❑
Explain:

Seizures last night/this morning: None ❑   Full ❑   Possible seizures ❑
Times: _____

Change in routine:

Initials:

Education and Learning

P.M. NOTE TO THE PARENT/CAREGIVER

Overall disposition and level of participation today: (check all that apply):

happy ❑   enthusiastic ❑   alert ❑   confident ❑   interacted with others ❑
worked hard ❑   deliberate choices ❑   coordinated movements ❑   quiet ❑
vocal ❑   irritable ❑   sad ❑   agitated ❑   lethargic ❑   difficulty responding
❑

difficulty concentrating ❑   sleepy ❑   inwardly focused ❑   wobbly ❑   silly
❑

other _____

Physical discomfort (explain):

Overall physical exertion: high ❑   medium ❑   low ❑

BM: Yes ❑   No ❑

Void on toilet: Yes ❑   No ❑

At toilet time, pants were: dry ❑   wet ❑   soiled ❑

Reflux problems: none ❑   belching ❑   lots of drooling ❑   vomiting ❑

Seizures: none ❑   full ❑   possible ❑   Times: _____

Eating: ate well ❑   ate so-so ❑   ate poorly ❑

Drinking: drank plenty ❑   drank little ❑   drank more ❑

Swallowed: well ❑   okay ❑   poorly ❑

Nap: Yes ❑   No ❑   Length of time: _____   When _____

TODAY'S ACTIVITIES

Physical therapy/walking ❑   ROM Exercises: Upper ❑   Lower ❑
Reading/Literacy ❑   Art ❑   Vocabulary/Symbol List ❑   Math Concepts ❑
Science ❑   Music ❑   Gym/Health ❑

Anything new at school today?

Skills to work on at home or things you might want to talk about at home:

Teacher comments:

Initials:

Education and Learning

HOME-SCHOOLING

SOME PARENTS CHOOSE TO HOME-SCHOOL their children. They may have had bad experiences with public school, or they may just feel they are able to provide a more quality program where she gets more time and attention at home. You will have to provide a letter from your daughter's primary care physician stating that a homebound program is best for your child. Most districts will provide the necessary therapies at home.

Nowadays, there are many educational computer programs and games that can be used at home. There is a ton of information on the Internet, including a number of Web sites where you can get curriculum and ideas for a small fee. Enchanted Learning Software includes interactive pages and a calendar with activities for every day of the month. It is easy to use and includes topics from the alphabet to science, with lessons in several languages.

Kristen is both homebound and regular schooled. At school, she has her own aide, who works with her all day. If Kristen misses more than two days, on the third day, her teacher/speech therapist will come out to our home for two hours each day until Kristen is ready to go back. There may not be a "perfect" program for her, but you must weigh all your pros and cons when it comes to home schooling. It may involve making sacrifices such as not having her socialize as much with other children because it may be more beneficial to her to be home-schooled.

Brittany learned very well at home, using DTT with no distractions. I feel that the best placement for her is in the home. That way, she can work on the DTT to acquire things and at the same time, devote more effort to activities such as her gross motor/fine motor program or physical activity with little time wasted or distractions.

I do a lot of unstructured teaching with Noi when she is alert and wanting to do things. We don't have a set block of time or set day of the week. She is usually more receptive to learning in the evening, so we work mainly from about 7-10 on reading and such. During the day, we fit subject matter into our everyday activities.

I just do whatever I feel Lissa can do each day. Some days, she loves to color hand-over-hand. She does a lot of eye gazing to make choices, what she wants to do (eat, drink, potty, etc.) I feel Lissa really needs to be able to communicate with others and let us know when she needs something or is hurting somewhere. We work with her on saying some words by saying and repeating them as she watches my lips. She uses a BIGMack switch. One advantage of home-schooling is that she doesn't have any set time to wake up or go to bed like when she was still in school.

We have chosen to keep Edie at home and it has worked out well. She does best in a 1:1 situation. We get OT twice a week, PT twice a week, special education twice a week, and speech twice a week. My house is a revolving door! Edie enjoys seeing everyone. This also allows me to keep a close eye on everything her teachers/therapists are working on. We have many outside activities so that she is able to socialize with other children. She plays baseball and soccer on a challenger league baseball team. She rides her horse once a week and goes to Sunday School on Sundays.

ALTERNATIVE THERAPIES

THERE ARE A NUMBER OF ALTERNATIVE THERAPIES that have been tried with varying results with girls with RS as well as with individuals with other learning and/or behavior challenges.

APPLIED BEHAVIOR ANALYSIS, DTT, AND THE LOVAAS METHOD

APPLIED BEHAVIOR ANALYSIS (ABA) is a systematic approach to understanding the relationship between the environment and behavior. ABA includes many types of instructional strategies and interventions including task analysis and Discrete Trial

Education and Learning

Training (DTT). Parents of young children with autism have popularized a specific curriculum and form of DTT, called the Lovaas Method. It is very fast paced and time intensive, taking from twenty to forty hours each week. Discrete Trials, as a teaching strategy, can be an effective teaching strategy with any child, however. It can be modified in time and intensity for the girl with RS. Using Discrete Trials, the child is asked to do a task, such as clapping, making a specific sound, or touching something, and, given a reward, which is usually food and praise, when she succeeds. At first, the responses are prompted by the adult moving her through the motions. The adult fades assistance over time, and the child is expected to do the task with responses that are close. In time, help is reduced completely. When the task has a high rate of correct responses, another task is selected which builds on the previous tasks. Like any other approach, it is not effective for all girls with RS.

We tried Lovaas for Leah when she was three and quickly modified it. We gave far fewer hours, since Leah needs rest and gets overload. We accepted a lower percentage of correct responses, since she can't always comply, even when she wants to and knows the answer. Also, we found that she became easily bored. Once she shows us she knows something, she doesn't see the point to constantly showing us. Her percent of correct responses increase while she is interested and then rapidly decrease as she becomes bored. We did, however, find benefit to Leah. The repetition and reward helped her in learning motor tasks such as pushing herself up from sitting and isolating her pointer finger. It has also been of benefit to us since it showed us how much she knows. She showed us she can identify different colors and letters, pick between big and small, and put an item into a category, such as food versus clothing. It convinced us that we do not have a severely mentally retarded child and to expect more from her.

ABA certainly isn't a one-size-fits-all answer to learning for any kid, regardless of disability. Even savvy, reputable ABA proponents agree with that. The beginning ABA, the repetitions of "show me circle," "show me circle," "show me circle" for eight out of ten trials are not appropriate for every child. The physical limits that slow my daughter down would unfortunately frustrate her and keep her locked at this level of non-interaction rather than support progress towards the more natural interactions. So instead, we keep things as close to "natural" and "age-appropriate" for her as we can, and she responds very well to this approach. She is quick to pick up new ideas and shuts down with repetition, so we have to be really careful to present things in new ways to keep her interest. There are some things she likes to repeat sometimes (favorite books and videos and repeating lines in stories), but overdoing it will burn her out. Keeping things new and stimulating within a predictable framework is our best strategy, and so she is able to thrive fully included in regular classes.

I have a couple of students with RS who are using ABA. It does become problematic when it is the whole program or the whole day at school, which the consultants tend to advocate. Any program that claims it will remediate a child in and of itself is not being honest, and autism consultants have often warned against this one-program-fits-all approach. No one program should ever be in place for a student. ABA misses very critical pieces of learning like interacting with the environment in a functional way and interacting with peers. It does, however, work wonders in many areas.

Kelsey had three years of ABA therapy using the discrete trial methods from age three to six. I think it's the best thing I ever did for her. I think she has a lot of skills now that she wouldn't have if we didn't do it. She can point to things she wants, and she can use a "yes/no" card communication system. She's got good enough hand skills to be able to hold her own sippy cup, and we used it a lot for desensitization programs (she used to be afraid of so many things, like stepping into the bathroom, going outside, cracks in sidewalks). The repetition and then immediate reinforcement with something that she likes worked the best for Kelsey compared to all her other therapies combined.

Education and Learning

A bit of advice: make sure you've got good, qualified people working with your daughter. That means that her discrete trial program should be headed up by a behavioral specialist, someone who has at least a master's degree in behavioral psychology or functional analysis. Then you need an experienced lead therapist, somebody who has been doing discrete trials at least three to five years. And lastly, make sure the people actually doing the discrete trials get the proper training, and that they get continued training with appropriate feedback. People doing discrete trials should be observed and critiqued at least every two weeks. The bad thing about DTT is that if it is not done right, its benefits can be completely ineffective.

Auditory Integration Training (AIT) was developed by French otolaryngologist Guy Berard in order to treat auditory processing problems. Berard claims that abnormal auditory processing results when there is discrepancies in how well someone hears different sound frequencies. He believes that this abnormality contributes to behavior and learning problems. Berard developed AIT as a way to reduce sensitivity to specific sound frequencies. AIT involves twenty sessions of thirty minutes where modified music is sent though a special modulating device into headphones. This device "exercises" the brain and inner ear until all the frequencies are perceived within a normal range.

Play Therapy is a type of intervention that uses play systematically to help children communicate, solve problems and learn acceptable behaviors. Play therapists are typically licensed mental health professionals. The therapist will choose toys or activities designed to address the individual child's need or goal.

Craniosacral Therapy (CST) was developed in the 1970s and 1980s by John Upledger, a doctor of osteopathy, when he was a clinical researcher at the University of Michigan. It is defined as "a gentle, hands-on method of evaluating and enhancing the function of the craniosacral system (head and spine) and the connective tissue (fascia) of the body." The craniosacral system includes the cerebrospinal fluid and the membranes within the cranium and spine, and their bony attachments. Craniosacral therapists are trained to feel this subtle motion in the body, and can use it to identify areas of congestion or restriction. Using the hands to reflect back to the body the pattern or restriction it is holding, the therapist provides an opportunity for the body to return to an easier mode of functioning.

Prism Glasses are used therapeutically to alter the visual midline concept of a person who has a neuro-motor imbalance physical disability. A person with this type of disability may have a shift in her concept of her visual midline. When the visual midline shifts, it causes the person to think, unconsciously, that her body center is shifted in the direction of the midline. In turn, she will lean toward the midline shift. Through the use of yoked prism glasses, the visual midline can be shifted. Yoked prism lenses have been used effectively through neuro-optometric rehabilitation in hospitals and rehabilitation programs throughout the United States. The purpose of these special prisms is to shift the visual midline thereby enhancing the effect of the physical and occupational therapy.

Sensory Integration Therapy (SIT) is a form of occupational therapy that comes from a body of work developed by A. Jean Ayres, PhD, OTR, in the late 1950s and early 1960s. Sensory integration is the neurological process of organizing the information we get from our bodies and from the world around us. In SIT, the child is guided through activities that are used to strengthen the child's sense of touch (tactile), sense of balance (vestibular), and sense of where the body and its parts are in space (proprioceptive).

Education and Learning

Jill Hess, Teaching Assistant, Nationview Public School, Ontario, submitted the following teaching program:

Novel/Subject Studies

The chapter or subject material is read twice to Kayleigh. If it is novel study, she is asked to tell where the setting of the chapter took place. She chooses between the symbols offered. The questions asked to her are both "yes/no" questions and fill in the blank questions. Example "Who was afraid when the snake came close?" Symbols of the characters in the novel are shown to her. "Was Susan happy to see her new brother?" "Yes/no" symbols were used. We always make the questions and symbols we use become a part of Kayleigh's life if possible. We are always expanding her "feelings"symbol list and use them where possible so she never forgets them. We try to use places, people, activities, etc., too. The questions always tell us if Kayleigh comprehended the chapter. Each chapter introduces four to five new symbols. Four to six questions are asked for each chapter. Kayleigh gets about 73 percent on all her novel studies and we are pleased with this.

In a grade six classroom, novel studies are a large part of the language arts curriculum. In order for Kayleigh to participate with complete understanding and success, the classroom novel needed to be modified. I began by consulting with the classroom teacher, asking for suggestions and ideas. After some brainstorming, I began to modify Kayleigh's novel.

Step One: I allowed myself enough time to pre-read the novel. At the end of each chapter I would record five to eight main points, which I felt Kayleigh would recall.

Step Two: After completing the novel myself, I rewrote the chapter's main points on its own piece of paper, pasting it then to colorful construction paper forming a mini-novel study of main points.

Step Three: Like the other students, Kayleigh was expected to answer questions at the end of each chapter. The teacher would provide me with a list of questions per chapter and I then would modify four or five questions for Kayleigh to eye gaze "yes" or "no." My assistance in modifying these questions came from the main points created at the end of each chapter.

Step Four: Using pictures from Boardmaker and Overlay Maker, I created symbols for all main characters and objects. As well, when possible, I created specific symbols to go along with each set of main points from each chapter. At this stage, Kayleigh is being introduced to new symbols and words as well as recalling "yes/no" questions throughout the novel.

We are now ready to begin our novel study. After reading chapter 1 to Kayleigh, I immediately go chapter 1 main points, allowing her extra preparation for the chapter questions. Chapter questions are answered using Kayleigh's "yes/no" communication symbols. I feel that Kayleigh is more attentive and demonstrates better understanding of the novel, proven by her average of three out of four correct answers per chapter.

Concept Learning (Science, Math)

1. Choose four concepts from the unit you would like Kayleigh to learn. Prepare the corresponding symbols. Teach the concepts to Kayleigh, presenting the symbols as they are referred to in your lesson.

Education and Learning

> 2. Presenting the symbols two at a time, using Intellikeys and/or eye gaze, ask Kayleigh to identify each symbol. "Kayleigh, look at/touch 'star.'" Record her answers. For each error follow error correction procedure from Sight Word Vocabulary. Continue at this level until Kayleigh correctly identifies the symbols three of four consecutive trials.
>
> 3. Prepare several questions about the concepts that can be answered by choosing from the symbols using Intellikeys or eye gaze, i.e. "Which one is hot?" Continue until Kayleigh answers correctly three of four questions per concept.
>
> 4. Prepare three fill in the blank sentences for each concept using the Intellikeys. Present each sentence and have Kayleigh choose the correct word to complete it. Print out the results as a record of learning.

EDUCATION HELPFUL HINTS

- Assume that she understands you.
- Understand that she may need a security symbol, such as a blanket or doll.
- Read to her.
- Let her see you use literacy.
- Maintain a good home and school relationship.
- Point out words, numbers, symbols, and pictures in everyday life.
- Show consideration for her fears and hesitancies.
- Limit outside stimuli to those that are necessary.
- Explain everything to her before you do it.
- Make situations meaningful.
- Choose activities that appeal to her emotions and her senses.
- Make sure activities are age-appropriate.
- Structure activities in a fixed sequence.
- Give her one task at a time.
- Schedule her activities with tangible reminders (bag by the door) (bib before lunch).
- Choose signals that she understands (words, signs, pictures).
- Combine several signals so that she gets more than one cue.
- Don't say it … sing it.
- Allow her to move about her environment; she learns from taking it in.
- Provide different sights and sounds.
- Allow ample time and opportunity for new experiences.
- Provide repetition of activities, but not to the point of boredom.
- Motivate her by creating anticipation for continuation or completion of a process or action … pause for her response.
- Give her the chance to participate at her own physical level.
- Make sure she is physically comfortable and well supported.
- Record activities in a daily communication book to share between school and home.

Education and Learning

- Instead of asking her to give a response, such as "Say hello," just give her a "hello."
- When trying to get her to act, don't ask her to act. Make comments on the activity or the object. Instead of saying "Pick up the candy," you could say, "You like candy." Instead of "Come sit at the table," try saying "Cookies are on the table." Here you encourage her to act incidentally, instead of having to plan her actions.
- Give her enough time to respond.
- Look for her body language to respond to you.
- When she gets "started," don't interrupt her by commenting on what she is doing. Her focus will shift to how she's doing it and she'll likely stop.
- Look for activities that are motivating. Most girls with RS like: cuddling, "roughhousing" play, music, books, television, swinging, riding in a car, bathing and swimming, outdoors, food, photos of familiar people and places, babies and small children (particularly voices), and men!

We follow Angela's lead, always with a vision for what we dream might be, yet never quite sure where her lead will take us. I just never know what to expect. It was Angela who wanted to try roller-skating. Good grief, the child doesn't walk, so why would I ever think to try it? Yet she loves it! It was Angela who demonstrated she does sound out words. We were hesitant to let her try last year's phonics-based reading program, because without being able to listen to her play with sounds we didn't know if she was tuned in to them. It is Angela who tries to speak out words every blue moon, even though we don't work on oral speech.

FINAL TIPS FROM SUSAN NORWELL, MA

- Everything you do should emphasize relationship first.
- You can't learn what you are not taught.
- Learn how to play!
- Think outside the box and stay there.
- Peer interaction is very important.
- Be prepared. Offer opportunity.
- Augmentative communication and technology are key.
- Verbal skills are NOT an indication of thinking.
- Watch those eyes.
- Be a meaning maker.

*"Good teaching is one-fourth preparation
and three-fourths pure theatre."*

– GAIL GODWIN

Therapeutic Approaches

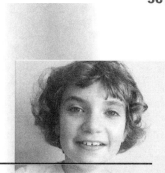

INTERVENTION STRATEGIES

MOTOR DEVELOPMENT IN RS is almost always delayed, but the extent of the delay can vary considerably. Some girls are never able to achieve independent sitting or standing, while others sit, stand, and walk at nearly the expected time. Her gait is often wide-based, unsteady, and asymmetrical. Specific motor problems which may need to be addressed are *hypotonia, ataxia, motor apraxia,* and *loss of transitional movements, spasticity, scoliosis* and/or *kyphosis, loss of ambulation, loss of hand function, foot deformities,* and *spatial disorientation.* (Oral motor dysfunction with feeding problems will be discussed in the chapter on nutrition. Speech and communication will be further explored in the chapter on communication.)

"The journey of a thousand miles begins with a single footstep."

– CHINESE PROVERB

The approach to treatment of motor problems in RS includes many disciplines including physical therapy, occupational therapy, speech therapy, music therapy, hydrotherapy, hippotherapy (horseback), and others. Each uses a combination of different interventions that are intended to maintain and maximize function in the girl with RS. While these therapies do not cure RS, they can maintain or improve function, prevent deformities, provide positioning and mobility, and help keep her in better contact with her environment. It is important to remember that while girls with RS share many similarities, their problems and responses to intervention may vary dramatically.

The sort of therapy is not the most important; it is the ongoing attention for stimulation and therapy, trying different approaches, all aiming for the same goals. There is a natural development in the girls with age, and we have to follow the tide, so to speak.

Overstimulating will not help. I had to learn over the years to be patient, to accept that changes come slowly. It was a hard lesson for me, for I am one of the world's most impatient persons, always focusing on results in all I do. This child has taught me patience and joy in achievements that count little or nothing in the "normal" world: We are euphoric when she fills her glass at the tap herself for the first time! But still it is often difficult to hold on to all the activities and attempts at teaching her certain things, when she does so often not respond. What keeps me going on is the thought of Karina at the age of three and four and the completely different girl she is now.

We just had a long conversation with Em's doctor about development, therapies, and her IEP coming up. I expressed some skepticism about the therapies, whether they really help, how much better Emma is a result of all this work. Her comments were helpful to me. She said that we are changing the natural history of the syndrome; that there is a difference for girls who are receiving early intervention and therapies in school. We cannot make Emma "well" medically and developmentally at this time, but we can help her have "better" outcomes, and what we want is for her to be able to function at whatever is optimal for her.

Therapeutic Approaches

WHAT EVERY PARENT SHOULD KNOW

JUST AS IT HAPPENS WITH OUR TYPICAL CHILDREN, we have to be careful not to over-schedule our girls with treatments and therapies. When too many therapies get out of balance, she cannot get full value from any one of them. It is tempting to do this in the beginning, because we feel an urgent call to do as much as we can all at once. Do consider her tolerance and fatigue level when scheduling appointments. Don't feel that you have to do everything at once, or that you have to do the same therapies as others. Make the best decisions for your own child, based on your own resources and her needs.

I think some parents look at what others are doing or have done and think they are being told or pushed to do the same when this is not the case. We all have a different child living with RS. We all have different family dynamics. We all have different supports systems, financial situations, government supports, doctors, and values, so our choices will be different.

Judgment of others should never happen. For us, therapy, communication, inclusion, and new medical treatments have all been a huge part of assisting our daughter through the challenges RS gives her each day. We are at peace with this and her smile each morning and the love she gives us and the joy she is to us are the most precious, spectacular gifts I can ever speak about. This is our journey and our choices within it. Yours will be different and that is right for you. Not wrong, just your journey.

WHAT EVERY THERAPIST SHOULD KNOW

THE GIRL WITH RS OFTEN APPEARS NONCOMPLIANT or uncooperative and disinterested. Actually, she knows quite well what she wants to do, but she is simply incapable of making it happen because of her severe apraxia. She knows what she wants to say, but cannot say it. Given proper support and encouragement, she can make active choices. Having control over what she does is powerful motivation, which leads to greater cooperation and success.

The therapist must capture her attention and maintain emotional contact with her throughout the therapy session. If she feels too much pressure, she will withdraw and the benefits of therapy will be limited. Verbal input from the therapist is vital and can help her motor planning. Don't talk down to her.

After being in therapy for about ten out of her eleven years of life, so far, every week of the year, and many days of every week, I certainly understand when Lyndie gives a therapist a hard time. She shows much more patience and perseverance than I know I would in the same situation. Like all of the rest of us, she just appreciates being treated with respect and then tries very hard to cooperate to the best of her abilities.

Emily does better with a full schedule. The input, stimulation and focus work are all good. The trick has been finding and working with really good therapists who can respond to her, recognize fatigue, build in breaks and nurture her even as they "push."

COMMON PROBLEMS

HYPOTONIA (DECREASED MUSCLE TONE) IS OFTEN DESCRIBED as "floppy" or "flaccid" tone. The muscles have limited readiness, and movement against gravity is difficult.

Therapeutic Approaches

Hypertonia (increased muscle tone) is referred to as "spasticity." Extension (movement in the opposite direction) is difficult and uncoordinated.

Soft tissue **contractures** are caused by abnormal shortening of muscle tissue, which causes the muscle to be very resistant to stretching. Contractures can lead to a complete loss of function of the body part. Contractures can come as the result of improper support and positioning of joints. Contributing factors are neurological damage which causes brain responses to stimuli to be different from the average person, and the force of gravity. Contractures are treated with active or passive exercise and supporting the joints to prevent constant shortening or stretching of the muscles and tissues which surround them.

Frogleg deformity occurs when the hips *abduct* (pull out) and externally rotate with some hip and knee flexion (bending). This deformity is usually seen with low muscle tone.

Windswept deformity is most often seen in the legs, although it can be seen in the arms. The child appears as though a strong wind has blown the extremities to one side of the body. In the legs, it causes abduction and external rotation of one hip and internal rotation of the other hip. Both legs will show some hip and knee flexion.

Scoliosis is a lateral curvature of the spine which varies in severity and location. The curve can be in the thoracic (upper back) region or in the lumbar (lower back) region. With the passage of time, the body compensates for the original curve by developing a secondary curve (usually higher than the original curve). This results in an "S" shaped curve. The cause of scoliosis is increased muscle tone. Specific positioning, bracing, and surgery are used to treat scoliosis.

Kyphosis is a forward curvature of the spine, often called "hunchback." Over time, kyphosis becomes more immobile and fixed. In RS, kyphosis seldom reaches a serious degree requiring surgery.

Decubitus ulcers (pressure sores) pose a risk for the child with RS because of decreased circulation, particularly in the lower extremities (and strong hamstring fixing). Skin breakdown, especially around the heels, must be anticipated whether casting because of a fracture or surgery. Both the PT and parents must be sure that whoever is applying the cast understands this risk.

CAUSES OF DEFORMITY

NEUROLOGICAL DEFICITS AND GRAVITY RESHAPE the structure and function of the body. Here is a list of some contributing factors:

- lack of appropriate position variety
- lack of active and passive movement
- use of inappropriate structural supports (such as positioning equipment)
- lack of adequate sensory stimulation
- lack of appropriate treatment

RESULTS OF DEFORMITY

THE MUSCULOSKELETAL SYSTEM PROTECTS and provides housing for internal organs. Each organ is arranged in a specific place within the skeleton and abdominal cavity. Changes in the shape of the skeleton or lack of upright orientation and normal movement patterns will have a direct impact on organs and their function.

Therapeutic Approaches

RESULTS OF IMMOBILITY

MUSCLE TONE AND BONE STRENGTH ARE MAINTAINED by normal movement. The results of immobility can be contractures, osteoporosis and skin problems (*decubitis* ulcers). It can also lead to primary changes in the cardiovascular system, including low blood pressure when changing positions, increased cardiac workload, and an increased number of blood particles adhering to the inside of vessels (*thrombus* formation). Gastrointestinal functions such as ingestion, digestion and elimination may be affected. Respiration becomes slower and shallower and lung secretions decrease. Urinary function, designed to work best when a person is upright, is compromised. Hormone secretion is reduced.

TREATMENT ASPECTS

THERAPISTS AND PARENTS SHOULD BE REALISTIC about treatment goals, but not hopeless. Too often, goals are based on outdated literature that refers to RS as a degenerative disorder. We have come a long way in realizing that RS is not degenerative, and girls can continue to learn and gain skills throughout their lives. RS is no longer seen as a disorder with a progressively downward turn. Therapies are essential for the development and maintenance of skills.

We know that the greatest handicap for the girl with RS is the enormity of her physical impairments. This often overshadows her ability to prove her knowledge and understanding. The girl with RS understands far more than what meets the eye. She is capable of taking in much more information than she can give out. Until recently, girls and women with RS have been classified as mentally retarded with little or no room for improvement. Intuition has always told us that she understands a lot. Recent scientific studies have illustrated this point.

With many disorders, repetition of the same activities over and over is reinforcing and, in time, will be "learned." However, in RS, no amount of repetition will completely restore hand function. It is not a matter of learning; it is a matter of making the brain connection necessary to carry through the required movement. Providing a variety of activities can lessen boredom and motivate her.

It is important to recognize that girls and women with RS have a severe delay in processing information. Apraxia makes it impossible for her to both think about it and do it. She does far better when she acts instinctively, without trying to figure out the movement or action in her head. It will take her longer to respond, so be patient with her efforts.

Finding positive and motivating activities that appeal to her emotions works best. Be patient. Giving verbal directions that call for her to think before she acts, may interfere with her ability to do so.

Since she seems to use one sensory channel at a time, looking and touching at the same time are as difficult as doing math and calisthenics at the same time. Choosing one impression at a time can greatly enhance her ability to concentrate.

Therapists should know that many of the behaviors seen in RS, particularly hand movements and breathing irregularities, are not under her control. They are happening *to* her, not *by* her. She can no more stop her hand movements, tooth grinding or hyperventilation at will that we can stop our hearts from beating at will. These behaviors increase when she is stressed and under pressure to perform. Instead of making demands, a positive approach

Therapeutic Approaches

with strongly motivating materials can help her temporarily "overcome" the severe apraxia and succeed. This is one reason why she is so successful at picking up pieces of food when she is incapable of picking up other objects, and why she can scratch her nose or rub her eyes when they hurt.

Katie hyperventilates when she is stressed, and her breathing gets heavier as demands are placed on her. I have felt when a demand is being placed on her, she knows what she is supposed to do, but at that moment, can't get her hand to move, as she knows we are expecting her to "perform."

TYPES OF THERAPY

THERAPY DOESN'T ALWAYS TAKE PLACE in a formal setting. Many daily activities can be therapeutic and fun as well.

We have always looked at therapy as a way to assist our daughter with the challenges RS gives her. We also feel therapy has given her a better quality of life than she would have had. This does not mean we do therapy ten hours a day. Never. It means we found a way to incorporate therapy into her daily life. Using her environment and buddy switches, she helps me make cookies. This could be thought of as practicing switch use (an OT goal) but we think of it as plain old fun. Mother and daughter time. Just seeing the big smile she gives and her chest pushed out with pride when Dad makes a fuss over the cookies she helped baked is enough.

Having her stand twice a day in a standing frame is therapy, but it is also done watching TV, listening to music and is so good for her. She smiles and sighs with relief when she is finally standing up straight. It is good for her back, her bones due to weight bearing, and great for the bowels. And she loves looking at me straight in the eye. She giggles when I tell her she is as tall as me.

Sometimes it's hard to keep up with therapy appointments. There are never enough hours in the day to do all that we want to. Don't get so busy running from one appointment to another that you forget the most important therapy of all, *love therapy.* It comes from your heart, your touch, your voice, all the things that say "I love you just the way you are."

Love therapy embodies all of the things that are so basic and important, such as acceptance, protection, patience, tolerance and understanding. All of the expensive and complicated therapies in the world cannot work without it. It starts with recognizing her as an important part of her family, her community, her world, our world. It wraps her up in the warm embrace of our belief that she is valuable and loved, no matter what she may ever achieve. It hears her cries and gives comfort, patiently awaits her sunny smiles with joy and tucks her in gently at twilight. It raises its fists for her when obstacles arise, and cradles her tenderly during long sleepless nights. Love does not give up in the face of adversity. It grows stronger.

Coordinating thirty hours of therapies with four therapists at home nearly killed me. I quit my part-time job, and pulled both kids out of day care so we could afford for me to stay home. Our lives revolved around all of her appointments at home and away. It was more than a full-time job. On the positive side, I learned a lot about working with her and supporting her. On the downside, I spent a year and a half acting as de facto case manager, coordinating her team. In retrospect, I'd rather have spent more time as Mom, less as case manager. I'm not sure it was the best situation for Emma's sister, either, though no real harm done.

Therapeutic Approaches

THE MOVE PROGRAM

THE PHILOSOPHY AND ATTITUDE of the MOVE program is, "Some things must be believed first before they can be seen," based on the idea that all children can progress in motor skills. The goal of the program is to start intervention early to try to eliminate some of the posture and positioning associated with scoliosis. In this program, every child is upright regardless of disability. The upright position allows the hips and lower body to straighten, the upper body to attain normal positioning, the diaphragm to lower, lungs to expand, and the intestines and all internal organs to remain in place. All of these aspects contribute to greater comfort. Visit the WE MOVE Web site at www.wemove.org.

I believe in the MOVE program because the curriculum is available to all. The beauty is that it does not need to be done by a special education teacher. When our daughter was included for the first time at her neighborhood school, the MOVE program was done by our general education teacher and aides. We had a MOVE mentor come out and help whenever needed. The program is so logical and the curriculum is very concise and easy for anyone to understand. It can be carried out while a child is simultaneously working on a computer, or doing other things on an IEP. For example, we incorporated MOVE while working in the classroom, and we also had Lani sometimes use the walker at recess so that she could play independently with the students, and not require an adult at her side. The kids decided they wanted to teach her football, and they devised their own method of teaching her. She got the MOVE program, peer interaction, occupational therapy (encouraging her to hold the ball), and fun all at once! The MOVE staff is so positive in looking at the children's strengths and expanding on them. Although not all children may actually result in being able to walk independently, I firmly believe that all benefit from the program in that at least their health improves significantly as long as they're encouraged to be upright. Our daughter's respiratory problems ceased once we had her upright, and everything just got better after that. Lani did learn to sit, stand, and walk. Folks who saw her six years ago, before we began the MOVE program are surprised to see how well she looks now. Before MOVE, her body was so atrophied, and she was very sickly, always on antibiotics. Today, her hips and legs have filled in beautifully and her physical stamina is always increasing.

PHYSICAL THERAPY

THE GOALS OF PHYSICAL THERAPY ARE TO MAINTAIN or increase motor skills, develop or maintain transitional skills, prevent or reduce deformities, alleviate discomfort and irritability, and improve independence. The physical therapist may assess and improve walking and sitting patterns, and monitor changes over time. The kind of approach taken will depend on her place in the staging process of RS. A physical therapy program must be individualized for each girl.

Stage 1 is usually overlooked. Many girls experience motor gains before a decline in hand function, play skills and communication emerges. Other girls are delayed in achieving motor milestones. As soon as a problem is detected, it is important to begin treatment in a physical therapy program aimed at independent sitting, standing, and walking.

Stage 2 is characterized by a loss of developmental milestones. This may happen over a short period of time, but more often occurs gradually. Gross motor skills continue to be significantly better than fine motor skills. The beginning of physical problems such as toe-walking or scoliosis may be seen. An emphasis should be placed on range of motion and ambulation. If she has severe *ankle pronation* (turning in), shoe inserts or ankle *foot orthoses* (AFOs) are recommended. Using assistive devices for walking is sometimes difficult due

Therapeutic Approaches

to her lack of hand control. Sometimes, arm/hand/elbow splints may be helpful to decrease stereotypic movements and increase functional use of the hands for gross motor activities. In this stage, her movements take on an ataxic quality, marked by lack of balance and jerky tremors. She is often very apraxic and fearful of movement that she does not initiate. Great care must be taken to comfort her, telling her how you will move her before doing so. She experiences problems with depth perception and often fears going down stairs or even changing floor textures from tile to carpet. She may always be fearful of movements, but your understanding will go a long way toward making her more at ease. Her constant hand movements interfere with using her hands for support and protection. Give her opportunities to use them.

In **Stage 3**, deformities and contractures may develop. *Kyphosis* or *scoliosis* may become more obvious. Seating equipment should be adapted to her needs for postural alignment and comfort. She may continue to walk and remain in Stage 3 for the rest of her life. If she does not walk, effective methods for lifting and transporting are essential.

Stage 4 is defined by loss of mobility. She may be able to continue to participate in a supported transfer (from bed to chair, etc.). Scoliosis and contractures may worsen as she loses mobility. She will most likely have circulatory problems, particularly in the hands and feet, which become cold, bluish and swollen. Feeding problems may increase with difficulty chewing and swallowing. In this stage, therapy should focus on range of motion, transfer skills, positioning and lifting, and evaluation for adapted or custom seating. Some girls with RS do not progress to Stage 4.

AIMS OF PHYSICAL THERAPY

PHYSICAL THERAPY is used to:

- reduce apraxia
- stimulate hand use to assist in mobility
- achieve better balance reactions
- promote better coordination and balance
- reduce ataxia
- improve body awareness
- influence scoliosis
- give better range of motion in the joints
- reduce muscle pain
- maintain and improve mobility
- counteract spasticity
- increase protective responses

The therapist must carefully evaluate her movement patterns to determine any obstacles to her motor function. These patterns can be modified with the use of a therapy ball, facilitation of movement, tone reduction activities and eliciting balancing responses. The girl's tolerance must always be considered, recognizing that she will probably resist being moved or manipulated.

Scoliosis and kyphosis often begin with tone problems, which are brought on by her inability to judge her own body's place in space (*orientation in space*). Tone altering activities, active exercise, and *passive range of movement* (ROM) exercises are helpful.

Therapeutic Approaches

Maintaining spinal alignment is important and can be facilitated by activities designed to provide *proprioceptive* (position in space), *kinesthetic* (sensations received from joints and muscles), and *tactile* (touch) awareness. Kinesthetic awareness combines proprioceptive and tactile input to give information on how the body is moving.

Girls who can walk should be encouraged to walk often. This stimulates the joints and muscles and helps her to better observe the environment. Patience is called for; she walks slowly and often stops or changes directions abruptly. Girls who do not walk should be encouraged to do weight bearing exercises and practice walking.

WHY PHYSICAL THERAPY?

In the twenty or so years since Rett syndrome has become more well known, incredible progress has been made, not only in discovering the gene responsible for the disorder but in management of daily life and health care for affected individuals. While cure is our goal, we must utilize all the tools available presently to make the best life possible. Physical therapy (PT) is an important one of these tools because of the motor problems that manifest in RS.

So, the next question is, "What constitutes a good life? Career? Wealth? Success?" Many of us define ourselves by the work that we do. If you ask me who I am, I am likely to say a physical therapist. Yet, since I retired nearly a year ago, that is not my defining role. Does that mean I find life less fulfilling, less fun, less challenging? Not in the least. Even those of us who love the work we do would name the fun times as those spent not at work, but in activities with people we are close to. We look forward to the evenings, the weekends, the vacations. In reality, our avocations define us as much as our vocations, maybe more. And, there are many who have lived happy lives without working at all.

We know that most children with RS will not grow up to work in the traditional sense, but whether this is cause for mourning or celebration depends largely on our attitudes and our planning. How do those who do not work stay active, happy, and healthy? To play one's way through life is not such a bad thing, and it gives us time for the truly important things in life, our relationships. After all, who is better at drawing people to them than our daughters? They have extraordinary skills in this area, and this is their joy and a major contribution they make to the lives of those they touch.

And what do we do to establish and develop relationships? We join groups of people with similar interests. We go out to eat or bowl or see a movie or sporting event, and we entertain. Can a person with RS plan a party? Of course. She can make choices of theme, food, activities, and guests. Swimming, bowling, horseback riding, walking, and other physical activities are possibilities. Collecting is an accessible hobby and an entrance to clubs and events. Shopping! Sports. Visits to the hairdresser, a concert, movies, bird watching, and various studies. Don't sell individuals with RS short. Explore their interests.

So, how is all this tied into physical therapy? Well, to do all these things, the person with RS is going to need help. The easier it is for the helper, the more likely it will be for the activity to take place. What makes it easy? Mobility. Lifting an adult is very difficult and it becomes more difficult as the helper gets older. Physical therapy can

Therapeutic Approaches

help identify skills that, if learned, can reduce the lifting necessary and increase independence. And if the necessary skills can't be learned, the PT can help devise compensatory equipment and methods to assist mobility and make doing things as easy as possible. Physical comfort will also influence a person's willingness to get out and do, so limiting deformities that cause discomfort improves the quality of life.

PT can't change the facts of RS, but it can mitigate the effects. Working from what we know of the diagnosis, we can anticipate problems to help guide us in the development of a physical therapy program. We know RS is a motor problem, actually a combination of several motor problems: Apraxia, hypotonia, ataxia, increased tone, rigidity, and involuntary movement.

Apraxia or dyspraxia, is the inability or difficulty to motor plan movement. The person knows what she wants to do, understands what you have asked her to do but can't pull together the sequence of moves to make it happen. It is not a conscious thing but something our brains do automatically. As we learn an activity, motor memory or a pathway is laid down and the more it is practiced, the easier it is to access or initiate that sequence of moves.

We seem to come preprogrammed to acquire basic motor skills. A baby does this in a fairly predictable sequence and recognizable movement patterns. But even with this preprogramming, a baby will practice a move over and over. The child with RS has a much harder time laying down these pathways, probably because of the scarcity of neuronal connections. In the typical brain with its plethora of connections, many neurons connect with many others, giving a wide path for the signal to travel. In the same physical area in the Rett brain, far fewer connections are made, leaving a very narrow path with many fewer options for transmission, alteration and adaptations and a much greater risk of interruption of the signal. This can also explain the loss of motor skills in this non-degenerative condition. Through normal pruning or dying off of neurons, connections are broken and there are no detours available to substitute. Much of physical therapy is directed to providing and assisting the practice needed to lay down the necessary pathways.

Involuntary movement takes many forms, the most common being hand wringing, hand to mouth, and body rocking. These repetitive movements are not under voluntary control and can so dominate the movement repertoire they block functional activity. Some folks, with major concentration and effort, can stop the stereotypies, but the moment their attention shifts to something else, the movements start again.

Ataxia is the loss of balance and regulation of trunk or limb stability. It produces the wide-based staggering gait and marked tremor often seen in those with RS. Intervention specific to this problem includes *balance practice, segmental rolling* (rolling over with a strong twist in the body), and *joint compression* when the body or limb is in the desired position. Some interesting success has been seen using a compression suit of neoprene covering trunk and hips.

Increased tone, fixing, and repeated motion become **rigidity** and/or structural deformity. This is a circuitous and complex process. For instance, in the child who hand wrings strongly, her hands are clenched together, usually near her chest (especially if she also has her hands going into her mouth). Her elbows are bent continuously, and her shoulders are rounded forward and pulled together, producing

Therapeutic Approaches

strong contractions of the muscles in the front of the chest and neck and arms. If there is asymmetry, the spine may be curved or rotated as well. Without intervention, the body tends to get locked in the position it assumes continually. Muscles and tendons shorten and bones may even deform. *Mobility* of the chest wall and shoulders must be maintained.

Fixing is a semi-voluntary movement or holding of the body in an effort (usually) to stabilize. Our faces twist when we concentrate on a fine movement with our hands; our knees flex when we walk on a slick surface; we brace all or part of our body against an actual or anticipated pain. Children with movement disorders will fix in an effort to function. They are usually unaware they are doing this and often cannot stop voluntarily. Braces are often necessary to reduce the resulting deformities. The most commonly used are ankle-foot orthoses and knee braces to increase extension.

Sensory disturbances, so closely paired with motor problems, are also present, and include alteration of orientation in space, depth perception, body awareness, and possibly parasthesias.

The purpose of PT is to develop and preserve function. So with all the things above to consider, how do we determine what to work on? This must be a collaborative effort between the family, the child and the therapist. The PT program for the infant and toddler should consist of maximum exposure to the basic movement patterns and variations, so that when interruptions occur, perhaps the break won't be total and the signal can still be transmitted. As the child ages and difficulties appear, practice should be directed to the most critical skills.

First, careful analysis is done of what skills are present and under what circumstances. We must try to determine what skills will contribute most to the child's quality of life and ease of care. What skills will support her interests? What skills are necessary now and in the future? Next, we must try to identify what is interfering with the child's use of a particular skill, and see if there is a way we can change it.

As an evaluation is done, it is important to remember that the child with RS has a long *latency* period and *often cannot perform on request.* Efforts at processing verbal information and trying to plan a movement and then initiate it make most responses take a very long time. It is easy to think the individual is not responding. *We must give them time.*

As for critical skills, here are some ideas to consider. You must evaluate these in terms of your own needs and lifestyle and decide which are most important to you.

Sit safely, with the least support possible. Ideally, individuals should be able to sit down and maintain position and balance with no back or side support, no seat belt, and even no foot support. They should be trustworthy to sit for a minimum of five minutes.

Stand; independently is best, but standing with help is nearly as useful. Standing while holding on or leaning against a wall increases independence. This skill allows for easier dressing, pulling up pants, smoothing dresses, and even changing diapers in a public restroom. Secure standing also allows one person to easily assist transfers from chair to car and bed and other furniture. This means increased comfort as the individual won't spend as much time in a wheelchair. It also makes it more likely the individual will get to go along on even quick outings.

Therapeutic Approaches

> **Walk independently or with assistance.** If this can get to be pretty easy, it cuts down on the number of times a wheelchair must be loaded and unloaded.
>
> **Independent movement of any means.** Crawl, bunny hop, walk, power chair or toy.
>
> The next consideration is how to compensate or substitute for the absence of critical skills. The PT can work with you to devise methods of moving that maximize the individual's participation and minimize the assistant's effort. This increases safety and frequency of movement. Equipment can substitute for lack of mobility or ability to maintain a position. Equipment can also be used to control or correct deformities. There are a plethora of things to help and a great variety of equipment out there. Talk to your therapist.
>
> There are several additional concerns with which physical therapy can help. The deformity which is the most problematical in RS is scoliosis. The incidence of scoliosis in those with RS is very high, 60-90 percent in different studies. To some extent, it is age dependent and the older the group, the higher the percentage affected. Unlike *idiopathic scoliosis* (of unknown origin), the progression of the curve in RS does not necessarily stop with the cessation of growth. Since this problem affects so many of this group, the safest approach is to expect it to show up. All activities should be done *symmetrically*, that is, as much to one side as the other should. Alternate sides so that she is not always fed from the same side or turning the same way to the TV. Encourage sleeping on alternate sides.
>
> A huge part of the therapist's job is to provide information to parents. The PT can help you learn how to do a lot of things. Ask questions; state you needs as well as your child's. Problem solving is part of the PT's job.

TRANSCUTANEOUS ELECTRICAL NERVE STIMULATOR (TENS)

DAILY EXERCISE SHOULD BE DONE TO GET THE HANDS over the head and out to the side. Using a TENS unit helps to get relaxation in the upper body. This may work because the hand motion might be due to *parathesias* in the hands. Parathesias are abnormal feelings like having your hand fall asleep, itching without reason or hurting when there is no damage, or a crawling sensation or tickling. Basically, it is any sensation that is perceived that has no stimulus creating it. Of course, this sort of problem may occur elsewhere in the body as well, and a full assessment of joint range should be done regularly.

PT HELPFUL HINTS

ENCOURAGE HER TO PARTICIPATE IN PHYSICAL ACTIVITY so she can learn how her body moves and reacts.

- Use stroking and massage to increase body awareness and relaxation and to decrease hypersensitivity.
- Name the parts of the body as they are being stroked or massaged.
- Tell her what you are about to do, or how you are going to move her.

Therapeutic Approaches

- Put her joints through full range of motion to prevent contractures and the decline of mobility.
- Provide weight bearing exercises that encourage protective responses in the arms.
- Provide appropriate seating at all times.
- Try to keep her as active as possible.
- Keep her moving with the physical support she needs.
- Use a ball pit/pool, waterbed, or trampoline for her to lie on to provide sensory stimulation if she is immobile.
- Allow adequate time for transition to a different activity or position.
- Provide gross motor activities that involve the entire body.
- Provide vestibular (balancing) movements like swinging, which stimulates other sensory systems.
- Provide strong gross motor stimulating activities, which open her senses.
- Integrate music into the PT program to keep her attention for longer periods of time.
- React with sound echoing her sound when she tries to express an emotion.
- Listen for and respond to any words she says appropriately.
- Using elbow splints may free her hands for functional support in gross motor skills such as walking or creeping.
- Foot deformities can be minimized by using exercise and short leg and ankle splints.
- Use a mirror to let her see her movements.

THINGS TO REMEMBER

1. Spinal mobility must be maintained. Structures on the *concave* (sunken) side of the curve are stretched, and those on the *convex* (arched) side are straightened.

2. The person's orientation in space must be evaluated. If her perception of upright has been altered by what is happening in her brain, she will adjust her posture to the upright she perceives. She will lean to align herself and strongly resist efforts to bring her back to actual midline. To correct her perception of midline, she must be leaned the other way to overcorrect her position. The trick is to convince her that it is OK to be there and get her to stay there fifteen to twenty minutes or more. It takes a lot of talking and physical assistance. Spinal flexibility and mobility must be worked on at the same time. Not only her position in space must be corrected, but body alignment as well.

3. If bracing is needed, the rest of the program needs to be followed as well. Acclimation to the brace may be easier than you expect. Another problem that has recently come to light is *osteoporosis*. X-ray bone density studies and bone biopsies have shown *osteopenia* (deficient bone mineralization) and osteoporosis (bone loss). While we have not studied the frequency of fractures clinically, it certainly appears that there is a higher incidence. This is all the more reason to maintain walking and physical activity while taking the necessary care.

IEP GOALS FOR PHYSICAL THERAPY

- Improve mobility in a variety of school settings including halls, classroom, playground
- Improve ability to get on and off the school bus
- Improve ability to access playground equipment

Therapeutic Approaches

- Improve ability to perform transfers and/or transitional movements in a variety of school settings.

- Improve strength and endurance needed for active participation throughout the school day.

- The physical therapist can make recommendations for positioning equipment, develop standing programs if appropriate, and serve as a consultant for adaptive physical education.

TYPES OF THERAPY

OCCUPATIONAL THERAPY IS IMPORTANT IN ADDRESSING problems our girls often have with functional performance. Occupational therapy provides ways to help her increase use of her body, particularly her hands. The byword of the OT is "adapt," whether it is the activity, materials, or the environment. The OT is very skilled at making an unattainable goal achievable. Since the girl with RS has so much difficulty using her hands, occupational therapy is essential for most of her activities of daily living. Increasing her hand use gives her satisfaction, confidence and great joy.

One important area for OT concentration is eating. Some girls do not lose feeding skills altogether, while others do. It may take intensive effort for her to relearn to feed. The most effective approach is giving physical assistance with a long-range goal to decrease the level of assistance over time. It is helpful to provide an adapted spoon, cup, and dish with plate guard or inner lip plate. There is a wide range of adaptive feeding equipment available that can make at least some independent feeding possible for almost any girl with RS.

Another area addressed by the OT involves the use of adaptive equipment and switches. With the appropriate technology and some switch training, most girls can achieve some control of their environment, play with toys, and become more fully integrated in school and community life. The OT can help determine what devices are appropriate, how they can be modified, and how the girl can be taught to access them. The OT is also useful in identifying specialized equipment and home modifications that can make life easier for the caregiver.

At Molly's private occupational therapy program, the people seemed more in touch with her than anyone else we had ever dealt with. The staff was incredibly tuned in to where she was at when she arrived. They would look at her and decide what she needed that day based on the way she was acting. Of all the people who ever worked with Molly, these were the ones I trusted the most. The people at this program gave me the feeling that the brain could improve, that there was the hope of improvement. This was one of the most positive environments Molly was ever in. No matter what she did, it was wonderful—even when she picked her nose! These people were so positive about everything that Molly did, I thought they were total Pollyannas. Little did I realize then that this would see me through years of public school when so often I was only told what Molly could not do. They gave me the confidence to realize just how together Molly was. They gave me back a perfect child.

Week after week, the OT would have Lyndie do often frustrating fine motor activities, such as trying to put blocks in a bucket or pick up puzzle pieces. This is such a tall order for Lyndie. Sometimes the therapist would put her on the computer, and sometimes she would enjoy it, sometimes not. At times, she would put Lyndie on a bolster swing, much to her delight. Other times the swing made her scream. Needless to say, no one ever knew what kind of a session would be in store for the therapist, or for Lyndie.

Therapeutic Approaches

Occupational therapy can also address problems with sensory processing. In RS, the sensory information coming into the brain is not well organized, making it difficult for the girl to respond appropriately to the information she is receiving from her environment. Sensory integrative therapy, using techniques such as brushing, swinging, tactile activities, and joint compression, can help her organize the information so that she is better able to respond.

Occupational therapists are some of the most creative people in the world. Sometimes, it is amazing what they can come up with—a simple solution to a very complicated problem. An attitude of warmth and caring can work wonders.

A helpful suggestion coming out of an OT assessment of Kim's balance and walking was tying bells on her shoes. This was so that she could hear when her feet hit the ground, since she could not feel her feet hit the ground. Many people, including teachers, have commented that she walks better with the bells.

We've been very fortunate to have therapists who really enjoy working with special needs children and love them for who they are. I believe this is the key factor in how Kara responds during her sessions. She currently has an OT who seems to struggle with her personal feelings. She's harsh, impatient, and rushes her through the session. I strongly believe Kara is able to pick up on this and therefore, doesn't respond to her very well. I've heard repeated stories from her PT and classroom teacher whereby the OT will ask Kara to do something and she won't do it. The PT will then ask her to perform the same task and Kara will respond positively.

Kara's very first OT was harsh in her mannerisms but yet was very encouraging and always praised her whenever she did something positive. Kara made great gains. I believe the attitude and approach taken with our girls, coupled with lots of praise, are the passports as to whether we experience positive or delayed results.

When a girl with RS is able to achieve a new movement or say something, it comes from her heart, not her head. So, when she does succeed, it is a real cause for celebration. She may say an appropriate phrase or perform a motor movement that is never repeated again. When this happens, she has broken through the apraxia to give us a rare glimpse of what she is capable of understanding.

OT HELPFUL HINTS

- Try to minimize distractions at first, gradually moving the situation closer to reality (less secluded).
- Look for what she intended to do with her hands, not just the end result.
- Provide physical assistance in the amount needed at first, gradually moving the situation closer to reality (less secluded). Guide her through the motions with your hand over hers.
- Restrain or hold the nondominant hand down to increase function in the dominant hand during functional activities.
- Weighted vests can be calming and decrease ataxia in some girls.
- Splints can be used to hold the thumb in a better position for picking up objects.
- During the regression stage, do not place primary importance on fine motor skills. Instead, provide hand activities that give enjoyment, such as splashing water or beating a drum.
- Adapt objects, materials and equipment so they are easier to grasp or maneuver.
- Use utensils with special cuffs or loops; plates with an edge to rest the spoon, and cups with a semicircle cutout for the nose.

Therapeutic Approaches

- Use switches for battery-operated toys or devices which can be operated by simple pressure or touch.
- Switches can also be used to achieve independence by activating any electrical appliance, operating computers, turning lights on and off, starting the TV/VCR, running a mixer or blender, etc.
- Place and hold objects of varying weight and texture in her hands.
- Fix objects to her hands with Velcro, masking tape or an Ace bandage.
- Put her hands in a pan of water, sand, snow, shaving cream, Jell-O, beads, beans, balls … whatever she might like to feel with her fingers.
- Massage her hands with a vibrator, brush, or lotion.
- Promote arm extension movements by progressively increasing the distance she has to reach for an object.

IEP GOALS FOR OCCUPATIONAL THERAPY

- Identify and encourage use of head, elbows, or other body parts over which she may have better control.
- Maximize hand use for functional activities.
- Develop ability to access communication devices.
- Develop ability to access a variety of assistive technology.
- Improve ability to assist with dressing.
- Improve ability to perform independent feeding skills.
- Improve ability to assist with grooming activities.
- Improve ability to tolerate sensory input in the school setting.

The occupational therapist can also serve as a consultant, recommending classroom modifications needed to improve the girl's ability to participate in school-related activities and with peers. The OT can also monitor the need for adaptive equipment and make recommendations.

COMMUNICATION THERAPY

RS IS KNOWN TO AFFECT *EXPRESSIVE LANGUAGE* (communicating with others) far more than it affects *receptive language* (understanding). Apraxia and more basic motor difficulties which involve chewing and swallowing combine with a lack of words or effective body language to make finding ways a girl can communicate functionally quite challenging. Speech-language therapists sometimes want to work on "speech readiness" skills such as making and imitating different sounds for several years before turning to other methods. In RS, however, these speech readiness skills may be absent and remain so. The girl with RS may demonstrate her potential for communicating in other ways, such as showing her ability to understand language.

In addition, therapists sometimes spend hours preparing the girl to use a communication device by asking her to touch pictures or objects named over and over or to match pictures with objects. She may rebel at this, possibly thinking, "I already showed her I could do that. Why is she asking me again?" Other girls are simply inconsistent in their responses from day to day, so that it is impossible to obtain a goal of 90 percent accuracy three days in

Therapeutic Approaches

a row, as is sometimes stated in IEPs. Therapists should assume that the concept is understood with a couple of correct responses and be willing to move on. Because her frustration comes much more from her inability to express herself than to understand, therapy should focus on increasing expressive communication.

> *Katie's cognitive abilities are pretty good. I cannot get through to therapists and teachers about her need to communicate. They want to start at such a small step with picture communication. I see so many of the girls catch on so fast. I believe a lot of Katie's tantrums would decrease if she had a means of communication.*

If she does not recognize pictures at first, she will learn the meaning through successes. For example, when using a voice output device, the message for the picture is heard each time, and someone responds in a way that teaches its function and usefulness. When you think you hear her say a word, you did! Respond appropriately.

Speech-language therapists need to work together with other therapists, staff, and families to explore potentially successful means of communication, effective positioning and needed vocabulary.

When new methods or devices are tried, it may be best to limit their use to specific times of the day or specific activities. It is better to enrich a single activity really well, than to water things down in a way which is never really helpful.

Sessions may best take place in the classroom or throughout the school or home, to practice and make the use of new communication methods both fun and functional. Additional time for developing systems, programming devices, and training staff and families may need to be built into a therapist's scheduled time. Sessions might also be combined with those of other therapists so that movement, sequencing, and communication all occur together. The girl with RS should be seen regularly, although frequency may vary, for the amount of time she can stay focused. Frequency of sessions may need to increase when a new communication method is introduced and tried until the girl, staff and family are familiar with it and comfortable using it in functional settings.

IEP Goals for Communication

- Utilize individualized communication strategy (AAC, FC, "yes/no," etc.)
- Communicate information
- Communicate knowledge
- Make choices
- Increase socialization with peers
- Communicate health feelings
- Increase class participation

More information is available in the chapter on Communication.

MUSIC THERAPY

MUSIC HAS ALWAYS HAD A STRONG INFLUENCE on behavior. It provides a powerful means to express emotions, thoughts, and experiences. As the famous composer Johann Sebastian Bach said, music has the power to "restore health to our souls."

Therapeutic Approaches

Studies have shown that hearing and making music have a positive effect on the brain, increasing blood circulation, glucose and oxygen. These changes stimulate learning.

Music therapy (MT) is the structured use of music or musical activities under the direction of a trained music therapist. These activities influence changes in behavior patterns that lead to specific individual goals that have been set for the child. Music therapy intervention focuses on acquiring non-music skills such as communication, socialization, choice making, and motor skills.

We know that girls with RS can communicate and express their feelings through music, but the music alone cannot do it. There needs to be a person behind the music, a messenger, a facilitator who acknowledges her feelings. People with RS are extremely sensitive to the quality of music and to the person who is behind the music. They know when they are being communicated to. Listening to music occurs on a *receptive* level, where she listens and enjoys, and also on a more *interactive/communicative* level. At this level, she can express her emotions and will have a partner to share those emotions with. The therapist is attuned to her and the music becomes meaningful.

The music can be either structured music, such as songs, or it can be improvisational music, music that is made up on the spot. Giving her a way to express herself through music opens her to opportunities for learning. Music therapy is such a motivating mode and through it, therapists are enabled to find those undiscovered channels, build confidence, and work toward independence. It is important to recognize that people with RS only cooperate when the activity is meaningful and interesting. Music therapy allows choice making and encourages initiation of hand use. Letting her know that you are there for her and that she can take her time will reduce her anxiety level. The more she has opportunities and the more she practices, the faster she will become, again only if it is meaningful. Music therapy can increase the level of awareness, elicit vocalization and increase focus, attention and eye contact.

For girls with RS, music therapy is an excellent supplement to other forms of therapy. Music provides a sense of perception and movement rhythm, and the therapist creates musical "curves of excitement," calling on her to respond to the music with her own actions. She learns to feel and understand time and space, quality, quantity, and cause and effect. Provided in a trusting, non-threatening atmosphere, music therapy can yield:

- the stimulation of a variety of musical experiences: texture, pitch, mood, pace, intensity, idiom-style.
- opportunities to enjoy making music spontaneously.
- experience of movement and playing instruments that can promote body awareness and a more purposeful use of her hands.
- musically induced relaxation to facilitate freedom of movement and expression.
- opportunities for communication and self-expression.
- stimulation for meaningful eye contact.
- motivation for the extending of attention and concentration span.
- a basis for increased memory/recall.
- a stimulus for decreasing the "delayed response."
- facilitation in grasping/holding.
- improvement in self-image and self-esteem.
- impetus for sensory-motor development.

Therapeutic Approaches

- favorable settings for social and emotional growth.
- an increase in vocalization.

The length and frequency of music therapy sessions will depend on the therapist or the school where it is provided, and the limits of what insurance will pay. She should get MT as often as she can. Some music therapists recommend two thirty-minute individual sessions a week and once or twice a week group music therapy. Sometimes they are limited to fifty to sixty minutes per week. However, most music therapists will consult with teachers and other team members on how to most effectively use music throughout the day.

Whether your child receives group or individual music therapy or whether she does not have any formal program with a registered music therapist, it is important both at school and home to integrate music to cue, soothe, and motivate, for music is powerful for girls with RS.

You may want to ask your daughter's physician or neurologist for a recommendation for music therapy. Remember to stress the fact that girls with RS are very motivated by music. It calms them when they are anxious, and allows them to communicate feelings they cannot otherwise express. To have music therapy provided through your daughter's IEP, you may need to be persuasive. Be prepared with written materials supporting the importance of music therapy for girls with RS. You may need to find a registered or certified music therapist to do the initial music therapy assessment. You will probably have to pay for it and may be able to be reimbursed by the school system. The assessment will include a recommendation for treatment.

FINDING A CERTIFIED MUSIC THERAPIST

LOCATING A GOOD THERAPIST MAY BE A CHALLENGE. In some parts of the country, music therapists are more difficult to find. Use contacts in the disability community to find someone who may qualify. Contact the music therapy consultant for the school district, the department of music therapy at a college or university, professionals in other fields who may know of a music therapist. Mental health care facilities may be a source. Contact the American Music Therapy Association, (301) 589-3300.

MUSIC THERAPY HELPFUL HINTS

- The setting for music therapy sessions should be quiet, without distractions. Sessions should be held about the same time of day in the same room.
- It is very important to establish a relationship between therapist and child. Establish a connection through eye contact, finger movement, a smile, or a look. This may take some time, as she becomes adjusted to the surroundings of the music therapy setting.
- The therapist should nurture contact with the child. It is essential to see her contribution to the session as valuable.
- Each girl has her own taste for music and sound. It is good to use short, repetitive, rhythmical songs when she is young. The repetition makes it familiar, and this provides confidence and security.
- Use music with a strong rhythm. It organizes her inner pulse and rhythm.
- Use movement songs, beginning with hand over hand assistance, then modeling, encouraging her to try and copy your movements.

Therapeutic Approaches

- Remember her delayed response and always give her plenty of time to respond.
- Make a page or card for each song, and slowly introduce the songs with the card. Fold the card in two parts, one with a picture (symbol) of the song, and the other with a word describing the song. Then let her choose the song she would like to play or hear.
- Sing familiar songs.
- Sing in a high pitch.
- Sing softly close to her ear.
- Make up your own songs with the appropriate text. Use her name and familiar things and people in the song.

IEP GOALS FOR MUSIC THERAPY

STRESS THAT MUSIC WORKS on the development of the following skills:

- to enhance purposeful hand use while playing instruments.
- to develop vocalization through music.
- to build independence choosing songs and activities.
- to communicate in musical activities through picture symbols.
- to increase cognition by raising the level of focus, attention, anticipation and imitation.
- to improve gross motor movements through movement songs.
- to increase socialization through participation.

MASSAGE THERAPY

BODY MASSAGE IS SOOTHING AND RELAXING. It may take her some time to adjust to lying down if she is very mobile, but in time she will love it.

We take Joanne for massage therapy about every two weeks. We have been doing this for over a year and have found it to be very helpful. Often it's hard for us to know if she is feeling pain in a certain area but our massage therapist can tell us if particular muscles are tight. It's nice to be able to know where it hurts, so to speak! Also massage therapy has helped Joanne to be more comfortable in any physical activity, as her muscles are not feeling too tight. Plus there's always the added benefit of relaxation! To be honest, Joanne loves her massage therapist and is always quite excited when she gets her turn!

HYDROTHERAPY

HYDROTHERAPY (MOVEMENT IN WARM WATER) IS ESSENTIAL for the girl with RS. Due to her apraxia, she is unable to plan and carry out movements she would like to make, and walking is always insecure. When other forms of mobility are decreased or lost, movement in water is still possible. Spontaneous movement is much easier in water and hydrotherapy increases range of motion and reduces spasticity. Sensory and perceptual difficulties which she feels on the ground are not present when she is in water, so she is able to achieve better balance without hesitation and fear. Viscosity and pressure provide proprioceptive and tactile stimulation. The water provides support for her limbs, giving her the confidence she needs to bear weight. This helps her to increase muscle bulk, strength and flexibility. The warmth of the water helps to calm the involuntary

Therapeutic Approaches

movements, hand stereotypies, and breathing irregularities and increases passive range of motion to a greater degree. Flexibility of the water allows her to move in all planes and allows symmetrical movement which may be difficult on the ground. Buoyance relieves her of her weight, and allows the therapist to provide treatment with greater and less effort by lifting her into desired positions. It also provides her with support for movement, allowing her to move more easily. Hydrotherapy contributes to the health of muscle and nerve, which her inactivity on ground impairs. It promotes her overall health and well-being, which greatly add to her capacity to learn.

HYDROTHERAPY HELPFUL HINTS

- The water should be warm, from 96 to 100 degrees.
- If she is thin, she may chill easily. Keep her wrapped in a towel before and after she enters the water. A neoprene vest can help prevent heat loss.
- Keep movements gentle and subtle until she adjusts to the water.

HIPPOTHERAPY

HIPPOTHERAPY (HORSEBACK THERAPY) is a treatment which utilizes the movement of the horse or activities on the horse to address impairments, functional limitations and disabilities. The therapist treats the participant in approximately forty-five minute individual treatment sessions. The therapy sessions take place in a highly structured environment with the use of additional assistants for safety and optimum results. Techniques may include gross/fine motor coordination via neuromuscular re-educating or therapeutic activities, gait training, sensory integrative activities, therapeutic exercise, and soft tissue mobilization.

Great care must be taken to be sure the child or adult is centered exactly on the horse and that the horse is not limping. This activity helps promote balance and torso strength, and requires the use of her hands, thus minimizing hand stereotypies and increasing functional hand use. She gains a sense of control, which gives her confidence and satisfaction. Being on the back of a moving horse also helps her experience the rhythm she needs to walk. The program provides the participant with a variety of sensorimotor experiences through changes of position on the horse. These changes develop body awareness, improved posture and balance, coordination and motor-planning.

Kara truly loves participating in therapeutic horseback riding through the North American Riding for the Handicapped Association (NARHA). The program includes a certified riding instructor or, at times, a physical therapist who provides direct handling and cuing. To participate in the program, Kara was first evaluated by a physical therapist. Since the sessions are due to her physical needs, a prescription for physical therapy services was needed. The program is currently not reimbursable through insurance, but we're working toward that goal.

While Kara is on the horse, a physical therapist walks next to the horse in addition to two other adults, one on either side of the horse. She has been on the horse frontward, backward, both legs on the left and both on the right side. They have also had her on her back which she tolerates, but not for long. While Kara was on backward, they practically had her in the crawl position with her hands toward the back of the horse.

The therapist observed that Kara uses the wrong muscles to breathe, and she feels the therapy will make her become aware of the appropriate muscles to be used. Kara also treats her entire upper body as one unit, and the therapy should help her make more isolated movements that are more natural for others.

Therapeutic Approaches

HIPPOTHERAPY GOALS

- Further development of head and trunk position control
- Further development of equilibrium reactions in the trunk and pelvis
- Mobilization of the pelvis, lumbar spine and hip joints
- Improve dissociation of body parts
- Improve body symmetry
- Improve body awareness
- Improve sensorimotor integration
- Improve proximal stability and/or co-contraction
- Improve vestibular reactions
- Improve eye-hand coordination and/or spatial orientation
- Improve motor planning skills
- Improve strength and/or endurance
- Improve ambulation skills
- Improve timing and rhythm
- Improve transfer skills

Taylor is very comfortable on the pony and shows excellent balance. Her normal hand mouthing activity is virtually stopped while she is riding. She has a huge smile and lets out periodic bursts of happiness with her voice. Two people work with her at a time. One leads the pony and the other walks along side with an arm around Taylor's backside. She especially likes it when they trot. The instructors occasionally spin her around backward on the saddle, to stimulate different muscle groupings. She is a little nervous when they are repositioning her, but she is just as happy forward and backward as long as they are moving. Taylor has begun to hold the reins all by herself instead of holding just the saddle knob. The instructors press her legs into the pony when starting from a stop. I'm sure that in time, Taylor will learn the correlation they are patiently teaching her. This is a wonderful activity and something Taylor can enjoy forever.

Chelsey smiled almost the whole time she was riding. She even held on to the saddle most of the time. They walked her up to a huge mirror in the arena and told her to look at herself and Mr. Snipper, and she looked and smiled. That really surprised me! Chelsey has never been one to look in a mirror.

Karina rides forty-five minutes without putting her hand in her mouth! From the beginning, we warned her that she had to stop riding if she did not hold on to the saddle. When she started to take off her protective cap, we did the same. She learned quickly after she had to dismount a couple of times. Now the teacher is teaching her to sit upright, as she tends to let her head hang low.

I can still remember the first day of riding, a month or so before her third birthday. I put my little girl on top of this massive animal and watched them walk away. When she was on the far opposite side of the ring 150 feet away, I realized that was the first time in her life she had ever been that far away from both parents at once. Over the time she has been riding, we have seen Naomi make tremendous strides in her awareness and responsiveness.

Kim has been riding for about two years with Riding for the Disabled. She was assessed, and now rides the police horses which are very big (many were once racehorses). They are very well trained and don't frighten easily. They are trained to tolerate people jumping out of trees at them! Once the horse moves her balance is excellent. Her holding on to the saddle is inconsistent unless the path of the horse keeps changing! So they never walk her in a straight line! She cannot manage to hold reins. Sometimes she has to trot, but as she cannot rise up and down she rather goes "plop plop plop" or "flop flop flop" with people on each side holding her on and running along beside her! Kim shrieks with excitement.

Therapeutic Approaches

THERAPIES AT SCHOOL

SCHOOL SYSTEMS VARY IN THEIR REGULATIONS not only from state to state, but often from county to county, so there is no one method for success. Most allow for private evaluations to determine eligibility for therapies given at school. Payment for services often comes from more than one source, including the school district, Medicaid, children's services, and private medical insurance.

Parents often disagree with the amount of time allowed, and must rely on their child's doctor's recommendations and other advocates to try to persuade the system to increase therapy time. One argument used to deny services is that RS is a degenerative disorder and the child will not be able to improve. This is untrue. RS is not degenerative and all kids can benefit from therapies. It may be necessary to copy a page from this book or get a statement from the doctor.

The best situation is when teachers and therapists form a team approach to treating the child with RS. Many of the goals for different therapies overlap, so that sharing information and co-treating are the keys to success.

Now that Emma is in pre-school, it is better for all of us, and I volunteer in her classroom in the morning each week, so feel like I am well connected. I do notice that her care and therapy are much better coordinated now that she is in a setting where all her providers function as a team.

Generally, the school is only mandated to provide therapies which are "educationally relevant." Therefore, the IEP The goal will not be to maintain or improve a motor skill. Instead, it should state the educational goals: good communication, good functional skills, and good motor skills. If abilities are lost, those IEP goals won't be reached, therefore therapeutic services will be needed.

For example: "Susie will walk to the office each day to deliver daily attendance sheets, choosing the correct location with minimal assistance. She will greet office staff by looking at them, and then return to her classroom." If Susie does not have good strength and balance skills, she will need PT services to achieve this goal.

Another example: "Jane will use hand switches in order to participate in classroom activities." If Jane does not have good range of motion, she will need OT to achieve this goal.

Music therapy is one therapy that is often challenged. Again, IEP goals must refer to the educational benefits of MT. One parent wrote the following request:

Melinda is presently receiving group music instruction three times a month. Music is a very strong motivator for her. We believe it is the best teaching tool to reach Melinda in her educational setting to achieve her maximum potential.

Music therapy helps Melinda to promote positive social responses and cognitive awareness, as well as eliminating her stereotypic hand movements so that she is more capable of focusing. It also helps in developing a basic understanding of cause and effect relationships, which is a goal we have been working on, but doesn't seem to be getting through using other traditional methods.

Therapeutic Approaches

> Music therapy is recognized as one of the related services in the IDEA that can be used to assist the learning of a child with a disability. Dr. Andres Rett has pointed out that the music center is a primitive part of the brain, which seems to be preserved in girls with RS. Therefore, learning experiences presented through the medium of music therapy may be more easily received and comprehended by girls with RS.
>
> We feel Melinda's educational goals would have a greater chance of being achieved if she had individual music therapy. For this reason, we are requesting an assessment to be done by a certified music therapist to determine if this would benefit her special education needs. Please contact me to set up a date for an assessment. Thank you.

POSITIONING AND SEATING

GIRLS WITH SEVERE PHYSICAL CHALLENGES require positioning, handling, and seating techniques which will improve and optimize their physical health and well-being. It is important to be vigilant in recognizing when changes in quality of positioning are necessary. When a range of positioning options is not used, gravity reshapes the body into the predominant position.

Symmetry (when divided in half, the two parts of the body are mirror images) is important, particularly in resting positions. Passive positioning in an *asymmetrical* (unbalanced) position for long periods should be avoided.

POSITIONING OPTIONS

SUPINE AND ELEVATED SUPINE (lying on the back) can cause muscular deformities and it makes the flowing of food very difficult. Eating and drinking should never be done when lying down because gravity drags the facial and oral structures into positions that are unsafe for swallowing. Stomach contents have to climb uphill to get to the small intestine. However, it is a good resting position if there are no abnormal reflexes present. Backlying can be used to give joint extension when the joints have been flexed for a long time. In this position, the individual must work harder against gravity and to coordinate eye-hand activity, especially at eye level. Using a wedge to elevate the head up to about forty-five degrees can eliminate the problem with gravity and the difficulty using the arms.

Prone resting (lying on the stomach) is a good resting position. Monitor the position by making sure the pelvis is level and flat on the resting surface. The head and trunk are straight, the navel, knees, and toes are pointed down, the face is turned to one side, and the knees and ankles are slightly bent with support and separated. The head should be resting on a comfortable surface.

Prone on forearms (lying on the stomach propped by forearms) is a working position. Without using a wedge, this position is difficult to maintain. This position stimulates head righting and increases head and neck extension, flexion, and rotation. It also allows weight bearing through the shoulders and arms, increasing their stability. It helps weight shifting and decreases abnormal reflexes. The position encourages reaching, assists with oral alignment and stimulates gastric emptying.

Quadruped on forearms (hands and knees position) calls for supporting the arms directly under the shoulders with the head free. It is a hard-working position and should

Therapeutic Approaches

be limited. This position increases hip flexion and adduction, and allows weight bearing through the arms and legs. It encourages a wide range of controlled head movements and stability and a weight shift through the shoulders and hips.

Sidelying (lying on the side) is the most frequently used position for sleep. This position promotes stomach emptying (lying on the right), helps breathing, and brings the head, arms and legs to midline gradually. It helps normalize muscle tone and can be used for eating if the head is elevated above the stomach. It also helps decrease gastroesophageal reflux.

Kneeling and supported standing is used to encourage weight bearing, which helps prevent hip dislocation and strengthens bones. An upright posture helps the function of internal organs, and helps with head and trunk balance. The use of upper extremities is improved.

SEATING OPTIONS

ACTIVE SEATING IS MORE EFFECTIVE in combating scoliosis than fully supportive seating. But a child can not sit actively all the time, so supportive seating must be correct and the child positioned exactly each time it is used. Once scoliosis appears, treatment must intensify. Stroller type wheelchairs are not indicated for girls with RS, as they do not provide the correct back support. Some of these travel-type chairs do come with additional back support.

Whether the seating is in a regular chair or a wheelchair, if the seating is proper, some important benefits are gained:

- safe eating, digestion and better chances of good elimination
- helps balance the head and gives freedom of movement when turning
- improves visual field
- allows mobility
- stabilizes the pelvis with more freedom of movement of the arms and hands
- increases trunk control

Basic Rules for Seating

- The pelvis should be maintained in a slight anterior pelvic tilt, level and parallel to the supporting surface of the back.
- The seatbelt stabilizes the pelvis. It should be snug over the pelvis.
- All body parts that are not perpendicular to the line of gravity (feet and forearms) should be supported.
- Trunk weight should be spread equally on the bottom of the pelvis.
  The seat-to-back angle should not be less than 100 degrees, to put body's center of gravity over the pelvis. A lesser angle pushes the center of gravity in front of the pelvis, which requires significant extensor activity to stay upright. It will cause fatigue and discomfort, and may increase muscle tone and reflexes.

Alignment

- The pelvis should be at a slight anterior tilt and de-rotated. You should be able to slide a flat hand into the small of the back. The buttocks should be in contact with the back chair surface.

Therapeutic Approaches

- Make sure the *anterior superior iliac spines* (landmarks used to monitor the position of the pelvis) are level and parallel to the back chair surface.
- The trunk should be straight, with the nose, navel and pubic bone pointing in the same direction.
- The shoulders should be level and the head should be erect. You should be able to put a flat hand comfortably between the back of the neck and chair.
- A weight bearing surface should be provided for the forearms.

MEDICATIONS

THE FOLLOWING LIST CONTAINS MEDICATIONS which parents of girls with Rett syndrome have tried and recommended. It is important to remember that different individuals vary in their response to different drugs.

- **Please discuss any medications with your child's physician.**
- Please disclose any supplements you may be using to your physician.
  Drug interactions can occur between medications and herbal supplements.
- All meds, including supplements, may have side effects that are unacceptable to you.
- Very few of these medications have been evaluated in a scientific (double blind placebo controlled) fashion, therefore, this list is the result of collective and sometimes anecdotal experience.
- None of these (except Revia) has been systematically studied in girls with Rett syndrome. We extrapolate from studies on children with global developmental delays, autism, cerebral palsy or mental retardation for possible usefulness in Rett syndrome.

Aggression

Clonidine

Anxiety/Agitation

Buspar, Ativan, Seroquel, Risperdal

Apnea

Buspar, Revia, Ritalin, Magnesium Citrate

Bowel Irritation

Bentyl, Levsin

Constipation

Miralax, Milk of Magnesia, Senekot, Lactulose

Depression

Prozac, Celexa, Nortriptylene, Zoloft

Drooling

Atropine Drops, Levsin, Robinul, Scopolamine patch, Botox injections

Therapeutic Approaches

Dystonia

Valium, Klonopin, Neurontin, Baclofen, Artane, Sinemet, Zanaflex

Gastroesophageal Reflux

Prilosec, Prevacid, Reglan, Carafate, Nexium, Protonix, Bethanecol

G-Button granulation/irritation/infection

Silver Nitrate, Zincofax, Tea Tree Oil, Maalox, Eucalyptus oil, 1% Hydrocortisone cream, Nystatin, Bactroban

Hyperactivity

Clonidine

Intestinal Gas

Gas-X, Maalox, Mylanta, DiGel, Bean-O.

Osteoporosis

Fosamax, Pamidronate, Calcium supplements

Note: Pamidronate has been used in children with osteogenesis imperfecta on study protocol, particularly because of the severity of fractures in children with this disorder. In some girls with RS who have had four and five fractures, Pamidronate would be a consideration, but would require very careful monitoring. There are many uncertainties about the use of this class of drugs.

Seizures

Tegretol, Keppra, Klonipin, Neurontin, Valium, Tranzene, Ativan, Depakote, Depakene, Zarontin, Lamictal, Luminal, Dilantin, Mysoline, Topamax, Zonegran, Trileptal, Versed

Self-Abuse

Seroquel, Revia, Risperdal

Sleep

Ativan, Trazadone, Melatonin, Clonidine, Cyproheptadine syrup (2 mg/5ml) (increases appetite), Remeron, Ambien, Atarax, Chloral Hydrate

Spasticity

Valium, Botox, Baclofen

Stomach Emptying

Reglan, Motilium

Tooth Grinding

Magnesium supplement

Therapeutic Approaches

Vitamin and Mineral Supplements
Flintstones Complete, Bugs Bunny Complete, Centrum Complete

"There are only two ways to live your life. One is as though nothing is a miracle. The other is as though everything is a miracle."

– ALBERT EINSTEIN

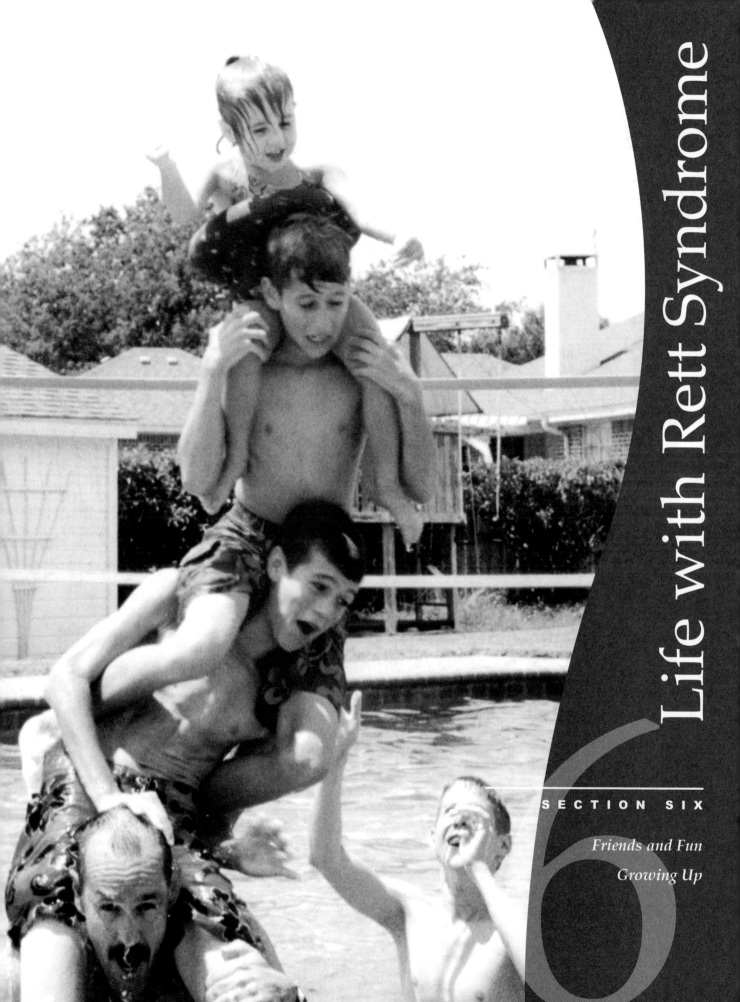

6

SECTION SIX

Friends and Fun

Growing Up

Life with Rett Syndrome

Growing Up

Friends and Fun

Friends and Fun

GIRLS JUST WANNA HAVE FUN

YOUR DAUGHTER may be a child with RS, but first and foremost, she is a child. She may need therapies, braces, and adapted equipment. Often, she may need medicines and special foods. She may need lots of patience from time to time. Now and then she may need extra attention. But always and forever, she needs friends. And she needs fun! Remember that your daughter is more like other children than unlike them. Fun is good for everyone.

One of the best ways to make sure your child is having fun is to let go and have fun yourself. It doesn't have to be expensive or complicated; it is mostly an attitude. Everyone needs some playfulness in their life. Laughter, having a good time and playing are very worthwhile pursuits. Make sure than fun is way high on your priority list.

Friends make fun even more fun! Look for ways to include others in your daughter's life, whether through school, church or the neighborhood. It is these friends who will develop into caring relationships–after all, these are the kids who will grow up to vote for laws and programs to support her. Most of all, they will learn to respect and value her.

You may think some things are impossible until you try them. Take a look at what some families and friends have come up with.

> *"Don't walk behind me; I may not lead. Don't walk in front of me; I may not follow. Just walk beside me and be my friend."*
>
> – ALBERT CAMUS

Initially, we felt some hurdles to getting out and doing things. All the packing just to go to the mall, or a trip to Grandma's: a cooler with pureed food, thickened liquids, a large bag with diapers, wipes, changing pad, emergency meds, change of clothes, etc. Once you get over this and get out enough, you no longer think of these things that you have to do as hurdles; they just become habit, second nature. And you become more efficient at it. Now, we just keep a backpack in the van with all the stuff we need. It's all in your mindset and attitude.

GETTING OUT AND ABOUT

GETTING OUT MAY BE TWICE AS HARD as the average family, and your time may be cut short when things just don't work out. It is a matter of hoping for the best and being prepared for the worst. You have to figure out what works and how to do it, but the effort you put into getting out is definitely worth it in the long run—for the whole family.

Catherine is messy and loud and does not always cooperate. I always have someone with me when we go to eat. She sits in a portable seat and we sit in a booth. We now bring a portable DVD player with us; it helps so

Friends and Fun

we don't have to rush. We try to go at the slower times and we tip a little extra. I always order her food when they take the drink order and I do bring in a few snacks just in case.

One hint for restaurant trips is to bring "new" toys with you. If it is fast food, I buy the kids' meal, which usually comes with a toy. I also keep a bag of toys in my car. Then when we go to a sit down restaurant, I surprise good manners with new toys. A radio and headphones are also great.

FINDING TIME

WITH ALL OF THE DAILY CARETAKING, SCHOOLING, therapies, and other family responsibilities, sometimes it's hard to make the time it takes to keep your child involved. At school, she may have a 1:1 aide who keeps her engaged, entertained, and busy all day long. Weekends may bring boredom when she has to wait for her share of attention.

During these times, it's natural to have her watch TV or listen to music. No one expects you to provide stimulating activities all the time. It helps when you can recruit others to join in the fun. Check out the kids in your neighborhood or school. They may be interested in getting to know your daughter and enjoy the same things she likes. You just have to keep your eyes open and then ask.

We kept busy with other kids' sports as well as their friends. As she got a bit older and went to school, she also had friends over. Amazing, they thought of the coolest things to do and didn't even need my help. They played hide and seek, did wheelchair races with old spare tires, swimming, told stories and jokes, and dressed her up in different outfits. They sometimes played games including her as a team member. As they got older, they would all go on trips to the movies, shopping, to the beach, out to eat, or whatever was going on. Non-disabled kids have the same problems of being bored sometimes, but don't need the intense assistance that our girls do. She still had some of these days but I didn't feel that it was up to me to keep her constantly entertained.

WHERE TO START

PAY ATTENTION TO WHAT OTHER CHILDREN HER AGE seem to like. Her interests may differ depending on her mood and her physical health on any one day. You don't have to plan activities for long periods of time.

We are lucky. We have several children in the neighborhood with disabilities (it is a new development and many people built ranch homes for the kids). We get together for walks, dinner, etc. We also have kids who are not disabled who like to push Erin in her wheelchair or help her in her gait trainer. We set up the sprinkler with Erin at the edge and the other kids run through. We set up the inflatable pool. Erin sits in the pool on a chair with the other kids playing around her.

Our family does a number of things for fun, from swimming with Joanne in the hot tub to going to the park and helping Joanne go around the garage on her scooter! One of the things we love to do is just be silly. We sing a lot of songs, imitate the voices of the characters in Joanne's favorite movies, and we take Joanne bowling!

You have to be a friend to make a friend. Remember that you might have to be the first one to include other kids in an activity. It will help show them how your daughter has fun and enjoys many of the same things they do.

Be able to "aid and fade." Be there to support but back off when others are interested or can offer the support.

Friends and Fun

For years I supported Joce in most of her activities, especially when she was little. But I often did it from a lit-tle distance, letting her friends and peers help her and support her while I was there doing something else but staying available if needed and to answer questions. As she got older and was in junior high school, this was even more important. Kids that age don't want to hang around adults. As kids spend time together and get to know each other better, they have more in common and develop their own special bonds.

As a teacher or parent, you can support positive interactions with peers by modeling positive behavior. Don't use baby talk. Be respectful and treat the individual age-appro-priately. It is very important to model the perceived competence of the kids, even if they can't be tested to "prove" their understanding. Talk about things that others are interest-ed in to help include your student/child into conversations. Girls with RS may not be able to speak, but they can communicate just fine when interested and when they are included in a conversation. If they know someone is really interested in what they think, it is also much more motivating to be actively involved. Brainstorm with peers to see what others are interested in and doing for fun. Then you can figure out how to support your child/student to be included. Now the other kids are part of the solution and they have an interest in making the plan work.

SOMETIMES IT'S HARD

SOME ACTIVITIES MAY BE TOO DIFFICULT OR INAPPROPRIATE for your child. Lifting her on to the jungle gym or in and out of the swimming pool may take more than two hands. Or she may chill too easily or swallow too much water in the pool. Her mood may change abruptly. Some days, you just plain don't feel in the mood for fun yourself! The best thing you can do is to match your resources and her health and interests, and don't expect it to work every time.

There is just no possible way for the two of us to shop for groceries together without someone else to push the gro-cery cart. There are days where my back is sore and I just don't have the physical energy to get the wheelchair in and out of the van. There are times where I know I'm up to the getting out part but the parking and the bathroom accessibility are so frustrating that I just don't want to deal with it. There's nothing worse than trying to get a child into a wheelchair accessible van in the middle of a snowstorm when someone has parked twelve inches from your side door, or when your child indicates that she needs to go to the bathroom now but there isn't a large wash-room stall to be found.

Joanne is on a bi-pap machine when she sleeps, so we are not able to let her fall asleep when we are out with-out packing all of it up. We try to plan our activities around her sleepy times. We have also bought a portable TV and VCR for our van. The TV keeps her awake 95 percent of the time, so it can buy us a little extra time to get her home for sleep when we are out.

TO GO OR NOT TO GO

IT MAY SEEM MUCH EASIER TO JUST STAY AT HOME some days. Gearing up for an outing may take some time and energy. This is not one of those decisions that anyone else can make for you. Some people feel obliged to take their children every-where while others are more comfortable leaving them home, especially when they would not get enjoyment from being out or if it would compromise their health.

Friends and Fun

I sometimes feel it is difficult to do some activities with our Erin but I really think I am the barrier. If I just get over my fear and also get more creative, we can make it work and make it enjoyable for the family. For example, we would not have dreamed of taking Erin on rides at an amusement park until our respite providers took all the kids to our local park. The kids loved the rides! I was too fearful. This taught me to get out there and not let my fear hold her back.

We go everywhere with our kids in tow: dinner out, shopping, apple picking, camping, long car trips, museum outings, etc. And, we still have a very active social calendar. We go to friends' homes quite a lot for dinner, bar-beques, etc. Usually, Kendall hangs with the adults, but sometimes, she can participate in the activities with the other kids. The other children like to take turns "helping" her by pushing her on the swing, helping her down the slide, etc.

We include Jacky in everything we do. She goes out to eat with us, to church functions, school functions, parties, and even to ball practices and ball games that her brothers are involved in. I never left her at home unless we all stayed home. As she gets older, it is harder for me to lift her. Other people are used to lending us a helping hand, like guys pushing her up and down steep hills so that we can be closer to the game, or sitting with her if I need to get drinks.

We take Samantha only if she will enjoy or benefit from the activity. For the most part, she goes wherever her sister gets to go. Her sister just started playing soccer and I am one of the coaches. We brought Samantha to two games because we thought she would enjoy it. She didn't. The cool wind and the sun were bothering her and it was very boring to her so she shut down and fell asleep. So now, when we don't bring her, she gets to stay home and do something fun with Daddy. Now that the fall soccer season is over, we will all start going to Samantha's aquatic therapy on Saturdays, where we can all get in the pool as a family.

When Gina was little, we took her everywhere, to all of the other kids' band and choir concerts, and any other school functions. We went to the movies, shopping and out to eat and on vacation. But over the last five years, she has started having crying spells and outbursts and we haven't been able to take her out as often. Sometimes we get take out food and eat in the park so it doesn't matter if Gina is loud.

A TEAM APPROACH

IT IS GREAT WHEN YOU HAVE OTHERS WHO CAN HELP, but all too often this isn't the case.

Having family members pitch in can teach them responsibility and help them understand that they receive in proportion to what they give.

Our family is committed to participating in the activities we enjoy. Everyone pitches in to help in order to do the activity that the family has planned. If everyone doesn't pitch in, we don't go. Even as toddlers, our kids knew that they would have to help in order to do something fun. It only took once or twice of not going somewhere for the entire family to understand that we are a team and we need to work together to accomplish our outing.

FOSTERING FRIENDSHIPS AT SCHOOL

HERE ARE SOME THINGS to consider when fostering friendships with peers.

- Is she fully included in all aspects of school, family, and community life? Shared time, space, and activities are essential in order for friendships to develop. Most friendships result from common experiences and interests.

Friends and Fun

- Does she have an adequate means to communicate with others? While not essential, it is harder for two people to become friends without the ability to communicate with one another. All forms of communication (body, gestural, behavioral) should be respected.

- Materials and conversations should approximate the individual's chronological age, especially among fellow students. Interaction should always be respectful of her age and grade.

- Are there opportunities in the classroom for her to give as well as receive support from classmates? Friendships often arise from mutual admiration and respect.

- Are supports brought into the classroom instead of the student always being "pulled out" of the classroom? When the student is always leaving the classroom, it sends a signal that she is "different."

- Is people-first language used? Referring to her as "the Rett girl," puts the greatest emphasis on her label. She is "the girl with RS" who sits next to the "boy with red hair."

- Do the people in her circle make dignity and respect high priorities? Referring to her in childish terms, or using "baby talk" is disrespectful.

Many wonderful school staff members also helped play an integral role in Lindsey's social circle. Their support included everything from identifying peers as potential friends to actually setting up a circle of friends for Lindsey throughout her elementary school years and to creating social interactions for Lindsey within the school day.

Lindsey and Bridget met in first grade. Lindsey was fascinated with Bridget's red hair and would often give it a pull. Now as eighteen year-olds, they are still good friends. They share movies together, baking, playing games, and, of course, Lindsey's favorite, eating pizza. Now that Lindsey's friends can drive, some of them take Lindsey out with them to the mall, or to movies. Lindsey and our family are truly blessed to have several friends in Lindsey's life. She even has several guy friends who like all the attention and flirting Lindsey does.

Samantha has a friend in school named Nellie who likes to watch out for her. She always wants to sit next to Samantha at lunchtime and she gets upset if Samantha is not sitting next to her for lunch. There are two boys who want to push her wheelchair when she is in it. During gym these same two boys, and other kids from her class help out and bring her whatever they are playing with.

Classroom friends can take your child out at recess, sit with her during reading time or music or play with her on the big ball or other equipment. You can have her classmates over to your house for birthdays, or just to hang out, watch a movie, etc.

What does it take to foster friendships?

- Commitment
- Time
- Creativity
- Initiation
- Persistence
- Being a Role Model

The Institute on Disability has made an excellent video which includes a girl with RS called *Voices of Friendship*. The video is available for purchase through the Web site at www.iod.unh.edu.

Friends and Fun

THE VALUE OF FRIENDSHIP

A DICTIONARY DEFINITION OF FRIEND is "one attached to another by affection and esteem." For the individual with RS, having friends helps them better fit into school, the neighborhood and the greater community. With friends, they belong to a larger group than just family. Not only are friends therapeutic, but these same friends will grow up to be future potential employers, co-workers and the taxpayers who will support the services that individuals with RS need.

EVERYONE LOVES FUN

FUN IS FUN, WHATEVER THE ACTIVITY. Whether it is a formal outing or just being silly in the backyard, your daughter can have fun! She can enjoy many of the same things her peers enjoy. It may take some preparation or a little extra help, but the important thing is that she enjoys the activity.

Activities

Bubbles

Cause-and-effect toys

Blocks, dolls and other manipulatives

Park or Beach

Swimming

Zoo

Movies

Music

Organized activities

    School

    Religious activities

    Girl Scouts, Indian Guide, Indian Princess

Recreational Activities

    Park district

    Special recreation programs

    Special Olympics

Beauty shop

Baking

Bowling

Miniature golf

Arcade

Roller skating

Adaptive skiing and biking

Trampoline

Sleepover

Birthday party

Friends and Fun

Crafts
  Painting
    Finger painting with paint, shaving cream or pudding
    Sponge painting
    Dabbers
    Swirl art
  Clay or Play-Doh
  Stamps and stickers
  Beads
  Sand Art
    Pictures
    Bottles
  Stationery, Scrapbooking and Photo Albums
  Fabric Paints
    Clothes, hats, bottles, candle holders
  Beauty products
  Candy making
  Flower pots
  Candles
  Rubber crafts
  Tie dye and reverse tie dye
  Miscellaneous crafts
  Invent it yourself
Games
  Adapt with hand-over-hand assistance:
    Go-Go Worms   Ages 5 and up
    Trouble   Ages 5 and up
    Guess Who?   Ages 6 and up
    Connect Four   Ages 7 and up
    Yahtzee   Ages 8 and up
  Adapt with A-B-C choices:
    N'Sync   Ages 8 and up
  Adapt with facilitation or switch:
    Mall Madness   Ages 9 and up
  Adapt with a handle for stamp:
    Sealed with a Kiss (Rose Art) Ages 9 and up
  Adapt with switch, Touch Window and
  other adaptive hardware:
Computer, video or portable electronic games

Friends and Fun

Our family has visited all of our local attractions as well as traveled across the country on vacations. We have researched numerous places that provide accommodations for the disabled, including recreational activities such as skiing, whitewater rafting, hiking, etc. Adapted recreational opportunities are available to people within all levels of ability. In addition to annual events we also have mandatory family dinners, at least once a week, and mandatory family traditions, which include visiting the zoo at the holidays, camping trips, family movie night, family games, etc. Even our twenty year old still participates. All of our kids know that these traditions will continue into the next generation.

There is a place by our house called Giggles. It's one of those indoor play places. We have to help Kendall do the games with hand-over-hand techniques. We love to have Kendall do things that other kids her age are doing. I paint her toenails in the summer and she got her ears pierced for her fourth birthday. She loves to go on carnival rides with her older brother.

Noi's friend, who was the same age, was a cheerleader and Noi often went with her to practice. She made sure that her friends included Noi for a sleepover. Noi's caregiver went with her and stayed out of the way. The girls, who had met her several times before, helped her. They all had cake and ice cream, made lip gloss, painted toenails and slept on the floor. When I went to pick her up, she was lying in the middle of a tangle of giggly eleven year-olds watching Princess Diaries.

MAKING PLAY DATES

OUR KIDS' LIVES ARE SO ORGANIZED these days. Between school, clubs, sports, and therapies, we often have to schedule play times for them.

Our daughter's very best friend does not have a disability and so we try to arrange weekly get togethers with her, sometimes with her family and sometimes just her. The girls love to swim, play with their toys, do crafts, and hang out. The greatest thing is that the girls have been friends for a few years now so they just don't think about it. Jana doesn't hesitate to get Joanne's picture symbols and ask her what she wants, and she knows how to read her facial expressions and respects her preferences.

On the way to my other child's play date, it occurred to me that my daughter with RS had never had a play date before. It made me feel so good when I arranged it to know that for once, my daughter with RS had a friend, even if it was another girl with RS. They enjoyed playing together and watching movies.

AGE-APPROPRIATE ACTIVITIES

TRY TO FIND ACTIVITIES THAT ARE AGE-APPROPRIATE. Other children will be more willing to join in if they think it is not "babyish."

It's hard to find age appropriate activities and peers. Noi's an only child, so it's even harder since she doesn't have siblings or cousins. I've found ganging up with other special needs families brings in a clan of compassionate siblings who introduce their friends to the mix. Noi has a friend who is a few years older, kind of her mentor. They enjoy going shopping, to the movies, out for lunch and to Disney on Ice.

ADAPTING THE FUN

WHEN CHOOSING ACTIVITIES, remember that you can break down or adapt almost any activity for partial participation. You can also make changes to equipment, toys and games which make them easier and doable.

Friends and Fun

We adapt all of our activities as much as possible to include Samantha, within reason given her limitations. We went to an amusement park this summer and we saw a river type ride. My husband was panicked when I said we were getting on this ride with Samantha and Allison. He said, "How?" I said, "Just pick her up and sit her down next to you or on your lap and hold her." He didn't think she would be able to sit up on the ride. You should have seen her face! She was so happy and excited to be on that ride and she sat just fine. Well worth it. Sometimes, it's not a lot of adaptation, it's just doing it, and getting over the "hurdles" we see in our minds.

The majority of our time is spent as a family and so we just choose activities that she can do or figure out ahead of time what to do to make it work. We also tend to spend the greater majority of our time with people who "get" our situation. We try very hard to have Joanne do things that other kids are doing, even if that means more modification on our part, or more hand over hand assistance on our part. We are really very adamant that she live as normal a life as possible.

Our family does a lot of camping in the desert. We recently bought a toy box trailer to better accommodate my daughter's needs, and we built a dune buggy with a comfortable seat for her to ride in, so we can all go on rides together.

OUTDOOR FUN

We got our daughter a skychair. It is adult-sized, but is somewhat like a hammock or a sling, so Gracie fits really well in it. We have it hanging from a tree in our backyard, but you can hang it from a swingset or even indoors. It hangs from a single rope so it swings in every direction, which Gracie loves.

We have a trampoline with an enclosure around it. Caitlin loves to jump and loves roughhousing with her brother on it. It was the best outdoor item we have bought her yet. It's also good for rolling around on. She also has a sandbox, but we have trouble keeping her from putting the sand in her mouth.

We have a play structure that my husband modified by closing in three sides rather than the standard two and he put a small stairway up to the playhouse rather than having Rachel climb the ladder. Another addition that we put on were handles at the top of the stairs and also at the top of the slide so she could help herself climb up and lower herself down as required.

In the summer, we buy a cheap plastic pool to put at the bottom of the slide and both my girls would have a great time sliding into it. Just make sure the plastic slide is wet.

Leah enjoys a "water table" where we fill a tub type container with water, put it on a low table and fill it with things Leah can grab and then drop.

We built a play structure where she can practice walking up and down stairs (it has small stairs and close side rails, a bouncy bridge which hangs and moves when she walks on it. It is good for balance.

FACILITATING FRIENDSHIPS

GIRLS WITH RS DO NOT USUALLY HAVE THE ABILITY to go out and get friends on their own, but they are often drawn to others, and may have favorites.

I believe that the key to Lindsey's successful long-term relationships lies in the commitment our family made several years ago to have at least one friend over every week for at least two hours. We learned to adapt games and activities to meet the needs of both Lindsey and her friends. Many of the friends she engaged over the years have also helped foster other friendships.

Friends and Fun

We invite Brooke's friend and her family to go camping with us, to ride our horse with us, and to go out shopping, to the movies and carnivals, etc. They are usually willing to try since we take Brooke with us all the time.

Our church has done something very special for our daughter and other children with special needs. They created a Sunday school class for children with special needs. There are always plenty of helpers (one adult to one or two children). They have specially adapted equipment for the kids. Just recently, we came to church and there was a chair in the classroom that is adjustable and has a tray. It was purchased with our daughter in mind so she could sit at the table with the other children more safely.

Carol has several girlfriends. Three of the girls and two boys have been friends since elementary school and they've all settled into the same adult program. Most of them competed in Special Olympics on a coed bowling league. All our families just kinda blended together. The "kids" would travel together and those times formed friendships. We'd all travel to a state tournament and book a block of rooms that were across the hall from each other. Then we'd take baby gates and block the hall off, open the room doors and let the "kids" do their thing. Each parent had "hall duty." Some nights I'd just have Carol at bedtimes and other nights, I'd have everyone in our room. We still get away one weekend a year.

CLUBS

CLUBS LIKE THE GIRL SCOUTS can be an excellent source of learning and fun. The troop can even earn a badge by becoming more aware of RS and others with disabilities. Girls with RS get companionship and fun, and typical girls learn responsibility, generosity, gratitude, and how to appreciate what they have.

At Brownies and Girl Scouts, Jaime's friends sat with her and helped her work on crafts. They included her in all activities, often figuring out as a troop how to best meet her support needs in the activity.

Girl Scouts has been such a wonderful experience for Chelsea and me. We have been camping, sailing, kayaking, horse back riding, roller skating (the girls pushed Chelsea on the rink in her wheelchair) and the girls came together to help organize our first annual Run For Rett in San Diego. I am very proud of those girls and the friends they have been to my sweet girl. They also will attend middle school with Chelsea next year, so it helps for me to know that she'll have friends to look out for her and be there for her when I am not. Chelsea truly perks up, as all kids do, when she is with her friends. They bring out the best in Chelsea.

Lindsey has been in Girls Scouts, Partners Club, and numerous recreational activities within the community, including swimming, summer day camp and horseback riding. The many kids who have been a part of Lindsey's life have renewed our faith in kids. Kids see others for who they are as people, not the disability they have.

PARTY TIME

WHETHER IT IS FOR A BIRTHDAY OR JUST FOR FUN, who doesn't like a party? It doesn't have to be elaborate or costly.

I try to have several pool parties and art parties in the summer. One time we had about fifteen kids with glue, paint and scissors everywhere. My dining room table has never recovered! All the kids have to help each other in making a project.

A friend of Noi's, who also has RS, had a roller skating party. They rented out the roller skating rink and invited children with or without disabilities. It was a fantastic party and the kids all intermingled and took turns taking the girls in wheelchairs out on the rink. It was so beautiful!

Friends and Fun

How about a swimming party at the Y? That would get everyone involved. You can also have a party during off hours at a place like Jeepers or Chuck E. Cheese. They are pretty good at keeping the stimuli down if you explain the party is for children with special needs. IKEA even does it for free!

We had a tile painting party at a ceramics shop. The children all decorated two tiles that were fired in the kiln. One tile is to decorate Noi's bedroom in a wall mural, and the other they got to keep. The children with disabilities did hand print pictures.

FUN FOR EVERYONE

WATER FUN

MANY GIRLS LOVE WATER ACTIVITIES. Check to see if you have a YWCA program or local community pool. Some schools allow their therapy tanks to be used by families after school hours. Make sure the water is warm enough, and towel her off quickly when she gets out so she doesn't get chilled.

Korie loves to swim. In order to give her total freedom in the pool, she wears a ski belt which we ordered from a sportsmen's catalog and water wings on her arms. The water wings can be purchased at any toy, discount, or pool store. With this equipment, Korie is completely free and swims all over the pool. The belt and water wings force her to keep her body upright and in order to move in the water, she needs to kick.

Stacie learned to swim wearing a Swim Sweater, which is an inner tube inside a tank top. She always loved having her face in the water and kicking around in the deep end. When she was about six, we took off the tube, and she just continued paddling around the pool! We were astonished, but so happy she mastered swimming. She loves being in water, and even being gently "pushed" off the diving board (sitting). She laughs and screeches as soon as she sees the water. Stacie has kept this skill for more than twenty-five years. It is a great sport for breath holders! She can swim the width of the pool, then reaches for the side and catches her breath.

GET CREATIVE

FAMILIES ARE VERY CREATIVE in finding ways to have fun together.

On skit night at camp, "Melinda and the Merrills" got on stage and presented "Brush Your Teeth." Mom and Melinda did the Raffi song accompanied by the audience, and then Melinda activated her BIGMack switch which said "No Mom, I want to do it a different way!" So Melinda and her siblings put on their baseball caps and shades, and waved their toothbrushes to a rap version of "Brush Your Teeth" (Rappin' Raffi). The crowd loved it! It was really fun!

How about a boom box with a switch hooked up to it so she can turn on her own music? Or a beautiful snow globe that plays music? I found gloves with Velcro on them so when you throw a ball at her hand it will stick. She thinks that is very funny. We also get books to read to her. Books on tape are another option. Cassette tapes are a standard for us. I just got a catalog in the mail from a company that makes puzzles with big sticks projecting from each piece. Some of the girls may enjoy a Mr. Potato Head massager. Some of the older girls may like a regular back or foot massager.

We do finger-painting on the tub walls with chocolate pudding. It's great fun, edible, and washes away easily. You can also do this on a kitchen table. Instant dessert!

Briana and I play with a variety of different textured toys and foods. Sometimes playtime is also learning time. I play music, and march her back and forth through the living room, or we march up and down the stairs. We

Friends and Fun

play dress up and sometimes even do baths for fun. In the summer it is hard to get Briana away from her pool, so I make the tub her winter pool and we splash, and play, and giggle.

Edie's "first love" has always been books. She would love to have someone read to her round the clock. I have recorded my voice on tape reading her favorite stories. It seems to help calm her when she gets over stimulated as well as providing entertainment. Her tape recorder is small and has a strap on it. It's perfect to hang on the handle of her wheelchair when we're out and about.

NEVER UNDERESTIMATE HER

THE VARIETY OF THINGS YOU CAN DO IS ONLY LIMITED by your imagination. Reach for the moon; the worst that can happen is that you get stuck in the stars somewhere.

Noi competed in a children's pageant last June and took a title. When I tell people they assume it was a pageant for children with disabilities. She competed against thirty-seven other typically developing girls in her age category. I never told them that she had a disability when I sent her application in. She was accepted on her model photos and application. When we got there we expected to get some resistance. They were great and went out of their way to ensure she enjoyed the day just like all the other girls.

FOR THE THRILL OF IT

YOUR DAUGHTER WILL SET THE PACE for how much excitement she wants. Some girls are very cautious about sudden movements, while others just love the action.

Heather doesn't crawl and can only walk with her hands held, but she is a real daredevil. She loves motion! Her favorites are swinging real high, Go-Kart cart rides, ferris wheels, and lately, the umbrella ride at fairs. She also enjoys swimming, horseback riding, music, and of course anything Disney!

One of the ski resorts in our area had a program in which they guaranteed they could get anyone skiing. Well, this was just too much of a challenge to pass up! We decided to give it a go. The equipment that was selected for Jocelyn was called a bi-ski. Basically it is a seat with rests for the feet mounted on a pair of short skis that are connected to each other. She is strapped in very securely and wears a helmet for additional protection. She is able to go up all the ski lifts, except gondolas, including the chair lifts and can ski on any part of the mountain. The bi-ski is controlled by an instructor specially trained in using this equipment. The instructor skis behind Jocelyn guiding the bi-ski down the slope with two tether straps. On her first time out we all skied all over the mountain, even down a race course. Jocelyn and I raced. I won! I was surprised that not only did skiing with this equipment not slow us down, but with an experienced instructor I actually had to work to keep up with them! Jocelyn likes to go fast and does not like waiting in line at the bottom for the lift at all.

ANIMAL FUN

PETS ARE A GREAT SOURCE OF COMPANIONSHIP and love. Finding the right pet depends on your preference and how the animal reacts around children.

Amber has a wonderful Cocker Spaniel, Avery, who has slept with her every night since we bought him five years ago. He sits on her lap and lets her pull on his ears. She even bit his ear when he was little. He has never snapped at Amber and is quite tolerant of her! Avery knows it is bedtime when he sees me carrying Amber, and then jumps into bed and waits for her! If he doesn't get in her room fast enough, he will cry at the door until we let him in. Then when we get her all covered up he curls himself up in the crook of her legs and keeps her feet warm. In the morning, he waits fifteen minutes by the door until the bus shows up five days a week.

Friends and Fun

We are bird lovers and have four bird feeders outside. We have stick-on feeders in both windows, which Melissa really loves to watch. In the summer, we have two hummingbird feeders.

Ashley has a Beagle, a Cocker Spaniel and a Red Bone Hound. She loves all three. It is so interesting that these dogs can be frisky but when they are around Ashley or visiting her in the bed, they are calm and careful with her. They love to sit by Ashley when she is being fed, hoping she will drop a morsel for them.

Bailey's dog is a rescued black Lab. She learned that if she pulled her apnea monitor wire loose, the dog would drag people into her room, kind of like room service. He also taught himself to know when she is having or going to have a seizure. He sleeps on her floor and when she is home, he is with her.

Ashlyn has a Saint Bernard and two Golden Retriever puppies, along with four horses at her Nana's house and two cats at her Grandma's. She loves animals. She loves to pet them and look at them very close. They also sense her. The horses are so gentle around her when she is there or on them. When you call for the dog or the puppies, she laughs hysterically. She thinks they are coming to kiss her. It is so fun to see her light up.

Corinne has a Cavalier King Charles Spaniel. We looked for a breed that would be everything we wanted, a good lap dog for Corinne, a dog that would be small, but not delicate, and smart. He regularly sits near her, his head on her lap and she breaks her hands apart and "pats" him, sometimes roughly, but most of the time quite gently, patting several times before bringing her hands together again, and sometimes resting one hand on him for a while. It is wonderful to see. She is also very entertained by him when he is playful, she laughs almost to the point of crying sometimes, whenever she sees him running around, playing fetch, etc. We took pains to teach him to NOT lick faces. This way he's not all over Corinne's face when we're not right there to shoo him away.

Katie has a zoo: two dogs, a cat, two chickens, and three ponies. She loves her animals. She likes to go sit outside her pony's corral, and he puts his head over the fence and nuzzles her hair. They'll sit like that, indefinitely, "talking." We take Katie on long pony rides (one person leads the pony and one walks beside to spot Katie) through the woods. She loves her dog, Ellie, and they have a conspiracy going when we're not looking. Katie will throw her food to Ellie. When she gets caught, she'll put the food in her mouth, and walk over to the dog, take the food out of her mouth and "slip" it to the dog. Either way, Ellie gets most of Katie's meals if I'm not watchful. How the dog taught Katie to do this, I'll never know.

IN THE SWING OF THINGS

WHETHER INDOORS OR OUTDOORS, swinging is a pleasant pastime. From baby jumpers to door swings and hammocks, most girls like to swing.

We have a large swing with a mirror, platform swing, slide and trampoline in our house.

We made Korie a platform swing and she likes to swing and bounce. We started with a 3' × 3' piece of plywood, covered it with foam and plastic upholstery and drilled holes in each corner to put rope through. Three feet above the swing, we put a 3' × 3' frame made from PVC pipe, and attached the rope to it. The swing is secured with a heavy-duty spring to a hook in the ceiling. She holds herself upright, which strengthens her torso muscles. This swing provides both enjoyment and therapy.

THE BALL GAMES

The round, multicolored, plastic balls like you'd see in kid's sections at amusement parks, are one of Korie's favorite toys at school, so we ordered some for home. I bought a large inflatable pool and put the balls in it. It worked out great, until we got a dog. Dog nails and inflatable pools do not go together. However, Grandpa

Friends and Fun

came to the rescue. He went to Toys "R" Us and found a circus tent made for the plastic balls. In addition to the section that holds the balls, the tent sits up off the ground on a trampoline. Korie absolutely loves it. She not only gets to play with the balls, but she gets to bounce around at the same time.

We bought an inflatable moon bounce at Wal-Mart and filled it with a box of ball pit balls. Shanda loves this. She can play in there by herself or with her little brother and sister.

BIKING FUN

We wanted a bike for Korie, but she can't support herself on a regular bike. We didn't let this stop us. We took one and a half inch wide flat stock aluminum and secured it to the base of a tricycle. We then attached a go-cart seat and headrest to the aluminum for a backrest and headrest. We placed two inch wide Velcro to the aluminum and backrest for hip and chest support. To allow Korie to pedal, adjustable roller skates, minus the wheels, were fastened to the foot pedals. A pulley was added to the handle bars with a rope through it and attached to the pedals keep her feet in the correct position. The handle bars were welded to the frame to keep the front wheel straight and along with a long, upright handle in the back for me to push her. Aluminum was used for added support from the bike to the handle. For that personal touch, we put a bike basket on the back support so we can take a drink and snacks with us on our walks. The total cost of the adapted tricycle was one hundred dollars. In the nice weather, Korie and I take nightly walks when she rides her tricycle. She not only gets exercise, but she also has a good time.

Stacie just loves to ride on the back of our Harley. We have a special seat that wraps around her for safety, and an extra harness. She has her own helmet and loves to throw caution to the wind!

BOUNCING

One day I was thinking that Korie might enjoy a Jolly Jumper since she enjoys bouncing so much, not to mention the benefits to her leg muscles. I made a pattern for the seat from her walker, cut it out of heavy material and sewed it together. I constructed the square frame from PVC pipe. After we were sure it would fit, we glued the pipe to the elbows and attached the rope and spring. We then hung it from a hook in the ceiling, the same hook we used for the platform swing. We found out that the swing was a great toy for one of our other granddaughters, too.

Abby loves being outside. Swinging and bouncing on the trampoline were favorites. We bounced with her at first, but now she jumps independently. I'm convinced that the trampoline work has kept her walking skills going.

ROCKING

Mary used her rocking horse until she was twelve. She also was a master at jumping on beds and loved the glider swing. She seemed to seek her own vestibular stimulation, though she gave the rest of us heart attacks along the way.

RIDING

Kori's aunt and uncle dropped off a large cardboard barrel which we carpeted, hoping she would crawl through it. While she doesn't crawl through it, she does ride it like a horse. We made an activity box from a square wooden box which we covered with carpeting. We placed Velcro on the back of some of her favorite toys and stuck them on the box. If she wants to play with the toys, she has to use her arms or hands to get at or activate the toys.

Jessica would rather be out mowing the yard (she rides on the riding lawnmower) with her daddy than eating (and believe me, she loves to eat). If she is in the house when he starts it up, she goes to the door and stands there and

Friends and Fun

if I don't get the message, she comes to me and starts fussing louder and louder, until I finally understand what she wants. When she gets on the mower she looks down to see if any grass is coming out the chute. And you can see her watching it all around the yard. To us, it's funny to see a little girl enjoy stuff like that. She also loves to ride four-wheelers, but not as much as the lawnmower.

BOATING

Jocelyn has been on several canoe trips with different youth groups. We usually sit her in a short beach chair in the middle of the canoe. This way she is stable and comfortable. Then at different stops along the river, she can sit in the chair either on the beach or even in the water.

MUSIC

Karina loves music and also shows interest in playing instruments herself. I asked an acquaintance who gives private piano lessons if he was interested in teaching Karina. Karina sat at the piano with the teacher next to her. She started to play with one finger of her left hand. She touched the keys very well. The teacher played with her, following her rhythm. She then began to use her right hand, to my utter amazement (she never uses that hand) and played with both hands! It was not just hitting, she was deliberately touching, as she listened to her own music. I asked her to play from low keys to high keys. She played a tone ladder as good as you or I would have done. She played with one finger at the time, and then with several fingers at once, imitating chords. When the teacher stopped playing, she stopped too, took his hand and replaced it on the piano to say, "Come on!" We decided that she will have a lesson every two weeks for forty-five minutes. The teacher was impressed, and he is making plans for teaching her to play simple songs, something I would have laughed at just one day ago. I was taken by surprise, and realized once more that it is easy to underestimate my daughter. I tell that to her teachers, and to everyone around her.

THE MOVIES

At our house we all love going to the movies. Stacie is no exception. She loves the popcorn most, and we have to watch that she doesn't swipe a handful from someone else while we're standing in line. We find it best to go on off-times when it is not crowded.

I call ahead to management and ask for the best time, and ask them to please make other patrons of the show aware that the theater accommodates all abilities including those who may be less than perfect listeners. I have yet to have a theater ask us to leave.

DOWN DAYS

SOMETIMES, FRIENDS ARE NOT SO MUCH FUN after all. There will always be "off" days when things don't go the way we want them to. It's all a part of life.

When I think Sherry's feelings might be hurt, I talk to her about it. After all, everybody gets their feelings hurt sometimes. When somebody insults or teases our "normal" child, don't we acknowledge it and try to explain why people can be that way? Once a little child came over and was playing with a huge ball that Sherry has. He tossed it to everybody in the house, but when it came to Sherry, he wouldn't do it. He would start to, but back off. After he left, I talked to Sherry about it. I said, "It bothered you that he wouldn't play ball with you, didn't it?" I explained I thought he was probably afraid, and he was just a little kid. But I think it would have been wrong to

Friends and Fun

force him. I think that would have done more harm than good. Besides, who wants to play with someone who is forced to play with you? Or interact with you? There are plenty of willing players. At a family gathering a while back, a second cousin that we don't see very often was there. She was tossing the ball to everybody and she very naturally included Sherry in the fun. Sherry had a blast. And so it goes.

VACATION

IT WON'T BE LONG BEFORE SCHOOL IS OUT for the summer and you might be thinking of taking a little vacation. When you think of all the things you have to do to make it happen, you might think it's a lot easier to just stay home. But staying home is not nearly as much fun as getting away! Besides, your special child will see new places, learn new things, and your other children will be able to do something other families often take for granted, going on vacation.

With some planning and a few practical tips, your trip can be a lot more pleasant for everyone. You will find that a vacation provides great rewards for everyone in the family. You may want to vacation with relatives or another family, and you might even consider another special needs family. This allows you to take turns with child care and get the most out of a trip aimed at rest and relaxation. You can share the fun and the work.

It might seem overwhelming to even think about all of the equipment you'll need to pack, but some careful organization and planning can go a long way to making the trip easier. Do as much as you can in advance. Find out where the nearest hospital will be, take a list of your child's doctors and phone numbers with you, and take a list of her medications with you. This way, you start your trip with some peace of mind.

To save space in your luggage, don't pack a week's worth of diapers if you can buy them when you get there. Most people pack twice as many clothes as they really need. Pack your bags, then unpack and put half of it back. You can always find a laundromat or a Wal-Mart if there is something you've forgotten.

Most of us have Plans A and B for everywhere we go with our girls. If you don't plan ahead, R&R (rest and recreation) can all too easily change to W&W (work and whining).

CARS, TRAINS AND AIRPLANES

IF YOU ARE TAKING A FLIGHT, CONTACT THE AIRLINES as early as possible for special assistance, or use a travel agent who is familiar with making special reservations. The airline will provide a wheelchair for transport around the airport. If you need boarding assistance, plan to get on the plane first and get off last, when the crowded plane has emptied. The airline will check your child's wheelchair at the door of the aircraft, and will wheel her to her seat in a special wheelchair designed to fit down the airplane aisle. Request bulkhead seating, which gives extra leg room and more space for you to tend to your child. An aisle seat affords easier transfer.

If possible, ask for a non-stop flight so you can avoid more airport shuffle. If it is not possible, double the usual connection time to allow yourself plenty of time to get to the next flight. If you are taking a long trip, you may want to consider an overnight flight, or "red eye" as it is called, to allow your child to sleep all the way.

If you use a car seat, check with the airline in advance to make sure it is certified for air travel. Folding wheelchairs have priority over other carry-on luggage for cabin storage and are allowed in addition to your other carry-on bags. Make sure to label all equipment with your name, address, and phone number. If your child's wheelchair is checked,

Friends and Fun

remind the flight attendant before landing so that she can make a radio inquiry to make sure the chair is delivered promptly.

Special meals are available on most airlines, but you must make these arrangements in advance. Do take along some of your child's favorite snacks and drinks. The small juice boxes with a straw are nice, even if she can't suck from a straw. Just squeeze the box for a sip; it's much better than a cup which might spill.

Be sure to confirm your special requests about forty-eight hours before departure. Arrive early before your flight, and reconfirm your special requests with the airline representative or gate attendant. If you have problems, ask to see the complaint resolution officer.

Take your child to the toilet or change her diaper before the flight. Airplane bathrooms are very small! Wet wipes last longer in a sealed bag.

Invest in a Walkman or DVD player and a good set of barrettes to anchor the headset. Tape the sound track of her favorite TV shows on a long-playing audio tape. For the noisy airport, get some soft earplugs to soften the noise and confusion. Do take her favorite blanket or stuffed animal. Take some chewing gum for landing if she is able to chew, to lessen ear-popping. Or, offer her something to eat on the way down. Pressure on the eardrum is bothersome and can be painful in little children.

If you need a car from the airport, make arrangements in advance with a car rental service which provides accessible service to the lot. Accessible cars and vans can be rented from most major car rental agencies. Or, you may be able to rent an accessible vehicle from a local car dealer; check the yellow pages under "Automobiles, Handicapped" or "Automobiles, Disabled Equipment." Sometimes it is cheaper to rent from a dealer than from a rental agency. Make sure to request a car large enough to accommodate the equipment you'll be carrying; most compact cars will not be large enough.

Before you leave home, get a disabled parking placard that can be used everywhere. As a safety precaution, ask for two sets of keys to avoid locking your child in the car accidentally.

Check with the hotel before you book a room to make sure the facilities are accessible. Inquire about the bedroom, bathroom, lounge, restaurant and pool. If your child uses a wheelchair, request the lowest floor possible. Remember that in an emergency, elevators will be turned off and you'll need to use the stairway.

TAKING TO THE ROAD

LONG AUTOMOBILE TRIPS CAN BE MUCH MORE PLEASANT if you plan frequent short stops to stretch. A portable television or video player come in very handy for helping to pass the time. Some come with ear jacks so you don't have to listen to Barney from coast to coast. Take a cooler with drinks and refreshments, and bag some wet washcloths in case of hot weather.

Tourist Attractions

Many tourist attractions make special accommodations for disabled patrons, including special parking or ways to avoid standing in lines. Some amusement parks allow their handicapped visitors to ride twice before getting off. Most include a first aid station where you can change diapers with much more room than a restroom. Don't be afraid to ask.

ENJOY!

WITH A LITTLE PLANNING, SOME ORGANIZATION, an adventuresome spirit and a good sense of humor, you can have lots of fun on vacation. From the

Friends and Fun

simple (tying the dog's leash to the wheelchair and letting her hold it) to the sublime (accessing attractions and childcare options through resorts like Disneyworld) vacation is a complex but essential part of living together for the long term. You'll make memories you'll never forget.

A couple of years ago, I would have never dreamed of vacationing, but we started small. We started with a weekend camping trip in the state, in a cabin with amenities. This past summer we went to Puerto Rico for ten days! It was a lot of planning, packing, sending things ahead, but well worth it. Now, I feel we can go just about anywhere.

A REAL VACATION

GIVE YOURSELF PERMISSION TO TAKE A VACATION ALONE here and there. Families who do the best are those who make time for themselves while still managing to provide the very best for their child. When we overextend ourselves we end up tired and resentful. Our girls will have very special needs for all of their lives, and we need to best preserve ourselves for the long haul if we're going to endure. We may have to make some trade-offs. She may not be as happy while we are gone and she may wear stripes with polka dots, but she'll survive. Finding care will take some extra energy and some creativity (ask your church, club, school, swap kids with a friend or neighbor). It might cost something, but consider the cost of *not* doing it. Give yourselves permission to be special to yourself for a time. It is possible and wonderful. Make it happen. You'll be glad you did.

This summer, we took a three-day trip to Florida with our best friends. They left their infant daughter home with family and we left Kendall and our infant daughter home with a friend. That way, we had just our six year-old children and we could go on all the rides and attractions. I knew Kendall wouldn't like the intense heat of Florida in August and my infant daughter wouldn't get much out of riding around in the stroller all day. As a rule, we include Kendall in everything from a trip to the grocery store, to her brother's games, to a family vacation, unless the trip is going to be something where she would be miserable the entire time.

Throughout the years, we've almost always made time for a short vacation during the summer months. Even when the bills were high and time was short, we managed to pile the kids into the station wagon and head off for a couple of days "away from it all." Most of our vacations were spent in a six-man tent which we shared with some pesky mosquitoes and other crawling critters. Our unlimited entertainment budget included fishing, swimming, shell hunting, cooking marshmallows by the fire and relaxing in damp sleeping bags by the light of the Coleman lantern. Most people don't understand why it is that we almost always come back from vacation tired. I never wondered why! Keeping Stacie happy and occupied was always a challenge, even in familiar surroundings. Pushing a wheelchair in the sand is work, if not impossible. As I look back, however, I remember that Stacie has had many good experiences with us and we all benefited in a number of ways. Even considering all the vacation time hassles, there were many precious memories in the making and I wouldn't trade any of them. But there is one thing I would change: as hard as it might seem, I would find, borrow, or make time to have at least one vacation a year without the work. Most folks do not realize how much of our time goes into cultivating an ordinary life in spite of some extraordinary stressful circumstances. Not to mention, balancing our energies to meet the demands of caring for our girls and their brothers and sisters. We all need time away, real vacation time. And that's what I would change if I could do it all over. I would still go camping in the tent that leaks. I would still include Stacie in our activities and outings most of the time. But I would make it a priority to plan some time alone without her to restore, refresh, and revitalize. This might include taking a caregiver along or finding a baby-sitter during vacation time, or it might mean leaving her alone in someone else's competent hands. It might be hard to arrange, but it is not impossible.

Friends and Fun

GOING TO CAMP

SUMMER CAMP

SUMMER CAMP CAN PROVIDE NEW EXPERIENCES, promote social skills, and bring lots of fun. Most families are a bit reluctant to "let go," but once they feel confident that their girls will be in good hands, they are more at ease. There are a limited number of overnight camps that serve disabled children, so finding a suitable camp for a child with RS may require searching outside the immediate community. Parents are the best experts on what their daughters need to function at their optimum levels. Your child's teacher and therapists can help to locate camps that will continue to promote the growth your child has made during the school year.

LETTING GO

IF YOUR CHILD IS YOUNG or has never been to camp before, the thought of letting her go is frightening. You may want to start out with a day camp close by. You might even consider going with her for part of the time. This allows you to show the camp staff how to best interact with your daughter and also enables you to join in the fun. Eventually, you may gain confidence to allow her to go unaccompanied. Once you have passed that milestone, you may want to consider an overnight camp close to you.

SPECIAL OR REGULAR CAMP?

SOME CAMPS ACCEPT ONLY THOSE WITH SPECIAL NEEDS while others will include special needs campers with typical campers. You are the best judge of your child's skills and needs in determining which is better. Some kids will enjoy being with a diverse group, while others have needs that might be more manageable in a specialized group.

A camp should have a broad range of activities, and a staff with the knowledge and experience to include children with disabilities in these activities.

I first sent Jocelyn to summer day camp when she finished fourth grade. She had been included in regular classes with her typical peers and I felt that sending her to the extended summer program offered for special education students would be a step backward, so I chose to send her instead to a local summer day camp in town. I asked the school to help support this in lieu of her summer program and it helped by funding part of her aide support (the same amount they would have spent on her aide for the summer program). I then used some respite money to cover the rest of the support person's salary and I paid the camp fees. She went to camp two days a week for most of the summer and she had a ball. She was the only camper with special needs there at the time and knew several other campers from school. The kids adored her and welcomed and included her easily. It worked so well that the school district ran the summer program from this camp the following year. The following year, Jocelyn went to the Boys and Girls Club summer camp two days a week. She was again included and her participation welcomed by the other students. A few of the counselors were a little skeptical, but the kids soon showed them how easy it could be. While she was "warned" by some of the counselors to watch out for some of the "tough kids," we found these were some of the most helpful and sincere kids when it came to Jocelyn.

DAY CAMPS

Samantha attends a daytime summer camp for special needs children and young adults. There are three two-week sessions and Sam attends all three. The DDA pays for her summer camp and a 1:1 aide. She's had the same

Friends and Fun

aide for two years now, so that makes it even more reassuring for me to send her. The camp is great, and they do activities with the kids such as swimming in the therapy pool, community outings, and other really fun things. Sam seems to really enjoy being around other children during the summer. She's made some really special friends.

OVERNIGHT CAMPS

Roselyn has been going to summer camp for seven summers now. About six special needs participants, ranging in age from ten to thirty years and at least two "typical" pals for each, together with counselors and a registered nurse, make up a group of about thirty. Roselyn is the only one with RS and using a wheelchair. One of Roselyn's pals is always a respite worker who is familiar with her. The first summer she went, we stayed in a hotel ten minutes from the camp. The next summer we went on a holiday six hundred miles away! Obviously, it was a good experience for her.

Katie has gone to camp since the age of seven. A very special case worker made that first summer easier, although I cried off and on for eight days. Those first few summers were a mixed blessing and my emotions ran wild. The last few years have been great. Once I got over camp syndrome, we had wonderful vacations. Katie rides the camp bus and it is about a two-hour ride. I am told she grins all the way. As soon as the bus comes, Katie is only good for one kiss. Then, it is, "Bye Mom. You can go now!" Each cabin has a bathroom and there is a dining hall, infirmary and arts and crafts building overlooking a scenic lake. Camp activities include, sports and games program, arts & crafts, nature program, fine arts, swimming, boating, campouts and field trips. In each cabin, there is a group of eight to ten campers and four counselors. Depending on the needs of the camper, 1:1 is provided with additional staff. The staff rotates each summer, and gets to know the kids well.

Stacey attends a camp provided through the Exceptional Needs Network. I was terrified the first year. It was her first time away from home and I didn't know what to expect. Stacey is ambulatory, her speech is limited, and she requires assistance with all self-help skills. That didn't stop her from having a wonderful time. Stacey's aides from school have gone with her which has made all the difference. They know her and have been able to assist with all her needs. The camp is a state-of-the-art handicapped accessible facility. The staff is volunteers who are trained to handle an array of situations. There is an RN there around the clock to handle medication or anything that comes up. There is a lifeguard on duty while the children are swimming. The food is handled by the local hospital, and they handle any food issues the children may have. They have a night shift staff for those who have trouble sleeping.

Christi is part of a cabin of seven girls, and I have always asked if she and her worker can stay in the side bedroom that is off the main room where all the bunks are, for privacy and the fact that Christi often needs more sleep than the rest of the gang. The camp facilities are amazing, and they are equipped to integrate ten kids each week into their program of about one hundred kids weekly. We figured that it was well worth the extra cost to be sure that Christi was well taken care of. The kindness that this camp has shown to our family has overwhelmed me. They have so embraced Christi, and treated her with such dignity and respect. Because of this, I have once again reaffirmed my belief that Christi does belong in the community. There are moments that we all face, when our children are not understood or are discriminated against. However, I have seen a model that works, and my faith has been restored.

FINDING THE RIGHT CAMP

MOST CAMPS ARE EXPENSIVE, even when they are not solely for kids with special needs. It helps to connect with other parents who have taken part in camp programs to get their recommendations. Ask the camp for the names and addresses of former campers. Other families are the best source of information about what camp life is really like.

Friends and Fun

Meet with the camp director and other camp counselors to get a "feel" for their attitudes and an outline for the camp's program. The opportunity to interact with camp personnel ahead of time, and to see movies or slides of camp life will go a long way toward making you feel comfortable. However, bear in mind that camp brochures and other visual aids usually show the camp on good days, when everything is at its best. Ask what happens when the weather is bad.

A good way to measure whether a camp program is right for your child is the staff's ability to understand and answer your questions and concerns. Ask for the policies on parent visits, homesickness, illness and any other concerns you may have. Ask about the training and experience of the counselors and other personnel. See if you can eat there, so you can judge the quality of the food. Visit the cabin where the child will sleep and the building where the child's program will take placed to judge the safety and cleanliness of the facilities. Take your child along, and see how the staff responds to her.

Amy went to her first summer camp when she was nine years old. I was frantic. I made a picture album of Amy and her family. I included pictures of what she did and how she did it. I put pictures of her teacher and classroom. I put pictures of her animals. I put captions on all of the pages and used it as a way to communicate to her camp counselors that Amy was a real person with a family who loved her. It also gave them something to talk to Amy about that would be familiar to her. She is thirty-five now and has never missed a summer of camp. She loves going. She always brings home an award and we make a really big deal out of it. I always wrote really clear instructions on her medications and her little ways of communicating to us. I left all of our contact numbers and circled myself with phones. They never called. She was just fine.

CAMP DIRECTORIES

THE EXCEPTIONAL PARENT MAGAZINE Web site (www.eparent.com) has a directory of schools, camps and residences for people with special needs, listed by state. The National Easter Seal Society also provides a list of camps for children with disabilities, free of charge. Call (800) 221-6827. The American Camping Association has a national guide of camps for children of all abilities for $19.95 (800-428-2267).

COMMUNITY RESOURCES

YOUR COMMUNITY MAY HAVE RECREATIONAL PROGRAMS in place. Check with your local parks and recreation department, YMCA, or your local ARC. Joining the program is just the beginning. Find ways to connect with others and help her participate, even if it is only partially. Look to other members of the group to help figure out how she can participate and how they can help support her in the activity. Including others helps them see the child's strengths and encourages them to reach out with confidence. It works both ways. The peer helper feels more important and gains responsibility, and the child who needs help gets support.

In junior high school, Jocelyn participated in parks and recreation trips, with her friends along to support her. They would go to the beach, shopping at the malls, and waterslides. They went on several trips that summer. The Parks and Recreation Department provided transportation for all kids for these trips and the girls figured out how to get Jocelyn's wheelchair on and off the bus through the emergency door in the back. I would drop them off and make sure they were all set and the bus driver would also be around to give them a hand if they needed it. When not out having adventures, the girls would come over and hang out either at our house or

Friends and Fun

have Jocelyn go to one of their houses and they would hang there. She followed this summer schedule for the next three summers.

Getting involved in community based programs like Special Olympics, T-ball, swimming, kickball teams and camping are the real key to forming friendships.

Parents have to get involved to facilitate the connections. For Carol's group of five friends, it has been the parents who have all committed to keeping this group together. The parents aren't all best friends, but our kids are, so we stay in contact and keep the traditions in place.

GOLDEN ACCESS PASSPORT TO FUN

THE GOLDEN ACCESS PASSPORT IS AVAILABLE only to citizens or permanent residents of the United States, regardless of age, who have been medically determined to be blind or permanently disabled. It is a lifetime entrance pass to those national parks, monuments, historic sites, recreation areas, and national wildlife refuges that charge an entrance fee. Golden Access Passports are free to eligible persons. The Golden Access Passport also provides a 50 percent discount on federal use fees charged for facilities and services such as camping, swimming, parking, boat launching and cave tours. (It does not cover or reduce special recreation permit fees or fees charged by concessionaires.) The Golden Access Passport admits the pass holder and any accompanying passengers in a private vehicle. Where entry is not by private vehicle, the passport admits the pass holder, spouse and children. You may obtain a Golden Access Passport by showing proof of medically determined blindness or permanent disability and eligibility for receiving benefits under federal law. A Golden Access Passport may be obtained in person at any federal area where an entrance fee is charged or at one of these agencies: U.S. Army Corps of Engineers, Pittsburgh, PA; National Park Service, Washington, D.C.; Forest Service, Washington, D.C.; Fish and Wildlife Service, Arlington, VA; and Bureau of Land Management, Washington, DC.

I love you. You love me. We're a happy family.
With a great big hug and a kiss from me to you,
won't you say you love me, too?

— BARNEY THE DINOSAUR

Growing Up

CARE FOR THE WOMAN WITH RS

AGE HAS ITS REWARDS

GROWING OLDER WITH RS has some rewards. The regression is over, school days are complete, yet the woman with RS continues to learn and enjoy life. She is more engaged with those around her and her ability to communicate improves. She can draw on her experience and wisdom to help her better understand things. Many families tell us that in many ways, the older girl and woman with RS is more settled and mellow, better than she has been her whole life. She makes better eye contact, is less irritable and has fewer panic attacks, seizures and breathing problems. She may sleep better. The sweeping mood changes that characterized her early years are gone and she enjoys activities that once frustrated or angered her. Her hand movements may become less complicated and less intense.

"The future comes one day at a time."

– DEAN ACHESON

In spite of the tendency to develop deformities, many older girls and women with RS continue to walk for decades. Those who lose ambulation remain alert and still keep a close watch on what's going on around them and stay connected to those they love. It is important to keep her in the mainstream of life, allowing important long-term relationships to continue and flourish. While she may slow down, it is important to include her in activities and events she loves.

Most of us find it hard to see our daughters as grown ups; they still look like small children and still need us for so much of their daily existence. Yet, it is true. They are women with RS.

In many ways, I have found that dealing with Ashley at twenty-five years is much easier than when she was younger. She now seems so peaceful. There is a calmness about her that was never present when she was younger. Ashley smiles now from the moment she wakes up until her eyes close in the evening, unless she is having a problem. She is quite healthy so that is a blessing. Ashley is now out of school so her weekdays are spent at home. Consequently, I rarely have to worry about what might be happening to her, which also gives me peace of mind. Ashley loves people, loves to travel, loves hotels, loves to go out into the community to restaurants and movies, loves festivals and music. We call her our party girl because she is always up for a party! Ashley is absolutely delightful and a real joy to live with.

Lyndie is eighteen years old. She walks very well in familiar territory, but needs to feel a hand of support when venturing in an unfamiliar environment. She goes up and down one step with little to no assistance, but the more the steps, the more the level of difficulty she has. Although Lyndie walks well, she is lousy at transitions. She needs quite a bit of help getting into and out of most chairs, bed, etc., though once her feet are both on the ground, she's off and walking. Although Lyndie's walking has always been fairly good Rett-wise, it actually improved after having her scoliosis surgery done three years ago. That was certainly a bonus of a blessing we were not anticipating!

LIFE EXPECTANCY

DUE TO THE RARITY OF RS, very little is known about long term prognosis and life expectancy. Most of those who have been identified are under eighteen years of age. It

Growing Up

is often difficult to identify older girls and women due to the frequent lack of complete infant and childhood developmental records. However, studies have determined that a girl with RS has a 95% chance of surviving to age 20-25 years. This compares to a 98 percent survival probability for the general U.S. female population. Between the ages of 25-40, the survival rate drops to 69 percent in RS, compared to 97 percent in the general US female population. The average life expectancy of a girl given the diagnosis of RS may exceed 47 years. While there are probably many women in their forties and fifties with RS, there have been too few women identified and studied to make reliable estimates beyond age 40. While these statistics show that life expectancy is less in RS, it is not nearly as low as other similar neurological disorders. While sudden death in sleep does occur, most women with RS can continue to live well into their forties and fifties with good medical care, nutrition and therapy.

I feel so blessed that my daughter has lived thirty-three years. She grows more precious and beautiful as the years go by and with each additional day I feel blessed with her presence.

QUALITY OF LIFE

WHEN SCHOOL IS NO LONGER a daily activity, maintaining friendships can be harder than in the past. Having graduated from the school routine, more emphasis must be placed on finding ways to keep her busy and comfortable.

The wonders of current medical technology have given Jenn a quality of life, and an extension of life, that we didn't think she would ever have. Jenn was so medically fragile in her youth we didn't think she'd make it to her sixteenth birthday. And here she just celebrated her twenty-third!

KEEPING BUSY

DEPENDING ON HER STATE OF HEALTH and local resources, there are many ways to keep her active such as park programs, swimming at the YMCA, trips to the zoo, walking, bowling, craft shows, movies, plays, concerts, visits to the pet shop or animal shelter, shopping, lunch at a restaurant … the list is as long as your imagination and energy.

Jenn remains pretty healthy, gets hydrotherapy three times a week, and volunteers twice a week during the school year listening to students practice their verbal reading skills. She works with a special needs dog in-training to assist individuals in wheelchairs. She helped out in two music classes the year before. We're aiming to start private music therapy and PT. If time, energy and financial resources are available, we may finally get into augmentative communication.

Shelley does what we do. She goes for walks and has her bird and squirrel watch outside the kitchen window. She prefers to walk in the neighborhood or walk in town for short trips. We have learned that too much stimulation does not make for a happy Shelley. We do not overdo. If we eat in a restaurant, we always tell the waitress to be prepared to box everything up in case Shelley does not want to sit.

Project Sunshine is a wonderful organization of university volunteers. They have monthly parties and each participant has at least one 1:1 volunteer who spends at least one hour each week with Ashley. The students come over weekly and they spend about four hours together. She loves this time with her friends.

We have a garden that we planted to attract hummingbirds. I bought those interlocking rubber mats, so Carol is able to w-sit and get her hands in the dirt and help. We also made bird feeders out of pie pans or paper cups

Growing Up

covered in peanut butter and rolled in bird seed. We're doing a scrapbook of all her adventures from last year. We make hats, which is great fun, and we go fishing. At home, we pile all the blankets in the middle of the floor, pile in and eat popcorn. Carol has this whole other social thing she does with her dad. He took her to dinner last week, without me!

I take one day off each week in the winter and we go skiing. Jocelyn has a used bi-ski and we modified it so that she is more comfortable. We have a regular ski date and friends at the mountain an hour away. We also volunteer at the theater in town and usher together and take tickets to about twenty shows each year. After we finish with the tickets, we see the shows. Jocelyn joined a social club and meets a few times a month for dinner, movies, etc., whatever we can figure out how to include her and fit in our schedule. I am starting to work on developing a network of people who would be comfortable supporting her in mutual interest activities. Jocelyn goes to the beach and loves the water. She can even ride on the jet ski. We bike on her adapted bike. She goes to as many of her brother's' hockey and baseball games as she can; she loves sports.

AGE-APPROPRIATE ACTIVITIES

IT IS TEMPTING TO KEEP HER HAIR in ponytails with ribbons and dress her in cute overalls. After all, she still looks like a child, and the selection of clothing which fits is generally limited to the children's department. But dressing her in age-appropriate clothing, similar to what ladies her age might choose, will help her assimilate into her adult peer group, whether typical or special needs. Give her some choice in how her hair is styled and the clothing she wears. You may be surprised at what she likes!

Some of the items used in therapy are actually cause and effect toys, because they are easy to adapt and easier for her to manipulate. But those same switches can be adapted to do other things, such as the hair dryer or the mixer, radio or computer. Provide her with age-appropriate books and magazines. If she is like the typical RS female, she will love posters and magazines of handsome guys.

There are many age-appropriate activities which your daughter may enjoy. How about the movies, shopping, or visiting friends? The list is endless.

With all this said, sometimes too much importance is placed on making sure everything is age-appropriate. Is a Barbie doll an inappropriate gift for a woman with RS? What about the collector? How about a Beanie Baby or stuffed animal? Many typical adults buy toys, bears, and dollhouses and entertain themselves for hours with them. Many adults love cartoons. It's important not to get carried away with the idea that everything must be age-appropriate.

FINDING RESPITE

ONCE YOUR DAUGHTER HAS AGED OUT of the school system, adult programs should be sought out. Too often, there are too few available programs to fill the gap. This calls for more caregiving at home, and more stress on families. It is important to find respite programs to help. After all, parents are aging too, and the burdens of lifting, bathing, feeding and dressing take greater toll.

We just admitted Sara to a nursing home for an eleven-day stay. She has a bath daily, goes on outings and has a private room. I call her daily and sing to her just to hear her giggle. When we admitted her, I asked if I could bring her home if I felt she was in distress. I thought she might try to tell me by moaning or her eyes would tell us that she was unhappy. It was just the opposite. Her eyes just sparkled and when the familiar faces would

Growing Up

> *come to greet her she would belly laugh so hard. I do this yearly so that we can function as a normal family and go on outings, just a little break from doing everything that has to be done for Sara.*

For the adult, funding respite care is often the easy part. Funds are generally available through Medicaid, Community Supported Living Arrangements (CSLA) or other adult services. However, finding a suitable caregiver may be another story. It may take some persistence and resourcefulness to find the right person.

HEALTH CARE

PEDIATRICIAN OR ADULT PHYSICIAN?

AS YOUR CHILD GROWS INTO ADULTHOOD, you may be faced with the decision to change her primary care from the pediatrician to an adult primary care physician. In some cases, insurance requires the switch. Often, pediatricians are willing to keep those over eighteen on their caseload. However, when illness or surgery requires hospitalization, the pediatrician may only be able to admit patients to a children's hospital.

AGE HAS ITS PROBLEMS TOO

THE WOMAN WITH RS FACES THE SAME ISSUES of aging as the typical population. It is important to follow up with routine health checkups and screenings, including colonoscopy, mammography, and pelvic examinations as well as screening for heart disease and diabetes.

MUSCLE TONE AND CONTRACTURES

THE WOMAN WITH RS MAY CONTINUE TO WALK well into adulthood, but as she gets older she may face other problems. Her muscle tone may increase, causing contractures of her joints that limit mobility. Girls with RS who have the least muscle tone (hypotonia) when they are children become the most rigid or spastic (hypertonic) in adulthood. Elbow contractures may prevent her from doing the stereotyped hand movements so common in childhood. Ankle and foot contractures may limit her ability to bear weight.

SCOLIOSIS

SHE MAY HAVE INCREASED KYPHOSIS OR SCOLIOSIS and intermittent muscle spasms. If her scoliosis has not been surgically corrected, she may experience back pain and will need to be repositioned often. Good seating and positioning is important, not only for comfort but to allow her to breathe as well as possible.

BREATHING

APNEA AND HYPERVENTILATION SEEN IN THE EARLIER YEARS may no longer be an issue, but if her scoliosis is severe or has not been surgically corrected, her breathing and lung capacity may be compromised. Internal organs may be compressed due to displacement from the spinal curve, and scarring in the lung from previous episodes of pneumonia may lead to shallow breathing. Each episode of pneumonia weakens the lungs and leaves her vulnerable for the next episode.

Growing Up

FOOT DEFORMITIES

WHEN TIGHT MUSCLES PULL HER JOINTS into abnormal positions, she may develop foot deformities which make it more difficult to walk and even to find shoes that fit. *Dystonia* may begin with the foot turning in and over time, and may advance and worsen with movement. Decreased blood flow to her legs and feet may cause the feet to be cold, reddish-blue, and swollen. All of these factors can lead to decreased mobility.

To minimize deformities:

- Promote good standing and sitting posture.
- Encourage active movement through walking and exercise.
- Use hydrotherapy.
- Do passive range of motion exercises.
- Use hand, elbow and/or foot splints.
- Treat rapidly progressing scoliosis with bracing or surgery.
- Correct foot deformities before they cause discomfort.

DYSTONIA

DYSTONIA CAN BEGIN AT ANY AGE, but is more common in older girls and women. The cramps caused by dystonia can be very painful. Treatment commonly consists of using medications, such as Klonipin/Clonazepam, which is very effective. Dystonia can range from mild to very severe and debilitating.

LONG Q-T SYNDROME

AS DISCUSSED IN THE DAY TO DAY LIFE chapter, Long Q-T syndrome is a disruption of the heart's rhythm. Long Q-T often first appears or worsens with age. If abnormalities are seen in the electrocardiogram indicating the presence of Long Q-T, the cardiologist may prescribe medications such as beta blockers (propanolol, Inderal). One contraindication for use of propanolol is asthma, but there are other medications that the cardiologist may choose to treat Long Q-T syndrome.

APPETITE AND WEIGHT

IF HER WEIGHT IS WELL BELOW what it should be for her height, measures should be taken to increase her weight. If this cannot be accomplished by adding calories through extra meals and snacks in her diet, inserting a G-button may be necessary.

If loss of appetite is sudden, it is advised to have her checked for gastroesophageal reflux, a very common cause for refusal to eat and discomfort.

Despite being very thin as children, many women gain sufficient weight in late adolescence or early adulthood, even without intervention. Some women become overweight, which poses a challenge to her when it comes to walking, moving, and transitioning.

FATIGUE

AS SHE GROWS OLDER, SHE MAY TIRE MORE EASILY than as a youngster. Her body size and weight put more challenges on her central nervous system. She may not have the stamina she once had, and may need to rest more often. L-Carnitine can be helpful as a daily supplement.

Growing Up

SLEEP

IN GENERAL, SLEEP IMPROVES WITH AGE. She may require several short naps during the day. Research studies show that as they age, women with RS have less nighttime sleep and more daytime sleep.

SEIZURES

SEIZURES OFTEN COME LESS FREQUENTLY or even disappear in adulthood. In women who continue to have seizures, they are usually well-controlled with medication. If she has not had seizures for a considerable period of time, it may be possible to reduce or gradually stop antiseizure medications. This should always be done very slowly, and only with a doctor's permission.

BREATHING

AS SHE GETS OLDER, the disorganized breathing patterns she had as a child may decrease. Hyperventilation usually decreases, although she may continue to have breath holding episodes. While sometimes difficult to watch, these episodes do not seem to cause pain or distress. They may occur rarely at night, but they do not seem to contribute to a drop in blood oxygen supply. If you notice long breath holding at night or breath holding that produces a color change, it may be important to see an ear, nose and throat specialist to rule out a simple obstruction caused by enlarged tonsils and/or adenoids. In rare cases, surgery is necessary and helpful.

CRYING

WHILE WE DO NOT UNDERSTAND WHY, some women return to the crying and irritability which characterized their early years. This is frustrating for everyone concerned. Sometimes the source can be traced to a toothache, constipation, heartburn, headache, menstrual pain, or muscle aches. Sometimes it can be identified as anger, frustration, or boredom. Unfortunately, at other times these crying spells cannot be understood. It is very important to rule out obvious physical causes for pain, such as mentioned above. Some of the remedies which worked in childhood may work again. If not, sometimes giving her comforting words and some quiet space to recover is what she needs most.

However, it is most important to consider physical causes for crying and to take them seriously. Gall bladder disease in RS is a recent finding, and can cause a great deal of discomfort. Thyroid disease can cause depression and crying. Dystonia can cause severe muscle cramps. Urinary tract and vaginal infections can be very distressing. Don't give up until you identify the cause of her distress.

Carol had always been a gentle silent soul, taking RS in stride, until she turned twenty. For the next two years, she became this person I didn't know. The episodes seemed to have no precursors and were a sudden burst of violent behaviors that included self-abuse serious enough to draw her own blood and screaming spells, kicking, pinching, food throwing. However, there were periods of hours (not days) where Carol would reappear and be her normal, gentle self. We did every possible test from EEG, CT, MRI, gastro, ortho and all other points in between, including dental. We made changes in seizures meds ... things got worse. Changed diet ... no change. We looked for environmental problems, like allegeries. The closest we came to an explanation was dystonia, which I still believe played a role, however it didn't explain everything. This period was the first time I ever

Growing Up

considered a group home placement. It was a frightening and difficult period, because she had made so many improvements to her skill sets. Then, almost magically, the episodes stopped. Literally one day, I realized we had slept through a night and then another. The school wasn't calling. Her hair started to grow back from where she had pulled it out. She started to regain weight. The smiles came back to her little face and then happiness. To this day, I've never completely understood what happened. I just know it was an awful period.

Lisa screamed a lot for several years, we knew we'd have to leave any place we took her or take turns going. Her screaming slowed down when she was in her mid-twenties. Now she doesn't scream at all.

ADULT RESOURCES

ELDERLY/DISABLED WAIVER (E&D WAIVER)
CONSUMER-DIRECTED PERSONAL ASSISTANCE SERVICES WAIVER (CD-PAS)

WHEN QUALIFYING FOR THESE WAIVERS, one can receive attendant and respite care plus Medicaid benefits (co-pays on prescriptions, medical equipment and therapies paid, co-pays on hospital and doctor bills paid, incontinence supplies paid, insurance premium paid for your whole family, etc).

MEDICAID HOME-AND-COMMUNITY BASED SERVICES WAIVER (HCBW)

THE HCB SERVICES WAIVER PROVIDES IN-HOME SERVICES to people who, without in-home care, would have to go to nursing homes. The program can be used to access a broad range of home and community services and supports for people of all ages with disabilities, and to promote consumer satisfaction and control. These Home and Community Based Waiver (HCBW) programs can be used to fund services not otherwise authorized by the federal Medicaid statute such as respite care, home modifications, and nonmedical transportation. Waivers can also be used to provide optional Medicaid services for waiver participants not offered to other adult Medicaid beneficiaries, such as case-management and personal assistance services. HCBW programs allow states to waive three specific Medicaid requirements: state-wideness, comparability of services, and community income and resource rules. Through these waivers, states can elect to cover a limited number of individuals, offer different groups different sets of services, offer the services in only certain geographic locations, or waive deeming requirements to allow more individuals to be Medicaid eligible. HCBW programs provide states the flexibility to design a waiver program offering a mix of waiver services that meet the needs of the group the state wishes to serve. Federal regulations permit HCBW programs to serve the elderly, and persons with physical disabilities, developmental disabilities, mental retardation, or mental illness. States may also target programs by specific illness or conditions, such as technology-assisted children or individuals with AIDS. States can also make home and community-based services available to individuals who would otherwise only qualify for Medicaid if they were in an institutional setting. States may limit the number of Medicaid beneficiaries who may participate in a HCBW program. Currently, 240 HCBW programs operate across the country.

COMMUNITY SUPPORTED LIVING ARRANGEMENTS (CSLA)

ONE FUNDING STREAM FOR SUPPORTED LIVING is the Community Supported Living Arrangements (CSLA) program, an initiative to provide supported living

Growing Up

services to Medicaid-eligible adults with developmental disabilities in eight states. CSLA provides individuals with the support necessary to enable them to live in their own homes, apartments, family homes, or rental units with no more than two other nonrelated recipients of these services; or members of the same family regardless of the family size. Covered services include assistive technology, adaptive equipment, environmental modifications, case management services and respite care.

- The person/guardian, through a person-centered planning process, identifies the supports and services which best meet his or her needs. If provider agency staff and the person receiving the services have a parting of ways, it is the agency that must be replaced, not the person.

- The person must live in his or her own home (including an apartment, condominium or house, owned or rented) where the setting is controlled by the person/guardian and not a service provider. Control may be shared with other people who live in the home. No more than three unrelated people excluding live-in care givers may reside in the home for it to qualify as an allowed living arrangement for CSLA. Participants may also reside with their families or with a relative.

Supplemental Security Income

WHEN YOUR DAUGHTER REACHES HER EIGHTEENTH BIRTHDAY, she becomes eligible for Supplemental Security Income (SSI) automatically. There is no financial formula, and the parents' income is not counted. She can probably qualify for the highest amount of benefits. It is best to apply a month or so before she turns eighteen so that her benefits will not have to be retroactive. If you do not apply, she does not receive the benefits. These funds are to be used to pay for her lodging, food, clothing, recreation and other needs. The Social Security Administration uses a mathematical formula to calculate her benefits. If she lives at home, you should assign an amount for her to pay "rent" to access the higher benefits. If she lives away from home, her SSI check is sent to her residential placement to help pay for her needs. You should expect a six-month wait for the bureaucracy to get all the paperwork approved. They will still back-date payments.

Jane just purchased her first accessible van. She is able to pay for this with money from her SSI check that she became eligible for at age eighteen. So she and friends have transportation to get where they need to go. Hopefully by the time she needs to worry about paying for housing, her van will be all paid up!

DAY HABILITATION PROGRAMS

Transition to Adult Services

AROUND THE AGE OF FOURTEEN the public school system begins the process of transition to adult life and adult services with a transition IEP. The options available when the school years are over will depend in large part where you live. Adult programs are not mandated and therefore, availability is tied to local funding. Programs may not be available in rural areas. Your state Developmental Disabilities Agency should be able to assist you with identifying appropriate programs.

Growing Up

WHEN THE SCHOOL BUS DOESN'T COME ANYMORE

IN MOST CASES, EDUCATION IN THE PUBLIC SCHOOLS can continue until at least age twenty-one. After this time, the availability of programs varies vastly from one area to another. Programs range from respite and in-home care to sheltered workshops and day centers. Residential programs present another option. More recently, some girls with RS have been able to attend college classes with assistance or work at community jobs with a job coach.

The woman with RS needs an appropriate adult program that meets her own special needs. A number of different programs may be found in the community, which should be explored for the one best suited to her. Often, these programs are a carry-over of the developmental approach used in the public schools. However, while the structure of the program is important, the most crucial aspect is finding caregivers who understand her and are knowledgeable about RS. They will make the biggest difference in her life. She needs to continue therapies that will help her remain as mobile as possible, and she needs a communication system that allows her to relate her wants and needs and to make choices. She should have good medical care by professionals who are aware of the changes which take place as she advances in age and stage of RS. She should have opportunities to participate in community activities and experiences that enrich her social life. Her parents are getting older too, and may not be able to continue to provide the same quantity and quality of care as in earlier years. It is wise to seek help so that she is allowed the continuity of good care.

When Shelley finished school it was a day of celebration for us. At first I wondered what she would do, but it worked out fine. My other children moved into their own lives and Shelley became our main focus. She adjusted to her siblings being gone and loved knowing she didn't have to go anywhere. She was happy to be done with school and the pressure was off her. She doesn't get sick as much, less colds. She loves just being home and feels very secure with Mom and Dad. We bought a motor home and off we go into the wide blue yonder whenever we want.

STARTING YOUR OWN PROGRAM

IF A DAY PROGRAM DOES NOT EXIST IN YOUR AREA, it may be possible for you to start a local program, pooling the energy of other families of adults and accessing local resources.

Four families started talking with our school district about this "idea." We spent two years working out the details and one week following graduation, the Partners in Adult Living (PAL) program started. We were fortunate to get a state grant to help purchase a bus, van and other equipment. The families hold an annual fundraiser each year to raise funds for any shortfall we have in the budget and purchase the extra items we need for the program. We have monthly partnership meetings to review standards, and purchasing of equipment and work on all other issues. Our ongoing challenge is to have the program fully staffed all the time. For those interested in starting their own programs, here are some ways to start:

- *Begin planning two years in advance.*
- *Find three or four committed parents who are strong advocates and have common goals.*
- *Try to get services for all of the attendees coordinated by one agency.*
- *Do a fundraiser prior to the startup date to demonstrate your commitment to the project.*

Growing Up

- *Encourage parents to donate personal money to the program.*
- *Apply for Medicaid waivers at least one to two years in advance.*
- *Get a local legislator to advocate for you.*
- *Ask people in the Office of Special Education to help identify possible grants.*

ALTERNATIVES TO DAY PROGRAMS

EVEN IF THERE ARE FORMAL DAY PROGRAMS in your area, you may choose not to use them, instead utilizing help from a home health agency to take advantage of community resources.

My daughter has been out of school for seven years now and we have not yet utilized any type of adult program. She has a support person through a home health agency who comes to our home weekdays from 8-4. Together, they cook, play games, go out for walks and to the pool, sit and swing in the sun, read, have lots of discussion about stuff going on in their lives, the newspaper etc. They work on projects, have friends over, have pampering "girlie days" with manicures, bubble baths etc. She also does regular bathing and hygiene duties, feeds her, and does range of motion stretches. The particular agency we work with does not allow their employees to transport clients, so they keep busy at home and have friends over. The previous agency had made an exception and she was able to get out regularly to go shopping, find volunteer employment, utilize the rehab pool in town, go to movies, take classes, go to the beach, mountains, etc. She still gets out a lot but mostly I take her out and support her in her involvement in the community.

Lynn took part in Community Supported Living Arrangements (CSLA) for a number of years, but nobody told me that I could have the money to do her program myself. Basically, it is the sum of money that's given to the placement for her education/placement at a day facility. So, after finding out, I got the sum of money myself (thru a payroll) and I administer her day activities myself. I hire aides to do it with her at ten dollars an hour, six hours a day, five days a week, which comes out of the sum allotted for her for the year. That way she does what she can do, instead of the day center taking all the money and giving her what it wants, which in my experience has not met Lynn's needs. It was a struggle at first trying to arrange activities and plan her day, but now three years later, it runs quite smoothly. I have no problem finding help. It is a good alternative to what is available in adult workshops and day centers.

COMMUNITY-BASED RESOURCES

MONEY IS AVAILABLE TO YOUR DAUGHTER for programs when she is over twenty-one. All you have to do is submit a plan for the program. Workshop facilities have persons who will write up a plan for you (but beware it comes with a cost, which comes out of her total money for the year and quite frankly, you can do quite easily yourself).

FINDING A JOB

WHILE THERE ARE A LIMITED NUMBER OF JOBS available, some girls do have supported employment, either through a workshop or other habilitation program.

I have been working on developing a job with junior high age kids in an alternative school placement. These kids are "troublemakers" in school so are in a different environment, working on skills they need to develop to succeed in life. Hopefully she will "work" with them on projects one afternoon a week, by giving them opportunities to

Growing Up

think of ways of helping her to help them. This calls for problem-solving skills, positive attitudes, compassion, and understanding. I think these are things she can help to teach them very effectively.

HOME AWAY FROM HOME

SOMETIMES A FAMILY FEELS THEY CAN NO LONGER CARE FOR their daughter at home full-time. Parents may be getting older or have health problems that limit their ability to provide the quality care their daughter needs. The physical and emotional strain on the family may be too much to cope with, especially for the single parent. There may not be adequate support or respite care from the extended family or through the community. In some cases, the family feels that she will do better in a residential setting which can provide twenty-four hour care. Whatever the reason, making a decision to find an alternative living arrangement can be painful and difficult. Finding the right home is often hard, and sometimes impossible. The family must choose to either remain in the same situation and feel drained, or place their daughter somewhere else and feel guilty. There is often no choice that is good for everyone. Parents may face criticism and judgment from others, and they will probably always feel some sadness.

It is easy to say that you would never do this or never do that, but when the choices are out of your control for any number of reasons, for health, income, or safety, you may just find yourself looking at an alternative placement for your child.

I don't have family, so the caregiver role falls squarely on my back and it gets heavier every passing year. I have started realizing that my dreams are gone and it all becomes a snowball rolling down hill at breakneck speed. It's comforting to know that there are people out there who do care, even in nursing homes and hospitals. We are not alone, there is help, and sometimes we need to reach out for it.

It is not easy for families who have found other options. Many times there is a great deal of contemplation over the decision and self-guilt. My support goes out to those who work hard to keep their children at home as well as those who have had the courage to know that they are unable to give the level of care that their child needs and have found alternative placements.

I thought Heather would never have to go anywhere after something happens to me, but that isn't the way life goes. When my two nieces were younger, they said they would take her and now they have families of their own, and don't visit any more. I have made an application to a very nice group home but I'm not ready yet. Heather needs twenty-four hour care. I wish I could live and care for her as long as she is on this earth but as she ages, so do we and we have no one that comes in to care for her.

If I've learned one lesson in life with Carol, it is that nothing ever stays the same. There will come a day when her needs are going to outwit my body. The emotional stress takes its toll. Carol lives at home only because I took an early retirement from my career. I spend every day trying to make her life meaningful. I am forced to re-evaluate my ability to physically care for Carol. In the big picture of life, I would rather emotionally connect longer than to burn out physically.

I know there are many of you who cannot fathom having your child cared for by anyone but you. At the moment that is how we feel, too, but I have learned through the years to never say "never." I have two older daughters and their welfare to consider, so while Tori does get the bulk of our attention, they deserve to have a life as well. My husband and I are also getting to an age where our parents are getting older and we may need to help shoulder

Growing Up

some of that responsibility as well, so we really don't know what our future holds. We plan to keep Tori at home, but we can't rule out other options for the future. You just never know what curve balls life is going to throw you or for sure how you will be able to deal with them when the time comes.

To those of you who have had to make the gut wrenching decision to have your child cared for by someone other than yourself, don't let other people add to your guilt by criticizing your decision. I believe a lot of soul searching goes into each decision that is made and that the welfare of the child is of utmost priority.

Mary was placed in an institution, then later moved to a group home. As a single parent, I had to rely on baby-sitters, and Mary's behavior had become so bad that I could not keep a sitter and she was kicked out of every school, including the one that took the worst of the worst. My guilt sent me into therapy until I accepted that none of us can be everything to our children. Mary moved into a group home and I have never been out of her life. I go to every treatment planning session. I fight all the battles all of us do, and bring Mary home for weekends. She never lost me. She just has me in a more loving capacity because I am not doing the hard work of training her. We can enjoy each other much more. Mary is thirty-seven and I'd say I've done a darn good job of hanging in there with her.

How easy it is to judge others. I think we are trained to be cautious and are primed to defend our situations and our daughters. When the majority of us hear the word "institution" we envision the cold, heartless, horrible places of years past. Every family is different and I feel does the best it can and makes the right choices for the individual situation. I can see it from both sides of that fence as I am the parent of a girl with RS and the foster parent of a young lady with cerebral palsy. She was "placed" with me when she was six. People always ask me that nasty question, "Why?" I answer them with the truth. The parents knew that to allow her to live with my family and me was the best for Melissa. It broke their hearts to let her go and to not be a part of her everyday life. But they did it purely out of love for their daughter and her needs.

THE RIGHT TIME

SOME FAMILIES KEEP THEIR DAUGHTERS AT HOME for all of their lives. If sufficient resources allow for good support and respite services, this can work well. However, the life expectancy in RS is well into the forties. When parents are in their sixties and seventies, it is difficult for them to maintain the level of physical care and attention she requires. They also must face the fact that their daughter may survive them. Parents should plan ahead for when they can no longer care for her at home.

As time goes on and your life patterns change you will make different decisions. I am also faced with very fragile aging parents who need a lot of support and help. I haven't had a vacation in eighteen years that hasn't been to care for someone else. I am not complaining. I feel blessed that I have the skills to give comfort to others. But I am tired. And on the days that we feel less than perfect we should be able to say so.

Amy is in a group home and has been for eight years. She went there when she was nineteen. I share her care. Amy gets tremendous support and love at her other home. It was the best decision we ever made. You have to protect your family unit and marriage and learn to let go at some point and trust that all of this is somewhere in God's plan. I remain Amy's guardian and she is home every weekend and holiday. I attend all doctor's appointments and take her to the Rett Clinic every year for evaluation.

We have a contingency intervention program and Carla was "placed" at a nearby regional center. Carla had a number one priority because I was a single parent and not getting any younger! If I said "No," there was no guarantee of placement in the near future. Furthermore, since this was her last year at school, there was no guarantee that there would be a day program available if she were still living at home. So, after many restless nights,

Growing Up

I decided to give it a try, especially since I was told I could change my mind at any time during the transition. I made my list of pros and cons. The pros included the following: it was a small facility with six beds to a unit and four units to a building designed with two units on each level; it was two miles from home, which was a big plus; the staff were warm and caring people who had worked there several years; and another girl with RS who was twenty-five years old would be Carla's roommate. All the cons were Mom related: I didn't want her to go; I wasn't ready; and maybe I should do this next year. I spoke to family, friends, Carla's teachers, therapists, and clergy. I had to do it! So the transition began. For two months, I brought Carla to the center after school for visits. The visits got easier and then we had our first overnight. I stayed until she was asleep and then cried all the way home and most of the night. I was there when she woke up the next morning. She seemed a little confused, but happy. The overnights became more frequent, but not easier—for me, anyway. Then, she moved in. I tried to think of it as going to camp. She spent Monday through Thursday nights there, attended summer school at her regular school, and was home from two to seven each day. Then, she was officially admitted. I was devastated. I heard myself talking at the meeting, but what I said was not what I felt. I knew what I had to do, but it wasn't what I wanted to do. I had to believe it was best for Carla, but I wasn't convinced. I felt I was giving her away. I had never experienced such pain even though I had gone through a divorce and lost a parent. Those events didn't even come close to the pain I experienced that day. I was awake and up all that night. I cried and cried, a full-box-of-tissue cry. Morning arrived and zombielike, I went about my chores. Carla was fine, though, and I got one of her "Don't bother me" looks when I visited her. That same day, I was involved in an auto accident. When they say that God works in mysterious ways, I believe it. I had been praying for guidance and this accident was an answer to my doubts in a way. It made me realize that if I had been seriously injured or killed, there was a place for Carla with people she knew and with those who knew how to care for her. For the first time in four months, I felt OK with the decision. I had mourned my loss and now it was time to celebrate Carla's new life. If I said everything was wonderful now, I'd be lying. It still hurts bringing her there Sunday nights. It's wonderful bringing her home weekends. We share only quality time together now. I'm beginning to enjoy my new freedom. For the first time in twenty-one years I can do things like making appointments without making arrangements for a sitter or like working my daily events around Carla. I visit her daily; they asked if I wanted a part-time job since I spend so much time there. She enjoys the constant activity and attention.

What is my advice to parents who might be in this stage? Do it! Do it while your daughter is still in her regular school program, if possible. It's easier for you and for her too. Don't let her see that you're upset. Be happy for her and her new "independence." Don't get upset with friends who say it's just as if she were away at college. They could never understand the pain of letting go of a child who is still so dependent on you. Kids choose to go to college and choose the college as well. They can tell you what's happening. In our case, we're making all the decisions and hoping and praying that they are the right ones. Carla has a new family now, and I have, too. I keep thinking that if I won the lottery, I'd bring Carla home, and have live-in help. But would Carla like that arrangement? Finally, pat yourself on the back for being such super parents. You've won all the awards for best parents and now it's time to enjoy life. Let others do the daily caregiving. Be there to love her, have fun with her, and keep an eye out for her. There's no place like home, but your daughter can have two homes. Try to view the new setting through your daughter's eyes. She is blind to situations that may not be pleasing to you. Isn't it better to be the one in charge of finding your daughter a new home and family than waiting until it is too late and letting strangers make the decisions?

FINDING THE RIGHT PLACE

IT IS PROBABLY BEST TO CONTACT YOUR STATE Developmental Disabilities Administration (DDA). Today, children are not placed into state facilities (institutions). All of the agencies participate in a review of each case. If she is over eighteen, she automatically qualifies for Medicaid, which provides assistance in the home at crucial hours, foster care in a family especially trained to deal with her problems or a group home.

Growing Up

HOW TO START THE PROCESS

THE PROCESS FOR PLACEMENT IS DIFFERENT from state to state but a cry definitely needs to go out to the social worker or caseworker. Talk to other parents who are in your area. The local ARC is a good starting point.

FOSTER CARE

People should not discount foster care when they are looking for placements. I know the feeling is sometimes that "if our family can't do it anymore, then how can another family?" Well, the other family hasn't been doing it all these years. They also may have different family situations than your family that may make providing care a possibility for them. I've met some pretty amazing foster families who have done marvelous things for some people with some severe disabilities. Every situation is different, just as every person is an individual.

HOW TO EVALUATE A RESIDENTIAL SETTING

DESPITE THE BEST REVIEWS by state case managers, you will never "trust" the quality of the residential setting without making a personal visit and speaking with the staff. There is no other way. And probably the bottom line will be an instinct, a gut feeling, that this is a good place. Certainly, ask the tough questions such as: Are your staff trained? Is the facility licensed? How often is it inspected by government agencies? Can I see your last report? Would it be OK for my family or my daughter's advocate to visit her and take her out occasionally? And, of course, the big questions. How much and what do we receive for this amount?

Whether she lives at home or away from home, those who care for her must be given adequate support and respite in order to meet her many needs. Caregivers need regular time off and some holidays without responsibility for the woman with RS. Caregivers should be provided with ample information about the woman with RS, and any problems, aids or adaptations that are necessary for her success. If she lives away from home, the caregiver should be contacted regularly by family members, who will always be her foremost guardians and advocates.

ADJUSTMENT TO A NEW LIFESTYLE

MANY PEOPLE THINK THAT MOVING THEIR DAUGHTER to a residential placement solves all of the problems. It does not. While the physical stress of caring for her at home is eliminated, it is often replaced with emotional stress over making sure she gets the same kind of care away from home. Parents find themselves helping to raise money, volunteering, and cheerfully spending more time than they had planned at the "new home." The sadness which follows placement tugs at the heart. Adjustment to a new and less demanding lifestyle that once was so overburdened by her care can take time. But eventually, as she convinces you that she is doing well, you can begin to adapt. There will always be a yearning for the way things might have been. You will always want to remain vigilant about her care, and in close touch with her new caregivers.

RESIDENTIAL OPTIONS

OPTIONS FOR RESIDENTIAL PLACEMENT will differ according to where you live. There are various types of residential living arrangements whose housing and/or supports are funded in full or part or are provided by the Division of Mental Retardation and

Growing Up

Developmental Disabilities (DMRDD). The DMRDD contracts directly with the person or family providing direct support to the individual, rather than contracting with an agency.

Large institutional settings are no longer an option for people with disabilities. Small group homes are a least restrictive alternative, providing a homelike atmosphere in the community. Some families prefer to combine resources and benefits to provide her own house or apartment close by with full-time caregivers.

Some options include:

Group Homes

The DMRDD contracts for residential habilitation services with agencies that may provide live-in and/or shift staff arrangements. A single base rate is established for the support of each resident. Regular group homes have four to eight residents. Residential Care Centers are group homes with more than eight beds.

Semi-Independent Apartment Living

The DMRDD licenses and contracts for semi-independent apartments. Each resident has his or her own apartment and support staff live in close proximity.

Home Ownership

For information on the Home of Your Own program (sometimes referred to as HOYO), contact: Michael Renner, Missouri Planning Council on Developmental Disabilities, 59th & Arsenal, Suite 1B, St. Louis, MO 63139, (314) 877-0068, or e-mail at mjrenner@aol.com.

Habilitation Centers

The DMRDD operates various habilitation centers, ranging from small (forty bed) to large (three hundred fifty bed) campuses. Residents primarily have significant and multiple disabilities.

Division of Aging Licensed Facilities

These include Residential Care Facilities (RCF I and RCF II), Intermediate Care Facilities (ICF) and Skilled Nursing Facilities (SNF). A program license from the DMRDD is also required if 50 percent or more of the residents have a diagnosis of mental illness or if one person has a diagnosis of mental retardation. Rates for these facilities are set by the Division of Aging, not the DMRDD.

SUPPORTED LIVING

THE OPTION OF SUPPORTED LIVING ALLOWS A PERSON with a disability to live in and become integrated into the local community. It provides the ongoing supports necessary for an individual to live in her own home, allowing control and personal choices. It occurs in your own home and community and gives you the chance to choose where, how and with whom your daughter will live. This service is offered around the country, with some differences from state to state. General eligibility requirements are: 1) eighteen years or older; 2) client of the Developmental Service Program; 3) desire to live in your own home; and 4) the need for ongoing supports and services to do so. An eligible person requesting supported living is not expected to demonstrate total independence or attain

Growing Up

a predetermined level of skills. Even individuals with the most severe or complex disabilities can live in their own homes, if adequate support is provided.

Supported living tailors supports and services to the needs of the individuals instead of making them fit into the system. It transfers control from the service providers to you. Supported living is different for everyone, just as every person is different. Individuals in supported living can live all over the community, in rented/leased homes and apartments, or in homes they own.

Supported living separates housing from support. A person does not have to live in a particular area to get needed supports and services. The intensity of the supports and services provided are designed to meet the individual's requirements. If an arrangement doesn't work, another is tried.

A supported living coach is provided through the Developmental Disabilities Program, Home and Community Based (Medicaid) Waiver. The coach enables your loved one to live in her own home or apartment by providing the help and training necessary. Help that a coach may give includes:

- finding an affordable house or apartment
- setting up and maintaining a household
- planning and preparing meals
- shopping for groceries, clothing and household necessities
- taking part in leisure and recreational activities and other life skills

Functions of a supported living coach are teaching new skills in the context of everyday life, helping with tasks and doing things with or for your loved one. Some people in supported living may need help with certain activities or need things done for them. A coach may also help by locating community resources and natural supports for your loved one.

Your *support coordinator* is your family's main contact with the developmental services system. It is the responsibility of your support coordinator to be sure you understand all available residential options and possibilities that can be created for you.

If you choose supported living, your support coordinator is responsible for:

- assisting your loved one in the process of selecting a supported living coach or provider
- coordinating all the supports and services your loved one needs, both paid and unpaid
- facilitating communications among various providers of supports and services
- advocating for your loved one by helping communicate likes, dislikes, hopes, and dreams
- monitoring your loved one's ongoing health and safety in the supported living arrangement

Just as every person's life circumstances are unique, her supported living arrangement will be unique also. Some people need only the assistance of a supported living coach. Others need the kind of intensive help with daily tasks that can only be provided by a personal care assistant or a homemaker. Still others have more complex needs that involve several service providers along with the coach. The support plan that will specify and authorize those services that your loved one needs will be as unique as that individual.

INDIVIDUALIZED SUPPORTED LIVING (ISL)

ISL IS A COORDINATED SYSTEM OF SUPPORTS centering on the individual which is designed to facilitate each person's choices to live, work, learn, and actively

Growing Up

participate in their community. Supports may include training, protective oversight, her own personal assistant services or environmental adaptations. It could be a person living alone with little support or a person living with several roommates, with or without disabilities, with a lot of support. This is NOT independent living, but supported living, based on the individual's needs. Supported living is one option in the range of choices in residential services.

IN-HOME SUPPORTED LIVING

AN INDIVIDUAL AND HER FAMILY may choose to have supports provided in the natural home; this is called In-Home Supported Living.

LIVING AT HOME

IF YOU CHOOSE FOR YOUR DAUGHTER to continue to live at home, you can still receive supports to help with her care, fund home modifications and equipment, and provide respite services.

SHARING YOUR HOME

ONE DRAWBACK TO RECEIVING SERVICES at home is the fact that you will be sharing your living space with support providers who come and go. This can be a huge invasion of privacy if your home is small, or if you are not fully at ease with her support staff. One alternative is to choose times to do errands or have a regular standing day or two out of the house during the week. If your caregiver is allowed to transport your daughter, encourage her to get out into the community as often as possible. You could set aside a specific room or area in the house for your daughter's activities to take place. Some people choose to close in the garage or add a room on to make space for caregiving.

FINAL THOUGHTS

CREATING A POSITIVE FUTURE

IN A NUTSHELL, THESE ARE THE IMPORTANT THINGS to strive for:

- Excellent health care
- A good place to live
- A place to work if desired
- Friends and fun
- Community resources
- Family support

How blessed we are in Jenn and how blessed we are in her gracious handling of RS. We are always being touched by the goodness of others.

Heather did not learn to walk independently until she was eighteen. Now, she often crawls into the living room, pulls up on the couch, turns around, and walks back into her room. She will repeat this several times, and I'm certain it is just something she's enjoying doing because she's discovered she can. She has also made small progress in other things. She actually watches TV now, when she used to never be interested in it at all, and loves classical and semiclassical music programs like the Boston Pops on TV. She's always liked classical music, but is

Growing Up

clearer in her preferences now. She is more assertive, more demonstrative about what she does and does not like than when she was younger. All in all, she is becoming more observant and seems more "with it" than she was when she was younger.

It seems the older Mary gets, the better she has been doing. Lately, we've noticed that when she reads a book, she is turning the pages on her own, which is a skill lost years ago. She is hooked on the television game show, Wheel of Fortune and becomes agitated when a contestant chooses a wrong letter or guesses wrong. Many of her physical skills have improved.

I know I'm getting old. I have more gray hair, my back aches and my knees make sounds like gravel. There's a strange little trick Mother Nature is playing. I see my friends who have children Carol's age and they seem so much older. They talk of retirement and downsizing … they've moved on. But I have come to realize that having Carol has allowed time to stand still for me. I'm still doing all the things I did twenty-seven years ago. I enjoy the little things and having a retirement fund isn't important to me, because I'm still having fun and acting too young for my age. I know all the words to every Disney movie, I'm an expert at coloring inside the lines, and no one can dance with Carol like I can. One day, I suppose I'll have to grow up, but not today.

"In three words I can sum up everything I've learned about life: it goes on."

– ROBERT FROST

Resources

7

SECTION SEVEN

Equipment and Ideas
Where to Go for Help

Resources

Where to Go
for Help

Equipment and Ideas

Equipment and Ideas

CHOOSING EQUIPMENT

THE INITIAL EVALUATION IS very important in determining what kind of equipment to choose. It should be done by your child's local physician, physical, occupational or speech therapist, or a local medical center representative, who may consult with vendors (equipment supply stores) to find the right piece of equipment for your daughter. Please see the Communication chapter for more information about choosing augmentative communication or assistive technology equipment.

"Necessity is the mother of invention."

– GEORGE FARQUHAR

It is also good to do your own research. Call or compose a form letter requesting catalogs from a variety of rehabilitation equipment vendors. Browsing through the catalogs will educate you as you comparison shop for styles, features, models, colors, and prices, all in the comfort of your own home. Some vendors will bring the equipment to your home or will allow you to keep it on a short trial basis. There may or may not be a rental fee associated with borrowing the equipment; be sure to ask.

It is helpful to talk to other families of girls with RS and ask how they feel about their daughter's equipment. Just remember that the piece of equipment should be suited to your daughter's individual needs. When you meet with the equipment representative, ask questions about items that otherwise might not have been explained. Vendors often have their favorite pieces of equipment and companies with whom they deal. Once you are an informed consumer, you will be an active participant in the evaluation process.

FUNDING EQUIPMENT

BE SURE TO CONTACT YOUR INSURANCE COMPANY and check out your policy thoroughly. Follow any required procedures to the letter. Any deviation could result in a reduction of benefits. You may need pre-approval. If so, take care of it right away. It may be too late to do it after you have already purchased the equipment. If you need a prescription for the equipment, get the forms you need from the insurance company and take them to your physician to complete. Some vendors may provide you with a prescription form to take to your physician as well. After an evaluation, the PT or OT will write a prescription describing the recommended equipment, along with a letter of justification from the physician. Here is what to include in the letter of justification:

- Include name, age, sex, and diagnosis of RS. Include a brief and simply worded explanation of the diagnosis with symptoms and prognosis. For example: "Susie Q., six years, female with RS, a neurological disorder which leads to loss of speech, gross and fine motor skills and muscle weakness, seizures, and breathing irregularities."
- Add a description of her functional skills. For example, "Susie is non-ambulatory, non-verbal, incontinent and dependent for feeding, bathing, and dressing."

Equipment and Ideas

- Describe the durable equipment she already has and explain why the new equipment is needed.
- Describe the piece of equipment prescribed now and why it has been requested. For example:
  - "Susie needs a light weight manual wheelchair because she can't walk. She must have a properly supported seating system to prevent scoliosis and avoid pressure sores."
  - "Susie needs a stroller because she can't walk long distances. She tires easily over long distances and runs greater risks of falling. She does not have purposeful hand use and cannot self-propel a wheelchair. She does not need the complex positioning support system of a wheelchair at this time."
  - "Susie needs a toilet chair because she can't sit independently on the toilet. She cannot be toilet trained without appropriate equipment for her to be successful. Toilet training reduces long-term damage to her skin and relieves the cost of diapers."
  - "Susie needs a bath chair because she can't sit or stand independently for bathing or showering. She has an increased risk of serious injury if an accident occurs while bathing without appropriate equipment."
- Include the name and phone number of someone the funding agency can call if there are questions. Signatures should include the person writing the letter and the prescribing physician if possible.
- Document why the equipment is medically necessary, as this can be the source for a denial.

Here is the process of insurance funding: the vendor (equipment supply company) provides a quotation of cost. The vendor sends it along with the doctor's prescription and letter of justification to the funding agency or insurance company. Insurance and governmental agencies generally pay the vendor directly. If families choose to deal directly with the funding source, it becomes their responsibility to work closely and communicate with the vendor regarding funding approvals or denials.

You should start early, especially for large or custom items. It may take four to six months to get a new wheelchair. If your request is denied, follow up with an appeal. Find out your insurance company's process for appeals, and get assistance from a therapist or parent who has been through this process (as this person may be able to help you use insurance-friendly wording). You may have to make some phone calls and get more documentation. *Always write down who you talked to, what they said, and when the call was made.* You may have to get a second medical opinion, but the extra work often pays off.

Keep in mind that while you may want a "Cadillac" chair, the insurance company will be more likely to fund a "Ford." The vendor will bill the insurance company for each part of the chair, from the anti-tippers to the seating system. Medicaid may not approve all parts of the chair and may require more documentation of need. Be prepared with all the necessary documentation when you order the chair.

OTHER FUNDING SOURCES

THERE ARE A NUMBER OF FUNDING SOURCES FOR DEVICES and services and it is important to go through them in proper order. First, try insurance or Medicaid, your child's school or the vocational rehabilitation agency. Each source has its own

Equipment and Ideas

procedures and policies. Do your homework first and check to find out what has worked for others. Some vendors have funding departments that will assist you with this entire process; it doesn't hurt to ask.

Insurance/Medicaid: A claim of medical necessity is a must. Denial is not the end of the story. Make it clear you will appeal.

Schools: Schools may purchase communication devices to enable the student to participate in a normal academic setting. However, the device belongs to the school, not the student.

Vocational Rehabilitation Programs: Vocational rehabilitation programs may fund equipment if the lack of it is the main obstacle to employment. Eligibility requirements vary from state to state. Look in the white pages of your local telephone book.

Private Corporations: Businesses can take a tax write-off for a charitable contribution and will get good public relations benefits at the same time.

Trust Funds: Check with the trust division of banks in your area to see if a trust fund exists for the purpose of helping people with disabilities. Banks don't often advertise the availability of this source.

Service Clubs: Local civic organizations such as the Lions Clubs, Kiwanis, and Rotary often contribute to the purchase of equipment.

Fundraisers: Churches and other organizations are often helpful in putting on a fundraiser in your community, such as a car wash, bake sale, dinner, or raffle.

Wish-makers: These organizations grant wishes to people with specific needs. Contact the Sunshine Foundation at 4010 Lefick St., Philadelphia, PA 19135 or call the Make-a-Wish Foundation at 1–800–722–9474.

Public Appeals: Contact local media to help get the word out in the community.

TYPES OF EQUIPMENT

EVERY PERSON'S CIRCUMSTANCE IS UNIQUE, and the kind of equipment needed will vary. It is important to develop a close working relationship with therapists and medical professionals who are best qualified to help select beneficial equipment and to advise in its application, daily use, and possible adaptation. Following are some types of equipment your child might need:

Arm Support Chair: Chairs with arm supports are helpful for ambulatory girls, allowing them to tuck their legs under a table. The chair and table must be the right size for them.

Bath/Shower Chair: For the individual who cannot sit independently, a bath chair provides support, promotes proper postural alignment, and improves overall safety in the tub. Chairs are adjustable to different angles so the seat can be repositioned to accommodate individual support needs, including reclining. Optional lateral pads provide additional support to the trunk to promote upright sitting in the bath chair. Additional straps can be used to offer support at the chest, hips, or legs. Many bath chairs can be ordered with attachable stands, which provide additional versatility. The chair alone can be placed down into the tub so that the child can soak. It can also be placed up on its stand and used in combination with a handheld shower so that the caregiver doesn't have to bend over during bathing.

Equipment and Ideas

Shower chairs come in roll-in models which also provide proper positioning, safety, and support and can be wheeled into the shower. Some bath and shower chairs also function as commode chairs, eliminating the need for multiple pieces of costly equipment.

Car Seat: These are essentially the same as the ones used with young children, but bigger. Some come with optional features such as a mobility base or an activity base. These features make it possible to remove the seat from the car and use it as a stroller or as a positioning chair.

Corner Chair: Corner chairs provide trunk support for children with mild trunk weakness while encouraging a functional positioning of the shoulders during sitting. Some models are elevated and have legs with casters while others sit directly on the floor. Floor sitters have the advantage of allowing a child to be down on the floor with her peers. They also encourage long sitting, which is great for stretching tight hamstrings. These chairs typically come with attachable trays.

A corner chair with tray and added padding for support allows a child to be down on the floor with the other children while providing support. It also frees up the teacher or therapist to work with other children, and provides her with the independence the other students have.

Commode Chair: Toileting equipment varies from over-the-toilet models to freestanding toilet chairs. Most come with lateral trunk sections to provide added support for children with more moderate to severe involvement and leg supports and footrests for comfort. Optional soft padded support cushions increase comfort and conform to the individual's shape without the cold and hard surface characteristics of the hard plastic. This results in better positioning control and longer tolerance for sitting.

Gait Trainer: The gait trainer provides the opportunity for the child to bear weight while providing more comprehensive upper and lower body support. It helps to improve the quality of movement and helps to increase lower body strength. The gait trainer also helps improve endurance and overall gross motor abilities. It adds to the child's daily activities and enhances learning through exploration.

Mobility Stroller: Mobility strollers fold easily and can be placed in the trunk of a car. They are a lighter weight than wheelchairs and can be convenient for short trips and running errands. However, they don't provide the degree of support offered by a wheelchair and shouldn't be used as a substitute. Due to their construction, they aren't able to provide the vertical up and down positioning and support that are needed to prevent deformities. Some mobility strollers have optional insertable "spines" for better back support. However, much better seating and positioning can be achieved in a wheelchair.

Positioning Chair: The positioning chair is used to allow the child to be arranged in a healthy and therapeutic position while at home, during therapy and in the classroom. Correct positioning helps to maximize her functional performance and independence in daily activities. Some chairs allow you to adjust the height and angle of the chair at different table and desk surface levels. Some also have the option of being able to "grow" with the child.

Stander: Standers are essentially standing frames that hold an individual upright, helping to improve bone density through weight bearing and improve circulation, digestion, and muscle tone. In general, there are both prone and supine standers, although there are models that can be positioned either way.

Walker: The walker is used to improve motor skills and balance. It stimulates walking movements, improves opportunities for social interaction, and serves as a link to more

Equipment and Ideas

advanced walking aids. It is used for a child with milder physical involvement who requires minimal support while walking. In general, walkers require a girl to inhibit her hand wringing and to sustain a grasp. Modifications, however, are always possible.

Wheelchair: A wheelchair must be custom-fit for the child's size and special needs. It provides a good sitting position when fit correctly and provides mobility for the child who has limited ability to walk. Moving from a stroller to a wheelchair is not giving up on walking. A wheelchair can provide the freedom to go and do things with the family, at school, and in the community.

Wheelchair Tray: Wheelchair trays provide a structure to give proprioceptive feedback to the individual and make access to materials much easier. The tray provides the support to either tuck one arm under, hold one arm gently down to increase dominant hand accuracy, and/or simply place materials. The tray allows positioning of any type of voice output and allows the individual to rest her elbow to access it, which is very important.

WHERE TO FIND IT— RECOMMENDED PRODUCTS AND MANUFACTURERS

ADAPTED CLOTHING

Adaptations by Adrian	www.AdaptationsByAdrian.com (877) 6-ADRIAN
Adrian's Closet	www.adrianscloset.com
One Step Ahead	www.onestepahead.com (800) 274-8440
Gabby's	www.gabbys.net (888) 442-2297
Special Clothes for Special Children	www.special-clothes.com (508) 385-9171

ARTS AND CRAFTS

Electric Scissors	www.ablenetinc.com (800) 322-0956
Switch-Activated Swirl Art	www.enablingdevices.com (800) 832-8697
Universal Art Tool Holder	www.sammonsprstonrolyan.com (800) 323-5547

BATH CHAIRS

Columbia Bath and Shower Chairs	www.columbiamedical.com (800) 454-6612
Dolphin Bath Chair	www.adaptivemall.com (800) 371-2778
Fortuna by Aquatec **Laguna by Aquatec** **Ventura by Aquatec**	www.clarkehealthcare.com (888) 347-4537

Equipment and Ideas

Robby Bathing Support Seat	www.ottobockus.com (800) 323-5547

BEDS

FINDING THE RIGHT BED can be a challenge. It needs to provide comfort, convenience, and safety, and be attractive as well as affordable. Special beds are expensive, but will often be covered by insurance or Medicaid when medical necessity is shown.

Enclosure Beds

Pedicraft Bed	www.pedicraft.com (800) 223-7649
S-Cape Bed	www.electropedicbeds.com (800) 528-3974
Sleep Safe and Sleep Safer Beds	www.sleepsafebed.com (866) 852-2337
Vail Enclosure Bed[1]	www.vailbed.com (800) 235-VAIL
Vivax Soma Safe Enclosure Bed	www.vivaxmedical.com (866) 847-7890
Volker Bed	www.nursingbeds.co.uk (800) 321-4240

Other Beds

Hospital Bed

Gives the option of bed rails and a mattress that adjusts to different heights. From your local medical supply store.

Select Comfort Adjustable Bed	www.selectcomfort.com (888) 637-8170
Tempur-pedic Mattress	www.tempurpedic.com (888) 811-5053

Water Bed with Heater

From your local retailer; build up the perimeter for safety. A water bed does not provide firm support or a stable surface and may not be appropriate for the individual with poor muscle control who cannot change positions. However, it does help prevent skin breakdown.

Bed Bolsters

Sammons Preston	www.SammonsPreston.com (800) 542-9297

Bed Risers

Linens 'N Things	www.lnt.com

---

[1]*Note:* In 2005, the US government branded this product inadequately labeled and unsafe.

Equipment and Ideas

BIBS

Assisted Living Store	www.assistedlivingstore.com (888) 388-5862
Babes in Paradise	www.Babes-In-Paradise.com
Crumb Catchers	www.crumbcatchers.com
Kangaroo Bibs	www.kangaroobib.com (800) 334-0442
Practical Creations	www.practicalcreations.com (315) 276-0505

CAR SEATS

Britax Traveler Plus	www.britax.com 44 (0)1926 400 040 (UK)
Columbia Car Seat	www.columbiamedical.com (800) 891-3857
Sit-n-Lift Power Seat by GM	www.GMMOBILITY.com (800) 323-9935
Snug Seat 1000	www.snugseat.com (800) 336-7684

COMMUNICATION EQUIPMENT
Catalogs

Ablenet	(800) 322-0956	BIGmack, Sequencer, PowerLink Wolf, Hawk Super Hawk
Adaptivation, Inc.	(800) 723-2783	VoicePal, Sequencers
Attainment Co.	(800) 327-4269	Talkers, prevocational pictures
Creative Communicating	(435) 645-7737	Adapted stories
Crestwood Communication	(414) 352-5678	Eye gaze bard and mount options
Don Johnston	(800) 999-4660	Discover switch, single switch, RE software
Dynavox Systems	(800) 344-1778	MT-4, DV-4
Enabling Devices	(800) 832-8697	Cheap Talk, switches, toys
Flaghouse	(800) 793-7900	Switch toys, switches, headpointer
IntelliTools	(800) 899-6687	IntelliKeys keyboard and software
Laureate Learning Systems	(800) 562-6801	Software for language, learning
Mayer-Johnson Co.	(619) 550-0084	Boardmaker, Speaking Dynamically Pro, Touch Windows
Puente Romich Co.	(800) 262-1990	Vanguard II, Pathfinder
RJ Cooper	(714) 240-4853	Biggy, computer software, Switch-activated mouse
Sammons Preston Rolyan	(800) 323-5547	Switches, communication devices

Equipment and Ideas

Technology for Education	(800) 370-0047	Special equipment, software
Words+, Inc.	(800) 869-8521	TuffTalker, Freedom 2000 series
Zygo Industries	(800) 234-6006	MACAW, Dialect, LightWRITER

If you have a Mac operating system, there is a free resource for downloading all kinds of switch-operated programs. There are programs for coloring pages, random spinners for game playing, simple switch versions of games like Memory and Bingo, a music maker, and more at www.switchintime.com/FreeStuff.html.

Vendors

Adaptivation, Inc.
Products: Switches, VoicePal, Sequencer
www.adaptivation.com
(800) 723-2783

AbleNet, Inc.
Products: Communication devices, switches, environmental control
www.ablenetinc.com
(800) 322-0956

Assistive Technology, Inc.
Product: Mercury Communication Device
www.assistivetech.com
(800) 793-9227

Attainment Company
Products: Communication devices, resource books
www.attainmentcompany.com
(800) 793-9227

Crestwood Communication Aids, Inc.
Products: Eye Gaze Board, communication devices, switch toys
www.communicationaids.com
(414) 352-5678

Don Johnston
Products: Software, USB Mouse, USB Switch Interface, switches
www.donjohnston.com
(800) 999-4660

DynaVox Systems, Inc.
Products: Series 4 Communication Devices (DV-4; MT-4)
www.dynavoxsys.com
(888) 697-7332

Enabling Devices
Products: Communication devices, eye gaze board, switch operated items
www.enablingdevices.com
(800) 832-8697

Flaghouse Special Populations
Products: Headpointer, communication devices, switches, switch toys, seating and positioning equipment, sensory motor items
www.FlagHouse.com
(800) 793-7900

IntelliTools, Inc.
Products: IntelliKeys keyboard, software
www.intellitools.com
(800) 899-6687

Laureate Learning Systems
Products: Software
www.llsys.com
(800) 562-6801

Mayer-Johnson, Inc.
Products: Boardmaker, Speaking Dynamically Pro, software, resource books
www.mayer-johnson.com
(800) 588-4548

RJ Cooper & Associates
Products: Computer software and hardware
www.rjcooper.com
(800) 752-6673

Equipment and Ideas

Sammons Preston Rolyan   (800) 323-5547
Products: Switches, communication devices,   www.sammonsprestonrolyan.com
adapted materials, seating and positioning
items, sensory motor items

Technology for Education   www.iste.org
Products: Special equipment, software   (800) 336-5191

Zygo   www.zygo-usa.com
Products: TuffTalker, Freedom 2000   (800) 234-6006

Web Sites

Augmentative and Alternative   www.aac.unl.edu/yaack
Communication (AAC)
Connecting Young Kids

ACC Intervention   www.aacintervention.com
(Caroline Musselwhite)

Technology Integration (Linda Burkhart)   www.lburkhart.com

Creative Communicating   www.creativecommunicating.com
(Patti King DeBaun)

GAIT TRAINERS/WALKERS

Ablegaiter   www.ablegaitor.com
                                       (888) 858-5289

Bronco Walker   www.snugseat.com
                                       (800) 336-7684

Meywalker   www.petergo.com/sales.html
                                       petergo@odyssey.on.ca
                                       (519) 235-2725

Pony Walker   www.snugseat.com
                                       (800) 336-7684

Rifton Pacer   www.rifton.com
                                       (800) 777-4244

Walkabout Gait Trainer   www.mulhollandinc.com
                                       (800) 543-4769

HEAD POSITIONING

Hensiger Head Support   www.abledata.com
                                       (800) 227-0216

HOME LIFTS

CHECK WITH YOUR DAUGHTER'S PHYSICAL THERAPIST to recommend the type of hydraulic lift that would be best for her needs.

Barrier Free Lift   www.horcher.com
                                       (800) 582-8732

Equipment and Ideas

Guardian Voyager Portable Ceiling Lift	www.susquemicro.com (888) 730-5463
Liko Light Lift	www.liko.com (888) 545-6671
Molift Lifter	www.molift.co.uk 0161 476 2413 (UK)
Porto-Lift Deluxe Pediatric Lift	www.americandiscountmed.com (800) 877-9100
Stair Lifts	www.accessind.com (800) 925-3100
SureHands Lift and Care Systems	www.surehands.com (800) 724-5305

INCONTINENCE PRODUCTS

EVERY INDIVIDUAL HAS DIFFERENT NEEDS. Personal trial and error is required to find what works best. Don't assume that the first product you use is the best one for your child. The following products have been recommended by parents.

Abriform	Promise
Attends	Protection Plus Ultra
Depends	Reassure
First Quality Youth Briefs	Select Disposable Underwear
Goodnites Pullups	Serenity
Kendall Wings ClassicSleep Pants by Curity	Sleep Pants by Curity
Luvs	Tena Ultra
MoliCare Superplus	Tranquility Slimline
Pampers Cruisers	Walgreens Private Label
Pampers Pull Ups	Wal-Mart Private Label

Disposable Diaper Vendors

Absorbent Solutions, Inc.	www.absorbentsolutions.com (800) 869-1275
Allcares	www.allcares.com (877) 613-6424
BAIP	www.baip.com (888) 401-5311
Diapers America	www.diapersamerica.com (800) 262-8670
Direct Medical, Inc.	www.directmedicalinc.com (800) 659-8037
Duraline Medical Products	www.dmponline.com (800) 654-3376
HDIS	www.hdis.com (800) 269 4663

Equipment and Ideas

Incontinence Resource Center	www.incontinencesupport.org briand@dcr.net
Magic Medical	www.adultdiapermagicmed.com (877) 245-7148
MOMS	www.momscatalog.com (800) 232-7443
MedCare Central	www.medcarecentral.com (800) 893-9371
Principle Business Enterprises Inc.	www.gopeach.com (800) 467-3224
Pant and Pad Systems **Humanicare**	www.humanicare.com (800) 631-5270

MISCELLANEOUS

Acid Reflux Pillow	www.acidrefluxpillow.com (800) 221-9105
Mother's Third Arm A device that holds a cup/bottle **Slant Board**	www.enablingdevices.com (800) 832-8697
NUK Massage Brushes	www.equipmentshop.com (800) 525-7681
Podee Hands Free Baby Bottle	www.nossgalenbaby.com (505) 400-4700
Oral/motor/chew items	www.integrationscatalog.com (800) 850-8602

POSITIONING CHAIRS

Corner Chair	www.SammonsPreston.com (800) 542-9297
Jenx Lion Chair	www.jenx.com (800) 547-5716
Kid Kart	www.usatechguide.org techguide@unitedspinal.org
Leckey Easy Seat	www.leckey.com (800) 626-020 (UK)
Leis Tech Orthopedic Positioning Chair	www.adaptivedesignlabs.com (800) 293-4ADL
Odyssey Chair	www.theradapt.com (800) 261-4919
Rifton Positioning Chair	www.rifton.com (800) 777-4244
Symmetrikit Tiltrite Chair **and Sleep System**	www.helpinghand.co.uk 01531 635 678 (UK)

Equipment and Ideas

Tiger Positioning Chair	www.snugseat.com
	(800) 336-7684
Tomato Multi-Positioning Chair	www.adaptivemall.com
	(800) 371-2778
Transition Chair	www.theradapt.com
Tumble Forms Floor Sitter	www.tumbleforms.com
Tumble Forms Feeder Seat	(800) 371-2778
Wombat by Snugseat	www.snugseat.com
	(800) 336-7684

PRONE STANDERS

Chattanooga Dynamic Stander	www.fasequipment.com
	03-95876766 (Aus)
Easy Stand Magician	www.easystand.com
	(800) 342-8968
Jenx Monkey Stander	www.jenx.com
	(800) 547-5716
Leckey Freestander	www.leckey.com
	(800) 626-020 (UK)
Quest 88	www.quest88.com
	44(0) 1952 463050 (UK)
Rifton Stander	www.rifton.com
	(800) 777-4244
Tumble Forms Tristander 45	www.tumbleforms.com
	(800) 371-2778
Youth 5000	www.adaptivemall.com
	(800) 371-2778
Superstand	www.primeengineering.com
	(800) 827-8263

SOFTWARE

Attainment Company	www.attainmentcompany.com
	(800) 327-4269
Edmark	www.riverdeep.net/edmark
	(800) 362-2890
Laureate Learning Systems	www.laureatelearning.com
	(800) 562-6801
MarbleSoft Online	www.marblesoft.com
	(763) 862-2920
RJ Cooper & Associates	www.rjcooper.com
	(800) 752-6673
SofTouch Inc.	www.softouch.com
	(877) softouch

Equipment and Ideas

SPECIAL FOODS

HAVE YOUR DOCTOR WRITE A VERY SPECIFIC LETTER as to the medical necessity for special foods and formulas. Be sure to make the insurance company aware that use of thickeners will avoid choking and that special formulas are your daughter's main source of nutrition. Both will enhance her health and prevent unnecessary illness.

Crescent Frutex	www.gicare.com (717) 761-0930
Fruit Eze	www.fruiteze.com (888) REGULAR
SimplyThick	www.simplythick.com (800) 508-2990
Thicken Up	www.tchomemedical.com (516) 326-4999
Thick It, Thick It 2	www.precisionfoods.com (800) 333-0003

SPLINTS

ArmBraces	www.Armbraces.com (316) 529-3698
Comfy Splints	www.comfysplints.com (800) 582-5332
Pedi-Wrap Splints	www.pediwrap.com (888) 463-3543

STROLLERS AND PUSHCHAIRS

Pixi Pushchair	www.sammonspreston.com (800) 323-5547
Otto Bock Kimba Stroller	www.ottobockus.com (800) 323-5547
Kid Kart	www.usatechguide.org techguide@unitedspinal.org
Special Needs Baby Jogger	www.joggingstroller.com (800) 887-0218

SWIM PRODUCTS

Adult Swim Diapers	www.urincontrol.com (888) 254-8780

Aqua Force Coast Guard Suit
  Alexis Play Safe Suit
  Pool Pal Flotation Suit
  Swim-sters Undergarments
	www.mypoolpal.com
	(888) 766-5725

Bema Schwimmflugels Buoys	www.splashinternational.com (888) 775-2744

Equipment and Ideas

Pool Pant Diapers	www.swim-diapers.com
	(888) 4GABBYS
Swimsuits and Undergarments	www.specialclothes.com
Wet Wrap Swim Vest	(508) 385-9171
Thera-Swim Undershirts, Wet Suits	www.sprintaquatics.com
Swim Diapers, Swim Tubes	(800)235-2156
Tushies Swim Diapers	www.swimdiapers.com
	(800) 344-6379

SWINGS

Full Support Swing	www.tfhusa.com
Wheelchair Platform Swing	(800) 467-6222
All types of swings	www.southpawenterprises.com
	(800) 228-1698

SWITCHES

One Step Communicator	www.ablenetinc.com
Step-by-Step Communicator	(800) 322-0956
Big Red Switch	
Jelly Bean Switch	
Koosh Switch	www.dragonflytoys.com
	(800) 308-2208
Say it Rocking Switch Plate	www.enablingdevices.com
	(800) 832-8697

TOOTHBRUSHES

Collis Curve Toothbrush	www.colliscurve.com
	(800) 298-4818
Infa-Dent Finger Toothbrushes	www.apexdentalproducts.com
Swallow Safe Toothpaste	(800) 959-8517
Radius Toothbrush	www.radiustoothbrush.com
	(800) 626-6223

TOYS, GAMES, AND FUN

The National Lekotek Center recommends considering these factors when buying toys for children with disabilities:

Multisensory appeal: Does the toy respond with lights, sounds, or movement? Are there contrasting colors? Does it have a scent? Is there texture?

Method of activation: Will the toy provide a challenge without frustration? What is the force required to activate? What are the number and complexity of steps required to activate the toy?

Equipment and Ideas

Where toy will be used: Can the toy be used in a variety of positions such as side-lying or on wheelchair tray? Will the toy be easy to store? Is there space in the home?

Opportunities for success: Can play be open-ended with no definite right or wrong way? Is it adaptable to the child's individual style, ability and pace?

Current popularity: Is it a toy most any child would like? Does it tie in with other activities like TV, movies, books, clothing, etc?

Self-expression: Does the toy allow for creativity, uniqueness, and choice-making? Will it give the child experience with a variety of media?

Adjustability: Does it have adjustable height, sound volume, speed, level of difficulty?

Child's individual characteristics: Does the toy provide activities that reflect both developmental and chronological ages? Does it reflect the child's interests and age?

Safety and durability: Consider the child's size and strength in relation to the toy's durability. Are the toy and its parts sized appropriately? Does the toy have moisture resistance? Can it be washed and cleaned?

Potential for interaction: Will the child be an active participant during use? Will the toy encourage social engagement with others?

Game and Toy Vendors

AbleNet	www.ablenetinc.com (800) 322-0956
Abilitations	www.abilitations.com (800) 850-8603
Alliance for Technology Access	www.ataccess.org (707) 778-3011
Center for Creative Play	www.center4creativeplay.org/adapted.htm (412) 371-1668
Come Play with Me	www.comeplaytoys.com (888) 798-2855
Crestwood Company	www.communicationaids.com (414) 352-5678
Dr. Toy	www.drtoy.org
Dragonfly Toy Company	www.dragonflytoys.com (800) 308-2208
Exceptional Parent Recommends	www.exceptionalparent.com/toys (800) 372-7368
Flaghouse Special Populations	www.flaghouse.com/special.htm (800) 793-7900
Freedom Concepts	www.freedomconcepts.com (800) 661-9915

Equipment and Ideas

Funtastic Learning	www.funtasticlearning.com (800) 722-737
Innovative Products, Inc.	www.mobility4kids.com (800) 950-5185
Lakeshore Learning Materials	www.lakeshorelearning.com (800) 421-5354
Laureate Learning Systems	www.laureatelearning.com (800) 562-6801
Leap Frog	www.leapfrog.com (866) 334-5327
Oppenheim Toy Portfolio	www.toyportfolio.com (800) 544-8697
Special Needs Toys	www.tfhusa.com (800) 467-6222
Tools for Life	www.gatfl.org (912) 681-5961
Touch Heal Feel	www.tfhusa.com/us_home.html (800) 467-6222
Toy Directory.com	www.toydirectory.com/specialneeds.htm (310) 979-4330
Toys for Special Children & Enabling Devices	www.enablingdevices.com (800) 832-8697
Toys "R" Us *Toy Guide for Differently-Abled Kids*	www.toysrus.com
Other Switches/Toys	www.enablingdevices.com (800) 832-8697
For Mac Computers free switch operated programs	www. Switchintime.com (978) 486-9433

VAN LIFTS

HandiRamps	(800) 876-RAMP
Braun ULV	www.braunlift.com (800) THE-LIFT

VAN RESTRAINTS

Q-Straint System	www.abledata.com (800) 227-0216
EZ-Lock	www.ezlock.net (225) 214-4620

WEIGHTED PRODUCTS

Southpaw Enterprises	www.Southpawenterprises.com (800) 228-1698

Equipment and Ideas

Achievement Products	www.specialkidszone.com
	(800) 373-4699
Active Blankets	www.ActiveBlankets.com

WHEELCHAIRS

Convaid Cruiser with back supports	www.convaid.com
Convaid Safari Tilt Chair	(888) 266-8243
Convaid Scout	
Convaid Rodeo	
Invacare Solara	www.invacare.com
Invacare Spree	(800) 668-5324
Libre Tilt-in-Space	www.abledata.com
	(800) 227-0216
Quickie Iris	www.quickie-wheelchairs.com
Quickie Zippie	(800) 236-4215
WheelchairNet	www.wheelchairnet.org
Zippie Tilt-n-Space Chair	www.phc-online.com
	(866) 553-5319

GENERAL EQUIPMENT VENDORS

Abledata	www.Abledata.com
	(800) 227-0216
Adaptive Mall	www.adaptivemall.com
	(800) 371-2778
Allegro Medical	www.allegromedical.com
	(800) 861-3211
American Discount Medical	www.americandiscountmed.com
	(800) 877-9100
National Seating and Mobility	www.nsm-seating.com
	info@nsm-seating.com
Planet Mobility	www.planetmobility.com
	(866) 465-4387
USA Tech Guide	www.usatechguide.org

DO IT YOURSELF

BEDS

- Use a daybed and make a removable tapestry or lattice panel.
- Make an enclosure bed from plywood cutouts for a mattress on the floor.
- Make a pipe "ladder" that slips between the vertical posts of the head and footboards.
- Have a bunk bed company make a custom version of a twin bed with safety slats and padding.

Equipment and Ideas

- Use a thick futon mattress with an egg crate mattress on top.
- Use a standard captain's bed (a taller bed with drawers underneath), and make rails out of two-by-eight boards.
- Use a sleigh bed with a headboard at each end and two bunk bed side rails that run the full length of the bed. Use crib bumper pads to pad the rails.
- Use a juvenile bed which has a very low setting for the rails. Use a bunk bed board instead of a box spring to keep the bed low.

BIBS

- Make a cardboard pattern and trace on a thick bath towel. Sew binding around the edges and put Velcro at the neckline. Use vinyl with flannel backing for a waterproof lining.
- Buy colorful bandanas that sell for a dollar. Make a triangle, and tie around the neck.
- Knit a scarf with very soft cotton yarn. They are soft, absorbent, and trendy.
- Use colorful kitchen hand towels and use a piece of elastic with a clip on each end.
- Sew each end of a four or five-inch length of wide, soft sheeting elastic onto the corners at the narrow end of pretty hand towels. They slip over the head and the neck come up nice and high under the chin. You don't even need to use a sewing machine.
- Turn a sweatshirt inside out and sew a line the size you want the bib to be, and then cut around it. Cut around the back of the neck about two inches down, and turn right side out. Stitch the back bib to the front and hem the back neckline. It then slips right over the head easily.
- Use a plastic barber's cape.

EYE GAZE FRAME
Materials

- 8-10 feet of 2-inch diameter PVC pipe
- 4 caps
- 4 T-shaped connectors
- 6 elbow shaped connectors
- saw or pipe cutters
- PVC pipe cleaner
- PVC glue
- strip of self stick Velcro-at least 24 inches

Directions

1. Using a saw or pipe cutters, cut pieces of PVC pipe to the lengths shown in the diagram. Note: feel free to make dimensions smaller or different to fit your child's needs.
2. Put pieces together as shown in the diagram using connectors and using caps on ends of the "feet" of the frame.
3. Clean ends where connected using the pipe cleaning liquid, then glue together (optional).
4. Stick on strips of the fuzzy side of the Velcro on the top, sides, and bottom of the frame so that pictures or objects can be attached.
5. Use small pieces of the hook side of the Velcro on whatever you want to attach.

Equipment and Ideas

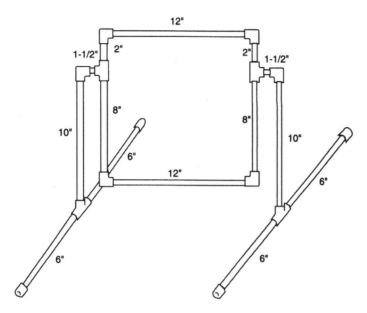

Eye gaze-frame

EYE GAZE VEST
Materials

- Plain, lightweight material
- Lining material if desired
- 1 yard of clear plastic (found at sewing stores)
- Sew-on Velcro

Directions

1. Cut out and sew vest to the dimensions shown in the diagram, making a hole for the neck and opening on one side of the neck.
2. Cut out and sew on plastic pockets, making each about 3.5 inch square, and spreading them apart evenly. Pockets are placed on both the front and back to allow the wearer to have two sets of pictures and simply turn the vest around to change topics.
3. Sew on Velcro to make an easy neck closure.
4. (Optional) On the inside, you can sew Velcro strips so that you can make the vest reversible and attach small toys or other objects and allow a child to reach for them or use eye gaze while your hands are free.

   A Communication (eye gaze) vest is also available through Mayer-Johnson.

LIFTS

We installed a metal beam to the ceiling rafters with large long bolts. We then bought an electric wrench and have that running on the track. I found a sling with a spread bar on the Internet, and with this, we can move Ashley from the bed to bathtub easily. My husband wired Ashley's room to a generator so if power goes out we can still use the lift.

Equipment and Ideas

SPLINTS

- Make elbow restraints with washcloths with a rubber type material inside secured with tennis elbow wraps.
- Use wrist weights either on both hands or just one on the dominant side.
- Use padded orange juice or potato chip cans.
- Use rolled-up magazines secured with tape or Velcro, covered by a long sock.

"There's a way to do it better—find it."

– THOMAS A. EDISON

Where to Go for Help

FINANCIAL CHALLENGES

FINDING SUPPORT

THE DIAGNOSIS OF A LIFELONG disorder brings financial challenges that might never have been considered before. The cost of doctors, nursing care, therapists, medications, supplies, and equipment might stagger any reasonable budget. There are financial supports available to help pay some of these costs; however, sometimes they are well embedded in the system and difficult to locate on your own. Perseverance is the key, whether dealing with an insurance reimbursement or acquiring funding from an outside source. Don't give up easily.

ADVOCACY

YOU ARE THE BEST ADVOCATE your daughter could possibly have. No one understands her condition and knows her needs better than you do. As her only voice, it is important for you to take this role seriously. Make sure you attend meetings, hearings, workshops, and seminars that relate to services that will affect her life. Look closely at what is being offered, proposed, or on the chopping block. Look between the lines and scrutinize language, analyze, and question changes in the provision of supports and services. Being careful and watchful are part of the advocate's territory.

"When one door of happiness closes, another opens; but often we look so long at the closed door that we do not see the one which has been opened for us."

– HELEN KELLER

WHAT THE LAW PROVIDES

FEDERAL AND STATE LAWS ARE IN PLACE to help you get the supports and services your child needs. It is important that you understand your rights and responsibilities under the law.

Public Law 94-142 is the primary federal legislative act involving the education of children who have educational disabilities. Called the Education for All Handicapped Act of 1975, this law aims to assure the availability of a "free appropriate public education" for every eligible child. It sets forth a range of school and parental responsibilities as well as procedural safeguards to ensure the due process of law.

The **Individuals with Disabilities Education Act** (IDEA) is a law which guarantees a free, appropriate, public education to all eligible children with disabilities. A child cannot become eligible for special education and services until an evaluation has been done. This evaluation must be provided by your state and local school district, but you may have to request it.

Where to Go for Help

If your child is under three years of age, she is eligible for early intervention services, which include any supports an infant or toddler may need to help her development. These programs differ from state to state. After the age of three, she is eligible for a free, appropriate, public education.

The IDEA provides support for special education and related services in many different settings, including child care, preschool, and kindergarten through high school. The philosophy of IDEA is to provide a way for children to be educated as much as possible with children who do not have disabilities.

Section 504 of the Rehabilitation Act of 1973 is a law which prohibits discrimination against individuals with disabilities. The law applies to all programs and activities which receive federal funds, including local school districts and Head Start programs. Any program which gets federal funds must provide a free public education to children with disabilities. Section 504 provides legal rights for children with disabilities. Some states also provide mediation services, which are useful in settling disputes about eligibility and the kind of services your child should get.

The **Americans with Disabilities Act** (ADA) is an important law for people with disabilities. It prohibits discrimination in employment, public transportation, services provided by state and local governments, services and accommodations offered by private businesses, and telecommunications. The ADA is intended to remove barriers that prevent individuals with disabilities from getting an equal opportunity to share in and contribute to American life, such as in restaurants, theaters, child care centers, and other community resources.

Parent Training and Information Centers (PTI) are located in each state. These centers are run by parents to provide education and training to all parents on their rights under the law.

GOVERNMENT ASSISTANCE PROGRAMS

MEDICAID

MEDICAID IS A COMBINED STATE AND FEDERAL assistance program for people aged 21 and over who are low income, over sixty-five and blind, disabled, or recipients of *Aid to Families with Dependent Children* (AFDC) or *Supplemental Security Income* (SSI). Eligibility requirements vary from state to state. In some states, the state may pay private insurance premiums to keep you off Medicaid. Benefits include inpatient care and may include limited outpatient services.

Medicaid Waivers

States may apply to the *Health Care Finance Administration* (HFCA) to set aside the income restrictions for Medicaid. This allows services to take place in the home or community for some patients who would otherwise have to be hospitalized or institutionalized for care. Medicaid waivers are targeted to individuals with mental retardation or developmental disabilities, the elderly, or disabled. A number of states also have programs specifically directed at other populations such as those who are medically fragile or technology dependent. Programs and services can vary greatly from one state to another.

Types of Waivers

The Model Medicaid Waiver removes the income requirements for Medicaid (in most states) and allows services to take place in the home or community.

Where to Go for Help

The Regular Home and Community Based Medical Waiver covers services typically covered by Medicaid and additional expenses not usually paid for by Medicaid (waivered services). If your daughter is under eighteen years, she may be eligible for one of these waivers, which are intended to offer what is needed to keep the child at home. Recognize that many individuals who are at risk of being placed in a medical facility can be cared for in their homes and communities, preserving their independence and ties to family and friends at a cost no higher than that of institutional care. A waiver may provide for assistance in the home at crucial hours, foster care in a family especially trained to deal with her problems, or a group home.

Eligibility for the waiver is determined by the child's degree of disability (requiring twenty-four hour care as in RS). But you do not need to have a twenty-four hour nurse available. The hours of assistance you are eligible for can vary according to the needs of the family.

There are seven services which may be provided in Home and Community Based Service waiver programs:

- case management
- homemaker services
- home health aide services
- personal care services
- adult day health
- habilitation
- respite care

Here are some items which can be provided through the waiver:

- skilled nursing care in the home, including overnight if necessary
- medical care not covered by insurance
- wheelchair
- car seat
- bath chair
- hospital bed
- gait trainer
- walker
- AFOs
- kangaroo pump, IV pole
- suction machine
- diapers and wipes
- some home modifications

Other services requested by the state because they are needed by waiver participants to avoid being placed in a medical facility (such as transportation, in-home support services, meal services, special communication services, minor home modifications, and adult day care) may also be provided, subject to approval.

The **State Medicaid Plan Option** allows states to provide medical services without permission from the federal government to certain designated categories of children who would

Where to Go for Help

otherwise have to be hospitalized or institutionalized. A state plan certifying these categories may be approved and applications are open only to children under the age of eighteen. This is known as the **Tax Equity and Fiscal Responsibility Act** (TEFRA) option.

Application for Medicaid

Contact your local Social Security office or Medicaid agency in your state to see whether there is a **Home and Community Based Service** (HCBS) waiver program which would meet the needs of your daughter. In most states, when you apply and receive Supplemental Security Income (SSI) for your daughter, she automatically qualifies for Medicaid. However, if your daughter is under eighteen years of age, your income is considered in the determination, so she may not get SSI. Your local Social Security caseworker may not know about this special waiver. Mention it during your appointment, and as with all dealings with the social security office, be persistent. You have a great chance of winning your appeal. The waiting lists for the waiver is typically long but it makes sense to get screened and on the list immediately.

Our first application was denied because of income. The second time around we had our tri-county representative send a letter detailing Nicole's condition and we were approved. The program pays for Nicole's prescriptions and doctor visits that our insurance won't cover. We also get diapers delivered to the house each month free of charge.

I contacted a home health agency, someone came to our home and did an assessment, then told us to go to the Department of Human Resources for the medical card portion of the waiver. We were first turned down because Ann wasn't disabled enough. I asked if you had to be dead! I appealed and we got through that stage. Then the papers went to the Medicaid office, which also denied it, saying that Ann did not qualify. I said that was unacceptable and took it to a hearing. The hearing officer ruled in our favor because a state office or clerical staff cannot override the medical professionals who had already made a level of care determination. It has been wonderful for us. Currently we have the attendant care portion of the waiver and have a caregiver forty-five hours a week as well as diapers and the medical card to pay for medical care not covered by our insurance.

Kristas has been on the waiver for the past nine years. At the time we applied for the waiver, we were denied because we were seen as "foster parents." However, with a couple of years of fighting and threatening institutionalization, and then a great lawyer who previously worked for Medicaid, we got it.

Every Monday I called and said we couldn't survive another weekend without help. I told them we had no energy left, we couldn't continue to care for Amanda and have any family left. I know I looked pretty tired. Of course you couldn't separate Amanda from my hands while I'm still breathing, but they didn't need to know that. I just told them how tired we were, how we were running out of money, how it was so consuming. I didn't whine or repeat myself, I just kept it to the difficult things. They don't need to know about the positives. Anyway, we qualified in one day after I finished all the paperwork based on need and not income.

We also have a supported living grant, which is funding we use to keep and pay a qualified person with her while we work. The caregiver goes with us on vacations so we can participate with our son in things our daughter just cannot do.

SUPPLEMENTAL SECURITY INCOME (SSI)

SUPPLEMENTAL SECURITY INCOME (SSI) is a federal program which provides regular income to individuals with mental or physical disabilities who meet disability and income limit requirements. Because of the income requirements, many middle income disabled children do not qualify. However, if the child is hospitalized more than

Where to Go for Help

thirty calendar days, she is not considered part of the family and can qualify on her own income limitations. Upon discharge from the hospital, SSI is discontinued unless she is part of a waiver program.

Those who are covered by SSI or AFDC (Aid to Families with Dependent Children) are automatically covered by Medicaid, so that even though there may be little income from SSI, the Medicaid benefits may be great. To reach the number for your local state Social Security Administration, call 1-800-772-1213. It is important to remember that first applications for SSI are routinely rejected, even though half are eventually approved. It may take some time, but the trouble is worth it because of the Medicaid benefits which can be obtained.

All individuals over the age of eighteen years qualify for SSI, because they are considered adults and the parents' income is not considered. It is important to make application for SSI benefits a few months before her eighteenth birthday, so that monthly payments can begin as soon as she turns eighteen.

STATE PROGRAMS FOR CHILDREN WITH SPECIAL HEALTH CARE NEEDS

PREVENTIVE, DIAGNOSTIC, OR TREATMENT SERVICES for children with disabilities vary with each state. Each state has a Children with Special Health Care Needs office, which makes these determinations. Copayments may be made for families with greater financial need, even though their income exceeds the eligibility.

GENETIC SERVICES

MEDICAID MAY COVER THE COST OF GENETIC SERVICES, which may vary from one state to another. Although some genetics programs are supported by state and federal funding, most charge a fee for services. For information about genetic services in your state, contact your state Genetic Services Coordinator.

EARLY PERIODIC SCREENING, DIAGNOSIS AND TREATMENT (EPSDT)

ALL STATES OFFER *Early Periodic Screening, Diagnosis and Treatment* (EPSDT) for children under the age of twenty-one who are eligible to receive Medicaid (whether through AFDC, SSI, waiver, or TEFRA). Screening must be done by a qualified provider, and many different providers may participate in screening. Screens must include a health, development and nutritional assessment, an unclothed physical exam, immunizations, and vision, hearing, dental, and lab tests (including blood lead level tests). If the screening identifies a problem, Medicaid must pay for the treatment, even if it is not approved for funding under the state Medicaid plan. The state can require prior approval for expensive medical services, but they must provide the services.

PUBLIC SCHOOL SYSTEM REQUIREMENTS

PUBLIC SCHOOLS MUST PAY FOR SPECIAL EDUCATION and any related services for children with disabilities, including medical services for diagnostic or evaluation purposes, occupational, physical and speech therapies, and psychological services. Any service which is needed by the child and identified on the IEP must be provided at no cost. If a service is identified on the IEP but is not available, the public school, a court, or hearing officer may order the school district to pay for the services at a private facility.

In limited situations, the school district can ask your private insurance to pay for special education services, but the Office for Civil Rights has established that schools cannot

Where to Go for Help

require parents to use their own health insurance. If you do consider using your own health insurance to pay for school services, look carefully at your policy for additional costs, higher premiums, limitations on lifetime or yearly limits, co-insurance requirements, deductibles, documentation of a pre-existing condition or transmission of information to the Medical Information Bureau. If any of these requirements exist, the school district cannot require you to use your own insurance.

SECTION 8 HOUSING

EVERY COMMUNITY HAS ITS OWN HOUSING AUTHORITY that handles applications and approval. It allows for the eligible family to pay thirty percent of the household income toward the rent. The housing authority is responsible for the difference. The family is responsible for finding housing that will pass inspection. The waiting list can be several years. Priority is given to victims of violence, and, applicants who are enrolled in an educational/training or upward mobility program and demonstrate that they are meeting the goals of the program, those currently working, or those in which the head of the household is disabled.

OTHER SOURCES OF SUPPORT

CHARITABLE SERVICE GROUPS SUCH AS ELKS, Lions, Kiwanis, Rotary, and Junior League often hold fundraisers for individuals in their communities who need help. Offer to give a presentation to the group on RS and ask if the group will help fund a particular item, travel to an IRSA conference or therapy.

We wrote a letter to our local Kiwanis Club, Rotary, and other local nonprofit organizations for the request of a van and/or assistance with getting a conversion van donated. We had our van conversion fully funded by various local organizations.

Shriners Hospitals and Clinics offer excellent free services and care for children under the age of eighteen with orthopedic needs. Located throughout North America, Mexico, and Canada, these Centers of Excellence serve as major referral centers for children with complex orthopedic problems. There is never a charge to the patient, parent or any third party for any service or medical treatment received at Shriners Hospitals. For information, call 1-800-237-5055. In Canada: 1-800-361-7256.

INSURANCE

THE COST OF HEALTH CARE HAS SKYROCKETED to crisis dimensions in recent years, and paying for health care is an additional burden to families of children with special needs. For many people, obtaining insurance coverage is difficult, if not impossible. Once obtained, the insurance may not pay for all of the child's needs. Others may find their policies dropped when they move to a new job or have their child's special needs deemed "pre-existing," and ineligible for coverage.

TYPES OF INSURANCE

THERE ARE A NUMBER OF DIFFERENT TYPES OF INSURANCE protection available. Sometimes the decision is made by your employer, and sometimes you

Where to Go for Help

have a choice in selecting healthcare coverage. Often, the type of insurance available is a variation or combination of the following:

Basic Protection: may include hospitalization, hospital services, supplies, and surgery. There are often specific limitations to this coverage.

Major Medical: supplements basic coverage, and covers long-term illness or injury, paying a major portion of expenses over and above basic protection policies.

Comprehensive Medical: a combination of basic, major medical, and catastrophic insurance. After a deductible amount is paid by the insured, a major percentage of costs is covered. There may be no limit on the maximum benefit, or the limit may be high.

Disability Insurance: does not pay the hospital or doctor, but ensures a regular cash income to someone who becomes disabled from illness or injury. Benefits vary widely from one policy to another.

Supplemental Policies: additional coverage which is purchased for catastrophic illness such as cancer or for nursing home care. Be cautious of solicitations for this type of insurance through the mail, by telephone, or door-to-door. They may not be legitimate.

ADDITIONAL POLICIES

Minimum Pediatric Life Insurance: from infancy to seven years of age, available without a physical examination. This type of insurance is helpful for those who have a family incidence of more than one child with RS.

Hospitalization Income Supplement Plans: provide a payment for every day spent in the hospital. This may not be economical, but may be helpful when frequent hospitalizations are necessary. Often, there is a one-to-two-year waiting period to fulfill preexisting condition qualifications.

PRIVATE INSURANCE OPTIONS

Group Plans: costs are shared by the insured and employers.

Preferred Provider Organizations (PPOs): services are provided with specific health providers, with an option to see nonparticipating doctors at a higher per visit cost.

Self-Insured Programs: businesses pay all or part of the medical expenses without using insurance. These programs are not subject to state regulation and have very limited legal protection.

Health Maintenance Organizations (HMOs): groups subscribe to these plans, which provide preventive, ongoing, and hospital coverage, usually with a set fee for service. These plans require that physicians who are members of the HMO are used. This sometimes restricts choice and specialized care. There is usually a small copayment and often a referral from the primary care physician is necessary for specialists.

Individual Plans: provided by an insurance company, with more restricted benefits than group plans.

THE PRE-EXISTING CONDITION PROBLEM

IF THE DIAGNOSIS OF RS IS MADE before the policy is in place, the insurance company has an option to reject the coverage if the policy has a "preexisting" clause. If RS is not disclosed on the application for coverage, the insurance company can deny

Where to Go for Help

benefits when a claim is made, or may cancel the policy and refund the premium. Many insurance companies have clauses that limit coverage for a condition which has been treated within three to six months of the start of the policy. Some companies exclude particular conditions for one year or even for the life of the policy. When the insurance company asks when the RS first began, it is attempting to determine if the condition pre-existed the purchase of the policy. This can give the company space to deny the claim.

HMOs are prohibited from excluding pre-existing conditions, but they may limit the coverage offered. Most large group plans may go into effect after a specified time period of employment, and may not have limitations on pre-existing conditions.

The Americans with Disabilities Act of 1999 (ADA), prohibits employers from discriminating against people with disabilities. Under this act, employers are prohibited from discriminating against an employee because a family member has a genetic disorder. However, the law does not prohibit employers from refusing to cover pre-existing conditions.

Prenatal testing which determines that a child will be born with a genetic disorder causes the condition to be considered pre-existing. This must be disclosed to health insurers. Therefore, if you are planning to have more children, it may be wise to obtain or change health insurance in advance.

The effect of this clause traps people in jobs for fear they will not be able to obtain insurance when they move. Make sure to consider this issue carefully before switching jobs or insurance companies.

I work in an insurance agency and, unfortunately, it is impossible to insure either health or life after a diagnosis of RS. If you have a life policy on yourself with a children's term rider you may be able to convert some coverage for her at the end of the term, usually twenty-five years. I have a policy with State Farm and when Ann is twenty-five I can convert up to five times the amount of CTR without proof of insurability.

GETTING INSURANCE TO PAY

FIND OUT THE INSURANCE COMPANY'S DEFINITION of "medical necessity," and ask for it in writing. Always write down the name of the person you speak with, and the date and the time. You may need this later! Every insurance company has its own definition for medical necessity. For communication equipment, point out the medical necessity of being able to communicate illness and pain so that prompt and accurate assessment and treatment can be started and extra costs avoided. For diapers, medical necessity is the avoidance of skin breakdown. For wheelchair and seating equipment, the medical necessity is determined by the need for proper support to avoid scoliosis and subsequent surgery.

If your insurance plan is inadequate, ask your employer if an extension to the policy can be granted. This may be done without a lot of additional cost.

WHEN YOUR CHILD IS NO LONGER A CHILD

WHEN YOUR CHILD REACHES ADULTHOOD, she may no longer be covered under your policy. Some insurers will cover a totally disabled child through adulthood, and others will allow you to convert the policy to an individual policy in her name. When the insurer will allow coverage to continue for a totally disabled child, you may have to make a formal written declaration of total disability (at least three months before her eighteenth birthday). Be sure to apply to your local Social Security office for Supplemental

Where to Go for Help

Security Income (SSI) when your child reaches her eighteenth birthday, so that medical assistance will be put in place. It is best to have both private health insurance and Medicaid.

REIMBURSEMENT STRATEGIES

FOLLOWING ARE SOME TIPS FOR AVOIDING time delays and hassles with insurance:

- Always pay by check so that you have proof of payment.
- Review your policy carefully after you purchase it. Most states allow ten days to cancel with a full refund.
- Every year, review the policy to make sure your coverage meets your needs.
- Keep a record of all expenses related to health care, including nonprescription items.
- Keep receipts for all payments you have made on the policy.
- Make copies of everything you send to the insurance company or the government.
- Always get the name of the person you speak to on the telephone. Follow up calls with a written letter sent by certified mail confirming the phone conversation.
- Even if your policy says it will not pay for a specific service or item, file anyway. Appeal if your claim is rejected.

AVOIDING DENIAL OF CLAIMS

YOU CAN AVOID DENIAL IF YOU MAKE SURE TO READ your policy carefully so that you know what is covered and what is not. Tell the doctors and service providers about your financial situation and what your policy covers. If prior authorization or a second opinion is required, make sure you follow through. Don't ever assume that everything will be covered just because the doctor ordered it.

APPEALING REJECTIONS

DON'T EVER TAKE "NO" FOR AN ANSWER. Statistics show that the majority of appeals are successful. Find out your insurance carrier's appeal process and follow these requirements carefully. Most companies have a three-stage appeal process: 1) informal; 2) formal; and 3) legal. Make sure to involve the service providers in appealing a denied claim, as they will be able to justify the expense. Often, a well-written letter of necessity from the physician or the rehabilitation team can be effective. File your appeal in a timely manner, within the policy deadline. Make sure your appeal is mailed to the correct person at the correct address.

KNOW THE LAW

THERAPIES ARE SOMETIMES DENIED ON THE BASIS that they are not "medical treatment." Insurance Code 10123.15 states that major medical benefits must be extended to pervasive developmental brain disorders if the same benefits are extended to other types of brain disorders, such as those caused by stroke or brain trauma or brain tumors. Health insurers cannot deny major medical early intervention rehabilitation benefits (i.e. speech, occupational, cognitive, psychiatric and neurological therapies) to victims of stroke, brain trauma or brain tumors based upon the "educational services" exclusion.

Where to Go for Help

INCONTINENCE PRODUCTS

HAVE THE PHYSICIAN WRITE A PRESCRIPTION for the necessary items (diapers, wipes, gloves and bed pads). Take the prescription to the pharmacy or supply house. It will contact your insurance company. If it is approved, the supply house will set up a delivery schedule. If the claim is denied, the supply house can help with an appeal. Be sure to keep receipts for these items while the claim is pending, so that you can be reimbursed if allowed. Medicaid may only pay for specific brands of diapers. Check with your supplier to make sure you are purchasing the approved ones when you are paying out of pocket so that you can be reimbursed.

Unfortunately, some insurance companies and some state waiver programs do not allow payment for diapers. If this is the case, visit the manager of your local pharmacy to see if he will extend a discount based on the number of diapers you will use. This can result in substantial savings.

INCOME TAX

A NUMBER OF YOUR DAUGHTER'S EXPENSES may be tax deductible. You can only deduct the amounts not reimbursed through insurance. They are deductible if you itemize your tax return and exceed a certain percentage of your adjusted gross income. Tax rules are very complicated and subject to change. Contact your accountant or tax preparer to see if you qualify for the following deductions:

- health insurance premiums
- medical service and hospital fees
- physical, occupational and speech therapy
- medications, supplies, equipment, and assistive devices which were prescribed
- X-rays
- inpatient treatment and rehabilitations services
- ambulance services
- cost of improving access to your home
- transportation costs for medical care
- costs for one parent for transportation, meals, and lodging for medical visits
- examination fees and costs for eye wear
- costs for attendance at workshops and conferences related to her condition
- cost of prescribed disability publications
- cost of prescribed special camps and schools
- cost of conferences with physicians
- out-of-pocket costs which may be associated with meeting your deductible and co-insurance premiums

HOME MODIFICATIONS

MODIFYING YOUR HOME to accommodate your daughter's needs can make caring for her much easier. Ramps, wider doors, bathroom renovation, and moving her room

Where to Go for Help

to the main floor of the house are just a few helpful suggestions. With today's technology, you can even have doors, drawers, and windows built so that your daughter can open and close them with a switch. You can also have temperature and lighting done that way so they are easier for you to program. Of course, all of this comes with a price tag.

Here are some ideas to keep in mind when buying or building an accessible home. The lists begin with the necessities and end with the more expensive options.

Exterior:
- accessible parking area/garage
- spacious flat concrete porches
- handicapped entrance: subtle concrete flair or "ramp" that is not noticeable, and does not require you to step up or down
- ramped at two exits in case of fire
- auto-sensored door openings
- screen/security door
- knee level lighting at door entry

Interior:
- wider doors, 32-36 inches
- levered door handles
- room/door entrances with flat thresholds
- lowered light switches
- carpeting, flat and efficient or hardwood/tile/stone floors
- stair lift or elevator

Bathroom:
- large roll-in shower
- non-skid shower floor surface
- higher toilet, for toileting from shower chair/toileting chair
- higher sink for roll up to/under
- detachable faucet/sprayers
- locking medicine cabinet
- bidet toilet seat
- changing table
- anti-scald control
- hot water recirculator
- support/balance grab bars
- secondary holder for shower head
- storage shelf built into shower design
- shower head with spray control

Bedroom:
- closet space with shelving
- room for lift

Where to Go for Help

- nanny camera
- good overhead lighting
- built-in storage shelving, bolted to wall
- small refrigerator and microwave
- extra bed for caregiver

We got help from the ENDependence Center of Northern Virginia. We have used this center as a resource for securing low-interest loans for house renovations for our daughter, but its utility extends way beyond this and can be a helpful resource for folks nationally. Go to www.ecnv.org.

AUTOMOBILES

SOME AUTOMOBILE COMPANIES OFFER DISCOUNTS for the installation of special equipment such as lifts, ramps, and running boards. Be sure to ask if discounts apply.

We found it less expensive to buy a full-sized conversion van (no raised roof, no fancy stuff) and have a lift installed locally than to buy a minivan from a company that does big-time conversions for handicapped use.

GUARDIANSHIP

GUARDIANSHIP IS A LEGALLY RECOGNIZED RELATIONSHIP between a competent adult and an adult with a disability (*ward*) who is incapable as determined by a court of law managing her affairs. In this relationship, the guardian has the duty and right to act on her behalf to make decisions which affect her life and to promote and protect her well-being.

According to law, guardianship for those with developmental disabilities "shall only be ordered to the extent necessitated by the person's actual mental and adaptive limitations." After she turns eighteen, it is important to consider guardianship because of her unique needs. If she is capable of making her own decisions, then no formal guardianship is required. If the family feels that she will need guidance in making decisions or she is incapable of making them, guardianship should be considered. It is a very difficult decision, because her rights are taken away. However, the family has to ask the very simple question, "If she cannot make decisions, who will?" While you may trust your local or state case managers, do you trust them enough to carry out this heavy responsibility? When you consider the fact that there is a high turnover in this case management area and your favorite social worker may leave, you may want to provide that personal support yourself.

Parents can be guardians once the child turns eighteen. In fact, many parents carry out this role without the formal legal guardianship by the simple fact that the person continues to live at home and most agencies respect the parents' informal position as advocate (someone who assists the person without the legal authority to make decisions). It is only when someone or an agency refuses to recognize the parents' decision that things can get complicated. For example, your daughter may need surgery and the hospital will only accept her signature for consent. The hospital attorneys may simply refuse to accept her signature because they do not believe she can give "informed consent," so everyone is stuck in

Where to Go for Help

limbo. Legal guardianship can avoid this problem because the parents can act on her behalf. While we usually speak about the parents acting in this role, any sibling or relative can do so. Even good friends can serve as guardians.

GUARDIAN RESPONSIBILITIES

THE GUARDIAN IS RESPONSIBLE FOR THE WARD'S CARE. The courts or an appointed social service agency will/should check on the person on a regular basis. This is not always done, however. If the case manager suspects any abuse or neglect, he must report it. The guardian could lose custody. There are laws in place to protect the person. However, the bureaucracy doesn't always keep up. Therefore, it is essential for families to recommend people they trust.

The guardian does not assume financial liability for his charge. Therefore, it is essential that you set up a trust or other account so there will always be funds available for your daughter. The guardian is not legally responsible for any debts incurred by the person. However, if the guardian incurs the debts, he or she is responsible. If the person charges a TV on a credit card, the guardian does not have to pay. If the guardian charges a TV for the person, then the guardian must pay. Without this safeguard, few people would take on guardianship. They would be sued for things the person did.

HOW TO ESTABLISH GUARDIANSHIP

DEPENDING ON YOUR STATE, the process can be easy or extremely difficult. The first thing you must do is consult an experienced attorney. Find someone who does guardianships on a regular basis. The attorney will file a motion with the local court. The court will appoint an attorney who will act on behalf of your daughter. Generally, the court will send an investigator to meet with you. In some states, the local or state agency will also conduct an investigation. Everyone goes to court on the appointed day, at which time the judge will review the reports and ask questions. Again, it depends on the state, but many of these guardianship hearings are held in smaller courts or even in the personal chambers of the judge.

TYPES OF GUARDIANSHIP

THE TYPES OF GUARDIANSHIP which should be considered are:

- **Full guardianship:** All rights are taken away and given to the guardian.
- **Limited guardianship:** no rights are taken away; however, the courts may give certain responsibilities to the guardian, i.e., sign contracts, handle finances, make housing decisions, etc. Approximately thirty states recognize limited guardianship.
- **Coguardians and backup guardianship:** It is always a good idea to obtain a coguardian or a backup. For instance, the court may appoint the mother as the primary guardian. The father would be appointed as the coguardian to act with the mother or as a backup if anything happened to the mother, such as illness or death. Many states permit the guardianship papers to include successor guardians. In a situation where an elderly mother is the guardian and she has to go into a nursing home, the court could approve the siblings as successor guardians at the same time they approve the mother's guardianship. In this way, the minute the mother goes into a nursing home or dies, the siblings have legal authority to take over.

Where to Go for Help

PREPARING FOR THE FUTURE

GUARDIANSHIP IS IMPORTANT, but it does not replace a good, well-written life plan.

LETTER OF INTENT

PARENTS NEED TO PUT IN WRITING what they would like for the future. This document, which is not legally binding, is called a letter of intent. It gives future care-givers insight into how your daughter should be provided for. Unlike a detached analytical report written by a caseworker, the letter of intent is a warm personal document which gives information on how to provide the best possible care. This letter of intent combined with a life plan or strategy for providing guardians, advocates, housing, etc. will be the difference between basic care in an institutional setting and a warm, loving lifestyle. Comprehensive planning will assure that adequate funds will be in place if you die first.

THE TEAM

THE TEAM SHOULD INCLUDE AN ESTATE PLANNER, an attorney and a certified public accountant (CPA). Look for an estate planning team that is experienced with special needs families. They should have a good working knowledge of government benefit programs and the service delivery system for the disabled person from birth to death. The team must take the necessary time and feel comfortable working with special needs families. The National Institute on Life Planning, dedicated to serving the needs of disabled persons, recommends the following approach to developing a life plan.

DEVELOPING A LIFE PLAN

- Decide what you and your loved one wants. The person with the disability is the key member in the decision-making process. It is her life. Look at all areas: housing, employment, medical care, etc.

- Put your desires in writing. Prepare a letter of intent which will let future care providers know what you want.

- Decide on an advocate or guardian, someone who will look after, fight for your child and be her friend.

- Determine the cost of your life plan and find the resources.

- Do the necessary legal work, which might include last wills and testaments, special needs trusts, durable powers of attorney, etc. Consult a qualified attorney for this specialized work.

- Develop a good record keeping system to keep all of your materials in one place. When there is an emergency (such as your death or nursing care), people need to find this information quickly. Let others know where you keep your records.

- Review and update your life plan at least once a year. Keep it current.

WILLS

THE WILL IS A LEGAL DOCUMENT which permits you to name a guardian for your minor children until they reach adulthood, allows you to select the person who will be responsible for the administrative tasks after your death, and permits you to decide how

Where to Go for Help

your property will be distributed when you die. *One mistake to avoid is leaving money in your will for your daughter with RS, because a financial inheritance can result in a reduction or elimination of benefits.* This extends not only to parents, but grandparents or any other relative who may want to put your daughter in their wills. A better avenue is to establish a trust in her name.

I have made a plan in my will for money to be set aside for Amy's extras. Leaving money to Amy directly would upset her SSI. I do not want her sister or brother to feel that they are responsible for her, but they will look after her and continue to be her advocate.

SPECIAL NEEDS TRUSTS

ONE WAY TO PROVIDE FOR THE LONG-TERM NEEDS of our kids without putting their SSI resources at risk is to establish a special needs trust. Any assets of the child and any gifts or bequests she might receive need to be redirected into the trust, which then "owns" them instead of the child. The trustees of the trust make the decisions about how and when to spend any of the money, but it does not get in the way of any of the governmental services the child is entitled to. Trust money can be used for clothing, outings, vacations, etc. at the discretion of the trustee(s). The trust will get its own tax ID number, and will have to file a separate return with the IRS each year. This is a fairly specialized type of trust and you might want to seek out someone who has specific knowledge about special needs trusts to guide you in setting one up. One potential hazard is an inheritance in which the benefactor leaves money to the child, rather than the trust.

We have designated a portion of our estate to be given to the trustees (executors) to be held in trust, in their names, for the care of our daughter. It is important that the trust fund is not in your daughter's name, as she would have to use up all those funds before she would receive the normal social assistance she is entitled to.

First, we talked to as many people as we could. Not surprisingly, most other parents hadn't made any provision. We talked to three separate lawyers and two trust companies before settling on the public trustee. We were looking for stability with similar families, and a secondary consideration, their fee structure for ongoing administration. Some have an hourly rate, and some take a percentage for every year. We purchased a second house and rented it out so that the rent helped pay off the mortgage. We had mortgage repayment insurance so that if we died prematurely, Rebecca would have had steady income. This kept us poor! You could probably get the same effect from some good life insurance but there were tax benefits for us to buy a house, and also we rather hoped that it would provide some retirement income. We wrote into our wills our desired standard of care: heaters, TV in her room, holiday every year, most comprehensive medical insurance, nice haircuts, trendy clothes, maintain activities. We also said we would prefer she lived in our family home with caregivers, preferably a family if she was younger, or with able-bodied roommates if she was older. We left all our assets to a discretionary trust to be created on our deaths. Because it was "discretionary," it did not affect any Social Security benefits Rebecca would be entitled to (it did not belong to her and she could not depend on any regular income from it). The trust was to be administered by the Public Trustee which is an organization that manages people's estates. It would pay all her bills, in return for an hourly rate. They have a number of clients with disabilities.

Our objectives were:

- *financial independence for Rebecca*
- *good lifestyle (not hand-to-mouth on Social Security) with all the niceties of life*
- *experienced advocate to oversee her care and provide a parental figure*

Where to Go for Help

- *experienced administrators to do all the bill paying*
- *ongoing life in the community—same one she grew up in, familiar house*
- *ongoing family involvement, without them being required to spend hours on administration*
- *spreading power over Rebecca across three different groups. The family is not able to conserve her estate in anticipation that they would inherit more*

COMMUNITY RESOURCES

CHECK WITH YOUR LOCAL ARC, Developmental Disabilities Administration (DDA) or other special needs families in your area to see what community resources exist.

FREE NATIONAL PARK ACCESS

THE GOLDEN ACCESS PASSPORT IS A FREE LIFETIME entrance pass to national parks, available to citizens or permanent residents of the United States regardless of age who have been determined to be permanently disabled. You may obtain a Golden Access Passport at any entrance fee area by showing proof of medically determined disability and eligibility for receiving benefits under federal law. The pass admits the pass holder and any accompanying passengers in a private vehicle. Where entry is not by private vehicle, the passport admits the pass holder, spouse, parents and children. The passport also provides a fifty percent discount on federal use fees charged for facilities and services such as fees for camping, swimming, parking, boat launching, or cave tours. For information, contact the Department of the Interior, (202) 208-3100.

RONALD McDONALD HOUSE

RONALD MCDONALD HOUSES ARE PUBLICLY SUPPORTED lodges built to meet the needs of families during a child's hospitalization. Families can stay overnight for a nominal daily charge. Transportation is often provided between the hospital and the Ronald McDonald House. The houses have facilities for storing food and cooking. For information, call (630) 623-7048.

FREE MEDICAL TRAVEL

AMERICAN AIRLINES HAS A PROGRAM CALLED **Miles for Kids in Need,** which offers free round-trip airfare for eligible children and their parents for air travel related to medical reasons. You must submit two letters. The first letter, from a charitable organization, must include an explanation of the need and verification of need for financial assistance with airfare. The second letter must come from a physician and must include the name of the parents, place of residence, type of illness, and necessity for treatment at the requested destination, age of the child, proof that the child is medically stable to fly, dates of travel, and place and origin of destination. These letters must be sent by mail to American Airlines, Frequent Travelers Special Programs, MD 1394, P.O. Box 61916, Dallas-Fort Worth Airport, TX 75261-9616 or sent by fax to (817) 931-6890.

Continental Airlines has a program known as **Continental Care Force,** which allows discounts on travel for diagnosis or treatment. Each participating hospital has a referral code, which must be obtained and submitted to the program. For details, call 281-360-5314.

Where to Go for Help

Angel Flight is a nonprofit organization. Pilots are volunteers who fly general aviation aircraft and donate their skills and their planes to fly children and adults to long-distance medical treatment centers. There is no cost to patients. Six Angel Flight regions help patients throughout the country reach their destinations. Angel Flight can accommodate a patient and a companion. If the patient is a child, both parents can come. Pilots fly during the day. Each pilot can fly about 300 to 350 miles. Patients must live within 1,000 air miles of their destination. Depending on where the patient lives, a trip may take one, two, or three planes. The patient needs to be medically stable enough to climb in and out of a small plane. Angel Flight is great for some patients. However, it's not for everyone. Some patients may not like the confined space or the noise of a small plane. Some may be anxious flyers. Most patients, though, have found Angel Flight to be a positive experience.

RESOURCES

CATALOGS

MAKING LIFE BETTER IS THE CATALOG OF CATALOGS, a one-stop access to low-tech assistive equipment for people with disabilities. Published by Easter Seals, the catalog features forty-eight of the top suppliers of assistive and adaptive equipment in sections geared specifically to the needs of children and sections devoted to increased mobility, medical supply services and more. Send a check or money order for $5.00 to Making Life Better, National Easter Seals Society, PO Box 06440, Chicago, IL 60606-0440.

BOOKS AND MAGAZINES

Exceptional Parent Magazine
(877) 372-7368

Enable Magazine
American Association of People with Disabilities (AAPD)
(800) 436-2253

Anderson, Winifred
Negotiating the Special Education Maze: A Guide for Parents and Teachers
Rockville: Woodbine House, 1990
269 pages, $12.95

Bernstein, Jane
Loving Rachel: A Family's Journey from Grief
Boston: Little, Brown, 1988
279 pages, $17.95

Brat, Bernie
No Time for Jell-O: One Family's Experience with the Doman-Delacato Patterning Program
Cambridge: Brookline Books, 1989
210 pages, $17.95

Crossley, Rosemary
Annie's Coming Out
New York: Penguin, 1980
256 pages, $6.95

Where to Go for Help

Crossley, Rosemary
Speechless: FC for People without Voices
EP Dutton, 1997
272 pages, $24.95

Crump, Iris
Nutrition and Feeding of the Handicapped Child
Boston: Little, Brown, 1987
163 pages, $22.50

deVinck, Christopher
The Power of the Powerless
New York: Doubleday, 1988
153 pages, $14.95

Dickman, Irving
One Miracle at a Time: How to Get Help for Your Disabled Child
New York: Simon & Schuster, 1985
351 pages, $17.95

Featherstone, Helen
A Difference in the Family: Life with a Disabled Child
New York: Penguin, 1982
288 pages, $6.95

Fountas, Irene and Pinnell, Gay Su
Matching Books to Readers
Dublin: Heinemann Company, 1999
39 pages, $32.00

Freeman, John
Seizures and Epilepsy in Childhood: A Guide for Parents
Baltimore: Johns Hopkins University Press, 1990
287 pages, $16.95 softback

Gill, Barbara
Changed by a Child
Honesdale: Main Street Books, 1998
336 pages, $11.95

Goldfarb, Lori
Meeting the Challenge of Disability or Chronic Illness
Baltimore: Paul H. Brookes, 1986
181 pages, $16.00

Grant, Russell and Fee, Richard
Planning for the Future
Evanston: American Publishing Co., 1993
420 pages, $24.95
1-800-247-6553

Where to Go for Help

Hagberg, Bengt
Rett Syndrome: Clinical and Biological Aspects
London: Cambridge University Press, 1993
120 pages, $49.95

Rett Syndrome: A Medical Dictionary, Bibliography, and Research Guide to Internet References
(Paperback)
Icon Health Publications, 2003
236 pages, $48.95

Jones, Monica
Home Care for the Chronically Ill or Disabled Child
New York: Harper & Row, 1985
306 pages, $12.95

Kelly, Jane and Friend, Teresa
Hands-on-Reading
Mayer-Johnson, 1993
430 pages, $34.00

Kerr, Alison
Rett Disorder and the Developing Brain
Oxford University Press, 2001
139 pages, $125.00

King-DeBaun, M.S., CCC-SLP, Patti
Storytime, Just for Fun
Creative Communicating, 1993
352 pages, $29.00

Klein, Stanley and Shive, Kim
You Will Dream New Dreams: Inspiring Personal Stories by Parents of Children with Disabilities
Kensington Publishing, 2001
278 pages, $13.00

Kupfer, Fern
Before and After Zachariah
Chicago: Academy Chicago Publishers, 1988
241 pages, $7.95

Lavin, Judith
Special Kids Need Special Parents: A Resource for Parents of Children With Special Needs
Berkeley Publishing, 2001
319 pages, $26.95

Levin, Jackie
Breaking Barriers: How Children and Adults with Severe Handicaps Can Access the World Through Simple Technology
Minneapolis: Ablenet, 1986
66 pages, $13.95

Where to Go for Help

Lewis, Jackie and Wilson, Debbie
Pathways to Learning in Rett Syndrome
London: David Fulton Publishers, 1998
133 pages, $31.95

LINC Associates
The Specialware Directory, 2nd Edition: A Guide to Software for Special Education
Columbus: LINC Associates, 1986
160 pages, $22.50

Lindberg, Barbro
Understanding Rett Syndrome, Rev. 2nd Edition
Toronto: Hogrefe & Huber, 2006
200 pages, $34.95

Mantle, Margaret
Some Just Clap Their Hands: Raising a Handicapped Child
New York: Adams Books, 1985
263 pages, $16.95

Male, M.
Technology for Inclusion: Meeting the Special Needs of All Students
Needham: Allyn and Bacon, 1993
191 pages, $36.80

Marsh, Jayne
From the Heart: On Being the Mother of a Child with Special Needs
Rockville: Woodbine House, 1995
149 pages, $14.95

Naseef, Robert
Special Children, Challenged Parents: The Struggles and Rewards of Raising a Child with a Disability
Baltimore: Brookes Publishing, 2001
288 pages, $21.00

Nordic Committee on Disability
The More We Do Together: Adapting the Environment for Children with Disabilities
New York: World Rehabilitation Fund, 1985
84 pages, $5.00

Nordoff, Paul and Robbins, Clive
Therapy in Music for Handicapped Children
London: Gollancz; distributed by David & Charles, 1985
191 pages, $13.95

Osborn, Susan and Mitchell, Janet
A Special Kind of Love: For Those Who Love Children with Special Needs
Broadman & Holman Publishers, 2004
192 pages, $14.95

Where to Go for Help

Okzal, Abide
The Silent Angel (RS Story)
ABC Matbaacilik, 2004
159 pages
abideozkal@hotmail.com

Ohio State University Research Foundation Staff
Toilet Training: Help for the Delayed Learner
New York: McGraw-Hill, 1978
106 pages, $17.60

Pages, Xiomara
Mi Cruz Ilene de Rosas: Cartas a Sandra Mi Hija Enferma
(My Cross of Roses: Letters to Sandra, My Sick Child) (RS Story)
Miami: Editorial Universal, 1996
83 pages, $9.95

Penner, Irma
The Right to Belong: The Story of Yvonne (RS Story)
Canada: Unipress, 1997
244 pages, $12.00

Perske, Robert
Circles of Friends
Nashville: Abingdon Press, 1988
94 pages, $9.95

Perske, Robert
Hope for the Families: New Directions for Parents of Persons with Retardation or Other Disabilities
Nashville: Abingdon Press, 1981
96 pages, $9.95

Perske, Robert
Mealtimes for Persons with Severe Handicaps
Baltimore: Paul H. Brookes, 1986
136 pages, $17.50

Powell, Thomas
Brothers and Sisters–A Special Part of Exceptional Families
Baltimore: Paul H. Brookes, 1985
226 pages, $16.95

Pressman, H. and Dublin, P.
Integrating Computers in Your Classroom
New York: Harper-Collins, 1994
384 pages, $12.95

Pressman, H. and Dublin, P.
Accommodating Learning Styles in Elementary Classrooms
Orlando: Harcourt Brace, 1995
308 pages, $88.00

Where to Go for Help

Pueshel, Siegfried
The Special Child: A Source Book for Parents of Children with Developmental Disabilities
Baltimore: Paul H. Brookes, 1988
368 pages, $22.00

Putman, J.
Cooperative Learning and Strategies for Inclusion: Celebrating Diversity in the Classroom
Baltimore: Paul H. Brookes, 1993
288 pages, $29.95

Richman, Linda G.
This Is the One I Want
Mayer-Johnson Co., 1987
1-800-588-4548
$29.00

Rose, Harriet Wallace
Something's Wrong with My Child!
Springfield: Charles C. Thomas, 1987
196 pages, $26.75

Russell, Mark and Grant, Arnold
The Life Planning Workbook
Evanston: American Publishing, 1995
272 pages, $24.95
1-800-247-6553

Schleifer, Maxwell
The Disabled Child & the Family: An Exceptional Parent Reader
Boston: The Exceptional Parent Press, 1985
183 pages, $15.95

Sienkiewicz-Mercer, Ruth
I Raise My Eyes to Say Yes: A Memoir
Boston: Houghton Mifflin, 1989
225 pages, $17.95

Simon, Rachel
Riding the Bus with My Sister
Boston: Houghton Mifflin Books, 2002
256 pages, $15.00

Simons, Robin
After the Tears: Parents Talk About Raising a Child With a Disability
Orlando: Harcourt Brace Jovanovich, 1987
89 pages, $4.95

Witt Engerstrom, Ingegerd
Rett Syndrome in Sweden
Goteborg: 1990
114 pages, $16.00

Where to Go for Help

Yurk, Amy
The Language of Sisters (RS Story)
Accent, 2002
256 pages, $13.95

Zimmermann, Susan
Keeping Katherine (RS Story)
New York: Three Rivers Press, 2004
237 pages, $14.95

BOOKS FOR CHILDREN

Brown, Tricia
Someone Special, Just Like You
New York: Henry Holt, 1984
64 pages, $14.95 (Ages 3-6, on multiple disabilities in the classroom)

Cohen, Floreva
My Special Friend
New York: Board of Jewish Education, 1986
64 pages, $5.95 (Ages 9-12, on having a "special" sibling)

Choldenko, Gennifer
Al Capone Does My Shirts
New York: J.P. Putnam's Sons
225 pages, $16.99 (Ages 9-12, on having a "special" sibling)

Emmert, Michelle
I'm the Big Sister Now
Niles, IL: Albert Whitman, 1989
32 pages, $12.95 (Ages 7-10, on being the "bigger" little sister)

Exley, Helen
What It's Like to Be Me
New York: Friendship Press, 1984
127 pages, $10.95 (Ages 9-12, on thoughts and feelings of children and teenagers with disabilities)

Meyer, Donald
Living With a Brother or Sister with Special Needs: A Book for Sibs
Seattle: University of Washington Press, 1985
110 pages, $4.95 (Ages 6-11, on sibling feelings and experiences)

Moss, Deborah
Lee, the Rabbit with Epilepsy
Rockville: Woodbine House, 1989
23 pages, $12.95 (Ages 3-7, on what it's like to have seizures)

Muldoon, Kathleen
Princess Pooh
Niles, IL: Albert Whitman, 1989
32 pages, $12.95 (Ages 7-10, on learning what it's like to be disabled)

Where to Go for Help

Prall, Jo
My Sister's Special
Chicago: Children's Press, 1985
31 pages, $4.95 (Ages 4-8, on being an important part of the family)

Quinsey, Mary Beth
Why Does That Man Have Such a Big Nose?
Seattle: Parenting Press, 1986
26 pages, $4.95 (Ages 4-7, on fostering positive attitudes)

Rosenberg, Maxine
Finding a Way: Living with Exceptional Brothers and Sisters
New York: Lothrop, Lee & Shepard, 1988
48 pages, $11.95 (on the special nature of sibling relationships)

Rosenberg, Maxine
My Friend Leslie: The Story of a Handicapped Child
New York: Lothrop, Lee & Shepard, 1983
$13.00 (Ages 5-8, on kindergarten experiences)

Schwier, Karin
Keith Edward's Different Day
Downsview, Ontario: G.Allan Roeher Institute, 1988
28 pages, $4.95 (Ages 4-7, on learning different isn't bad)

Shalom, Debra
Special Kids Make Special Friends
New York, NY: Association of Children with Down Syndrome, 1984
43 pages, $5.00 (Ages 3-6, on similarities/differences)

Shriver, Maria
What's Wrong with Timmy?
Little Brown & Company, 2001
4 pages, $14.95

Stein, Sara
About Handicaps: An Open Family Book for Parents and Children Together
New York: Walker, 1974
47 pages, $6.95 (Ages 4-8, preparation for realities)

Wolf, Bernard
Don't Feel Sorry for Paul
New York: Harper & Row, Harper Junior, 1974
96 pages, $18.50 (Ages 5-8, physical differences)

Wright, Betty
My Sister Is Different
Milwaukee: Raintree, 1981
31 pages, $15.35 (Ages 5-8, on feelings)

Where to Go for Help

DISABILITY ASSOCIATIONS

The ARC of the United States	www.thearc.org
Association for the Care of Children's Health (ACCH)	www.acch.org
Association for Persons with Severe Handicaps (TASH)	www.tash.org
Council for Exceptional Children	www.cec.sped.org
Nat'l Association of Developmental Disabilities Councils	www.igc.opc.org
Nat'l Association of State Directors of of Special Education	www.nasde.org
National Parent to Parent Network	www.netnet.net
National Parent to Parent Network (UK)	www.parenttoparent.com
WE MOVE	www.wemove.org

RETT SYNDROME ASSOCIATIONS/FOUNDATIONS US

International Rett Syndrome Association (IRSA)	www.rettsyndrome.org
Minnesota Rett Research Foundation	www.mrsra.org/
Northwest Rett Syndrome Foundation	www.nwrettsyndrome.org
Rett Syndrome Association of Illinois	www.rettillinois.org
Rett Syndrome Association of Massachusetts	www.orgsites.com/ma/rsam
Rett Syndrome Research Foundation	www.rsrf.org

RETT SYNDROME ASSOCIATIONS/FOUNDATIONS WORLDWIDE

International Rett Syndrome Association (IRSA)	www.rettsyndrome.org
Rett Syndrome Association of Austria	www.rettsyndrom.at
Rett Syndrome Association of Australia	www.ichr.uwa.edu.au/rett/aussierett
Rett Syndrome Association of Belgium	www.rettsyndrome.be
Rett Syndrome Association of Bosnia	www.rettsyndrome.com/bosnia.htm
Rett Syndrome Associations of Canada Manitoba Rett Syndrome Association Ontario Rett Syndrome Association Saskatchewan, British Columbia, Alberta, Quebec	www.rettsyndrome.mb.ca www.rett.ca/ontario www3.telus.net/rettsyndrome/Cancontacts
Rett Syndrome Association of the Czech Republic	www.rettsyndrome.com/Czech.htm
Rett Syndrome Association of Denmark	www.rett.dk
Rett Syndrome Association of Estonia	www.rettsyndrome.com/Estonia.htm
European Association for Rett Syndrome	www.rettsyndrome.com

Where to Go for Help

Rett Syndrome Association of France	www.afsr.net
Rett Syndrome Association of Germany	www.rett.de
Rett Syndrome Association of Greece	www.rettsyndrome.com/greece.htm
Rett Syndrome Association of Hungary	www.rettsyndrome.org/main/rsaoh.htm
Rett Syndrome Association of India	www.retindia.org/
Rett Syndrome Association of Ireland	www.rettsyndromeireland.com
Rett Syndrome Association of Israel	www.rettisrael.org
Rett Syndrome Association of Italy	www.airett.it
Rett Syndrome Association of Japan	www.rett.gr.jp
Rett Syndrome Association of Korea	www.rettsyndrome.org/main/rsaok.htm
Rett Syndrome Association of Malta	www.rettsyndrome.com/malta
Rett Syndrome Association of Mexico	www.rettsyndrome.org/main/rsaom.htm
Rett Syndrome Association of Norway	www.rettsyndrome.com/norway.htm
Rett Syndrome Association of New Zealand	www.nzord.org.nz
Rett Syndrome Association of Poland	www.rettsyndrom.gd.pl
Rett Syndrome Association of Portugal	www.rettsyndrome.com/portugal.htm
Rett Syndrome Association of Russia	www.rettsyndrome.com/russia.htm
Rett Syndrome Association of Scotland	www.guide-information.org.uk/guide
Rett Syndrome Association of Slovakia	www.rettsyndrome.com/slovakia.htm
Rett Syndrome Association of Spain	www.rett.es
Rett Syndrome Association of Switzerland	www.rettsyndrome.com/switzerland.htm
Rett Syndrome Association of Turkey	www.rettsyndrome.org.tr/english.htm
United Kingdom Rett Syndrome Association	www.rettsyndrome.org.uk

HOTLINES AND INFORMATION LINES

Americans with Disabilities (ADA) Information Line	(800) 514-0301
International Rett Syndrome Association (IRSA)	(800) 818-RETT
National Health Information Clearinghouse	(800) 336-4797

GOVERNMENT SUPPORTED ORGANIZATIONS

Education Resources Information Center (ERIC)	www.eric.ed.gov
Disability Information and Resources	www.makoa.org
DisabilityInfo.gov	www.disabilityinfo.gov
National Information Center for Children and Youth with Disabilities	www.nichcy.org

Where to Go for Help

National Organization for Rare Disorders (NORD)	www.rarediseases.org
National Rehabilitation Information Center (NARIC)	www.naric.com
United Cerebral Palsy Association	www.ucp.org

DISABILITY RESOURCES

ARC Sibling Support Project	www.thearc.org/siblingsupport
Archives and Library on Disability	www.cu.edu/ColemanInstitute
Beach Center on Families and Disability	www.beachcenter.org
Council of Parent Attorneys and Advocates	www.copaa.net
disABILITY Resources on the Internet	www.disabilityresources.org
Family Village	www.familyvillage.wisc.edu
Internet Resources for Special Children (IRSC)	www.irsc.org
National Early Childhood Technical Assistance Center	www.nectac.org
National Fathers Network	www.fathersnetwork.org
National Parent Network on Disabilities	www.npnd.org
National Early Childhood Transition Research and Training Center	www.ihdi.uky.edu/nectc
National Clearinghouse of Rehabilitation Training Materials	www.nchrtm.okstate.edu
National Information Center for Children and Youth with Disabilities	www.nichcy.org
National Rehabilitation Information Center	www.naric.com
Quality Mall	www.qualitymall.org
State Parent Training and Information Centers	www.taalliance.org
State Special Education Departments	www.yellowpagesforkids.com
Special Education Resources	www.specialednet.com
Special Education Resources on the Internet	www.seriweb.com
Social Security Administration Home Page	www.ssa.gov/history/history.html

SUPPORT FOR COMMUNITY LIVING

The Center on Human Policy	www.thechp.syr.edu
The Institute for Community Inclusion	www.communityinclusion.org
The Institute on Community Integration	www.ici.umn.edu

NATIONAL ORGANIZATIONS

Developmental Disabilities Administration	www.acf.dhhs.gov

Where to Go for Help

North American Riding for the   www.narha.org
  Handicapped Association

WISH-GRANTING ORGANIZATIONS

WISH-GRANTING ORGANIZATIONS have individual requirements, but most will grant wishes to those under the age of eighteen. Most require a physician's letter stipulating that the child's condition is life threatening.

Make a Child Smile (MACS)   www.makeachildsmile.org
Make-A-Wish Foundation   www.wish.org
                                (800) 722-9474

Believe in Tomorrow National Children's   www.dreamsurger.org
  Foundation   (800) 933-540
Starlight Foundation   www.slsb.org
                                (310) 479-1212

Sunshine Foundation   www.sunshinefoundation.org
                                (215) 396-4770

The Dream Factory   www.dreamfactoryinc.com
                                (800) 456-7556

Believe in Tomorrow National Children's   www.grant-a-wish.org
  Foundation   (800) 933-5470
Children's Hopes and Dream Foundation   www.childrenswishes.org
                                (973) 361-7366

Children's Wish Foundation International   www.childrenswish.org
                                (800) 323-9474

Brass Ring Society   www.brassring.org
                                (800) 666-WISH

Where to Go for Help

FORMS

USE THIS FORM to track symptoms and treatment.

RETT SYNDROME RECORD FORM

NAME: _____ DATE OF BIRTH: _____

TESTS AND RESULTS:

AGE AT DIAGNOSIS: _____

MUTATION: _____ X-INACTIVATION RATE: _____

DATE OF TEST: _____ LABORATORY: _____

PHYSICIAN: _____

OFFICE PHONE: _____

TYPE OF RETT SYNDROME

Classic Form _____   Preserved Speech Form _____

Congenital Onset Form _____   Male Form _____

Late Onset Form _____

ONSET OF SYMPTOMS

Early normal development
  to what age? _____

Regression of motor skills

  Highest motor skill _____

  Age lost skill _____

Regression of verbal skills

  Babbling   What age?   _____

  Single words   How many?   _____

  Two-word phrases   How many?   _____

  More than two-word phrases How many?   _____

Eye contact

  Poor eye/social contact   What age?   _____

  Good eye/social contact   What age?   _____

Lack of sustained interest in toys   Yes/No   _____

Irritability, crying tantrums   What age started? _____

                                          What age stopped? _____

Overactive   Yes/No _____

Over passive   Yes/No _____

Where to Go for Help

Does not reach for objects or people   Yes/No _____

Does not follow verbal commands, acts deaf   Yes/No _____

LATER SYMPTOMS

Breathing
    Hyperventilation (overbreathing)   Yes/No _____
    Apnea (underbreathing)   Yes/No _____
    Air-saliva expulsion/drooling   Yes/No _____
    Oxygen needed?   Yes/No _____

Gastrointestinal
    Reflux   Yes/No _____
    Constipation   Yes/No _____
    Impaction   Yes/No _____

Seizures   What age started? _____
    What age stopped? _____

    Tonic Clonic   Yes/No _____
    Partial   Yes/No _____
    Absence   Yes/No _____

Tooth Grinding   What age started? _____
    What age stopped? _____

Apparent insensitivity to pain   Yes/No _____

BEHAVIOR

Self-mutilation/pulling hair or ears, scratching, etc. Yes/No _____
Aggressive behavior (head banging, biting, spitting) Yes/No _____
Masturbation Yes/No _____

MOTOR SKILLS

Hand clumsiness   Yes/No _____
Wide gait   Yes/No _____
Ataxia/apraxia (gait & trunk)   Yes/No _____
Truncal rocking/shifting weight   Yes/No _____
Muscle Tone
    Hypotonia   Yes/No _____
    Hypertonia   Yes/No _____
        Spasticity   Yes/No _____
        Rigidity   Yes/No _____
    Dystonia   Yes/No _____
Hypomimia (loss facial expression)   Yes/No _____

Where to Go for Help

ORTHOPEDICS

Toe walking	Yes/No	_____
Scoliosis	Yes/No	_____
Kyphosis	Yes/No	_____
Myoclonus	Yes/No	_____
Cold Feet/Hands	Yes/No	_____
Hip Abduction	Yes/No	_____
Foot Deformities	Yes/No	_____

HAND STEREOTYPES

Mouthing of hands & objects	Yes/No	_____
Hand wringing/washing	Yes/No	_____
Hand clapping	Yes/No	_____
Hand tapping/patting	Yes/No	_____
Pill rolling/kneading movements	Yes/No	_____

NUTRITION AND FEEDING

Feeding difficulties

Chewing difficulties	Yes/No	_____
Swallowing difficulties	Yes/No	_____
G Button	Yes/No	_____
Supplements	Yes/No	_____
Vitamins	Yes/No	_____
Oral Therapy	Yes/No	_____

MEDICATIONS

Seizures _____
_____
_____

Anti-Reflux _____
Muscle Relaxants _____
Mood Control _____
Birth Control _____
Urinary Tract _____
Constipation _____
_____
Anxiety _____
Anti-depressants _____
Sleep _____

Where to Go for Help

DENTAL

First exam   _____

Bruxism   What age started? _____
     What age stopped? _____

Cavities   _____

Fillings   _____

SLEEP

Sleep latency   Yes/No _____
Waking during night   Yes/No _____
Early-morning waking   Yes/No _____
Cries at night   Yes/No _____
Laughs at night   Yes/No _____
Naps during daytime   Yes/No _____

EQUIPMENT

Bath chair   Yes/No _____
Car seat   Yes/No _____
Wheelchair   Yes/No _____
Walker   Yes/No _____
Prone stander   Yes/No _____
Lift   Yes/No _____
Special chair   Yes/No _____
Braces/AFOs   Yes/No _____
Splints   Yes/No _____
Oxygen   Yes/No _____
Bi-pap machine   Yes/No _____
Apnea monitor   Yes/No _____
Special bed   Yes/No _____
Toilet chair   Yes/No _____

OTHER

Crossed eyes   Yes/No _____

Toilet trained
     Urine _____   What age? _____
     Bowels _____   What age? _____
     Incontinent   Yes/No _____

Allergies   Yes/No _____
     To what _____

Use this form as a record of your child's history.

Where to Go for Help

ANNUAL RETT SYNDROME EXPENSE RECORDS

EDUCATION/THERAPY

Therapies
(not covered by insurance or school)

Physical $_____
Occupational $_____
Music $_____
Horseback $_____
Water $_____
Vision $_____
Speech $_____
Applied Behavior Analysis $_____
Patterning $_____
Other $_____

Education (your costs)

School tuition $_____
Adult day program $_____
Transportation $_____
Other $_____

EDUCATION/THERAPY
  Subtotal: $_____

EQUIPMENT

Communication Equipment

Books $_____
Computer hardware $_____
Computer software $_____
Switches $_____
Augmentative device $_____
Other $_____

Home Adaptation

Doorways $_____
Bathroom $_____
Bedroom $_____
Ramp $_____
Other $_____

Equipment

Adapted feeding
  equipment $_____
Specialized blender $_____
Wheelchair $_____
Walker $_____
Splints $_____
Specialty bed/mattress/
  linen $_____
Special toilet $_____

Special chair $_____
Feeding table $_____
Whirlpool $_____
Specialized car seat $_____
Stroller $_____
Bath chair $_____
Transfer lift $_____
Stair lift $_____
Suction machine $_____
Oxygen $_____
Nebulizer $_____
Air purifiers $_____
Disposable parts and filters $_____
Other $_____

Special Clothes

Adapted Clothes $_____
Bibs $_____
Alteration of regular clothes $_____
Shoes $_____
Other $_____

Equipment Repairs $_____

EQUIPMENT Subtotal: $_____

Where to Go for Help

HOME CARE

Special Foods
Gastrostomy formulas $_____
Non-allergenic foods $_____
Nutritional supplements $_____
     Special formulas or foods)
   Thickening agents $_____
   Other $_____

Incontinence Products
Special underwear $_____
Diapers, pads $_____
Disposable bed pads $_____
Rubber gloves $_____
Disposable wipes $_____
Air fresheners $_____
Skin ointments and
   creams $_____
Other $_____

Home/Health Aid/Nursing
   Services $_____

Respite Care $_____

Day Care
To allow parent/s to work $_____

Nursing Staff Incidentals
Food and drink $_____
Gifts $_____

HOME CARE Subtotal: $_____

MEDICAL

Diagnostic Testing
Blood Tests $_____
Geneticist $_____

Medications
Prescription $_____

Insurance
Medical (extra costs) $_____
Over-the-counter
   (includes enemas, suppositories,
   and vitamins) $_____
Other $_____

Dental Visits $_____

Dental Surgery $_____

Surgery
Anesthesia $_____
Physician fees $_____
Hospital costs $_____
Other $_____

Hospitalizations
Hospital bills $_____
Physician fees $_____
Other $_____

Travel
To doctors, hospital, therapies,
   drugstore (gasoline, wear on car)
   $_____

Mental Health Services
Family counseling $_____
Marriage counseling $_____
Sibling $_____

MEDICAL Subtotal: $_____

Where to Go for Help

MISCELLANEOUS

Advocacy
  Purchasing materials for teachers,
    therapists $_____
  Hiring an advocate to assist in
    educational plans $_____
  Other $_____

Lost Wages
  Caring for a sick child $_____
  Unable to work due to child's
    condition $_____

Insurance
  Life (extra costs) $_____

Recreation
  Special bike $_____
  Adaptive ski equipment $_____
  Adaptive swimming devices and
    floats $_____
  Jogger stroller $_____
  Beach wheelchair $_____
  Horseback riding $_____
  Other $_____

Vehicle
  Adapted doors $_____
  Lockdown equipment $_____
  Lift $_____
  Other $_____

Telephone Costs
  Out-of-town specialists $_____

Support/Groups
  Membership $_____
  Travel to meetings and
    conferences $_____
  Cost of conferences $_____
  Other $_____

Furniture/Carpet Wear and Tear
  From equipment $_____
  From body fluid stains $_____
  Other $_____

Laundry
  Extra loads of wash $_____

Legal Fees
  Inclusion/services $_____
  Guardianship $_____
  Special estate planning $_____

Miscellaneous
  Extra health costs for caregiver
    (back strain/depression)
    $_____
  Lost savings for retirement $_____
  Extra electricity for equipment
    $_____
  Other $_____

MISCELLANEOUS Subtotal:
  $_____

"As long as you derive inner help and comfort
from anything, keep it."

– MAHATMA GANDHI

The Future

8

SECTION EIGHT

Research

The International Rett Syndrome Association

The Future

Research

IRSA

Research

EARLY LITERATURE ON RS described it as a degenerative disorder. Research has shown, however, that RS is not a progressive disorder with continuing downhill degeneration, so this definition has been replaced with one of developmental arrest. Currently, researchers are exploring the theory that neurons do not die, but instead do not reach a stage of developmental maturation necessary for proper central nervous system development and maintenance in RS. Studies which reversed the previous hypothesis of brain degeneration have made way for new studies which are exploring the role of neurotrophic (growth) factors in RS. New studies on all aspects of RS from the basic biology to the complex genetics of the disorder hold great promise for expanding our knowledge and furthering understanding that will lead to treatments and cures.

"In the middle of difficulty lies opportunity."

– ALBERT EINSTEIN

RETT SYNDROME: A SLICE OF HISTORY

In 1954, Dr. Andreas Rett, a Viennese physician, first noticed this syndrome in two girls as they sat in his waiting room with their mothers. He observed these children making the same repetitive hand-washing motions. Curious, he compared their clinical and developmental histories and discovered they were very similar.

Dr. Rett checked with his nurse and learned that he had six other girls with similar behavior in his practice. Surely, he thought, all of these girls must have the same disorder. Not content with studying his own patients, Dr. Rett made a film of these girls and traveled throughout Europe seeking other children with these symptoms.

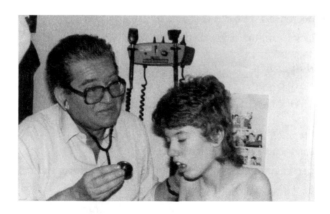

Dr. Andreas Rett with a patient

Research

Meanwhile, in 1960, young female patients in Sweden with quite similar symptoms caught the eye of their own physician, Dr. Bengt Hagberg. Dr. Hagberg collected the records of these girls and put them aside, intending to return to them when he had more time to study this curious phenomenon.

Then, in 1966, Dr. Rett published his findings in the German language in several Austrian medical journals, which, however well-known in that part of the world, were hardly mainstream reading for much of the rest of the world's medical community. Even after Dr. Rett published a description of the disease in English in 1977, RS remained in the backwaters of medical concern: the pre-Internet world lacked the electronic information highways taken for granted in the 21st Century.

But in 1983, an article on RS appeared in the mainstream, English-language journal, *Annals of Neurology*. Written by none other than Dr. Hagberg and his colleagues, the report finally raised the profile of RS and put it on the radar screen of many more investigators. This article was a breakthrough in communicating details of the disease to a wide audience, and the authors honored its pioneering researcher by naming it Rett syndrome.

WHAT WE KNOW

EARLY RESEARCH IN RS FOCUSED ON developing a natural history of the disorder. Information collected at the Rett Centers and through brain tissue donation has substantiated the following basic findings:

Neurobiological Findings
- small brain (12-33 percent reduction)
- no malformations, storage, demyelinization, infection, or gliosis
- dendritic arborizations, cell differentiation and neuronal growth are affected
- small neurons with increased neuronal packing, migration not affected
- thinning of hippocampus
- significant involvement of caudate nucleus
- decreased melanin (pigment) in substantia nigra
- lack of mature olfactory (smell) neurons

Immunochemical Findings
- early cholinergic deficits result in defective dendritic differentiation (branching)
- MAP 2 decreased or absent in inner layer of cortex

Neurochemical Findings
- early cholinergic deficits
- decreasing levels of CSF dopamine and norepinephrine with age
- elevated levels of beta-endorphins
- transient elevation of lactic acid and alanine in plasma CSF

Cardiovascular Findings
- atrio-ventricular conduction system immaturity

Research

Autonomic Findings
- agitation
- disorganized breathing
- vasomotor changes (blue hands and feet)
- vacant spells
- constipation (90 percent)
- abdominal distention (bloating) (50 percent)

Neuropathological Findings
- Morphologic (anatomical) features are unique, with only decreased brain weight being consistently present. The brain is preferentially involved in this altered growth; other organ weights are appropriate for the individual's height.
- There is no consistent evidence of a degenerative, inflammatory or ischemic process.
- There is no evidence of a progressive change in brain morphology over time. MRI and EEG studies support this observation.
- There is no recognizable disease process. RS seems to be the result of a maturational arrest of brain development.
- Golgi studies suggest that arrested brain development affects dendritic size in selected brain regions, namely the frontal, motor, and limbic regions.
- Alterations in numerous neurotransmitters have been observed, but there does not yet appear to be consistent data suggesting that the primary defect is in any of them. Rather, neurotransmitter defects can be seen as an outcome of malfunctions in other systems and can be used to trace back the source of the malfunction.
- Neurobiologic research is directed toward identifying possible deficiencies in neurotrophic factors which could initiate the apparent arrest of brain development.

Epidemiology and Survival
- The prevalence of RS is estimated at 1 per 22,800 (0.44/10000) females aged two to eighteen years of age as determined in the Texas Rett Syndrome Registry. In a similar study done in Sweden, the prevalence has been recorded at 1:10,000 females.
- RS has been reported in all races, ethnic groups, and socioeconomic classes worldwide.
- Individuals with RS have an estimated 70 percent survival at age thirty-five years. This contrasts sharply with an estimated 27 percent survival at thirty-five years for individuals characterized as "severely retarded."
- The majority of Rett syndrome deaths are either sudden and unexpected or secondary to pneumonia.

Additional information on brain findings in RS is located in the Nervous System chapter.

ROSETTA STONE OF NEUROLOGICAL DISORDERS

RETT SYNDROME WAS LONG RELEGATED to obscure articles and the fervent concern of parents, but it has now been adopted into a family of higher profile neurological disorders. This change from medical oddity to the focus of avid researchers reflects

Research

the exciting discovery of genetic similarities between RS and disorders as disparate as autism, mental retardation, bipolar disorder and schizophrenia. And if this early promise holds true, RS will no longer be a medical trivia question. Rather, it could become a medical Rosetta stone for translating a tangle of genetic and biochemical evidence into a real understanding of a number of other neurological conditions.

An ancient slab of writing, found in the Nile delta area in 1799, was inscribed in multiple languages—Egyptian hieroglyphics, a simpler form of Egyptian writing, and Greek. By comparing how the same messages were written in these different languages, a French scholar was able to decode the language of hieroglyphics by 1822. This monumental breakthrough in understanding an important age in ancient history occurred because the Rosetta stone shed light on the similarities between known and unknown languages. Likewise, medical scholars are now decoding the mysteries of certain brain disorders by comparing them to RS.

SCOPE AND AIMS OF RESEARCH

IN ORDER TO SHARE WITH YOU THE STRIDES that have been made and predict where research will take us, it is important to first make sure we can all speak the same language. You will find a glossary in the back that should simplify some of the more scientific jargon as well as clarify some common terms that might mean different things to different people. Words in italics in this chapter are further defined in the Glossary.

Many different kinds of research can contribute to finding *treatments and cures* for RS. Typically, when people think of research they envision folks in white coats and a room full of microscopes, flasks, and bubbling beakers. Certainly, all of these are found in a biomedical research lab where scientists seek to understand how RS works at the molecular, genetic, or other biological level. But there are other kinds of research which can lead to the discovery of improved systems and technologies in the quest for further understanding of RS and its many clinical symptoms.

It is important to remember that treatment is more than a pill or a shot. Treatment can be anything that improves the outcome of conditions caused by RS. With that perspective, we can consider a number of areas to be included in the research category. For instance, *educational research* can help optimize learning for people with communicative disorders and conditions such as apraxia. *Technology research* and development can create and improve needed tools, like new or improved computer programs that work on eye gaze, or better assistive devices that could help in lifting, dressing, or bathing. *Applied research* in these areas can be very beneficial in the development of specific treatment and therapy regimes. We can even imagine the creation of some high-tech external devices. Based on the enormous success of cochlear implants to help the hearing impaired (see illustration), perhaps something similar could be made for neurons that fits like a hairnet and could improve communication between nerve cells. While this last example lives only in our imaginations now, that is the first step that brings dreams to reality.

We must find the means to support "good" research in all of these areas in addition to our investments the biomedical arena. "Good" research produces good data, and good data can be relied upon as the foundation supporting the development of new treatments,

Research

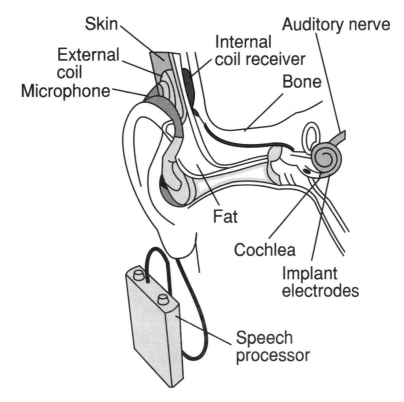

Cochlear implant diagram

therapies and educational approaches. So what makes "good" research? Typically, good research rests on having a testable hypothesis, or theory. There also needs to be a set of well-defined experiments that will challenge the hypothesis, minimize the confounding variables and be able to report the answer with a big enough sample set to demonstrate some quantifiable statistical rigor. This means that, when the experiments are repeated, they produce about the same results, so the data identify something that is a real phenomenon, and not just a fluke of one or two observations. In cases where sufficient data support the hypothesis, improvements will be seen. In cases where the data does not support the hypothesis, people can chose to forgo the original exercise in favor of something known to produce beneficial results. That way, we maximize our access to things that will work and minimize wasted time, energy and money.

Research aimed at daily methods of care is one type of research that is less likely to be funded by traditional funding sources. Common questions on the effectiveness of different therapies are often left to parents for empirical answers. A general sense of whether something is good or not-so-good develops from shared observations. This anecdotal approach to knowledge is a good beginning. But imagine if we could fund real research projects that could definitively answer some of these questions and come up with a plan to optimize results for that particular situation. Maybe we would find that one particular type of therapy would be more effective in one age group but less effective than another therapy in a different age group, for example pre- and postpuberty. Wouldn't you want to know that, and help your daughter use her time and your money most effectively? Moreover, wouldn't

Research

you want your educators, therapists, and policy makers to know that there is real research out there that could influence your child's IEP, PT, or, very importantly, the amount of public funds available for local, state or federal programs supporting education, therapy, and development for your child?

Good research in any arena gives reproducible results, and reproducible results encourage the development of and investment in programs that maximize the benefits of those results for our kids. Whether it's biomedical, educational, therapeutic, applied, or technological, research is a particular way of approaching a problem that is based on defining the *variables*, making sure you know what is positive and what is negative (called *controls* in the world or research) and being able to reproduce your results, given the same variables and controls, again and again. That's why it's called *re*-search instead of just *search!*

CLINICAL AND LABORATORY RESEARCH

MOST OF THIS CHAPTER focuses on the white-coat, pocket-protector realm of biomedical research. While no more important than any other aspect of RS research, biomedical research grabs the headlines and our heartstrings because life-changing treatments and cures are there, waiting to be discovered in this laboratory realm of flasks, beakers, microscopes and high-tech paraphernalia.

The goal of biomedical research is to make the unknown known so that steps can be taken to repair, replace, or restore an interrupted function. Researchers look for patterns. They see how something works when it's ABC and then, systematically, they change a component: AB_; A_C, _BC and see what's different from what they originally saw. When they can predict what happens in one situation, they challenge it with another variable until they can predict what will happen in this new scenario, and so on, until all possible outcomes are known and an informed decision can be made that will change the medical outcome in a controlled, repeatable, and reliable way. This is the path that will find treatments for the medical conditions that plague our children and find cures that will eliminate the issues caused by RS.

The tools of the research scientist—knowledge, technology, creativity and patience, hold the promise of treatments and cures for RS. We already know that RS is a complex disorder, with many variations in the severity, onset, and types of medical conditions that all fall under this single diagnosis. This complexity both intrigues and challenges geneticists, molecular biologists, neurologists, and other specialists who spend their professional lives trying to fill in the pieces of this most difficult puzzle. Each time there is a "Eureka!," each time even a tiny piece falls in place, the road to understanding how RS works becomes a little smoother. Each breakthrough paves the way for a new level of understanding, a little more known, a little less left to find out.

DISCOVERIES OLD AND NEW

IT IS NOT REALLY POSSIBLE TO ENUMERATE all of the research that has occurred since the first edition of the Handbook. There is simply too much, so this chapter is aimed at giving you a flavor of the scope and type of biomedical research that continues to accelerate the study of RS. Even as this chapter is being written, we are poised at

Research

the threshold of many more discoveries that will be significant not only to those with RS, but which will inform research strategies for many other neurological disorders as well.

LABORATORY MODELS

FOLLOWING THE DISCOVERY OF THE ROLE of the *MECP2* gene, scientists concentrated on the creation of laboratory models, animals manipulated by science to include special "designer genes." Easy to say, hard to do. But within two years of finding the gene, independent labs in Scotland (Dr. Adrian Bird), Boston (Dr. Rudolph Jaenisch) and Houston (Dr. Huda Zoghbi) had each created mouse strains with different parts of their *MECP2* genes changed, added (*knock-in*) or removed (*knock-out*). Knock-out mice, while the condition is not known to occur in any real person, are a valuable lab tool for exploring the outer edge of what *MECP2* (or lack thereof) does. Mice were also challenged by having a whole *MECP2* gene reinserted via gene therapy. It was discovered that too much *MECP2* led to unhappy consequences for the mice just as much—albeit somewhat later in their lives—as having part of the *MECP2* genes missing. This important piece of information shows scientists that adding just the right amount of *MECP2* and in the right place will be a consideration in the development of treatments.

The mouse models permit researchers to chart the course of events in the various *MECP2* scenarios and work on ways to alter the outcomes. Interestingly, it was found that early attempts to create mouse models caused male mice to develop symptoms within four weeks of life, have an advanced form by week seven, and die by week ten. The female mouse, on the other hand, developed an RS-like disease within six months of life, well into adulthood for that animal, and still, today, no successful female mouse model mimics what is seen in our children. Clearly, there are elements in leading a human life that further differentiate *MECP2* mutations in mouse and man.

Nevertheless, the mouse models let researchers probe how variations in the MeCP2 protein affect brain function at critical stages in development.

> "As development progresses, what we encounter—our experiences—may also change how the brain responds. This may account for individual variation in disease severity. It may be that enrichment of the environment or exposure to certain stimuli may give affected children more milestones. I could envision that with interventional studies in mice, we may identify pathways that could lead to behavioral or pharmacological approaches that may provide at least symptomatic relief." ~ Huda Zoghbi, M.D.

SOME ANSWERS, MORE QUESTIONS

RESEARCH IS OFTEN DESIGNED AS A SET OF "contrast and compare" exercises. As we've discussed, scientists ask questions like: "If you've made a mouse without any MeCP2, what happens when you use gene therapy to put a whole *MECP2* gene in?" "What happens if you add parts of the *MECP2* gene, but leave out others?" Answers to these kinds of questions help to set the stage for the development of treatments, preventions and cures for people, but this stage of research is still, as this edition of the Handbook goes to press, in its infancy. There are many twists and turns before you can move from *treating*

Research

or *curing* a mouse—and we are still a long way from that—to *treating* or *curing* a human, and those differences illustrate the chasm between laboratory research and clinical research.

CLINICAL TRIALS

CLINICAL TRIALS IN RS HAVE BEEN CONDUCTED in a number of areas, mostly on single medical issues and after extensive planning and hurdle-jumping. There are numerous federal, state, and even local laws as well as ethical considerations that can apply to clinical trials that aren't concerns in animal model experiments. Clinical researchers need to get extensive approvals from their institutions for any trials that use human subjects. It often takes more than a year to receive approval from the Institutional Review Board (IRB) at a university or other public research facility to perform clinical studies. Frequently, IRB approval requires extensive rewriting of protocols and consent agreements before even the first steps of organizing the trial can begin.

These important safeguards can often seem insurmountable, but when the time is right and the research is ready, they must be conquered. It is this clinical step that brings real answers about the efficacy of a treatment. Clinical trials are the bridge between the lab bench and the bedside. But clinical trials are still research. That means that, just as at the lab bench, many experiments simply will not yield positive results, may refute earlier beliefs, or may answer an as yet unasked question. All of these situations occurred when the *neurotransmitter* folate was reexamined in detail after some preliminary analyses suggested a closer look was warranted.

When we heard the story in 2004 about a little girl with a deficiency in her folate neurotransmitter who underwent a significant transformation by the simple addition of folic acid, there was quite a buzz. Many believed that we had a possible answer for at least some of those in the "gray area" of an RS diagnosis. Perhaps some percentage of the nearly 20 percent* of those without observable *MECP2* mutations actually had something other than RS. If some of that 20 percent really had a folate transport deficiency disorder (FTDD), they could receive immediate benefit from treatment with some form of folic acid.

Shortly after this case was aired, doctors from Germany published a paper announcing that the cerebrospinal fluid (CSF) of four patients with RS were also deficient in folate. The researchers reported small but perceptible subjective improvements in these girls including increased engagement, better muscle tone, and reduced frequency/duration of seizures. The lead author, Dr. Vincent Ramaekers, also presented additional data at a conference showing a total of eight patients with RS who all had very deficient folate levels. According to his data, the girls with RS had lower folate levels than those patients with identified FTDD! You don't argue with 100 percent (eight out of eight girls)! You jump on it!

Upon hearing these results, Dr. Alan Percy from the University of Alabama re-examined the data from the folate-betane study he performed with many participants over several years. This was a blind study where participants were given folic acid, betane, or a harmless placebo, but no one knew who was getting what, including the researchers. This "blind study" method is tried and true in science and keeps people from unconsciously biasing the results (called "the placebo effect").

---

*The figure of 20 percent for those without an observable *MECP2* mutation is based on the traditional *MECP2* mutation testing that was available at the beginning of 2004. By 2005, new and more sensitive testing had reduced that percentage to about 15 percent, and new advances are likely to uncover still other hidden *MECP2* differences.

Research

When Dr. Percy "unblinded" his study, he found parents whose children were receiving folic acid reporting similar subjective improvements as those seen by Dr. Ramaekers' group. Reports showed those receiving folic acid to be more alert, have better muscle tone, and experience fewer/shorter seizures than those on either betane or placebo. The difference in reports between the three groups was statistically significant. In research, statistically significant results indicate that something has happened that is beyond mere chance alone, so it seemed that something was going on with the addition of folic acid that wasn't happening otherwise.

Because of the Percy and Ramaekers findings, Baylor College of Medicine and the University of Alabama, with support from IRSA, organized a larger scale study to analyze CSF folate levels from more that seventy courageous volunteers. Participants from all age groups and many of the mutations, including all seven common forms, were part of the study. There were long waits, frustration, some pain, and some risks taken by the many volunteers.

This study, led by Dr. Jeffrey Neul, revealed that CSF folate levels were normal in all but one of the more than seventy people studied, and were only borderline low in one girl. Thus, while the subjective improvements seen in both earlier studies remain valid empirical observations, their underlying biological cause has not been elucidated.

These studies serve as a reminder that the road on which research drives is unmarked. What can we learn about the road to discovery from this experience? Was it a worthless detour that falsely raised hopes, or an interesting side trip that gave some helpful, if not dramatic, results useful in the development of treatment regimens for some people with RS?

You'll need to decide if the effort was worth the results. Because of this research, parents can be confident that their daughters are unlikely to be suffering from severe chronic folate deficiency. They can also know that a multivitamin which includes folic acid may bring some subjective but statistically measurable improvements in their daughters' lives. These are small but useful findings, and sometimes that's all a heap of work finds—or less.

But there is more to this story beyond laying to rest an unconfirmed, extraordinary observation that RS leads to severe folate deficiency. Dr. Neul and his colleagues examined the other neurotransmitters in the CSF to fully exploit the data so valiantly volunteered by the RS community. He found there was a significant reduction in some of the **biogenic amines** in a number of the samples. This actually verified the initial studies done in the early eighties, although others were unable to reproduce the same results in the earlier experiments because of limitations in the technologies of the times. Because the finding of Dr. Neul and his colleagues was statistically significant, it suggests the cause is biologically correlated to RS rather than a chance occurrence. The new finding leads to a new set of experiments to make sure that the correlation can be verified and, if so, better understood.

Biogenic amines are compounds derived from ammonia in which hydrogens are substituted by organic radicals. They are frequently involved in *signaling,* an area we know is disrupted in RS. This observation has allowed Dr. Neul and his colleagues to re-examine dopamine and serotonin in their mouse models to help determine the mechanism for the observed reduction. Although this phase of the work is still preliminary as we go to press, there have been some positive results in the mouse models which, if they hold true, will lead us full circle back to a clinical investigation. So begins another round of *re*-search.

Research

PARTICULAR PROBLEMS FOR CLINICAL RESEARCH ON RARE DISORDERS

IT IS IMPORTANT TO HAVE A RESEARCH STRATEGY that can take results from the lab bench to the clinic as quickly as safely possible. As we discussed above, this is often the most difficult step in research for any disorder. But it is an even thornier problem for a rare disease when drug companies are reluctant to make the development investments needed to create new medicines because small user-base limits their ability to recoup those investments. Fortunately, in the United States, the federal government recognized this disparity and created some safety nets for those with rare or orphan diseases. These nets are just now being activated and RS is one of the fortunate few early recipients of this outreach.

Congress mandated the Rare Disease Act of 2002 directing National Institutes of Health (NIH) to develop and support "regional centers of excellence for clinical research into, training in, and demonstration of diagnostic, prevention, control, and treatment methods for rare diseases." With a frequency of approximately 1 in 10,000 to 1 in 25,000 live female births, RS meets the criteria of a "rare (or orphan) disease," which the US Congress defined in the Orphan Drug Act as:

- a condition affecting fewer than 200,000 in the United States or
- a more common disease, for which no reasonable expectation exists that the costs of developing or distributing a drug can be recovered from the sale of the drug in the United States.

There are about six thousand disorders or conditions that fall into the first category, and about twenty-five million people in the US who collectively fall into the second category.

In order to fulfill the above-mentioned congressional directive, the NIH created an opportunity for doctors to develop proposals seeking to establish clinical research centers focusing on rare disease types. Further, NIH wanted to support those centers with a dedicated "informatics" (computer storehouse of data, web resources, etc.) component. In addition to the usual requirements for scientifically sound proposals outlining the clinical approaches the applicants would take to diagnose and treat these rare disorders, how they would collect data and handle new clinical trials, and so on, there was a requirement that the clinicians also include a partnership with a patient advocate group.

Of the more than one hundred applications vying for the funding, the proposal by Dr. Art Beaudet and his colleagues from Baylor College of Medicine and the University of Alabama, and IRSA was one of the ten awarded. We are now in the early stages of the Rare Disease Clinical Research Network (RDCRN) with our center focusing on three rare neurological disorders: Prader-Willi, Angelman, and Rett syndromes. These three disorders were selected as targets not only because of the particular expertise of the applicants on those disorders, but also because all three all had known genes. The reviewers who scrutinized this application agreed with Dr. Beaudet and his collaborators that these three disorders seemed particularly likely to provide some near-term clinical approaches.

In addition to the nine clinically based centers, the federal investment has included a center dedicated to the development of shared informatics. The Data Technology Coordinating Center (DTCC) is a critical component to the study of rare diseases because it will let us paint a big picture from the tiny parts.

SEEING THE BIG PICTURE

THE BIG PICTURE IS A CRUCIAL ELEMENT in the study of rare diseases. It is the very rarity of the events that makes it so difficult to collect the information into a

Research

cohesive whole. Imagine that RS is an enormously complex jig-saw puzzle with thousands of tiny pieces, each with its own complex shape and shading, just like each of our children. Imagine, too, if the pieces were as spread out as our children are across this country and the world. When the puzzle is complete—when all the pieces are fit together—we will get a clear understanding of what that picture really is and knowing that will help us to solve other puzzles as well. But unless we can see many, many of the pieces at once—if each piece remains an isolated event—we won't be able to solve the puzzle. The RDCRN offers the opportunity to see scores more puzzle pieces. The enormous informatics capabilities of the DTCC lets the information be stored and retrieved—in this analogy the exact shapes, shadings, and patterns of each piece—in a way that will permit the puzzle to be virtually assembled when enough pieces have been collected. Being able to see the big picture brings the power of reliable prediction and enables treatments to be targeted and interventions to be effective.

WHAT DO WE KNOW?

WHILE CLINICAL SUCCESSES RELY ON BEING ABLE TO SEE the big picture, the steps leading up to even beginning to consider a big picture are still built on the knowledge gained from working on the very smallest corner of one tiny picture at a time. For that reason, it is important to go back to the bench to share a small snapshot of some of the laboratory advances that have been made since the gene was found. Following research is a little like taking a road trip without a map, but with a final destination in mind. You never know which road you'll be on, but it can be spectacular trip.

Some of the most significant recent breakthroughs that move us to new stages of understanding include abundant data on the relationship between neurons and synapses, the role and function of MeCP2, the relationship of MeCP2 to other important developmental proteins like Brain Derived Neurotrophic Factor (BDNF), and the relationships that are emerging between *genotype* (mutation status) and *phenotype* (clinical presentation). Many lines of evidence are converging that allow researchers the luxury of synthesizing data from a wide range of sources and issues that make up the Rett condition. Things are beginning to fit together, patterns are emerging, and events we thought were unique are beginning to coalesce with other observations to form a cohesive story.

Take, for example, the 2004 discovery that the *MECP2* gene creates a general MeCP2 protein and a neuron-specific MeCP2 protein. This discovery, published first by the North American team led by Toronto researchers Drs. BA Minassian and JB Vincent and then independently corroborated by identical findings in the laboratory of Dr. Adrian Bird in Scotland, let us see a clearer picture of how *MECP2* (the gene) and MeCP2 (the protein) work together. It also helps to draw a map that could permit scientists to develop new, targeted reagents—from experiments to treatments—to create bridges for those with improperly functioning proteins and genes that could alleviate symptoms, as well as being able to screen for problems before they arise.

The roads of scientific discovery are often not straight, linear speedways, but curves, some of which, yes, lead to deadends, but others of which can offer the most breathtaking views just around the curve. One such collective gasp for our community is caused by the vistas shown by the work of Dr. Jaenisch's graduate student, Sandra Luikenhuis, in 2005. For her dissertation research, Dr. Luikenhuis fashioned a designer gene for the *MECP2*-deficient mice created by Dr. Rudolph Jaenisch's lab to help understand RS. In a series of complex, careful, and elegant experiments, Dr. Luikenhuis was able to fuse usable MeCP2 protein

Research

onto a genetic vehicle that drove it directly to the mouse's neurons. Using this tactic, genetically engineered mice without any *MECP2* gene exhibited none of the Rett-like symptoms seen in mice who did not receive the *transgene* treatment.

> "Understanding how to circumvent the clinical issues reliably before they are expressed will lead to a better understanding of potential therapies for mice (and eventually people) in whom expression of a clinical phenotype has occurred, but that is still in the future." ~ Dr. Rudolph Jaenisch

Another recent discovery occurred when a second gene on the X chromosome gave us new insights into the symptoms of RS. Dr. John Christodoulou and his colleagues and Dr. YF Tao et al simultaneously discovered the presence of another gene near but independent of *MECP2* in which mutations cause clinical features that fit within the broad Rett phenotype. This is important to us for a number of reasons. The most obvious is that some portion of those clinically diagnosed with RS but without an observable genetic mutation despite repeated analyses using all known methodologies may, in fact, have a mutation at this newly defined genetic locus. Because of this discovery, these researchers and their colleagues and collaborators have created a new tool to hone the diagnosis of Rett syndrome. Is a mutation at the newly defined CDKL5 locus still Rett syndrome? No decision has been made on that yet, but it is likely that there will be some gene-specific treatment differences that will be important to consider, even in the face of clinical presentation overlap. As in so many situations, the devil is in the details, and knowing this distinction is an important step allowing further clarification and discrimination of the RS condition.

ROADBLOCKS, DETOURS AND FLAT TIRES

It's probably safe to say there isn't anyone whose life has been touched by RS who doesn't wish they could turn back the hands of time to those days before we knew "something was wrong" and take a different path at that crossroad. It's been said before in this book, but it can't be said enough–there really were no "choices" about the road to take, as much as people question themselves. You did not "do" anything or not "do" something that made RS happen to your child. You did not pick RS. It picked you.

But the landscape is significantly different for those with RS today than it was even ten years ago, and those benefits have accrued and will continue to accrue because of the strides made in research. Earlier diagnoses, thanks to greater awareness among medical professionals, and more sensitive mutation testing mean earlier interventions, greater proactive supplementation, and earlier identification of potential problems. But a magic bullet without consequences is a very unlikely event, despite the hype of certain approaches that may suggest otherwise. These final thoughts are meant to keep hope, faith and belief in the promise of research in a perspective that is reasonable and keeps the safety of our children who have RS today as a primary objective.

We can all expect important advances to occur in the near term (usually defined in development terms as three to five years). RS is hard to erase. That doesn't mean that

Research

some treatments can't make some people with RS appear to the world to be symptom-free, although they will still carry the mutated gene and could pass it on to their children. There is likely to be a wide range of biomedical treatments with an equally wide range of effectiveness, but each biomedical treatment breakthrough for one mutation type and level of X-inactivation will light the path for new breakthroughs for other mutation types and X-inactivation ratios. Drastic treatments that predominantly mask symptoms for some are certainly a possibility, but we'll hedge those bets for the more drastic outcomes and look in a near to mid-term time frame, given the current pace of research (three to ten years). Time will tell if we've predicted well. As Einstein showed us, time is relative. Another day is too long for any parent. A decade is a modest investment in a scientific career.

Is treatment the same as a cure? When we say "cure," we mean the complete eradication of Rett syndrome so that no symptoms are discernible, even by a doctor and a battery of tests, and no impact will be felt in future generations. When we say "treatment," we mean interventions that cause a reduction in clinical manifestations that improve the medical/cognitive outcome of Rett syndrome. Treatments can occur at any time in a person's life and have impacts as dramatic as we propose above so that RS seems to disappear—but "seems to" and "does" are two different biomedical situations. Now, maybe those definitions are too pure, and if treatments that erased all or most visible effects of RS were available, even if your grandkids would also need the same treatment, and that would suit you just fine, then you have every reason to be encouraged. It's important to stress that not every treatment will lead to such dramatic benefits, but it is likely to see important improvements for most with RS, even if they are not in the "dramatic" league. Even with some dramatic treatment breakthroughs, the level of benefit is likely to vary with different mutation/X-inactivation status, but, again, one breakthrough creates a segue for others.

There isn't a person whose life has been touched by RS who doesn't believe with all their heart that biomedical research will find a way to make this better. We dream of it, we work toward it, we strategize and plan and support and spend every waking minute trying to stimulate, elicit, convince, and cajole everything possible out of each research dollar we raise and each project we fund, because we know that it is that research that will make the difference. The real issue is the time frame.

We have already made incredible strides in understanding RS since the gene was found in 1999—amazing, exciting information that will move us forward to treatments and cures. With all of us working together, we will get there—but we can't sacrifice our children to our hopes and premature results that could harm them in the long run. We must all be realistic watchdogs to keep our children safe while we get to the right place, where interventions won't come with a price tag none of us can afford.

The future for people with RS is full of hope. The incredible gene breakthrough now allows us to make an early and accurate diagnosis, leading to better care and management. More scientists than ever are interested in this disorder that was nearly unknown two decades ago. For the first time, researchers in the field speak realistically of treatments and cures.

Research

FUTURE DIRECTIONS

THE TARGETS FOR RESEARCH in RS over the next five years can be divided into two categories: clinical and basic science; each with subcategories.

CLINICAL RESEARCH
Gene Studies

CONTINUED ANALYSIS OF MUTATIONS in the *MECP2* gene must be pursued to include regions of the gene not previously explored. These studies are in addition to routine diagnostic studies and are designed to understand the gene more fully.

Phenotype-Genotype Correlation Studies

Correlation of disease expression, (severity of RS symptoms) with the type of mutation has given limited results thus far, mostly because the number of individuals in each study has been small. The creation of IRSA's international mutation database (RettBASE) and clinical database (InterRETT) will allow this information to be pooled. As discussed, this approach is expected to yield a big picture to assess the relationship between the specific disruption of the gene and the medical outcome of RS. The role of X chromosome inactivation must also be explored more fully in this relationship.

For individuals who have the clinical features of RS but who have not to date had a mutation in *MECP2* identified, this database may help us understand how they differ and lead to refinements in clinical diagnoses.

Finally, for individuals who have mutations in *MECP2* but who do not have the clinical features of RS, study of the specific mutations may help us understand why such varied clinical expression is possible and that too can lead to the development of treatments in RS. These varied disorders include non-specific mental retardation, developmental delay, learning disabilities, and autism.

Basic Research

Animal Models

Ongoing creation of more mouse models of RS based on specific mutations is an important effort. Existing models, which result from deletion of the entire gene, are important as well but do not appear to be truly representative of RS. These models will allow understanding of why this gene is some important for brain function and what specific targets it has, and will be critical for evaluation of treatment strategies.

Identifying Gene Targets

MECP2 produces a protein product (MeCP2), which is critical for the regulation of many different types of other genes, so-called downstream genes, responsible for brain function. Scientists do not yet know how many other genes are impacted by disruptions in MeCP2. It is essential that these targets be identified. This will provide fundamental new information and offer potential avenues for treatment by directly attacking these other genes or their targets.

MECP2 Function

The MeCP2 protein is known to recognize specific elements in DNA, but the mechanism of recognition has not yet been discovered. This mechanism must be fully understood,

Research

which would permit the development of mechanisms for replacing or supplementing the defective gene.

Neurobiology

The mechanism of action of the "downstream" genes will provide important information on the development, maturation, and maintenance of connections between nerve cells. This appears to be the fundamental problem in RS and one which is completely open to study.

THE IRSA COMMITMENT TO RESEARCH

THE INTERNATIONAL RETT SYNDROME ASSOCIATION continues its commitment to excellence in research. As it has for the last two decades, IRSA will continue to fund world-class biomedical, clinical and treatment oriented research. Our basic research path forward is to fund, foster, and organize this type of innovative collaborative and multidisciplinary thinking. The ultimate outcome of this integrated basic research will eventually be successful treatments, prevention and cures for people with RS.

- **International Dissemination of Clinical and *MECP2* Mutation Data**
  The IRSA *MECP2* database is an Internet-accessible database providing a list of all published *MECP2* gene variations, including *polymorphisms* (benign mutations). This extremely flexible database contains an extensive search engine, with added features allowing clinicians and scientists to submit new and unpublished variation data. IRSA was very excited to designate support for the development of the IRSA Clinical Database, RettBASE, which contains extensive clinical data from RS patients worldwide. Now linked to the *MECP2* Variation Database, InterRETT, this dual database system will also provide an invaluable research tool for the examination of phenotype/genotype correlations.

- **Building Relationships in the Rett Syndrome Scientific Community, and Fostering Collaborations among Clinical and Research Professionals**
  With the recent discovery of *MECP2* mutations in other disorders such as autism, X-linked mental retardation, and schizophrenia, we feel it is imperative to develop an open dialogue among professionals working on these increasingly linked disorders. As such, we encourage collaborative efforts in our grants and fellowship programs at both the basic and clinical levels. In addition, we are very proud to foster collaborations through IRSA's Professional Advisory Board, an international membership comprised of the foremost authorities and leading innovators in RS research and related disorders. Finally, we work closely with institutes within the NIH, including the National Institute for Neurological Disorder and Stroke and the National Institute for Child Health and Human Development, to identify researchers requiring support for generating the pilot data necessary for successful federal funding of innovative and high-risk projects.

- **Supporting Rett Syndrome Tissue Banks**
  IRSA partners with the Harvard Brain Bank to collect, maintain, and curate the precious gift endowed to science by families whose children have died. Autopsy is the ultimate gift of hope because it helps to build understanding about the most detailed functions of the brain in Rett syndrome. As part of the research effort, an autopsy protocol has been designed that uses a uniform procedure so that scientists are assured that the results from one tissue sample are comparable to another. This banked tissue has been the foundation of critical discoveries about the role of MeCP2 in the brain. Without these noble contributions, progress in these areas would be slowed, possibly by

Research

decades, and our optimism about the near-term possibilities for treatments and cures would be limited. Families who participate in this legacy know that their child's contribution is an integral part of important research. We believe that each contributor to the brain bank is a collaborating scientist whose work will lead to new ways to prevent the ravages of RS from those yet to be born with *MECP2* mutations. No preplanning is necessary. The IRSA provides detailed instructions for parents to follow in advance of their child's death, and at the time of death. For a packet with questions and answers on this sensitive and important issue, call IRSA at 1-800-818-RETT. To report a death, call IRSA at 1-800-818-7388 or the Harvard Brain Bank at 1-800-Brain-Bank (1-800-272-4622).

• **Dissemination of Current Research Information**
If a tree falls in the forest and there's no one there to hear it, does it make a sound? Families suffered the bewilderment of not knowing what was wrong with their children for a decade between the time Dr. Rett discovered RS and the time the rest of the medical community learned of the link that could focus study and research on this constellation of medical conditions. Timely dissemination of research information is a critical component that needs to be shepherded by groups like IRSA. New studies with promising results, or results that need debunking, the coordination of patient volunteers, and other important messages need to get through the network to all the stakeholders and the world-at-large. IRSA often acts as the conduit for the dissemination of important research news by hosting:

  ○ *scientific symposia:* IRSA sponsors and supports professional meetings where scientists convene to share recent information and restrategize about research directions and priorities in light of what they learn at these high-level meetings.

  ○ *family conferences:* IRSA hosts an annual national meeting and is a frequent presenter at numerous local and regional meetings that inform families about the latest progress, its significance to their children now, and its potential tomorrow.

  ○ *professional conferences:* IRSA attends national and international conferences in relevant areas of scientific inquiry (i.e. Child Neurology Society, Society for Neuroscience, American Academy of Neurology, Society for Human Genetics, etc.) both as an active exhibitor there to educate the meeting attendees on RS and as a participant by presenting talks, sponsoring panels, and reviewing presentations to summarize for our membership.

  ○ *community outreach:* IRSA serves the entire RS syndrome community by supporting RettNet—an online list-serv open to all seeking dialogue about issues relating to RS and by providing IRSAlerts, e-mail news flashes that tell the community about important occurrences in close to real time.

  ○ *public awareness:* We know that the research that gives us hope in the future for better lives for our children will also have critical impacts on many other neurological disorders. It is important for the rest of the world as well. IRSA disseminates information through testimony about our disorder and the scientific advances we've made in the halls of Congress, in news releases that we blanket across the news and television wires, and through many other public venues to spread the word, gain support, and raise awareness.

THE ROAD TO RESEARCH IS PAVED WITH FUNDING

ALL OF THE GREAT STRIDES BEING MADE on the research frontiers show us brightly lit roads to a future of pre- and antenatal screening with promising outcomes

Research

akin to those seen in other conquered disorders such as PKU (phenylketonuria). They give us more reason than ever to hope that such advances can lead to ameliorating treatments for those who already live with the consequences of RS. But we know that the road to research is paved with funding. In partnership with the RS community, IRSA has committed millions of dollars to stimulate advances, not only in biomedical research but in translational, quality of life research as well, including educational, psychological, and technological research and development to help those with RS harness their ranges of possibilities and potentials. And, because of that commitment, and IRSA's commitment to using those hard-earned, hard-baked, -washed-, -run-, -golfed, yard-saled, gala-ed and other donated dollars you've raised, we've worked to leverage those dollars against federal funds.

This has happily paid off with help from friends like Congressman Steny Hoyer and Academy Award-winning actress Ms. Julia Roberts. Because of these advocacy efforts, the National Institutes of Health—the lead science agency in the United States—now provides funding for a targeted program in RS research. We continue to make the argument to Congress that because RS is a multifaceted disorder, the results from a wide range of research involving the orthopedic, respiratory, gastrointestinal, circulatory, and cardiac systems in addition to severe seizures, and scoliosis, will stand to benefit millions of Americans suffering from any of these conditions, as well as improve the lives of those with RS who endure all of them, often simultaneously. With the recent strides made by those studying RS, the commitment of the NIH to support the best and most promising leads as they develop, and the dedication of IRSA's families, we know our tax dollars will continue to be put to work building the roads to research needed to navigate Rettland.

"In order to be a realist you must believe in miracles."

— HENRY CHRISTOPHER BAILEY

The International Rett Syndrome Association

IT BEGAN WITH TWO little girls …

… in 1954. Dr. Andreas Rett, of Vienna, Austria, noticed them sitting with their mothers in his waiting room, both compulsively moving their hands as if they were washing them. His curiosity was piqued, but his subsequent research into the disorder went unnoticed. Six years later, Dr. Bengt Hagberg of Sweden observed the same tendencies in several of his patients. Many years went by before Drs. Rett and Hagberg found each other and joined forces. In 1983, their findings were finally reported in an English language article; that year, the American medical community recognized the disorder known as Rett syndrome (RS).

Shortly afterward, the International Rett Syndrome Association (IRSA) was born as families joined together. IRSA was established as a 501(c)3 organization of parents, physicians, therapists, researchers, and friends, dedicated to promoting and funding research efforts and quality-of-life issues for children with RS. IRSA was incorporated in 1984 with a three-part mission:

"Never doubt that a small group of committed citizens can change the world. Indeed, it is the only thing that ever has."

– MARGARET MEAD

- to support and encourage research to determine the cause, treatments and cures for RS;
- to increase public awareness of RS;
- to provide informational and emotional support to families of children with RS.

IRSA has become the largest and most respected organization devoted to RS compassionate care and groundbreaking research for those living with RS. It is the only international clearinghouse providing vital and timely information to medical, scientific, and educational institutions, policy makers, the pharmaceutical industry, and advocacy organizations as well as families and caregivers. Members include parents, relatives, physicians, therapists, researchers and friends from all fifty states and seventy foreign countries. A

The International Rett Syndrome Association

national board of directors is complemented by an international professional advisory board comprised of highly skilled and respected experts in the fields of pediatric neurology, genetics, developmental pediatrics, orthopedics, education, and physical, occupational and music therapies.

RESEARCH FOR THE TREATMENT AND CURE

IRSA SUPPORTS PROMISING RESEARCH through its Permanent Research Fund. The fund played a pivotal role in the breakthrough discovery of the Rett gene, *MECP2*. Current research priorities include the *IRSA MECP2 Variation Database*, a central repository containing all Rett gene information gathered from laboratory analyses worldwide, and the *IRSA Clinical Database* which, when linked to the Variation Database, will allow researchers to quickly and thoroughly compare patients' mutations with their clinical symptoms, providing exciting opportunities for treatment discoveries.

THE CIRCLE OF ANGELS RESEARCH FUND is a major private donor fundraising campaign to ensure higher levels of support for IRSA's most aggressive research agenda to date.

Income from the fund and its endowment will provide ongoing and enduring support for a wide range of research services, programs, education and outreach.

Circle *of* ANGELS Research Fund

PRIORITIES OF THE CIRCLE OF ANGELS RESEARCH FUND

1. Ground breaking research to discover the means to eliminate Rett syndrome as well as new therapies to enhance lives today while we search for a cure.

2. "On call" programs that unite families, clinicians and researchers across the country. Not only does the program support individual families in need of advice, but also encourages research collaboration and promotes awareness and understanding.

3. Rapid dissemination of the latest in biological and treatment information, as well as promising research updates. In addition, providing continued maintenance of the IRSAlert, a valued resource for families, friends, researchers and clinicians.

4. Convening conferences to bring families together with members of the scientific and medical communities, promoting the most diverse array of first-hand clinical information for incorporation into treatments and enhancing researchers' understanding for the most targeted research design.

5. Supporting think tanks that bring together top researchers in the field of Rett syndrome and other relevant fields to encourage the stimulation of new ideas, new insights, and new research.

6. Underwriting IRSA's strong "AAA" programs—activism/awareness/advocacy emphasizing lobbying Congress and increasing public awareness of Rett syndrome through documentaries such as "Silent Angels." IRSA's efforts in this arena are already credited with generating substantial federal research funding.

The International Rett Syndrome Association

In addition to creating long-term tools like the databases to be mined by researchers and clinicians seeking to improve the lives of those with Rett syndrome, IRSA has raised millions of dollars to support seed grants and foundational research. Through these pilot projects, IRSA encourages investigators to attempt novel approaches to treatments, care and cures of those with Rett syndrome. When new breakthroughs occur through these cutting edge experiments, scientists can leverage their proof-of-concept knowledge into larger, federally-funded research programs, bringing understanding about Rett syndrome to a new level.

Often called a "Rosetta stone" by the medical community, RS holds the key to unlocking and understanding an array of neurological disorders.

EDUCATION/PATIENT AND FAMILY SUPPORT SERVICES/PUBLIC AND PROFESSIONAL INFORMATION

IRSA IS COMMITTED TO PROVIDING TIMELY, accurate, and objective information on RS to constituencies, thereby improving awareness and an image of those with RS as individuals who are capable of understanding, learning and growing in spite of their numerous handicaps. This effort includes annual conferences, newsletters, a resource center, video and audiotapes, an extensive web site, an Internet forum, and a parent network. IRSA also funds seminars for scientists, doctors, and other researchers to share new information, and provides materials for educators and therapists.

Family support is crucial to IRSA's mission. Recognizing that peer contact is perhaps the most invaluable means of support for those caring for their children with RS, IRSA creates opportunities to help families find and reach out to each other. Examples include RettNet, a free internet forum and help line designed to encourage and enable open discussions on the many facets of RS, and IRSA Regional Representatives who are appointed to provide emotional support and information to the families of their region by telephone, mailings, informal meetings, picnics etc., and to the parents of recently diagnosed children looking for information and contact.

In addition to providing advice and resources on everything from the often overwhelming health insurance issues to the details of how to make hand splints, IRSA also provides financial aid to families via its Angel Fund.

IRSA increased awareness of RS to unprecedented heights with the making of *Silent Angels: The Rett Syndrome Story*, hosted by actress Julia Roberts and featured on the Discovery Health Channel. Articles on RS and IRSA have appeared in numerous journals, *Marie Claire, Woman's Day, Ladies Home Journal, Redbook, Family Circle, People, Prevention, Seventeen, Wired* and *Good Housekeeping*, and have been read by millions.

ADVOCACY AND THE ADVANCEMENT OF PUBLIC POLICY

IRSA SUPPORTS A HIGH PROFILE and continuing active public policy program that includes targeted federal advocacy as well as extensive grassroots efforts. To date, IRSA's advocacy has resulted in nearly $70 million in federal research funds. Between the federal fiscal years of 1986 to 2003, the RS research budget for the National Institute of Child Health and Human Development increased from a low of $10,000 per year to $2.9 million. In the same period of time, the National Institute of Neurological Disorders and Stroke's RS yearly research budget grew from $434,000 to $1.3 million. Actress Julia Roberts joined forces with IRSA to testify before Congress for increased funding. All of these efforts led

The International Rett Syndrome Association

to a skyrocketing of interest in the scientific study of Rett syndrome, and resulted in targeted, multi-year research programs funded by the National Institutes of Health, considered to be the premier scientific research organization in the United States.

THE INTERNATIONAL RETT SYNDROME ASSOCIATION (IRSA)

www.rettsyndrome.org • 1-800-818-RETT

ORGANIZATIONAL PROFILE

- Non-profit organization founded by parents in 1984, incorporated in 1985
- Partnership with physicians, researchers, educators and therapists
- Parents and researchers with representatives in all 50 states and 70 countries
- Management by elected Board of Directors who serve four-year terms and:
  - determine IRSA's mission and purposes
  - ensure effective planning and adequate resources
  - design and monitor IRSA programs
  - enhance IRSA's image while ensuring legal and ethical integrity
- Professional Advisory Board of International Medical, Educational and Allied Health Professionals
- Funding through membership fees, donations, fundraising events, private grants, the Combined Federal Campaign, America's Charities, and the United Way

MISSION

- Support and encourage medical research to find the cause of, and develop effective treatments for, Rett Syndrome
- Increase public awareness of Rett Syndrome
- Provide informational and emotional support to families of children with Rett Syndrome
- Assist in identifying individuals with Rett Syndrome to ensure proper care and support

Collaboration with researchers

- research grants
- patient referrals
- international mutations database of gene mutations related to Rett Syndrome, RettBASE
- patient database
- clinical database to catalog syndromes, *InterRETT*

Membership services

- publication of state-of-the art literature
- publication of a newsletter, *Rett Gazette*
- maintenance of a professional library of materials on RS
- coordination of family network to provide mutual support and sharing of information
- coordination of annual conferences and seminars on RS

The International Rett Syndrome Association

- extensive website, www.rettsyndrome.org
- participation on Rettnet, online list-serv
- publication of online newsletter, *IRSAlert*

When we learned that our daughter had RS, we found IRSA and that helped us a lot. We began to share our experiences and we learned a lot from parents who walked the Rett road before. It filled our solitude and gave us support. Our tears turned into a fortress to help our daughter to live better.

I just don't know where we would be without IRSA. We found help and hope there, and we learned not only how to care for our daughter, but how to care for ourselves. We are forever grateful for the dedication and support IRSA provides.

Without IRSA, we wouldn't have known where to begin. We felt surrounded by care and went from complete despair to hope. Their support of research has led to new understanding that will help my daughter to have a better life. IRSA has helped us with the everyday challenges and has given us the gift of hope for a better future. We couldn't ask for more.

"The purpose of life is a life of purpose."

– ROBERT BYRNE

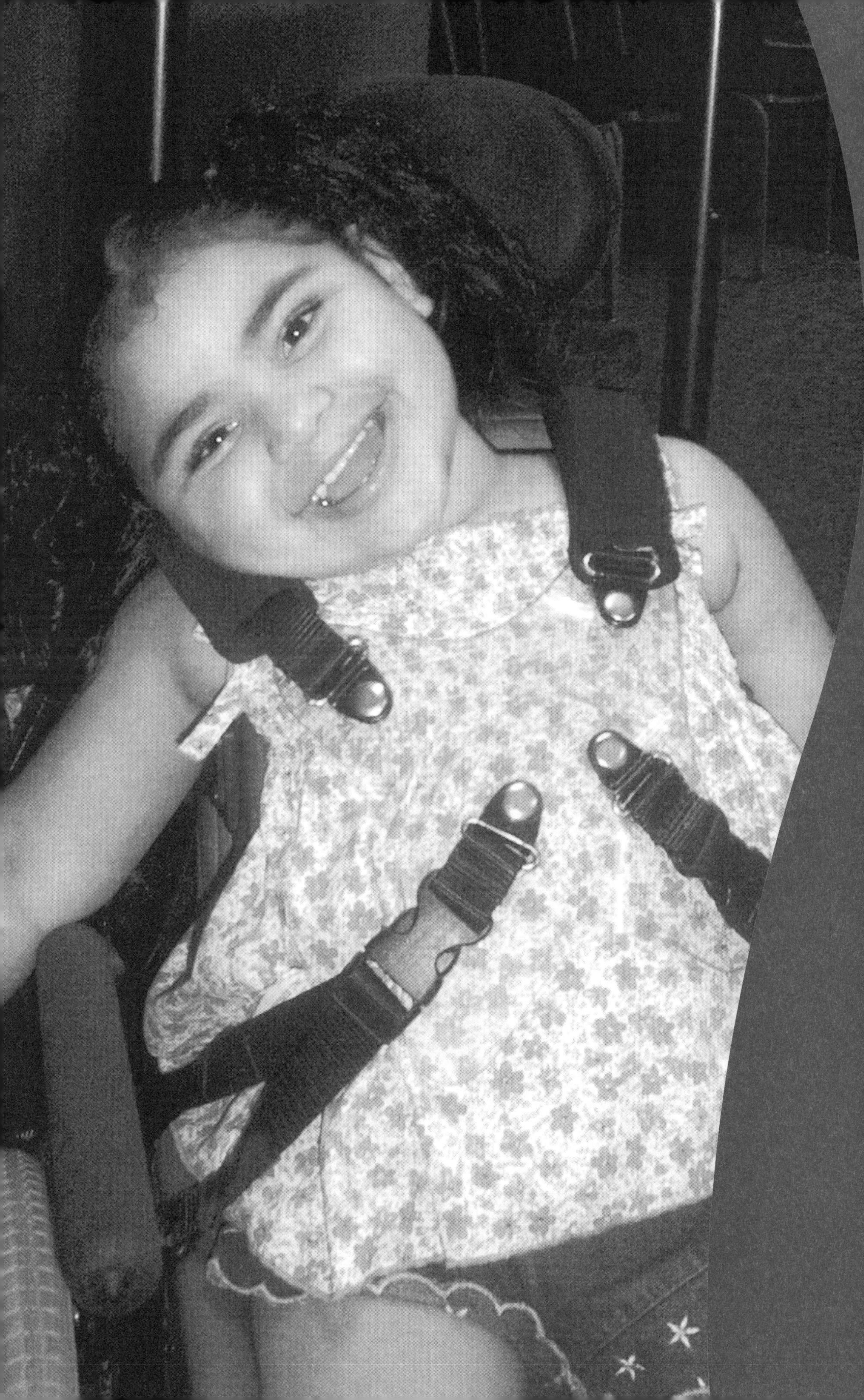

Glossary

Glossary

FOLLOWING IS A LIST of common terms that you may come across in your search for information. Some of these terms are used to describe conditions that explain Rett syndrome. Other terms are used to rule out Rett syndrome.

Abduction: movement of a limb or any other part away from the midline of the body.

Absence seizure: a generalized seizure in which consciousness is altered, formerly called "petit mal."

"Only a few things are really important."

– MARIE DRESSLER

Acetylcholine: a neurotransmitter chemical.

ADA (Americans with Disabilities Act): federal legislation enacted in 1990, intended to protect all people with disabilities from discrimination.

Adaptive behavior: skills needed by a child to function effectively and appropriately for her age in the school, family, and community settings.

Adduction: movement of a limb or any other part toward the midline of the body.

Aerophagia: swallowing of air.

Alternative communication: a method which replaces traditional forms or methods already used by someone to communicate.

Ambulatory: able to walk.

Amino acids: the building blocks or chief structure of proteins; several are essential in human nutrition.

Anecdotal: Report of clinical experiences based in individual cases, rather than an organized investigation with appropriate controls.

Angelman Syndrome (Happy Puppet Syndrome): AS is a neurodevelopmental disorder caused by loss of paternally derived gene(s) on chromosome 15. It has many features that are similar to RS including ataxia, lack of speech, seizures and microcephaly. The majority of cases can be detected by an analysis of chromosome 15.

Ankle-foot orthosis (AFO): an orthopedic apparatus, most commonly a splint or brace, used to support, align, or correct deformities or to improve the function of the ankle/foot.

Annual review: a review of a child's special education program to be held at least once a year to assess progress and determine whether any program changes are necessary in the following year.

Anorexia: a severe loss of appetite.

Anticonvulsant: any medication used to control seizures.

Apnea: episodic arrest of breathing, seen during waking and not usually during sleep in RS.

Glossary

Appropriate education: a program that is capable of meeting the educational needs of a child who has an educational disability.

Apraxia: difficulty with the usually automatic planning done by the brain to execute voluntary movements.

Asphyxia: interference with circulation and oxygenation of the blood that leads to loss of consciousness.

Aspirated: inhaled.

Aspiration: entry of liquids (saliva or drink) or solids into the airway.

Aspiration pneumonia: a lung infection caused by inhaling a foreign body, such as food, into the lungs.

Assay: a method or way of measuring chemical or biological compounds.

Ataxia: imbalance or lack of coordination of voluntary and involuntary muscles; shakiness on reaching or moving the trunk that is associated with malfunction in the cerebellum; unbalanced gait and jerky, uncoordinated movements.

Atom: a particle composed of a nucleus (protons and neutrons) and electrons. Atoms differ from one another by having different numbers of protons, neutrons and electrons. Groups of atoms bonded together are called molecules.

Atonic seizures: generalized seizures in which body tone is suddenly lost and the child falls to the ground or her head slumps forward.

Atrophy: wasting, from disuse; implies normal tissue to begin with.

Atypical: not typical; different.

Auditory evoked potential: a test to evaluate the processing of sound by the brain stem.

Augmentative communication: all forms of communication that enhance, replace or supplement speech and writing.

Aura: the start of a seizure; a peculiar feeling, sense of fear or unusual sensation in one part of the body.

Autism: a developmental disability that results in impairments in social interaction, verbal, and nonverbal communication and unusual behaviors and responses to the environment.

Automatisms: purposeless automatic movements that accompany a complex partial seizure, such as smacking the lips, chewing, or picking at the clothes.

Autonomic nervous system: the part of the nervous system that regulates certain automatic functions of the body, for example, heart rate, temperature, and bowel movements.

Autonomic responses: body functions that happen involuntarily, such as breathing, sweating, blood pressure, heart rate, and flushing of the face.

Autosome: any of the first twenty-two pairs of chromosomes; all chromosomes are autosomes, except for the sex chromosomes, X and Y.

Autosomal dominant trait: a genetic trait carried on the autosomes. The disorder appears when one of a pair of chromosomes contains the abnormal gene; statistically, it is passed on from the affected parent to half of the children.

Glossary

Autosomal recessive trait: a genetic trait carried on the autosome. Both asymptomatic parents must carry the trait to produce an affected child. This child has two abnormal genes. The risk of recurrence is 25 percent. RS is not felt to be autosomal recessive.

Axon: a nerve fiber.

Babinski reflex: extension of the big toe upon stimulation of the sole of the foot. This abnormal response is found in individuals with pyramidal tract damage.

Barrett's esophagus: damage to the normal skinlike lining of the esophagus, which is replaced with a lining that resembles that of the stomach. It is caused by persistent reflux of acid from the stomach. The new lining can resist the gastric reflux, but inflammation at the upper end of the new lining may narrow the interior passageway of the esophagus.

Basal ganglia: several large masses of gray matter embedded deep within the white matter of the cerebrum.

Base: a flat ring structure, containing nitrogen, carbon, oxygen and hydrogen, that forms part of one of the nucleotide links of a nucleic acid chain. The four different bases are adenine (A), thymine (T), guanine (G), and cytosine (C).

Base pair: two bases, one in each strand of a double-stranded nucleic acid molecule that are attracted to each other by weak chemical interaction. Only certain base pairs form: A-T (or T-A), G-C (or C-G), A-U (or U-A).

Behavior modification: the systematic application of the principles of learning theory to change behavior by modifying events that precede or follow the behavior.

Beta endorphins: the body's own morphine-like substance.

Binding: attaching.

Biogenic amines: neurotransmitters dopamine, norepinephrine (also known as noradrenaline), serotonin, and a few others.

Biological marker: a scientific test which proves the presence of a condition.

Body jacket: a molded, padded thin plastic brace designed to apply gentle pressure in the proper areas to straighten the spine.

Bolus: clump; term used in tube feeding to indicate feeding given at one time.

Brain stem: the primitive portion of the brain that lies between the cerebrum and the spinal cord.

Brain stem auditory evoked response (BAER): a test to evaluate the processing of sound by the brain stem.

Breathholding: quick inspiration of a single full breath, followed by delayed expiration during which breathing stops.

Bruxism: tooth grinding, common in RS.

Carnitine: an amino acid which helps to transport long-chain fatty acids.

Cell: the smallest unit of living matter capable of self-perpetuation; an organized set of chemical reactions capable of reproduction. A cell is bounded by a membrane that separates the inside of the cell from the outer environment. Cells contain DNA (where information is stored), ribosomes (where proteins are made), and mechanisms for converting energy from one form to another.

Cell membrane: the membrane that contains the cell components and the substance in which they float.

Central apnea: cessation of breathing movement at the end of expiration.

Central nervous system (CNS): the portion of the nervous system that consists of the brain and spinal cord. It is primarily involved in voluntary movement and thought processes.

Cerebral cortex: the outer part of the cerebrum.

Cerebral palsy: a disorder of movement and posture due to a non-progressive defect of the immature brain.

Cerebrospinal fluid (CSF): the normally clear fluid that surrounds the brain and spinal cord.

Cerebrum: the largest region of the brain, made up of four lobes and connected by the corpus callosum.

Child Find: the continuous efforts of a school district to identify all children from birth to age twenty-one in its area who may have educational disabilities and need special education.

Chiropractic: a system of treating diseases by manipulation, mainly of the vertebrae of the backbone. It is based on the theory that nearly all disorders can be traced to the incorrect alignment of bones, with consequent malfunctioning of nerves and muscles throughout the body.

Chromatin: chromosomes in their less compact state. During this stage, they appear under a microscope as long tangled threads.

Chromosome: a subcellular structure containing a long, discrete piece of DNA plus the proteins that organize and compact the DNA.

Chromosome analysis: a study of the forty-six potential chromosome structures that consist of the genetic code for our physical and biochemical traits.

Chronological age: the child's actual age in years and months.

Classic: typical.

Clone: 1) noun, a group of identical cells, all derived from a single ancestor. 2) verb, to perform or undergo the process of creating a group of identical cells or identical DNA molecules derived from a single ancestor.

Code (genetic): the system in which the arrangement of nucleotides in DNA represents the arrangement of amino acids in protein.

Clinical diagnosis: a conclusion based on findings from the patient's history and physical exam, usually not as definitive as a laboratory-made diagnosis would be.

Clonus: alternate muscle contraction and relaxation in rapid succession.

Cognitive disability: an educational term usually synonymous with the medical term, mental retardation.

Glossary

Cognitive skills: thinking abilities, most often represented by IQ scores; difficult to assess in Rett syndrome.

Complex partial seizure: a seizure which involves only part of the brain and which alters consciousness or awareness.

Computerized axial tomography (CAT scan): an X-ray which is used to examine soft tissues in the body. The technique involves the recording of "slices" of the body with an X-ray scanner and then integrating them by computer to give a cross-sectional image. Within the skull, it can be used to reveal the normal anatomy of the brain, and to distinguish pathological conditions such as tumors, abscesses, and hematomas.

Congenital: present at or before birth.

Constipation: a condition in which bowel evacuations occur infrequently, or in which the feces are hard and small, or in which passage of feces causes difficulty or pain.

Contracture: irreversible shortening of muscle fibers that causes decreased joint mobility.

Controls: study subjects; individuals without disease who are used to compare normal values.

Convulsion: older term for a seizure; it most commonly involves a series of involuntary contractions of voluntary muscles.

Corpus callosum: the bridge of white matter connecting the two hemispheres of the brain.

Cortex: the gray matter that lies at the outer portion of the cerebrum.

Cure: the complete eradication of symptoms so that no symptoms are discernible, even by a doctor and a battery of tests, and no impact will be felt in future generations.

Cyanosis: a bluish discoloration of the skin and mucous membranes resulting from an inadequate amount of oxygen in the blood.

Cytoplasm: the jellylike substance that surrounds the nucleus of a cell.

Cytological: relating to the study of cell structure, often using microscopy. A commercial cytology laboratory examines the structure of chromosomes for genetic disorders.

Deceleration: reduced velocity. In RS, deceleration often refers to slowing of the growth rate of the head (circumference).

Degenerative CNS disorder: a condition leading to progressive disability and death, usually associated with significant, identifiable changes in the brain. Rett syndrome is no longer thought to be a degenerative CNS disorder.

Deletion: loss of genetic material from a chromosome.

Dementia: marked decline in intellectual ability; loss of cognitive skills. In RS, loss of cognitive skills will have a different mechanism than aging-related dementias like Alzheimer's.

Dendrite: one of the shorter branching processes of the cell body of a neuron, which makes contact with other neurons at synapses and carries nerve impulses from them into the cell body.

Glossary

Deoxyribonucleic acid (DNA): a fundamental component of living tissue; it contains the genetic code.

Developmental arrest: after normal development, a complete cessation of developmental progress.

Developmental delay: a delay in the development of skills and abilities which usually would have developed by a certain age.

Diagnostic test: a test that provides an in-depth assessment of a skill area, including strengths and weaknesses and error patterns.

Differential: a list of conditions that could possibly cause the patient's presenting problem. Differential diagnoses for RS include cerebral palsy and autism.

Diffuse: widely spread, as in diffuse cerebral impairment, which means that many areas on both sides of the brain are affected, not a localized problem.

Distal: situated away from the organ or point of attachment or from the median line of the body.

DNA: Deoxyribonucleic acid. DNA is a spiraling, ladder-like(helical) molecule that is the carrier for the genetic code. It is usually found as two complementary chains and is often hundreds to thousands of times longer than the cell in which it resides (it is tightly wrapped to fit inside). The links or subunits of DNA are the four nucleotide (deoxyadenylate, deoxycytidylate, deoxythymidylate, deoxyguanylate). The precise arrangement of these four subunits is used to store all information necessary for life processes. DNA is also found in mitochondria, the rod-like structures outside the nuclei of cells that function as a primary source of cellular energy.

Dominant: a "strong" gene whose effect will appear whether its partner gene is of the same type or different.

Dorsiflexion: backward flexion of the foot or hand or the toes and fingers.

Due process: a system of procedures designed to ensure that individuals are treated fairly and have an opportunity to contest decisions made about them. The due process requirements of Public Law 94-142 and Section 504 are intended to safeguard the right of children who have disabilities to a free, appropriate, public education.

Duodenum: upper part of the small intestine.

Dysmotility: impaired movement, usually used in reference to parts of the body that work automatically, e.g., gastric dysmotility refers to impaired emptying of the stomach.

Dyspraxia: partial impairment of the ability to perform coordinated motor movements.

Dystonia: alteration in muscle tone, usually referring to muscle cramps/spasms of muscles close to the midline of the body (neck, shoulders, hips).

Early intervention: the provision of educational services at an early age for children with learning difficulties to avoid more serious problems later in life.

Electrocardiogram (EKG or ECG): the tracing made by an instrument for recording the changes of electrical potential occurring during the heartbeat.

Glossary

Electroencephalogram (EEG): a test to measure and record brain waves. In Rett syndrome, the EEG is almost always abnormal, although clinical seizures are not always present.

Electromyelogram (EMG): a test in which wire probes which detect muscle contraction are inserted into a muscle. The muscle is then stimulated electrically to initiate a contraction and the response is recorded. The test allows monitoring of muscle contractions, timing, and efficiency of the response to a known stimulus.

Electronic communication device: a communication system which is computer chip based and contains messages which are words or phrases designed for the user of the device. Pictures, small objects, or words are placed on the device as cues to where messages are located.

Empirical: Pertaining to, or founded upon, experiment or experience.

Encephalopathy: an indication that something is wrong in the brain.

Encode: to contain a nucleotide sequence specifying that one or more specific amino acids be incorporated into a protein.

Endometrial ablation: a laser procedure to remove the lining of the uterus, which results in total or partial cessation of menstrual bleeding.

Endorphins: the body's natural opiates, probably involved in the perception of pain and pleasure.

Endoscopy: the use of an instrument to visualize the interior of a hollow organ, such as the esophagus; used to detect gastroesophageal reflux (GER).

Enzyme: a protein molecule specialized to accelerate a biological chemical reaction without itself being consumed. Generally, enzyme names end in -ase.

Epiglottis: a lid-like structure that hangs over the entrance to the windpipe and prevents aspiration into the lungs during swallowing.

Epilepsy: recurrent seizures, excluding ones caused solely by fever.

Epileptiform patterns: patterns which resemble those of a seizure.

Equilibrium: balance.

Equinus: involuntary extension of the foot downward, due to a tight or overactive heel-cord.

Esophagitis: inflammation of the esophagus.

Esophagus: tube extending from the pharynx to the stomach.

Etiology: cause.

Evaluation: the process by which a team of professionals gathers information about a child's skills, deficits, aptitudes, interests, and personality variables from a variety of sources including testing, observation, and other procedures to guide decisions about the child's educational program. Often used interchangeably with "assessment."

Exon: a region of RNA that encodes a portion of a protein.

Expressive language: communication that is given out to others.

Glossary

Fine motor coordination: the ability to use the small muscles to accomplish tasks requiring precision.

Flexion: the bending of a joint so that the bones forming it are brought toward each other.

Flexor: a muscle whose primary function is flexion at a joint.

Formal test: a standardized evaluative measure which has explicit methods for administration and scoring and for which norms are available.

Forme fruste: incompletely expressed (a frustrated form), as in a RS variant who has most but not all of the classical characteristics.

Fortunate activation: females usually randomly inactivate one of the two copies of the X- chromosome in each cell. Fortunate activation refers to a situation where a female who carries an abnormal gene on one X-chromosome silences the abnormal copy, leaving the normal copy to function. It protects her from symptoms of the X-linked disease, but does not prevent her from passing it on.

Frontal lobe: front part of the cerebrum; important for voluntary muscle movement and memory.

Fundoplication (fundal plication): an operation in which the opening from the esophagus to the stomach is closed.

Gagging: voluntary or involuntary rhythmic movements of the back of the mouth near the epiglottis; protects airway from a bolus; usually triggered by food near the back of the tongue that does not trigger the swallowing reflex.

Gait: manner or style of walking.

Gastroesophageal reflux disease (GER): the backward flow of stomach contents from the stomach back into the esophagus.

Gastroenterologist: a doctor who specializes in disorders of digestion.

Gastrostomy (G-tube): a surgical creation of an artificial opening into the stomach through the wall of the abdomen.

Gel electrophoresis: a method for separating molecules based on their size and electric charge. Molecules are driven through a gel by placing them in an electric field. The speed at which they move depends on their size and charge.

Gene: a small section of DNA that contains information for construction of one protein molecule.

Gene cloning: a way to use microorganisms to produce millions of identical copies of a specific region of DNA.

Gene expression: the process of making the product of a gene; information is transferred, via messenger RNA, from a gene to ribosomes, where a specific protein is produced.

Generalized seizure: a seizure involving the whole brain.

Gene therapy: a process of altering genes in living persons through the administration of specific regions of DNA.

Glossary

Genetic engineering: the manipulation of the information content of an organism to alter the characteristics of that organism. Genetic engineering may use simple methods such as selective breeding or complicated ones such as gene cloning.

Genetic map: a representation of DNA in which the relative position of regions is determined by the frequency of genetic recombination between observable traits.

Genome: the genetic information of an organism or virus; for organisms with two pairs of each chromosome, the genome refers to the information in one set.

Genotype: genetic profile or makeup of an individual.

Germ cells (gametes): reproductive cells. Male gametes are called sperm. Female gametes are called eggs.

GI: gastrointestinal.

Global: affecting all areas, e.g., *global developmental delays*.

Grand mal: old term for tonic-clonic; a form of seizure in which there is a sudden loss of consciousness immediately followed by a generalized convulsion.

Gray matter: the parts of the brain that contain the cell bodies of nerve cells (neurons).

Gross: on a large scale; not to be confused with the common term for "yucky." "Grossly normal," means "after less than in-depth inspection, this appears to be normal." "Gross anatomy" refers to the study of organs as they appear to the naked eye, without the benefit of a microscope.

Gross motor coordination: the ability to use the large muscles in a coordinated, purposeful manner to engage in such activities as walking and running.

Grossly normal: usually implies a less than detailed evaluation of the body part or function being described.

Gyri: convolutions of the surface of the brain.

Habilitation: teaching of new skills.

Handicapped child: the term used in federal and state law to designate a child who has a specific cognitive, physical, or emotional disability to the extent that specially designed instruction is necessary for her to learn effectively.

Head circumference: the size of the head, usually plotted on a growth curve to compare with other children of the same age; the increase in the head circumference in infancy and early childhood is a reflection of normal brain growth.

Heredity: the genetic transfer of characteristics from parents to offspring.

Hip dislocation: occurs at the ball and socket joint of the hip, when the ball is completely pulled out of the socket.

Hippotherapy: therapeutic horseback riding.

Hip subluxation: occurs at the ball and socket joint of the hip, when the ball is partially pulled out of the socket.

Glossary

Histones: members of a small class of eukayotic chromosomal proteins that wrap DNA into ball-like structures called nucleosomes.

Homebound instruction: temporary instruction at home, provided if a child is unable to attend school for medical reasons or if the school is in the process of arranging a special education placement.

Human genome: the information content of one set of human chromosomes.

Hydrotherapy: water therapy, such as provided in a whirlpool bath or warm pool.

Hypertonia: high muscle tone, muscle tightness, or spasticity.

Hyperventilation: exaggerated inspirations followed immediately by equally exaggerated expirations (fast, deep breaths), contributing to a central apnea at the end.

Hypoplasia: underdeveloped tissue. Both atrophy and hypoplasia can lead to smaller than normal amounts of tissue, but atrophy implies that normal tissue was once present and hypoplasia implies that normal tissue never developed. Both processes appear to occur in the brains of girls with RS.

Hypotonia: low muscle tone, not to be confused with muscle strength, implies a certain amount of looseness or floppiness of joints.

Hypothesis: A supposition that appears to explain a group of phenomena and is advanced as a basis for further investigation, a proposition that is subject to proof or to an experimental or statistical test.

Hypoxia: reduction of oxygen content in body tissues.

Hypsarrhythmia: an abnormality of the EEG, a wildly chaotic pattern with multiple spikes and slow waves.

Ictal (ictus): an event. A seizure of any type is referred to as an ictus.

IDEA (Individuals with Disabilities Education Act): passed in 1997, this law was written to strengthen academic expectations and accountability for the nation's 5.4 million children with disabilities, and bridge the gap that has too often existed between what those children learn and the regular curriculum.

Idiopathic: of unknown cause.

Ileum: lower portion of the small intestine.

Incidence: the number of cases of something in a given population over a specific time (e.g., the number of cases of lung cancer in the United States in one year).

Inclusion: the placement of a child who has an educational disability in an instructional setting in which most students do not have disabilities, in a manner that is educationally and socially beneficial to the child.

Incontinence: absence of bowel or bladder control.

Independent evaluation: evaluation of a child by one or more professionals who have no formal relationship with the school district. Parents can request this evaluation if they disagree with the school's evaluation.

Glossary

Independent living skills: skills needed to care for oneself and to function effectively in a community setting (including for example, personal hygiene, money management, cooking, and use of public transportation).

Individualized education plan (IEP): a written plan that a team composed of school staff, parents, and the child, if appropriate, develops for every special education student. Must include, at a minimum, the child's current educational strengths and weaknesses, goals and objectives, educational services, start-up dates for those services, and procedures for program evaluation.

Individualized habilitation plan (IHP): a written plan for someone over school age; used in adult programs.

Intelligence quotient (IQ): score on an intelligence test for which 100 is the mean. Indicates a child's test performance relative to other children of the same age.

Intelligence test: a test used to measure overall capacity for learning. In RS, an adequate intelligence test has not been devised that can accurately measure understanding.

Intussusception: the slipping of a length of intestine into an adjacent portion, usually producing obstruction.

Intubation: the insertion of a tube through the nose or mouth into the trachea to provide artificial ventilation.

In utero: before birth.

Invasive test: a procedure or examination that requires that the body be entered in some way, either through a needle or with a tube.

Joy: what you experience when your daughter lights up the room with a smile.

Karyotyping: photograph of the chromosomal makeup of a cell. In humans, there are twenty-three pairs of chromosomes in the sex chromosomes, in this case, female. A few girls with RS have had abnormal results. Karyotyping is a chromosome analysis, which looks for visibly missing or extra pieces of whole chromosomes; not the same as looking for a specific gene.

Ketogenic diet: a diet which provides the minimal amount of protein necessary for growth, no carbohydrates, and most of the calories from fats. The diet is used in seizure control.

Ketosis: the buildup of acid in the body due to starvation; important in the ketogenic diet.

Kindred cases: recurrences of RS in a family, for example, sisters, cousins, etc.

Kinesthesia: the unconscious awareness of body parts in relation to movement.

Kyphosis: a spinal curvature as seen from the side, often termed "hunchback".

Least restrictive environment (LRE): a standard established by Public Law 94-142 for special education placement. A child who has an educational disability must be allowed to participate in as much of the regular education program as is appropriate in view of her educational needs. The law holds that children with special needs must not be separated from students who do not have disabilities any more than is educationally necessary.

Lumbar puncture (spinal tap): the tapping of the subarachnoid space to obtain cerebrospinal fluid from the lower back region for examination.

Glossary

Lysosomal enzymes: enzymes normally involved in the process of digestion.

Magnetic resonance imaging (MRI): imaging procedure that uses the magnetic resonance of atoms to provide clear images on interior parts of the body.

Mediation: a process for settling disputes between parents and school districts through the intervention of a neutral third party who tries to negotiate an agreement acceptable to all.

Medulla: the brain stem.

Melatonin: hormone which determines skin pigmentation. In humans, it is believed to play a role in the establishment of circadian rhythms.

Meiosis: the form of cell division that occurs during formation of reproductive cells to reduce the number of chromosomes from two to one of each type.

Meninges: the three connective tissue membranes that line the skull and vertebral canal and enclose the brain and spinal cord.

Mental age: a form for expressing a child's performance on an intelligence test. A child who receives an MA of 8-4 has achieved a score comparable to an "average" child of eight years, four months.

Mental retardation: a significant delay in the development of cognitive (problem-solving) skills that is associated with a significant delay in adaptive (use of intelligence in daily living) skills that occurs during childhood. The term "significant" refers to "statistically significant" when compared to other children of the same age. Usually measured by intellectual functioning at least two standard deviations below the mean, or average.

Messenger RNA: RNA used to transmit information from a gene on DNA to a ribosome, where the information is used to make protein.

Metabolites: the products of metabolism; in RS articles, often seen in the phrase "biogenic amine metabolites," which refers to the normal breakdown products of the neurotransmitters dopamine, norepinephrine and serotonin. These can be measured in the cerebrospinal fluid directly.

Metabolic disorder: also referred to as an "inborn error of metabolism," these conditions are caused by impairment in a person's ability to process the breakdown products of protein, fat or carbohydrates. Your daughter may have had a metabolic workup when she first regressed or developed seizures.

Microcephaly: head circumference below normal for age (two standard deviations below the average); usually reflects lack of brain growth.

Mitochondria: a specialized intracellular structure that converts the chemical energy stored in food into a more useful form as molecules called ATP.

Mitosis: the type of cell division that results in exact duplicates of the original cells.

Molecule: a group of atoms tightly joined together.

Mucopolysaccharides: product of metabolism that may accumulate in cells and cause a progressive neurological disorder known as mucopolysacharidosis; usually ruled out before the diagnosis of Rett syndrome is given.

Glossary

Music therapy: the use of music by someone (music therapist) who is trained to use musical activities to teach non-music skills, such as communication, socialization, choice-making, and motor skills.

Mutation: a change in a gene, such as loss, gain, or substitution of genetic material that alters its function or expression by an incorrect amino acid sequence. This change is passed along with subsequent divisions of the affected cell. Gene mutations may occur randomly for unknown reasons or may be inherited.

Myelination: the production of a coating called myelin around an axon, which quickens neurotransmission.

Myoclonic: repetitive contraction of muscles; occurs in infantile spasms.

Myopathy: condition affecting the muscles.

Nasogastric tube (NG tube): a temporary plastic feeding tube placed through the nose down the esophagus and into the stomach for introduction of high caloric foods.

Negative test result: the test was normal (usually perceived by the patient to be a "positive" event).

Neurologist: a physician skilled in the diagnosis and treatment of disease of the nervous system.

Neurons: the nerve cells of the brain.

Neuropathy: any disease of the peripheral nerves, causing weakness and numbness.

Neurotransmitters: the chemicals used by nerves to "talk" to each other; released at the synapse that permits transmission from one nerve to another.

Neurotrophic: involved in the nutrition or maintenance of neural (brain) tissue. A classic example is nerve growth factor.

Nociception: the perception of pain, impaired in girls with RS.

Nonspecific findings: those physical or laboratory results that can be seen in a variety of conditions, for example, seizures are a nonspecific finding because they occur in many neurologic diseases, not just Rett syndrome.

Nucleotide: one of the building blocks of nucleic acids. A nucleotide is composed of three parts: a base, a sugar, and a phosphate.

Nucleotide pairs: two nucleotides, one in each strand of a double-stranded nucleic acid molecule, that are attracted to each other by weak chemical reactions between the bases.

Nucleus: the cell control center. It houses the chromosomes containing the genes.

Nystagmus: rapid involuntary movements of the eyes.

Obstipation: severe and obstinate constipation; leads to fecal impaction.

Occipital lobe: one of the major divisions of each cerebral hemisphere.

Occupational therapy: treatment by an occupational therapist to improve an individual's ability to integrate different mental and motor processes in a purposeful and efficient manner. The occupational therapist concentrates on promoting, maintaining or restoring use of the body for daily living skills.

Glossary

Opthamalogical: anything related to the eye.

Organic acids: error in metabolism of organic acids that can cause the child to develop symptoms of acidosis, coma, developmental and psychomotor retardation. Some forms of this disorder have been successfully treated by vitamin therapy both before and after birth.

Organomegaly: enlarged internal organs, not seen in RS.

Oropharyngeal dysfunction: improper function of the mouth and pharynx.

Orotic acids: excessive excretion of orotic acids is indicative of a genetic metabolic disorder, characterized by physical and mental retardation; ruled out in Rett syndrome.

Orthopedic: relating to bones or joints.

Orthosis: an orthopedic appliance used to support, align, prevent, or correct deformities or to improve the functioning of movable parts of the body.

Osteotomy: surgical realignment of the bone; used for hip subluxation.

Osteoarthritis: inflammation of joints characterized by degenerative changes and sometimes increasing bulk in the bone and cartilage.

Osteopenia: deficient mineralization of bone.

Osteoporosis: loss of bone minerals.

Palmar grasp: immature hand movement in which the palm rather than the fingertips makes contact with an object.

Paresis: weakness, e.g., *quadriparesis* means weakness in four extremities. Technically, quadriplegia means paralysis of all four extremities, but often the terms are used interchangeably.

Parietal lobe: one of the major divisions of each cerebral hemisphere, lying behind the frontal lobe, above the temporal lobe, and in front of the occipital lobe. It contains the sensory cortex and association areas of the brain.

Pathologic fractures: when minor trauma results in broken bones.

Pedigree: chart showing how members of various generations are related. Also known as a family tree.

Peripheral nervous system: the parts of the nervous system that are outside the brain and spinal cord.

Petit mal: old term for absence seizures.

Pharynx: a muscular tube lined with mucous membrane which extends from the beginning of the esophagus up to the base of the skull.

Phenotype: the clinical appearance of a patient, her historical and/or physical findings; in contrast to a patient's genotype, which is the genetic profile of a patient. Patients with the same phenotype can have different genotypes. Or, just because patients share the same clinical findings doesn't mean that they were caused by the same thing.

Phenylketonuria (PKU): Congenital absence of phenylalanine hydroxylase (an enzyme that converts phenylalanine into tyrosine). Phenylalanine accumulates in the blood and

Glossary

seriously impairs early neuronal development. The defect can be controlled by diet and is not serious if treated in this way.

PhProbe: a test for gastroesophageal reflux (GER), in which a probe is placed near the esophageal sphincter, and acid reflux is measured.

Physical therapy: Treatment by a physical therapist to improve an individual's motor skills and increase the strength and endurance of body parts.

Pincer grasp: refined, mature hand movement in which the thumb and first finger are used to pick up a small object.

Plantar flexion: bending of the toes or fingers downward toward the sole or palm.

Placement: the educational setting in which a student receives instruction.

Pneumonia: An acute infection of lung parenchyma including alveolar spaces and interstitial tissue.

Polymorphism: a normal variation in a gene.

Prenatal: before birth.

Probe: a DNA or RNA molecule, usually radioactive, that is used to locate a complementary RNA or DNA by hybridizing to it.

Protein: a class of long, chainlike molecules often containing hundreds of links called amino acids. Twenty different amino acids are used to make proteins. The thousands of different proteins serve many functions in the cell. As enzymes, they control the rate of chemical reactions, and as structural elements they provide the cell with its shape. Proteins are also involved in cell movement and in the formation of cell walls, membranes and protective shells. Some proteins also help package DNA molecules into chromosomes.

Positioning: physical management of posture and body alignment for daily living skills such as eating and standing up.

Positive findings: an abnormal test or finding (although usually not a positive event from the patient's point of view, a consistently positive test result in girls with RS would lead to a diagnostic test for this disorder).

Positron emission tomography (PET scan): imaging study which uses radioactive labeled chemical compounds to study the metabolism of an organ.

Prevalence: the number of cases of something in a population at any given time (the number of girls with RS in a country at any given time).

Procedural safeguards: legal regulations intended to safeguard the right of a child who has an educational disability to a free, appropriate, public education, and to ensure that both child and parents receive the due process of law.

Prognosis: what is likely to happen.

Progressive: the problem gets worse with time. In RS, this means that symptoms continue to develop over time; it is not clear whether or not the underlying disease process is actively getting worse with time or whether the new symptoms represent the result of previous involvement of the brain.

Glossary

Prolonged Q-T syndrome: when the resting period between heart beats is elongated. *See* Q-T interval.

Pronation: turned inward.

Prone stander: a piece of equipment that holds a person upright in a standing position. The support is under the front of the body and the individual is tipped forward slightly.

Proprioceptive input: unconscious information from the muscles and joints about position, weight or pressure, stretch, movement, and changes of position in space.

Pseudobulbar palsy: weakness of muscles coordinated by nerves originating in the brainstem; generally refers to coordination of mouth/throat muscles.

Public Law 94-142: the primary federal legislative act involving the education of children who have educational disabilities. Called the Education for All Handicapped Act of 1975, this law aims to assure the availability of a "free appropriate public education" for every eligible child. It sets forth a range of school and parental responsibilities as well as procedural safeguards to ensure the due process of law.

Pseudo arthritis: failure of bone to fuse, sometimes requiring bone graft.

Pulmonary: pertaining to the lungs.

Pyramidal tract: a collection of nerve tracts in the brain stem.

Range of motion: the amount of movement available in a joint, measured in degrees. May be reduced in RS, as seen in spasticity (as in tight heel cords) or by the rigidity or fixing (as in the shoulders and elbows). The motion may be temporarily reduced. If motion is limited for a long time, the limitation becomes structural because muscles and tendons become shortened.

Q-T interval: a measurement from an EKG (electrocardiogram) that tells how long electricity takes to get through a portion of the heartbeat; a *prolonged Q-T interval* means that the impulse takes longer than expected and may be a factor in sudden, unexpected death. A *Qtc* interval means that the time has been corrected for how fast the heart is beating. (EKG = ECG)

Receptive language: communication that is received.

Recessive: a "weaker" gene whose effect will only appear when its partner gene is the same type.

Recombination: the breaking and rejoining of DNA strands to produce new combinations of DNA molecules. Recombination is a natural process that generates genetic diversity. Specific proteins are involved in recombination.

Related services: support services needed by a child to benefit from special education.

Residential placement: a placement, usually arranged and paid for by a state agency or the parents, where a child with special needs resides and typically receives academic instruction.

Restruction mapping: a procedure that uses restriction endonucleases to produce specific cuts in DNA. The positions of the cuts can be measured and oriented relative to each other to form a crude map.

Glossary

Retinopathy: disease of the retina (the back of the eye that registers visual signals); NOT seen in RS.

Righting response: ability to return to upright after tilting.

Rigidity: abnormal stiffness of muscle.

RNA (ribonucleic acid): long, thin chainlike molecules in which the links or subunits are the four nucleotides adenylate, cytidylate, uridylate, and guanylate (A,C,U,G). The precise arrangement of these four subunits is used to transfer and sometimes store genetic material.

Rotation: turning of a body part about its long axis as if on a pivot; i.e. of the head to look over the shoulder.

Rumination: after swallowing, the regurgitation of food followed by chewing another time.

Salivation: the secretion of saliva by the salivary glands of the mouth, increased in response to the chewing action of the jaws or to the thought, taste, sight, or smell of food.

Scoliosis: curvature of the spine that includes a twisting component; in RS, usually due to neurologic factors.

Section 504: a federal civil rights law passed in 1973 to eliminate discrimination against people with disabilities in federally funded programs. Requires that children with disabilities receive educational services and opportunities equal to those provided other children.

Segmental rolling: rolling over where there is rotation (twisting) between the shoulders and hips, often difficult for the child with RS.

Seizure: an episodic electrical discharge of nerve cells in the brain resulting in alteration of function or behavior.

Self-help skills: skills related to the care of oneself such as eating, dressing, and grooming.

Sensory modalities: specific channels through which a person receives information about the environment, including sight, sound, touch, taste, and smell.

Serial casting: a series of casts on the feet to correct shortened heel cords.

Sequence: the order of; in reference to DNA or RNA, the order of nucleotide.

Sex chromosomes: those chromosomes that determine gender; the X and Y chromosomes.

Short-term instructional objective: precise statement, described in terms of overt behavior, of what a child is expected to accomplish over a short period in a specific educational area. An intermediate step between the student's current skill level and the annual goal.

Siblings: the other kids who live at your house. Before you had a daughter with RS, they were called brothers and sisters.

Sidelier (sidelyer): a piece of equipment that supports and stabilizes the child on her side. It may be used to provide change of position for the very inactive child or may be used as part of a therapy program to correct scoliosis.

Simple partial seizures: local seizures involving a single area of the brain.

Sleep myoclonus: sudden massive jerks of the body when going to sleep. These are normal.

Glossary

Somatic: pertaining to the body. When referring to a type of cell, somatic means body cell rather than a germ (sperm or egg producing) cell. Somatic cells contain two pairs of each chromosome, while germ cells contain only one.

Sporadic: occurrence by chance with little chance of recurrence.

Spatial disorientation: when a person's perception of where she is in space is distorted and not accurate. This is observed in RS when the girl's perception of midline is disturbed, causing her to lean.

Spastic: increased muscle tone so that muscles are still and movements are difficult.

Special education: specialized instruction for children who have educational disabilities based on a comprehensive evaluation. The instruction may occur in a variety of settings, but must be precisely matched to their educational needs and adapted to their learning styles.

Splint: a material or device use to protect or immobilize a body part.

Sporadic: occurring by chance, with little risk of recurrence.

SSI (Supplemental Security Income): federal and state funded program that provides money to offset expenses for children with disabilities who come from low-income families under the age of 18, and all individuals with disabilities after the age of eighteen.

Static: unchanging; a static encephalopathy refers to a brain disorder that does not get worse with time. It does not mean or imply that the child will remain static or unchanging. A child with a static encephalopathy, such as cerebral palsy, can continue to learn and develop.

Stereotypies: repetitive, patterned movements; in RS, usually referring to the hands.

Storage diseases: a number of metabolic diseases in which some material, usually a breakdown product of normal tissue, cannot be further metabolized and is stored within nerve cells of the brain, which produces malfunction.

Strabismus: inability of one eye to attain binocular vision with the other because of imbalance of the muscles of the eyeball.

Stem cell: a cell type that has not specialized to carry out particular functions and retains the ability to divide and differentiate to form a variety of cell types.

Subluxation: partial dislocation.

Substrate: the molecules on which an enzyme acts.

Sulci: crevices on the surface of the cerebrum.

Synapse: the minute spacing separating one neuron from another; neurochemicals breach this gap.

Syncope: fainting; dizziness, pallor, sweating, and loss of consciousness.

Systemic illness: illness affecting the body as a whole instead of one part.

Temporal lobe: one of the main divisions of the cerebral cortex in each hemisphere of the brain, lying at the side within the temple of the skull and separated from the frontal lobe by a cleft (sulcus).

Glossary

Tonic: continuous increased muscle tone.

Tonic-clonic seizures: once called grand mal seizures; seizures associated with stiffening followed by rhythmic jerking.

Tongue thrust: oral-motor feeding problems; voluntary tongue motions are not controlled; tongue extends in front of the lips when touched with spoon or food; interferes with moving food from the front of the mouth to the back for swallowing.

Transcription: the process of converting information in DNA into information in RNA. Transcription involves making an RNA molecule using the information encoded in the DNA. RNA polymerase is the enzyme that executes this conversion of information.

Transgene: DNA integrated into the germline from transgenetic organisms.

Transgenetic organisms: organisms that have integrated foreign DNA into their germline as a result of the experimental introduction of DNA.

Transitional movements: movements which allow us to change position. For example rolling, pulling to stand.

Translocation: the transfer of a fragment of one chromosome to another chromosome.

Treatment: interventions that cause a reduction in clinical manifestations that improve the medical/cognitive outcome of a disorder.

Trophic foot disturbances: poor growth of the feet, likely resulting in poor circulation.

Truncal ataxia: ataxia is poor coordination resulting most often from poor function of a part of the brain called the cerebellum. Truncal ataxia describes limitation or exaggeration of the symptoms to the muscles of the torso. If the torso is unsteady and poorly balanced, the limbs have to overwork to maintain posture.

Unconditional love: love with no conditions, as seen through your daughter's eyes.

Unfortunate activation: females usually randomly inactivate one of the two copies of the X- chromosome in each cell. Unfortunate activation refers to a situation when a female who carries an abnormal gene on one X-chromosome silences the normal copy of the gene. This allows females to manifest symptoms of X-linked recessive diseases like Duchenne muscular dystrophy or hemophilia.

Upper motor neuron: refers to the nerve cell that starts in the cerebral cortex, winds its way down through the brain and then into the spinal cord and that carries information about movement to the lower motor neuron. Damage to the upper motor neuron results in spasticity and deep tendon flexes (like the knee jerk) that are too brisk, while damage to the lower motor neurons results in weakness and decreased reflexes.

Vacant spells: may be confused with seizures, but are usually associated with irregular breathing patterns instead.

Vagal tone: impulse from the vagus nerve.

Vagus nerve: the tenth cranial nerve which supplies motor nerve fibers to the muscles of swallowing and parasympathetic fibers to the heart and organs of the chest cavity and abdomen.

Glossary

Valgus: turned outward, usually referring to the ankle in Rett syndrome.

Valsalva's manoeuver: long inspirations (breath holds) capable of raising blood pressure and heart range changes.

Varus: turned inward, usually referring to the ankle in Rett syndrome.

Vasomotor disturbance: relating to the nerves or the centers from which they arise that supply the muscle fibers of the walls of blood vessels, which regulate the amount of blood passing to a particular body part or organ. In Rett syndrome, used to describe cold, bluish hands and feet.

Vestibular: movements which give the body input about posture and movements in space which allow coordination and balance.

Vestibular input: unconscious information from the inner ear about equilibrium (state of balance), gravity, movement, and changes of position in space.

Video EEG: the use of video cameras to capture visually the onset and characteristics of seizures while simultaneously monitoring the EEG to see electrical changes.

Volvulus: a twisting of the intestine upon itself which causes obstruction.

Weight-for-height: a term that refers to the appropriateness of a child's weight compared to her height; one measure of nutritional status. "Low weight-for-height" would mean "underweight."

Weight shift: the movement of the body's center of gravity in any direction. Most movement sequences are initiated by this and it is a significant concern because this may be very difficult for the girl with RS to do.

White matter: the parts of the brain made up of axons, the long "extension cords" of the nerve cells that carry messages from one cell to another. These extensions are wrapped in an insulating substance called myelin and when the axons are grouped together, they appear white.

X-inactivation/random: because females have two X chromosomes, yet only one functioning copy is necessary, a percentage of X chromosomes with the mutated gene may not be expressed. As a result, females with X-linked disorders often have less severe symptoms than affected males. In contrast, because males have one X chromosome from the mother and one Y chromosome from the father, those who inherit an X-linked dominant disease trait typically fully express the mutated gene on the X chromosome, causing a more severe form of the disorder that may result in lethality before or shortly after birth. Fathers with an X-linked dominant trait transmit the gene to their daughters but not to their sons. Mothers with a single copy of an X-linked dominant gene have a 50 percent risk of transmitting the gene to their daughters as well as their sons.

X-linked dominant disorder: a disorder caused by a gene located on the X chromosome; also called sex-linked; passed on by one parent.

X-linked dominant trait: human traits, such an individual's specific blood group, eye color, or expression of certain diseases, result from the interaction of one gene inherited from the mother and one from the father. In X-linked dominant disorders, the gene muta-

Glossary

tion for the disease trait is transmitted as a dominant gene on the X chromosome and therefore may "override" the instructions of the normal gene on the other chromosome, resulting in expression of the disease.

Zero reject: all children are to be provided a free appropriate education.

Index

Index

Index

Index

Index

Index

Index

Index

Index

Index

Index

Index

Index

Index

Index

Index

Index

H

Index

Index

Index

Index

Index

Index

Index

Index

Index

Index

Index

Index

Index

Index

Index

Index

About the Author

KATHY HUNTER FOUNDED THE INTERNATIONAL RETT SYNDROME ASSOCIATION following the diagnosis of her then ten year-old daughter, Stacie, in the spring of 1984. After working several years in special education, she was honored to serve two terms on the National Board of Directors of the National Organization of Rare Disorders (NORD). She accepted a Congressional appointment to the National Advisory Neurological Disorder and Stroke Council (NANDS), and appointment to the Leadership Council of WE MOVE, representing national, regional and international patient advocacy organizations and foundations. Kathy has received several honors including selection as one of the *Maxwell House* 100 Real Heroes and she was featured by *Family Circle Magazine* in their Women Who Make a Difference series in 1996. Under Kathy's leadership, IRSA was honored to receive the First Annual Advocacy Group Award of Merit from the Child Neurology Foundation in 2001. She was selected as a *Baltimore Business Journal* Health Care Pioneer in 2003. Kathy's work has been featured in a number of national newspapers and magazines. She has authored several publications on Rett syndrome, including *Share the Journey*, *Bridges*, *Raindrops* and *Sunshine*, and *The Rett Syndrome Handbook*, *Edition One*, which was translated to seven different languages. Kathy currently lives in Maryland with her husband Scott and daughter Stacie.

"You cannot kindle a fire in any other heart until it is burning in your own."

– BEN SWEETLAND

"How deeply humanly you have put the destiny of Rett syndrome in the lives of so many parents, physicians, teachers and therapists. It is going to help offset so many heartbreaks and will help thousands of girls live more comfortable lives. We advise all our students to read The Rett Syndrome Handbook, *as there is so much good advice and healing attitude in its pages that is immediately applicable to understanding and working with children with other disabilities."*

> - CLIVE ROBBINS, DMM, FOUNDING DIRECTOR, NORDOFF-ROBBINS CENTER FOR MUSIC THERAPY AT NEW YORK UNIVERSITY

*"*The Rett Syndrome Handbook *is a tremendous resource guide for those interested in knowing more about Rett syndrome—therapists and teachers who need specific questions answered, and to parents who need guidance and suggestions from other parents about what works."*

> - JUDY FRY, MOTHER TO ASHLEY, 27

"The handbook is like having all the RS experts in the world holding your hand and safely guiding you."

> - MAUREEN WOODCOCK, MOTHER TO TIFFANY 39, ERIKA, 35, AND GRANDMOTHER TO ARI, 1 AND PAIGE, 13

"Thank you for taking on the monumental task of writing and putting together the many facts for the handbook. As I have thought about our journey, the thing we missed most was a road map. Thanks for providing one for those who have come behind you."

> - CAROL COX, MOTHER TO JENNIFER, 32

*"*The Rett Syndrome Handbook *is so full of knowledge, wisdom and love. I can quickly find the answers to questions on everyday care and treatment, and locate the resources my granddaughter needs. On the difficult days, I can find hope and inspiration. The handbook helps me survive today and prepare for the future. It is must reading for any family."*

> - PENNY HORSFALL, GRANDMOTHER TO ALEXIS, 7

INTERNATIONAL RETT SYNDROME ASSOCIATION
9121 PISCATAWAY ROAD, SUITE 2B
CLINTON, MARYLAND 20735
PHONE: (800) 818-RETT
(301) 856-3334
FAX: (301) 856-3336
WWW.RETTSYNDROME.ORG